H A N D B O O K S

IDAHO

JAMES P. KELLY

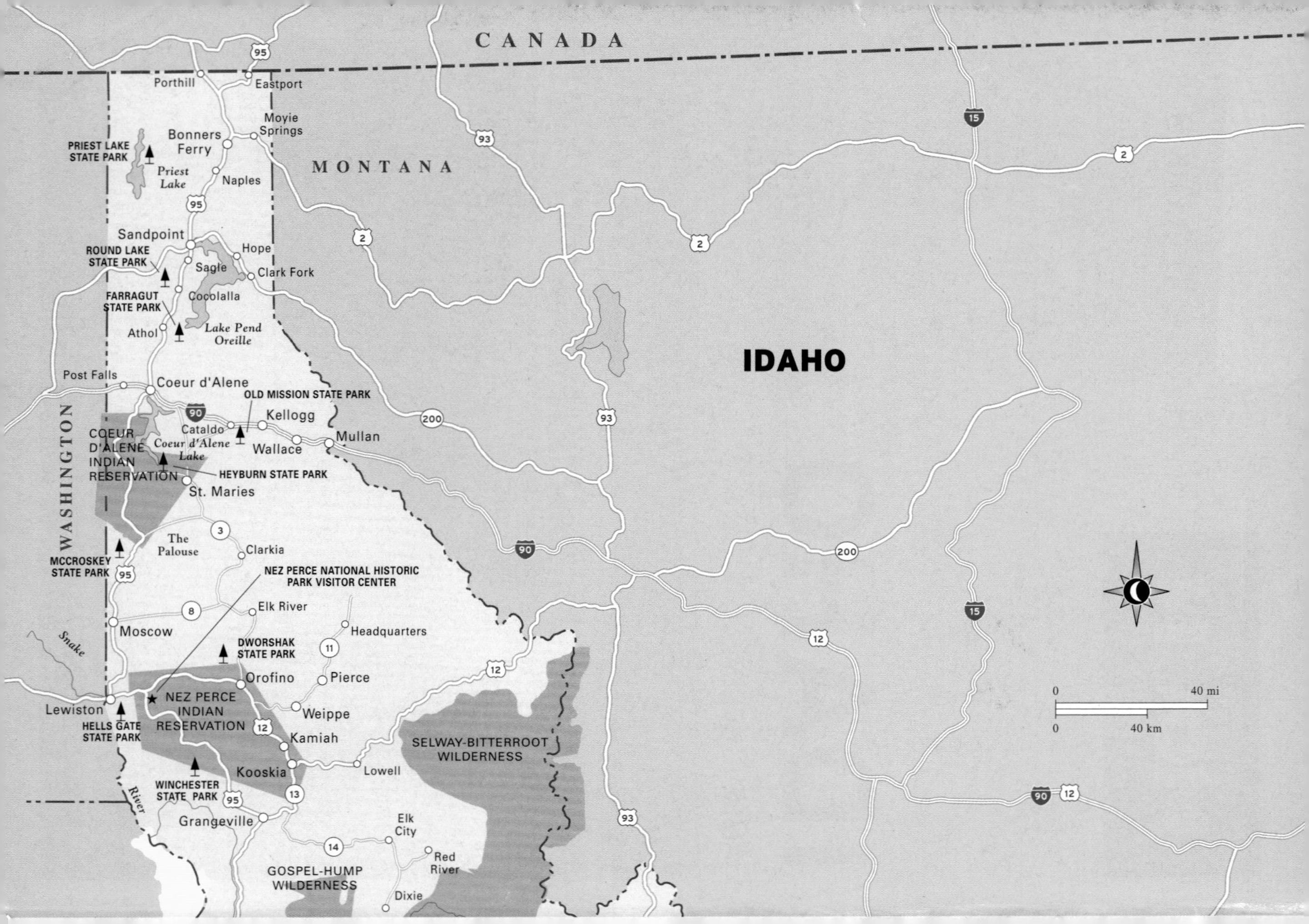

CANADA

MONTANA

IDAHO

WASHINGTON

40 mi
40 km

Eastport
Porthill
Movie Springs
Bonners Ferry
Naples
Sandpoint
Hope
Clark Fork
Sagle
Coolalla
Priest Lake
Lake Pend Oreille
Athol
Post Falls
Coeur d'Alene
Cataldo
Coeur d'Alene Lake
Kellogg
Wallace
Mullan
St. Maries
Clarkia
The Palouse
Moscow
Lewiston
Snake River
Orofino
Pierce
Weippe
Kamiah
Kooskia
Grangeville
Headquarters
Elk River
Lowell
Elk City
Red River
Dixie

PRIEST LAKE STATE PARK
ROUND LAKE STATE PARK
FARRAGUT STATE PARK
OLD MISSION STATE PARK
HEYBURN STATE PARK
COEUR D'ALENE INDIAN RESERVATION
McCROSKEY STATE PARK
HELLS GATE STATE PARK
NEZ PERCE NATIONAL HISTORIC PARK VISITOR CENTER
DWORSHAK STATE PARK
NEZ PERCE INDIAN RESERVATION
WINCHESTER STATE PARK
SELWAY-BITTERROOT WILDERNESS
GOSPEL-HUMP WILDERNESS

2   15   95   93   200   12   3   8   11   14   13   90

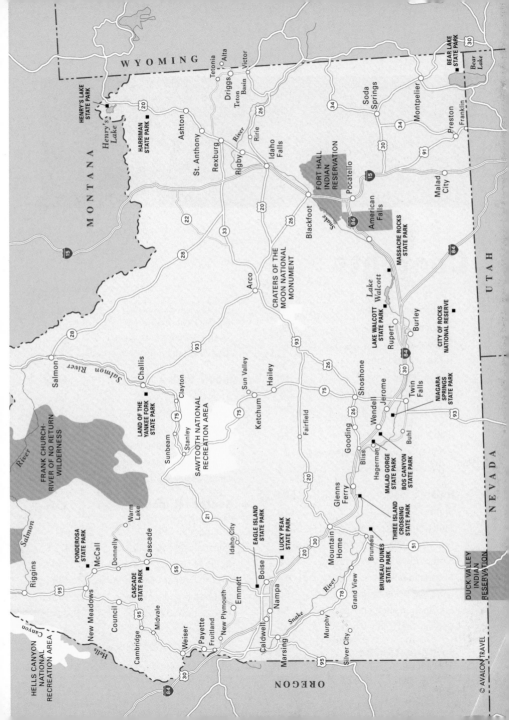

Contents

Discover **Idaho**

Idaho is often misunderstood. When this rugged North-western state is not being confused with Iowa, it's usually the brunt of some bad potato joke. True, farmers here do grow more spuds than any other state in the country, but Idaho goes beyond russet potatoes.

It's hard to fathom the varied landscapes of Idaho and the events that caused such a geologic spectacle. I strive to compre-hend this beautiful state every time I head out in search of the perfect fishing hole in Hagerman Valley or when I'm crunching across a frozen lake in the Sawtooths on my snowshoes. The intense volcanic activity and major floods that helped to shape Idaho are evident at almost every bend. The basalt-hemmed cliffs along the Snake River Canyon seem like a different planet than the cedar-ringed glacial lakes in the northern Panhandle.

Central Idaho's Rocky Mountains have numerous wild rivers that vein the largest roadless area in the Lower 48. The few roads that do exist in the Frank Church–River of No Return Wilderness are jaw-chattering routes better suited for mountain bikes and bighorn sheep than they are for the family minivan. This craggy terrain poses the same challenges for modern-day explorers, decked out in high-tech clothing and holding GPS devices, as it did for the Lewis and Clark expedition more than 200 years

ago. But in today's world, the Salmon River is praised by white-water rafters and not cursed for its turbulence, as it was by those early explorers in their primitive dugout canoes.

Juxtaposed with Idaho's remote wilderness are thriving urban areas. Boise, the state capital, has a surprisingly mellow vibe for a city with the third largest metropolitan population in the Northwest. The City of Trees has an exciting arts and entertainment scene, and it has the largest Basque population outside Spain. The Basque Block, a thriving ethnic enclave with restaurants, bars, and a museum, adds greatly to the city's cultural identity. Not far from Boise is the Snake River Valley, one of the country's newest wine-producing appellations.

The people of Idaho are as varied as the land itself. Conservative farmers, intellectual liberals, eco-rednecks, and antigovernment types may not have much in common, yet their adoration for the remarkable landscape that surrounds them is the only common thread they need.

Planning Your Trip

▶ WHERE TO GO

Boise

This little river city has grown leaps and bounds in recent years. Boise boasts a hip downtown area, lots of parks with big shade trees, and a major urban university. The newly developed BoDo and Linen Districts mesh well with the beautifully preserved historic neighborhoods. Folks are active thanks to the Boise River Greenbelt, a 25-mile recreational path, and Bogus Basin Ski Resort, which is only 16 miles north of town.

Southwest Idaho

Mountains, cities, remote desert, and vinifera grapes: This diverse region has it all. The Snake River Valley wine country is the focal point for oenophiles who come to taste remarkable vintages made from grapes grown in the Sunny Slope area. Downtown Nampa's historic Belle District has a profusion of used bookstores, antiques shops, coffeehouses, and contemporary restaurants.

IF YOU HAVE . . .

scenic Sun Valley in summer

- **THREE DAYS:** Visit Boise and Snake River Valley wine country.

- **ONE WEEK:** Add Fairfield and Sun Valley-Ketchum.

- **TWO WEEKS:** Add Stanley and Salmon.

- **THREE WEEKS:** Add Lava Hot Springs, Pocatello, Driggs, and Island Park.

- **FOUR WEEKS:** Add McCall, Coeur d'Alene, Wallace, and Priest Lake.

Boise's famous trees put on a colorful fall show.

Snake River Canyon near Swan Falls Dam, in southwest Idaho

Magic Valley

South-central Idaho is a strange and wonderful place. The Snake River defines the arid landscape. At Thousand Springs, water from an ancient aquifer gushes out of the cliffs like a faucet left on full blast. Hagerman Valley is a high-desert oasis with lots of shady fishing spots and commercial hot springs. And rock climbers will surely enjoy the massive granite pinnacles at the City of Rocks near Oakley.

Southeast Idaho

Framed by the majestic Tetons looming just over the border in Wyoming, this spectacular region is a veritable playground for anglers, backpackers, and skiers. The fabled Henry's Fork of the Snake River is pure fly-fishing paradise. Pocatello and Idaho Falls offer travelers urban amenities within a few miles of remote back-country. This part of the state also boasts the largest potato farms in North America.

Sawtooth Country and Beyond

The high country of Idaho's Central Rockies is an excellent place to get away from it all, but not before you go through the ritzy Sun Valley-Ketchum area. This world-famous

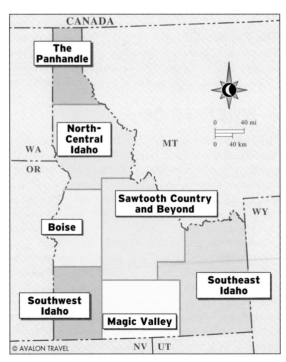

resort community has excellent skiing, top-notch restaurants, and attractive lodges. A few miles north, the buildings become few and far between as jagged mountain ranges dictate the scenery. The loveably rustic town of Stanley is a fun base camp for outdoor excursions.

North-Central Idaho

Hells Canyon marks the spot where the Snake River is furiously funneled through the deepest river gorge in North America en route to its confluence with the Columbia River. A few miles east, the resort town of McCall enjoys prime real estate on the southern shores of Payette Lake. Just outside town, Brundage Mountain beckons skiers and snowboarders to its powdery slopes. Traveling north on U.S. 95, the mountainous terrain eventually straightens out, giving way to a patchwork quilt of dryland farms near Moscow.

hiking in the Seven Devils Mountains above Hells Canyon, in north-central Idaho

The Panhandle

The tip-top of Idaho is home to the state's largest lakes, Coeur d'Alene and Pend Oreille. This region may only be 45 miles wide at its skinniest point, but recreation abounds. The bustling resort towns of Coeur d'Alene and Sandpoint give travelers a place to relax after ripping through fresh powder at the Silver Mountain and Schweitzer Mountain ski resorts. During summer, the lakes buzz with activity as people flock here for boating, fishing, and general aquatic fun.

▶ WHEN TO GO

Idaho offers year-round fun. Summer activities include white-water rafting, backpacking, fishing, mountain biking, and boating on the state's many scenic lakes. Wintertime brings tons of snow to the mountains, making Idaho a popular destination for skiers and snowboarders.

Summer is peak season in most resort communities in Idaho. Places like Coeur d'Alene, the Sawtooths, and Island Park in southeast Idaho are quiet during the winter months. As a matter of fact, most fishing and backcountry lodges are closed in winter due to heavy snow. Coeur d'Alene, on the other hand, may be slow in the off-season, but many of the hotels offer reduced rates and special package deals.

Mountain resort communities with skiing and snowboarding, like Sun Valley, McCall, and Kellogg, have two distinct peak seasons, winter and summer, when rates are at their highest. The ski season generally runs from Thanksgiving weekend to around the end of March. Hotels, lodges, and restaurants are usually open year-round in these places. If skiing is not your thing but you like biking, fishing, and hiking, spring and fall are also good times to visit the mountain resort towns, when the streets are less crowded and room rates can drop as much as 25–30 percent.

► BEFORE YOU GO

Getting There and Around

Since Idaho is bordered by six states (Washington, Oregon, Nevada, Utah, Wyoming, and Montana) and one country (Canada), many people get here by car, especially along the I-84, I-15, and I-90 corridors.

Folks coming from areas outside the region generally fly into Boise, Salt Lake City, and Spokane. Renting a car makes the most sense and offers the most freedom because public transportation can be spotty in Idaho. Not to say there aren't shuttles to and from the airports to popular resort destinations, but you're on your own after that. Ketchum and Coeur d'Alene have good local transit systems, but that won't help much if you plan on exploring the hinterlands.

With winter snow comes hazardous driving conditions. Getting to Idaho's numerous ski resorts and other winter recreation areas is generally not a problem, but it's important to check current weather advisories and road reports before embarking on a winter trip to the Gem State. Road conditions aren't a major consideration during the warmer months, except a few errant rangeland livestock and an occasional late-spring snowstorm.

What to Take

Once the mercury drops in Idaho, it's imperative that you bring along a snow parka, wickaway thermal underwear, gloves, and a warm hat. And regardless of where you are in the state, a well-insulated pair of snow boots will get you a long way during the frigid winter months, as will a sturdy pair of hiking boots in summer.

It doesn't rain much in Idaho as it does elsewhere in the Northwest, so rain gear isn't a necessity for those visiting the arid Snake River Plain and Idaho's Central Rockies. But the Panhandle does receive measurable annual rainfall, so you might want to pack a rain-resistant jacket if you're headed to north Idaho during the fall and spring months.

In general, the dress code is decidedly casual in Idaho, meaning you can get away with wearing a Carhartt jacket with your John Fluevog boots.

Sun Valley in fall

Explore Idaho

▶ THE BEST OF IDAHO

It's nearly impossible to take in all of Idaho in 10 days. You truly need more time to fully appreciate the Gem State in its entirety. But here is a recommended travel plan to see some of Idaho's top spots in one fell swoop. Since the Gem State has a blend of upscale lodging and more rustic accommodations, this day-by-day planner offers a variety of options.

Day 1

Speaking of fell swoops: Once you arrive in Boise, take in a summer play under the stars at the Idaho Shakespeare Festival after touring the Basque Block and the downtown museums. After filling up on the bard, have a late-night dinner at Red Feather Lounge before calling it a night at the Modern Hotel.

Day 2

Go east on I-84 and get on U.S. 20 at Mountain Home, which will lead you 108 miles to the Ketchum–Sun Valley area. Check into the lodge at Sun Valley Resort and take a walk to downtown Ketchum, where you can peruse the art galleries, shop for souvenirs, and grab dinner at the Vintage Restaurant.

Day 3

Drive north on the Sawtooth Scenic Byway toward Stanley. Before you get to town on Highway 75, stop and take a day hike to Cabin Creek Lakes. Later you can grab a pizza and some beers at Papa Brunee's, and then rest your sore muscles at Salmon River Lodge.

Day 4

Travel west from Stanley on Highway 21, also known as the Ponderosa Pine Scenic Byway. Stop at Kirkham Hot Springs near

Idaho Shakespeare Festival in Boise

Lowman for a quick soak. In Lowman, head west on Banks-Lowman Road for about 35 miles until you come to Banks. Go north on Highway 55 for 65 miles to McCall and check into your reserved cabin at Ponderosa State Park.

Day 5

Get up early and take Highway 55 to the U.S. 95 junction at New Meadows. Head north for about 35 miles to Riggins, where you can arrange to take a half-day white-water rafting trip down the Salmon River. Grab an elk burger and a microbrew at Shelly's Back Eddy Grill. The Riggins Motel is a good place to bed down.

Day 6

Travel north on U.S. 95 past Grangeville until you come to the Clearwater River near Lewiston. Here you'll find the interpretive center for the Nez Perce National Historic Park, adjacent to the Spalding Mission site. Head southeast on U.S. 12 along the banks of the Clearwater River, a stretch of road known as the Lewis and Clark Highway.

rafters navigating rapids on the Salmon River

GEM STATE FESTIVALS

The Trailing of the Sheep Festival

There's no doubt that Idaho has a flavor all its own. The quirky personality of the Gem State is exemplified every year with a bevy of wacky and wild festivals. Here's a look at several events that are quintessentially Idaho.

- **Riggins Rodeo:** If you thought the Wild West was dead, visit Riggins the first weekend in May, when the town brings it back to life with a ruckus rodeo and big parade celebrating all things cowboy and cowgirl. The two-day event also features a big cowboy breakfast.

- **Moscow Renaissance Fair:** Don ye medieval garb and head to this fun festival that happens the first weekend in May at East City Park in Moscow. You'll be treated to a themed parade, food and grog (honey mead, perhaps?), crafts, and live music ranging from Celtic to bluegrass to acoustic "rawk" folk.

- **Salmon River Testicle Festival:** This homespun festival takes place at the end of June on a private ranch near Salmon. The event, as the name suggests, pays homage to Rocky Mountain oysters – served up with potato salad and other traditional side dishes. Plus there's live music and plenty of Western dancing.

- **Atomic Days:** Arco celebrates its nuclear history every July with a three-day festival, which includes a rodeo, carnival rides, food, crafts, and a glowing parade.

- **Soul Food Extravaganza:** Soul food in Idaho? This tasty festival comes to Julia Davis Park in Boise the first Saturday in August. A large array of Southern food is dished up under the park's big shade trees. Expect to see fried catfish, barbecued chicken, sweet potato pie, saucy black-eyed peas, and delish peach cobbler.

- **Lavapalooza:** This fun twist on a popular music festival happens the first Saturday after Labor Day with a benefit motorcycle ride that leaves Ogden, Utah, and heads for Lava Hot Springs in southeast Idaho. After the Harleys roar into town, several bands take to the stage for a blistering good time.

- **The Trailing of the Sheep Festival:** Every October in the Wood River Valley the entire community celebrates its woolly heritage with a three-day festival, culminating with sheepherders bringing home their flocks from the high country and herding thousands of sheep down Ketchum's Main Street.

- **McCall Winter Carnival:** How about Mardi Gras in the snow? This annual festival in McCall takes place at the end of January and the beginning of February. Thousands of revelers converge on this mountain resort town for 10 days of wintry fun, including a world-famous ice sculpture contest, live music, fireworks, and a wacky Mardi Gras-themed parade.

Grab a riverside cabin at Three Rivers Resort in Lowell, about 100 miles from Lewiston.

Day 7

Continue back to Lewiston on U.S. 12 and take U.S. 95 northbound, which rises dramatically above the Clearwater River Valley and into the Palouse. Once in Moscow (about 30 miles from Lewiston), take a leisurely stroll through the beautiful University of Idaho campus or play a round of golf. Treat yourself to dinner at the Red Door.

Day 8

Go north on U.S. 95 for 82 miles until you reach the shores of Coeur d'Alene Lake. Chill out in Coeur d'Alene and take a hike on Tubbs Hill. After frolicking in the lake all day and checking out the cool downtown shops, have dinner at Scratch before turning in at the Flamingo Motel.

Day 9

Head east on I-90 for 59 miles to Lookout Pass near the Montana border, where you can park your car and jump on your mountain bike (or rent one at Lookout Pass) for a 15-mile ride along the Route of the Hiawatha trail. Later, grab a hotel room in nearby Wallace and cruise the funky antiques shops, museums, and saloons in this Victorian-era mining town.

Day 10

Go back to Coeur d'Alene on I-90 and head north on U.S. 95 toward Sandpoint. Along the way you'll pass by Silverwood Theme Park, the only amusement park in the Northwest. Once in Sandpoint (about 48 miles from Coeur d'Alene), let Lake Pend Oreille Cruises take you on a boat ride around the scenic lake. Reserve a room at the Inn at Sand Creek, which also has one of the best restaurants in town.

along the Route of the Hiawatha bike trail

▶ WINE COUNTRY WEEKEND

Snake River Valley wine country is an astonishing 8,263 square miles, but most of the state's 40-plus wineries are on the west side of the appellation. The high-desert terrain boasts rich volcanic soil, which makes for exceptional fruit. Wines produced in this region have pronounced tannins and well-balanced acidity. Syrah, cabernet sauvignon, malbec, viognier, chardonnay, and riesling are the leading varietals in the Snake River Valley.

It's important to keep in mind that most tasting rooms are typically open Friday–Sunday spring–fall, and some wineries are only open by appointment. Make sure to have a designated driver, or just sign up for a guided winery tour.

Friday

Start your Idaho wine country tour in the Sunny Slope area of Caldwell. This is the epicenter of winemaking activity in the Snake River Valley. Most of the vineyards here are situated on south-facing steps near the Snake River. Koenig Vineyards turns out remarkable syrah, viognier, cabernet sauvignon, and ice wine made from riesling grapes. Just up the road is Bitner Vineyards, which makes bone-dry riesling, cabernet sauvignon, and an excellent chardonnay. The winery also has a small bed-and-breakfast inn where you can call it a night after exploring wine country. East of Highway 55, you'll find Ste. Chapelle Winery, a large corporate operation, and Hells Canyon Winery, a relatively small winery that produces top-notch estate wines, including syrah, cabernet sauvignon, merlot, and chardonnay. Continue wine tasting in Nampa at Brick 29 Bistro, a contemporary Northwestern restaurant with lots of Idaho labels.

Sunny Slope, the winemaking epicenter of the Snake River Valley

the tasting bar at Cinder Wines

Saturday

Start out the day in Eagle (about 30 miles east of Sunny Slope), where you can taste wines at Woodriver Cellars and 3 Horse Ranch Vineyards, an organic winery specializing in syrah, merlot, and an extremely drinkable roussanne-viognier blend. Next, head to nearby Boise and sample vintages at the Snake River Winery tasting room in BoDo. This small winery produces syrah, grenache, barbera, malbec, and chardonnay, to name a few. Across town, over in Garden City, is one of the best wineries in the state, Cinder Wines. Here you can taste syrah, chardonnay, viognier, and nearly perfect dry rosé. Nearby, you'll find Syringa Winery, which turns out small lots of merlot, cabernet sauvignon, primitivo, and sauvignon blanc. After checking out the wineries, head to the Basque Block for croquetas and a solomo sandwich at Bar Gernika. Grab a room at Leku Ona Hotel.

Sunday

To get to the east side of the Snake River Valley, take I-84 eastbound past Mountain Home to Hammett (about 62 miles from Boise). This is where you'll find Cold Springs Winery, a small operation that makes varietal wines and blends like Hot Rod Red. Then continue east on I-84 to Glenns Ferry and stop by Carmela Vineyards, a good place to sample wines and have brunch at the winery's full-service restaurant. Get back on I-84 eastbound and head to Bliss, and jump on U.S. 30 southbound. Take this scenic drive through the Hagerman Valley en route to Buhl, home to Holesinsky Winery, which makes excellent organic wines, and Snyder Winery, where you can taste cabernet sauvignon, syrah, chardonnay, and riesling. Spend the night at Billingsley Creek Lodge in Hagerman.

▶ AVIAN ADVENTURE

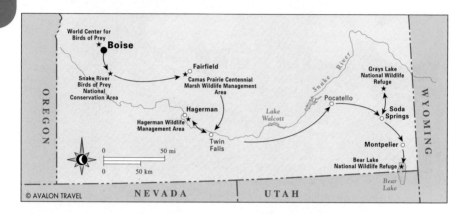

Idaho offers wing-watchers a multitude of beautiful spots to view birds in their natural habitats. Make sure to have your binoculars and plenty of batteries for the camera.

Day 1

With Boise as your base camp, check out the raptor exhibits at the World Center for Birds of Prey, and then take the short drive south of town along the Western Heritage Historic Byway en route to the Snake River Birds of Prey National Conservation Area. Here, along the tall cliffs above Swan Falls Dam, you can watch red-tailed hawks, golden eagles, and peregrine falcons snatch little critters off the rocks by the river.

Day 2

Camas Prairie Centennial Marsh Wildlife Management Area near Fairfield has a profusion of wildflowers and chattering birds. It's easy to find. Head east on U.S. 20 toward Sun Valley, and about 10 miles before Fairfield you'll see the marshlands on the south side of the highway. This place explodes with color each spring and in early summer when the bright blue camas lilies blossom. Equally as colorful are the western tanagers, red-winged and yellow-headed black birds, curlews, and blue herons that frequent the area. Fairfield is a good place to bed down for the night.

a peregrine falcon up close as you might see it at the World Center for Birds of Prey

Day 3

If viewing large waterfowl is your thing, go south on Highway 75 to Twin Falls (about 81 miles from Fairfield) and get on U.S. 30 heading west to the Hagerman Wildlife Management Area. Right before Hagerman is the state fish hatchery, where white pelicans, blue herons, and sandhill cranes like to hang out in the little lakes that dot the parklike grounds. You'll also see these big birds nearby along the Snake River, along with golden eagles, prairie falcons, and turkey buzzards. Spend the night in Hagerman.

Day 4

Grays Lake National Wildlife Refuge is one of the best places in Idaho to view birds, and it's delightfully off the trodden path. To get here, take I-84 eastbound from Twin Falls to the I-86 interchange and head for Pocatello (about 122 miles). Once in Poky, go south on I-15 to U.S. 30 and travel east to Soda Springs. Jump on Highway 34 northbound and go 27 miles to this gorgeous refuge. Expect to see a waterfowl extravaganza in the marshlands, and don't be surprised to

blue lilies swaying in the wind on the Camas Prairie

spot some bald eagles, harriers, hawks, and kestrels as well. Soda Springs offers basic accommodations.

Day 5

To see one of the largest nesting grounds for Canada geese in the western United States, check out Bear Lake National Wildlife Refuge in Idaho's extreme southeast corner. To get here, travel south from Soda Springs on U.S. 30 for 29 miles to Montpelier, and then go southwest on U.S. 89 for about three miles until you come to Airport Road. Located on the marshy north end of Bear Lake, this refuge has terns, wrens, short-eared owls, trumpeter swans, and the country's largest population of white-faced ibis. Spend the night in Montpelier.

Bear Lake National Wildlife Refuge

▶ REST AND RECREATION IN SOUTHEAST IDAHO

You can cover a lot of ground in southeast Idaho in a week's time. Here's a fun itinerary that allows you to see some of the region's top spots without feeling too rushed.

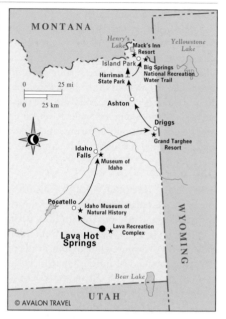

Day 1

Start your journey in Lava Hot Springs, just off U.S. 30. This is where you'll find the Lava Recreation Complex, a sprawling facility with three large geothermal swimming pools surrounded by a shady picnic area. After relaxing in the water and playing a few games of volleyball, retire to the Royal Hotel, which also has a good restaurant.

Day 2

Take U.S. 30 west to I-15 and head north to Pocatello. Tour the Idaho Museum of Natural History on the Idaho State University campus. Afterward, jump on a bike and cruise along the Portneuf Greenway, a 13-mile recreational path that runs through town. Grab a pizza at Pie Hole and call it a night at the Thunderbird Motel.

Day 3

Go north of Pocatello on I-15 for 52 miles to Idaho Falls. This sparkling clean city has several good museums, including the Museum of Idaho and The Art Museum of Eastern Idaho. And it's hard not to miss the Mormon Temple, which punctuates the sky near the Snake River. Try some inventive cuisine at Rutabaga's before turning in at the Red Lion Hotel on the falls.

Day 4

Head east from Idaho Falls on U.S. 26 toward the Wyoming border (about 66 miles from Idaho Falls to Victor). Take Highway 33 north to Driggs, a recreational haven and

Idaho Falls

THE QUEST FOR PERFECT POWDER

The Gem State boasts some of the best skiing in the country. Skiers and snowboarders love Idaho for its killer powder and relatively short lift lines. Here's a look at several ski resorts worth checking out.

Hands down the most popular ski destination in Idaho is the ultrachic **Sun Valley Resort,** which has more than 2,000 acres of skiable runs and a vertical drop of 3,400 feet. The only bummer about this place is the long lift lines and crowded slopes during peak season.

Nearby, you'll find excellent powder and much shorter lift lines at **Soldier Mountain Resort.** This small winter resort, just off U.S. 20 near Fairfield, has a vertical drop of 1,425 feet and 1,150 skiable acres.

Just over the Idaho border in Alta, Wyoming, **Grand Targhee Resort** boasts some of the fluffiest powder in the region. This beautiful resort has 1,500 acres of lift-served skiable terrain, with a 2,212-foot vertical drop and a base elevation of 8,000 feet.

Sixteen miles north of Boise is **Bogus Basin Ski Resort,** which has 2,600 acres of skiable runs and a vertical drop of 1,800 feet. The resort can get crowded at times, but the views of Boise from the top are spectacular.

For remarkable powder and great views of Payette Lake, head to **Brundage Mountain Resort** just outside McCall. This small resort, which can be somewhat empty if you come mid-week, has a vertical drop of 1,800 feet and 1,500 skiable acres.

The Panhandle has become well known for its ski resorts. While **Lookout Pass Ski Area,** just off I-90 near the Montana border, may not get much press, it still offers shredders lots of fresh powder and beautiful alpine views. Here you'll find uncrowded slopes, 540 skiable acres, and a vertical drop of 1,150 feet.

Nearby in Kellogg, it's hard not to miss **Silver Mountain Resort,** mostly because the gondola – the longest of its kind in the world, at 3.1

skiing at Grand Targhee Resort

miles – comes down the mountain right into town. The resort boasts 1,590 acres of skiable runs and a vertical drop of 2,200 feet.

Eleven miles north of Sandpoint is **Schweitzer Mountain Resort,** which earns the award for the ski resort with the best view in Idaho. From the top, you'll be treated to a 2,400-foot vertical drop, 92 excellent runs, and breathtaking panoramas of Lake Pend Oreille and a ring of mountain ranges.

Henry's Lake

all-around fun place nestled up against the Tetons. Check out Grand Targhee Resort, where you can play according to the season and have dinner at the Branding Iron Grill. Stay the night at the Teton Valley Cabins.

Teton Mountains in winter

Day 5

Take Highway 33 about 40 miles west to Sugar City, and then go north on U.S. 20 to Ashton, a good place to stock up on groceries and other provisions. Stay the night in a reserved yurt at Harriman State Park. Here you can fly-fish for cutthroat trout on the Henry's Fork, hike or mountain bike along the nature trails, and decompress away from the trappings of modern society.

Day 6

Take the short drive up U.S. 20 to Mack's Inn Resort, where you can stay in a rustic cabin and enjoy a canoe trip along the Big Springs National Recreation Water Trail. This scenic float trip down the Henry's Fork affords spectacular views of Mount Two Top and the chance to spot meandering moose and bald eagles hanging out in the trees along the river.

Day 7

Continue northbound on U.S. 20 for about 10 miles to Henry's Lake and try your luck at catching a few rainbow-cutthroat hybrids in the lake's shallow depths. Grab a cabin at Jared's Wild Rose Ranch, a full-service fishing lodge with boat rentals, a tackle shop, and a restaurant. You might even have time for a scenic horse ride at Meadow Vue Ranch.

▶ HIGH COUNTRY ODYSSEY

Sawtooth Country in Central Idaho is a dreamland for outdoor enthusiasts. With a profusion of choices for backpackers, whitewater rafters, mountain bikers, and anglers, this gorgeous mountain region has got you covered. Here's a suggested summer trip that's guaranteed to raise your heart rate and soothe your soul.

Day 1

Start your high-country adventure with a two-day backpacking trip (or bring your mountain bike) in the White Clouds near Stanley. To access the Boulder Chain Lakes, head east on Highway 75 for about 30 miles until you come to East Fork Salmon Road, and then travel southwest on this road for 22 miles, where you will come to the Little Boulder Creek trailhead. Don your backpack and follow the trail, which ascends next to the creek for about seven miles to the lakes. Scoop Lake is a great place to camp, and fishing is excellent at this postcard-perfect spot.

Day 2

First thing in the morning, cast a line in the tranquil lake for some rainbow trout. After a healthy breakfast of pan-fried trout and eggs, explore a few of the 13 subalpine and alpine lakes that dot the map near majestic Castle Peak. After getting a strenuous workout and enjoying the remarkable scenery, set up camp at Castle Lake, where you can do some more fishing and sing campfire songs.

Day 3

Strike camp and make your way back to the trailhead. Travel north on Highway 75 for about 20 miles to Challis. Get on U.S. 93 northbound and go about 60 miles to

the Sawtooths near Stanley

the stunning view along the main Salmon River

Salmon. Check into the Sacajawea Inn and take a much-needed hot shower before heading over to the Sacajawea Interpretive Cultural and Educational Center, which pays homage to the legendary Shoshone woman who was integral to the success of the Lewis and Clark expedition. After a history lesson, grab a microbrew and a burger at Bertram's Brewery.

Days 4-6

Book a white-water trip (well in advance) down the main Salmon River with Kookaburra Rafting in Salmon. A two-night, three-day rafting excursion will take you along a 45-mile stretch of this wild and scenic river, where you will be treated to rapids galore, stunningly beautiful riparian campsites, and hearty meals. The trip starts at North Fork, just north of Salmon, and ends three days later at Corn Creek. Since you won't get back to Salmon until around 5:30 P.M. on the last day, it's best to grab a hotel room there. And, once again, a hot shower will never feel so good.

Day 7

Get up early and head south on U.S. 93 to Challis, and take Highway 75 south for 115 miles to Ketchum. Continue southbound on Highway 75 for another 12 miles to Hailey. The Big Wood River, one of Ernest Hemingway's favorite fly-fishing holes, runs alongside the highway near town. Try your luck for trophy-sized brown trout at one of the many access spots, but be forewarned: it's mostly catch-and-release in this area. After a peaceful afternoon of casting woolly buggers, have dinner in Hailey at CK's Real Food before calling it a night at the Wood River Inn.

BOISE

Boise's metro population is fast approaching the 700,000 mark, making it the third largest city in the Northwest behind Seattle and Portland. It's hardly the little river city that it used to be, but this burgeoning capital city hasn't forgotten its storied past, as evidenced by the attractive historic districts that flourish alongside ongoing urban renewal. Several gentrification projects and recently constructed high-rises have remarkably changed the city's look in the new millennium.

Boise (pronounced BOY-see not BOY-zee) is home to a thriving high-tech industry anchored by Micron Technology, a worldwide manufacturer of semiconductor devices. Boise State University is another local institution where great minds collide, and its football team has become one of the best Division 1-A programs in the country.

The City of Trees is also a hotspot in the region for entertainment, shopping, and dining, and there are a bevy of new tasting rooms where Snake River Valley winemakers strut their vintages for all to taste. Or you can stick with the old standbys, like noshing on Basque cuisine on the Basque Block, catching up with Bard at the Idaho Shakespeare Festival, or enjoying a free Wednesday-night concert at The Grove as part of the city's summer concert series.

Boise may be an urban mecca, yet it still has a mellow vibe and a relatively low crime rate. You are more likely to be panhandled by transients than fall victim to street crime, unless you're out stumbling the streets at 3 A.M.

© IDAHO DIVISION OF TOURISM

HIGHLIGHTS

(The Basque Block: Boise is home to the largest Basque population in the United States. This vibrant cultural group has its own enclave in downtown Boise, with a cultural center, a museum, and a handful of Basque eateries (page 31).

(Idaho State Capitol: The state capitol building recently underwent major renovation, adding two underground wings and restoring much of the original interior construction. It's open to the public for self-guided tours (page 33).

(MK Nature Center: Area residents adore this 4.6-acre wildlife preserve and botanical garden near downtown Boise. Stroll along the shady walkways and peek through glass windows at several fish species in various stages of life (page 37).

(Old Idaho Penitentiary: The Old Pen is one of only four U.S. territorial prisons still standing. The inmates are long gone, and you can tour this medieval-looking penitentiary that's surrounded by an imposing sandstone wall (page 38).

(Boise River Greenbelt: Join the locals for bicycling, running, walking, and fishing along this paved recreational path that hugs the Boise River for more than 25 miles (page 43).

(Bogus Basin: Skiers and snowboarders flock to this nearby winter recreation area for tons of fresh powder and spectacular views of Boise and beyond (page 54).

(Idaho Shakespeare Festival: Fans of the bard converge every summer season at an outdoor theater near the Boise River. With a spectacular desert backdrop, the talented troupe brings to life Shakespeare's comedies and tragedies as well as contemporary plays (page 57).

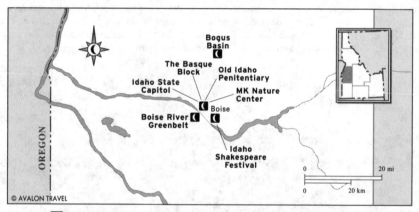

LOOK FOR (TO FIND RECOMMENDED SIGHTS, ACTIVITIES, DINING, AND LODGING.

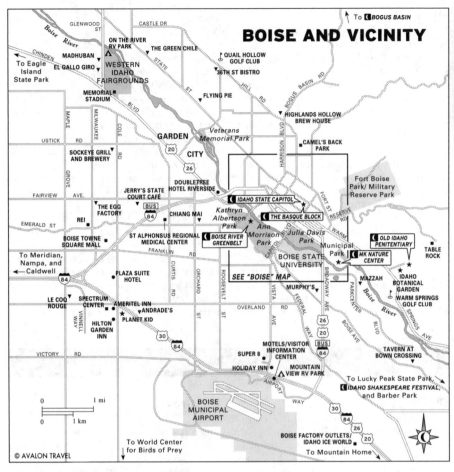

The lines between town and country definitely blur in Boise due to its close proximity to backcountry fun. Locals are active and would often rather ride bicycles than drive cars. They also stay fit by kayaking, mountain biking, skiing, and hiking in the nearby Boise Mountains and Owyhee Canyonlands.

Spend the morning fly-fishing on the Boise River before jumping on a mountain bike and hitting the labyrinth of single-track trails in the Foothills. Play a round of disc-golf at Ann

Morrison Park, and then take a leisurely stroll along the Boise River Greenbelt at sunset.

Year-round recreation abounds because Boise boasts a moderate climate and more than 300 days of sunshine per year. Sure, winter brings a little snow and ice to the valley floor, but that generally melts away by noon. For those wanting to frolic in deep snow, head up to nearby Bogus Basin for steep alpine runs, cross-country ski and snowshoe trails, and one helluva ride down the massive tubing hill.

BOISE

HISTORY

Early-19th century French-Canadian fur trappers were among the first nonnatives to see the location of present-day Boise, where the sprawling high desert gives way to the Boise Front of the Rocky Mountains. Can you imagine their surprise when they dropped into this scenic valley after laboring for days in the wide-open terrain of the Snake River Plain? An oft-told story is that members of this ragtag group reportedly said, *"Les bois! Les bois!"* ("The woods! The woods!") upon seeing the clusters of cottonwoods and other indigenous trees that skirted the Boise River.

About a half-century later, around 1863, Fort Boise was relocated here from near present-day Parma, and these first settlers started to plant a large variety of nonnative trees that the city is now known for. These early residents seeking shady reprieve from the blazing desert sun are why Boise is called "The City of Trees." The Oregon Trail ran right down Main Street, but most of those folks were headed for the greener pastures of Oregon's Willamette Valley.

In 1865, Boise became the official capital of the Idaho Territory, designated by President Abraham Lincoln two years earlier. The City of Trees wrestled the distinction away from Lewiston, which had served as the capital for a little more than a year. Some people in the north part of the state are still sore about this shift of power.

During this period of the mid-19th century, Boise grew tremendously, from a fur-trading post to a bustling center of commerce for the nearby boomtowns in the Boise Basin and Silver City mining districts.

PLANNING YOUR TIME

It takes at least three days to enjoy all the sights in and around Boise. In one day, you could tour the state capitol and the museums, take a walk on the Greenbelt, and still have time to enjoy a nice dinner. The extra days will make it possible for you to hit the slopes at Bogus Basin or go mountain biking in the Boise Front.

Sights

DOWNTOWN

Most of Boise's worthwhile sights are in or near the downtown corridor, meaning you can walk or ride a bike to these places without breaking much of a sweat. The transit system around town is in dire need of an overhaul, but during the day you can find a fairly steady stream of buses going to popular destinations. Check out www.valleyride.org for routes and schedules.

Besides the historic Old Boise and Hyde Park districts, Boise has several new districts to explore, including BoDo, Bown Crossing, and the Linen District.

And don't forget about venerable destinations like the Basque Block, Boise State University, and the Idaho State Capitol, which was recently renovated.

The Grove

South of Main Street between 8th and 9th Streets is The Grove, a large brick plaza surrounding a central water fountain where kids often splash to beat the summer heat. By day, impromptu Hacky Sack games are a common sight; by night, benches host late-night folk guitarists, cooing couples, and socializing high-school kids too young to make the bar scene. The plaza fills with revelers every Wednesday evening in summer for Alive After Five—an open-air festival with live music and dancing, not to mention a liberal amount of beer-quaffing.

On one corner of the plaza is the **Grove Hotel** and **Qwest Arena,** a huge multipurpose venue that accommodates concerts and home games of the Idaho Steelheads pro

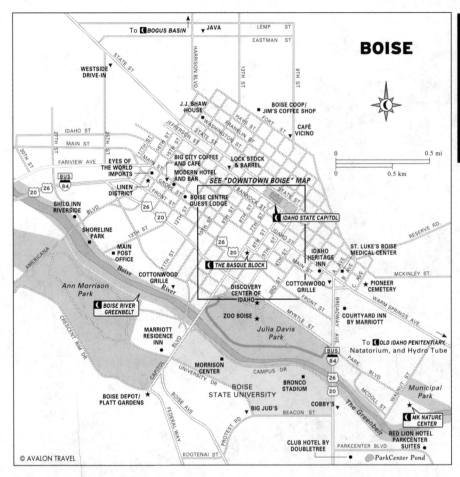

To **C** *BOGUS BASIN* ▼ JAVA LEMP ST
EASTMAN ST

BOISE

WESTSIDE
DRIVE-IN

HARRISON BLVD

STATE ST

13TH ST

8TH ST

J.J. SHAW
HOUSE

BOISE COOP/
JIM'S COFFEE SHOP

HAYS ST
FRANKLIN ST
FORT ST

CAFÉ
VICINO

JEFFERSON ST
STATE ST
WASHINGTON ST

IDAHO ST

27TH ST

25TH ST

MAIN ST

30TH ST

FAIRVIEW AVE

EYES OF
THE WORLD
IMPORTS

BIG CITY COFFEE
AND CAFÉ

LOCK STOCK
& BARREL

27TH ST
16TH ST
13TH ST

MODERN HOTEL
AND BAR

SEE "DOWNTOWN BOISE" MAP

BUS
84

20 26

LINEN
DISTRICT

GROVE ST

BANNOCK ST

STATE ST

SHILO INN
RIVERSIDE

26

BOISE CENTRE
GUEST LODGE

FRONT ST

10TH ST
9TH ST
8TH ST
7TH ST

20

C *IDAHO STATE CAPITOL*

RESERVE RD.

SHORELINE
PARK

13TH ST

20

26

6TH ST
5TH ST
IDAHO ST

IDAHO
HERITAGE
INN

ST. LUKE'S BOISE
MEDICAL CENTER

AMERICANA

MAIN
POST
OFFICE

14TH ST

20

C *THE BASQUE BLOCK*

MAIN ST

A AVE
B AVE

MCKINLEY ST.

Boise

COTTONWOOD
GRILLE ▼

3RD ST

COTTONWOOD
GRILLE ▼

PIONEER
CEMETERY

Ann Morrison
Park

River

DISCOVERY
CENTER OF
IDAHO

FRONT ST

WARM SPRINGS AVE

C *BOISE RIVER
GREENBELT*

ZOO BOISE ★

*Julia Davis
Park*

MYRTLE ST

BROADWAY AVE

COURTYARD INN
BY MARRIOTT

CRESCENT RIM DR

MARRIOTT
RESIDENCE
INN

BLVD

BUS
84

PARK BLVD

To **C** *OLD IDAHO PENITENTIARY,*
Natatorium, and Hydro Tube

CAPITOL

MORRISON
CENTER

UNIVERSITY DR

CAMPUS DR

26

20

MCDOLL ST

WALNUT ST

*Municipal
Park*

BOISE DEPOT/
PLATT GARDENS ★

BOISE AVE

BOISE
STATE UNIVERSITY

BRONCO
STADIUM

COBBY'S ▼

The Greenbelt

RED LION HOTEL
PARKCENTER
SUITES ●

FEDERAL WAY

PROTEST RD

BIG JUD'S ▼

BEACON ST

C MK NATURE
CENTER

© AVALON TRAVEL

KOOTENAI ST

CLUB HOTEL BY
DOUBLETREE

PARKCENTER BLVD

● *ParkCenter Pond*

0   0.5 mi
0   0.5 km

hockey team and Idaho Stampede pro basketball team. Just across the way, it's hard not to notice the gargantuan **Boise Centre on the Grove,** a 85,000-square-foot convention center that brings in thousands of people annually for conferences and local gala events.

BoDo

Boise's latest entertainment and shopping district consolidates the historic 8th Street Marketplace with an array of newly constructed buildings that house upscale boutiques, restaurants, and specialty shops. The name BoDo is an abbreviation of Boise and downtown.

BoDo is as glitzy as it gets in Boise. Big-name boutiques such as **Ann Taylor Loft, Urban Outfitters,** and **Helly Hansen** bring in droves of people looking for an urban shopping experience. Corporate restaurants such as **P. F. Chang's** and **Bonefish Grill** anchor the restaurant scene, but you will also find several independent eateries and bars such as **Happy Fish Sushi** and **Ha' Penny Bridge Irish Pub.**

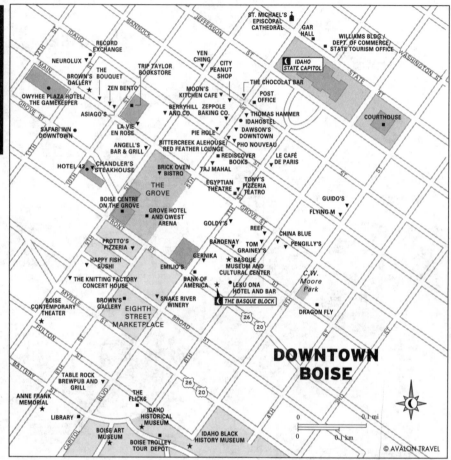

DOWNTOWN BOISE

© AVALON TRAVEL

Just down the brick-clad alley, the **Knitting Factory** books an endless flurry of national touring bands.

Connoisseurs of wine and chocolate will definitely get their fix at the **Snake River Winery** tasting room and **Carre Chocolates,** an importer of delicious Belgian truffles and fondant candies. Sample some syrah and dark chocolate before catching a flick at Bodo's theater complex, **Edwards Cinemas Stadium 9.**

Old Boise Historic District

On the east end of downtown, centered around 6th and Main Streets, is the Old Boise Historic District, one of the best preserved and most enjoyable "old towns" of any city in the West. Shortly after the city was founded in 1863, its premier commercial and residential district developed here. Back then you could hop on a streetcar that ran down Main Street and out Warm Springs Avenue to the Natatorium.

Today Old Boise remains a beautiful and vital district—a testimony to both the quality of the original construction and loving restoration efforts. Coffeehouses, restaurants, bars, art galleries, and shops hum with activity day and night in buildings that once housed the city's pioneer businesses and residents.

❰ The Basque Block

Basques began settling here in significant numbers in the late 1890s. Today, Boise's Basque population is the largest in the world outside the Basque region of Spain. Locals call the 600 block of Grove Street the "Basque Block." On the corner of Grove and 6th Streets is the **Basque Center,** built by Basques for Basques in 1952. The building serves as a center for Basque culture and a social center for older Basques who play cards and converse in their native tongue.

The **Basque Museum and Cultural Center** (611 Grove St., 208/343-2671, www.basquemuseum.com, 10 A.M.–4 P.M. Tues.–Fri., 11 A.M.–3 P.M. Sat., closed Sun. and holidays, $4 adults, $3 seniors, $2 ages 6–12, free under age 6) is two doors down, adjacent to the Cyrus Jacobs-Uberuaga House, Boise's oldest surviving brick building. The house was built in 1864 by Cyrus Jacobs, an early Boise

merchant who eventually became mayor, and later purchased by Jose Uberuaga, a Basque who turned the residence into a boardinghouse for Basque sheepherders. Famous Idaho statesman William Borah, a longtime friend to the Basques, was married here in 1895. The museum's exhibits, including musical instruments, crafts, and other items unique to the Basques, provide a historical overview of the Basque culture in their homeland and in the United States.

On the end of the block is **Bar Gernika,** one of Boise's classic pubs. It's a great place to get a taste of Basque cuisine and culture intertwined with a hip modern scene.

Linen District

Located in a former laundry district on the industrial fringe of downtown, the aptly named Linen District blends trendy with everyday useful. Mixed in with the carpet warehouses and industry supply stores are hip restaurants, bars, specialty shops, and the **Modern Hotel,** an ultracool boutique hotel. Bounded by Main and

© IDAHO DIVISION OF TOURISM

the Basque Block

EUSKERA IKAZI!

Euskera ikazi means "learn Basque" in the Basque language. If you spend much time in Boise, you'll be wanting to do just that. Idaho is home to about 12,000 Basque Americans; a large percentage of them live in Boise. A Basque bar, Basque restaurants, Basque dancers, and a Basque block add cultural spice to Idaho's capital city.

Euskadi, the Basque homeland, lies in northeastern Spain and southwestern France. The region straddles the Spanish-French border from around Bilbao in the west to Bayonne in the east. To the south, the Basque country spreads into the Pyrenees Mountains and the foothills on either side. The seven Basque provinces — four in Spain, three in France — are home to about 2.5 million Basques. Populations of emigrant Basques can be found throughout the world, with the largest concentrations being in North and South America and Australia. In the United States, most Basques live in the Western states of California, Nevada, Wyoming, Oregon, Utah, and Idaho.

The Basque language, Euskara, is unique. Hard as they try, linguists are unable to relate it to any other language in the world. As a result, some have suggested that the Basques might be the survivors of the lost continent of Atlantis, although a less fanciful theory holds that the Basques are a unique evolutionary branch that split off from the Cro-Magnon tree some 10,000 years ago.

Although Basque territory was invaded at different times by different groups, the Basque language and culture have survived intact, perhaps due to the Basques' noted courage and strength in defending their homeland. The *irrintzi,* a Basque war cry likened to an eerie cross between a wolf howl and a horse whinny, was reputedly enough to send all but their fiercest enemies running in the opposite direction.

Besides their skill at raising livestock and farming, Basques established a reputation early on as premier shipbuilders and mariners. As early as the 14th century, Basque fishermen and whalers pulled a harvest from the Bay of Biscay and crossed the Atlantic to pursue their catch off the Grand Banks; they probably landed on the coast of North America about a century before Columbus. A Basque named Lokotza was Columbus's navigator, while another named Elcano took over and completed Magellan's circumnavigation of the earth after Magellan died en route.

Basques first began coming to Boise soon after the city was founded; by 1910 the city's Basque population was sizable. In traditional Basque culture, only one child inherits all the family wealth. The others — drawn by stories of goldfield bonanzas and high wages — made their way to the western United States. Many found work as miners, others as ranch hands. A large number became sheepherders, though it wasn't their experience back home that got them that job. Some of them had never tended sheep before; others had run small herds in their homeland, but nothing the size of the operations common to Idaho and the West. But it was a job that they could get without needing to speak English and that few others were willing to take because of its solitary nature. The Basque shepherds quickly gained a reputation for hard work and reliability.

Basques eventually assimilated into American culture and today are found throughout Boise's establishment. Famous Basques in history include painter Francisco Goya (1746-1828); Simon Bolívar (1783-1830), the "George Washington of South America," who helped the countries of Venezuela, Colombia, Ecuador, Panama, Peru, and Bolivia win their independence from Spain; and legendary modern-day bicycle racer Miguel Indurain, five-time winner of the Tour de France.

In Boise today, you can taste Basque cuisine at **Gernika, Leku Ona,** and the **Basque Market;** see traditional Basque dances performed by the **Oinkari Basque Dancers;** and get an overview of the unique culture at the **Basque Museum and Cultural Center.** If you're in town for the annual **Festival of San Inazio** at the end of July, you can get a full-blown introduction to Basque life. And if that suits your fancy, make plans to attend the next **Jaialdi** in 2015 — it's an international Basque cultural festival organized by the Basque Museum (208/343-2671, www.jaialdi.com) held in Boise every five years.

Front Streets and 13th and 16th Streets, the focal point is along Grove Street, where you will find a great cup of joe and house-baked goodies at **Big City Coffee** and big burgers and a fun atmosphere at **Donnie Mac's Trailer Park Cuisine.**

◖ Idaho State Capitol

Just after the turn of the 20th century, prominent Boise architect J. E. Tourtelloutte was commissioned to draw up plans for the state capitol. He came up with a neoclassic design modeled after the U.S. Capitol, albeit on a smaller scale. Construction began in 1905 and was completed in 1920. It's the only capitol building in the country heated with geothermal hot water.

Outside, the building is a rather drab tan color thanks to the exterior use of Boise sandstone; multiton blocks were quarried behind the old Idaho State Penitentiary and hauled to the site by convicts. Inside, however, the impressive rotunda sports vast amounts of marble from Alaska (gray), Georgia (red), Vermont (green), and Italy (black). Sixty-foot-high faux-marble pillars support the dome, the very top of which is painted on the underside with 43 stars—Idaho was the 43rd state—against a blue background.

Around the four-story interior are changing exhibits put together by many state agencies and special-interest groups as well as several sculptures, mostly by Idahoans. A replica of the *Winged Victory of Samothrace,* a gift from the French following World War II, is prominently displayed just inside the main entrance. The first floor holds a portrait gallery of Idaho's territorial governors—beards were apparently in vogue back then—while the fourth floor displays tapestry murals depicting elements of the state's history and culture. Also on the fourth floor are the entrances to the House and Senate galleries, where you can watch Idaho's lawmakers in action when the legislature is in session. The second and third floors house the executive-branch offices and the legislative chambers, respectively.

Back outside, a circuit of the grounds reveals some interesting finds. Across Jefferson Street stands a bronze statue of former governor Frank Steunenberg, assassinated in 1905, supposedly in retaliation for his use of federal troops to squelch the Silver Valley mining riots some six years earlier. On the front steps of the capitol is a replica of the Liberty Bell, sans crack, while to the west is a seacoast cannon of the type used by the Confederacy in the Civil War. Legend has it that before the state plugged the cannon with concrete, some enterprising Boise youths actually managed to pack it with shot and gunpowder and set it off, blowing out all the windows in the building across the street.

The capitol is open for self-guided tours 6 A.M.–6 P.M. Mon.–Fri., 9 A.M.–5 P.M. weekends. A free walking-tour booklet is available at the visitor information desk on the first floor. One-hour guided tours (208/332-1012, 10 A.M.–1 P.M. Mon.–Fri., minimum 10 people, maximum 100 people, reserve at least two weeks in advance) are also available.

Around the Capitol

If you're done touring the capitol but aren't ready to get back in the Buick, take a walk around the neighborhood, past the expansive, freshly mowed lawns and large mostly government buildings in the vicinity.

The namesake of the 1897 **Moses Alexander House** (304 W. State St.) served as mayor of Boise and governor of Idaho; he was the nation's first Jewish governor. The state renovated the beautiful Queen Anne in 2001, and plans are to turn it into a museum of the state's governors.

The **Idaho Supreme Court Building** (451 W. State St.) features opulent touches such as travertine-limestone walls and granite-chip floors, which made it an expensive project. Critics of such extravagance refer to the building as the "Palace of Justice."

It's hard to miss the **Joe R. Williams Office Building** (700 W. State St.): Its mirrored glass windows reflect the capitol dome, creating a perfect photo opportunity. Inside is the Idaho Department of Commerce, where you can pick up visitor information on all parts of the state.

EXTREME CAPITOL MAKEOVER

In 2010, a major capitol restoration project was completed at the cost of $120 million to state taxpayers. Besides extensive renovation to the original exterior, the interior was given lots of love, including refinished marble and wood flooring, upgraded lighting, hardware restoration, and the addition of a new passenger elevator. Speaking of elevators, construction workers found a nice surprise when they tore down a wall-sized bookcase on the first floor, unveiling a beautifully preserved electric elevator from the early 20th century. The shaft was plugged long ago, but the birdcage-like elevator is now part of the capitol tour.

There was much more than restoration going on while the building was closed to the general public for two years. The project also included the construction of two 25,000-square-foot underground wings. These subterranean structures (barely visible from the street) are used for additional legislative offices and hearing rooms. The only downside to the construction was that eleven century-old trees had to be cut down to make way for the digging. Unfortunately, these included an oak tree planted by Benjamin Harrison and an Ohio buckeye planted by William Taft.

A creative caveat to this tree felling is that more than 4,000 board feet of wood was made available to local artists for various projects. Idaho State Rep. Max Black, an ardent woodworker and Republican lawmaker who spear-

Idaho State Capitol after major renovation

headed the drive, carved out a wooden replica of an Oregon Short Line steam engine, now exhibited in the Statuary Hall on the fourth floor. A permanent Idaho history exhibit was also installed four flights down the marble steps on the garden level.

Continuing west on State Street, the tiny 1892 **GAR Hall** (714 W. State St.) once held meetings of the Grand Army of the Republic—the bluecoat veterans of the Civil War.

Capital City Public Market

Eighth Street in downtown Boise explodes in a flourish of color every Saturday April–October. The Capital City Public Market (www.capitalcitypublicmarket.com, 9:30 A.M.–1:30 P.M.) is the state's largest Saturday market. Here you will be able to score fresh organic produce, farm-fresh duck

eggs, local farmstead cheese, and prepared goodies such as crepes and flaky breakfast pastries. There is also a plethora of nonfood artisans selling handcrafted soap, photography, pottery, jewelry, and fused-glass art. The Market, as locals call it, also sets up 4:30–8:30 P.M. Thursday May–September on a smaller scale in the same location.

NORTH END AND HYDE PARK

Some of Boise's most appealing architecture is found in the city's quiet North End, between State Street and the foothills. The

© DANA HOPPER-KELLY

The Capital City Public Market flourishes on Saturdays.

tree-canopied streets are lined with Victorian beauties and craftsman-era bungalows.

Bounded by 8th and 14th Streets and Hays and State Streets, numerous churches vie with one another for eye appeal. Seemingly around every corner a different spire draws the eye toward heaven, and nearly every one is a uniquely beautiful work of art. The ivy-covered sandstone walls of English Gothic **St. Michael's Episcopal Cathedral** (518 N. 8th St. at W. State St.) draw a congregation that was first organized in 1864, just after the city itself was established.

Within the beautiful redbrick arches of **First United Presbyterian Church** (10th St. and State St.) are the original church furnishings brought to the city by covered wagon in 1878. **Congregation Beth Israel Synagogue,** among the West's oldest, was recently moved from 11th and State Streets to Latah Street near Morris Hill Cemetery, southwest of downtown. The red and white **First Baptist Church** (13th St. and W. Washington St.) is a relative newcomer;

services began in 1948, but the steeple wasn't erected until 1960.

The magnificent **First United Methodist Church** (11th St. and W. Franklin St.) is called the "Cathedral of the Rockies." The modern Gothic steeple and its ornate stonework can be seen from some distance in all directions, and it's an impressive edifice from any angle. Across 11th Street, the **Bush Mansion** (1020 W. Franklin St.) was built for James Bush, a Boise hotelier and businessman. When it was built in 1892 it was considered one of Idaho's finest homes. The price tag? A whopping $6,000.

Continuing east, you'll see the octagonal dome of **Central Christian Church** (9th St. and W. Washington St.), dating from 1910; heading north and east from there you'll come to **St. John's Catholic Cathedral** (804 N. 8th St.). Built in 1921, it's the spiritual center for Boise's Basque population. The interior of the sandstone cathedral features vaulted ceilings, marble floors, and beautiful stained-glass windows. Behind the cathedral, a 1905

Tudor house now serves as the church rectory. Finally, around the corner to the northeast is the Immanuel Evangelical Lutheran Church, most of which consists of a relatively modern and unremarkable brick edifice. But next to it is the church's handsome **Augustana Chapel** (701 Fort St.), an old stone-and-shake affair dating from 1906.

Boise's coolest "neighborhood," **Hyde Park,** lies farther north, up 13th Street—a nice long walk from downtown, or you can hop a bus (Rte. 14). Hyde Park simply exudes charm. Its main drag—North 13th Street between Alturas and Brumback Streets—is just about two blocks long, but it is home to a concentration of interesting restaurants, coffeehouses, and antiques shops.

JULIA DAVIS PARK AND VICINITY

Thomas Jefferson Davis was one of Boise's earliest pioneer settlers. He and his brother homesteaded 360 acres here in 1863, raising vegetables that they sold to the Boise Basin mining communities. On July 7, 1863, Davis and a handful of men got together in Davis's log cabin to lay out the city of Boise. In 1871, Davis married Julia McCrum of Ontario, Canada. The new couple's agricultural empire grew over the years, and they continued to add to their real estate holdings in the valley. In their retirement they offered the city about 40 acres along the river for a park. It took a while to settle the arrangements, but in 1907 Julia Davis Park (700 S. Capitol Blvd.) became a reality. Julia died shortly thereafter; Tom died the following year. Their simple graves can be seen in Pioneer Cemetery along Warm Springs Avenue. Today, the park is the queen of Boise's park system, home to many of the city's major attractions and plenty of open space. Plus, the park has the most beautiful rose garden in town, hands-down.

Boise Art Museum

Beautiful inside and out, the Boise Art Museum (670 S. Julia Davis Dr., 208/345-8330, www.boiseartmuseum.org, 10 A.M.–5 P.M. Tues.–Sat., noon–5 P.M. Sun., closed Mon. and holidays, $5 adults, $3 seniors and college students with ID, $1 children grades 1–12, free to BAM members and under age 6) is growing in reputation with each passing exhibit. Major traveling exhibitions have been shown here over the years, including sculptures by Edward Degas, landscape paintings by Georgia O'Keeffe, and blown-glass art by Dale Chihuly. Its permanent collection includes the Glenn C. Janss collection of American realism, featuring some absolutely amazing photorealist works. A small store sells arts and crafts, art-related books, and art postcards. In addition to providing Boiseans a visual feast, the museum also hosts events year-round, plus the big Art in the Park festival each September.

Idaho Historical Museum

Stories of Idaho's people and progress since ancient times are illuminated in grand style at the Idaho Historical Museum (610 N. Julia Davis Dr., 208/334-2120, www.idahohistory.net, 9 A.M.–5 P.M. Tues.–Sat., 1–5 P.M. Sun., $5 adults, $4 seniors, $3 ages 6–12 and students with ID, free under age 6), also in Julia Davis Park. Artifacts illustrate the lives of Idaho's indigenous people as well as the fur traders, prospectors, and pioneer settlers who later claimed the land. The exhibits will give you a better understanding of the state's ethnic diversity, particularly of the Native American, Basque, and Chinese cultures still glimpsed today throughout the state. Outside the museum in the Pioneer Village are some of the earliest structures built in Boise. The Coston and Pearce cabins were built in 1863, the year of the city's founding. The Mayor Logan Adobe was built in 1865 for Boise's four-term mayor, Thomas E. Logan.

Zoo Boise

Zoo Boise (355 N. Julia Davis Dr., 208/384-4260, www.zooboise.org, 9 A.M.–7 P.M. Mon.–Tues., 9 A.M.–5 P.M. Wed.–Sun. May–Aug., 10 A.M.–5 P.M. daily Sept.–Apr., $6.50 ages 12–61, $4 over age 62, $3.75 ages 4–11, free under age 3) is no threat to the preeminence of the San Diego Zoo, but if you enjoy zoos, it's worth a stop. The more than 80 species include Amur tigers, penguins, zebras, giraffes, meerkats, and birds of prey. The zoo is open year-round but many of the larger animals are moved inside and not available for viewing. But the steamy indoor rain forest exhibit is not a bad place to hang out on a frigid day.

Discovery Center of Idaho

On the park's northern fringe is the Discovery Center of Idaho (131 Myrtle St., 208/343-9895, www.sciidaho.org, 9 A.M.–5 P.M. Mon.–Thurs., 9 A.M.–7 P.M. Fri., 10 A.M.–5 P.M. Sat., noon–5 P.M. Sun., closed Mon. winter, $6.50 adults, $5.50 seniors, $4 ages 3–17, free for members and under age 2). More than 100 wild, wacky, and amazing hands-on exhibits—a spelling robot, an air-brake chair, and a seven-foot tornado, to name just a few—fill this huge, mad-scientist-in-training's classroom. Sound, light, fluids, electricity—who needs a stuffy old book to learn about these things when you can come here and experience the phun of physics phirsthand. Kids love this place, and it's popular with adults too.

WARM SPRINGS AVENUE

This was one of early Boise's most prestigious addresses, and home after stately turn-of-the-20th-century home can be seen as you cruise down the shady tree-lined avenue. The street didn't get its name for nothing: Boise's abundant geothermal resources were developed early in the city's history. Today, many of the homes here continue to be heated with naturally hot water, as is the state capitol.

Pioneer Cemetery

Boise founders Julia Davis and Thomas Jefferson Davis, early Idaho governor George Shoup, and pioneer notables and nobodies alike share this final resting place near the intersection of Warm Springs and Broadway Avenues. The simple, poignant graves remain unadulterated by modern historical plaques or keep-away-from-the-history barriers. It's a nice spot for a picnic amid the ghosts of Boise's forefathers and foremothers.

【 MK Nature Center

Squirrels chatter in the trees, rainbow trout cruise sheltered pools, birds practice avian arias, and brightly colored flowers face the sun

© DANA HOPPER-KELLY

The MK Nature Center offers a fish's-eye view.

to shout off the morning dew. It's all at the MK Nature Center (600 S. Walnut St., 208/334-2225 or 208/368-6060, trails sunrise–sunset, free; visitors center 9 A.M.–5 P.M. Tues.–Fri., 11 A.M.–5 P.M. Sat.–Sun., free)—a miniature 4.6-acre wildlife preserve and botanical garden a couple of blocks south of Warm Springs Avenue. Trails lead past a rushing stream and a tranquil glade to unique exhibits like the fluvarium—a cutaway glass-walled stream where you can watch many of Idaho's native fish species cavorting in their underwater realm. The visitors center holds additional exhibits and a gift shop.

Natatorium and Hydro Tube

Well, it used to be a natatorium (indoor pool), and a fancy one at that. The big, elaborate building, built in 1892, had removable flooring over the pool, and dances and social functions were often held there. In 1934 a massive storm blew it apart, and now it's an outdoor pool (1811 Warm Springs Ave., 208/345-9270, 1:30–5:30 P.M. and 7–9 P.M. Mon.–Sat., 1:30–5:30 P.M. Sun. summer, pool $3.50 adults, $2.50 ages 12–18, $2 under age 12, free for seniors). The hydro tube, a waterslide popular with kids of all ages, costs $8 for an all-day pass, or you can get a book of 10 tickets for $6.

◖ Old Idaho Penitentiary

The Old Pen (2445 Old Penitentiary Rd., 208/334-2844, 10 A.M.–5 P.M. daily summer, noon–5 P.M. daily fall–spring, $5 adults, $4 seniors, $3 ages 6–12, free under age 6) is one of only four U.S. territorial prisons still standing. It was built in 1870 and remained in use for more than a century. Among its famous tenants: Harry Orchard, convicted for the 1905 assassination of Governor Frank Steunenberg; and Lyda "Lady Bluebeard" Southard, convicted of killing her fourth husband for insurance money and suspected of doing away with the first three as well.

It's hard to imagine that a 19th-century cellblock with no internal plumbing ("night buckets" were used) served inmates until the 1970s.

Not surprisingly, the antiquated conditions led to a riot in 1973 that resulted in the gutting of a couple of buildings. That event helped convince the powers that be to move the prison to a new facility more appropriate to the 20th century. Now you can tour this State Historic Site, pondering Sartre in "Siberia" (solitary confinement) and smelling the roses in the prison rose garden, where the original prison gallows once sent unfortunate convicts to their final resting place. The self-guided walking tour takes approximately 90 minutes. This prison is certainly more interesting architecturally than its famous cousin, Alcatraz. While the latter resembles nothing so much as a WPA project gone to seed, the Old Pen looks like something from another time—part Wild West hang-'em-high hoosegow, part medieval castle.

In 2002, the Old Pen added the J. Curtis Earl Memorial Exhibit, featuring 5,000 years of arms and weaponry. The artifacts, dating as far back as 3500 B.C., were accumulated over some 60 years by the late J. Curtis Earl, a part-time Boise resident. You'll see daggers and arrow points from the Bronze Age, medieval arms and armor, Civil War artifacts, and an 1883 Gatling gun on its original carriage. Admission is included in the Old Pen entry price.

Idaho Botanical Garden

Adjacent to the Old Pen you'll find the Idaho Botanical Garden (2355 Old Penitentiary Rd., 208/343-8649, www.idahobotanicalgarden.org, 9 A.M.–5 P.M. Mon.–Fri., 10 A.M.–6 P.M. Sat.–Sun. Mar. 16–Nov. 15, 9 A.M.–5 P.M. Mon.–Fri. Nov. 16–Mar. 15, $4 adults, $3 seniors, $2 ages 6–12, free under age 5). One species or another will be in bloom late April–mid-October. A humble labor of love relying heavily on memberships and volunteer efforts, the gardens provide an always-welcome oasis of tranquil greenery. Various trails snake around the grounds, with picnic tables and benches placed strategically. The Idaho Botanical Garden has turned into a popular summer concert venue in recent years, booking big-name acts like Willie Nelson and Bob Dylan.

And during the holiday season, Winter Garden aGlow beautifully illuminates the desert.

BOISE STATE UNIVERSITY

More than 20,000 students pursue undergraduate and graduate degrees at the 153-acre Boise State University (BSU, 208/426-1011, www. boisestate.edu) campus lining the Boise River, making BSU the state's largest-enrollment university and one of the West's fastest-growing schools. It's also a hub of activity for students and city residents.

Campus Highlights

On the west end of campus along the river is **Morrison Center for the Performing Arts** (tickets 208/426-1609 or 208/426-1110). Considered one of the country's most acoustically perfect performance halls, the award-winning Morrison Center hosts musical and cultural events year-round. Tours of the 2,000-seat facility are offered by advance arrangement.

The **Hemingway Western Studies Center** (208/426-1999) focuses on the works and study of Western writers and other artists. The center also holds Hemingway memorabilia, including pictures of Papa's Ketchum home and a magazine article reprinting a letter Hemingway wrote to his editor grousing about young wannabe writers dropping by uninvited and interrupting his work. It also houses the **Idaho Film Collection,** an archive of films made in the Gem State that includes the complete works of silent filmmaker Nell Shipman. A small art gallery (10 A.M.–5 P.M. Mon.–Fri., noon–5 P.M. Sat., free) presents student projects and exhibits related to the West.

Centennial Amphitheater is a delightful open and grassy 800-seat amphitheater within earshot of the Boise River. If you brought a sack lunch with you, this would be a great spot to stop and devour it. The adjacent road heading away from the river into the heart of campus leads to the huge orange-sided **Taco Bell Arena** (tickets 208/426-1494, www.broncosports.com) which students humorously refer to as "Taco Ballerina." A variety of events—from

BSU Broncos basketball games to national touring concerts—are staged in this 13,000-seat arena.

Looking east from the arena, you can't miss **Bronco Stadium** (tickets 208/426-1494, www. broncosports.com) on the east edge of campus. For better or worse, this 33,500-seat stadium is known throughout the country not only as the home of the BSU Broncos football team but for its bright blue artificial turf, affectionately known as "Smurf Turf." Thanks to the incredible success of the university's football team, the stadium recently underwent a major expansion project—adding glitzy skyboxes, more season ticket seating, a 97,000-square-foot indoor practice facility, and a **Bronco Shop** (208/426-4887), a ground-level store with shelves full of blue-and-orange BSU gear. Also on the ground level of the stadium is the **World Sports Humanitarian Hall of Fame** (208/343-7224, www.sportshumanitarian. com, 9 A.M.–5 P.M. Mon.–Fri. or by appointment, donation). This unusual museum honors the efforts of "those who go beyond the game." Founded in 1994, the Hall of Fame showcases such benevolent sports stars as Arthur Ashe, Roberto Clemente, Mary Lou Retton, and the Harlem Globetrotters. Two or three newcomers are inducted each year. The Hall of Fame is affiliated with Boise's annual post-Christmas Humanitarian Bowl football game.

The newly remodeled and expanded **Student Union Building,** the on-campus social hub, contains the university bookstore (208/426-2665), an art gallery, food courts, pool tables, and even a small bowling alley. Adjacent is the **Special Events Center,** a theater used for seminars and performances, and across the parking lot on the first floor of the Liberal Arts Building is the **Visual Arts Center Gallery** (daily during the school year, free).

In 2002, BSU opened its brand-new 86,000-square-foot recreation center (1515 University Dr., 208/426-5641). Unfortunately, most of it is only open to Boise State students, employees, and alumni—though there are exceptions, like the climbing wall and the outdoor program's equipment rental center.

Tours and Information

Tours leave the New Student Information Center (208/426-1820) in the Student Union Building at 10 A.M. and 1 P.M. Monday–Friday during the school year. The center can also provide campus maps and further information about the university.

Parking

Metered parking is available all around campus, and pay parking is available for visitors in front of the Administration Building (Joyce St. and University Dr.) and in two newly constructed parking garages (University Dr. and Lincoln Ave.; University Dr. near Capitol Blvd.). For more information, call the **Parking Office** (208/426-7275). The BSU campus is a short walk from downtown, and the city transit system operates a shuttle bus around campus.

EAST BOISE

East of the university, ParkCenter Boulevard runs close to the Boise River Greenbelt. Here you will see the headquarters of two corporations that helped to define Boise's reputation in the business world: URS Corporation (formerly Morrison-Knudsen) and the Albertsons grocery chain. Near these corporate campuses there are several restaurants, hotels, and other businesses, as well as the **ParkCenter Pond,** a popular urban fishing hole consistently stocked with rainbow trout.

Bown Crossing

Travel southeast on ParkCenter Boulevard and you will eventually come to Bown Crossing, a startup district that places an emphasis on pedestrian traffic. This new 35-acre development has nearly 100 residences—craftsman patio homes, townhouses, and apartment lofts—amalgamated with fun restaurants, boutiques, and specialty shops.

Satiate your sweet tooth at **Powell's Sweet Shoppe,** an old-time candy store. Feed your shoe fetish at **Bown Shoes,** which sells some of the hippest footwear in town. Eat local at **Locavore** or grab a burger and an ale at the **Tavern at Bown Crossing.**

Leaving Bown Crossing, cruising north, you cross over the Boise River on the new

Bown Crossing favors pedestrian traffic.

© DANA HOPPER-KELLY

ParkCenter Bridge. Immediately on the right is **Marianne Williams Park,** a new public green space that debuted in 2011.

Harris Ranch

Heading north on East ParkCenter Boulevard, you will soon come to the newish Harris Ranch neighborhood (on E. Warm Springs Blvd.), where upscale homes have replaced a sprawling cattle ranch that once dominated Barber Valley. Besides lots of upscale houses, Harris Ranch also has a small strip with coffeehouses, retail shops, and one extremely popular local restaurant, **Lucky 13,** a venerable pizza and sandwich joint that recently relocated here from Hyde Park.

Hang a right (east) on Warm Springs Avenue and it will lead you past the **Idaho Parks and Recreation Department** (5657 Warm Springs Ave., 208/334-4199) and the **Idaho Shakespeare Festival** en route to Highway 21.

OTHER SIGHTS

Idaho Anne Frank Human Rights Memorial

In 2002, Idaho dedicated this moving tribute to the teenage author whose family hid from the Nazis during World War II. A statue of Anne Frank is next to the United Nations Universal Declaration of Human Rights and powerful quotes from human rights advocates through history. A series of educational voice boxes were recently installed that can be heard in English and Spanish. The monument is accessible from the Greenbelt between Capitol Boulevard and 9th Street, or by walking behind The Cabin Literary Center (801 S. Capitol Blvd.).

Boise Depot and Platt Gardens

The city of Boise owns the beautiful old Union Pacific Depot (2603 Eastover Terr., 208/384-9591, 12:30–8 P.M. Mon., 10 A.M.–6 P.M. Sun. June–Sept., free) perched on a bench at the south end of Capitol Boulevard. The Amtrak route that once stopped here was abandoned in 1997. The depot's Great Hall holds railroad memorabilia. Climb up into the bell tower for a great view of the capitol and downtown.

© DANA HOPPER-KELLY

Take a minute for reflection at the Anne Frank Human Rights Memorial.

Outside the depot you'll see "Big Mike," a Japanese-made steam engine from the early 20th century, as well as Platt Gardens, a small landscaped hillside with fountains, koi ponds, and trees.

Peregrine Fund World Center for Birds of Prey

The World Center for Birds of Prey (5668 W. Flying Hawk Lane, 208/362-3716, www.peregrinefund.org) lies six miles south of I-84 (take S. Cole Rd. south to the end and continue straight ahead a bit further; look for the sign on the right). It's on a hilltop only 15 minutes from the city but a world away—worth the trip just to experience the wind blowing across the sage and grasses, unimpeded by gas stations and shopping malls.

The Peregrine Fund started in 1970 from efforts to save the peregrine falcon, whose populations were on the decline before this nonprofit organization decided to step in. The peregrine was removed from the endangered species list in 1999. The Peregrine Fund continues its work to restore viable populations of other endangered raptors worldwide.

The **Velma Morrison Interpretive Center** (9 A.M.–5 P.M. daily Mar.–Oct., 10 A.M.–4 P.M. Tues.–Sun. Nov.–Feb., $7 adults, $6 seniors, $5 ages 4–16, free under age 4) has slide presentations to fill you in on the status of endangered raptors worldwide as well as the fund's efforts to preserve them. You'll see a couple of individuals up close and personal, perhaps a harpy eagle headed for the jungles of South and Central America, or a huge California condor. Outside are several birds of prey species, all incapable of surviving life in the wild for one reason or another.

SCENIC DRIVES

Boise is such a great outdoors city, it'd be a shame not to get out of your car and take advantage of it. But it's possible to get a flavor of the city from behind the windshield. Drive up to **Table Rock,** on the northeast edge of town, for an aerial view. More like a table mountain than a rock, this natural feature can be seen from many parts of Boise. To get there, take Reserve Road northeast from Fort Street, turn right on Shaw Mountain Road, and follow it up the hill. At the top of the hill, bear right onto Table Rock Road when the road forks. Continue past the end of the pavement about 0.5 miles to the top. The road is a little bumpy but passable in the family sedan.

A couple of Boise's original avenues show off the trees that gave the city its nickname and also provide a glimpse of some fine old homes. **Warm Springs Avenue** is the commonly cited example—you drive down it on the way to the Old Pen and Botanical Garden. Perhaps even more beautiful than Warm Springs, thanks to a

wide green median divider planted with shade trees, is **Harrison Boulevard,** which leads out to Bogus Basin Road. The quiet residential streets on either side of Harrison hold many tidy, well-cared-for old homes. Another good view of the city can be had from **Crescent Rim Drive,** which curves along the lip of the Boise Bench above Ann Morrison Park. From here the park and the city spread out before you, and behind them the hills and mountains of the Boise Front rise steeply. The snow-covered peaks up at Bogus Basin provide the icing on the cake in winter.

SIGHTSEEING TOURS

Boise Trolley Tours

Boise Trolley Tours (602 Julia Davis Dr., 208/433-0849, www.boisetrolleytours.com, 11 A.M. and 1 P.M. daily, $18 adults, $16 seniors and ages 13–18, $8 ages 3–12, $4 under age 3) provides a reasonable way to get an overview and background on some of the key parts of the city. It's not actually a trolley on tracks but a bus that's gussied up to look like a trolley. It'll take you around Boise for a one-hour narrated tour, introducing you to Julia Davis Park, the historic Warm Springs neighborhood, the Old Idaho Penitentiary, the capitol area, and the Old Boise Historic District. An informative narration reels off the history and fun facts of the city. You'll find the little depot where tickets are sold just east of the Idaho Historical Museum.

Flightseeing

SP Aircraft (3815 Rickenbacker St., 208/383-3323), a scenic and charter air service based near the airport, will take passengers up in a Cessna 172 on a one-hour air tour for $255 per hour (up to three people).

Sports and Recreation

This is an outdoors-oriented town. As soon as the spring rains end, Boise's hills come alive with a profusion of wildflowers and the sounds of ratcheting derailleurs. Mountain bikers are everywhere—up on the Boise Front, along the Greenbelt, in the streets downtown. Warm spring and summer evenings find the streets crowded with walkers and joggers, getting after-work exercise or just enjoying the City of Trees. And come the dog days of summer, the Boise River and local reservoirs draw water-sports enthusiasts by the thousands. You can float the Boise right through downtown, past park after verdant park. Or go white-water rafting on the Payette River less than an hour outside town. When winter snows blanket the Boise Mountains, the skis come out of the closets, bound for Bogus Basin Ski Area. Both alpine and cross-country skiing there is close enough to get to after work or even on a long lunch hour.

CITY PARKS

No matter which part of town you're in, you'll almost certainly be near one of the more than 90 parks maintained by the City of Boise. The parks range in size from the grand Julia Davis and Ann Morrison Parks to smaller pocket parks dotting the city. Several of the most popular parks are described below. For a complete list of parks and their respective facilities, contact the Boise Parks and Recreation Department (1104 Royal Blvd., 208/384-4240, www.cityofboise.org/parks).

All city parks are open sunrise–sunset. Dogs must be kept on a leash and are not allowed at Municipal Park off Warm Springs Avenue or at Platt Gardens adjacent to the Boise Depot. (Dogs can play off-leash in a designated dog park at Fort Boise Park, as long as they're under your control.) Beer and wine are permitted at most of the parks, except where expressly prohibited. (Hard alcohol and glass containers are not permitted.) The Parks Department asks that you not feed the waterfowl or any other wildlife you might encounter.

(Boise River Greenbelt

The beautiful, modestly sized Boise River flows through the heart of the city. Its lushly

© DANA HOPPER-KELLY

The Greenbelt is Boise's beating heart of recreation.

lined banks have been preserved as the city's signature park, the 25-mile Boise River Greenbelt that connects 850 acres of parks and riparian wetlands. Here you will find paved trails on either side of the river that wind along the banks, drawing strollers, bicyclists, joggers, and skaters. Several small piers jut out into the river in places, some half hidden by luxuriant greenery, while benches overlooking the water provide ideal places for quiet contemplation.

Wildlife also enjoys this riparian oasis. You'll see abundant waterfowl, and if you get lucky, you might spy bald eagles, blue herons, great horned owls, muskrat, beavers, deer, or foxes. At some points along the trails, the downtown skyline comes into view, reminding you just how close this tranquil escape is to the urban core. The Greenbelt runs from Garden City in the west (with plans to expand onto Eagle Island) to the Discovery Unit of Lucky Peak State Park in the east. Other major access points include Veterans Memorial Park, Ann Morrison Park (enter from Americana Blvd.), and Julia Davis Park, off Capitol Avenue. But head down to the river anywhere in town and you should be able to find the Greenbelt trails with no difficulty.

Ann Morrison Park, lining the south side of the Boise River

© DANA HOPPER-KELLY

Ann Morrison Park

This 153-acre spread lines the south side of the Boise River between Americana and Capitol Boulevards. It's mostly level and grassy, suitable for kite-flying and pickup soccer games. There's also an 18-hole disc-golf course, plus nice picnic areas and a big playground. Tubers generally haul out here after floating down from Barber Park.

Julia Davis Park

This is the "sights" park, home of Zoo Boise, the Boise Art Museum, Idaho Historical Museum, Idaho Black History Museum, a rose garden, and a band shell. The tennis courts here see a lot of use, as do the pedal boats you can rent for a cruise around the park's pond. The park is bounded by Capitol Avenue on the west, Front Street on the north, Broadway

Avenue on the east, and the Boise River on the south.

Kathryn Albertson Park

You can't miss the entrance sign for this tranquil, 40-acre wildlife preserve just across Americana Boulevard from Ann Morrison Park; its name is chiseled into 11 huge sandstone boulders that look like something out of *The Flintstones* or *Jurassic Park*. Paved trails wind around ponds, where many species of birds and other animals can be seen. The park was specifically designed to encourage wildlife—if you're quiet and lucky, you might find yourself within mere feet of a great blue heron or other waterfowl. This park is a great spot for quiet meditation, a relaxing picnic, or an outdoor wedding. Swimming and fishing are prohibited, and dogs must be kept on a leash.

Marianne Williams Park

The newest in the string of Boise's female-named parks, fondly referred to as the "Ribbon of Jewels," this 70-acre spread is scheduled to open in 2011 near Harris Ranch on East ParkCenter Boulevard. Prominent Boise businessman Larry Williams, who once operated a lumber mill on the site, donated the property to the city; the park is named after his wife, Marianne. Expect to find lots of green space, paved walkways, picnic areas, and a fishing dock. As an added bonus, the Greenbelt runs right through it.

Camel's Back Park and Reserve

North of Hyde Park out along 13th Street, Camel's Back Park has two components. The corner lot at 13th and Heron offers an expanse of green grass with a soccer field, tennis courts, trees, and a large children's play area with some neat equipment. Behind this area is the camel's back itself—a couple of humps of hills rising up about 100 feet. Hike up to the top for a great view of the city; this is a popular place to watch fireworks. On the other side of the humps, trails continue down to the 8th Street trailhead.

Fort Boise Park and Military Reserve Park

Fort Boise was built in 1863 as a base from which the U.S. 9th Cavalry could protect Oregon Trail emigrants from attack by hostile Native Americans. The guardhouse at 5th and Fort Streets is the original sandstone structure. In addition to the many original buildings, a number of newer government buildings have been added, including Veterans' Hospital and the Idaho Veterans' Home. This is also the hub of Boise Parks and Recreation activities. The **Fort Boise Community Center** (700 Robbins Rd., 208/384-4486) houses the city recreation office, a community weight room and gym, an art center, and lots more. Fort Boise Park also has a skate park, tennis courts, and ball fields. The Boise Little Theater (100 E. Fort St., 208/342-5104) is here too.

Military Reserve Park encompasses 466 acres of brush-covered foothills behind Fort Boise Park. Only a few dirt roads cross the park, but dozens of hiking and biking trails lace the hills. It's a quick-access wild area just

three blocks from the city. Sagebrush scents and some great city views make the park a good place for a day hike, a trail run, or quality time with Fido, who can run off-leash.

ParkCenter Pond

This eight-acre pond amid the hotels and offices of ParkCenter is a favorite spot for float-tube fishing and windsurfing. Sand volleyball courts and picnic tables round out the offerings.

Municipal Park

Your basic picnic venue, Muni Park has large grassy areas that make it a natural for family reunions or employee get-togethers. But anyone can enjoy the shade and tranquility. Off Warm Springs Avenue, it's near the MK Nature Center.

Veterans Memorial Park

As schizophrenic a park as ever there was, the front half of Veterans Memorial Park (36th St. and State St., west of town, sunrise–sunset) has neatly trimmed lawns, stately evergreens, a small amphitheater, and a solemn memorial to Idaho's fallen veterans. But head down to the back half and the park turns wild: The river flows through it, bringing swamps and riverine jungles that attract would-be Huck Finns with fishing poles as well as bicyclists and joggers who work up a sweat doing laps on the cool, quiet trails. A large lake separated from the river by a narrow isthmus provides calm water for swimming or floating around on a raft.

COUNTY AND STATE PARKS

Barber Park

East of town, 87-acre Barber Park (Eckert Rd., off Warm Springs Ave., 208/343-1328) draws tubers in summer for the six-mile float down the Boise River to Ann Morrison Park. You can rent tubes and rafts (208/577-4584) in the summertime. In addition, the park offers fishing access, trees and grass, and shaded picnic areas. A $5 parking fee is charged in the summer floating season to offset the cost of keeping this tidy, well-maintained Ada County park in such good shape. The park is on the Greenbelt bike path and makes a nice destination for a half-day bike ride out from downtown.

Lucky Peak State Park

Lucky Peak Reservoir, about a 15-minute drive east of downtown, is Boise's premier place to escape the heat of summer. Lucky Peak State Park (208/334-4199, day-use only, Memorial Day–Labor Day) comprises three different units, one on the reservoir and two downstream from Lucky Peak Dam.

Coming from downtown Boise, take Warm Springs Avenue east. Eventually it turns into Highway 21. The first part of the park, about eight miles from town, is the **Discovery Unit** (day-use $5). The beautiful grassy park along the riverbank offers plenty of sun and shade, picnic tables, and some barbecue grills. No lifeguards are on duty, and some tricky currents in places make swimming potentially dangerous and certainly not recommended for small children.

Take the kids instead a bit farther upstream to the 25-acre **Sandy Point Unit** (208/334-2679, 7 A.M.–9 P.M. daily summer, lifeguards on duty 11 A.M.–6 P.M. daily summer, day-

use $5), right below the dam. A calm cove here surrounds a fountain and makes a great place to float around on tubes or rafts, both of which can be rented from the concessionaire. Sunburning on the beaches is the most popular summer activity, but you'll also find abundant grass for Frisbees or Hacky Sacks. A snack bar means you can leave the picnic basket at home if you want, but picnickers will find plenty of tables to further their experiments in ant- and yellow jacket–attraction techniques. Don't bring Spot—no pets are allowed, and fishing is also prohibited.

You may find it a little disconcerting to be loafing in the sun right below a dam that is holding back several gazillion gallons of water, but if you set up your lawn chair facing downstream, this won't bother you at all.

Finally, the **Spring Shores Unit** (day-use $5) is nine miles farther up the highway toward Idaho City on Lucky Peak Reservoir. The road curves over Highland Pass, past hillsides blanketed with arrowleaf balsamroot—brilliantly yellow in spring—and then drops down to the reservoir (turn right off the highway just across Mores Creek Bridge). This is the boaters' unit of the park—water-skiers, Jet Skiers, bass

© IDAHO DIVISION OF TOURISM

Sandy Point swimming area at Lucky Peak State Park

boaters, sailboarders, and even a few sailboaters come here to do their thing in the high-desert lake rimmed by mountains. Anglers try their luck at pulling trout, smallmouth bass, kokanee, perch, and whitefish from the glimmering waters. The large **marina** (208/336-9505) offers numerous slips and a boat-launching ramp. The concessionaire also runs a small grill (burgers and such), sells boating supplies, and rents multipassenger personal watercraft ("spud tubs"). A few picnic tables line the shore.

BICYCLING

Boise is a great bicycling town. In addition to the **Greenbelt,** the "Ridge to Rivers" trail system (www.ridgetorivers.org) provides for on-road and off-road cyclists alike and continues to expand under municipal planning efforts. Boise also has plenty of bike lanes to offer cyclists an added margin of safety and comfort by keeping them a little farther away from traffic.

Mountain biking claims a big niche, and no wonder. Just north of the city lies the **Boise Front,** a vast tract of foothill wilderness— part Bureau of Land Management, part Forest Service land—laced with both primitive roads and single-track trails. You can ride right from downtown and in minutes be out in the sage and rabbitbrush with no other sound than the wind whistling through your ears. This is an immensely popular after-work and weekend destination for Boiseans, and the heavy use is beginning to result in some erosion problems in the area's fragile soil. With the increased bike traffic, collisions at blind corners are not unheard of; ride responsibly.

To get there from downtown, head north on 8th Street and just keep going. Other access points in the same general area include Crestline Road (off Brumback St.) and Bogus Basin Road, just past the Highlands Hollow brewpub. A little farther south, Military Reserve Park, Rocky Canyon Road (at the end of Shaw Mountain Rd.), and Table Rock Road are other gateways to the Front's trail system. Military Reserve Park has many trails that are well used in summer.

BOISE: BICYCLE CITY USA

It doesn't take long after arriving in Boise to figure out that those who live here have bicycles on their brains. You'll see people whizzing around on cool cruisers, tricked-out mountain bikes, and really nice road bikes.

If lucky, you might even spot Olympic gold medalist Kristin Armstrong, who lives in Boise, taking a morning ride along Hill Road. (Armstrong is no relation to Lance Armstrong or his ex-wife, who also happens to be named Kristin.) She is a University of Idaho graduate and three-time national champion road racer. Her biggest achievement came at the 2008 Summer Olympics in Beijing when she earned gold in the Women's Time Trial. Needless to say, she came home to a hero's welcome and a grand bike parade in downtown Boise.

On the benevolent side of biking, the **Boise Bicycle Project** (1027 Lusk St., 208/429-6520, www.boisebicycleproject. org) is a nonprofit community-run bicycle cooperative that fixes up donated bikes and gives them to low-income families. BBP also offers bike repair workshops, teaching people how to work on their own rides.

Boise hosts several exciting bicycling events, like the July **Twilight Criterium,** which brings in more than 100 professional road racers for a nighttime sprint through the streets of downtown Boise. Twenty thousand screaming fans line the sidewalks for this annual race, which has a Kid's Ride (led by Kristin Armstrong, no less) earlier in the day. If you like suds and bikes, check out **Tour de Fat-Boise,** a beer and bicycle blowout, sponsored by New Belgium Brewing Company, that happens every August in Ann Morrison Park. The costumed bike parade is a hoot.

A couple of Boise's bike laws are worth a mention. Bicyclists must slow down and use caution at stop signs, but need not stop if it isn't necessary for safety. Bicyclists must stop

BOISE

at all red traffic lights. Also, it's legal to ride on the sidewalks unless specifically prohibited by signs; pedestrians have the right-of-way, however.

FISHING

How many cities this size—how many state capitals—offer good fishing right within the city limits? Start with the **Boise River** that flows through town. Its cold waters hold rainbow and brown trout and whitefish. Popular access points include (west to east) Glenwood Bridge, Veterans Park, Capitol Bridge, and Barber Park. The river is stocked with rainbows monthly.

In addition to the river, many urban ponds are frequently stocked. Near the Glenwood Bridge, **Riverside Pond** holds rainbow trout and bluegill. **Veterans Park Pond** holds rainbows, largemouth bass, crappie, bullhead, and bluegill. **ParkCenter Pond** provides a home to rainbow trout, largemouth bass, crappie, bluegill, bullhead, and channel catfish. The ponds make ideal spots for youngsters to try fishing for the first time.

A couple of reservoirs not far from town also draw anglers. Large **Lucky Peak Reservoir,** full of fat rainbow trout, is eight miles east of Boise on Highway 21. Summer smallmouth bass fishing is reportedly good as well. Other species inhabiting the reservoir include perch and whitefish along with small populations of bull trout and chinook. Finally, 19 miles east of town you'll come to **Indian Creek Reservoir,** on the south side of I-84. Here you'll find an array of fish, including cutthroat trout, largemouth bass, bluegill, bullhead, channel cats, and the ubiquitous rainbow trout.

For more information on fishing the waters in and around town, pick up *Fishing Urban Boise* from the Idaho Department of Fish and Game office (600 S. Walnut St., 208/334-3700). Among the several fishing supply stores in town are **Anglers** (7097 Overland Rd., 208/323-6768), **Idaho Angler** (1682 Vista Ave., 208/389-9957), and **Stonefly Angler** in The Benchmark mountain-sports shop (625 Vista Ave., 208/338-1700).

GOLF

Several courses in the vicinity keep Boise golfers swinging year-round, weather permitting—usually about 325 days a year. All the major courses offer club and cart rentals.

Boise Ranch Golf Course (6501 S. Cloverdale Rd., 208/362-6501, $20–35) is an 18-hole, par-71 course with staggered tees providing course lengths of 5,206–6,574 yards. Seven manmade lakes provide water traps galore. To get there, take Victory Road west from Cole Road to Cloverdale Road and turn left (south).

A perennial local favorite for its course, pro shop, and 19th hole is **Shadow Valley Golf Course** (15711 Hwy. 55, 208/939-6699, $25–42). Length for the 18-hole, par-72 course runs 5,514–6,433 yards. Many Boise golfers pick Shadow Valley's short, scenic, and unforgiving hole 2 as the best in town. Also look out for holes 13 and 14 on the back nine. Hole 13 is a 525-yard, par-five dogleg with what many consider the most difficult drive in the city, while hole 14's green has water on either side and both water and trees behind it. To get there, take State Street northwest from downtown and turn right on Highway 55 toward McCall.

On the north side of town you'll find **Quail Hollow Golf Club** (4520 N. 36th St., 208/344-7807, $15–30) Hole one at this challenging 18-hole course sets the tone for what could be a very long afternoon; it's a 293-yard, par-four nightmare that seems to be made up of equal parts sand, water, and grass. Hole 7 provides a great view of the city. The length of the par-70 course runs 4,557–6,394 yards.

On the east side of town you'll find **Warm Springs Golf Course** (2495 Warm Springs Ave., 208/343-5661, $25–29). One side of the picturesque municipal course runs alongside the beautiful Boise River—also known as "Old Man Watertrap" to those who hook left on hole 2. The 18-hole, par-72 course runs 5,660–6,719 yards.

HIKING

Most bike trails in the Boise Front are open to hikers as well as bikers, and the **Hull's Gulch**

National Recreation Trail is open to hikers exclusively. Of the two Hull's Gulch trailheads, the lower one is 3.5 miles from the end of the pavement at the north end of 8th Street; the upper trailhead is three miles farther up the road. The primitive road is easily traversed in the Oldsmobile; just take it slowly. Both trailheads are on the right and well marked. From the lower trailhead, the 3.5-mile Bureau of Land Management (BLM) foot trail rounds a ridge and drops into Hull's Gulch—a deep, brushy canyon sliced down its center by the proverbial babbling brook. In spring, the wildflowers and butterflies try to outdo each other for your attention. Watch out for ticks during the spring months. The gradually ascending trail eventually reaches the lower limit of the pines, where a few magnificent ponderosas inhabit the sunny slopes.

All along the way, BLM signs identify some of the common botanical species and offer some basic ecology lessons. Among the plants you'll see: willow, rabbitbrush, Rocky Mountain maple, chokecherry, and syringa, the state flower. In spring, wildflowers brightening the gulch include arrowleaf balsamroot, phlox, lupine, and larkspur. Among the animals you might catch a glimpse of: rabbits, lizards, porcupines, badgers, and coyotes. A 2.5-mile loop at the top lets you come back on a slightly different path, or you might want to leave the gulch behind at the upper trailhead and just hike back down the dirt road. This route doesn't have quite the same wilderness feel, but it's atop the ridge and provides great views of Boise, the Owyhee Mountains, and a large chunk of southwestern Idaho. For more information on the Hull's Gulch Trail, contact the BLM's Boise District office (3948 Development Ave., 208/384-3300).

HOT-AIR BALLOONING

Dawn over the Treasure Valley, the perfect desert stillness broken only intermittently by the blast of a propane burner lighting off a couple of feet over your head. Ah, the magic of ballooning. Several companies in the area offer rides. Try **Footelights** (11269 W. Reutzel Dr., 208/362-5914) or **Idaho Hot Air Lines** (4049 W. Plum St., 208/344-8462).

ROCK CLIMBING

Good boulder fields are scarce in the Boise area, but several climbing gyms in town and a good top-rope area out near Lucky Peak help keep the local climbers in shape. On the **BSU campus** you'll find a state-of-the-art climbing gym in the Student Recreation Center (1515 University Dr., across from the Student Union, 208/426-1946, 6–10 P.M. Mon.–Thurs., 3–7 P.M. Sun., closed school holidays, $13 nonstudents); equipment rental is available. Climbers must pass a mandatory belay test ($5); free belay classes are offered periodically throughout the week.

Urban Ascent (308 S. 25th St., 208/363-7325, www.urbanascent.com, 4–10 P.M. Mon., Wed., and Fri., noon–10 P.M. Tues. and Thurs., noon–7 P.M. Sat.–Sun., day pass $7.50–14) is near downtown, just off the Connector. Climbers can belay up the massive climbing walls away from the outside elements. Shoe, harness, and chalk-bag rentals are available.

Both the **West Family YMCA** (5959 N. Discovery Pl., 208/377-9622) and the downtown **Boise Family YMCA** (1050 W. State St., 208/344-5501) have climbing walls.

The most popular outdoor climbing area in the vicinity is **Black Cliffs,** a 1–2-pitch basalt outcropping on the north side of Warm Springs Avenue (Hwy. 21), across from the Diversion Dam. You can't miss the roadside cliffs, a little less than a mile past the Beaver Dick and Oregon Trail twin historical markers, about seven miles east of downtown. Other popular areas include the old quarry behind the Old Pen, and Rocky Canyon—a small but scenic area north of Table Rock. To get to Rocky Canyon, take Reserve Road to Shaw Mountain Road as if you were going to Table Rock, but at the Y at the top of the hill, bear left on Shaw Mountain Road. A blue sign at the Y reads "To Rocky Canyon Road." Follow the road to the end of the pavement and continue about another 0.25 miles on a good gravel road.

BOISE SPORTS OUTFITTERS

The great outdoors is at your doorstep in Boise, and you'll want to get out there and enjoy it. Here's a list of some outfitters that rent the gear you'll need. First look up the type of gear you want to rent in the chart on top, then match the numbers listed there to the outfitter list.

Backpacks: 2, 6, 10
Bikes: 3, 6, 8
Canoes: 7
Inner tubes: 1
Kayaks: 4 (inflatable), 7
Rafts: 1, 4, 7
Rock-climbing shoes: 2, 6, 10
Skates: 8, 9

Skis:
  Alpine: 5, 8
  Cross-country: 2, 6, 8, 10
  Telemark/backcountry: 2, 6, 10
Snowboards: 3, 5, 6, 8, 9
Snowshoes: 2, 5, 6, 8, 9, 10
Tennis rackets: 8
Tents: 2, 6, 10

1. **Epley's Boise River Rentals** (Barber Park on Eckert Rd., upstream end of the Greenbelt, 208/577-4584), July 1–Labor Day
2. **The Benchmark** (625 Vista Ave., 208/338-1700)
3. **Bikes2Boards** (3525 W. State St., 208/343-0208, www.bikes2boards.com)
4. **Boise Army-Navy** (4924 Chinden Blvd., 208/322-0660)
5. **Sports Authority** (1301 N. Milwaukee St., 208/378-9590)
6. **Idaho Mountain Touring** (1310 W. Main St., 208/336-3854)
7. **Idaho River Sports** (3100 W. Pleasanton Ave., 208/336-4844)
8. **McU Sports** (822 W. Jefferson St., 208/342-7734, 2314 Bogus Basin Rd., 208/336-2300, www.mcusports.com)
9. **Newt & Harold's** (1021 Broadway, 208/385-9300)
10. **REI** (8300 W. Emerald St. at Milwaukee St., 208/322-1141)

Boise State University's Outdoor Program, located in the Student Recreation Center (1515 University Dr.), has a mind-boggling selection of four-season rental gear. If you're a BSU student, staffer, or alum, or if you're attending a BSU conference, you qualify to rent gear here. For more information on equipment rentals or eligibility, call 208/426-1946.

RUNNING

The city is full of great places to go jogging. Start with the Greenbelt, where you can enjoy a car-free workout of up to 25 miles, past the rushing waters and lushly vegetated banks of the Boise River. At any time of year, you'll find Boiseans out for exercise on the Greenbelt's paths. All the major parks are great places to run. You can loop through Ann Morrison Park, using the Greenbelt as one side of the loop and the park's walkways as the other side. Or head over to Veterans Memorial Park on the west end of town—trails there wind down to the Boise River and around a marsh and a large pond.

Racers will find an event scheduled almost every weekend April–October; this is a runner's town. Among the best-known races in Idaho is mid-April's **Race to Robie Creek,** a brutal 13.1-mile ordeal from Fort Boise Park up Rocky Canyon and over Aldape Summit. That may sound like self-inflicted punishment, but upward of 2,000 people have taken up the challenge in recent years.

SKATEBOARDING

On weekends, boarders and in-line skaters head to **Rhodes Park** (Front St. between 15th St. and 16th St., next to Reel Foods Fish Market), a concrete slab under The Connector freeway. The park is the brainchild and labor of love of retired contractor Glenn Rhodes, who thought the kids of Boise needed a safe and secure place to skateboard away from the streets of downtown and away from the inevitable complaints of city merchants. Rhodes created this veritable haven for youth, which is absolutely free. The park has quarter pipes, a half pipe, and rail slides as well as basketball hoops. **Fort Boise Skate Park** is another option, located off Reserve Street past the baseball field.

Board shops in town include **The Board Room** (2727 W. State St., 208/385-9553) and **Newt & Harold's** (1021 Broadway, 208/385-9300).

SKATING

The hard-core in-line skaters go to **Rhodes Park** (15th St. and Front St.) to fly up the quarter pipes just like the skateboarders. **Fort Boise Skate Park** and the **Greenbelt** are prime skating territory too.

Those who prefer skating on ice can head to **Idaho Ice World** (7072 S. Eisenman Rd., 208/331-0044, $7 adults, $6 under age 13 and over age 59) next to the Boise Factory Outlets. Public skating sessions are held daily; call for times. Skate rentals are $3, and lessons are available. Idaho Ice World also offers curling (7–10 P.M. Sun. Nov.–Apr.).

SKIING

Skiers and snowboarders head to the Bogus Basin recreation area north of town.

SWIMMING

The Boise River and Lucky Peak Reservoir are suitable for summer swimming, but Boise offers a number of swimming pools too. For indoor swimming, the **Boise Aquatic Center** at the West Family YMCA (5959 N. Discovery Pl., 208/377-9622, $9 adults, $4 children, family rates available) has a 50-meter pool for lap swimming as well as a children's pool, a waterslide, and a hydrotherapy pool.

Outdoor city swimming pools can be found during the summer months at **Borah Park**

(801 Aurora Dr., 208/375-8373); **Fairmont Park** (7929 W. Northview St., 208/375-3011); **Ivywild** (2250 Leadville Ave., 208/384-1697); **Lowell School** (1601 N. 28th St., 208/345-7918); and the **Natatorium/Hydrotube** (1811 Warm Springs Ave., 208/345-9270). Admission varies from pool to pool but averages $3.50 adults, $2.50 ages 12–18, $2 under age 12, free for seniors.

TENNIS

Tennis courts are located in about two dozen of the city's numerous municipal parks, including **Ann Morrison** (off Americana Blvd.), **Camel's Back** (13th St. and Heron St.), **Fort Boise** (Fort St. and Reserve St.), Julia Davis (700 S. Capitol Ave.), and the **Willow Lane Sports Complex** (4650 Willow Lane) in west Boise.

TUBING AND FLOATING

Each summer, some 300,000 people start at Barber Park and float their way down the Boise River to Ann Morrison Park, a six-mile trip that takes about an hour and a half. You can bring your own gear (air is available at Barber Park 10 A.M.–7 P.M. daily) or rent it at the park's rental office (208/577-4584, noon–5 P.M. Mon.–Thurs., noon–6 P.M. Fri., 11 A.M.–6 P.M. Sat.–Sun. and holidays summer, tubes $12, rafts $45–55, inflatable kayaks $35). A shuttle bus (1–8 P.M. Mon.–Fri., 1–9 P.M. Sat.–Sun. and holidays, $3 pp per trip) leaves Ann Morrison Park every hour on the hour and Barber Park every hour on the half-hour. Neither the rental office nor the shuttle operates if forecast temperatures fall below 80°F. It's important to note that alcohol consumption has been banned for those floating the Boise River, and it's strictly enforced by Boise's finest. Also, Idaho law states that rafters ages 14 and under must wear a life vest. Tubers are exempt from this law, but wearing a life vest is strongly recommended. It's also recommended that rafters and tubers take out at Ann Morrison Park because there's a dangerous diversion dam just past the park that has claimed a few lives in recent years.

WALKING

One nice aspect about walking in Boise: By and large, the city is flat. The **Greenbelt,** Boise's premier walking path, meanders along the lush banks of the Boise River, providing plenty of spots along the way for quiet contemplation of the natural beauty. It also connects a string of parks from one end of town to the other and passes by Boise State University. BSU students often park off-campus and walk to class on the Greenbelt. You can pick up the path just about anywhere—just head for the river—but Julia Davis Park and Ann Morrison Park are two of the most popular access points.

One particularly wonderful spot on the Greenbelt for a stroll is at the east end, where you'll find the **Greenbelt Wildlife Preserve** (ParkCenter Blvd. and River Run Dr.), open only to pedestrians and wildlife. You can't park at the access point, which is located in a residential area; park on ParkCenter Boulevard somewhere, or just budget enough time to mosey down the Greenbelt from points farther west.

Downtown itself is generally a safe and pleasant place to walk, day and night. Evenings are especially nice here, after all the business traffic has migrated back to suburbia and the setting sun casts a warm glow on the numerous beautiful buildings.

WHITE-WATER RAFTING AND KAYAKING

The **Payette River,** less than an hour outside Boise, drops down out of the mountains in world-class white water that draws thrillseekers from all over the country. Summer weekends see hundreds of rafters and kayakers on the river. The rapids here range from moderate Class III all the way up to unrunnable Class VI.

Construction is under way at the **Ray Neef River Recreation Park** (208/384-4240) near Quinn's Pond (near State St. and 31st St.). Boise Parks and Recreation will operate this in-town paddling park slated to open in 2012.

ATHLETIC CLUBS

YMCAs

Boise has two YMCAs, both open to the public for a day-use fee ($13.25 adults, $6.75 ages 7–18). Here's a hot tip for road warriors on a tight budget: the Y charges just $2 for use of its showers, but you'll need to check the schedule to find out the available times.

The extensive facilities at the downtown **Boise Family YMCA** (1050 W. State St., 208/344-5501, 5 A.M.–10 P.M. Mon.–Fri., 7 A.M.–8 P.M. Sat., 10 A.M.–6 P.M. Sun.) include pools, basketball and racquetball courts, cardio equipment and free weights, a climbing wall, and child care. The pool closes a half-hour earlier.

The **West Family YMCA** (5959 N. Discovery Pl., south of W. Chinden Blvd. and west of Cloverdale Rd., 208/377-9622) has racquetball courts, a gym, a teen center, a climbing wall, a child-care center, basketball and volleyball courts, and an indoor running track. The facility also houses the Boise Aquatic Center.

Other Clubs

Several private athletic clubs are also open to the public for a day-use fee. **Idaho Athletic Club** has two locations in Boise: Black Eagle (1435 S. Maple Grove Rd., 208/376-6558) and State Street (2999 N. Lakeharbor Lane, 208/853-4224), where you can work out for $10.

Boise Racquet & Swim Club (1116 N. Cole Rd., 208/376-1052) has indoor and outdoor tennis courts, a fitness center with exercise bikes, Nautilus equipment, and free weights as well as an outdoor heated pool, saunas, and spa facilities.

SPECTATOR SPORTS

Baseball

Memorial Stadium (5600 Glenwood Ave.), adjacent to the fairgrounds, is home to the Single-A **Boise Hawks** (208/322-5000, www.boisehawks.com, mid-June–early Sept., $6–12), a farm team of the Chicago Cubs.

Basketball

Idaho Stampede (tickets 208/331-8497, www. qwestarenaidaho.com, Nov.–Mar., $7–20) is an NBA Development League team that plays its home games at Qwest Arena. They are affiliated with both the Portland Trailblazers and the Denver Nuggets.

Hockey

The **Idaho Steelheads** (208/424-2200, tickets 208/331-8497, www.idahosteelheads.com, Oct.–Mar., $15–50), affiliated with the Dallas Stars, bring East Coast Hockey League action to Qwest Arena.

Boise State University Sports

BSU fields intercollegiate athletes in seven men's sports and 10 women's sports, most competing in the Mountain West Conference as of the 2011 season. **BSU football** is the big

COLLEGE FOOTBALL MANIA: BRONCOS ON THE BLUE TURF

© THE ARBITER, BOISE STATE UNIVERSITY

the Boise State Broncos at Bronco Stadium

The Boise State Broncos have made quite the dent in college football since joining the Division 1-A ranks in 1996. Bronco Stadium, which is known for its blue artificial turf and incredibly loud fans, is not an easy place for visiting teams. As a matter of fact, the Broncos maintained an astonishing 59-2 home record from 1999 to 2009, knocking off big-name schools like Oregon and Iowa State on the blue carpet. Boise State dominated the Western Athletic Conference from 2001 to 2010, with a 68-4 league record. The school joined the Mountain West Conference in 2011.

The Broncos appeared in nine bowl games from 1999 to 2009, including two exciting BCS Bowl wins at the Fiesta Bowl (a barn burner against Oklahoma in 2007, and an equally exciting victory over Texas Christian University in 2009). The Broncos have consistently been in the Top 25 since 2002, and they started the 2010 season in the top five in both major polls. Accolades like these make for excitable fans come football season.

draw, with autumn games at the often sold-out Bronco Stadium. The BSU athletic ticket office (208/426-4737, www.broncosports.com) is on the south end of Bronco Stadium.

Humanitarian Bowl

The annual Humanitarian Bowl (208/426-4737, www.humanitarianbowl.org) is Boise's single biggest sporting event, held at Bronco Stadium during the post-Christmas football bowl season. The bowl game draws its name from the Boise-based World Sports Humanitarian Hall of Fame, which champions athletes' involvement in the community as well as on the field. Tickets are available through the BSU ticket office or Select-A-Seat (208/426-1494, www.idahotickets.com), a major local ticket broker with outlets at all Albertsons stores.

Treasure Valley Rollergirls

If you like hard-hitting women on roller skates, definitely check out the Treasure Valley Rollergirls (208/342-1726, www. treasurevalleyrollergirls.net), who host bouts throughout the year at Qwest Arena. These tattooed ruffians take on clubs from other cities in the region. You can buy tickets ($10–25) at the door or at various locations around town, like The Record Exchange (1105 W. Idaho St., 208/344-8010).

☾ BOGUS BASIN
Skiing and Snowboarding

Boise skiers are spoiled by a superb ski resort just 16 miles north of town. **Bogus Basin Ski Resort** (2600 Bogus Basin Rd., 208/332-5100 or 800/367-4397, snow report 208/342-2100, www.bogusbasin.org, lifts 10 A.M.–10 P.M. Mon.–Fri., 9 A.M.–10 P.M. Sat.–Sun., full-day lift tickets $42 adults, 4–10 P.M. lift tickets $20 adults) has a base elevation of 5,800 feet and rises to a peak of 7,582 feet—high enough to provide featherweight powder when a cold front blows through. On the resort's 2,600 acres are two quad chairs, a triple chair, four double chairs, and a rope tow, serving 52 trails with a maximum vertical drop of 1,800 feet

sliding down Bogus Basin's tubing hill

© IDAHO DIVISION OF TOURISM

and a longest run of 1.5 miles—not bad for Boise's "local hill." Snowboarders are welcome anywhere on the mountain, and a separate snowboard park offers a mogul field, half-pipes, quarter-pipes, and rail slides. There's also an 800-foot tubing hill ($5 for one hour, $10 for two hours) that's accessible by a rope tow.

Night skiing here is one of the resort's high-lights, with 165 acres open until 10 P.M. nightly. Weather can often be better at night than during the day, and a peaceful, uncrowded feeling settles over the area. The views on a clear night are something special.

Down near the lower day lodge, a **cross-country ski area** offers skating and traditional cross-country tracks on more than 12 miles of developed trails. Snowshoers will also find lots of trails that skirt the ridge, most of which offer great views of a major chunk of southwestern Idaho, from the Boise Front foothills in the foreground out across the Snake River Plain to the Owyhee Mountains in the background. Backcountry telemarkers who don't mind

some hiking should ask the staff about Mores Mountain (trail fee $12 adults, $7 ages 7–11, free under age 7 and over age 69). A snowshoe trail ticket will cost you $5. Rentals and lessons are available. For more information, call the Frontier Point Nordic Lodge (208/332-5390).

The resort's skier-service facilities include two day lodges, cafés, rental and retail shops, a ski school, a racing program, ski programs for children and physically challenged skiers, and day care.

The season here usually starts around Thanksgiving or early December and continues through the end of spring break.

Buses (208/459-6612, $13 round-trip, $8 one-way) serve the mountain from Boise and some neighboring communities; call for routes and schedules.

Sleigh Rides

Bogus Creek Outfitters (7355 S. Eagle Rd., Meridian, 208/887-7880, www.boguscreek. com) will bundle you up in wool blankets and take you for a horse-drawn sleigh ride

© IDAHO DIVISION OF TOURISM

skiing at Bogus Basin

from the Bogus Basin Nordic Area to a cozy cabin a mile deep in the woods. There you'll be served hot drinks by a roaring fire followed by a three-course dinner. The 2.5-hour dinner rides (6 and 8:30 P.M. daily, $74 pp) are offered November 28–mid-March.

Mountain Lodging

Sure, it's only a half-hour drive back to Boise, but to guarantee first crack at that untracked powder, you might want to book a room in the **Pioneer Condominiums** (208/332-5200, www.pioneercondos.com, $129–149, reserve in advance), which lie at mid-mountain, just steps from the slopes—you could ski right to your door if you wanted. Many of the plush yet unpretentious units offer fireplaces, with kindling and firewood provided. A hot tub and sauna can work après-ski wonders on those knots in your quads. Other amenities include free laundry and free transportation to the lower base area in ski season. You can get special rates for weekly stays and large groups. The condos are immediately adjacent to Pioneer Lodge—the upper day lodge of the alpine ski area—where the bar and grill is open until 11 P.M. nightly.

Bogus Basin also operates a yurt (208/332-5100, sleeps up to 12, $125), but reservations need to be made far in advance because it's popular during the winter months. No maid service here—you pack it in and pack it out.

Entertainment and Events

Boise has an always-evolving arts and entertainment scene, with several outstanding mainstays leading the way. The City of Trees boasts a high-concentration of actors, dancers, writers, and visual artists, giving it an artsy feel. Musicians flourish here too; indie superstars Built to Spill hail from these parts, and the city has long had a vibrant jazz scene, led by the late great Gene Harris and current rising star Curtis Stigers.

PERFORMING ARTS

Tickets for many Boise-area performing arts events, especially those at Boise State University's Morrison Center and Taco Bell Arena, are available through **Select-A-Seat** (208/426-1494, www.idahotickets.com), or stop at any of the dozens of outlets, which include the BSU Student Union Building (1700 University Dr.) and Albertson's stores across southern Idaho and eastern Oregon.

Boise Philharmonic

One of the Northwest's premier symphony orchestras, the Boise Philharmonic (ticket office in Esther Simplot Performing Arts Academy, 516 S. 9th St., 208/344-7849, www.boisephilharmonic.org, $10–35) is the state's largest performing arts organization and the oldest as well, dating back more than 100 years. Symphony season runs mid-September–mid-April, with performances at the Morrison Center on the BSU campus, Swayne Auditorium at Northwest Nazarene University in Nampa, as well as other venues around town. Numerous internationally acclaimed guest artists perform with the symphony each year.

Opera Idaho

See Madame Butterfly get the shaft! See Don Giovanni meet his just reward! Opera Idaho (513 S. 8th St., 208/345-3531, tickets 208/387-1273, www.operaidaho.org, $11–69) performs several masterworks throughout the year. Boise performances usually take place at the Egyptian Theatre (700 W. Main St.).

Other Musical Organizations

The 110-member **Boise Master Chorale** (100 W. State St., 208/344-7901, Oct.–Apr.) performs at various venues during its season. The **BSU Music Department** has a busy schedule of recitals, master classes, concerts, and more. For the schedule and performance venues, call

208/426-1596 or see the events calendar at www.boisestate.edu.

Ballet Idaho

Squeeze into those toe shoes and plié on down to the Morrison Center for a performance by Ballet Idaho (501 S. 8th St., 208/343-0556, www.balletidaho.org, tickets 208/426-1494, www.idahotickets.com, Oct.–Apr., $20–50). The company teams up with the Boise Philharmonic in December for the perennial holiday favorite, *The Nutcracker*.

Oinkari Basque Dancers

The story of the Oinkari Basque Dancers starts in 1949 with Basque Boisean Juanita "Jay" Uberuaga Hormaechea, who could dance the *jota* like a house afire. She decided that all Basque American children should have the chance to learn the dances of the old country and began teaching them. In 1960 a group of her students went to Europe to see the homeland firsthand. In San Sebastian they met and studied with a local troupe named Oinkari, loosely translated as "check out those flying feet!" The two groups danced together a few times a week, developing close bonds.

When the Boiseans were ready to return to the United States form their own troupe, the San Sebastian Oinkaris asked the Boiseans to do them the honor of naming the fledgling American troupe Oinkari as well, in effect creating sister dance companies.

Boise's Oinkari Dancers (208/336-8219, www.oinkari.org) went on to perform at four World's Fairs and in the rotunda of the nation's Capitol in Washington, D.C. Today the company performs at the international Jaialdi festival, at the annual Festival of San Inazio, and at other times throughout the year. Members wear traditional Basque costumes and dance the *jota*—a quick-step that has been around in one variation or another since the 12th century—and other traditional dances. The company remains a vital part of Boise's Basque community; dancers must be of Basque descent to join the troupe.

◖ Idaho Shakespeare Festival

Boise's bard-based Idaho Shakespeare Festival (box office 208/336-9221 or 208/429-9908, www.idahoshakespeare.org, $12–39) troupe ranks among the city's shiniest cultural gems. From mid-June through September, Will's

© DKM PHOTOGRAPHY/IDAHO SHAKESPEARE FESTIVAL

the Idaho Shakespeare Festival's outdoor amphitheater

works and other dramatic delights come alive in an outdoor amphitheater (5657 Warm Springs Ave.) along the river east of downtown. The festival grounds are a wonderful place to picnic before the show; bring your own or sample fare from Café Shakespeare.

Other Theater and Dance Troupes

Boise now has about 10 professional and community theater groups, so drama fans often have several playbills to choose from each week. The venerable **Boise Little Theater** (100 E. Fort St., 208/342-5104, www.boiselittletheater.org, Sept.–June, $8–12.50) company was organized in 1948. Performances take place at the Boise Little Theater in Fort Boise Park.

As its name implies, **Boise Contemporary Theater** (854 Fulton St., 208/331-9224, www.bctheater.org, four productions Oct.–May, $12–32) presents fare by such current-day playwrights as David Sedaris and Steve Martin as well as classics by the likes of Lanford Wilson and Samuel Beckett, all in an intimate "black box" environment at the Fulton Street Theater.

Also of note, the Hailey, Idaho–based **Company of Fools** (208/788-6520, www.companyoffools.org) brings its productions to the Fulton Street Theater several times each year.

Boise has a thriving modern dance scene as well. Check out **Idaho Dance Theatre** (405 S. 8th St., 208/331-9592, www.idahodancetheatre.org, Nov.–Apr.), a local troupe that puts on performances at the Special Events Center on the BSU campus. The **Trey McIntyre Project** (775 Fulton St., 877/867-2320, www.treymcintyre.com) is another troupe helping to define modern dance in Boise. This stylish dance company tours the country throughout the year and performs at various venues in the Boise area.

LITERARY ARTS
Writers in Residence

Many notable writers have made Boise their home over the years. Most come to Idaho to teach at BSU's Master's of Fine Arts Creative Writing program. In the past, Robert Olmstead and Elise Blackwell have taught classes at the university. Currently, fiction writer Brady Udall (*The Lonely Polygamist, Letting Loose the Hounds*) and poet Janet Holmes (*F2f, The Green Tuxedo*) teach the fine art of wordsmithery.

Up-and-coming literary star Anthony Doerr also lives in Boise. He is the author of several short-story collections, novellas, and a popular creative nonfiction book, *Four Seasons in Rome*. Doerr is a recipient of the O. Henry Prize and the Pushcart Prize for fiction.

The Cabin

Considered to be the beating heart of Boise's literary world, The Cabin (801 S. Capitol Blvd., 208/331-8000, www.thecabinidaho.org) is based in an old log cabin next to the Idaho Anne Frank Human Rights Memorial. The literary center offers writing workshops and hosts a continuous stream of readings and author discussions. Famous writers such as T. C. Boyle and Elizabeth Gilbert have read excerpts from their books here in recent years.

VISUAL ARTS
Galleries

Gallery open houses take place on the first Thursday of every month. **Brown's Gallery** (408 S. 8th St., 888/342-6661, www.browns-gallery.com) is one of Boise's more established venues and carries a mix of Western art, landscapes, and some good local artists. Nothing here will shock or upset you—it's a comfortable gallery for comfortable Boiseans.

At the other end of the art-world spectrum is **J Crist Gallery** (420 Main St., 208/336-2671, www.jcrist.com), an attractive space that exhibits and sells the works of local and regional artists. Expect to find lots of contemporary paintings, eye-catching sculptures, and mixed-media pieces. Another noteworthy gallery in the downtown area is **Boise Art Glass** (530 W. Myrtle St., 208/345-1825, www.boiseartglass.com), a blown-glass studio that offers classes and sells jewelry, marbles, vases, bowls, and lighting fixtures. The in-house gallery exhibits a rotating selection of fused and hand-blown glass art.

All the hipsters hang out at the **Visual Arts Collective** (VAC, 3638 Osage St., 208/424-8297, www.visualartscollective.com), just off Chinden Boulevard in nearby Garden City. Here you will find a constantly changing display of locally produced contemporary art, ranging from surrealistic paintings to bizarro mixed-media offerings. The VAC also has a bar, and it features live music and cutting-edge performance art on a weekly basis. You must be 21 to enter.

Boise State University has several galleries scattered around campus, including one in the Liberal Arts Building, one in the Student Union, and another in the Hemingway Center. For current shows, see www.boisestate.edu/art.

Boise Public Art

One of the treats of exploring Boise is the discovery of art where you least expect it. Boise has about three-dozen pieces of public art in an ever-growing collection that spans the city from the airport to downtown nooks and alleys.

The Grove is a good place to start looking. *Great Blues* (David Berry, 1990) is a bronze rendering of the magnificent Idaho-native birds, one of which is captured in mid-flight. You'll find it on the south side of the Brick Oven Bistro. Just to the east is a nostalgic local favorite—*Keepsies* (Ann LaRose, 1985)—depicting a trio of innocent youngsters playing marbles on the plaza.

Homage to the Pedestrian (Patrick Zentz, 2002) is an interactive walkway where motion detectors set off sounds. It's on the west side of The Grove. Across 9th Street in front of the Statehouse Inn, *Grove Street Illuminated & Boise Canal* (Amy Westover, 2003) offers some glimpses into local history through silk-screened vintage photos and engraved text that observers can see as they walk amid steel and cast-glass circles.

If you've flown to Boise, don't leave the airport without seeing some of the impressive art in the new terminal. Huge fish seem almost to jump out of a six-sided lenticular light-box

mural near the baggage claim. Meanwhile, the ticketing area boasts a gorgeous 50-foot mural by Idaho artist Geoffrey Krueger, who portrays a Boise River scene with the Boise Front foothills rising behind. It's a fitting send-off to passengers, whether they live here or hope to visit again soon.

CINEMA

The Flicks (646 Fulton St., 208/342-4222, www.theflicksboise.com, 8.50, $6.50 before 6 P.M. and for students with ID, seniors, and under age 13), near Capitol Boulevard and Myrtle Street, is Boise's art film house. Its four screens show independent and foreign films as well as some of the more intelligent first-runs. In addition to the theater, a deli-style café serves panini sandwiches, lasagna, and house-made soups. You can get a microbrew or glass of wine from the café and take it out onto the patio or even into the theater with you. You'll also find a good collection of art and foreign films for rent in the video shop (208/342-4288).

The restored **Egyptian Theatre** (700 W. Main St., 208/345-0454, www.egyptiantheatre.net) is the city's most historic and beautiful movie house. Built in 1927, its Egyptian design was inspired by the discovery of King Tut's tomb not long before. Check out the ornamental sphinxes up near the roof. In addition to first-run films, the Egyptian regularly screens black-and-white classics, and there are live music concerts too.

Elsewhere downtown, you can watch current-run movies in BoDo at **Edwards Cinemas Stadium 9** (760 Broad St., 208/338-3821, $9.50 adults, $7.50 matinee, $7 children, $6.50 seniors).

Hands down, the biggest Boise-area movie emporium is the **Edwards Boise Stadium 22 & IMAX** (7709 Overland Rd., 208/377-9603) in the Boise Spectrum entertainment complex at Cole and Overland Roads just off I-84.

For budget movies, head to **Northgate Reel Theatre** (6950 W. State St., 208/377-2620, www.reeltheatre.com), where a second-run flick will only set you back $1–3.

NIGHTLIFE

The local music scene in Boise is undeniably rich. The town has a lot of musicians and a lot of places for them to play. Boise fervently supports its homegrown musicians, to the extent that many locals can actually support themselves with their music. It's not uncommon for local bands to draw bigger crowds at the clubs than the nationally famous touring bands that come through town. And cutting-edge out-of-town bands show up in Boise with some regularity.

The **Knitting Factory Concert House** (416 S. 9th St., 208/367-1212, www.bo.knittingfactory.com) is the top live-music venue in town, with a never-ending onslaught of national touring acts. Don't be surprised to see bands like the Smashing Pumpkins, the Robert Cray Band, David Allan Coe, and The Misfits.

The Bouquet (1010 W. Main St., 208/345-6605, www.thebouquet.com, open nightly), formerly known as Blues Bouquet, is another great spot for live music from occasional touring bands and popular local acts that always pack the dance floor.

Neurolux (111 N. 11th St., 208/343-0886, www.neurolux.com, open nightly, cover charge for live music) is Boise's hippest watering hole. The bar's tattoo-clad clientele comes here to enjoy stiff drinks, a good jukebox, DJ music, poetry slams, and lots of local bands. Edgy touring acts, like Jerry Joseph and the Jackmormons and Guided by Voices, occasionally grace the stage.

Old Boise, near the corner of 6th and Main Streets, is the epicenter of nightlife in downtown. Here you will find several live music venues, including **Pengilly's Saloon** (513 W. Main St., 208/345-6344), a historic bar that features acoustic music in a nonsmoking setting, and **Tom Grainey's** (109 S. 6th St., 208/345-2505), which has a pair of bars, upstairs and down, that spotlight local rock bands. If you desire a tropical experience, check out the **Reef** (105 S. 6th St., 208/287-9200, www.reefboise.com), upstairs at the corner of 6th and Main Streets. This Polynesian-inspired restaurant and lounge has a palm-thatched roof over the bar and a spacious rooftop patio that's lit up with tiki torches. Besides tropical drinks and pupu platters, the Reef also has live music on weekends.

Across the street from the Reef, **China Blue** (100 S. 6th St., 208/338-6604) is perhaps Boise's swankiest DJ dance club. It's extremely popular with the risqué college crowd, meaning you'll most likely see some serious bumping and grinding on the dance floor.

Elsewhere downtown, get your groove on at **The Balcony** (150 N. 8th St., 208/336-1313), a happening dance club popular with both gays and straights (and everyone in between), with near-nightly DJ music. From its second-floor perch in the Capitol Terrace, it overlooks what surely is Boise's most fabulous block—even if there is a gaping hole in the landscape where the long-on-hold Boise Tower project languishes.

In BoDo, **Liquid** (405 S. 8th St., 208/287-5379, www.liquidboise.com), located in the alley between 8th and 9th Streets, is one of Boise's newest nightclubs. Expect to find lots of creative cocktails and live music at this hipper-than-hip hotspot.

FOR THE KIDS

Boise has been called one of the best places in the United States to raise children, and visiting families will have a ball. In addition to all the inexpensive things to do at the parks listed in this chapter, you'll find great attractions throughout the metro area.

Planet Kid (1875 Century Way, 208/375-8923, www.wingscenter.com, 10 A.M.–7:30 P.M. Mon.–Thurs., 10 A.M.–8:30 P.M. Fri.–Sat. summer, 10 A.M.–7:30 P.M. Mon.–Thurs., 10 A.M.–8:30 P.M. Fri.–Sat., noon–6 P.M. Sun. fall–spring, $7.75 ages 4–12, $4.75 ages 1–3, free under age 1), on the south side of I-84 off South Cole Road, is an incredible indoor soft playground for kids ages 1–12. Its agenda is appealing: no arcade or video machines, no silly tickets or prizes, no mall traffic. Part of the Wings Center complex, Planet Kid stresses fitness and fun. Kids can challenge themselves mentally and physically on such play elements as the Rings of Infinity, Cyborg Swing, and Trapdoor Transporter.

Pojo's (7736 Fairview Ave., 208/376-6981, www.pojos.com, 10 A.M.–11 P.M. Mon.–Thurs., 10 A.M.–midnight Fri.–Sat., 11 A.M.–10 P.M. Sun.) is another huge (20,000 square feet) fun center, with indoor bumper cars, high-tech interactive games, redemption games, a nickel arcade, kiddie rides and games for the toddler set, and a café. Admission is free, but it's pretty easy to go through a mess of quarters.

EVENTS
Year-Round
Boise is a party town, and one event or another happens just about every weekend year-round. The delightful **First Thursday** series (5–9 P.M. first Thurs. of every month), run by the Downtown Boise Association (208/472-5200, www.downtownboise.org), turns downtown Boise into a street fair. Galleries hold open houses, musicians play on the sidewalks, and seemingly all of Boise is out strolling downtown.

Spring
In mid-April, the **BSU/Gene Harris Jazz Festival** (www.geneharris.org) pays tribute to the late great Idaho jazzman, with various performances by international acts around town. Mid-April also brings more than 2,000 runners to the **Race to Robie Creek** (www.robiecreek.com), a 13.1-mile test of strength and will that starts in Fort Boise Park and climbs Rocky Canyon up and over Adalpe Summit—a gain of 2,000 vertical feet followed by a loss of more than 1,000 feet. A spring tradition in Boise since the 1970s, it's considered the toughest half-marathon in the Northwest.

You know summer's on the way when **Alive After Five** (www.downtownboise.org, 5–8 P.M. Wed.) kicks off in early June at The Grove, which becomes a city party. Crowds pack the outdoor plaza to sample microbrews and food from local restaurants while listening or dancing to live bands. The concert series runs through September.

The first weekend in June is the **Greek Festival** (St. Helen's Church Park, 27th St. and Bannock St., behind the church, 208/345-6147) sponsored by Saints Constantine and Helen Greek Orthodox Church. More Greek food than you can possibly imagine—dolmas, souvlaki, spanakopita—will be spread out by Boise's Greek community, while Greek dancing and revelry continue all weekend. Foodies will also like **Savor Idaho** (visit www.savoridaho.org), a local food and wine showcase that takes place in mid-June at the Idaho Botanical Garden. This new celebration features more than 25 Idaho wineries and about 20 area restaurants and food artisans.

Later in the month, hundreds of triathletes come to town for the **Ironman 70.3 Boise** (www.ironmanboise.com) competition. These buffed athletes push their bodies to the limit with a 1.2-mile swim at Lucky Peak Reservoir, a 56-mile bike ride through the Foothills, and a 31-mile run that ends in downtown Boise.

Summer
At the end of June, Boise's Jewish community sets the table for **Deli Days,** held at the Ahavath Beth Israel Synagogue (11 N. Latah St., 208/343-6601). Here you can nosh on potato knishes, delicious baked goods, and fat pastrami sandwiches served with a pickle that actually has a crunch. Also at the end of the month is **Boise Rec Fest** (www.boiserecfest.com), a new event in Ann Morrison Park that celebrates outdoor sports. Expect to find lots of exhibits and workshops relating to mountain biking, skiing, backpacking, and white-water rafting, to name a few. There's plenty of food and drink to whet your appetite.

Boise celebrates **Independence Day** on July 4 with fireworks and a parade. The last weekend of July, Boise's Basque community comes out in force for the **Festival of San Inazio of Loyola;** St. Ignatius, a native of Spanish Basque country, died July 31, 1556. The festivities include a performance by the Oinkari Basque dancers, Basque athletic contests, and an abundance of local Basque food and drink. For more information, call the Basque Museum (208/343-2671). **Jaialdi,** an international Basque festival, is held every five years at various locales around town; the next one is in 2015.

Fans of chitlins, fried catfish, black-eyed peas, and sweet potato pie won't want to miss the **Soul Food Extravaganza** (www.boisesoulfoodfestival.com), the first Saturday in August at Julia Davis Park.

The **Western Idaho Fair** (208/287-5650) comes to the Expo Idaho fairgrounds (Chinden Blvd. and Glenwood St.) for 10 days in mid-August, bringing with it a carnival midway, livestock shows, eclectic exhibits, food galore, and lots of entertainers.

Dozens of hot air balloons take to the air over Ann Morrison Park on four mornings in early September for the **Spirit of Boise Balloon Classic** (www.spiritofboise.com). This is probably Boise's most colorful event.

Fall

Autumn brings colorful trees and the opening of a colorful cultural calendar as the Boise Philharmonic, Ballet Idaho, and Opera Idaho open their seasons.

The weekend after Labor Day brings **Art in the Park,** run by the Boise Art Museum (208/345-8330) and one of Idaho's largest and most elaborate arts and crafts shows, with hats, drums, candles, toys, fine arts, and lots of food. The "gallery" for this event is beautiful Julia Davis Park.

One of the coolest neighborhood bashes in the Northwest can be found in mid-September at the **Hyde Park Street Fair** (www.northend.org), a weekend full of live music, kids' activities, and community conviviality. It's at Camel's Back Park in the city's North End.

In late September, look for the **Women's Fitness Celebration** (www.celebrateall.org), which brings the largest road race in Idaho and the second-largest women-only run and walk in the country. More than 8,000 women and girls typically participate.

Winter

Late November through January, the Idaho Botanical Garden's **Winter Garden aGlow** (208/343-8649) features thousands of

dancers performing at the Jaialdi Basque festival

© IDAHO DIVISION OF TOURISM

twinkling lights decked artistically amid the garden grounds, along with bonfires and hot beverages.

Kids and adults alike will enjoy the collaborative efforts of Ballet Idaho and the Boise Philharmonic in bringing performances of Tchaikovsky's masterpiece *The Nutcracker* to Morrison Center. Call 208/426-1110 for schedule and ticket information. Christmas shoppers can find **gift shows** at Expo Idaho (www.expoidaho.com) and The Grove early in December. And if you're lucky, you might hit The Grove at the right time for **Tuba Christmas** (www.tubachristmas.com) where upward of 60 tuba and baritone horn players oompah their way through traditional Christmas music and more. Check the website for this year's date.

Shopping

MALLS

Boise Towne Square mall (350 N. Milwaukee St., 208/378-4400, www.boisetownesquare.com, 10 A.M.–9 P.M. Mon.–Sat., 11 A.M.–7 P.M. Sun.) is off I-84 at the Franklin Road exit. Sears, Macy's, JCPenney, and Dillard's are the anchor tenants, and in between you'll find a plethora of clothing stores, places to eat, jewelers, shoe stores, sporting-goods stores, ATMs, book and music stores, and much, much more.

Boise Factory Outlets (208/331-5000, 10 A.M.–8 P.M. Mon.–Sat., 11 A.M.–6 P.M. Sun.) is east of town past the airport— take I-84 Exit 57 at Gowen Road. The mall complex offers dozens of stores selling name-brand merchandise at 30–70 percent off—Reebok, Eddie Bauer, Levi's, Van Heusen, and more.

BOOKS

When it comes to new books, Boise doesn't have many options beyond corporate bookstores. **Barnes & Noble Booksellers** (1315 N. Milwaukee St., 208/375-4454), near Boise Towne Square mall, offers a typical selection of book titles, stationery, and CDs. Ditto for **Borders Books** (350 N. Milwaukee St., 208/322-6668) on the ground level of the mall.

The **Boise State Bookstore** (1910 University Dr., 208/426-2665, 8 A.M.–7 P.M. Mon.–Tues., 8 A.M.–5:30 P.M. Wed.–Fri., 10 A.M.–5 P.M. Sat. year-round), in the Student Union Building on campus, not only has textbooks, it stocks other books (Idaho authors, recreation, travel guides), stationery, and office supplies.

For used books, check out **Trip Taylor Bookseller** (210 N. 10th St., 208/344-3311). This downtown bookstore has lots of used books and rare editions. The **Rediscovered Bookshop** (180 N. 8th St., 208/376-4229) is another place where you can find good dog-eared books.

OUTDOOR GEAR

If you need a new carabiner or hiking boots, **REI** (8300 W. Emerald St., 208/322-1141, www.rei.com, 10 A.M.–9 P.M. Mon.–Fri., 9 A.M.–7 P.M. Sat., 11 A.M.–6 P.M. Sun.) can help you out. This Seattle-based cooperative outdoor store has everything from maps to clothing to skis to tents and much more.

Hunters and anglers will find everything they need at **Cabela's** (8109 W. Franklin Rd., 208/672-7900, 9 A.M.–9 P.M. Mon.–Fri., 8 A.M.–9 P.M. Sat., 10 A.M.–6 P.M. Sun.) near the mall. Besides having fishing rods, tackle, and hunting gear, this giant store also carries clothing, accessories, and a large selection of cast-iron Dutch ovens and other outdoor cooking supplies and food. It's something of a museum and nature center too, meaning you'll find wall tanks filled with live trout and sturgeon, and there's an impressive "mountain" with taxidermy wild game animals. Watch out for bears!

BOISE

SPECIALTY SHOPS

Downtown Boise has a profusion of local stores where you can spend your hard-earned cash. **Eyes of the World Imports** (1576 W. Grove St., 208/331-1212), in the Linen District, sells "cool stuff from cool places"—handcrafted items from around the world. And it's also where you can score a box of Nag Champa incense.

The Record Exchange (1105 W. Idaho St., 208/344-8010) occupies the corner of the funky block that also holds Neurolux. It's the oldest music seller in town, where you'll find new and used CDs, old vinyl, and a friendly, knowledgeable staff who can fill you in on the latest chords in the Boise music scene.

Dragonfly (414 W. Main St., 208/338-9234) is a fun boutique and gift shop in Old Boise that stocks hippy-chic clothing, funny greeting cards, and various figurines, like Gumby and Buddy Christ.

Satiate your sweet tooth at **The Chocolat Bar** (805 W. Bannock St., 208/338-7771), a little shop that specializes in handcrafted truffles, turtles, barks, and dipped fruit. Nearby you'll find the **City Peanut Shop** (803 W. Bannock St., 208/433-3931). This old-school store turns out freshly roasted nuts, caramel corn, handmade brittles, and such.

Accommodations

Boise has an abundance of corporate hotels and motels, most toward the high end of the $50–100 price range. The major hotel areas are: downtown; around the university; around the airport; around the Boise Towne Square mall; and the ParkCenter business district. The downtown places are mostly upscale, though a few less-expensive independents are available there as well. The university area is close to downtown and both Ann Morrison and Julia Davis Parks, though most of the lodgings here tend to be along busy thoroughfares. The airport area is convenient to I-84 and is where most of the national chain motels are located, but it's a long walk to downtown. The ParkCenter area is hoofable from downtown for those with time and a reasonable fitness level, and it's close to the Boise River. The mall area is on major bus routes. If you have a favorite chain, call its 800 number and chances are it'll have a place in Boise. A number of possibilities, including historic bed-and-breakfast inns, are listed below.

UNDER $50

Boise doesn't have many lodging options in this price range. A handful of budget corporate hotels exist around town, though, including

Motel 6 (2323 Airport Way, 208/344-3506 or 800/466-8356, www.motel6.com, from $49 d) near the airport and **Budget Inn** (2600 Fairview Ave., 208/344-8617, about $40 s, from $65 d) on the fringe of downtown. Trekkers can find inexpensive refuge at **Idahostel** (280 N. 8th St., 208/703-0161, www.idahostel.com, $19–22). Located in the historic Idaho Building (8th St. and Bannock St.), this new hostel has three dormitory rooms, a communal kitchen, and showers. If you don't mind driving a few miles west, check into **Hostel Boise** (17322 Can-Ada Rd., Nampa, 208/467-6858, www.hostelboise.com, $20–45) is friendly and inexpensive.

$50-100

Downtown, the **Owyhee Plaza Hotel** (1109 Main St., 208/343-4611 or 800/233-4611, www.owyheeplaza.com, from $89 d) was built in 1910, but renovations have kept it up to modern standards. The exterior won't win any awards for architecture, but the interior is elegant. This is a full-service hotel popular with visiting dignitaries and executives. Amenities include shoeshine, a valet, a barber and beauty shop, a courtyard pool, and a small café. Across the street you can find clean and comfortable lodging at the **Safari**

THE IDANHA

Although you can no longer stay here, the grande dame of downtown buildings remains the 1901 **Idanha Hotel** (pronounced EYE-din-ha, 928 W. Main St.), whose tall corner turrets are an impressive sight from blocks away. Famed architect W. S. Campbell designed the French château-style masterpiece, Idaho's first six-story building and the first in the state to have an electric elevator. When it was completed it was considered the finest hotel west of the Mississippi and featured bay windows, claw-foot tubs, and the finest furnishings. In the hotel's glory days, Teddy Roosevelt, John and Ethel Barrymore, Buffalo Bill, William Borah, and Clarence Darrow all spent nights here. The Idanha's rooms were converted to apartments, but the ground-floor Indian restaurant and European bakery are open to the public.

Inn Downtown (1070 Grove St., 208/344-6556, www.safariinndowntown.com, from $89 d). This old-school motor inn has amenities like high-speed Internet, free continental breakfast, and an outdoor pool and spa. Also downtown is the small **Leku Ona Hotel** (117 S. 6th St., 208/345-6665, www.lekuonaid.com, $65–85), a Basque-run establishment that's next door to the Leku Ona, restaurant and bar. The rustic hotel may only have five guest rooms, but it's smack-dab in the middle of Boise's nightclub district. You could literally crawl back to your room after a night of reveling.

The best thing about staying at the somewhat scruffy **Shilo Inn Riverside** (3031 Main St., 208/344-3521 or 800/222-2244, from $74 d) is its location right on the Greenbelt. Avid walkers and cyclists will have no trouble making it downtown or to BSU; by car it takes five minutes. Amenities include a big indoor pool and a small continental breakfast.

If you're into historic bed-and-breakfast inns,

the downtown area has two worth mentioning. The **(** **Idaho Heritage Inn** (109 W. Idaho St., 208/342-8066, www.idheritageinn.com, $75–120) more than lives up to its name. It's an exquisitely lovely lodging in a turn-of-the-20th-century home that once belonged to Governor Chase Clark and later was the residence of his daughter Bethine and son-in-law Senator Frank Church. How's that for heritage? Needless to say, the inn is listed on the National Register of Historic Places. The location can't be beat, within walking distance of Old Boise, BoDo, and the capitol; to help you extend your explorations, mountain bikes are available for rent. The inn's six guest rooms all have private baths, queen beds, air-conditioning, and in-room phones. A full gourmet breakfast is included in the price, as is an evening glass of wine—weather permitting, either may be enjoyed out in the shaded courtyard. No smoking or pets are allowed.

Another early-20th-century gem, the 1907 **J. J. Shaw House** (1411 W. Franklin St., 208/344-8899 or 877/344-8899, www.jjshaw. com, $79–129) enjoys a great North End location. The quiet neighborhood and beautiful house and grounds almost guarantee you'll unwind fast. Each of the five guest rooms and the separate guest cottage, with a kitchenette, has a phone, a private bath, and air-conditioning. The romantic third-floor suite, Shaw's Retreat, features its own private staircase and a shower built for two. Rates include full breakfast. Smoking is allowed outdoors only, and pets and children under age 10 are not allowed.

Boise has a multitude of corporate hotels in this price range. On the eastside of the BSU campus and across Broadway is **Courtyard by Marriott** (222 S. Broadway Ave., 208/331-2700 or 800/321-2211, from $99 d). It's a big newish place about a mile from downtown and has an indoor pool, a hot tub, and a fitness center. Nearby in the ParkCenter area is the **Doubletree Club Hotel** (475 W. ParkCenter Blvd., 208/345-2002 or 888/222-8733, from $89 d), a pet-friendly hotel near the Greenbelt. Expect to find all the modern amenities.

Near the mall there are now several options for lodging, including the **Hyatt Place**

Boise Towne Square (925 N. Milwaukee St., 208/375-1200, www.hyattplace.com, from $69 d) and **AmeriTel Inn** (7965 W. Emerald St., 208/378-7000 or 800/600-6001, www.ameritelinns.com, from $89 d), both newish hotels with all the bells and whistles.

Other hotels near downtown and the mall area include the **Rodeway Inn** (1115 N. Curtis Rd., 208/376-2700 or 800/727-5002, $59–100) near St. Alphonsus Regional Medical Center, and **Harrison Plaza Suite Hotel** (409 S. Cole Rd., 208/375-7666 or 800/376-3608, from $79 d), a tucked-away place just off Franklin Road that's popular with the business set.

A variety of places in this price range are out by the airport. Most are branches of the big chains, so they're predictable, comfortable, and entirely unremarkable. Among them: **Inn America–A Budget Motel** (2275 Airport Way, 208/389-9800 or 800/469-4667, from $69 d) and the **Best Western Airport Inn** (2660 Airport Way, 208/384-5000 or 800/727-5004, from $79 d).

$100-150

The **Grove Hotel** (245 S. Capitol Blvd., 208/333-8000, www.grovehotelboise.com, from $139 d) has the best location in town, adjacent to The Grove, but this high-rise hotel is an urban eyesore. The drab sandstone-hued edifice appears uninviting from the street, and it epitomizes a lack of pedestrian vision in architecture—the hotel and connected Qwest Arena don't offer much sidewalk space, and watch out for delivery trucks and tour buses around the building. That said, the guest rooms are pleasantly decorated and the lobby is luxe, with plenty of seating, a cocktail lounge, and Emilio's, one of the finest restaurants in town.

Also downtown, you'll find the newly constructed **Hampton Inn & Suites** (495 S. Capitol Blvd., 208/331-1900, from $149 d), an 11-story hotel in BoDo that has complimentary breakfast, a coin-operated laundry, and an indoor pool and fitness center. Its central location makes walking around town a breeze.

One of downtown Boise's swankiest new places to sleep is **Hotel 43** (981 W. Grove St., 208/342-4622 or 800/243-4622, www.hotel43.com, from $135 d). This boutique hotel, formerly the Statehouse Inn, boasts 112 stylishly renovated guest rooms with excellent views of the city. Expect to be pampered here with room service, free Wi-Fi and airport shuttle service, and valet parking. Chandler's Steakhouse, on the hotel's first floor, offers upscale contemporary dining and a top-notch martini bar. Nightcap, anyone? In the morning, head to the espresso shop near the lobby where you can score a morning cappuccino and freshly baked pastries.

For a B&B–type experience in this price range, go to the **Boise Guest House** (614 N. 5th St., 208/761-6798, www.boiseguesthouse.com, $90–200) near Fort Boise Park. The inn's location next to the Foothills makes for easy access to mountain biking and hiking, and it takes less than five minutes to walk downtown. The guest suites are literally apartments, with private showers, kitchens, and flat-screen televisions, not typical little B&B guest rooms. Besides waking up to a big breakfast, the place also offers free parking and high-speed Internet.

On the west side of Capitol Boulevard, backing up against Ann Morrison Park, is **Marriott Residence Inn** (1401 Lusk Ave., 208/344-1200 or 800/331-3131, from $99 d). Its 104 suites are more like apartments than motel rooms; all have full kitchens, and many have fireplaces and living rooms. The nicely landscaped complex sits just far enough off Capitol Boulevard to be quiet. Amenities and services include cable TV with HBO, a free airport shuttle, an outdoor pool, spas, and a sport court. A large complimentary breakfast buffet is served in the spacious lobby, and if that doesn't fill you up, you can head to Elmer's next door.

The **Doubletree Hotel Riverside** (2900 Chinden Blvd., 208/343-1871 or 800/222-8733, from $109 d) has good Greenbelt access west of downtown, in the same area as the Shilo Inn in the previous price category, but catering to a higher-end business clientele. (In fact, weekday rates sometimes top $150.) This is Boise's largest hotel, with 304 guest rooms.

Amenities include a nice outdoor pool and fitness center. Bikes are available for rent too.

Also on the fringe of downtown and in the same price range, but generally less expensive than the Doubletree is the seven-story **Red Lion Hotel Boise Downtowner** (1800 Fairview Ave., 208/344-7691 or 800/325-4000, $79–149), which is a popular spot for conferences and business meetings.

The Boise Spectrum entertainment complex south of I-84 Exit 50, about seven miles from downtown, has a pair of newer upscale hotels worth a mention: **AmeriTel Inn–Boise Spectrum Center** (7499 W. Overland Rd., 208/323-2500 or 800/600-6001, from $109 d) and **Hilton Garden Inn Boise Spectrum** (7699 W. Spectrum Way, 208/376-1000, from $109 d). Both have indoor pools and are steps away from a 22-screen multiplex and nearly a dozen restaurants.

$150-250

Boise doesn't have many hotels and inns that cost more than $150 a night. Of course, some of the aforementioned hotels have larger suites in the $175–225 range, but not many places exceed that limit. The **((Modern Hotel and Bar** (1314 Grove St., 208/424-8244 or 866/780-6012, www.themodernhotel.com, $97–200) in the Linen District, a revamped old-school Travel Lodge, is as posh as it gets in Boise. The Modern, as everyone calls it, has lots of post-postmodern touches, like contemporary Euro furniture and glass-tiled spa baths. All rooms are accentuated with splashes of bold color, and they have 32-inch flat-screen televisions, free Wi-Fi, and iPod docks. Grab a cocktail at the first-floor bar and take it outside to the hip fireplace seating area, where local artists often hang out.

The themed guest rooms at the **Anniversary Inn** (1575 S. Lusk Ave., 208/387-4900 or 800/324-4152, www.anniversaryinn.com, suites $139–249) are among the most expensive lodging options in town, but where else are you going to find a "Jungle Safari" room or a "Biker Roadhouse" room? There's also a room called "Bronco Nights"—for diehard Boise State football fans—all decked out in blue and orange. The hotel may be cheesy, but it remains popular for those desiring a fantasy getaway.

RV PARKS

Boise has some good in-town options for RV campers, though tenters will find slimmer pickings, with only one area park currently accepting them. Unfortunately, the nearby state parks are day-use only. But there is plenty of dispersed camping in the Boise Front; for more information, drop by the **Boise National Forest headquarters** (1249 S. Vinnell Way, 208/373-4100). Here are a few decent choices if you are driving an RV and want water and electricity hookups.

Tenters are welcome at **On the River RV Park** (6000 N. Glenwood St., 208/375-7432 or 800/375-7432, RVs $28–33, tents $25). The 215 spaces have Good Sam and AARP discounts. Amenities include a Greenbelt location, high-speed wireless Internet access, and a neat laundry and shower building. The park abuts the Western Idaho Fairgrounds and the baseball stadium where the Boise Hawks play, so expect a bit of noise when games or other fairground events take place.

Over by the airport is **Mountain View RV Park** (2040 Airport Way, 208/345-4141, $29–32). It seems like an odd place for an RV park—squeezed in between the airport and I-84—but it has the advantage of easy freeway access and easy maneuvering within the park itself; all of the park's 63 spaces are pull-throughs. Facilities include laundry and showers. Sites have full hookups; discounts are available.

Hi-Valley RV Park (10555 Horseshoe Bend Rd., 208/939-8080, $31) is on the way out of town heading toward McCall on Highway 55. The big park, about eight miles from downtown Boise, has 194 spaces with full hookups, and there are discounts for AAA and Good Sam members. No tents are allowed, but the park has two rental cabins ($75). The clubhouse has a large-screen TV, a full kitchen, spacious shower rooms, a laundry, and a billiard room.

Food and Drink

FINE DINING

Due to the ongoing economic downturn, Boise's fine-dining scene has experienced some setbacks in recent years, with several closures of upscale establishments. But there are still many venerable restaurants and some relatively new ones in the downtown area where you can enjoy a fine-dining experience, especially if you like steak and potatoes.

If you're into upscale dining in a swanky environment, head to **(Chandler's Steakhouse** (981 W. Grove St., 208/383-4300, www.chandlersboise.com, from 5:30 P.M. daily, appetizers $9–15, entrées $26–40) inside Hotel 43. Restaurateur Rex Chandler debuted this Northwest-influenced steakhouse in 2008 after relocating from Ketchum, where he ran Chandler's and Baci for many years. Success seems to follow Chandler because his Boise restaurant was met with resounding applause by those craving big steaks, seafood, and vintages from one of the best wine lists in town. The kitchen here likes to source Idaho foodstuffs, like Kobe-style beef, Kurobuta pork, Hagerman Valley trout, and local grass-fed lamb. Start out with house-made gravlax, baked oysters, clam chowder, and a delicious roasted artichoke. The entrée menu is mostly à la carte, but the restaurant offers a tasting menu that comes with three courses for around $30. The other route includes a large list of steaks, like New York strips, rib eyes, and filet mignon, served with chosen sides such as pommes frites and asparagus with hollandaise. Finish with a crock of delish berry cobbler. Chandler's Steakhouse also has a martini bar (from 4 P.M. daily) that puts out inventive cocktails in a lively setting. Local jazz musicians play in the lounge on a weekly basis.

Berryhill & Co. (121 N. 9th St., 208/387-3553, www.berryhillandco.com, lunch Mon.–Sat., dinner daily, brunch 10 A.M.–2 P.M. Sun., $14–35) is another high-end restaurant and bar downtown that's full of personality, thanks to a modern design and the eccentricities of its owner, chef John Berryhill. You'll often see him roaming the dining room, cracking jokes and schmoozing the guests. Sit on the happening patio and enjoy starters like baked escargot, wild salmon cakes, and a trifecta of sliders— washed down with a glass of local chardonnay from the eclectic wine list. Larger plates include offerings like London broil, shrimp linguine, honey-lavender rack of lamb, and a pan-seared Kurobuta pork chop smothered with brandied leeks.

A stone's throw away, under the One Capitol Center building, **Angell's Bar & Grill** (999 Main St., 208/342-4900, www.angellsbarandgrill.com, lunch 11:30 A.M.–2 P.M. Tues.–Fri., dinner from 5 P.M. daily, $18–29) has a unique layout—you walk from street level down an amphitheater-like grassy slope to the subterranean but open, not basement-like, restaurant. A patio outside offers some of the city's most enjoyable alfresco dining. The restaurant recently underwent renovation, adding contemporary upgrades to the dining room and bar, and the menu was retooled as well. Prime your palate with wild mushroom bruschetta, baked Pacific oysters, and crab cakes with Thai pepper aioli before committing to plates from the entrée menu, which has lots of globally-inspired pasta dishes, steaks, and seafood. Some standouts include the slow-roasted prime rib, trout amandine, and cedar-plank salmon with a bright citrus butter. The large wine list plays well with the menu.

On the ground floor of a modern office building, **Cottonwood Grille** (913 W. River St., 208/333-9800, www.cottonwoodgrille.com, lunch 11 A.M.–4 P.M. daily, dinner 5–10 P.M. daily, brunch Sun., lunch $8–13, dinner entrées $16–29) hides its charms from passersby. Inside, you'll discover that the dining room backs right onto the Greenbelt and the Boise River. In summer, the large patio, replete with pond and waterfall, offers a great place to dine in a natural setting (mist-makers keep alfresco diners cool in the dog days of summer). The extensive menu offers veggie dishes, soups and salads, pastas, seafood, and all the usual upscale meat dishes—many of which are made with local foodstuffs. The dinner menu has items such as olive tapenade served with local goat cheese, house-smoked trout, beef stroganoff, and a braised lamb shank with lentil ragout.

For inventive New American cuisine, check out **(Emilio's** (245 S. Capitol Blvd., 208/333-8002, www.emiliosboise.com, breakfast, lunch, dinner from 5 P.M. daily, entrées $16–28) at the Grove Hotel. This is a true hotel restaurant, and the nighttime menu really shines with a bevy of seasonal offerings. Expect to find appetizers such as lobster corndogs, artisanal cheeses, and wood-fired flatbread with Tasso ham, tomatoes, basil, and fresh mozzarella. Seal the deal with entrées like pan-seared Alaskan halibut with coconut rice risotto, Kobe beef pot roast with smoked cheddar grits, and a roasted rack of lamb with cipollini onion marmalade. The wine list spans the globe, with lots of Northwestern and European labels. You can also score sashimi and maki rolls from the sushi bar in the lobby.

Red Feather Lounge (246 N. 8th St., 208/429-6340, www.justeatlocal.com, lunch Mon.–Fri., dinner from 5 P.M. daily, brunch 8:30 A.M.–2 P.M. Sun., $8–25) is another downtown mainstay known for its excellent New American fare. Even though the place has a bar-like name, it's actually one of the better contemporary restaurants in town. Don't get me wrong, the Red Feather has a great lounge where you can indulge in creatively mixed cocktails, microbrews, and wines from the largest cellar in Boise (more than 5,500 bottles are kept in a towering glass wine storage area). But the seasonal cuisine takes center stage at this stylishly modern restaurant. Restaurateur Dave Krick, who also owns Bittercreek Alehouse next door, is passionate about sourcing locally produced and grown foodstuffs. One any given night, you might see dishes like grilled halloumi (squeaky Greek cheese) with basil and fresh tomato, braised lamb riblets with harissa (spicy North African sauce), wood-fired pizzas,

and fried chicken with savory corn waffles. The bar stays open till 2 A.M. most nights.

For more traditional steakhouse and seafood offerings, try these two venerable Boise restaurants. Prime rib is the claim to fame at **Lock Stock & Barrel** (1100 W. Jefferson St., 208/336-4266, www.lsbboise.com, lunch and dinner 11 A.M.–9 P.M. Mon., 11 A.M.–10 P.M. Tues.–Sat., 4–9 P.M. Sun., entrées $16–32), but a large variety of steaks, seafood dishes, and surf and turf combos add to the menu. All dinners include a trip to the salad bar, a bowl of clam chowder, and hot bread. If you still have room for dessert, try the LS&B variation on the traditional mud pie: the cow pie. The casual wood-and-brick decor with low lights and candles is suitable for dates and good conversation.

Murphy's Seafood & Steakhouse (1555 Broadway Ave., 208/344-3691, lunch at 11 A.M. Mon.–Sat., dinner from 4 P.M. daily, brunch 10 A.M.–2 P.M. Sun., $6–30) is a longtime local favorite. Appetizers like oysters Rockefeller or a pound of steamers start things off. Salads come with fresh-baked sourdough and garlic butter. Fresh seafood entrées might include Atlantic salmon mesquite broiled and basted with rosemary, sage, and thyme butter, or grilled Copper River salmon. Other seafood, chicken, and steak entrées are available. Most larger plates are in the $20 range. Murphy's also has an excellent Sunday brunch.

GASTROPUBS AND BREWPUBS

The City of Trees could easily be called the City of Pubs, yet most watering holes here miss the mark in the culinary department. Foodies need not fret, though, because there are a few pubs where the food is just as good if not better than the drinks. **(Bittercreek Alehouse** (246 N. 8th St., 208/345-1813, 11 A.M.–late daily, $6–14), next to the Red Feather Lounge and owned by the same people, has been extremely popular since it opened in 1995. Besides having more than 30 microbrews and imported beers on draft, the kitchen produces some of the best upscale pub grub in town.

Expect to find Northwestern offerings like grilled wild sockeye salmon with sweet hazelnut butter, clam chowder, and inventive burgers topped with local artisanal cheeses.

The **Tavern at Bown Crossing** (3111 S. Bown Way, 208/345-2277, www.tavernatbown.com, from 11:30 A.M. Mon.–Sat., from 9:30 A.M. Sun., $8–37), in southeast Boise, not only pours cocktails, microbrews, and wines, it also puts out a creative menu of upscale pub fare in a contemporary environment. Standouts include the pot roast nachos, fried calamari with Cajun aioli, warm artichoke heart dip, and grilled filet mignon with potatoes au gratin. Did I mention that it also has a sushi bar? The restaurant has a popular Sunday brunch as well.

While **Bardenay** (610 W. Grove St, 208/426-0538, www.bardenay.com, lunch and dinner daily, $8.50–23), with other branches in Eagle and Coeur d'Alene, may not be a pub per se, this microdistillery on the Basque Block has a stellar reputation for serving high-end pub fare to go along with cocktails mixed with its house-made vodka, gin, rum, and bourbon. The large menu spans the globe with offerings like Thai salmon cakes, bourbon-glazed pork chops, and grilled Hagerman Valley trout with balsamic reduction.

Boise's microbrew scene is a far cry from what's going on in Seattle and Portland, but there are some places where you can enjoy commendable handcrafted brews. **Highlands Hollow Brewhouse** (2455 Harrison Hollow Lane, 208/343-6820, www.highlandshollow.com, 11 A.M.–late daily), just off Bogus Basin Road, produces some extremely quaffable microbrews, including golden ale, pale ale, ginger wheat ale, and robust stout. The food here is above average as well, with appetizers like steamer clams, grilled polenta, and pan-fried oysters.

In Boise's Winstead Park neighborhood you'll find **Sockeye Grill & Brewery** (3019 N. Cole Rd., 208/658-1533, 11 A.M.–late daily, around $8), a little brewpub that turns out decent India pale ale, pale ale, espresso stout, porter, and various seasonal ales. The menu has a typical array of sandwiches, wraps, salads, and rice bowls.

Table Rock Brewpub & Grill (705 Fulton St., 208/342-0944, 11 A.M.–late daily), on the fringe of BoDo, has made microbrews for more than 20 years. This is a good spot to sample handcrafted ales and hang out with friends, or meet some new ones; after all, Boise is friendly.

WINE BARS AND WINERY TASTING ROOMS
Wine Bars

Situated on what's easily downtown Boise's busiest corner, 8th and Idaho Streets, the **Grape Escape** (800 W. Idaho St., 208/368-0200, lunch and dinner daily, brunch 10 A.M.–2:30 P.M. Sun., $8–17) has been a food-and-wine constant since 1997. The lively sidewalk patio is a great place to nosh on shared plates and sample vintages from one of the largest wine lists in town. You'll see more than 200 labels from Argentina, France, Spain, Italy, Australia, California, and the Northwest; 30 wines are offered by the glass. The wine-friendly menu includes artisanal cheese plates, flatbread pizzas, and various antipasto items. The Grape Escape also has live jazz with Sunday brunch.

Twig's Cellar (816 Bannock St., 208/344-8944, www.twigscellar.com, from 4 P.M. Tues.–Sat., $7–14), in the basement of the Garro Building, is a new wine bar that boasts a multitude of wines by the glass, many of which are from Washington, Oregon, and Idaho. The menu favors small plates such as seasonal bruschetta, crab cakes, and smoked salmon with dill pesto. Twig's features live jazz 6:30–9:30 P.M. Friday–Saturday.

Winery Tasting Rooms

Four local wineries have set up tasting rooms in the downtown area in recent years. These boutique-level producers grow their grapes in the Snake River Valley, Idaho's new wine appellation. In BoDo, you can sample some excellent vintages at the appropriately named **Snake River Winery** (786 W. Broad St.,

208/345-9463, www.snakeriverwinery.com, tasting room 10:30 A.M.–7:30 P.M. Tues.– Sat., noon–5 P.M. Sun.). This winery grows its grapes at Arena Valley Vineyard in Parma. Chef-turned-winemaker Scott DeSeelhorst produces several remarkable small-batch wines, including syrah, chardonnay, riesling, grenache, barbera, and malbec.

Fraser Vineyard (1004 La Pointe St., 208/345-9607, www.fraservineyard.com, tasting room by appointment only) operates a small tasting room by Ann Morrison Park. Winemaker Bill Fraser, who grows his grapes near Sunny Slope, makes superb cabernet sauvignon, viognier, and a fruit-forward syrah-malbec blend.

You can sample some excellent vintages in nearby Garden City at **Cinder Wines** (107 E. 44th St., 208/433-9813, www.cinderwines.com, tasting room noon–5 P.M. Sat. or by appointment) on Chinden Boulevard. Winemaker Melanie Krause opened this small winery in 2008, after cutting her winemaking teeth at Chateau Ste. Michelle in Washington. Considered one of the best winemakers in Idaho, Krause turns out chardonnay, syrah, viognier and a wonderfully dry rosé made from grapes grown at various Snake River Valley vineyards. Also in Garden City, you'll find **Syringa Winery** (3500 W. Chinden Blvd., 208/433-1616, www.syringawinery.com, tasting room noon–7 P.M. Thurs.–Sat.), a boutique operation that makes small lots of merlot, cabernet sauvignon, primitivo, and sauvignon blanc produced by winemaker Mike Crowley.

ETHNIC CUISINE
Basque

More than 15,000 Basques live in the Boise area, so Basque food is fairly embedded into the mainstream culture. In other words, your average Joe can easily identify a croqueta. You'll find two Basque eateries and bars as well as one import market on the Basque Block.

(Bar Gernika (202 S. Capitol Blvd., 208/344-2175, www.bargernika.com, 11 A.M.– 11 P.M. Mon., 11 A.M.–midnight Tues.–Thurs., 11 A.M.–1 A.M. Fri., 11:30 A.M.–1 A.M. Sat.,

$7–9.50), a tiny place that borrows its name from a city in the Basque region of Spain, is a popular hangout for people from all walks of life. You'll see bifocal-wearing college professors next to visiting Basquos (conversing in their tongue-twisting language) next to tattooed 20-something locals—all enjoying big glasses of Rioja (Basque red wine) and draft microbrews. But this bar focuses just as much attention on food as it does on drink. (The Basques love to eat, and talking about food and wine is a favorite pastime as well.) The vibe here is casual, and the kitchen puts out everything from Basque-influenced sandwiches and traditional dishes to American-style burgers and melts. Try an order of croquetas (crunchy fritters made with chicken stock and roux) and a solomo sandwich (marinated pork loin with pimentos) served with hand-cut fries. Other noteworthy dishes include the lamb dip (dripping with jus on a crusty roll), paella, and delicious braised beef tongue—the latter dish is only served on Saturday, and it usually runs out by midday.

Leku Ona (117 S. 6th St., 208/345-8887, www.lekuonaid.com, 9 A.M.–midnight Mon.– Thurs., 9 A.M.–1:30 A.M. Fri.–Sun., $8–30) bookends the eastside of the Basque Block. This newish establishment is in a historic brick building that used to be a Basque boarding house and social club. It's once again a social hub for Basques and non-Basques alike, now boasting three floors of restaurant and bar space: two separate lounge areas (one smoking, the other nonsmoking), a downstairs banquet room near the wine cellar, and an elegant third-floor dining room with a rooftop terrace overlooking the Leku Ona Hotel. Whether you're into tapas and Rioja in the bar or a full-service dinner upstairs, Leku Ona has got you covered with a gamut of traditional Basque dishes. Start the night with ham croquetas, shrimp-filled piquillo peppers, and escargot baked in zesty butter. Many of the entrées are also made with tried-and-true recipes from the homeland. Expect to see dishes such as a braised lamb shank, stewed beef tongue, and pepper-stuffed squid cooked in its own ink. The menu

© IDAHO DIVISION OF TOURISM

Leku Ona

also has lots of grilled steaks and pork chops. (The Basques love their meat almost as much as they adore seafood; there aren't many vegetarians in this culture.) If you're really hungry, go for the family-style dinner ($28 pp), a package deal that includes your choice of an entrée (lamb stew, roasted chicken, meatballs, or pork chops) served with soup, salad, and passable platters of fried cod, paella, and crispy fries.

Next door, **The Basque Market** (608 W. Grove St., 208/433-1208, www.thebasque-market.com, 10 A.M.–6 P.M. Mon.–Sat.) is the place to go for all things Basque, like imported wines, cured meats, cheeses, chocolate, good olive oil, house-brined green olives, and more. The market has shifted gears into the restaurant (or at least deli) realm in recent years. You can now score various tapas dishes and sandwiches and take them to a table on the sidewalk patio. The Basque Market also sells freshly baked bread and tubs of house-made soups as well as delicious rice pudding.

Italian

Boise has a typical profusion of corporate Italian places out in the burbs, yet here are two restaurants in the downtown area that make Italian food from scratch. **Asiago's** (1002 Main St., 208/336-5552, www.asiagos. com, lunch Mon.–Fri., dinner daily, $9–25), in the historic Gem-Noble Building, has earned a loyal following for its creative regional Italian offerings. The exposed-brick dining room and adjacent wine bar quickly fills up with those craving big glasses of Sangiovese and dishes like herb-crusted veal loin with sweet vermouth-lemon reduction and grilled flatbread with pesto, artichoke hearts, and arugula. Pasta is made fresh daily, and the list might include rosemary gnocchi, shrimp and clam linguine, and spinach fettuccine with smoked tomato cream sauce.

Café Vicino (808 W. Fort St., 208/472-1463, www.cafevicino.com, lunch Mon.–Fri., dinner from 5 P.M. Mon.–Sat., $6–30) in the city's North End dishes up remarkable Italian fare in a casual setting. The decidedly Mediterranean menu changes with the season. Expect to see entrées like cioppino, cheese ravioli with brown butter–sage sauce, and pan-seared New York strip steak served with a puffy Gorgonzola soufflé. Smaller plates might include prosciutto-wrapped figs, grilled shrimp on risotto cakes, and bruschetta with artichoke tapenade. The wine list has plenty of Italian and Northwestern labels, including some from Idaho's Snake River Valley.

Mediterranean

For fast Eastern Mediterranean fare, check out **Mazzah** (404 E. ParkCenter Blvd., 208/333-2223, and 1772 W. State St., 208/333-2566, lunch and dinner daily, entrées $8–11), a takeout restaurant that specializes in falafel sandwiches, gyros, lamb kabobs, and dolmas (stuffed grape leaves). Also expect to find tabbouleh salad, fatoosh, baba ghanoush, and hummus, served with warm flatbread. Finish with some jolting Turkish coffee and a wedge of flaky baklava.

Another good takeout place for gyros is the aptly named **Gyro Shack** (6631 W. Ustick Rd., 208/378-1325, lunch and dinner Mon.–Sat., most sandwiches under $5), where locals line up at the drive-through window for traditional Greek lamb sandwiches. The small restaurant, in the burbs of West Boise, also has an indoor seating area where you can enjoy lemonade and a "Super Gyro," a warm pita filled with shaved lamb, bacon, lettuce, tomato, and tzatziki (garlicky Greek yogurt sauce).

Chinese

At one time, more than a century ago, Boise had a large Chinatown with many Chinese restaurants. Now the city only has a few worth mentioning, unless you're into mediocre Chinese buffets.

Yen Ching (305 N. 9th St. at Bannock St., 208/384-0384, www.yenchingboise. com, lunch and dinner daily) is a local favorite. You can enjoy recognizable Chinese cuisine in a pleasant setting. The dining room is accented with stylish art and ornate Asian screens. Sit in a comfy booth and peruse the large menu of Hunan, Szechuan, and Cantonese offerings—cooked in the eye-catching Mandarin style. The dinner menu

FRENCH DINING IN A FRENCH-NAMED CITY

Considering the name Boise is French in origin, it only makes sense that the city have French restaurants.

Locals flock to ◖ **Le Café de Paris** (204 N. Capitol Blvd., 208/336-0889, www.lecafede-paris.com, 7 A.M.-3 P.M. Sun.-Wed., 7 A.M.-10 P.M. Thurs., 7 A.M.-11 P.M. Fri.-Sat., $5-21) near the state capitol for fresh baguettes, chocolate croissants, and specialty cakes and tarts. The café also puts out traditional Gallic dishes like onion soup gratinée, duck confit with pan-seared apple, and roasted pork loin with glazed morel mushrooms and savory bread pudding. Desserts are pretty spectacular here too; take care of your sweet tooth with the ultrasilky chocolate mousse or a flaky strawberry tart.

Also downtown, in the historic Idanha Building, is **La Vie en Rose** (928 W. Main St., 208/331-4045, www.lavieenrosebakery.com, 8 A.M.-5 P.M. Tues.-Sun., lunch $5-13). This European bakery and bistro has a decidedly French bent, with glass cases filled with everything from freshly baked lemon brioche to almond croissants and delectable cream puffs. The lunch menu focuses on house-made soups, salads, and Euro-inspired sandwiches. Standouts include the Mediterranean tuna salad, veggie melt with grilled eggplant and zucchini, and the croque monsieur, a classic French ham, Swiss cheese, and Dijon sandwich on crusty sourdough bread.

Up by the mall, Francophiles will surely like **Le Coq Rouge** (1320 S. Maple Grove Rd., 208/376-9463, 11 A.M.-9 P.M. Wed.-Sat., 10:30 A.M.-4 P.M. Sun., entrées $15-29), a small French café that sticks to countryside classics, like quiche Lorraine, escargot, duck confit, and coq au vin (chicken, bacon, and mushrooms cooked with red wine). But chef Franck Bacquet, who hails from France, also has some contemporary French dishes up his sleeve. Order a bottle of Bordeaux and dig into a plate of truffle-filled ravioli or some rack of lamb "lollipops." Make sure to save room for the delightful chocolate bread pudding.

© DANA HOPPER-KELLY

Le Café de Paris

($10–13) has barbecued spare ribs, egg drop soup, fried rice, and roasted duck. The twice-cooked pork and kung pao chicken are also good picks. Vegetarians won't feel left out; there are plenty of properly cooked tofu and vegetable dishes for them. Wash everything down with a cold Chinese beer or a cocktail from the lounge. The restaurant recently started dishing out dim sum, like barbecued pork buns and siu mai.

In the Bench Depot neighborhood, you can take care of that craving for Chinese food at **Panda Garden** (2801 Overland Rd., 208/433-1188, www.boisepandagarden.com, lunch and dinner daily, $8–12). This tiny Chinese restaurant, which also serves sushi and sashimi, puts out decent Cantonese and Hunan-inspired food. Expect to see lots of egg rolls, soups, stir-fried dishes, and moo shu in every conceivable form, as well as more Americanized fare like egg foo young and chow mein. Vegetarians should try the tofu and broccoli with brown rice. The service is friendly and swift, and they will deliver to your hotel room.

Thai

If you've got a hankering for nose-clearing curries and wok-seared noodles, head to **C Pad Thai House** (1473 S. Five Mile Rd., 208/375-6014, 11 A.M.–9:30 P.M. Sun.–Thurs., 11 A.M.–10 P.M. Fri., noon–10 P.M. Sat., $7–14) near the corner of Five Mile and Overland Roads. This popular Thai restaurant may be situated in an innocuous-looking strip mall, but the inside is beautifully designed with Thai woodcarvings and elegant furniture. Plus, service is incredibly friendly and efficient. The menu has Thai offerings from the country's four culinary regions, including coconut milk-infused curries (red, green, golden) and soups, charb salads, satay, and sweet and spicy pad thai as the name suggests. The honey-roasted duck and green papaya salad are also noteworthy dishes.

Chiang Mai (4898 W. Emerald St. at Orchard St., 208/342-4051, lunch and dinner daily, $7–14), puts out excellent Thai cuisine from the northern reaches of Siam. Besides fresh rolls, green papaya salad, and Panang curry, the menu also has dishes from other regions in Thailand, like chicken and pork satay, southern-style curries and soups, and a delicious beef salad redolent of lime, ginger, and red chili paste. Don't worry, though, Chiang Mai serves ice-cold Thai beer and creamy iced tea to put out the fire.

Vietnamese

Unlike Portland and Seattle, Boise is not known for having good Vietnamese food. (This may have something to do with the fact that only about 1,000 Vietnamese people live in the area.) But a few decent Vietnamese restaurants have opened here in recent years. **Pho Nouveau** (780 W. Idaho St., 208/367-1111, www.phonouveau.com, lunch and dinner daily, $6–14) is one of the city's only bona fide pho shops. Locals file in everyday for big bowls of beef noodle soup served with fresh basil, bean sprouts, and lime. The restaurant also dishes up other traditional Vietnamese specialties, like Saigon-style crepes, shaken beef salad, lotus root salad with shrimp, and crispy spring rolls (cha gio) sided with lettuce leaves and seasoned fish sauce (nuoc cham).

For Vietnamese-style sandwiches, check out the **Baguette Deli** (5204 W. Franklin Rd., 208/336-2989, lunch and dinner daily, sandwiches around $6) on the Bench—next to the Fred Meyer department store. This affordable restaurant specializes in banh mi, Vietnamese sandwiches (grilled beef, shrimp, pork loaf, roasted chicken, and veggie "ham") made on crusty baguette rolls with pickled radish, cilantro, and jalapeño. Besides banh mi, also expect to see pork and shrimp spring rolls, sweet pastries, Vietnamese coffee (with sweet condensed milk), and bubble tea. The Baguette Deli has plans to open a second location soon in the downtown area.

Japanese

For a city that's about an eight-hour drive from the nearest ocean, Boise sure has a lot of sushi joints, but not all of them are noteworthy. One sure bet is **C Shige** (100 N. 8th St., 208/338-8423, www.shigejapanesecuisine.com, lunch and dinner Mon.–Sat., $11–30) on the second-floor of the Capitol Terrace building. This downtown sushi bar is as authentic as it gets in Boise, and the interior design is straight out of Tokyo, with its wrap-around counter, rice-paper lanterns, and glass case packed with relatively fresh fish. Chef Shigeki Matsuzawa and his crew turn out a large array of sushi and sashimi, including maki rolls (traditional and fusion), hand rolls, nigiri, and Kumamoto oysters on the half-shell. If raw fish isn't to your liking, go for the hot dishes such as shrimp tempura, chicken tonkatsu, and miso soup. Expect the usual array of sake, rice lagers, and sweet plum wine.

Right next door, chef Matsuzawa also operates a dinner-only Japanese steakhouse (150 N. 8th St., 208/331-8202), with table-side teppanyaki grills where you can watch the shrimp fly.

In BoDo, **Happy Fish Sushi** (855 Broad St., 208/343-4810, www.happyfishsushi.com, lunch and dinner daily, $5–14), in the alley next to the Knitting Factory Concert House, is a popular hangout for young hipsters who come here for sushi, sashimi, and martinis. The menu has lots of fusion rolls, nigiri, and other Japanese specialties such as beef tataki and poke, a martini glass filled with cubed raw tuna and spicy sesame sauce. Hot items include rice bowls, tempura, miso-glazed salmon, and blanched soybeans (edamame) sprinkled with sea salt.

Only a few places in Boise get teriyaki right. **Zen Bento** (1000 W. Main St., 208/388-8808, www.zenbento.com, $7–9) is a downtown take-out place that focuses on teriyaki rice bowls and salads. Walk up to the counter and pick your protein (grilled chicken, beef, salmon, ahi, tofu) and they'll plop it in a bowl with steamed rice and crisp veggies. Sauces come on the side, and they include regular teriyaki, ginger-soy, and a zippy chili-garlic sauce, to name a few. There's also a Zen Bento (342 E. State St., 208/938-4277, 11 A.M.–6 P.M. Mon.–Fri., 11 A.M.–4 P.M. Sat.) in nearby Eagle.

Yokozuna Teriyaki (824 S. Vista Ave., 208/377-3064, lunch and dinner daily), near the Boise Depot, is another take-out restaurant that specializes in grilled teriyaki meats with all the fixings.

Pan-Asian

Chef Shigeki Matsuzawa recently debuted his latest contribution to Boise's fine-dining scene, **Shige's Red Carpet** (150 N. 8th St., 208/338-8423, 5–10 P.M. Mon.–Sat., entrées $12–59), next to his other restaurants on the second floor of the Capital Terrace building. Red Carpet is all about upscale Japanese-French fusion cuisine. Expect to see appetizers like Kobe beef carpaccio (slices of raw beef) with sweet onion jam and sea scallops with caviar and spicy mustard sauce. Larger plates might include pan-seared sea bass with shiitake mushrooms and a foie gras–crowned filet mignon with huckleberry-plum wine reduction. The wine list includes premium sakes and regional American labels, pairing well with chef Matsuzawa's inventive fare.

Ⅽ Ono Hawaiian Café (2170 Broadway, 208/429-6800, www.onocafe.net, 11:30 A.M.–8 P.M. Mon.–Wed., 11 A.M.–8 P.M. Thurs., 11 A.M.–9 P.M. Fri.–Sat., noon–7 P.M. Sun., entrées $7–15) is where people go for a taste of Polynesia. Hawaii is known to be a melting pot of Asian flavors, and this small restaurant delineates the islands well with a bevy of traditional offerings, including kalua pork, ahi poke, teriyaki, kimchi shrimp, and Spam musubi (nori-wrapped grilled canned ham and rice). And it wouldn't be Hawaiian cuisine without sides of coconut milk-infused rice and creamy macaroni salad, which the restaurant makes in big batches every day. Ono also has a popular catering business that specializes in luaus.

Indian

Boise has two noteworthy Indian restaurants. **Taj Mahal** (150 N. 8th St., 208/473-7200, lunch and dinner Mon.–Sat., $5–22), across the terrace from Shige, leans to Pakistan and northern India for inspiration. The menu has everything from saucy curry dishes to tandoori chicken specialties to flatbreads like naan, kulcha, and roti. Start out with samosas (little meat pies), kebabs, and pakora (crunchy veggie fritters) washed down with an Indian beer or aromatic chai tea. Standout main dishes include chicken biryani (seasoned basmati rice) and vindaloo lamb, a spicy Goan curry guaranteed to open your nasal passages. Cool your palate with a bowl of rice pudding spiked with cardamom and almonds (kheer). Like most Indian restaurants, Taj Mahal offers a lunch buffet that's packed with all the Indian standards.

Madhuban (6930 W. State St., near Glenwood St., 208/853-8215, lunch and dinner daily, $7–16) also serves good Indian cuisine. Here you can choose from a large selection of traditional dishes such as chicken tikka masala, lamb vindaloo, and shrimp cooked with spinach and fresh herbs. Noteworthy vegetarian dishes include aloo chana (chickpeas and potatoes) and tarka dal (lentils stewed with spices). There's plenty of freshly baked naan bread to soak up the sauces. Madhuban puts out an excellent lunch buffet spread daily.

Mexican and Southwestern

Most locals would agree that nearby Canyon County has the best Mexican food in the area thanks to a large Hispanic population in Nampa and Caldwell. In Boise, Mexican cuisine is hit or miss, but there are a few Mexican restaurants around town that don't melt orange cheese on everything. **Andrade's** (4903 W. Overland Rd., 208/344-1234, lunch and dinner daily, $7–12) serves fairly authentic Mexican fare such as chiles rellenos, tamales, torta sandwiches, seviche, and tacos galore. Carnitas (fried pork butt) and carne asada (marinated, grilled skirt steak) are good choices if you're into tacos. Most dishes include rice and refried beans, not to mention chips and salsa. The beverage list boasts a good lineup of Mexican beers and sodas.

El Gallo Giro (5285 Glenwood St., 208/321-0355, www.elgallogiroidaho.com, lunch and dinner daily), across from the fairgrounds, is another Mexican restaurant that isn't overly Americanized. Here you will find friendly staff and lots of Mexican standards, like menudo (tripe soup), campechana (shrimp and octopus cocktail), chicken mole, smothered burritos, and combination plates. This place is also known for its tasty beef tongue (lengua) and beef cheek (cabeza) tacos.

For a taste of Southwestern cuisine, head to **The Green Chile** (5616 W. State St., 208/853-0103, lunch and dinner Mon.–Sat., $8–11), a small restaurant that draws influences from New Mexico. This place has delicious chili (red and green), chiles rellenos, pork sopapillas, stacked enchiladas, and Tex-Mex burgers.

PIZZA

It wasn't long ago that Boise's pizza scene was controlled by corporate chains. Thankfully the city has recently undergone a pizza renaissance, with several notable restaurants (serving a variety of thin-crust pizzas) leading the way. **Casanova Pizzeria** (1204 S. Vista Ave., 208/331-3535, www.casanovapizzeria.com, 11 A.M.–10 P.M. Mon.–Sat., $7.50–21.50), in the Bench Depot neighborhood, will have you falling in love with their Neapolitan pies, blistered in a brick oven. Try a classic Margherita (tomato, basil, and fresh mozzarella) or the outstanding clam and bacon pizza. The pesto pizza with mushrooms, artichoke hearts, and pine nuts is a good pick too. Casanova also dishes up entrée-sized salads and hot sandwiches.

Pie Hole (www.pieholeusa.com) is a newish pizza joint that receives rave reviews from locals. With two Boise locations, one downtown (205 N. 8th St., 208/344-7783, open late daily) and one by the university (1016 Broadway, 208/424-2225, open late daily), Pie Hole serves whole pies and pizza by the slice (around $2). Expect to see New York–style pizzas, ranging from a tasty potato and bacon pie to a meaty creation called the "Tritalian," which has lots of pepperoni, salami, and Italian sausage. The meatless crowd will surely like the four-cheese and veggie pizzas.

Next to the Egyptian Theatre, you'll find **Tony's Pizzeria Teatro** (105 N. Capitol Blvd., 208/343-1052, lunch and dinner Mon.–Sat.). This tiny restaurant puts out excellent Naples-inspired pizzas, antipasto, and gelato. Nearby in BoDo, **Proto's Pizzeria Napoletana** (345 S. 8th St., 208/331-1400, www.protospizza.com, 11 A.M.–10 P.M. daily) also makes thin-crust pizzas with premium toppings like hearts of palm, kalamata olives, and prosciutto. For dessert, try the classic cannoli and lemon gelato.

Before all these other pizza joints opened, **Guido's Pizzeria** (235 N. 5th St., 208/345-9011, and 12375 Chinden Blvd., 208/376-1008, lunch and dinner daily) was the only place in town to get true New York–style pizza, served with a Big Apple attitude. Here you can score salads, sausage rolls, stromboli, whole pizzas (a 20-inch cheese pie is around $12), and pizza by the slice.

Another longtime local favorite is **Flying Pie** (6508 Fairview, 208/345-0000, and 4320 State St., 208/384-0000, lunch and dinner daily), a pizzeria that dishes up decent pizzas with typical toppings. It's a great place for families, and they deliver.

BURGER JOINTS AND SANDWICH SHOPS
Burgers
Without a doubt, **Big Jud's** (1289 Protest Rd., 208/343-4439, www.bigjudsboise.com, 11 A.M.–9 P.M. Mon.–Sat., under $10) makes the best and biggest burgers in town. Known for its one-pound and two-pound gut-bombs (made with hand-formed beef patties), this small restaurant near BSU is an institution in these parts. Don't worry, though, Big Juds also sells smaller burgers, served with hand-cut fries and real ice cream milk shakes.

Downtown, **Moon's Kitchen** (712 W. Idaho St., 208/385-0472, www.moonskitchen.com, burgers $7–11.50) is a traditional diner that serves breakfast, lunch, and dinner, but burgers, patty melts, and hand-spun shakes reign supreme. You can't go wrong with a chili cheeseburger and chocolate shake at this venerable Boise restaurant.

Westside Drive-In (1939 W. State St., 208/342-2957, lunch and dinner daily), in the North End, is a classic burger joint operated

by Lou Aaron, a local chef known for his great food and big personality. Expect to find lots of burgers, fries, and shakes, but the restaurant also sells prepared dinners to go, like enchiladas and beef stroganoff.

Over on Broadway, the **Boise Fry Company** (111 Broadway, 208/495-3858, www.boisefrycompany.com, 11 A.M.–9 P.M. daily, $3–8.50) specializes in hand-cut fries—twice-cooked in the Belgian style. Not only do you have to choose what kind of potato you want (russet, Yukon gold, sweet potato, white, Peruvian purple), you get to pick the cut, ranging from traditional to shoestring to curly to home-style. House-made sauces, like smoky chipotle and blueberry ketchup, are there for dipping. You would be remiss not to try the wonderful burgers as well.

Sandwiches
Like most cities, Boise has a multitude of sandwich shops. **Cobby's** (1030 Broadway, 208/345-0990, and 6899 Overland Rd., 208/323-0606, lunch and dinner daily, sandwiches $5–13) is the place to go for submarine sandwiches. Recommended are the hot meatball sub and Italian sandwich made with capicolla ham, Genoa salami, mortadella, and provolone. They also make a decent veggie sub.

Zeppole Baking Co. (217 N. 8th St., 208/345-2149, breakfast and lunch Mon.–Sat.) is a local bakery that turns out freshly baked baguettes and other loaves of artisanal bread. But they also have a café downtown that serves sandwiches (around $5), house-made soups, and salads. Most sandwiches are made on crusty focaccia rolls, and Zeppole is also known for its cookies and grissini—long breadsticks coated with pesto and such. The veggie sandwich (with roasted red pepper, spinach, olives, and feta and provolone cheeses) will keep you coming back.

Jenny's Lunch Line (106 N. 6th St., 208/433-0092, www.jennyslunchline.com, 11 A.M.–3 P.M. Mon.–Fri.) is a weekday-only lunch counter in Old Boise that changes its menu daily and with the seasons. The

BOISE

made-from-scratch soups (like gazpacho and curried red lentil) and salads are wonderful. Sandwiches (around $4) might include a turkey Cuban, veggie avocado, and chicken Waldorf salad (made with grapes, apple, celery, and pecans).

BISTROS

Brick Oven Bistro (801 Main St., 208/342-3456, www.brickovenbistro.com, lunch and dinner daily, about $10) on The Grove has been a local favorite since 1984. While the menu at this cafeteria-style restaurant is not overly exciting, it will comfort you with dishes like sliced turkey with cranberry relish, tender pot roast, and wild rice meatloaf. Open-faced hot sandwiches, soups, and salads are also available. In the North End, check out the **36th Street Bistro** (3823 N. Garden Center Way, 208/433-5100, 7 A.M.–8 P.M. Mon.–Sat., 9 A.M.–5 P.M. Sun.), in the 36th Street Garden Center just off Hill Road. This bright and open restaurant serves sandwiches, burgers, and salads. The brunch menu includes apricot-almond bread pudding, chorizo hash, and Nutella French toast.

BREAKFAST

Don't be surprised to see a line out the door on weekends at ◖ **Goldy's Breakfast Bistro** (108 S. Capitol Blvd., 208/345-4100, www.goldysbreakfastbistro.com, 6:30 A.M.–2 P.M. Mon.–Fri., 7:30 A.M.–2 P.M. Sat. and Sun., $6.50–12), kitty-corner from the Egyptian Theatre. This breakfast hotspot is known for its modern dining room (the balcony is a great spot to watch people) and creative menu, with dishes like banana French toast, red flannel hash, eggs Benedict, and a delish red potato–dill frittata. You can also fire up your morning with a plate of habanero sausage and eggs. They pour a mean cup of coffee too.

Another good place for eggs and such is **Jim's Coffee Shop** (812 Fort St., 208/343-0154, breakfast and lunch daily, $5–7) in the North End. It's easy to find: just look for the giant inflatable rooster on the roof. The no-frills menu, including ham and eggs, omelets,

pancakes, and waffles, is about as affordable as it gets in Boise. The likelihood that you will be called "honey" is pretty high at this friendly neighborhood diner, and no coffee cup goes unfilled.

Up on Fairview Avenue, you'll find two beloved restaurants that serve breakfast all day. **Jerry's State Court Café** (6767 Fairview Ave., 208/376-6767, 7 A.M.–9 P.M. daily, breakfast $7–9) has been around at some capacity since 1954. Originally located on State Street, hence the name, this homespun diner serves breakfast, lunch, and dinner, but the breakfast menu is what really brings in the masses. Expect to find biscuits and gravy, eggs Benny, fruit crepes, chicken fried steak, huevos rancheros, potato pancakes, and omelets galore. **The Egg Factory** (8061 Fairview Ave., 208/322-0191, 6:30 A.M.–3 P.M. daily, under $10), in a strip mall at the corner of Milwaukee Street and Fairview Avenue, is a relatively new restaurant that specializes in, you guessed it, egg dishes and other breakfast items. The expansive menu is full of food puns, like "Strawberry Fields Pancakes," "Buenos Dias Burrito," and "Are You Yolkin' Egg Sandwich." The list includes corned beef hash, stuffed omelets, crepes, and cinnamon French toast, to name a few.

If you're into corporate restaurants, head to **Elmer's** (1385 S. Capitol Blvd., 208/343-5714, 6 A.M.–9 P.M.) daily in the shadow of the Boise Depot. The usual array of breakfast offerings gets served here. There's nothing like a fat omelet at night.

COFFEEHOUSES

Corporate coffee chains (Starbucks, Tully's, and Moxie Java) are pervasive in the Boise area. But if you're looking for indie coffeehouses, The City of Trees has plenty of options.

The big, comfortable ◖ **Flying M Coffee House** (500 W. Idaho St., 208/345-4320, www.flyingmcoffee.com, 6:30 A.M.–11 P.M. Mon.–Fri., 7:30 A.M.–11 P.M. Sat., 7:30 A.M.–6 P.M. Sun.) features funky-chic decor: old grade-school tables and chairs, beat-up couches, and a chandelier in the phone booth. It's popular with locals who hang out here to read, study, or chat with friends. The menu has the usual array of coffeehouse concoctions as well as light breakfast and lunch fare. Expansive windows make for a bright interior and good people-watching. Part of the coffeehouse is given over to an artsy gift shop selling local crafts. Flying M, which also has a coffeehouse in downtown Nampa, features live acoustic music on occasion.

Dawson Taylor is a local coffee roaster with several locations in the Treasure Valley. The company's flagship coffeehouse, **Dawson's Downtown** (219 N. 8th St. near Bannock St., 208/336-5633, www.dawsontaylor.com, 6 A.M.–10 P.M. Mon.–Thurs., 6 A.M.–11 P.M. Fri.–Sat., 7 A.M.–9 P.M. Sun.), is a hip place that serves a wide variety of coffee made from fair-trade beans sourced throughout the world, some of which are organically grown. Expect to find espresso blends, Vienna roast, French roast, and several signature blends. Across the street, you'll find **Thomas Hammer** (298 N. 8th St., 208/433-8004, 6 A.M.–9 P.M. Mon.–Sat., 6 A.M.–6 P.M. Sun.), a Spokane-based roaster that serves organic fair-trade coffee in a stylish storefront. The busy-bee baristas here hammer out espresso drinks and drip coffee made from whole beans, like an ultrasmooth Columbian variety, French roast, and a bold espresso roast called the "Fireball Blend." Thomas Hammer also has a small gift shop that sells T-shirts and coffee mugs emblazoned with the store's logo: a simple construction hammer.

In the Linen District, **Big City Coffee & Café** (1416 W. Grove St., 208/345-3145, 6 A.M.–6 P.M. daily) has earned a reputation for making excellent espresso drinks and baked goods, like apricot scones, bear claws, cinnamon rolls, and pumpkin chai muffins. Big City also serves breakfast sandwiches and steamed egg dishes as well as soup and sandwiches during lunchtime. Another local favorite is **Java** (6 A.M.–9 P.M. Mon.–Fri., 7 A.M.–9 P.M. Sat., 7 A.M.–6 P.M. Sun.) with two Boise locations: downtown (223 N. 6th St., 208/345-0777) and Hyde Park (1612 N. 13th St., 208/345-4777). This Ketchum-based coffeehouse uses organic fair-trade beans for its espresso drinks that boast clever names like "Bowl of Soul," a Mexican mocha with a hint of cinnamon, and "Keith Richards," a four-shot concoction that will have you jittering like the rock star himself. Java isn't all about coffee, though. The place also dishes up breakfast sandwiches, huevos rancheros, steel-cut oatmeal, and tasty baked goods.

GROCERIES

The **Boise Co-op** (888 W. Fort St., 208/472-4500, www.boisecoop.com, 9 A.M.–9 P.M. Mon.–Sat., 9 A.M.–8 P.M. Sun.) in the North End is currently the only natural food store in town. In addition to organic produce, soymilk, yogurt, vitamins, and other staples of a healthy diet, you'll find a large selection of cheeses, artisanal bread, a deli offering sandwiches and salads, and Boise's best selection of microbrews. Expect to get gouged at the cash register, though, and the hippy-trippy employees can be a little snooty at times. Across the parking lot is the co-op's wine shop (915 N. 8th St., 208/472-4519, 10 A.M.–8 P.M. Mon.–Sat., 10 A.M.–6 P.M. Sun.), where you can choose from a large variety of labels from around the world.

Whole Foods Market recently bought a big chunk of dirt on Broadway between Myrtle and Front Streets. If all goes well, the store should be open by 2012.

For a good deal on garden-variety groceries, head to **Winco,** an employee-owned local grocery chain with two Boise locations (110 E. Myrtle St., 208/424-1634, and 8200 W. Fairview Ave., 208/377-9840).

Information and Services

TOURIST INFORMATION

Visit the **Boise Convention and Visitors Bureau** (1199 Main St., 800/635-5240 and 208/344-7777, www.boise.org, 8:30 A.M.–5 P.M. Mon.–Fri.). The **Boise Visitors Center** (850 W. Front St., 208/344-5338, 10 A.M.–5 P.M. Mon.–Fri., 10 A.M.–2 P.M. Sat. summer, 9:30 A.M.–4 P.M. Mon.–Fri. off-season) on The Grove provides racks of free literature.

The **Boise Metro Chamber of Commerce** (250 S. 5th St., 208/472-5200) can also tell you what's going on around town. The **Idaho Department of Commerce** (700 W. State St., 208/334-2470 or 800/842-5858, www.visitid. org) offers tourism information for all parts of the state.

The **Idaho Outfitters & Guides Association** (P.O. Box 95, Boise, ID 83701, 208/342-1438, www.ioga.org) can hook you up with various outfitters and guides throughout the state. The **National Weather Service** (3833 S. Development Ave., 208/334-9860) can keep you up to date with local weather conditions. Call 208/342-6569 for a current forecast.

MEDIA

The *Idaho Statesman* (1200 N. Curtis Rd., 208/377-6200, www.idahostatesman.com), part of the McClatchy Company, is the largest-circulation daily in Idaho. Particularly interesting are its Thursday outdoor page, especially Pete Zimowsky's columns; the human-interest musings of Tim Woodward; and the Scene entertainment tabloid on Friday. The *Boise Weekly* (523 Broad St., 208/344-2055, www. boiseweekly.com) is a good liberal rag that acts as a watchdog on the establishment; it'll also direct you to the heart of Boise's hip arts and entertainment scene. Bill Cope's sardonic columns are consistently outstanding. *The*

Arbiter (www.arbiteronline.com), Boise State's twice-weekly student newspaper, is available on campus and at many locations around town.

KBSU (www.radio.boisestate.edu), the city's NPR affiliate, has three signals: jazz and news at 90.3 FM, classical music, news, and information at 91.5 FM, and jazz at 730 AM. Programming schedules can be seen on the website. For local and national talk radio, dial up **KIDO** (580 AM) or **KBOI** (670 AM).

LIBRARIES

The main branch of the **Boise Public Library** (715 S. Capitol Blvd., 208/384-4114, www. boisepubliclibrary.org, 10 A.M.–9 P.M. Mon.–Thurs., 10 A.M.–6 P.M. Fri., 10 A.M.–5 P.M. Sat., noon–5 P.M. Sun.) is located across from the Boise Art Museum and Julia Davis Park. Boise State's **Albertsons Library** (1910 University Dr., 208/426-1816) is a good place to do some research and look at periodicals, but you can't check out anything unless you're a student or faculty. The **Idaho State Library** (325 W. State St., 208/334-2150) offers lots of resources as well.

POST OFFICES

Visit the **main post office** (770 S. 13th St., 800/275-8777) or the **Borah Station** post office (750 W. Bannock St.) in the old Federal Building.

HOSPITALS

If you pull an "endo" over your mountain bike handlebars and need to get stitched up, Boise has two main hospitals: **St. Luke's Boise Medical Center** (190 E. Bannock St., 208/381-2222), near the intersection of Warm Springs and Broadway Avenues, and **Saint Alphonsus Regional Medical Center** (1055 N. Curtis Rd., 208/367-2121) just off the Curtis Road exit on the I-84 Connector.

Getting There and Around

GETTING THERE
By Air

The **Boise Airport** (BOI, 3201 Airport Way, 208/383-3110, www.boise-airport.com) is on the southeast edge of town at I-84 Exit 53 (Vista Ave.). Its spacious and airy new terminal building opened in 2003.

Airlines serving the city include **Delta/SkyWest** (800/221-1212), which offers flights just about everywhere through its Salt Lake City hub; **Frontier** (800/432-1359), with seasonal service to and from Denver; **Southwest** (800/435-9792), offering direct flights between Boise and Salt Lake City, Portland, Reno, Las Vegas, Oakland, and Spokane; and **United** (800/241-6522), with direct flights to and from San Francisco, Chicago, and Denver.

Horizon Air (800/547-9308) is a commuter service affiliated with Alaska Airlines that offers nonstop flights between Boise and the Idaho cities of Lewiston and Sun Valley (Hailey), plus Denver, Los Angeles, Oakland,

Portland, Sacramento, San Diego, San Jose, Seattle, and Spokane.

The airport itself offers the usual restaurants and lounges as well as a business center with phones, fax machines, photocopiers, and both FedEx and UPS courier drops.

Car-rental companies with offices in the airport include **Avis** (208/383-3350 or 800/331-1212), **Budget** (208/383-3090 or 800/527-0700), **Enterprise** (208/381-0650 or 800/736-8222), **Hertz** (208/383-3100 or 800/654-3131), and **National** (208/383-3210 or 800/227-7368).

Those heading directly from Boise's airport to Sun Valley can catch the **Sun Valley Express** bus (208/342-7750 or 877/622-8267, $54 each way with advance purchase); the route operates year-round.

Many Boise hotels and motels run free shuttle buses to the airport. You can catch a cab out front if need be; cab fare to downtown costs about $10. The budget alternative is the **Valley**

Boise Airport

Ride city bus (208/345-7433); Route 3 connects the airport with downtown for $1. Call for bus schedules and information.

By Bus

Downtown, you'll find the **Greyhound** terminal (1212 W. Bannock St., 208/343-3681, www.greyhound.com), where three buses daily connect Boise with Portland as well as Salt Lake City. Sharing the Greyhound terminal is **Northwestern Trailways** (208/336-3300, www.northwesterntrailways.com), which offers one bus daily to McCall, Grangeville, Lewiston, Coeur d'Alene, and Spokane (with onward connections to Seattle).

By Car

I-84 runs east–west across southern Idaho, connecting Boise with Portland to the west and Salt Lake City to the southeast. Highway 55 leaves Boise headed north to New Meadows, where it joins U.S. 95, the only north-south route traversing the entire state. South of Boise, Highway 55 rejoins U.S. 95 for its run across the desert to Winnemucca, Nevada. For 24-hour **road conditions** in Idaho, dial 511 or visit www.511.idaho.gov.

GETTING AROUND
Driving and Parking

Driving around downtown Boise could give you fits; the one-way streets always seem to go the wrong way. It's best just to find a place to park and hoof it or bike around town. Both those nonpolluting modes of transportation are safe and practical downtown.

Municipal pay-parking lots are scattered throughout downtown; many downtown merchants validate parking. Metered spaces line the streets, and empty ones aren't too difficult to find, even in the heart of downtown. Look for a blue button on most meters; press it and you'll get 20 free minutes, which makes those quick trips much less of a hassle. And although the information printed on the meters says they operate 8 A.M.–6 P.M. daily except Sunday and holidays, actually you don't need to plug them on Saturday either.

Bicycling

Bicycling isn't just a Boise passion—it's probably the most efficient mode of transportation here. The city, even out to the limits of the greater urban area, is still small enough to get around by bike without requiring a major time commitment. In the downtown area, biking (or even walking) is often faster than driving for most trips. Many streets are designated bike routes, with wide lanes marked specifically for cyclists. Even better than the bike lanes is the Boise Greenbelt, a multiple-use car-free path that follows the beautiful Boise River from one end of the city to the other. Using the Greenbelt and the bike lanes, you can get around town in a jiffy.

City Bus

Valley Ride (208/345-7433, www.valleyride. org), part of the Valley Regional Transit system, operates 18 bus routes in Boise and Garden City—radiating out from the downtown transit mall bordered by Capitol Boulevard, 9th Street, Main Street, and Idaho Street. Adult fare is $1, seniors, students, and disabled pay $0.50. An all-day adult pass costs $2. You can pick up route brochures at Boise City Hall (N. Capitol Blvd. and W. Idaho St.) and at area Albertsons grocery stores.

SOUTHWEST IDAHO

Southwest Idaho's scenery is geographically diverse—colorful desert canyon lands and ponderosa pine-studded mountains—and it is the most densely populated area in the Gem State. It doesn't take long to go from busy streets to remote blue highways in this western swath of the Snake River Plain, commonly referred to as the Treasure Valley.

The Boise suburbs of Eagle and Meridian have recently experienced major growth as housing developments quickly replace old farms that once dotted the desert landscape. Downtown Nampa has a thriving historic neighborhood where you can nosh on cutting-edge cuisine and shop for used books and antiques.

Take a tour of the local wineries in the heart of Idaho's newly designated wine country around Sunny Slope while cruising through undulating orchards and vineyards along the Snake River Canyon Scenic Byway.

The ominous Owyhee Mountains loom in the near distance along the Oregon border, beckoning adventurous types who desire extreme desert remoteness. You would be hard-pressed to see another human being while taking a three-day rafting trip through these basalt-rimmed chasms long ago carved out by the gurgling Owyhee River and its tributaries.

To the north, the dry desert floor runs up against the shadowy foothills of the Boise Mountains, which rise dramatically to a panorama of granite peaks and ponderosa pine forests. This rugged region, known as the Boise Basin, was a hotbed of gold-mining activity during the mid-19th century.

© DANA HOPPER-KELLY

HIGHLIGHTS

◖ Sunny Slope Wineries: In 2007 the U.S. government approved the Snake River Valley American Viticultural Area, opening the door to major growth in the state's winemaking industry, especially in the Sunny Slope area of Caldwell (page 89).

LOOK FOR ◖ TO FIND RECOMMENDED SIGHTS, ACTIVITIES, DINING, AND LODGING.

◖ Deer Flat National Wildlife Refuge: This expansive wildlife refuge south of Nampa is one of the oldest of its kind in the United States, thanks in part to President Theodore Roosevelt. The 11,430-acre refuge is a watery safe haven for migratory birds such as mallards and Canada geese (page 95).

◖ National Oldtime Fiddlers' Contest and Festival: Thousands of people show up every June in the small town of Weiser for the best hoedown this side of the Mississippi (page 108).

◖ Silver City: To call Silver City a ghost town wouldn't be entirely accurate. This former mining town still has some year-round residents who live in the historic buildings, one of which is the operational Idaho Hotel (page 113).

◖ Bruneau Dunes State Park: Bruneau Dunes State Park is a spectacle to behold as two prominent sand mounds rise nearly 500 feet from the sagebrush-dotted desert floor. The park is also known for its night-sky observatory that boasts a 25-inch telescope (page 114).

◖ Idaho City: Travelers get a true Wild West experience in the heart of the Boise Mountains in this former boomtown, which has beautifully preserved its many historic sights (page 116).

◖ Thunder Mountain Line: An excursion railroad company based in Horseshoe Bend, the line offers several scenic train rides along the steep grades of the Payette River (page 123).

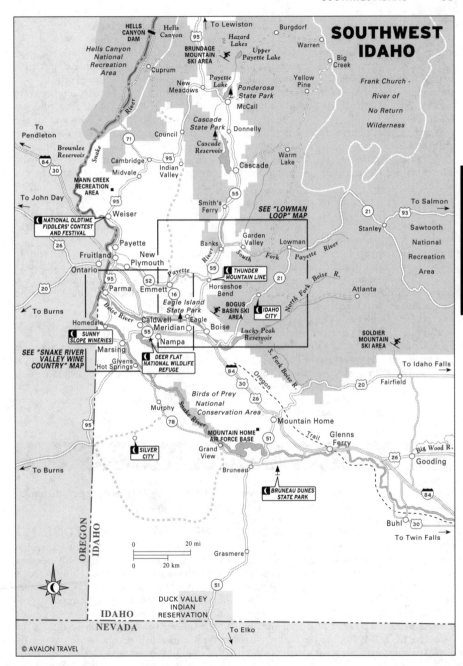

© AVALON TRAVEL

Idaho City for a spell was the largest city in the Northwest, before the boom ended and the miners left. Today, this colorful mining town wears its rough-and-tumble past like an old hat. Many of the rustic buildings still boast their original boardwalks and decorative wood facades. And yes, the kindly locals are colorful as well.

North of here, white-water rafters and kayakers converge every summer in the Lowman and Banks area, where the Payette River rushes toward its confluence with the Boise and Snake Rivers.

HISTORY

The Snake River has long been the lifeblood for those living in southwest Idaho. From 19th-century fur trappers to modern-day farmers who harness the big river's endless flow of water, the occupants of this region have always been integrally tied to the Snake. The first nonnative settlement appeared in 1834, when the Hudson's Bay Company built a fur-trading post close to the confluence of the Snake and Boise Rivers. This bustling British post was originally called Snake Fort, but the name was later changed to Fort Boise. The fur trade brought a constant stream of river commerce to the developing region.

The fort later became safe haven for the convoys of wagons navigating the Oregon Trail before it was moved to present-day Boise. The fur trade eventually fizzled out and the westward migration across this unforgiving portion of the Snake River Plain tapered off.

Twenty years later, human activity once again picked up in the region after gold was discovered in the Mores Creek area of the Boise Mountains. The Boise Basin mining towns of Idaho City, Placerville, and Centerville literally popped up overnight, and the frenzied rush lasted for the better part of 10 years until the pickings became slim. At this point, the miners shifted their attention to Silver City, nestled in the high-desert Owyhee Mountains on the southern fringe of the Snake River Valley.

After the mining heyday ended, farming and ranching became the primary business in the area during the early 20th century, when newly built irrigation canals brought water to the once-arid fields.

PLANNING YOUR TIME

You'll need at least three days to explore this region—two days to check out Eagle, Nampa, and Caldwell, taking in the sights and sampling wines around the Snake River Valley, and a day to venture into the nearby desert or mountains for hiking and white-water rafting.

Snake River Valley Wine Country

Even though the Snake River Valley Appellation spans nine southern Idaho counties, Canyon County is undeniably the heart of wine country. This agricultural area is known for its big crops of sugar beets, yellow onions, mint, hops, and sweet-corn seed. But area farmers also produce tons of apples, cherries, apricots, peaches, and pears. And where tree fruit grows well, so do vinifera grapes. Grape-growing and wine-making are hardly new concepts in the region, though. Winemakers have produced vintages here since the late 1970s, but the industry has grown tremendously in recent years thanks to

the Snake River Valley American Viticultural Area (AVA), created in 2007.

WINE TASTING AND TOURING

Most of Idaho's wineries (with the exception of the larger corporate ones) are only open on weekends for tours and wine tasting—generally spring–late fall. And many of the smaller boutique wineries are open by appointment only. It's also important to note that some of the smaller wineries are closed during the harvest and crush season, which typically runs mid-September–mid-October; all those

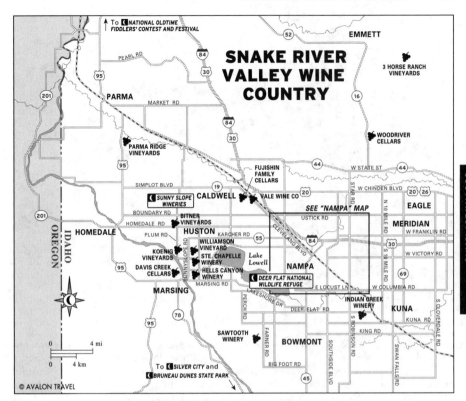

tractors and forklifts buzzing around can be dangerous for visitors.

Since Idaho's wineries are spread over a large area, you might want to leave the driving to someone else. **Idaho Winery Tours** (208/890-6627, www.idahowinerytours.com) conducts Snake River Valley wine country tours for those interested in just kicking back and enjoying the ride. The packages include half-day tours, full-day tours, and custom tours. Call George Condit for more information and prices.

CALDWELL

Caldwell (population 46,000) was called Bugtown in the late 19th century when Oregon Short Line Railroad trains frequently steamed through the area. The town acquired this unsavory name because it was known for having many mosquitoes, red ants, grasshoppers, and flies. Luckily the name didn't stick, but the bugs are still around in this part of Canyon County during the dog days of summer.

Situated near the hustle and bustle of I-84 (Exits 26–29), Caldwell hasn't offered much to visitors in the past, but the downtown sector is currently being restored to support the area's burgeoning wine tourism. (It's being modeled after Walla Walla, a wine boomtown in Washington state.) The quaint district boasts lots of new public art and a meandering path alongside Indian Creek. This is where you will find **Coyotes Fine Wines on the Creek** (217 S. Kimball Ave., 208/453-9463), a wine bar that acts as a tasting room for Bitner Vineyards. It also carries bottles

© DANA HOPPER-KELLY

downtown Caldwell

of other Snake River Valley wines as well as hosts educational events.

A few blocks from downtown, just off Blaine Street, is a top-notch liberal arts college and the **Steunenberg Residential Historic District,** a colorful neighborhood with more than 300 historic homes, many of which are on the National Register of Historic Places.

The Sunny Slope area of Caldwell, called "The Slope" by locals, has emerged as the epicenter of the Snake River Valley wine country. Eight wineries are clustered along this scenic stretch of Highway 55, about eight miles south of downtown Caldwell en route to Marsing, that has long been home to fruit orchards and vineyards. But now you will see acres upon acres of new vineyards situated on south-facing steps near the Snake River, mixed in with vines that were planted many moons ago.

College of Idaho

The College of Idaho (2112 E. Cleveland Blvd., Caldwell, 208/459-5011 or 800/224-3246, www.collegeofidaho.edu) enjoys a solid reputation and alumni who include grocery magnate Joe Albertson, two former governors, a Pulitzer Prize–winning historian, an Academy Award–winning musician, and many Rhodes Scholars. It's also the state's oldest four-year college, founded by the Wood River Presbytery in 1891. The name was changed to Albertson College of Idaho in 1990, but the college went back to using its original name in 2007—mostly to keep its benevolent alumni happy.

Among the buildings on the 43-acre campus are the 850-seat **Jewett Auditorium,** which hosts concerts, lectures, and meetings; the 54,000-square-foot **Langroise Center for the Performing and Fine Arts,** housing the college's music, drama, dance, and visual arts departments; the **Rosenthal Gallery of Art,** which presents a half-dozen exhibitions each academic year and also serves as a venue for poetry readings and performance art; and the **Orma J. Smith Museum of Natural History,** containing a sizable collection of animal and plant specimens, minerals, fossils, and Native American artifacts.

SNAKE RIVER VALLEY AVA: LEGITIMIZING IDAHO WINES

In 2007, the Alcohol and Tobacco Tax and Trade Bureau, the U.S. government agency responsible for designating regional wine appellations, approved the Snake River Valley's application to become an American Viticultural Area – the first official AVA in the Gem State.

This heightened status has paved the way for more wineries, both large and small, to set up shop in Idaho. The state now has more than 40 wineries, almost double the number in operation five years ago. The AVA designation has also greatly helped the marketing of Idaho wines.

In sheer size, the Snake River Valley AVA is one of the largest in the nation, an astonishing 5.27 million acres, nearly the size of New Jersey. It stretches from about 30 miles inside the Oregon border, on the western fringe of the Snake River Plain, well into south-central Idaho.

The Snake River Valley's high-desert terrain, with its long, hot days and cool nights, makes for exceptional fruit. When winemakers speak of *terroir* in this region, they usually talk about the high elevation at which the grapes are grown and the richness of the volcanic soil, lending itself to fruit-forward wines with pronounced tannins and well-balanced acidity. Hearty Rhône varietals such as syrah and viognier thrive, but this area has a long-standing tradition of growing Bordeaux-style varietals like cabernet sauvignon, merlot, and cabernet franc. Riesling and chardonnay grapes have also been grown in the Snake River Valley for more than 30 years. (Sorry, you won't find any potato wine, but there's a spud vodka made in the area.)

SOUTHWEST IDAHO

◖ Sunny Slope Wineries

Winemaking is a family affair at **Hells Canyon Winery** (18835 Symms Rd., Caldwell, 208/454-3300, www.hellscanyonwinery.org, tasting room noon–5 P.M. Sat., 1–5 P.M. Sun. Apr. 1–Dec. 1), where winemaker Steve Robertson and his daughter, assistant winemaker Bijou Robertson, turn out two labels: Hells Canyon and Zhoo Zhoo. This Sunny Slope–area winery, which has been in business since 1980, specializes in cabernet sauvignon, chardonnay, merlot, cabernet franc, and syrah, which you can sample for a small fee at the winery's tasting room. Hells Canyon Winery also has a spacious guesthouse that can be rented by appointment for large groups.

Koenig Vineyards and Distillery (20928 Grape Lane, Caldwell, 208/455-8386, www.koenigvineyards.com, tasting room noon–5 P.M. Fri.–Sun. or by appointment) produces wine, fruit brandies, and potato vodka. Winemaker Greg Koenig is a busy guy: Not only does he make wine for his own winery, Koenig Vineyards, he is also the head winemaker for three other local wineries. This Sunny Slope winery and distillery boasts an attractive Tuscan-inspired structure overlooking the Snake River. The winery is known for its exceptional vintages, including reserve syrah, viognier, Bordeaux blends, and ice wine made from riesling grapes. Greg's brother, Andrew, is in charge of making eau-de-vie–style fruit brandies and ultrasmooth potato vodka, produced in an ornate copper-pot still. A small tasting fee applies for large groups.

Bitner Vineyards (16645 Plum Rd., Caldwell, 208/899-7648, www.bitnervineyards. com, tasting room noon–5 P.M. Wed.–Sun. or by appointment) definitely has the best view in the Sunny Slope area. Ron Bitner, an entomologist turned vintner, was instrumental in landing Idaho's only American Viticultural Area (AVA). He was involved in writing the official application, first drafted in 2001. Bitner spent several years studying leaf-cutter bees in Australia, which might help to explain why his estate winery turns out bone-dry riesling and a cabernet-shiraz blend as well as excellent cabernet

SOUTHWEST IDAHO

© DANA HOPPER-KELLY

old chardonnay vines at Hells Canyon Winery

sauvignon, chardonnay, and a silky merlot–petit verdot blend—all made by his neighbor down the hill, winemaker Greg Koenig.

Bitner first planted chardonnay vines in the early 1980s, and since then he and his wife, Mary, have added a small bed-and-breakfast and hilltop tasting room with spectacular views of the Snake River and Owyhee Mountains. Bitner Vineyards also sells its wines at Coyotes Fine Wines (217 S. Kimball Ave., Caldwell, 208/453-9463) in downtown Caldwell. Foodies will like the fact that Bitner has hazelnut and oak trees on his property that have been in-oculated with black truffle spores; he will be harvesting his first crop soon.

Ste. Chapelle Winery (19348 Lowell Rd., Caldwell, 208/453-7843, www.stechapelle.com, tasting room 10 A.M.–5 P.M. Mon.–Sat., noon–5 P.M. Sun. year-round) is the oldest and largest winery in Idaho. It has produced an impressive array of wines since 1976. This corporate behemoth in Sunny Slope, on the west side of Highway 55, quickly became known for turning out lots of decent riesling. In recent times, head winemaker Chuck Devlin has added many other wines to the repertoire, including sauvignon blanc, ice wines, and various red varietals. The destination winery boasts a remarkable French-inspired château (with Gothic architecture, no less) that sits perched atop the hill. This is where you can find the gift shop and tasting room (small fee), and it's also the starting point for the winery tour. Ste. Chapelle Winery has beautifully landscaped grounds, making the grassy terraces a great spot for a picnic and enjoying the popular concert series held every summer.

Williamson Vineyard (19692 Williamson Lane, Caldwell, 208/459-7333, www.willorch.com, tasting room 10 A.M.–6 P.M. Mon.–Fri., 10 A.M.–4 P.M. Sat.–Sun. June–Dec.) is a small boutique winery affiliated with Williamson Orchards, a local fruit company and fruit stand next to Ste. Chapelle Winery. Roger Williamson is in charge of growing the grapes, which are then made into wine by Greg Koenig. Among the orchards and vines you can taste a lineup of exceptional estate wines that includes viognier, syrah, and cabernet sauvignon. The tasting room is situated in an old barn near the produce stand.

Fujishin Family Cellars (15593 Sunnyslope Rd., Caldwell, 208/573-0793, www.fujishinfamilycellars.com, tasting room 10 A.M.–5 P.M. Tues.–Sun.) is a relatively new boutique winery in the Sunny Slope area. Winemaker Martin Fujishin produces an array of fruit-forward wines, including viognier, syrah, merlot, petite sirah, and late-harvest chardonnay. The winery's tasting room shares space with Robison Fruit Company's produce stand, meaning you can score some peaches and a bottle of good wine in one fell swoop.

Vale Wine Co. (1904 E. Chicago St., Caldwell, 208/409-8950, www.valewineco.com) grows its grapes in Vale, Oregon, on the western fringe of the Snake River Valley AVA, but you can buy winemaker John Danielson's wines in Caldwell at Coyotes Fine Wines on the Creek (217 S. Kimball Ave., Caldwell, 208/453-9463) and at various wine shops around the valley. Expect to find dry riesling, syrah, chardonnay, cabernet sauvignon, and a robust red blend.

Produce Stands

The Sunny Slope area has several excellent produce stands that are packed with local fruit and vegetables early summer–late fall. **Symms Fruit Ranch** (14068 Sunnyslope Rd., Caldwell, 208/459-4821, www.symmsfruit.com, 11 A.M.–5 P.M. Mon.–Fri., 7 A.M.–noon Sat.), located on the east side of Highway 55 between Lowell Road and Williamson Lane, has been selling tree-ripened fruit for nearly a century. Even though the farm specializes in peaches, you can also find lots of cherries, nectarines, plums, pears, and apples as well as asparagus and onions in the spring and early summer. **Williamson Orchards** (19692 Williamson Lane, 208/459-7333, www.willorch.com, 10 A.M.–6 P.M. Mon.–Fri., 10 A.M.–4 P.M. Sat. June–Dec.) recently celebrated its 100th anniversary. This family-run orchard and winery sells a large variety of stone fruit, garden-fresh vegetables (tomatoes, eggplants, and pumpkins) and more than 20 varieties of apples that include Criterion, Honeycrisp, and Empire,

which it makes into delicious cider sold in plastic jugs.

Recreation

At **Luby Park** (off N. Illinois Ave., Caldwell, north side of I-84 Exit 28) you'll find ball fields, hoops, and tennis courts as well as the city's beautiful rose garden, which in full bloom presents a kaleidoscope of colors. Look for the **Greenway** along the Boise River on the west side of town; a jogging path and an Oregon Trail monument highlight the site, just west of I-84 at Exit 27.

Many golfers consider **Purple Sage Golf Course** (15192 Purple Sage Rd., Caldwell, 208/459-2223, year-round, $13–23.50) to be one of the state's finest courses. The 18-hole, par-71 course spreads over 6,754 yards. Cart rental is available. To get there, take I-84 Exit 25, turn east from the off-ramp onto Highway 44, go north on U.S. 30, and then east on Purple Sage Road to the course.

Events

The **Caldwell Night Rodeo** is one of the country's top 20 Professional Rodeo Cowboys Association–sanctioned rodeos, drawing almost 40,000 fans to the rodeo grounds (near Simplot Stadium) for a weeklong run in mid-August. For more information, call the Caldwell Chamber of Commerce (208/459-7493). On the last Saturday in September, College of Idaho hosts **Taste of the Harvest** (208/459-5011), an annual event that celebrates the area's prolific bounty. Nosh on creatively prepared seasonal dishes made with local foodstuffs washed down with select wines from the Snake River Valley.

Accommodations

Unfortunately the Caldwell–Sunny Slope area doesn't offer travelers much in the way of lodging beyond the corporate hotels that line the interstate.

Most of the hotels in the Caldwell area are located near I-84 Exit 29. **Best Western Caldwell Inn and Suites** (908 Specht Ave., Caldwell, 208/454-7225, www.bestwesternidaho.com, from $73 d) is a newer hotel with amenities such as an indoor swimming pool, a workout room, free Wi-Fi, and a hot breakfast buffet. Just down the road, **La Quinta Inn** (901 Specht Ave., Caldwell, 208/454-2222, from $69 d) offers clean guest rooms with all the amenities, including a complimentary breakfast.

Elegant bed-and-breakfast–style guest suites can be found at **Wild Rose Manor** (5800 Oasis Rd., Caldwell, 208/454-3331 or 866/399-3331, www.wildrosemanor.com, $139–189) just off I-84 Exit 17. This beautiful mansion, a popular spot for weddings, sits high atop a hill with commanding views of the Boise Front. Expect to be pampered with early-evening appetizers and wine, jetted tubs, and a multicourse breakfast.

In Sunny Slope, **Bitner Vineyards** (16645 Plum Rd., Caldwell, 208/899-7648, www.bitnervineyards.com, $149–169) operates a bed-and-breakfast next to the winery. Situated in the basement of the main house, this small inn has two guest rooms with queen beds and a private patio. Fill up on a farm-fresh continental breakfast before heading out to tour the wineries.

If you are driving an RV or towing a trailer, check out the **Ambassador RV Resort** (615 S. Smeed Pkwy., Caldwell, 208/454-8584, $31 with hookups) near I-84 Exit 29.

Food

The Caldwell area is known for its authentic Mexican restaurants. One such place is **Tacos Michoacan** (2904 Cleveland Blvd., Caldwell, 208/454-5577, lunch and dinner daily, $7–12), a regional Mexican joint that specializes in tacos, as the name suggests. Expect to find carne asada (grilled beef), carnitas (fried pork butt), lengua (beef tongue), and sesos (brains) plopped on warm corn tortillas and served with freshly made red and green salsas. If you are not in the mood for tacos, try a bowl of pozole (pork and hominy soup) or menudo (tripe soup), washed down with a cold Mexican beer.

Get your gyro fix at **Athena's Greek Grille** (2609 E. Blaine St., 208/454-9169, 11 A.M.–8 P.M. Mon.–Sat., $6–8) near the fairgrounds. This friendly little gyro shop serves more than delish lamb sandwiches (made with pillowy pita, feta cheese, garlicky yogurt, and fresh veggies); you also can enjoy other Mediterranean standards such as hummus and olives, souvlaki, Greek rice, and Greek salads.

Near the College of Idaho, **Bent Fork Bar and Grill** (2805 Blaine St., Caldwell, 208/454-8382, 11 A.M.–9 P.M. Mon.–Thurs., 11 A.M.–10 P.M. Fri.–Sat.) keeps it simple with a pub menu that spotlights dishes like fried green beans and a delicious black-and-blue burger. A nice array of draft microbrews and cocktails will surely quench your thirst.

The Orchard House (14949 Sunnyslope Rd., Caldwell, 208/459-8200, breakfast, lunch, and dinner daily, dinner entrées $13–23) is Sunny Slope's only bona fide restaurant, where you can score standard fare. Take reprieve from the scorching sun on the restaurant's shady patio, and enjoy some hand-cut steaks and a bottle of Snake River Valley wine. The dinner menu has plenty of appetizers, like bacon-stuffed mushrooms and salt-and-pepper prawns, alongside burgers and inventive salads.

Don't be surprised to see more dining establishments popping up in Sunny Slope as the wine industry continues to flourish.

In the morning, or any time of day, coffee-up near downtown Caldwell at **Moxie Java** (2904 Cleveland Blvd., Caldwell, 208/454-5577, www.moxiejava.com), a local coffee chain that roasts its own beans. Choose from a large selection of espresso drinks, teas, and Italian sodas.

Information and Services

The **Caldwell Chamber of Commerce** (704 Blaine St., Caldwell, 208/459-7493) is where to go for local tourist information, including pamphlets and area maps.

For current winery information, contact the **Idaho Grape Growers and Wine Producers Commission** (821 W. State St., Boise, 208/332-1538, www.idahowines.org). Commonly referred to as the Idaho Wine Commission, this agency provides maps and other resources. Just go to the website and download what you need.

NAMPA

Nampa (population 82,000), located between Caldwell and Meridian on I-84, has come a long way since its humble days as an Oregon Short Line rail stop. The town was originally platted in 1886 on land owned by Alexander Duffes, a pious man who refused to sell property to anyone planning to open a saloon. Financial pressures must have got the better of him because the town, mockingly called "New Jerusalem," eventually had a few drinking establishments. As a matter of fact, Duffes's house was moved 20 years later to make room for brewery.

Colonel William Dewey was another central figure in Nampa's history. This affluent mining baron, who made his riches in the nearby boomtown of Silver City, dumped oodles of money into the development of Nampa. In 1901 he built the luxurious Dewey's Palace, a grand hotel that was unfortunately torn down in 1963 after it fell into disrepair. Dewey turned Nampa into a major railroad town by establishing a busy terminus for the Boise, Nampa, and Owyhee Railroad.

Today, Nampa is the second largest city in Idaho and is still a busy railroad hub; the ground often shakes with train activity, and blasting horns are frequently heard in the downtown area, where you will find a vibrant historic neighborhood affectionately called the Belle District, in which there are lots of interesting antiques shops and used bookstores mixed in with hip coffeehouses and contemporary restaurants. Nampa is also home to a highly recognized Christian college and several museums. But the rest of the city is an unsightly blur of newer housing developments and big-box stores.

Hispanic Cultural Center of Idaho

Get an eyeful: Not only is the vibrant-hued building (315 Stampede Dr., 208/442-0823, www.hispanicculturalcenter.org, 9 A.M.–5 P.M. Mon.–Fri., free) a real architectural standout, it houses an impressive array of work by

SOUTHWEST IDAHO

© DANA HOPPER-KELLY

historic downtown Nampa

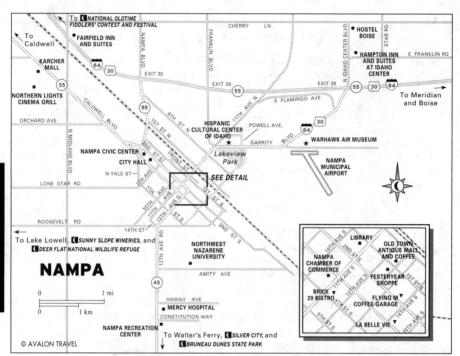

contemporary Hispanic artists. Check the website for upcoming events, or simply drop by.

Warhawk Air Museum

Fans of World War II–era aviation will enjoy this museum (201 Municipal Dr., 208/465-6646, www.warhawkairmuseum.org, 10 A.M.–5 P.M. Tues.–Sat., 11 A.M.–5 P.M. Sun., $10 adults, $8 seniors, military, and veterans, $4 ages 5–12), where you'll find two Curtiss P-40 fighters used in the movie *Pearl Harbor* along with many other vintage aircraft. Surrounding the planes are aircraft engines, armaments, uniforms, old photos, and other World War II memorabilia.

Nampa Train Depot Museum

Some dusty old historical museums are exciting only to dusty old historians, But the Nampa Train Depot Museum (1200 Front St., 208/467-7611, 11 A.M.–5 P.M. Wed.–Fri., 10 A.M.–2 P.M. Sat., donation), operated by the Canyon County Historical Society, is a great stop. The history begins with the building itself: The museum is housed in the beautiful old Oregon Short Line Depot, built in 1902. Its architecture is unique and impressive—an ornate design in dark brick with white trim. The building was abandoned in 1972 but saved and restored a year later; it is now listed on the National Register of Historic Places. Inside you'll find railroad memorabilia, old newspapers dating back to 1881, photographs from as early as 1891, and pictures of the old Dewey Palace Hotel in its glory days.

Northwest Nazarene University

Northwest Nazarene University (NNU, 623 Holly St., 208/467-8011 or 800/852-2978) is a top-rated four-year Christian liberal-arts school subscribing to the Wesleyan doctrines of the Church of the Nazarene, one of which is "that man is born with a fallen nature, and is, therefore, inclined to evil, and that continually." No keg parties here, I guess. The campus lies south of downtown on the east side of Highway 45 (12th Avenue Rd.) at Lake Lowell Avenue.

◖ Deer Flat National Wildlife Refuge

Birds and birdwatchers alike flock to this 11,430-acre refuge four miles southwest of town. The refuge, managed by the U.S. Fish and Wildlife Service, is a stop on the Pacific Flyway, an avian route for migratory species. During peak migration in early December, roughly 12,000 geese and 100,000 ducks honk and quack their way around the refuge's two units. The first unit—8,800-acre artificial Lake Lowell—was part of a 1906 irrigation project and was designated a national wildlife refuge by President Theodore Roosevelt in 1909. The second unit comprises the 107 islands in the Snake River between Swan Falls and Farewell Bend, Oregon.

Mallard ducks and Canada geese are the dominant species, but more than 200 other species have been observed on the refuge, among them loons, grebes, pelicans, cormorants, bitterns, herons, egrets, ducks such as the northern pintail and the cinnamon teal, raptors—bald eagles, red-tailed hawks, and peregrine falcons—and eight different species

THE AMAZING COMEBACK OF THE PEREGRINE FALCON

The peregrine falcon (*Falco peregrinus*) has bounced back from the cusp of extinction worldwide. Herbicides and pesticides were the main cause of the species' drastic decline, which started during the 1950s. By 1975 it was estimated that there were only 324 nesting pairs remaining in the world. Harsh chemicals, including DDT, caused the female falcons to lay eggs with paper-thin shells that easily broke, killing the embryos. DDT was banned in the United States in 1972.

With this harmful chemical reduced, peregrine populations have risen dramatically in recent years. It is believed that there are now 2,000–3,000 nesting pairs in North America, and the Peregrine Fund has released 4,000 captive-raised falcons in the United States in the last 25 years.

The peregrine, the fastest animal on the globe, reaching speeds up to 200 mph, has a wide distribution, from frozen tundra to the tropics. They have adapted specifically to cityscapes, where the tall buildings act as a safe haven and where they help to keep pigeon populations from getting out of control.

Idaho has a love affair with this colorful bird, which has a distinct yellow hue and a dark gray-and-white pattern. The peregrine is the state's official raptor, and it was recently commemorated on the state quarter.

© DANA HOPPER-KELLY

of sandpipers. A complete birding checklist is available at the visitors center.

Birding is just one of the many forms of recreation available here. Boating, swimming, waterskiing, fishing, horseback riding, mountain biking, cross-country skiing, and ice skating can all be enjoyed at one time of year or another, with certain restrictions in place to protect the refuge's winged inhabitants. No boating is allowed on Lake Lowell October 1–April 14, and fishing from the shores of the Snake River islands is prohibited February 1–May 31 when the geese are nesting.

The refuge headquarters and visitors center (13751 Upper Embankment Rd., 208/467-9278, 8 A.M.–4 P.M. Mon.–Fri. and 10 A.M.–4 P.M. Sat. mid-Apr.–Sept.) is on the northeast shore of Lake Lowell near the intersection of Lake and Lake Lowell Avenues. Lake Avenue turns south off Highway 55, on the way out of town toward Marsing; the turnoff is marked. Inside are informative exhibits focusing on the natural history of the refuge. Outside, a short self-guided nature trail winds down to the lakeshore and back; a pamphlet introduces some of the plant and animal species commonly seen along the way. The rest of the refuge is open dawn–dusk; no overnight camping is permitted.

Sawtooth Winery

Even though Nampa is smack-dab in wine country, it only has one winery to show for it. Sawtooth Winery (13750 Surrey Lane, 208/467-1200, www.sawtoothwinery.com, noon–5 P.M. Fri.–Sun.) is Idaho's second-largest winery in terms of production, and it has turned out superb wines since 1987. Sawtooth makes a large variety of estate wines, including cabernet sauvignon, merlot, chardonnay, riesling, syrah, and viognier. The winery sits high atop a hill overlooking Hidden Valley, Skyline Vineyard, and the foreboding Owyhee Mountains. It can be tricky to find if you are not from these parts. To get there, take Exit 36 off I-84 to 11th Avenue North, and then hang a right to 3rd Street South. Travel just one block to 12th Avenue South (Hwy. 45)

and turn right. Continue on Highway 45 for 8 miles to Missouri Avenue, where you take a right and follow the signs to the winery.

Recreation

Lakeview Park (Garrity Blvd. and 16th Ave. N.) isn't large but has a lot to offer, including a beautiful rose garden splashing bright colors across one corner of the park. Elsewhere you'll find softball fields; volleyball, basketball, and tennis courts; horseshoe pits; a pool, a water park, a playground, and a duck pond; and picnic tables. The park is also the venue for many of Nampa's annual events.

Raise your heart rate at the **Nampa Recreation Center** (131 Constitution Way, 208/468-5777, www.nampaparksandrecreation.org, 5 A.M.–10 P.M. Mon.–Fri., 8 A.M.–7 P.M. Sat., 11 A.M.–6 P.M. Sun., $8 adults, $6 seniors, $6 ages 6–17, $2 under age 6). The massive (140,000 square feet) building provides opportunities for swimming, basketball, racquetball, running, aerobics, dance, gymnastics, and more. The six different pools include a huge lap pool, a play pool, a kiddies' wading pool, a diving pool, a hydrotherapy pool, and a jetted tub. Near the pools you'll find a steam room and a sauna. The aerobics area offers an indoor running track, weight machines, NordicTracks, Exercycles, treadmills, and StairMasters. A large wall-climbing area offers more than 50 routes for all ability levels; climbers must provide their own belay, and rental equipment is available.

Entertainment

Grab dinner and a movie all in one spot at **Northern Lights Cinema Grill** (1509 Caldwell Blvd., 208/475-2999, www.northernlightscinemagrill.com) near the Karcher Mall. This new-concept establishment has two large theaters equipped for dining. Buy a ticket, order some food and draft brews, and it's delivered to you in the theater. Don't quaff too much ale, though, or you will miss half the movie making frequent trips to the restroom. The theater shows second-run movies and serves standard fare such as pizza, burgers, and burritos.

The **Idaho Center** (16200 Can-Ada Rd., 208/442-3232, www.idahocenter.com) has both an indoor arena and an outdoor amphitheater where major sports and entertainment events are held. The arena is home to the Snake River Stampede pro rodeo. Most of the big-name bands that come through the Boise area play this venue. The Rolling Stones even rocked the Idaho Center a few years back.

Events

The **Snake River Stampede** (208/466-8497, www.snakeriverstampede.com, $10–35) bucks into the Idaho Center every year around the third week of July. The Professional Rodeo Cowboys Association–sanctioned Stampede is one of the country's top 25 rodeos, attracting some 500 world-champion pros competing in bareback and saddle bronc riding, bull riding, steer wrestling, individual and team roping, and barrel racing. Even the rodeo clowns compete, in a "bullfight" competition, while kids ages 5–7 compete in Mutton Busting. The week kicks off with one of the West's largest horse parades and a buckaroo breakfast.

Shopping

Downtown Nampa is a veritable treasure trove of collectibles, used books, and antiques thanks to a profusion of shops in the Belle District. The **Yesteryear Shoppe** (1211 1st St. S., 208/467-3581) is a wonderful spot to lollygag in time. This spacious used bookstore has thousands of titles neatly arranged in easy-to-follow sections, including history, general fiction, science, and beyond. Rare editions are kept under glass near the front of the store beside an impressive collection of old vinyl records. The shop specializes in jazz and blues, but you can probably score an old Iron Maiden album too.

Across the street, grab an espresso drink and peruse the dusty rooms at the **Old Town Antique Mall and Coffee** (1212 1st St. S., 208/463-4555), where there is a multitude of 20th-century collectibles and antiques ranging from old G.I. Joes to cool poster art and retro dishware.

Karcher Mall (1509 Caldwell Blvd., 208/465-7845) is located on the "Boulevard," as locals call it, the bustling road that connects Nampa and Caldwell. The indoor mall, the first of its kind in Idaho, was recently given a makeover. Expect to find typical chain stores and restaurants.

Accommodations

With a country setting just a mile north of the Idaho Center, **Hostel Boise** (17322 Can-Ada Rd., 208/467-6858, www.hostelboise.com, $20–45) is a friendly and inexpensive base for exploring the area. A clean kitchen, a peaceful back patio, and a comfortable living room make guests feel at home, as does owner Elsa Freeman, who has practically made it her mission to bring this hostel, a Hostelling International affiliate, to southwest Idaho. Check-in is between 5 and 10 P.M., check out by 9:30 A.M. Reservations are advised.

Nampa has a string of motels near downtown along the Boulevard, but many of them are filthy and rife with illegal-drug activity.

For clean and safe lodging, check out the **Hampton Inn and Suites at the Idaho Center** (5750 E. Franklin Rd., 208/442-0036, www.hamptoninn.com, from $89 d) near I-84 Exit 38. This chain hotel is completely nonsmoking, and it offers all the amenities—an indoor swimming pool, a fitness room, and complimentary hot breakfast. A few miles west on I-84, near Exit 33, you'll find **Fairfield Inn and Suites** (16150 Midland Blvd., 866/539-0036, from $69 d), which offers clean guest rooms. There's no pool but there is a workout room, a business center, and complimentary breakfast.

Food

Nampa has experienced something of a restaurant renaissance in recent years. Of course, there is the typical gamut of corporate restaurants on the Boulevard, but the downtown area now has several remarkable indie eateries. ◖ **Brick 29 Bistro** (320 11th Ave. S., 208/468-0029, www.brick29.com, 11 A.M.–9 P.M. Mon.–Thurs., 11 A.M.–10 P.M.

Fri., 4–10 P.M. Sat., brunch 10 A.M.–2 P.M. Sun., dinner entrées $12–26) is the brainchild of chef Dustan Bristol, who opened the contemporary Northwest restaurant a few years ago in a former Masonic Temple on the edge of downtown. Locavores will love this place because Bristol has a penchant for sourcing local foodstuffs that end up on his seasonal menus. Brick 29 Bistro offers whimsical yet recognizable dishes, like pear pizza with pesto, braised lamb shank with smoked mushroom risotto, and a scrumptious Kobe beef burger served on a crusty bun with jalapeño aioli. There are lots of Snake River Valley wines and inventive cocktails to wash everything down.

La Belle Vie (220 14th Ave. S., 208/466-0200, www.labellevienampa.com, 11 A.M.–3 P.M. Tues., 11 A.M.–9 P.M. Wed.–Fri., 9 A.M.–9 P.M. Sat., 9 A.M.–3 P.M. Sun., $7–20) is a relatively new French café in an old house downtown. The restaurant sticks to French classics like Brie and baguette, Mediterranean-inspired salads, and grilled chicken with fresh herbs, but La Belle Vie has a decidedly American side, as evidenced by the burgers on the menu. Expect to see lots of labels from France, California, and Idaho on the wine list.

Hipsters will definitely get a kick out of the **Flying M Coffee Garage** (1314 2nd St. S., 208/467-5533, www.flyingmcoffee.com, 6:30 A.M.–11 P.M. Mon.–Fri., 7:30 A.M.–11 P.M. Sat., 7:30 A.M.–6 P.M. Sun.), a funky coffeehouse in a former tire shop. Surf the Web while enjoying an espresso drink and house-baked pastries. The walls are adorned with local art, and the place features live acoustic music now and then.

The **Nampa Farmers Market** (12th Ave. S. and 1st St., www.nampafarmersmarket.com, 9 A.M.–1 P.M. Sat. mid-Apr.–Oct.) is held in historic downtown Nampa. More than 20 produce vendors sell an assortment of impeccably fresh seasonal vegetables and fruit. Shoppers can also find artisanal bread, honey, fresh salsa, and locally roasted coffee. The market also has lots of crafts, like goat's milk soap, pottery, and stained glass. There is live music every weekend as well as chef demonstrations.

Information and Services

The **Nampa Chamber of Commerce** (312 13th Ave. S., 208/466-4641 or 877/206-2672, www.nampa.com) offers brochures, maps, and general information about the area. The **Nampa Public Library** (101 11th Ave. S., 208/465-2263), built in 1919, is beautiful and comfortable; the upstairs tables along the window-lined north wall make particularly fine places to read one of the library's 79,000 volumes.

The **Idaho Department of Fish and Game** (3101 S. Powerline Rd., 208/465-8465) has a few wildlife and nature exhibits, and right nearby are some stocked fishing ponds and a trout hatchery.

KUNA

Kuna (pronounced Q-nuh) is a charmless little hamlet located seven miles southeast of Nampa on the edge of Ada County. The downtown area is nothing more than a strip of ramshackle buildings that look like they were slapped together overnight. And they probably were, considering the town was once a whistle stop for the Union Pacific Railroad's Oregon Short Line. If you like real-deal cowboy and biker bars, though, Kuna is definitely the place to go; there are several beat-up saloons along the main drag known for warm beer and tremendous bar fights. Don't be surprised to hear, "Are you looking at me?" if you spend any time at these places.

Kuna still holds onto its small railroad-town roots, but the new housing developments surrounding the downtown core tell a different story. Many people who work in nearby Boise choose to live here because of its small-town feel. This may help to explain the profusion of drive-through espresso shops that have popped up here in the new millennium.

Head south of Kuna on the Western Heritage Historical Byway and it will feel like you're in the middle of nowhere. The desert hinterlands roll and dip as far as the eye can see until they reach the imposing basalt cliffs of the Snake River Canyon—home to the Snake River Birds of Prey National Conservation Area—and the remote Owyhee Mountains.

Indian Creek Winery

Kuna has turned out to be a harsh place to grow wine grapes because the area is prone to hard freezes in the winter that tend to kill the vines. This winemaking travesty happened a few years ago at Indian Creek Winery (1000 N. McDermott Rd., 208/922-4791, www.indiancreekwinery.com, tasting room noon–5 P.M. Sat.–Sun. or by appointment) when an extremely bitter winter wiped out most of the winery's vineyards. Yet Indian Creek Winery has made a serious comeback due to the dedication and tenacity of owner Bill Stowe and his family, who produce several remarkable wines such as pinot noir (yes, pinot in Idaho), chardonnay, cabernet sauvignon, malbec, and red blends. The winery has a tasting room and gift shop where you can sample wines free of charge. To get to the winery from Nampa, follow Greenhurst Road toward Kuna until you cross McDermott Road, and then turn right (south) and continue three miles to the winery.

Snake River Birds of Prey National Conservation Area

The southern border of Ada County is defined by the Snake River, and the river here and the undeveloped high desert surrounding its banks have been designated the Snake River Birds of Prey National Conservation Area (NCA). The chaparral along the riverbank is home to large populations of rodents and small mammals that constitute the prime diet for a variety of birds of prey. Among the raptors permanently residing here or just passing through are short-eared owls, burrowing owls, northern harriers, kestrels, Swainson's hawks, red-tailed hawks, sharp-shinned hawks, golden eagles, and the largest nesting concentration of prairie falcons in the country.

The NCA boundary is three miles south of Kuna on Swan Falls Road. On your way down to the river—another 16 miles farther—you'll see the raised lava butte of **Initial Point** on the east side of the road. In addition to being a great viewpoint over the vast plain and the Owyhee Mountains to the south, the point is

significant in that it marked the starting point for Idaho Territory's first official land survey, begun in 1867. The base meridian for the survey ran due north from here, through what would become the town of Meridian. It's just a short hike up to the top of the butte, which is a tranquil spot for meditation or a picnic (provided the locals aren't using the adjacent hillside for target practice, as they often do).

The road continues down to the canyon rim and a pullout parking area at **Dedication Point.** A 0.25-mile nature trail leads to the edge of the abyss, and interpretive signs provide information about the various birds of prey, flora, and geology of the area.

The road continues southeast for a moment before making a hairpin turn and dropping precipitously into the canyon, to the road's end at **Swan Falls Dam.** The dam was the brainchild of Colonel William Dewey, a pioneering southwest Idaho entrepreneur who intended to use the hydroelectric power generated at the dam to run an electric railway up to his mine near Silver City. His plan never materialized, but the dam did supply electricity to Murphy and to Silver City as well until World War II. The dam, built in 1901, was the first hydroelectric project on the Snake River. A grassy picnic area and restrooms make this a good place for a stop.

For more information on the Snake River Birds of Prey National Conservation Area, contact the Bureau of Land Management's Lower Snake River district office (3948 Development Ave., Boise, 208/384-3300).

GUIDED BIRDS OF PREY AREA TOURS

While it's possible to experience the Birds of Prey Area on your own, either by boating down the river or hiking through the canyon and along the rim, **Birds of Prey Expeditions/ Whitewater Shop River Tours** (4519 N. Mountain View Dr., 208/327-8903, www.birdsofpreyexpeditions.com) offers expert interpretive half-day ($75) or full-day ($95) tours of the preserve. Both trips include lunch. Various special tours are occasionally offered; call for updates on schedules and prices.

Recreation

Veteran's Memorial Park (Main St.) is Kuna's only true park, with a picnic area, a playground, and some scuffed-up skateboard bowls in the shadow of the water tower. Adjacent to the park is the **Indian Creek Greenbelt**, a short walking trail that meanders alongside a swift-flowing creek on the north side of the busy railroad tracks.

Falcon Crest Golf Club (11102 S. Cloverdale Rd., 208/362-8897, www.falconcrestgolf.com) is one of the nicest public golf courses in the area. With 36 holes of playable golf greens (one 18-hole course, two nine-holes, and a driving range), this expansive complex boasts incredible views of the Boise Front and vast desert landscape. Greens fees range $6–45, depending on the course and time of day.

Food

Kuna is not known for its haute cuisine, but the town does have a beloved Mexican restaurant that brings in people from miles around. ◖ **El Gallo Giro** (482 Main St., 208/922-5169, www.elgallogirokuna.com, 10 A.M.–10 P.M. Mon.–Sat., 10 A.M.–9 P.M. Sun., entrées $8–15) is a colorful place with great grub, cold *cerveza,* and exceptionally friendly service. This family-run restaurant puts out an extensive menu of Mexican offerings such as chicken mole, carnitas, chili verde, enchiladas, and the best damn beef tongue (simmered in a peppery tomato sauce) this side of the Rio Grande, or at least the Snake.

Peregrine Steaks and Seafood (751 W. 4th St., 208/922-4421, lunch and dinner daily, dinner entrées $12–24) is the nicest restaurant in Kuna. Located on the edge of town near the Sandstone Plaza, Peregrine offers standard steakhouse fare with an Idaho twist. Shrimp cocktail, slow-roasted prime rib, and grilled Hagerman Valley trout are the orders of the day. A decent wine list and cocktails (mixed at the full-service bar) round out the menu.

MERIDIAN AND EAGLE

Meridian (population 75,000), seven miles north of Kuna on Meridian Road and sharing a border with Boise to the east, is one of the fastest growing cities in Idaho, which has brought multilane boulevards dotted with big-box stores and corporate restaurants. Once a bustling milk hub, Meridian now is a hodgepodge of innocuous strip malls and office parks that have gobbled up the old dairy farms.

The behemoth Roaring Springs Water Park greets travelers at I-84 Exit 44. Take these off ramps and head north on Meridian Road, and it will lead you past the old Meridian Speedway and into an attractive little downtown area. Here you'll find an excellent Basque restaurant, among other good eateries and little shops.

It's hard to tell where Meridian ends and Eagle (population 19,000) begins as you travel north on Eagle Road. After crossing Chinden Boulevard, Eagle Road drops into a pleasant little valley and crosses the Boise River into downtown Eagle. This affluent river city, in the shadow of the foothills, has a multitude of locally owned restaurants and shops, many of which are along the cute downtown strip. These places cater to well-heeled customers who live in the nearby McMansions. Eagle also has two burgeoning wineries that have tasting rooms. Eagle Island State Park is another popular spot where you can take a dip or a shady hike in the trees near the Boise River during the sweltering days of summer.

Wineries

Spend the day at **Woodriver Cellars** (3705 Hwy. 16, Eagle, 208/286-9463, www.woodrivercellars.com, tasting room 11 A.M.–6 P.M. Thurs. and Sun., 11 A.M.–10 P.M. Fri.–Sat.) sipping wine and playing boccie ball on the winery's four courts. Winemaker Neil Glancey turns out crisp sauvignon blanc, chardonnay, Bordeaux-inspired reds, and a port dessert wine made from grapes grown on the property. Woodriver is a destination winery, with an 800-square-foot tasting room, beautifully landscaped grounds, and an outdoor amphitheater where the winery hosts its summer concert series. To get to the winery from downtown Eagle, head west on SR-44 (W. State St.) for about nine miles until you come to the

Highway 16 junction. Hang a right and head due north for about two miles; the winery is on the left side of the highway.

3 Horse Ranch Vineyards (5900 Pearl Rd., Eagle, 208/863-6561, www.3horseranchvineyards.com, tasting room 11 A.M.–6 P.M. Thurs.–Sun.) is relatively new to Idaho's winemaking scene. Owner Gary Cunningham started the small organic winery in 2003 after planting vines in the vast rolling hills west of downtown Eagle. Expect to taste robust syrah, merlot, riesling, and a superb roussanne-viognier blend (small tasting fee refundable with purchase). To get here, go north on Highway 16 at the SR-44 junction for about six miles until you arrive at West Chaparral Road. Take a right here and travel three miles. Hang a left at Pearl Road and go 2.5 miles to the winery. You'll see the vineyards and the three horses.

Recreation

Southern Idaho can get brutally hot in the summer, so **Roaring Springs** (400 W. Overland Rd., Meridian, 208/884-8842 or 877/420-7529, www.roaringsprings.com, 11 A.M.–8 P.M. daily June–late Aug., 11 A.M.–7 P.M. Sat.–Sun. late May and early Sept., full-day $27 over 48 inches, $22 under 48 inches) is understandably a huge draw, especially for kids. The park has a wave pool, a kids' play place, and a river for mellow tubing—plus thoroughly gonzo attractions like the Thunder Falls Family Raft Ride, Viper's Vortex, and the U-shaped Avalanche.

Next door to Roaring Springs, **Wahooz Family Fun Zone** (1385 S. Blue Marlin Lane, Meridian, 208/898-0900, packages from $13) has two miniature golf courses (one sporting a replica of Utah's Delicate Arch), bumper boats, batting cages, and go-karts outside, plus laser tag and a huge arcade indoors. Check the website for hours, which change with the season and day of the week.

Race fans should check out **Meridian Speedway** (335 S. Main St., Meridian, 208/888-2813, www.meridianspeedway.com, Apr.–Sept., $5–15), a 0.25-mile oval track that features winged sprint cars, late-model stock cars, and an occasional smash-up derby. The track has spawned many professional racers over the years, including Indy driver Davey Hamilton, whose family operates the speedway.

Summer brings something for everyone at **Eagle Island State Park** (2691 Mace Rd., Eagle, 208/939-0696, parking $5, pedestrians free), a beautiful spot about two miles west of downtown Eagle. A 15-acre lake makes a good swimming hole, and a nice sandy beach draws sun worshippers. Kids head right to the waterslide (noon–8 P.M. Thurs.–Sun., $7 for 10 rides, $12 all day), while picnickers will find expansive grassy areas and numerous picnic tables to lay out the spread. There's also an 18-hole disc golf course and more than five miles of hiking trails, which get shared with horses. The park boundaries extend far to the east—only 26 of the park's 546 acres have been developed. No pets are allowed in the park.

Events

Jazz on the River (208/321-4162, $40 adults, $20 students) happens every June in Eagle. This music festival features a bevy of semifamous jazz musicians, such as Bill Anschell, Brent Jensen, and Orrin Evans, who play at various locations around town. An art fair takes place concurrently, and a handful of local winemakers and chefs come together to give people a taste of their creations.

Pick up some seasonal produce and freshly baked bread at the **Eagle Saturday Market** (8:30 A.M.–1 P.M. Sat. May–Oct.) in downtown Eagle's Heritage Park. Besides local farmers and bakers, the market also has lots of locally raised natural and organic meat products that include Kobe-style beef, lamb, elk, chicken, and buffalo as well as booths with grab-and-go food. But the market isn't all about food; expect to find aromatherapy products, landscape photography, and funky birdhouses. There's also live music every week in the gazebo.

Shopping

Bargain hunters will surely like the **Sierra Trading Post** outlet store (530 E. Sonata Lane,

© DANA HOPPER-KELLY

Eagle Saturday Market

Meridian, 208/898-0261, www.sierratrading-post.com) next to I-84 Exit 44 in Meridian. This Wyoming-based company, specializing in online mail-order sales, has a cultlike following. The superstore has tons of great deals on name-brand clothes, hiking boots, GPS devices, and other outdoor gear.

Before hitting one of Idaho's many rivers, fill your tackle box at **Sportsman's Warehouse** (3797 E. Fairview Ave., near Eagle Rd., Meridian, 208/884-3000, www.sportsmanswarehouse.com), but beware: This is busiest intersection in the state. The large chain store carries all things related to fishing, hunting, and camping. There is row upon row of fishing poles, tackle, and accessories. It's easy to get tunnel vision.

If you are looking to buy wines from around the world, **Erickson Fine Wines** (150 E. Riverside St., Eagle, 208/938-3698, www.ericksonfinewines.com, 10 A.M.–7 P.M. Mon.–Sat.) near downtown Eagle is the place to go. This small yet well-stocked wine store next to Tully's Coffee has labels from Argentina, Chile, Spain, France, and Italy as well as California, Washington, Oregon, and Idaho. Owner Brian

Erickson is a knowledgeable guy who can steer you in the right direction.

Accommodations

Meridian is the land of corporate hotels, especially along I-84, where you will find a plethora of choices. Here are two good picks at Exit 46 (Eagle Rd.): The **Courtyard by Marriott-Boise West** (1789 S. Eagle Rd., Meridian, 208/888-0800, www.marriott.com, from $108 d) is easily Meridian's largest hotel. The four-story hotel has a nice indoor pool, a business center, an exercise room, and a complimentary breakfast buffet in the small restaurant just off the lobby. **Comfort Suites** (2610 E. Freeway Dr., Meridian, 208/288-2060, www.comfortsuites.com, from $89 d) is a shiny new place with the usual amenities. It's located on the north side of I-84.

Hilton Garden Inn (145 E. Riverside Dr., Eagle, 208/938-9600, www.hiltongardeninn.com, from $99 d) is currently Eagle's only lodging option, but with the local wine industry booming, don't be surprised to see some bed-and-breakfast inns and other hotels opening up here in the coming years. The hotel (six miles north of Exit 46 on Eagle Rd.) is set on the Boise River and has an indoor pool, a fitness room, and a hot breakfast buffet.

Food

Both Meridian and Eagle have a frenzied blur of mediocre corporate restaurants, but do yourself a favor and check out these independently owned gems. **((Epi's** (1115 E. 1st St., Meridian, 208/884-0142, dinner at 5 P.M. Tues.–Sat., entrées $15–25) offers outstanding traditional Basque fare in a bright, tidy, and very friendly atmosphere. Basque music fills the air, and Basque art and family photos line the walls. You can choose from dishes such as stewed beef tongue in a pepper-tomato sauce or baby squid in a sauce of its own ink. Or stick with something slightly less adventurous but equally as wonderful, like the lamb stew. This small, dinner-only restaurant is very popular; reservations are strongly recommended.

For a true taste of regional Italian fare, head to **Gino's Ristorante and Bar** (3015 W. McMillan Rd. at Ten Mile Rd., Meridian, 208/887-7710, 11 A.M.–10 P.M. Mon.–Sat., entrées $10–22), where chef Gino Vuolo puts out food with a southern Italian bent. Prime your palate with starters like beef carpaccio, antipasto, and bruschetta with smoked trout. Choose from a large selection of pasta and meatier dishes like a delightful braised boar shank and pan-seared veal chop. The wine list makes its way around Italy.

Sa-Wad-Dee (1890 E. Fairview Ave., Meridian, 208/884-0701, www.sawaddeethai. com, lunch and dinner daily, $7–19) is the best Thai restaurant outside Boise. This ornately designed place has great food and friendly service, and the menu runs the gamut of typical Southeast Asian offerings such as chicken satay, silky shrimp dumplings, fresh basil rolls, vibrant curries, stir-fried noodles, and colorful seafood dishes.

Locals adore **Bardenay** (155 E. Riverside Dr., Eagle, 208/938-5093, www.bardenay.

com, lunch and dinner daily, entrées $9–23), a micro-distillery and restaurant next to the Hilton Garden Inn. Walk past the towering still near the front door, and the large dining room opens up onto a comfortable riverside patio where you can try the house-made spirits and appetizers from the expansive menu. Noteworthy picks include spicy plum-glazed chicken wings, smoked trout spread, and an artisanal cheeseboard. If you are really hungry, try a burger, beer-battered cod and chips, or the beef tenderloin with smoked tomato sauce.

Everyone in town goes to **((Rembrandt's Coffee House** (93 S. Eagle Rd., Eagle, 208/938-1372, www.rembrandtscoffeehouse. net, 6:30 A.M.–9 P.M. Mon.–Thurs., 6:30 A.M.– 10 P.M. Fri., 8 A.M.–10 P.M. Sat., 8 A.M.–2 P.M. Sun.) for morning java, loose-leaf tea, and light breakfast fare. Located in a former church in downtown Eagle, this comfy coffeehouse has lots of big chairs and couches where you can kick back and sip an espresso drink made from fair-trade coffee beans while nibbling on a house-baked pastry.

Porterhouse Market (600 S. Rivershore Lane, Eagle, 208/938-1441, www.porterhouse-market.com, 10 A.M.–6 P.M. Mon.–Sat.) is a specialty food store, butcher, and deli near the intersection of Eagle Road and State Street. Besides cases filled with ready-to-grill Kobe-style beef, house-made sausages, seafood, and natural chicken and lamb, the market also keeps hot barbecue items such as Kansas City–inspired baby back ribs, pulled pork, and beef brisket in a small case by the deli. You can also score fat sandwiches and tasty salads.

Information

For more information on Meridian, contact the **Meridian Chamber of Commerce** (215 E. Franklin Rd., Meridian, 208/888-2817, www. meridianchamber.org). The **Eagle Chamber of Commerce** (597 E. State St., Eagle, 208/939-4222, www.eaglechamber.com) also provides visitor information and other resources about the area.

U.S. 95: North to Weiser

U.S. 95 is Idaho's main arterial linking southern Idaho to northern Idaho. This long and winding two-lane road skirts the Oregon and Washington borders on its way to the Panhandle. In southwest Idaho, out on the flats of the Snake River Plain, U.S. 95 leads through mile after mile of rural farmland. During the summer, you can smell the yellow onions in the air. Many of these pungent alliums are sold to Ore-Ida, a processing plant in nearby Ontario, Oregon, that makes them into onion rings.

The small town of Parma is the western starting point for the newly designated Snake River Canyon Scenic Byway, a beautiful route that winds its way along the big river en route to the Owyhee Canyonlands. Just up the highway on the north side of I-84 are the small towns of Payette and Fruitland, which are known for having large fruit orchards. Continue due north on U.S. 95, and you will eventually come to Weiser, a town that hosts a famous fiddle festival every summer.

PARMA

Even though Parma is in the Snake River Valley Appellation, there's not much going on here in terms of viticulture—at least not yet. Local farmers grow large cash crops of potatoes, wheat, hops, and table grapes. Raising cattle is also big business around this tiny town.

Fort Boise, four miles west of present-day Parma near the confluence of the Boise and Snake Rivers, was the first nonnative settlement in southwest Idaho. In 1834, good ol' Thomas McKay of the Hudson's Bay Company built this fur-trading post in an effort to compete with the brisk business being conducted at Fort Hall on the southeast edge of the Snake River Plain. By 1863, Fort Boise had been moved to what is now downtown Boise, and it quickly fell into disrepair and was eventually washed away by the spring's rushing waters.

Thirty years later, settlers started to file land claims in the area, one of whom was F. R.

Fouch, a man with a penchant for classical history: He named the town after Parma, Italy. Over the years, Parma has had several colorful residents, including Edgar Rice Burroughs, author of *Tarzan of the Apes,* who tried his hand at cattle ranching here during the early 19th century. He was even on the city council for a short time.

Today, Parma is home to a replica of Fort Boise, a winery, and it boasts one of the only operational drive-in movie theaters in the state.

Parma Ridge Vineyards

Parma Ridge Vineyards (24509 Rudd Rd., 208/722-6885, www.parmaridge.com, by

SNAKE RIVER CANYON SCENIC BYWAY

The newly designated Snake River Canyon Scenic Byway winds its way through 53 miles of bountiful agricultural land, ranging from near the Oregon border to Walter's Ferry in the Owyhee hinterlands. Parma is the western starting point for the byway. From this spot, the route meanders southeast along the Snake River on a series of well-marked rural roads, passing by family-run farms, fruit orchards, and vineyards. You'll go through the winery district of Sunny Slope before ascending onto a sagebrush-dotted bench that skirts the river canyon, where Map Rock near Walter's Ferry shows ancient petroglyphs. Up here, dormant cinder cones punctuate the landscape and the deep-canyon rim – long ago carved out by the Bonneville Flood – offers dramatic views of the Owyhee Mountains. Besides cattle, bison, and sheep, also expect to see abundant wildlife that includes mule deer, coyotes, badgers, and red-tailed hawks along this spectacular drive.

appointment only) is a boutique-level operation with a small vineyard south of town. The winery puts out chardonnay, cabernet sauvignon, merlot, syrah, viognier, and malbec. Owner-winemaker Dick Dickstein is a friendly guy who will gladly show you around his property.

Fort Boise Replica

Although the original Fort Boise long ago succumbed to the elements, a re-creation has been built along the U.S. 95 in downtown Parma. The new old fort contains a museum and a pioneer cabin. The Fort Boise Replica (1–3 P.M. Fri.–Sun. June–Aug., other times by appointment, admission free, donations appreciated) hosts **Old Fort Boise Days** in June, featuring a parade, a crafts fair, period costumes, and a chili cook-off. For further information or an off-season appointment to see the recreated fort, contact **Parma City Hall** (305 N. 3rd St., 208/722-5138). The adjacent Old Fort Boise Park has a picnic area, overnight RV parking, and a small campground ($13 RVs, $7 tents, fee box at the park) overseen by the Parma Police Department (105 N. 4th St., 208/722-5900), so behave yourself.

Recreation

At the site of the original Fort Boise is the 1,500-acre **Fort Boise Wildlife Management Area** (30845 Old Fort Boise Rd., Parma, 208/722-5888), a popular fishing and bird-hunting area managed by the Idaho Department of Fish and Game. To reach the site, take Old Fort Boise Road west off the highway, just north of town.

Drive-in Theater

Remember drive-in movie theaters? Well, one still exists in Parma. **Parma Motor-Vu** (29522 U.S. 95, 208/722-6401, www.parmamotorvu.com, $7, free for children under 12) is located northwest of town en route to Nyssa, Oregon. This classic drive-in, operated by the same family that opened it in 1953, gives people a blast from the past by showing current-run movies on its large screen during the summertime.

Go retro at Parma Motor-Vu.

Fans of all things retro will get a kick out of the cool neon sign that draws people in like a bug zapper. Speaking of bugs, the only downside to the theater is that mosquitoes tend to swarm around the marshy grounds. (Careful: Don't get bug spray in your popcorn.)

Food

Next to Old Fort Boise Park, you'll find **Boy's Better Burgers** (911 E. Grove Ave., 208/722-5463), a fast-food joint that brings in droves of locals for cheesy gut-bombs, fries, and shakes. In the quaint downtown area, try **Bistro 2 Fifteen** (215 Main Ave., 208/722-5444, 6 A.M.–2 P.M. Mon.–Fri., 8 A.M.–2 P.M. Sat.–Sun., under $10). This casual café—it's not really a bistro—serves espresso drinks, sandwiches, wraps, and house-made soups.

PAYETTE AND FRUITLAND

Soon after crossing over to the north side of I-84, you will hit the small towns of Payette and Fruitland near Ontario, Oregon. It's hard to tell the difference between these two agricultural towns while driving northbound on U.S. 95—they kind of blur together into one big burg along this stretch. The area is known for having several large fruit-packing companies and produce stands that sell sweet onions, corn, apricots, peaches, and apples.

Payette, the seat of Payette County, has an attractive downtown district with several buildings on the National Register of Historic Places, making it a worthwhile stop for lunch or simply to stretch your getaway sticks. Major League Baseball great Harmon Killebrew, who played 22 seasons in the big leagues for the Washington Senators and Minnesota Twins, hails from these parts. With 573 career home runs and a lifetime batting average of .256, he was inducted into the Baseball Hall of Fame in 1984.

Payette County Museum

Delve into local history at the Payette County Museum (90 S. 9th St., Payette, 208/642-4883, noon–4 P.M. Wed.–Sat., free), located in a former Episcopal church near downtown.

Beautiful stained glass windows refract the light in a kaleidoscope of colors as you walk through the front doors. The museum houses an array of local photos and artifacts, a Civil War–era cannon, and lots of Harmon Killebrew memorabilia such as old jerseys, bats, and photos from his high school days and time spent in the pros.

Recreation

Local golfers head to **Scotch Pines Golf Course** (10610 Scotch Pines Rd., Payette, 208/642-1829, www.scotchpinesgolf.com, $21–28), a challenging 18-hole course nestled in the foothills. East off U.S. 95, take 7th Avenue North, turn left on Iowa Avenue, and right on Scotch Pines Road. The course is sometimes closed in winter. After a game of golf, take refuge in the dining room at **Mulligan's Restaurant** (208/642-4866, dinner Tues.–Sat., reservations recommended), an air-conditioned 19th hole that puts out steaks, seafood, and stiff drinks.

Anglers can try their luck on **Paddock**

Payette County Museum, located in a former Episcopal church

© DANA HOPPER-KELLY

Valley Reservoir; take Little Willow Road off Highway 52, northeast of Fruitland or southeast of Payette. According to the Idaho Department of Fish and Game, the reservoir is renowned for excellent crappie fishing. Isn't that an oxymoron? You'll find a boat-launching ramp at the end of the road on the south edge of the reservoir.

Events

The **Apple Blossom Festival** happens annually in Payette in mid-May. You'll find a parade, arts and crafts, a carnival, and entertainment. The **Payette County Fair and Rodeo** comes to the fairgrounds in nearby New Plymouth in mid-August. Look for an Idaho Cowboys Association rodeo, agriculture and livestock exhibits, and food, food, food. For more information on these and other events, call the Payette Chamber of Commerce (208/642-2362).

Food

Spring through fall, stock up on locally grown fruit and vegetables at **Purdum's Produce** (U.S. 30 and Elmore Rd., Fruitland, 208/452-4098), right off the junction of I-84 and U.S. 95. This seasonal produce stand has a delicious bounty of sweet corn, tomatoes, peppers, squash, peaches, nectarines, plums, and apples, to name a few. **Moxie Java** (816 N. Whitley Dr., Fruitland, 208/452-5996, www.moxiejava.com) is a locally operated coffeehouse located next to a garden nursery on U.S. 95; just look for the big barn. You can open your eyes with an espresso drink and a fat scone.

In downtown Payette, locals convene at **Kloys Pizza** (120 N. Main St., Payette, 208/642-1877, lunch and dinner daily) for big pizza pies and hot sandwiches. It's a great place for kids.

Information and Services

Just past Fruitland, traveling north on U.S. 95, is the NW 16th Street junction. Take a left (west), and you will cross over the Snake River and enter into Ontario, Oregon. This humdrum town has lots of chain hotels, big-box stores, and fast-food joints. For more information

about the Payette and Fruitland area, contact the **Payette Chamber of Commerce** (711 Center Ave., Payette, 208/642-2362).

WEISER

The seat of Washington County, Weiser lies just north of the confluence of the Snake and Weiser Rivers. North of here the Snake rolls northwest toward its drop through Hells Canyon, while the highway bears north and east, climbing slowly up the Weiser River watershed.

Weiser, both river and town, were named for Peter Weiser, a Revolutionary War veteran and cook for the Lewis and Clark expedition of 1804–1806. In May 1806, the Corps of Discovery reached the confluence of the Snake and Clearwater Rivers, site of present-day Lewiston, and Weiser and two others were dispatched on an exploratory mission up the Snake. When they reached the Snake's confluence with the Salmon, they traveled up that river another 20 miles, becoming the first nonnatives to see the Lower Salmon Gorge. Clark subsequently named one of the Snake's tributaries for Weiser, perhaps in fond remembrance of his chef's particularly savory salmon steaks.

Weiser was once home to famed pro baseball player Walter "Big Train" Johnson, who pitched for the Washington Senators. Over the course of his 21-year pro career, Johnson won 666 games, making him the second-winningest pitcher in history behind Cy Young. But the town's biggest claim to fame is its world-famous fiddle festival and competition held every June.

Historic Buildings

Weiser's early wood-framed commercial district was rebuilt in brick after an 1890 fire reduced much of the town to ashes. Before the fire, the town core had been farther east, but rebuilding efforts centered the new downtown around the **Oregon Short Line Depot.** The Queen Anne-style depot at the south end of State Street was built in 1906–1907 and is currently being restored. The building that now houses

Matthews' Grain & Storage (Commercial St. and E. 1st St.) was once a house of ill repute known as the Clinton Rooms (no Democrat jokes, please). According to local legend, a mailman delivering a COD package to the Clinton Rooms was one day offered payment in services instead of cash.

A Welsh castle in southwest Idaho? Strange but true. The local Knights of Pythias began building the storybook **Pythian Castle** (E. Idaho St. between State St. and E. 1st St.) in 1904, modeling it after a château in Wales. The stone blocks of the facade were quarried north of town, hauled here by wagon, and cut on-site. You'll find the castle on. For a guide to these and other historic buildings downtown, pick up a free walking-tour pamphlet at the chamber of commerce office (309 State St., 208/414-0452).

Recreation

Mountain bikers, hikers, and cross-country skiers can get out on the **Weiser River Trail,** which follows an abandoned Pacific and Idaho Northern Railway right-of-way for 84 miles

from Weiser up to New Meadows. Some parts flank civilization, and other sections are blissfully remote. Some sections are in better shape than others; trail building and maintenance are ongoing.

At **Walter Johnson Park** (Hanthorn St. and 3rd St.), you'll find a baseball diamond, naturally, as well as tennis courts, picnic tables, barbecues, and a small stage.

Rolling Hills Golf Course (50 W. Indianhead Rd., 208/549-0456, $5–18) sits at the top of the hill on the north end of town. The tree-lined, 18-hole course ranges over 6,090 yards. Cart rentals are available. The course's restaurant, **The Loft at Rolling Hills** (208/549-2909, lunch Mon.–Sat., dinner Wed.–Sat.), was recently remodeled, and a new chef was brought in to upgrade the fare.

Events
(NATIONAL OLDTIME FIDDLERS' CONTEST AND FESTIVAL

Each year during the third full week of June, Weiser is occupied by an army of fiddlers and their fans, here to participate in the National

National Oldtime Fiddlers' Contest and Festival

© IDAHO DIVISION OF TOURISM

Oldtime Fiddlers' Contest (309 State St., 208/414-0255 or 800/437-1280, www.fiddle-contest.com), the most prestigious fiddle festival in the United States. All week long, all over town, the strains of fiddles, guitars, and banjos waft through the air. Schoolyards become makeshift campgrounds where hundreds of RVers circle the wagons, pull out their instruments, and play all day and into the night.

The competition itself is staged in the high school gym (W. 7th St. and Indianhead Rd.). Each contestant has four minutes to play a hoedown, a waltz, and a third tune of the contestant's choice. The competitors, ranging from preteen to octogenarian, are judged in a number of age categories.

Some of the oldest senior-senior players have played old-time fiddle since the Wilson administration and are predictably masterful. But as you wander through the warm-up rooms and campgrounds, what may impress you more are the kids, who play with the same passion and fury as the older folks.

Tickets to the daytime rounds are $2.50 adults, $1.50 children, and the nighttime rounds run $10–19. A full-week pass good for everything but the Saturday finals is $55 adults, $25 under age 13.

Accommodations

Indianhead Motel & RV Park (747 Hillcrest Ave., 208/549-0331), near the west side of the highway as you head north out of town, offers eight nonsmoking motel rooms ($60–95) and 12 RV spaces ($25) with water and electricity hookups. Amenities include a laundry room, a picnic area, showers, horseshoe pits, and a golf-practice cage. Tent camping and pets are not allowed. The RV park is closed in the winter.

Weiser has two attractive bed-and-breakfast inns that are both in historic homes. **Galloway House Inn Bed and Breakfast** (1120 E. 2nd St., 208/549-1719, www.gallowayhouseinn.

com, $90 with private bath, $70 shared bath) is in Victorian mansion near downtown. Relax in one of the many parlor-like common areas or sip iced tea on the shady patio. The **🄲 Liberty House Bed and Breakfast** (308 W. Liberty St., 208/549-1442, www.liberty-housebedandbreakfast.com, $70 shared bath) has five beautiful guest rooms and puts out an excellent home-style breakfast before sending guests on their way.

Food

The preferred fare in Weiser is diner food. Locals file into the **Beehive Family Restaurant** (611 U.S. 95 at E. 7th St., 208/549-3544, breakfast, lunch, and dinner daily, under $10) for big breakfasts and a never-ending flow of coffee. The homespun restaurant serves everything from chef salads to chicken-fried steaks. For comfort food with a Norwegian touch, head to **Synnove's Kitchen** (1095 W. 7th St., 208/414-5000, 5–9 P.M. Wed.–Sat.), a dinner-only restaurant.

Weiser Classic Candy (449 State. St., 208/414-2850, www.weiserclassiccandy.com, 10 A.M.–5:30 P.M. Mon.–Fri., 10 A.M.–4 P.M. Sat.) is a cool candy store located in a Bavarian-influenced storefront downtown. Satiate your sweet tooth with a bevy of freshly made chocolates and specialty candies, like chai tea truffles, champagne truffles, almond bark, fudge, and apricot bonbons. The place also has a full-service deli that puts out superb salads and sandwiches ($5–7). Try the delicious Monte Cristo.

Information

The **Weiser Chamber of Commerce** (309 State St., 208/414-0452) can tell you more about the town. For information about the area's recreational possibilities, drop by the Payette National Forest's **Weiser Ranger District** (851 E. 9th St., 208/549-4200).

Owyhee Mountains and Canyonlands

In many ways, life hasn't changed that drastically in Owyhee County in the last century or so. Ranchers now dial their trusty satellite phones (cell phone coverage is spotty out here) instead of riding their fastest horse into Murphy to dispatch an urgent message. But jackrabbits and rangeland cattle still outnumber people in this vast and desolate county, the second largest in the state at a 7,639 square miles.

If you are lucky, a herd of wild horses will cross the dusty horizon as the high desert unfolds in front of you. Expect to see bighorn sheep, coyotes, rattlesnakes, peregrine falcons, and possibly an occasional cougar hanging out in a creek bed, stalking a wild turkey for dinner.

Named for Hawaiian fur trappers that frequented the area in the early 19th century, the Owyhee (loosely translated from the word *Hawaii*) Mountains and Canyonlands was once a rough-and-tumble place. Many train robberies and murders occurred here in the 1800s. Even the Hawaiian fur trappers mysteriously disappeared without a trace.

The ruggedly beautiful Owyhee Mountains run like a granite spine from the north to southeast, all the way into northern Nevada, splitting Idaho and Oregon into two distinct high-desert valleys. The mountain range rises to 8,403 feet at Hayden Peak. Back in the day, nearby Silver City was a bustling mining town, and in some respects it is still alive.

A few miles to the southeast, the undulating lower valley starts to straighten out until it reaches a pair of giant sand dunes that seem rather out of place among the sage brush and basalt-streaked canyons.

MARSING

Marsing is a relatively new town, considering there was no bridge crossing the Snake River here until 1921. Before that, two different cable-ferries hauled travelers back and forth, and there wasn't much of a town here at all; it was actually platted about the same time the bridge was built.

Lizard Butte, a prominent basalt bluff that resembles a reptile's head, marks Marsing's north entrance, where the highway curves downward from Sunny Slope and crosses the Snake into the town. **Island Park,** on the up-river side of the bridge, offers a grassy area with picnic tables, barbecue grills, and some resident ducks. Anglers might try dropping a line in hopes of making the acquaintance of a small-mouth bass or two.

To say that Marsing is not visually appealing would be generous, yet it has a handful of decent eateries, a new winery tasting room, and the only grocery store and gas station for miles around. But don't expect any shiny Holiday Inns and corporate restaurants; in fact, you won't find any hotels or motels (at least ones I feel comfortable recommending). Instead, the downtown strip—Highway 55 slowed to a snail's pace—winds its way through the small town and up a big hill, eventually meeting U.S. 95 and continuing into the far reaches of southeastern Oregon.

Wineries

Thanks to Marsing's close proximity to Sunny Slope (it's about a mile away), a couple of small wineries have popped up here lately. **Davis Creek Cellars** (429 Main St., Marsing, 208/794-2848, www.daviscreekcellars.com, tasting room noon–5 P.M. Fri.–Sun.) is a Sunny Slope–based winery that found affordable rent in Marsing for its tasting room. Try winemaker-owner Gina Davis's line of small-lot wines, including tempranillo, viognier, cabernet sauvignon, syrah, and malbec made from grapes sourced at area vineyards. About seven miles southeast of town, along curvy Highway 78, you will come to **Miceli Vineyards & Winery** (8114 Owyhee View Lane, Givens Hot Springs, 208/896-5803, www.micelivineyards.com), a micro-winery that grows its own grapes. Owner-winemaker Jim Mitchell produces limited cases of cabernet sauvignon, zinfandel, chardonnay, and merlot.

© DANA HOPPER-KELLY

Jump Creek Falls

Recreation

Jump Creek cuts down through the Owyhee foothills, forming a spectacular steep-walled canyon where 60-foot **Jump Creek Falls** plunges into a deep pool. It's an idyllic spot for a cooling summer swim.

The site is managed by the Bureau of Land Management. Primitive camping is possible, but there are no developed facilities. To get here, take Jump Creek Road south from U.S. 95. At the Y just past the high-tension wires, go right. Just a little farther, at the base of a small ridge, go left. At the next Y you can go either way—from there on out, all roads lead to the parking area. I don't suggest parking in the lower lot after it has rained heavily because it can become extremely slick; there's ample parking in the upper lot. An easy trail leads up about 0.25 miles to the falls. Beware of poison ivy and rattlesnakes.

Entertainment and Events

The annual **Flower of the Desert Festival** in May is the town's biggest bash. Also in May

is **Fishing Day,** followed by a **Fishing Derby** in June. **Sprint boat races** take place on the river about once a month throughout summer, while a **Holiday Parade** livens up Main Street in December. For a complete schedule of local events and more information about the town, stop by **Marsing City Hall** (425 Main St., 208/896-4122).

Food

The Sandbar River House Restaurant (18 Sandbar Ave., 208/896-4124, www.sandbar-riverhouse.com, lunch and dinner Tues.–Sun., dinner $8–24, reservations recommended), in a converted house on the riverbank, serves more than the usual burgers and Budweiser. Lunch features several sandwiches ($7–13), while at night expect a large selection of hand-cut steaks and seafood paired with a substantial list of Idaho wines. The cool, shaded back patio is the spot to be in summer, offering views of the river and Lizard Butte. To get here, head toward the river from downtown and make the last left before you get to the bridge (across from Island Park). The restaurant is down a block on the right. You can't miss the place—it's the nicest looking building in town.

Alejandra's Mexican Restaurant (208 Main St., 208/896-5339, lunch and dinner daily) is the place to go for tamales, chili verde, carnitas, and enchiladas. This small restaurant on the main drag also has a *mercado* that sells chicharrones (crunchy pork rinds), fresh tortillas, and long-necked refrescos (Mexican soft drinks).

HIGHWAY 78 TO MURPHY
Givens Hot Springs

Nomadic Native Americans had been using the hot springs here for thousands of years when Oregon-bound Milford and Mattie Givens came upon the spot in 1879. The couple immediately abandoned their journey down the dusty Oregon Trail and set up housekeeping. In 1881 they built a home, and in the 1890s, with the help of their four sons, they added a bathhouse. Alas, marital bliss eluded the settlers, and they divorced. Mattie stayed in the

SOUTHWEST IDAHO

family home and remarried, this time to Gus Yanke. Gus helped expand the home into a travelers' oasis that eventually included a hotel, a restaurant, an ice-cream parlor, tree-shaded picnic grounds, a barbershop, and a post office. In 1907, a school was established that apparently doubled as a matrimonial service—three of the four Givens boys married girls who came to teach.

The resort became known throughout the area and was well used by Oregon Trail pioneers, Silver City miners, and residents of the Treasure Valley. The hotel burned down in 1939 and was never rebuilt. In 1952 a new bathhouse was constructed. Although only a small icehouse today remains of Milford and Mattie's handiwork, the resort is still owned by their descendants, who have renovated the property in recent years.

The present bathhouse (208/495-2000, noon–10 P.M. daily year-round) has an Olympic-size pool ($7 adults, $5 seniors and children, free under age 2 and over age 90), private soaking tubs ($7 pp per hour), and a small snack bar. Outside are picnic areas, horseshoe pits, and areas for baseball, volleyball, and fishing on the Snake River. Tent sites ($20) and RV sites ($25) are available, and cabins will cost you $55.

The resort is on the south side of Highway 78, 11 miles south of Marsing.

Accommodations and Food

Nothing screams "desert" like a giant log home. The **Snake River Log Bed and Breakfast** (11800 Snake River B&B Lane, 208/495-2288, www.snakeriverlog-bb.com, $175) is a posh place for this neck of the sagebrush. The three-story log home has three large guest suites with killer views of the Owyhee Mountains. Each room has its own bathroom, whirlpool tub, fireplace, king bed, and private balcony. Wake up to a large homespun breakfast before heading out to explore the desert. To get here, continue on Highway 78 one mile past the Walter's Ferry Bridge, the junction of Highway 45, and take a left when you see the sign; there's not much else out here.

Just down the way, continuing southeast on Highway 78 about 1.5 miles, you'll find another kind of desert oasis. **The Blue Canoe** restaurant (16479 Hwy. 78, 208/495-2269, www.thebluecanoerestaurant.com, 4–9 P.M. Fri.–Sat., 11 A.M.–7 P.M. Sun., entrées $11–26) shines like a brightly painted toenail on the dry, sagebrush-covered foot of the Owyhee Mountains. The large menu features prime rib (Fri.–Sat. night only) and crawdads from nearby C. J. Strike Reservoir.

Murphy

Although Murphy is the Owyhee County seat, it's not the largest town in the county. In fact, it's one of the smallest, with a population of around 50. In the mining boom days at the turn of the century, Silver City was the county seat, but when metal prices dropped and the mines began to play out, a new site closer to the Snake River was proposed. At that time, Murphy had the county's only railroad terminal, the end of the line for the Boise, Nampa and Owyhee Railroad. Colonel William Dewey had hoped to build an electric continuation of the railroad from Murphy all the way up to his mine near Silver City, to be powered by electricity from the Swan Falls Dam hydroelectric plant he'd built, but the railroad never made it past Murphy. In the meantime, the county's extensive cattle and sheep industries had turned Murphy into the largest livestock shipping point in the Northwest, securing it as the county seat in 1934.

Murphy is semi-famous for its single parking meter in front of the courthouse. The meter was originally an unsubtle hint by locals to discourage people from parking in front of the courthouse gate. Now the lone meter highlights the fact that this little hamlet could well be the smallest county seat in the country. Facilities are limited; the town has no motels and just one small restaurant.

The **Owyhee County Museum** (Bassey St., 208/495-2319, 10 A.M.–4 P.M. Tues.–Sat. year-round, donation), one block south of the highway (look for the sign by the courthouse), includes several transplanted structures and a small historical research library. Among the historic buildings is a one-room schoolhouse, a homesteader's log cabin, and the old Marsing depot, outside of which sits a Union Pacific caboose. Much of the museum's exhibit space is devoted to the history of the Owyhee mines and includes a recreated stamp mill. Library archives hold microfilmed newspapers dating as far back as 1865 as well as more than 4,000 historic photographs of Owyhee County. On the first weekend of each June, the museum sponsors **Outpost Days,** a festival of folk art, cowboy poetry, country music, parades, food, a Saturday-night dance, and the culminating Horny Toad races.

C SILVER CITY

Silver City lies in a draw on Jordan Creek, 6,200 feet high in the Owyhee Mountains. To get here, you have to negotiate a narrow winding road for 23 miles up from Murphy. The gravel and dirt road is usually blocked by snow more than half the year, and even in summer it's not recommended for trailers and large RVs. But if you think it's hard getting to Silver City today, just imagine what it was like trying to get here during the town's heyday, roughly 1860–1900. Back then, Silver City had a population of 2,500 along with some 75 businesses and 300 homes. Its prosperity led to its status as the county seat 1866–1934. By 1874 it boasted the first telegraph office and the first daily newspaper—*The Idaho Avalanche*—in Idaho Territory. Today, less than 10 people live here year-round. While modern-day residents are after nothing more than remote relaxation, the boomtown-era residents came for silver and gold.

The **Idaho Hotel** (208/583-4104, www.historicsilvercityidaho.com) is the gathering spot in Silver City. Built in 1863, it was falling down until it was brought back to life in 1972. The hotel has remained open since then under various owners. Go into the saloon, grab a cold one, and find your way across the sloping floor to a table by the back window. Besides microbrews you'd never expect to see in the boonies, the dining room offers snacks,

short-order food, and family-style meals. You can even rent a room ($75–150). The Ritz it ain't, but the 130-year-old hotel looks a damn sight better than you will at that age, and it's a fun place to stay.

Besides the hotel, the town has some rental cabins in various price ranges and various states of entropy. And just downhill from town, the Bureau of Land Management (BLM) oversees a free, primitive 12-site campground along Jordan Creek.

GRAND VIEW TO BRUNEAU
Owyhee Uplands National Backcountry Byway

If you're in need of solitude, the Owyhee Uplands National Backcountry Byway might be just the ticket. From east of Grand View, the gravel road loops out behind the Owyhee Mountains, leading back to Jordan Valley, Oregon, or Silver City. Along the way it passes through varied and spectacular high-desert terrain virtually devoid of people. The gravel road is easily passable in the Oldsmobile from as soon as it dries out in spring through the first snowstorm of late fall. Most of the land surrounding the road is public, managed by the BLM, so unless posted otherwise, you can set up your tent anywhere you want. Several creeks along the way provide an ample water supply, but much of this land is used for grazing cattle; make sure to boil or filter the water, or better yet, bring your own.

Heading south out of Grand View, you'll pass through arid ranchlands and then quickly leave civilization behind. Soon you'll reach the Owyhee foothills and begin ascending Poison Creek, where you'll find a small BLM picnic area. The road keeps climbing and it won't be long before you'll have a sweeping, eagle's-eye view of the Snake River Plain. Onward and upward, the higher elevation brings new flora—first hills of mountain mahogany, then high tablelands covered in dense juniper forest. Wildflowers brighten the interspersed grassy slopes until well into July. Keep your eyes peeled for wildlife. Mule deer, pronghorn, big-horn sheep, badgers, and coyotes inhabit this broad-brushed landscape, and looking skyward you might see golden eagles, red-tailed and ferruginous hawks, northern harriers, and short-eared owls.

The road continues relatively level for miles through beautiful rolling terrain before suddenly dropping down into the canyon formed by the North Fork of the Owyhee River. A small BLM campground along the river here is a great spot to stop for the day and get wet while you explore the area. Upstream, the river rounds a bend to a hidden valley where large gravel bars along the banks make secluded sunning spots. Downstream, the river enters a dramatic gorge with red rock walls rising vertically hundreds of feet above the water.

Continuing past the campground, you'll pass through more cattle country. It's open range out here—there are no fences to keep bovines off the road. Drive carefully to avoid inadvertent steak tartare. Plus, if you hit a rangeland animal in Idaho, you're legally obligated to pay for it. You'll pass the little ranch called Cliffs and then descend through irrigated farmland and ranchland into Oregon and the turnoff to DeLamar and Silver City (it's marked with a huge sign for the Kinross DeLamar mine). Continuing straight on will take you into Jordan Valley, Oregon, where you can hook up with U.S. 95 and head north back into Idaho. If you head to Silver City from here, you'll have good road up to the DeLamar junction, then rougher road for the last eight miles into Silver City. From Silver City, you can descend the north side of the Owyhee Mountains into Murphy. Don't head up this way if the roads are wet. You might make it up to the top, but coming down the other side is steeper, slipperier, and more treacherous.

The length of the byway from Grand View to Jordan Valley is 103 miles, and you can figure on traveling about 35 mph or less en route. The road is well marked with directional signs and the special Backcountry Byway route markers, but obviously there are no services along the way, so make sure to top off the fuel tank

before you set out. For more information about the route, contact the BLM's Boise Field Office (3948 Development Ave., 208/384-3300).

C. J. Strike Reservoir and Wildlife Management Area

Clifford J. Strike was the president of the Idaho Power Company from 1938 to 1948. The dam named after him, built in 1952, backs up 7,500-acre C. J. Strike Reservoir, a popular fishing hole with bass, bluegill, crappie, perch, catfish, and even the mighty sturgeon. The reservoir and the land surrounding it make up the 12,500-acre C. J. Strike Wildlife Management Area (WMA), protected habitat for migratory ducks and geese in winter. The WMA headquarters is near Jack's Creek, 12 miles east of Grand View on Highway 78. Several free BLM camping areas are spread along the southern shore of the reservoir. From east to west: **Jack's Creek** Sportsman's Access Area; **Cottonwood** Sportsman's Access Area; and **Cove** campground, with 26 sites, fishing, swimming, and hiking trails.

Bruneau

Residents of the little town of Bruneau are up in arms over a snail. It seems strange, but it turns out a certain tiny snail unique to these parts is an endangered species, and federal regulations to preserve it are seen by the locals as putting a serious crimp in their lifestyle.

If you pass through town and continue out on Hot Springs Road, it eventually turns into Clover–Three Creek Road and leads to a spur road to the **Bruneau Canyon Overlook,** where the Bruneau River has sliced a deep gash in the earth. You can see the river glimmering down at the canyon bottom, but you can't get down to it. The river is run by rafters and kayakers who put in southwest of here, across the river near Grasmere.

◖ Bruneau Dunes State Park

One of the state's larger parks, Bruneau Dunes State Park (27608 Sand Dunes Rd., Mountain Home, 208/366-7919) encompasses some 4,800 acres of southwestern Idaho desert. Two enormous interconnecting sand dunes—the tallest nearly 500 feet high—rise from the center of the park. Unlike most sand dunes, these don't shift much, thanks to prevailing winds that blow in opposite directions for roughly equal amounts of time. The pristine dunes are closed to motor vehicles, but you can hike right up to the top, where you'll find an interesting crater that the two dunes seem to spiral out of, along with great views across the Snake River Plain. Kids, and the more childlike adults among us, won't be able to resist rolling back down the giant sand hills. Various hiking trails lead around the base of the dunes, past a couple of lakes that attract both wildlife and anglers. Another feature of the park is an observatory with a 25-inch telescope and several smaller scopes. Public stargazing programs (9:30 P.M. Fri.–Sat. Mar.–Oct., $3, free under age 6). are offered.

The park has a grassy, 48-site campground charging the standard state park fees ($22 per night with hookups, $16 without), as well as rental cabins ($50) that can sleep up to five. Inside the small visitors center you'll find fossils, mounted specimens of species native to the area, a gift shop, and lots of information about how the dunes came to be.

The Lowman Loop

Up in the northeast corner of the Treasure Valley, the desert finally surrenders to the pine-forested Boise Mountains. Amazing panoramas can be found just a short drive from Boise as you travel north on Highway 21. This curvy drive, known to locals as the Lowman Loop, connects three nationally designated scenic routes: Ponderosa Pine Scenic Byway, Wildlife Canyon Scenic Byway, and Payette River Scenic Byway.

Idaho City is 38 miles northeast of Boise. You can lick an ice cream cone while taking a historic walking tour of the town's brick-clad buildings, many of which still have their original boardwalks. And Idaho City has the funkiest pioneer cemetery north of Tombstone, Arizona.

The South Fork of the Payette River near Lowman is a spectacular place to embark on a guided white-water rafting trip through a squeeze of impressive granite canyons. The area is also a hotbed of geothermal activity: Relax and take a soak in one of the many hot springs along this steamy stretch.

Leave the main highway at Lowman and head west through the deep recesses of South Fork Canyon on your way to beautiful Garden Valley. Continue west until you reach Banks and the North Fork of the Payette River, where you finish the loop by heading south to the small town of Horseshoe Bend, home to the Thunder Mountain Line.

HIGHWAY 21 TO IDAHO CITY
Arrowrock Reservoir and Middle Fork Boise River
Coming up Highway 21 from Boise, at the upper end of Lucky Peak Reservoir, a turnoff to the right (Forest Rd. 268) leads along the northern arm of Lucky Peak Reservoir to Arrowrock Dam. Beyond the dam, the road follows the north shore of Arrowrock Reservoir to its inlet and continues up the Middle Fork of the Boise River all the way to the old mining town of Atlanta, at the foot of the Sawtooths. It's a long way to Atlanta along bumpy washboard roads.

Numerous free Boise National Forest campgrounds are strung along the route. Heading upstream, these include **Cottonwood** (3 sites), **Willow Creek** (10 sites), **Badger Creek** (5 sites), **Troutdale** (4 sites), and **Ninemeyer** (8 sites). For more information on the campgrounds, contact the **Mountain Home Ranger District**

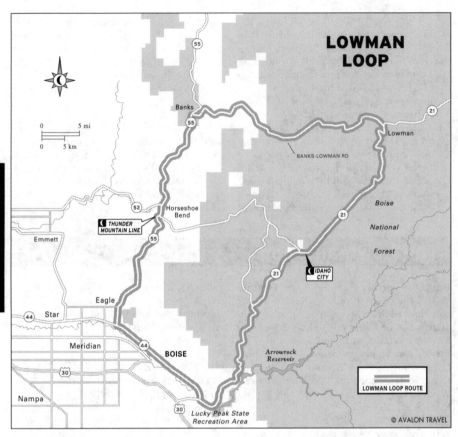

(2180 American Legion Blvd., Mountain Home, 208/587-7961).

◖ IDAHO CITY

After gold was discovered here in 1862, prospectors came flooding in seeking a share of the wealth, and many found it. More gold was mined from the mountains of this area than from all of Alaska. Along with the miners came gamblers, ladies of the evening, lawmen, and ne'er-do-wells. Looking at Idaho City today, it's hard to imagine that for a while this was the biggest city in the Northwest. By 1864 some 20,000 people inhabited the Boise Basin Mining District, with Idaho City the booming hub. Today the town's population is around 500, and the surrounding area—once full of mining camps—now has many more ghosts than people.

Historical Sights

Wandering through town on the many wooden sidewalks will take you past one historic "first" after another. Among them: the 1863 building where the *Idaho World*—Idaho's oldest newspaper—was first published; the 1864 **Idaho Territorial Penitentiary,** a hand-hewn log hoosegow that once held the killer of Idaho City's first marshal; the 1865 **Boise Basin Mercantile,** Idaho's first general store; and the

© DANA HOPPER-KELLY

Idaho City has a rough-and-tumble past.

1867 **St. Joseph's Catholic Church,** successor to an 1863 church that was the state's first Catholic church for nonnative settlers. Out past the west end of town is the **Pioneer Cemetery.** Of the first 200 men and women buried here, it's said that only 28 died of natural causes. To find out more about the town's Wild West history, visit the **Boise Basin Historical Museum** (Wall St. and Montgomery St., 208/392-4550, 11 A.M.–4 P.M. daily Memorial Day–Labor Day, $2 adults, $1.50 seniors and students, $5 families), featuring old photos, mining tools, and other artifacts and memorabilia.

Boise Basin Loop

Several old mining camps lie northwest of town in the Boise Basin, once the richest goldfield in Idaho history. You can make a loop trip past several of them in your Buick or, if you're ambitious, on your mountain bike. From Idaho City, take Forest Road 307 up Slaughterhouse Gulch and over the divide down to Grimes Creek. The creek is named for George Grimes, who discovered gold here in 1862 and was killed the same year by someone who wanted it. Turn right on Forest Road 382 and continue a couple of miles to **Centerville,** also founded in 1862 and named for its location halfway between Idaho City and Placerville. A bit farther down the road is **Pioneerville,** another important early mining camp. When you reach Route 17, turn left, head west to Garden Valley, and turn south again on Alder Creek Road (Forest Rd. 615). Follow this road to **Placerville,** founded by miners from California in December 1862; less than a year later the place boasted a population of 3,200. West of Placerville are **Granite,** site of the basin's first stamp mill, and **Quartzburg,** founded in 1864 around a hard-rock mine. Continuing south from Placerville on Forest Road 307 will take you to New Centerville Junction and on back to Idaho City.

Between August 1862 and December 1863 alone, the basin yielded more than $6 million in gold dust. By the time the miners were through, they'd reaped a glittering treasure estimated at $250 million (which would equate to around $4 billion today).

PANNING FOR GOLD IN THE BOISE BASIN

As a general rule, you can pan for gold anywhere on U.S. Forest Service land, unless it's on someone's mining claim, which are usually marked with small signs. The Idaho City area only has one location – along **Grimes Creek** – that is designated for the general public to pan for gold. To get here from Idaho City, head south on Highway 21 until you come to mile marker 29, where there is a small picnic area. Take a right at Grimes Creek Road and head northwest for about five miles until you reach the site, where Grimes Creek and Clear Creek come together.

You can buy supplies like pans, magnets, and sluice boxes in Boise at **Rosehill Coins &**

Jewelry (3506 Rose Hill St., 208/343-3220). Many folks use metal detectors in hopes of finding nuggets, but like panning, you can't search for gold with these electronic devices on an active claim. And it's also important to note that it's illegal to keep any old coins and other artifacts found on public land; these artifacts belong in a museum.

For more information about panning for gold and where to get mining claim maps, contact the **Gold Prospectors Association of America** (P.O. Box 891509, Temecula, CA, 92589, 909/699-4749, www.goldprospectors.org). For local advice, stop by the **Idaho City Visitor Center** (Main St. and Hwy. 21, 208/392-6040).

Recreation

Cross-country skiers and snowshoers will like the three Park N' Ski areas that lie along Highway 21 between Idaho City and Lowman. Thanks to their proximity to Boise—close enough for a day trip—the areas are the most heavily used and the best groomed in the state Park N' Ski system. Most of the trails are of intermediate difficulty. Both traditional and skating tracks are set, usually once a week on Thursday. That puts them in good shape for the weekend. By Wednesday they're usually pretty well thrashed. Park N' Ski permits ($20 for the season, $7.50 for three days) are required and are sold in Idaho City at Tom's Service (208/392-4426) and Idaho City Grocery (208/392-4900).

Eighteen miles north of Idaho City, **Whoop-Um-Up Creek Park N' Ski** offers four miles of marked but ungroomed trails. Two loops are set on the west side of the highway, three on the east side. This is the place to bring Fido, as dogs are not permitted on groomed trails. Another three miles up the highway, **Gold Fork Park N' Ski Area** provides eight miles of marked and groomed trails in loops on both sides of the highway. Finally, 3.5 miles farther north is **Banner Ridge Park N' Ski Area,** where you'll find 16 miles of marked and groomed trails.

The Banner Ridge and Gold Fork systems are connected by a groomed trail, and both trailheads provide access to **Beaver Creek Cabin** ($45), a two-bedroom Forest Service cabin you can rent by the night. Make reservations through the Idaho City Ranger District (208/392-6681). Telemarkers can also ask at the ranger station for directions to great slopes off the Gold Fork and Banner Ridge systems.

The Idaho Department of Parks and Recreation (208/334-4199, www.idahoparks.org) oversees three backcountry yurts ($60–72) in the area. (Just so you know, bears are fairly active in this area. I woke up one morning to find muddy paw prints all over my truck.)

For more information about the Park N' Ski trails, contact the Idaho City Ranger District (3833 Hwy. 21, Idaho City, 208/392-6681), west of Idaho City on Highway 21. There you can also pick up the brochure *Park N' Ski— Idaho City Area,* which describes all the trails in the three systems.

For hiking and mountain biking, check out the **Crooked River Trail** just off Highway 21. This relatively easy hike (2.6 miles round-trip) skirts along the gurgling Crooked River. Just past the trailhead, you'll see the remnants of an old miner's cabin right before the trail starts its traverse through the steep-walled canyon. At 1.3 miles, you can continue on for another nine or so miles across a newly built bridge, or turn around and head back out. This is a popular elk and deer hunting spot during the fall, so wear bright orange clothing.

To get to the trailhead, take Highway 21 north of Idaho City to Forest Service Road 384 (Crooked River Rd.), and then take a right and head past the Edna Creek Campground until you see the pullout on the right.

Events

Idaho City hosts cowboy poetry readings at various spots around town during the first week of May. For a raucous good time, check out **Frontier Days** in June. This annual blowout features a free rodeo and lots of food and wine booths. You might even see a staged gunfight. For more information about area events, contact the **Idaho City Chamber of Commerce** (208/392-4148).

Accommodations

The creaky old **Idaho City Hotel** (215 Montgomery St.) was built at the turn of the 20th century. Despite extensive renovations, the hotel's mining camp character has been preserved. The hotel is currently closed for yet another renovation, but it should be reopening soon under new ownership; ask the friendly folks at the visitors center about the current status of the historic hotel. Across town, the **Prospector Motel** (517 Main St., 208/392-9501, from $58 d) is a rustic place—just like everywhere else around here—that offers six guest rooms with old claw-foot bathtubs. Don't expect any frills, though.

Trudy's Cabins (3876 Hwy. 21, 208/392-4151, $79–99) are near town on the highway next to Trudy's Kitchen. Here you will find two standard rental cabins and a few RV sites ($21 with hookups).

Camping

Between Idaho City and Lowman you'll find several Boise National Forest campgrounds. **Grayback Gulch** (18 sites, $15–30) is about three miles south of Idaho City on Highway 21. About halfway between Idaho City and Lowman along the highway is a cluster of three fee campgrounds all within a couple of miles of one another: **Ten Mile** (16 sites, $15), **Bad Bear** (6 sites, $15), and **Hayfork** (6 sites, $15). Farther north, just past the Whoop-Um-Up Creek Park N' Ski Area, is **Edna Creek** (9 sites, $15). For more information, contact the **Idaho City Ranger District** (3833 Hwy. 21, Idaho City, 208/392-6681).

Food

Everyone in these parts dines at **(Trudy's Kitchen** (3876 Hwy. 21, 208/392-4151, 8 A.M.–8 P.M. daily, under $10), which makes its own desserts, including scrumptious huckleberry pie. Expect other homespun offerings such as biscuits and gravy, hot roast beef on white bread, and a big chicken-fried steak.

Head to the **Sarsaparilla Ice Cream Parlor** (205 Main St., 208/392-4484, 11 A.M.–6 P.M. Mon.–Fri., 11 A.M.–9 P.M. Sat.–Sun.) to get your licks on. This popular ice cream shop pumps out lots of cones, shakes, and sundaes.

There are several other eateries along the main drag that offer steaks and cold beer, the preferred local diet.

Information

The year-round **Idaho City Visitor Center** (Main St. and Hwy. 21, 208/392-6040) offers reams of information about the town and the area as well as a helpful staff member who can answer your questions. You can pick up a historic walking-tour map and inquire about a guided tour of the town.

LOWMAN

Lowman is about 35 miles northeast of Idaho City on Highway 21. While the mountainous area surrounding this tiny town abounds with recreational fun, it doesn't offer much in the way of services. There are several businesses along the South Fork of the Payette River that appear to be open but really aren't.

If you plan to continue driving on the Lowman Loop, this is where you leave

Highway 21 and turn left (west) onto Banks-Lowman Road, also known as the Wildlife Canyon Scenic Byway. If you stay on Highway 21, which is closed at times during the winter through this area, you will pass Grandjean en route to Stanley on the Ponderosa Pine Scenic Byway.

Do yourself a favor and hang out in Lowman for a day or so. The area has a plethora of hot springs, hiking trails, and white-water rafting possibilities. For information about recreation in the Boise National Forest, stop by the **Lowman Ranger District** (7359 Hwy. 21, 208/259-3361).

White-Water Rafting

Payette River Company (7655 Hwy. 21, 208/259-3702, www.payetterivercomapny.com) is a small outfit located along a stretch of the highway severely burned in 1989 when a lightning strike started a fast-moving fire that blackened 47,000 acres of pristine mountainscape. The rafting company's building is not easy on the eyes, but owners Sean and Ginger Glaccum have more than 20 years of combined experience as river-rafting guides. So who cares if the rafts are stored next to a rundown mobile home? You will be spending your time on the river anyway. Payette River Company offers half-day and full-day white-water rafting excursions ($60–103 pp); all-inclusive multiple-day trips range $300–775.

Accommodations and Food

Southfork Lodge was the nicest place to bed down in the Lowman area, but unfortunately it's currently closed and up for sale. This beautiful log lodge, with a restaurant, bar, and an assortment of log cabins, could be yours for a cool $3 million.

But all is not lost. **Sourdough Lodge** (8406 Hwy. 21, 208/259-3326, www.sourdoughlodge.com), 12 miles east of Lowman at mile marker 84, offers relatively clean lodging and friendly faces. This rustic resort has a full-service restaurant, a grocery store, a gas station, nine guest rooms ($64–245), three small cabins ($99–129), and four RV sites ($20 with

wildflowers near Lowman

© DANA HOPPER-KELLY

hookups). Beware the hot tub, though—during my visit it looked like a grizzly had crawled in, or perhaps a big hairy lumberjack.

Camping

Camping and hot springs go hand in hand in the Lowman area, considering that most of these steamy natural pools are next to established campgrounds. U.S. Forest Service campgrounds in the Lowman area include **Whitewater** (5 sites, $15) and **Pine Flats** (24 sites, $15), with hot springs, both a short distance west down the Banks-Lowman Road; **Park Creek** (26 sites, $8), three miles north of Lowman up Clear Creek Road (Forest Rd. 582); **Mountain View** (14 sites, $15), right in Lowman; and three campgrounds east of Lowman on Highway 21 heading toward Stanley: **Kirkham** (15 sites, $15), **Helende** (10 sites, $12), and **Bonneville** (22 sites, $15). Kirkham is right at the roadside Kirkham Hot Springs, while Bonneville is within walking distance of the more secluded Bonneville Hot Springs.

Forest Service Rentals

In winter, Boise National Forest offers several ski-in guard stations for rent in the area, such as the **Warm Springs Guard Station** (sleeps six, Nov. 15–Apr. 15, $40) near Bonneville Hot Springs, a mile north of Highway 21 at mile marker 91. For reservations and additional information about other rentals, contact the Boise National Forest offices in Boise (208/373-4100).

GARDEN VALLEY

Heading west on Banks-Lowman Road, back onto the Lowman Loop, you quickly traverse the steep grade of **South Fork Canyon,** a deep chasm with weeping walls and visible mine shafts next to the road. After climbing up and over Grimes Pass, the twisting road continues to hug the river until the landscape opens up into a gorgeous valley.

Garden Valley was named for its prolific vegetable gardens in the late 19th century. Because of the valley's surprisingly mild temperatures, endless geothermal water, and fertile soil, many Chinese growers set up shop and supplied fresh produce to the Boise Basin mining camps. Today, there are only a few newer hothouses that grow specialty blooms for Boise-area florists.

After passing through a nondescript business district, you come to Middle Fork Road. Hang a right, and you enter the tiny hamlet of Crouch. The downtown area boasts a frontier motif. Many of the wood structures have intentionally similar red-tin roofs and a rustic appearance. This is a great spot to grab a burger and a beer, and perhaps a history lesson reluctantly told by a surly local.

Recreation

White-water fanatics looking for a thrill ride will definitely find it on the South Fork Canyon stretch of the river, which drops 475 feet in 13 miles. Along the way you'll have the chance to soak in a riverbank hot spring, portage around a 40-foot waterfall, and paddle for all you're worth through a slew of Class IV crunchers. Scenery is outstanding as you

find yourself closed in by the canyon's steep granite walls.

Other boatable stretches on the South Fork in this area include a relatively easy float between Danskin Station and Garden Valley.

Idaho Whitewater Unlimited (208/462-1900, www.idahowhitewaterunltd.com) operates on this portion of the river as well as on the North and Main Forks of the Payette River. The rafting company has several half-day and full-day packages ranging $25–105.

Golfers will rejoice in the natural beauty of the golf links at **Terrace Lakes Resort** (101 Holiday Dr., Garden Valley, 208/462-3250, www.terracalakes.com, $13–38), four miles north of town. The 18-hole golf course is situated amid the pine trees and mountainous terrain, so don't be surprised to see elk grazing on the fairway as you're teeing off.

Getting to **Silver Creek Plunge** (2345 Silver Creek Rd., Garden Valley, 208/739-3400, www.silvercreekplunge.com, 9 A.M.–10 P.M. Thurs.–Tues., noon–10 P.M. Wed., $10 adults, $8 seniors, $8 under age 14) may be a long drive on washboard roads, but it's well worth the effort. Situated in Peace Valley, about 23 miles north of Crouch, this commercial hot springs resort is a great place to soak your sore muscles after fighting a current all day. Expect to find a 100°F outdoor swimming pool, cabins ($69–119), and several campsites ($12.50) along the meandering Silver Creek.

Accommodations

In downtown Crouch, within stumbling distance of the bars, you'll find the **Wander Inn Motel & Cabins** (486 S. Middle Fork Rd., Crouch, 208/462-2305, $55–65). This rustic yet well-kept place has two motel rooms and three cutesy rental cabins.

For a true ranch house experience, try **Walk on the Wild Side Bed & Breakfast** (69 River Ranch Rd., Garden Valley, 208/462-2732, www.wildsidebb.com, $95–145), an attractive inn on the banks of the Middle Fork that serves a big homespun breakfast.

If you're interested in renting a cabin or vacation home in the Garden Valley area, contact

Idaho Cabin Keepers (522 S. Middle Fork Rd., Garden Valley, 208/462-3451 or 877/322-2467, www.idahocabinkeepers.com) for listings and pricing information.

Camping

Past Crouch up Middle Fork Road (Forest Rd. 698), you'll enter the heart of Boise National Forest and find a number of hot springs and Forest Service campgrounds. Between Crouch and the Trail Creek Junction are **Tie Creek Campground** (8 sites, $10), **Hardscrabble Campground** (6 sites, $8), **Rattlesnake Campground** (10 sites, $10), and at the junction of Forest Roads 698 and 671, **Trail Creek Campground** (11 sites, $8). About 1.5 miles upriver from Hardscrabble Campground, across the river from the road, you may see the steam rising out of **Rocky Canyon Hot Spring.** If you decide to soak, be careful fording the Middle Fork.

A left on Forest Road 698 at Trail Creek Junction reveals, in less than 0.5 miles, a spur leading off to the left; take it down to the river and **Fire Crew Hot Springs,** a good place for a soak after the peak spring runoff has passed. Seven miles or so farther north on Forest Road 698 you'll find **Boiling Springs Campground** (9 sites, $8) near some riverside hot springs that bear the same name.

Food

Cowboy up at the **Longhorn Bar & Grille** (1049 Old Crouch Rd., Garden Valley, 208/462-3108, breakfast, lunch, and dinner daily). This venerable restaurant and bar in downtown Crouch has been here for more than 60 years and is under new ownership; it's now smoke-free. You can still smell the faint cigarette smoke from years gone by, but the haze is gone. Choose from a large selection of standard fare and strange creations like pizza topped with sauerkraut and elk sausage. And the bar has 16 brews on tap; need I say more?

Information

Load up on brochures and area maps at the

Garden Valley Ranger Station (1219 Banks-Lowman Rd., Garden Valley, 208/462-3241).

BANKS AND VICINITY

Not long after leaving Garden Valley, traveling west along the South Fork on Banks-Lowman Road, you will come to the junction of Highway 55 at Banks. This stretch of the road, known as the Payette River Scenic Byway, hugs the river like a wet sock—and you probably will have wet socks if you spend any time in the river. Banks doesn't have many facilities except for the small **Banks Store & Café** (7864 Hwy. 55, Banks, 208/793-2617), which doubles as a rafting company.

White-Water Rafting

Between Banks and Horseshoe Bend, the main Payette offers up the tamest water on the river, which isn't to say it's placid; three Class III rapids and several easier ones make for a thrilling ride, especially for white-water neophytes who might be a little nervous about offering themselves up to the river goddess. The river's highest flow rates are found here, peaking at around 8,000 cubic feet per second in June. That can make for some big waves. But the river is widest here as well, which tempers its ferocity. Between the rapids you'll find plenty of time for relaxation on sandy beaches or in good swimming holes.

The South Fork

At Banks, the two major forks of the Payette River meet. The South Fork, coming in from the east, is the most prized stretch of the river for most boaters. The **Lower South Fork,** between the Deer Creek put-in and Banks, offers a five-mile thrill ride through three Class III rapids, the Class III+ Bronco Billy rapid, and the awesome waves of the Class IV Staircase. In high water, Staircase will put you into adrenaline overload. Think of your blender on frappé. You need plenty of speed and concentrated paddling to make it through the string of waves nearly a boat-length high. And when it's all over and you're safely back in Banks, you'll thank your lucky stars you came through in one piece—then beg to do it again. The great thing about the Payette is that you *can* do it again: Access is easy because the Banks-Lowman Road parallels the river, and the stretch is short, so you can run it three times a day if you have the stamina.

The North Fork

Continuing north up Highway 55 past Banks, the North Fork of the Payette puts on quite a show. Incredible amounts of water funnel through the tight, rock-filled canyon in a raging flow no wider than a Winnebago. From just south of Smith's Ferry to Banks, the North Fork is, for all intents and purposes, just one long Class V rapid. Needless to say, it's not run commercially. Just looking at the river from the highway fills you with wonder that this river has ever been run at all. It has.

Above Smiths Ferry, the river returns to a descent once again suited to mere mortals. The **Cabarton run** from Cabarton Bridge to Smith's Ferry is a popular day trip through a canyon with some healthy but not too intimidating rapids. A bonus on this stretch is the abundant wildlife along the river, including bald eagles, ospreys, and deer.

River Guides

Many companies offer guided trips on the Payette River, among them **Bear Valley River Co.** (7864 Hwy. 55, Banks, 208/793-2272 or 800/235-2327), next to the Banks Store & Café, which guides all the Payette's major runs as well as the Grandjean stretch on the upper South Fork. **Cascade Raft & Kayak** (7050 Hwy. 55, Horseshoe Bend, 208/793-2221 or 800/292-7238) offers trips on all the major runs, and it has a kayak school.

Smiths Ferry

Smiths Ferry is about 25 miles north of Banks on Highway 55, up a rugged draw next to the rapid-laden river. Once you crest the top of the canyon, the road flattens out through a tranquil high-mountain valley. **Cougar Mountain Lodge** (9738 Hwy. 55, Cascade, 208/382-4464) is a cozy roadhouse restaurant—a nice place to duck in out of the weather—with five guest rooms ($48–60) available.

West of Smiths Ferry, small but scenic **Sagehen Reservoir** lies in a forested 4,800-foot-high basin; from Highway 55 at Smith's Ferry, take Forest Roads 644, 626, and 614. Forest Service campgrounds ring the lake, which offers good fishing for stocked trout. Small boats are permitted on the reservoir; Antelope and Sagehen Creek Campgrounds offer docks and ramps.

Counterclockwise around the lake from the southeast shore, campgrounds include **Hollywood** (6 sites, $15), **Eastside** (6 sites, $15), **Sagehen Creek** (15 sites, $15), and **Antelope** (20 sites, $15). All are open mid-May–mid-September. Reservations are taken for Antelope and Sagehen (877/444-6777); the others are first-come, first-served. Also here at the west side of the reservoir is the **Sagehen Dam Picnic Area,** which charges a $5 day-use fee.

Hikers will find a trail (Joe's Creek Rd., then Joe's Creek Trail 137) between Sagehen Creek and Antelope Campgrounds that leads north up Joe's Creek about five miles to great views at the top of West Peak (8,086 feet). In late spring, hikers should keep their eyes peeled for morel mushrooms, which grow profusely in the area.

HORSESHOE BEND

To complete the Lowman Loop, head south on Highway 55 along the main Payette River toward Boise. Eventually you arrive in Horseshoe Bend, a sleepy little community in a bowl-like valley. Here you will find a few restaurants and service stations as well as a popular scenic train ride.

(Thunder Mountain Line

Horseshoe Bend is the home depot for the Thunder Mountain Line excursion railroad (120 Mill Rd., 208/793-4425 or 877/432-7245, www.thundermountainline.com, $15–159, reservations advised). Three basic trips are offered: the *Horseshoe Bend Express,* a

© IDAHO DIVISION OF TOURISM

Thunder Mountain Line railroad

2.5-hour tour from Horseshoe Bend to Banks and back; the *Cabarton Flyer,* a 2.5-hour round trip from Cascade to Smiths Ferry; and the *Cascade Limited,* a five-hour trek from Horseshoe Bend to Cascade and back. Other offerings include murder-mystery trains, "river and rails" train-rafting combos, wine-tasting trips, and more.

Zip Idaho

Take a fast ride through the pine trees at Zip Idaho (101 Locust Ave., 208/793-2947, www.zipidaho.com, $75), a new zip-line company that offers several adrenaline-spiking tours. Scream your lungs out on the "Wild Turkey," a 1,700-foot zip-line that will have you reaching speeds up to 40 mph. You must weigh between 80 and 260 pounds to ride.

Food

Corner Café Bar & Grill (445 Hwy. 55, 208/793-3374, breakfast, lunch, and dinner daily, under $10) dishes up standard fare along the main drag. The restaurant has everything from fat breakfast burritos to saucy barbecue dishes.

If you're looking to load up on fresh produce, check out **Volcanic Farms** (457 Hwy. 55, 208/584-3383, May–Nov.). Here you can score a multitude of locally grown fruit and vegetables such as bing cherries, peaches, melons, onions, and red potatoes.

MAGIC VALLEY

Seen through a car window on I-84, the sprawling landscape of the Magic Valley in south-central Idaho may seem uninspiring, with miles and miles of agricultural flatlands spread out like a patchwork sheet across the Snake River Plain. But take any exit and you will find oases of geologic wonder tucked away throughout this great rift, caused by the monumental Bonneville Flood about 15,000 years ago.

Water, fed by an ancient aquifer, gushes in hundreds of streams falling from black-rimmed basalt cliffs. Bizarre rock outcroppings and boulders as big as minivans are strewn across the expanse. Shoshone Falls, called the "Niagara of the West," is a hydro spectacle when it roars full force each spring. The Magic Valley is aptly named, both for its natural features and irrigation marvels that helped to reshape the land.

Before this high-desert terrain was irrigated in the early 20th century with 2,600 miles of canals of water rerouted from the Snake River, a seemingly unending convoy of oxcarts and covered wagons passed through the arid region en route to greener pastures on the West Coast. It was here that these Oregon Trail emigrants faced some of their toughest challenges along the 2,000-plus mile trail: they had to get to the north side of the Snake River, but the region's deep gorges and turbulent waterfalls made the task perilous and nearly impossible; it wasn't a magic place for them at all. The wagons eventually found an easy spot to ford the river, at Three Island Crossing near present-day Glenns Ferry.

© IDAHO DIVISION OF TOURISM

HIGHLIGHTS

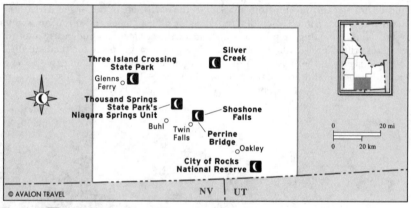

◖ Three Island Crossing State Park: The 614-acre state park commemorates one of the most important historic sites on the Oregon Trail. Big shade trees and the air-conditioned interpretive center now offer relief from the blazing desert sun (page 129).

◖ Thousand Springs State Park's Niagara Springs Unit: Here you will find an oasis in the desert, a magical place where high-rimmed canyon walls weep water at 250 cubic feet per second (page 139).

◖ Perrine Bridge: This 486-foot-high metal bridge spans the scenic Snake River Canyon in Twin Falls. It has become a top destination for BASE jumpers, who show up here in droves during the summer months (page 141).

◖ Shoshone Falls: Springtime is the right time to view these 212-foot-high falls, when a forceful torrent of water comes barreling over the giant rocks. It's a mere trickle the rest of the year (page 143).

◖ Silver Creek: These alkaline springs near Picabo entice fly-fishers from around the world. Elusive wild rainbow and brown trout scurry about in the crystalline waterways, surrounded by a high-desert wonderland that's teeming with other wildlife (page 154).

◖ City of Rocks National Reserve: This out-of-the-way preserve near Oakley is one of the country's top rock-climbing destinations. A city of monolithic granite rocks makes a veritable playground for the "on belay" crowd (page 159).

© AVALON TRAVEL

LOOK FOR ◖ TO FIND RECOMMENDED SIGHTS, ACTIVITIES, DINING, AND LODGING.

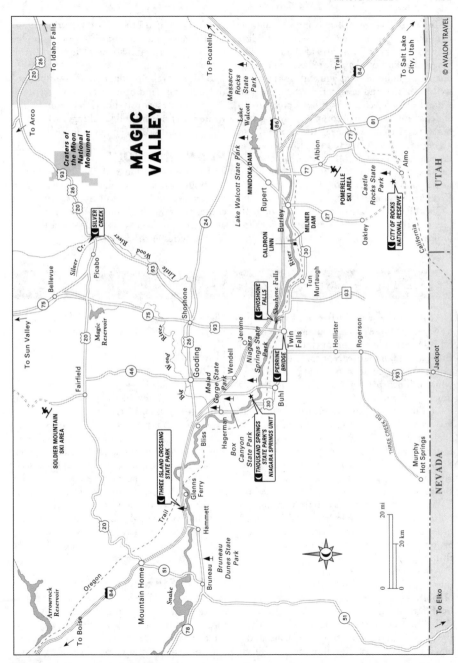

MAGIC VALLEY

© AVALON TRAVEL

Today, the Magic Valley is more hospitable to humans, thanks in part to a series of bridges that now connect both sides of the river. The Hagerman and Buhl areas are home to numerous fish hatcheries and aquaculture farms as well as dairies and creameries where you can score the best ice cream for miles around. As an added bonus, a string of commercially operated hot springs is situated near the Snake River, giving travelers a place to unwind after a long day behind the wheel. The area has also become a fruitful wine-producing region due to its position on the eastern fringe of the Snake River Valley Appellation.

Twin Falls, the largest city in the region, offers sojourners a wide variety of restaurants, lodging, and cultural activities. And thrill-seekers can leap off the 486-foot Perrine Bridge (with a parachute, of course), the only bridge in the United State where it's legal to BASE jump year-round.

Besides strapping on a chute, outdoor enthusiasts will find other exciting recreational opportunities throughout the region, like white-water rafting and kayaking, rock-climbing, downhill skiing, and premier fishing.

PLANNING YOUR TIME

You can explore most of the Magic Valley in about two or three days. Twin Falls and Hagerman, both close to I-84, are good base camps for your high-desert adventures. Go ahead—allow yourself a little extra time to tour wineries in the area.

The West Side

Getting to the western fringe of the Magic Valley from Boise takes about one hour by car on I-84 east. There's not much to see between Boise and Hammett except for miles of sagebrush, ancient cinder cones, and newly erected wind turbines that strikingly punctuate the flat desert landscape.

You'll pass by Mountain Home along the way. This lackluster military town, home to the Air Force's 366th Fighter Wing squadron, is a good place to stop and fuel up the SUV, but that's about it. Several gas stations and fast-food chains are at Exit 95, along with the junction for U.S. 20, leading to the Sun Valley–Ketchum area. It's also the jumping-off point for Bruneau Dunes State Park, about 15 miles south on Highway 51. The barren desert on the way to the big dunes will have you thinking *Area 51*.

After leaving Mountain Home, I-84 drops into a tight canyon with black-hemmed buttes on both sides of the highway. Soon you will be in Hammett, but you may not know it, because there's not much here besides a wide swath of the Snake River, a few family-run farms, and a newish winery. Keep traveling east on I-84 to Glenns Ferry (Exit 120), a cute little town that has a rich Oregon Trail and railroad heritage.

HAMMETT
Cold Springs Winery

This boutique winery (7853 W. Ringert Lane, 208/366-7993, www.coldspringswinery.com, tasting room noon–5 P.M. Sat. and Sun. or by appointment) is perched on a hill on the north side of I-84. At Exit 112 look to the left, and you'll see the winery's name plastered on a big potato-storage shed with an equally big arrow. Owner Bill Ringert, a former lawyer and Idaho state senator, operates the small winery on his 33-acre spread overlooking the Snake River. Winemaker Jamie Martin produces several varietal wines, like chardonnay, viognier, merlot, syrah, and "Hot Rod Red," a big blend of syrah, merlot, and cabernet franc.

GLENNS FERRY

In 1869, Gus Glenn built a ferry across the Snake River, putting an end to the dangerous ford that Oregon Trail emigrants had been forced to negotiate. By 1879, enough of a settlement had grown up around the ferry that a post office was established, but it wasn't until the arrival of the Oregon Short Line Railroad in 1883 that Glenns Ferry was formally platted into a town.

◖ Three Island Crossing State Park

At one of the most important historic sites on the Oregon Trail, settlers faced a decision that could have life-or-death consequences. Reaching this point from the south side of the river, they could either brave the ford—a dangerous undertaking in high water, but one that led to a shorter, easier route to Fort Boise—or continue down the longer, drier, more sparsely vegetated south bank. The three somewhat level islands in the river served as stepping-stones for those who attempted the crossing, and many wagons and their passengers were swept away by the swift current.

At the 614-acre state park (off W. Madison Ave., 208/366-2394), you'll find 82 campsites ($22 with or without hookups) and camping cabins ($50) with all the usual state park amenities; an Oregon Trail interpretive center featuring many historical exhibits about the trail and the indigenous Shoshone people

of this area; and an interpretive path leading down to the river past visible Oregon Trail wagon ruts. Of particular interest at the beginning of the trail is a beautiful replica of a Conestoga wagon.

Carmela Vineyards and Golf Course

Vines, wines, and a nine-hole golf course, all on a scenic stretch of the Snake River, makes Carmela Vineyards a great stop. The winery (1289 W. Madison Ave., 208/366-2313, www.carmelavineyards.com, tasting room 11 A.M.–8 P.M. daily) produces 16 varietal wines and blends, and there is a restaurant (lunch and dinner daily, brunch Sun., entrées $14–22).

Vineyard Greens Golf Course ($16) at the winery surrounds the vineyard with a par-34 course stretching 4,478 yards. Hard-core golfers can park the RV at **Vineyard RV Park** ($22 with hookups) across the street. The winery also has a few camping cabins ($90) near the links.

Glenns Ferry Historical Museum

In an early 20th century sandstone schoolhouse, the Glenns Ferry Historical Museum

MAGIC VALLEY

© DANA HOPPER-KELLY

wagon replica at Three Island Crossing State Park

Carmela Vineyards, offering both grapes and golf

© DANA HOPPER-KELLY

(200 W. Cleveland Ave., 208/366-2320, noon–5 P.M. Sat.–Sun. June–Sept., donation) has exhibits that provide insight into the town's early history as well as beautiful charcoal portraits by local artist Frank Clark.

Entertainment and Events

On the main drag near the railroad tracks, you'll see the historic **Gorby Opera House** (128 E. Idaho Ave., 208/366-7408, www.glennsferrytheatre.org), built in 1914. This classic theater house, designed by Tourtellotte and Hummel, the same architectural firm that designed the Egyptian Theatre in Boise, originally featured vaudeville acts and melodramas. Today, the theater still serves the community with a summer schedule of old-time musicals and plays (Fri.–Sat. night June–Aug., $7 adults, $6 seniors and under age 12, dinner show $22.50, reservations recommended). Whenever a train rumbles by (and this happens often), the performances stop momentarily, and everyone in the audience stands up and sings, "I've Been Working on the Railroad." It's definitely a fun experience.

It's too bad the **Three Island Pioneer Celebration** (www.glennsferry.org) doesn't have a river-crossing reenactment anymore, as it did for many years; but locals still celebrate the historic event in mid-August with a parade, wagon rides, live music, and food and crafts vendors.

Accommodations and Food

The **Redford Motel** (525 W. 1st Ave., 208/366-2421, $35–62) is a well-kept place on the way into town that has 11 guest rooms, some in the main building, and the rest across the street in an old-style motor inn.

River Roads Bed & Breakfast (1882 E. Little Basin Rd., 208/366-2974, $100) is east of town right on the river. It only has two guest rooms, but the view here is spectacular, and there's a hot tub. Wake up to a big homespun breakfast before heading out to explore the Oregon Trail. Pets are not allowed.

Besides the dining room at Carmela Vineyards, locals also eat downtown at the aptly named **Oregon Trail Café** (37 E. Idaho Ave., 208/366-2280, breakfast, lunch, dinner

© DANA HOPPER-KELLY

Gorby Opera House, on the main drag in Glenns Ferry

daily). This rustic diner boasts an exaggerated Western motif. Expect standard breakfast dishes ($4–10) such as biscuits and gravy, flapjacks, French toast, and "Three Eggs Garbage," a big egg-and-potato pileup. Hopefully you don't mind a little guff with your morning eggs and coffee, because the waitresses here can be surly at times. The dinner menu has buffalo steaks, gizzards and fries, and pan-fried oysters. The restaurant also has a cocktail lounge that stays open late.

Information

The **Glenns Ferry Visitors Center** (7 E. 1st St., 208/366-7345, www.glennsferry.org, 11 A.M.–4 P.M. Tues.–Fri.) and the chamber of commerce are one and the same. These friendly folks can give you the lowdown on what's going on around town.

Hagerman Valley

In Hagerman Valley, due east of Glenns Ferry, are huge rounded boulders that were carried along by the great Bonneville Flood and then dropped in place when the waters receded. The valley's chief topographic feature, however, is the series of springs gushing from the lava rock along the north rim. The springs are outflow from the Snake River Plain Aquifer, which begins some 100 miles northeast near Howe, where the waters of the Big and Little Lost Rivers, Birch Creek, and other smaller watercourses disappear into the lava of the Snake River Plain and begin a century-long journey to the Hagerman Valley. The water flows underground until the deep cut of the Snake River Gorge sets it free. Once this must have been a spectacular sight, when springs flowed unimpeded from mile after mile of canyon wall. Today, most of the springs have either been despoiled by hydropower facilities or diverted

MAGIC VALLEY

THE HAGERMAN HORSE WAS ACTUALLY A ZEBRA

Archaeological digs at the Hagerman Fossil Beds National Monument have yielded more than 125 full skeletons of a prehistoric, zebra-like horse from the Pliocene epoch that were found in one location. No hide samples made it through the last 3 million years, so we have no idea if the animals had stripes or not. Now called the Hagerman horse, *Equus simplicidens* is the earliest known member of the *Equus* genus and has been designated the Idaho state fossil. A local rancher first discovered the bones in 1928, and a major archaeological excavation led by paleontologists from the Smithsonian Institution began the following year. Two theories prevail as to why so many of these horses died in one place. One assumes the prehistoric watering hole turned into a mud bog, trapping the animals in sticky goo. The other holds that the horses drowned trying to cross the river during a flood. Either way, these ancient horses have been forever locked in local folklore.

to farmlands and fish hatcheries. Nevertheless, what's left still makes an unusual sight, well worth the detour off I-84.

At I-84 Exit 137 is the junction of U.S. 30, where you'll come to the blink-and-miss-it burg of Bliss, the first town along the 68-mile **Thousand Springs Scenic Byway.** After dropping down the hill into Hagerman, this curvy road begins to hug the river along U.S. 30, which used to be the main highway before I-84 was built. Now it's a sight-laden "back way" into Twin Falls. If you want to go directly to Twin Falls, continue east on I-84.

HAGERMAN

Shoshone people spearfished for salmon on the Snake River here for centuries, until the nonnatives showed up and drove off first the Shoshone, then the salmon. The Oregon Trail passed near the site—wagon ruts are still visible across the river from town—which later became a stagecoach stop. Present-day Hagerman began in 1892, when Stanley Hegeman applied for a post office. The Postal Department got Hegeman's name wrong and granted the post office under the present spelling.

In modern times, Hagerman offers anglers several good places to fish for trout and warm-water species like catfish, smallmouth bass, and yellow perch. The area also has two fish hatcheries—state and federal—and a few aquaculture farms that raise everything from rainbow trout to catfish and white sturgeon. Leo Ray, a local fish biologist who operates an aquaculture farm near Hagerman, also produces sturgeon caviar and alligators, sold for its tail meat. Hagerman Valley is also known for its sweet melons—honeydews, cantaloupes, and watermelons—that are grown here in the peak of summer.

Several famous people have made Hagerman their home over the years, including writer Vardis Fisher and Archie Teater, a renowned landscape artist who built a home here that was designed by master architect Frank Lloyd Wright.

Hagerman Fossil Beds National Monument

The 4,300 acres of this monument are not developed for visitor use, nor will they ever be. That's because the area is one of the world's foremost fossil beds, and indiscriminate trampling could destroy priceless archaeological remains. Unfortunately, a fast-moving brush fire in 2010 burned more than 75 percent of the national monument property, most of which was sagebrush and grass. Archeologists are still worried about erosion of the site.

In addition to the Hagerman horse, fossils of more than 140 other species have been unearthed, including waterfowl, otters, muskrats, and 3.5-million-year-old beavers.

Details on this fascinating historical site are found at the national monument visitor center (221 N. State St., 208/933-4100, 9 A.M.–6 P.M. daily Memorial Day–Aug. 31, 9 A.M.–5 P.M. Thurs.–Mon. Sept.–Memorial Day) in downtown Hagerman, across from the high school. When funding allows, rangers lead free tours of sites in the monument on weekends in summer; tours leave from the visitor center. Otherwise, a flyer describing a self-guided auto tour (22 miles, two hours) is available. The best view of the fossil area is from the Bell Rapids Sportsman's Access Area, on the Hagerman side of the river (follow the signs from U.S. 30). You won't see anything exciting, but your imagination can fill in the picture with thousands of prehistoric beasts.

You can also drive over to the other side of the river for a closer look. Continue south through Hagerman and turn right just after you cross the bridge over the Snake River. Alongside the fossil area you'll find a turnout with an interpretive sign, but you won't see giant dinosaur bones sticking out of the mud. Continue to the top of the hill, where a meandering trail skirts the ridge. You'll also see some well-preserved Oregon Trail wagon ruts nearby.

Snake River Pottery

Northwest of Hagerman on U.S. 30 lies the oldest pottery studio in Idaho. Established in 1947, Snake River Pottery (555 E. River Rd., 208/837-6527, 9 A.M.–5 P.M. daily year-round) sells handmade earthenware, stoneware, and terra-cotta pieces by a handful of regional potters, including founder Aldrich Bowler and resident potter Ned Swisher. Look for the rattlesnake logo on a sign. If you can't make it during business hours, you might swing by anyway—if someone's there, you're welcome to come in. From the studio's beautiful back deck

overlooking the river, you'll get a good view of the Archie Teater house.

Hagerman Valley Historical Society Museum

Like the national monument visitors center, the tiny Hagerman Valley Historical Society Museum (100 S. State St., 208/837-6288, 1–4 P.M. Wed.–Sun. year-round, free) in a historic brick building holds a full-size cast replica of a Hagerman horse skeleton. You'll also see a colorful mural and some historic photos of the Hagerman Valley.

Vardis Fisher Home Site

Hagerman writer Vardis Fisher was a permanent fixture in the valley until his death in 1968. With more than 30 published works of fiction and nonfiction, Fisher was hands-down the most prolific Idaho author of his generation. Sure, Ernest Hemingway and Ezra Pound had more name recognition, but they didn't spend most of their lives in the Gem State, as

Idaho writer Vardis Fisher's home site

© DANA HOPPER-KELLY

MAGIC VALLEY

Vardis Fisher's home site overlooks a pond known locally as Hidden Lake.

© DANA HOPPER-KELLY

Fisher did. He was born in 1895 near Rigby in southeast Idaho and raised in a Mormon household. Later in life Fisher became an avowed and outspoken atheist.

He's probably best known for his novel *Mountain Man,* the basis for the 1972 Robert Redford movie *Jeremiah Johnson.* But Fisher also wrote many other historical novels, including the epic series *Testament of Man* and *The Mothers: An American Saga of Courage,* depicting the tragic story of the Donner Party. He was also a columnist at the *Idaho Statesman* and the director of the Idaho Writer's Project for the Works Progress Administration, publishing *Idaho: A Guide in Word and Picture,* a 1937 history-laden travel book about the Gem State.

Fisher built his own home north of town on a secluded knoll overlooking a vodka-clear pond fed by cold springs. Sadly, the house fell into disrepair after his death, and it eventually burned down—only the lava-rock chimney stands today. The site is now managed by the Idaho Parks and Recreation Department as part of the Thousand Springs State Park system, although it's not yet fully developed. The pond, known to locals as Hidden Lake, is one of the best swimming holes in the Magic Valley.

To get here from downtown Hagerman, take a left (north) at Hagerman Avenue and head up Tupper Grade for about 1.5 miles, until the road drops into a bowl; a dirt parking lot is on the left. On foot, cross Billingsley Creek on the wood bridge, go past the University of Idaho's ramshackle-looking fisheries facility, and follow the path around to the pond, shaded by big Russian olive trees, cottonwoods, and some pine trees that Fisher planted himself. There is still an old cabin and other outbuildings on the property, offering a glimpse into the writer's private world.

Hagerman Wildlife Management Area and Fish Hatcheries

On the north side of the Snake River, two miles south of Hagerman, the Hagerman Wildlife Management Area (WMA) preserves 880 acres of riverine wetlands as wildlife habitat. Fed by the constant-temperature springwater, the area stays ice-free all year long. This makes it a winter haven for ducks and geese by the thousands, as well as ospreys, peregrine falcons, and bald and golden eagles. The river also supports a healthy population of river otters.

Within the WMA is **Hagerman State Fish Hatchery** (1060 State Fish Hatchery Rd., 208/837-4892), which raises millions of trout annually to be stocked in waters across Idaho. Six miles of walking trails loop from the hatchery past many lakes and ponds. You can get a close look at various species of fish, including rainbow trout, white sturgeon, and tiger muskie kept in cement raceways near the parking lot. There's even a gum-ball machine filled with fish pellets that you can feed the fish, but you may want to wash up afterward to get rid of the fishy smell on your fingers.

Fish-hatchery fans will find the **Hagerman National Fish Hatchery** (3059 National Fish Hatchery Rd., 208/837-4896) just down the road. This federal facility raises 1.5 million steelhead smolts each year. Visit in March–April for the best look.

Fishing

Anglers can try their luck at catching trout and bass at the Hagerman WMA, where there are several big ponds (July 1–Oct. 31) with easy access. Before you cast a line, check with the **Idaho Department of Fish and Game** (324 S. 417 E., Jerome, 208/324-4359) for restrictions and possible closures. If you like battling feisty bass, head to the **Bell Rapids Sportsman's Access Area** on the Snake River just south of Hagerman (follow the sign on U.S. 30). There are some restrictions at this year-round spot near the Lower Salmon Falls Dam: catch-and-release January 1–June 30, and a bag limit of two fish per day July 1–December 31, and they can't be 12–16 inches long. The river also holds some white sturgeon, but there's currently no harvest allowed on these massive prehistoric fish.

Near Vardis Fisher Park, you can fish for rainbow trout (some of which are the hybrid blue and gold variety) in Billingsley Creek and in the pond. You must use artificial flies or lures (no worms) and barbless hooks. There's a daily limit of two fish, and they must be at least 20 inches long.

Accommodations and Food

The 16-room **Hagerman Valley Inn** (661 Frogs Landing, 208/837-6196, www.hagermanvalleyinn.com, from $59 d) is a clean motel on the south side of downtown. All rooms are nonsmoking, and amenities include an upstairs deck, cable TV, and a covered patio area downstairs. Pets are allowed.

Billingsley Creek Lodge (17940 U.S. 30, 208/837-4822, www.billingsleycreeklodge.com) is on U.S. 30 about a mile north of town. It has been around since 1928 and boasts a distinguished literary history: Ernest Hemingway and Vardis Fisher both stayed here. Although it's right along the highway, the resort is well landscaped and has a tranquil little picnic area on the creek. Choose from six lodge rooms ($60–80) or five private cabins ($75–115).

Snake River Grill (611 Frogs Landing, 208/837-6227, breakfast 7–11:30 A.M. Tues.–Sat., lunch 11:30 A.M.–4:30 P.M. Tues.–Sat., dinner 6–10 P.M. Tues.–Fri., 5–9 P.M. Sat., dinner entrées $10–21), next to the Hagerman Valley Inn, is where to go in town for a fine-dining experience. Chef Kirt Martin, an all-around nice guy and graduate of Le Cordon Bleu in Paris, uses local foodstuffs on his menu, including grilled sturgeon, pan-seared rainbow trout, and Cajun-style fried alligator medallions. Expect to see plenty of Idaho labels on the wine list.

Also just off the main drag, you'll find the **Thunderbird Café** (120 E. Main St., 208/837-4949, 8 A.M.–8 P.M. Mon.–Sat.), a funky little place that boasts mission-style ambience. The decidedly Southwestern menu is supplemented with espresso and freshly baked pastries in the morning hours.

Camping and RVing

Hagerman RV Village (18049 U.S. 30, 208/837-4906) offers 60 RV sites with hookups

MAGIC VALLEY

© DANA HOPPER-KELLY

the weeping walls of Hagerman Valley

($22–25), five cabins ($25–50), and several tent sites ($15–20). Amenities include a laundry room, restrooms, showers, an exercise room, and a sauna.

Information
The **Hagerman Chamber of Commerce** (380 State St., 208/837-9131, 9 A.M.–noon and 1–4 P.M. Mon.–Fri.) can give you advice and information about the Hagerman Valley.

THOUSAND SPRINGS AREA
Along this stretch of the Snake River south of Hagerman, a torrent of waterfalls emerges from the black basalt cliffs on the river's north side. This extensive lineup of springs—there may be more than 1,000—gushes forth clean, crystal-clear water at a constant 58°F.

Thousand Springs State Park
This state park has five major units in the Hagerman and Buhl areas: **Malad Gorge, Billingsley Creek, Niagara Springs, Earl M. Hardy Box Canyon,** and **Ritter Island,** formerly the Nature Conservancy Thousand Springs Preserve. Be aware that the Thousand Springs State Park system (main office at Malad Gorge, 1074 E. 2350 S., Hagerman, 208/837-4505, day-use $5) can be confusing because it's always morphing into new units, and some of them are only open on a limited basis.

Near Hagerman, you'll find three units of the park, including the small but interesting Billingsley Creek unit (north of town), the Earl M. Hardy Box Canyon, and Ritter Island, a 400-acre spread that the Nature Conservancy recently turned over to the state. Ritter Island can be a challenge to find. From the west side of the river, you can look right across at the power plant and the unbridled springs on either side, but getting over to those springs is quite another matter. To get there from U.S. 30, first follow signs to the Hagerman National Fish Hatchery (on the north side of the Snake River bridge, three miles south of Hagerman), then work your way south along the rim. Once you get up on the river's rim, it's easy to get lost. Some roads lead out to the edge of the canyon only to dead-end. Now that it's an official park, the signage is a little better along the way.

The preserve occupies the former Minnie Miller ranch, purchased by businesswoman and dairy farmer Minnie Miller in 1918. For 36 years, Miller steadfastly protected her share of the Hagerman Valley springs from usurpation and development, and upon her death she deeded the property to an equally staunch environmentalist. The property was sold to the Nature Conservancy in 1986. Among the highlights of the preserve are Minnie Miller Falls, which pours forth from the canyon wall and cascades down nearly 200 feet into crystalline pools, and Ritter Island, site of Miller's 1920 home, now the park's office. A 0.25-mile trail on the island leads north to the falls, the only totally undisturbed springs along the entire 40-mile width of the aquifer. Due to budget cuts, this unit of the park is only open periodically; call 208/837-4505 for details.

The new Earl M. Hardy Box Canyon unit, which also used to be under the auspices of the Nature Conservancy, is east of town on the way to Wendell. This small horseshoe-shaped canyon boasts a 20-foot waterfall that drops into a beautiful cold springs pool, the 11th largest spring in North America. Lots of red-tailed hawks, falcons, owls, and eagles can be spotted perched on the cliffs, looking for little critters to munch on. The park is also home to an endangered snail species and the rare Shoshone sculpin, a spiny little fish with prehistoric ties. But this wide-open place doesn't offer much relief from the hot desert sun, so early mornings and late evenings are good times to a take a hike here. Watch out for poison ivy. To get to Box Canyon from Hagerman, take U.S. 30 south to Hagerman-Wendell Road, hang a left (east) and travel about four miles until you come to County Road 1500 East. Take a right on this road and go three miles to the signed parking lot on the right.

Thousand Springs Winery

The 10-acre Thousand Springs Vineyard and Winery (18854 U.S. 30, Hagerman, 208/837-4557, www.thousandspringswinery.com, tasting room by appointment only) just south of Hagerman turns out small lots of chardonnay (aged in Hungarian oak) and a cabernet franc–syrah blend.

Snake River Boat Tours

Several outfitters conduct guided boat trips down the Snake River through Hagerman Valley. You can cruise up the river on a motorboat or shoot down the rapids in a raft. Due to the influx of springwater into the river, this section of the Snake can be run nearly year-round.

1000 Springs Tours (208/837-9006, www.1000springs.com) offers two-hour cruises down the Snake River through Hagerman Valley aboard a 30-foot motorized pontoon boat. Along the way you'll see Blue Heart Springs, which gurgle their way up from the riverbed into a crystal-clear pool, and Riley Creek Falls. Tours (10 A.M. and 1 P.M. Tues.–Sun., $25 pp, reservations advised) are offered year-round, weather permitting, but prime season is April–October. Also available are elegant dinner tours ($58 pp) with a multicourse menu that includes prime rib; beer, wine, and cocktails are available. All tours leave from Sligar's 1000 Springs Resort (18734 U.S. 30, Hagerman), on the river six miles south of Hagerman.

For those who prefer a raft to a motorboat, the Hagerman Reach of the Snake River churns through challenging Class II–III rapids—exciting but not dangerous when you ride with a skilled skipper. Outfitters offering guided trips on the Hagerman Reach include **High Adventure River Tours** (1211 E. 2350 S., Hagerman, 208/837-9005 or 800/286-4123) and **Idaho Guide Service** (563 Trotter Dr., Twin Falls, 208/734-4998 or 888/734-3246). Plan on spending about $40–60 with lunch.

Commercial Hot Springs Resorts

The first of three resorts on the way south through Hagerman Valley is **Sligar's 1000 Springs Resort** (18734 U.S. 30, Hagerman, 208/837-4987 or 888/849-4181, pools

MAGIC VALLEY

11 A.M.–9:30 P.M. Tues.–Sat., noon–8 P.M. Sun. year-round, $6.50 adults, $5.50 ages 6–13, $3 under age 6). Sligar's offers a large, hot spring–fed indoor swimming pool, hot baths, and an RV park (year-round, $30 with full hookups, $20 without). Campers get a discount on the pools. Private hot baths are also available. Picnickers can drive in and use the grounds for a small fee.

The other two resorts are on opposite sides of the river but share the same turnoff from the highway. Turning left (east) will take you to a T intersection; turn right and follow Banbury Road for 1.5 miles over a small hill and down to **Banbury Hot Springs** (1128A Banbury Rd., Buhl, 208/543-4098, noon–9 P.M. Sat.–Sun. May 1–early June, noon–9 P.M. daily early June–Labor Day). The venerable resort offers a crystal-clear outdoor swimming pool ($8 adults, $7 ages 6–13, $4.50 under age 6) fed by continuously flowing hot and cold springs; five hot tubs ($8 pp per hour, jetted tubs $9 pp per hour) that are drained, cleaned, and disinfected before each use; and picnic grounds and campsites ($13 tents, $16–28 RVs), luxuriously shaded under a profusion of mature trees. A boat-launching ramp ($6) and dock are down on the river; restrooms, showers, and laundry facilities are available for campers. The popular area has a wholesome family atmosphere (no alcohol and no smoking are allowed on the premises). Tub rental here doesn't include admission to the swimming pool.

The relaxed, low-key **Miracle Hot Springs** (19073A U.S. 30, Buhl, 208/543-6002, 8 A.M.–11 P.M. Mon.–Sat. year-round, $9 adults, $7 over age 54, $4 ages 4–13, $1 under age 4 includes swim diaper), on the west side of the highway, is small but spunky—a personal favorite. Where else would you find alligators on the grounds? They are kept behind a fence, of course. In addition to the first-come, first-served soaking tubs ($2–10 pp), there are four reservable VIP tubs that are large, private, temperature adjustable, and open to the stars. The swimming pool has springwater continuously flowing through it. Massage is available by appointment. As with the other two

resorts, there's an RV park ($10–20); the sites are a little close to the highway but are nicely landscaped. Miracle also has several geodesic domes ($59–64) available that sleep two in big beds. Two "camping domes" ($39) can accommodate up to six people each; bring your own sleeping bags, but pads are provided.

BUHL AND VICINITY

Buhl was founded in 1906 and named after Frank Buhl, a bigwig in the Twin Falls Land and Water Company. It's an agricultural center where you'll find fertilizer stores, tractor lots, Farm Bureau Insurance, Farmers National Bank, and a big Green Giant vegetables plant right in the middle of town. But this is also one funky farm town, with a great arts center, many alternative-health practitioners, and lots of cool junk stores.

Eighth Street Center

A few blocks off Buhl's main drag, the Eighth Street Center (200 N. 8th St., Buhl, 208/543-5417, http://eighthstreetcenter.com) is home to the Buhl Arts Council and a cornucopia of arts classes, performances, and gallery space. "The arts" can mean everything from painting exhibitions to couples massage classes. A permanent labyrinth and butterfly garden is outside across the alley from the center. Check the website to see what else is happening.

Bordewick Sportsman's Access Area

Idaho is chock-full of Sportsman's Access Areas—you'll see numerous signs along every highway. This one is spectacularly notable for its location on a stunning stretch of the Snake River where several species of large waterbirds nest and congregate. Great blue herons, white pelicans, and Canada geese can often be seen soaring above the riffles and around the many verdant islands. You'll also find good fishing, toe-dabbling, and primitive camping at this beautiful site, or at several other possible campsites along this stretch of the Snake. A little farther down the road is the state's **Magic Valley Fish Hatchery** (208/326-3230), which raises millions of steelhead from roe to fingerling size for release back into the Salmon River drainage. To get to the access area and the hatchery, head out of Buhl on Clear Lakes Road and turn right just before you cross the river.

Trout Farm

The world's largest commercial trout farm is just north of Buhl on Clear Lakes Road (turn off U.S. 30 at the big Buhl water tower). **Clear Springs Foods** (1585 Clear Lakes Rd., 208/543-4316, www.clearsprings.com) produces millions of pounds of Idaho rainbow trout each year. Visitor facilities include a picnic area and a fish-viewing pond. The pond holds trout, of course, as well as a couple of big Snake River sturgeon. An underwater viewing window gives you a trout's-eye view of their riverine abode.

◖ Thousand Springs State Park's Niagara Springs Unit

On the river's north side, across the water from the reaches of the Bordewick Sportsman's Access Area, is the Thousand Springs State Park's Niagara Springs unit (2136 Niagara Springs Rd., 208/536-5522). A National Natural Landmark, the springs gush out of the canyon wall at 250 cubic feet per second. It's a roundabout route to get there from Buhl and much easier from Wendell, to the north. From Buhl, after crossing the river on Clear Lakes Road, the road ascends to the north rim. Turn right on the Bob Barton Highway and continue past four intersections (1600 E., 1700 E., 1800 E., and 1900 E.); the next intersection you'll come to should be Rex Leland Highway (1950 E.). If you travel south from Wendell, this is the road you follow straight down the whole way. From Bob Barton Highway, turn right and follow the road down to the river and the park. It's a steep drop of 350 vertical feet to the canyon floor; the gravel road is not recommended for trailers or motor homes.

Two different areas make up the park. The Emerson Pugmire Memorial Recreation Area (day-use $5) offers a picnic area and a campground ($12–16) that has bathrooms and running water but no hookups. If you camp, the $5 day-use fee is included in your camping fee. The area is well maintained and offers a large expanse of grass and a great location on a scenic stretch of the Snake River. Continuing a little farther down the road will take you to the Crystal Springs Area, where you'll find springs as well as a small pond for year-round fishing.

Niagara Springs Wildlife Management Area

Just west of Thousand Springs State Park's Niagara Springs unit, the Niagara Springs Wildlife Management Area (WMA) protects 957 acres of habitat for waterfowl and other wildlife. Wildlife viewing and fishing are the most popular activities; birdwatchers and others can follow trails both up on the canyon rim and down along the water, where sightings of songbirds and mule deer are common. In winter, waterfowl arrive in large numbers. Anglers can try for rainbow trout in the Thompson-Mays Canal or for trout, catfish, and sturgeon (catch-and-release) in the Snake River.

To reach the WMA from Buhl, cross the river on Clear Lakes Road, which ascends to the north rim. Turn right on the Bob Barton Highway and continue past four intersections to Rex Leland Highway (1950 E.). If you travel south from Wendell, this is the road you follow straight down the whole way. From Bob Barton Highway, turn right and follow the road to the bottom of the river gorge, then turn right into one of several parking areas. Hiking trails follow the river east past Boulder Rapids and a couple of ponds. For more information, contact the **Idaho Department of Fish and Game** (324 S. 417 E., Jerome, 208/324-4359).

Balanced Rock

This huge question mark–shaped rock, 17 miles southwest of Buhl and west of Castleford, is balanced on a small point and looks as though a strong wind would blow it over. Apparently the thought of that happening scared the county's lawyers, and the wondrous natural feature has been reinforced with concrete around its base.

Just down the hill from Balanced Rock is **Balanced Rock Park,** offering picnicking and swimming along Salmon Falls Creek. Rock climbers can find interesting climbing on the area's castle-like hoodoos—the formations that gave the town of Castleford its name. And across the road on the river's north side, hot springwater pours out of a pipe, creating a semi-natural hot tub.

Wineries

Buhl has two boutique wineries where you can taste varietal wines from the Snake River Valley Appellation. **Holesinsky Vineyard & Winery** (4477A Valley Steppe Dr., Buhl, 208/543-6940, www.holesinsky.com, tasting room by appointment only) is one of the only certified organic wineries in the state. Here, winemaker-owner James Holesinsky produces estate wines from organic grapes grown in his 18-acre vineyard. His lineup includes syrah, dry rosé, riesling, and merlot.

Snyder Winery (4060 N. 1200 E., Buhl, 208/543-6938, www.snyderwinery.com, tasting room 1–5 P.M. Thurs. and Sun., 1–9 P.M. Fri.–Sat.) boasts beautifully landscaped grounds and a dinner-only restaurant (5:30 P.M.–close Fri.–Sat.). Owners-winemakers Russ and Claudia Snyder started this small winery to give them something to do in retirement, and it has turned into a full-time gig for the former Salt Lake City residents, but they don't seem to mind the hard work. The "retirees" produce small lots of cabernet franc, chardonnay, syrah, cabernet sauvignon, and riesling. To get here from downtown Buhl, head west on Burley Avenue (the road name quickly changes to E. 4100 N.) and turn left (south) onto North 1200 East; look for the winery on the left.

Golf

Clear Lake Country Club (403 Clear Lake Lane, 208/543-4849, year-round, $26–30) offers a gorgeous 18-hole, 5,895-yard, par-72 course in the Snake River Canyon. The 13th green is shaped like a rainbow trout, and the 14th tee offers commanding canyon views. Cart rentals available, and there is a restaurant and bar. Hard-core hackers can park the Winnie at the club's RV park ($18 with electrical hookups). Nongolfers can go fly-fishing ($10 adults, $3.50 children) at the club's own private, no-license pond (catch-and-release only).

Accommodations and Food

Buhl has a few cutesy old motels around town. One good pick is the **Oregon Trail Motel** (510 S. Broadway, 208/543-8814, from $54 d), a tidy motor inn with 17 nonsmoking guest rooms within walking distance of downtown.

For barbecue and beer, head to **That One Place** (1003 Main St., 208/543-5334, lunch and dinner daily, around $9), a little barbecue joint that slow-smokes its meats with apple wood. Enjoy pulled pork sandwiches, beef brisket, and pork baby back ribs smothered with tangy barbecue sauce. Sides include garlic fries, coleslaw, and potato salad.

Remember when milk came in glass bottles? It still does at **(C** **Clover Leaf**

Clover Leaf Creamery, formerly known as Smith's Dairy

© DANA HOPPER-KELLY

Creamery (205 S. Broadway, 208/543-4272, 9 A.M.–7 P.M. Mon.–Fri., 10 A.M.–7 P.M. Sat., 1–7 P.M. Sun.), formerly known as Smith's Dairy. Besides all-natural milk, this classic creamery makes the best damn ice cream and milk shakes in southern Idaho. Choose from a large selection of flavors such as strawberry, peach, rocky road, and "Elk Tracks," a chocolate and vanilla swirl with peanuts and big chunks of dark chocolate. Clover Leaf also sells local farmstead cheeses, made by Ballard Family Dairy in Gooding, and frozen local trout.

Information
The **Buhl Chamber of Commerce** (716 U.S. 30 E., 208/543-6682) answers visitor inquiries.

Twin Falls

Twin Falls (population 44,000), seat of the county of the same name, was founded in 1904 as a hub for Carey Act settlers, who came flooding in to grab up 160-acre parcels for $25 per acre. The huge Snake River irrigation projects of the day turned the desert here into a livable, arable place. Potatoes, sugar beets, and alfalfa are among the crops grown locally, and cattle ranches and dairies also add to the ag scene. Yet Twin Falls is too big to be just a farm town. Diverse services, light industry, and a top-notch junior college with a nationally recognized basketball program contribute to the town's healthy mix of rural character and urban amenities.

The falls for which the city is named were supposedly once a sight, but dams have dimmed their glory. Just downstream, however, wide Niagara-like Shoshone Falls has been a tourist destination since the pioneer days and still is the city's prime sightseeing attraction.

Twin Falls perches on the rim of the Snake River Canyon, a spectacular gorge that offers recreational activities like rafting, kayaking, fishing, hiking, mountain biking, and golf on one of the wildest courses in the state.

Spending a summer day in Twin Falls will give you a clue as to why the westward-bound pioneers were so relieved to get to tree-filled Boise. Here the summer sun reflects off a city covered by miles of asphalt and concrete right up to the canyon rim and buffered by precious little shade. If you don't have air-conditioning in your Roadmaster, you'll regret it when the dog days of summer push the mercury past 100°F. The downtown area does have its charms, however, and several big shade trees.

SIGHTS
◖ Perrine Bridge
Coming from I-84, you enter Twin Falls over 1,500-foot-long Perrine Bridge. It is named for I. B. Perrine, the region's biggest pioneer-era promoter and the man most responsible

MAGIC VALLEY

© DANA HOPPER-KELLY

Perrine Bridge spans the Snake River Canyon.

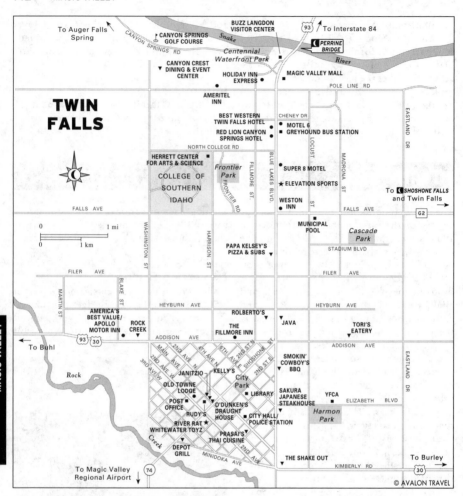

for bringing about the irrigation projects that turned much of the area green. The bridge ushers traffic across the river 486 feet above the glimmering waters. The town's main visitor information center is just across the bridge on the southwest side. From here, you can actually walk out onto the bridge on a pedestrian walkway—not for those with a fear of heights.

Hansen Bridge

Hansen Bridge crosses the Snake River east of the city. Until 1919 crossings were made via rowboat. Then a suspension bridge was built, and in 1966 the current bridge was put in. It's a 350-foot drop from the bridge to the river.

Evel Knievel's Jump Site

Besides the big earthen ramp directly east of the Perrine Bridge, there's not much to see at Evel Knievel's famous jump site. But you can let your imagination run wild. In 1974, Knievel attempted to fly a rocket-powered motorcycle across the 1,500-foot gap, but his parachute deployed prematurely, causing Knievel to drift rather anticlimactically into the deep canyon. The stunt did earn the city a claim to fame, though. Robbie "Kaptain" Knievel, Evel's daredevil son, recently solicited city officials to allow him to jump the chasm in September 2011. Considering the city's tolerance for daredevils (BASE jumping is legal at the Perrine Bridge), it looks they might grant the younger Knievel's wishes to take care of his father's unfinished business.

◖ Shoshone Falls

East of town, Shoshone Falls (7 A.M.–10 P.M. daily year-round, $3 per vehicle) has been called the "Niagara of the West." At 1,000 feet wide and 212 feet high, the horseshoe-shaped waterfall is 52 feet higher than Niagara. The falls are often a mere trickle, since much of the water is diverted to the region's irrigation system; spring is usually the best time to see some water going over.

Fortunately, there's more to do if the falls aren't falling. Twin Falls's 2004 centennial year is celebrated with a new trail leading out of the canyon from Shoshone Falls Park. Also part of the same park complex, **Dierkes Lake** is a favorite haunt for fishing, swimming, paddling, and rock climbing. The swimming areas employ lifeguards in summer, and trails provide some nice hiking opportunities if you can ignore the obnoxious trophy homes perched on the canyon rim. To get to Shoshone Falls and Dierkes Lake, take Blue Lakes Boulevard to Falls Avenue and go three miles east—to 3300 East Road—and two miles north, following the ample signage.

College of Southern Idaho

A two-year junior college offering associate and vocational degrees, College of Southern Idaho (315 Falls Ave., 208/733-9554, www.csi.edu) enrolls more than 7,000 students. One highlight for visitors to the 300-acre campus is the free **Herrett Center for Arts & Science** (www.herrett.csi.edu, 9:30 A.M.–9 P.M. Tues. and Fri., 9:30 A.M.–4:30 P.M. Wed.–Thurs., 1–9 P.M. Sat. year-round,

© DANA HOPPER-KELLY

Shoshone Falls at a mere trickle

MAGIC VALLEY

longer hours in summer), which boasts a collection of almost 20,000 pre-Columbian artifacts from North and Central America. The museum also has a gallery of contemporary art and the **Faulkner Planetarium** (shows $4.50 adults, $3.50 seniors, $2.50 children). You can also catch a music laserium show (8:15 P.M. Tues. and Fri.–Sat.) at the planetarium; expect to see shows like *U2: Feel the Music, Ride the Light.*

Numerous public events are held in the school's Fine Arts Auditorium, and the rest of the nicely landscaped campus makes a nice spot for a picnic lunch or a stroll.

RECREATION
Guided Recreation
Visitors with a hankering to get out for some serious adventure in the area can contact **Idaho Guide Service** (563 Trotter Dr., 208/734-4998 or 888/734-3246), which offers guided canoe, raft, and kayak trips as well as hiking and biking trips. Fishing excursions and powerboat tours are also available.

Parks
Although most of Twin Falls's prime canyon-rim real estate has been claimed by chain stores and tony professional offices, paved paths offer pedestrian and bicycle access much of the way. To find one especially nice stretch, take Pole Line Road west from Blue Lakes Boulevard, then north on Washington Street. Park in the small lot at the end of Washington Street and stroll east.

Centennial Waterfront Park (free) lies practically at the base of Perrine Bridge and offers a dock and a boat ramp in addition to splendid views and some big rocks to crawl around on. It's at the bottom of Canyon Springs Road, a scenic drive in itself past a waterfall gushing forth from the canyon's south

BASE JUMPING

Twin Falls draws BASE jumpers from all over the world. BASE stands for "building, antenna, span (bridge), earth" – and in the case of Twin Falls, the focus is on "span." BASE enthusiasts say the 486-foot-high Perrine Bridge over the Snake River Canyon is the only one in the United States where it's legal to jump year-round. BASE jumpers travel from around the world to plunge off the Perrine, and on summer holiday weekends as many as 150 people may be in town for the opportunity. Don Mays, whose Snake River Canyon Tours boat frequently shuttles jumpers from their target landing site beneath the bridge, estimates there have been 30,000 jumps – with two deaths and a few serious injuries – since he started his service in 1996.

BASE experts say would-be jumpers need to become proficient in sky-diving before attempting BASE jumps. After about 200 jumps from an airplane, parachutists should be ready for the more demanding BASE experience. (It's harder because you're closer to the ground and there's less room for error.) Would-be jumpers are also urged to take BASE jumping instruction. First-jump courses, many held at the Perrine Bridge, are offered by manufacturers such as Vertigo BASE of Moab, Utah, and Consolidated Rigging of Auburn, California.

Twin Falls is exceptionally friendly to BASE jumpers. Many jumpers stay at the KOA in nearby Jerome or at the motels within walking distance of the canyon. When night falls, you'll often find BASE enthusiasts swapping stories at restaurants near the bridge, especially the Outback Steakhouse and Johnny Carino's Italian Kitchen.

If you'd like to see BASE jumpers in action, stand on either end of the Perrine Bridge any day that has calm winds, and you're likely to spot some. You can also watch jumpers preparing their gear on the lawn at the Buzz Langdon Visitors Center and in the canyon at Centennial Waterfront Park.

rim. Photographers will find this an excellent place to get a shot of the bridge.

Also down in the canyon, about four miles northwest of Centennial Waterfront Park on Canyon Springs Road, you'll discover **Auger Falls Park** (free), a new 547-acre wilderness spread that's well-suited for mountain biking, hiking, and fishing—you can really get away from it all.

Downtown, **City Park** (Shoshone St. between 4th Ave. and 6th Ave.) was the original central-city park platted by the town founders in 1904. It's still a major venue for events throughout the year. The year-round **city pool** (756 Locust St., 208/734-2336), managed by the YMCA, is a swimming facility that's open to the elements in the summer and covered the rest of the year by a giant bubble.

For more information on the city's parks, contact the **Twin Falls Parks and Recreation Department** (136 Maxwell Ave., 208/736-2265).

Golf

Down in the canyon, offering great worm's-eye views of Perrine Bridge, is the 18-hole **Canyon Springs Golf Course** (199 Canyon Springs Rd., 208/734-7609, year-round, $19–37). The 6,770-yard, par-72 course is laced with rock and water traps. There are also a driving range, a pro shop, a restaurant, and a lounge. The course is open unless there's snow on the ground.

Another 18-hole course is the 5,234-yard, par-68 **Twin Falls Municipal Golf Course** (Grandview Dr., 208/733-3326, $15–23), two miles west of Blue Lakes Boulevard off Addison Avenue West.

ENTERTAINMENT AND EVENTS
The Arts

The **Magic Valley Arts Council** (195 River Vista Pl., 208/734-2787, www.magicvalleyartscouncil.org) is the clearinghouse for cultural information. Its new headquarters, near the south canyon rim, includes an art gallery that exhibits and sells local artwork.

The new facility also features a casual–fine dining restaurant, **Elevation 486** (208/737-0486, www.elevation486.com, 5–10 P.M. daily). The council also sponsors annual events like the **Arts on Tour** series with the College of Southern Idaho and **Kids Arts in the Park.**

Nightlife

Twin Falls's nightlife scene, such as it is, centers mostly around the Old Town area, south of downtown via Shoshone Street. **Woody's** (213 5th Ave. S., 208/732-0077, www.woodystwin.com, until late daily) is where to go for draft microbrews, DJ dancing, and live music.

Also downtown is **O'Dunken's Draught House** (102 Main Ave. N., 208/733-8114, 11:30 A.M.–late daily), a happening place with 25 draft microbrews, pizza and sandwiches, big flat-screen TVs, and the best sidewalk patio in town. It's not only for adults, though; this nonsmoking establishment is open to people of all ages.

Twin Falls has quite a jazz scene owing to a strong music department at the College of Southern Idaho. (The college is also the home of the Boise State University Radio Network's statewide jazz feed, 1450 AM.) But because there's no jazz club, you'll find trios and quartets playing at various coffeehouses and other venues around town. To find out who's playing where, keep an eye open for fliers, or call the CSI jazz studies program (208/732-6765).

Events

June is a busy month for events in Twin Falls. The week leading up to the first weekend in June brings **Western Days** to town. You can "Howdy, pardner" your way from the mock gunfight to the barbecue to the Western dance to the chili cook-off. Naturally, there's a parade. A week later, The **Snake River Canyon Jam** (www.snakerivercanyonjam.com) takes center stage at Centennial Waterfront Park, with a full day of live jazz music that includes a well-known headliner or two. Also in mid-June, **Art in the Park** is held at the Twin Falls City Park. This annual event features arts and crafts vendors, food, live music, and pottery and woodworking demonstrations. For more information about area events, call the Twins Falls Chamber of Commerce (208/733-3974).

SHOPPING

The 430,000-square-foot **Magic Valley Mall** (1485 Pole Line Rd. E., 208/733-3000, 10 A.M.–9 P.M. Mon.–Sat., 11 A.M.–6 P.M. Sun.), at Blue Lakes Boulevard just south of the Perrine Bridge, has more than 70 stores, including JCPenney, Sears, Macy's, and Barnes & Noble as well as a multiscreen movie theater.

Gear for all your outdoor adventures is the specialty of **Elevation Sports** (1170 Blue Lakes Blvd. N., 208/734-6635). For paddle-sports sales, rentals, and know-how, head to **River Rat Whitewater Toyz** (138 2nd Ave. S., 208/735-8697).

Foodies will enjoy **Rudy's: A Cook's Paradise** (147 Main Ave. N., 208/733-5477, 9 A.M.–7 P.M. Mon.–Fri., 9 A.M.–5:30 P.M. Sat.), a new shop downtown that specializes in all things food where you'll find kitchen cookware, wines, oils, and vinegars, plus a good lineup of local foodstuffs such as artisanal cheeses, grass-fed lamb and beef, and preserves. Rudy's also has wine tastings and cooking classes.

ACCOMMODATIONS

The two major motel districts in town are on the north end of Blue Lakes Boulevard and on the west end of Addison Avenue (U.S. 30). Both zones are busy thoroughfares. The Blue Lakes Boulevard accommodations are primarily the bigger chain motels, while the Addison Avenue establishments are mostly older but serviceable independents.

Under $50

The Twin Falls **Motel 6** (1472 Blue Lakes Blvd. N., 208/734-3993, from $49 d) offers 132 guest rooms, a pool, and guest laundry.

Near the heart of downtown, **Old Towne Lodge** (248 2nd Ave. W., 208/733-5630,

$25–55) offers basic but inexpensive rooms with cable TV. **Monterey Motor Inn** (433 Addison Ave. W., 208/733-5151, from $46 d) has 28 guest rooms—some nonsmoking—with queen and king beds. Amenities include cable TV and high-speed Internet.

$50-100

America's Best Value/Apollo Motor Inn (296 Addison Ave. W., 208/733-2010 or 888/315-2378, from $76 d) offers a complimentary continental breakfast, cable TV, a pool, and a hot tub.

On the Blue Lakes strip, **Weston Inn** (906 Blue Lakes Blvd. N., 208/733-6095, from $70 d) has relatively clean smoking or nonsmoking guest rooms and continental breakfast included. Family suites are available, and pets are allowed.

Super 8 Motel (1260 Blue Lakes Blvd. N., 208/734-5801, from $69 d) offers queen beds, nonsmoking and wheelchair-friendly guest rooms, cable TV, and free coffee and doughnuts in the morning.

Red Lion Hotel Canyon Springs (1357 Blue Lakes Blvd. N., 208/734-5000 or 800/325-4000, from $86 d) features spacious guest rooms, all with king or queen beds, irons, hair dryers, phones, and Wi-Fi, along with a restaurant and lounge and an outdoor swimming pool.

Best Western Twin Falls Hotel (1377 Blue Lakes Blvd., 208/736-8000 or 800/822-8946, www.bestwestern.com, from $85 d) is another typical chain hotel with standard amenities.

Near the Magic Valley Mall, you'll find the **Holiday Inn Express** (1554 Fillmore St., 208/732-6001 or 800/465-4329, www.hie.com, from $89 d), which offers 91 business-friendly guest rooms, each with Wi-Fi, hair dryers, and irons and ironing boards. Other amenities include free continental breakfast, an indoor pool and spa, cable TV with HBO, and an exercise room.

$100-150

AmeriTel Inn (539 Pole Line Rd., 208/736-9600, www.ameritelinns.com, from $99 d) has

101 guest rooms and amenities like an indoor pool, free breakfast, and high-speed Internet.

For a bed-and-breakfast experience, check out ◖ **The Fillmore Inn** (102 Fillmore St., 208/736-4257, www.thefillmoreinn.com, $99–160). This beautiful redbrick house boasts several guest rooms with hardwood floors and antique furniture. Wake up to breakfast and coffee served in the elegant dining room.

Camping

Oregon Trail Campground (2733 Kimberly Rd., 208/733-0853 or 800/733-0853, $25 RVs, $18 tents) is on the way out of town heading east on Kimberly Road (U.S. 30). The 75-site RV park features a playground, restrooms and showers, a game room, a snack bar, and 24-hour guest laundry. RV sites have full hookups and cable TV.

FOOD

Twin Falls has just about every kind of chain restaurant imaginable, especially along the Blue Lakes strip, but there are several places around town that are locally owned and operated.

Upscale Fare

The restaurant at ◖ **Canyon Crest Dining & Event Center** (330 Canyon Crest Dr., 208/733-9392, www.canyoncrestdining. com, lunch 11 A.M.–3 P.M. daily, dinner 4–9 P.M. Sun.–Thurs., 4–10 P.M. Fri.–Sat., entrées $15–40) is hands-down the swankiest place in town. The restaurant is right on the lip of the canyon overlooking Centennial Waterfront Park. Enjoy the view from the deck while trying the restaurant's upscale offerings, ranging from lobster cakes to trout amandine to prime rib and herbed rack of lamb. Finish with a big wedge of Kahlúa-chocolate cheesecake.

Rock Creek (200 Addison Ave. W., 208/734-4154, dinner daily, entrées $12–20) is a long-standing steak-and-seafood place west of downtown. With subdued lighting and a friendly bar, it makes a reliable stop for visitors to Twin.

Tori's Eatery (1924 Addison Ave. E., 208/733-1860, www.toriseatery.com, 5–9 P.M. Tues.–Sat., under $20), in a converted house east of downtown, is a dinner-only restaurant that dishes up pasta, seafood, and steaks with contemporary flair.

Ethnic Cuisine

Thai one on at ◖ **Prasai's Thai Cuisine** (428 2nd Ave. E., 208/733-2222, 11 A.M.–9 P.M. Mon.–Thurs., 11 A.M.–10 P.M. Fri., noon–9 P.M. Sat., $10–15), where you will find traditional dishes like sweet and sour catfish, assorted curries, and wok-seared noodles galore. Vegetarians won't starve here either. Wash everything down with a cold Thai beer.

For dinner and a show, head to **Sakura Japanese Steakhouse** (562 Blue Lakes Blvd., 208/736-2977, 4–11 P.M. Mon.–Sat., around $20), where silly teppanyaki chefs work the crowd over a sizzling hot grill. Watch them make onion-ring volcanoes and flip shrimp into people's mouths.

Twin has a multitude of Mexican restaurants, many of which are overly Americanized, but a couple of places are worth checking out. **Rolberto's** (275 Blue Lakes Blvd. near Addison Ave. E., 208/733-5516, 24 hours daily) seems to get it right with a large array of affordable Mexican fare served *mucho rapido*. Big burritos, tacos, tamales, and torta sandwiches are the orders of the day, and it has a drive-through.

If you're into a chips-and-salsa kind of place, try **Janitzio** (164 Main Ave. N., 208/734-9910, lunch and dinner daily, $8–12). This family-style Mexican restaurant is festive, with ranchera music blaring from the speakers. Sink into a big booth and munch on fajitas, enchiladas, smothered burritos, and combination plates. Try the flan and churros for dessert.

Burgers and Sandwiches

Locals flock to **The Shake Out** (1186 Kimberly Rd., 208/734-0300) for big burgers, tater tots, and milk shakes. The restaurant has more than 50 flavors of shakes, including huckleberry, apple pie, peach, chocolate chip, and butterscotch.

You can get decent barbecue-style sandwiches at **Smokin' Cowboys BBQ** (837 Blue Lakes Blvd., 208/735-1008, lunch and dinner Mon.–Sat., sandwiches $8), a place that packs doughy rolls with tri-tip, pulled pork, and smoked chicken. You can also get slow-smoked pork spare ribs and beef brisket served with baked beans, coleslaw, and mashed spuds and gravy. Close by is **Papa Kelsey's Pizza & Subs** (637 Blue Lakes Blvd. N., 208/733-9484, lunch and dinner daily), which has good pizza ($12–20) and oven-baked sub sandwiches ($5–10).

Breakfast

For a good breakfast downtown, **Ⓒ Kelly's** (110 Main Ave. N., 208/733-0466, 7 A.M.–2:30 P.M. Mon.–Sat., under $10) is a real find, and this author is fond of the restaurant's name. Great omelets bursting with fresh veggies and tasty home-fried potatoes with a minimum of grease are among the delights on the menu, and the coffee is pretty good too. The bright and cheery downtown eatery is a nonsmoking establishment, and it serves sandwiches, burgers, and salads at lunchtime.

Night owls and insomniacs head to the **Depot Grill** (545 Shoshone St. S., 208/733-0710, 24 hours Mon.–Sat., closes 9 P.M. Sun.)—a Twin Falls institution since 1927. The Depot serves breakfast around the clock, and the menu offers a delightful variety of pancakes, including dollar-sized buckwheat cakes. The Depot also serves lunch and dinner.

Coffee

Like its sister establishments in Hailey, Ketchum, Boise, and Coeur d'Alene, **Java** (228 Blue Lakes Blvd. N., 208/733-9555, 6 A.M.–9 P.M. Mon.–Sat., 7 A.M.–6 P.M. Sun.) has good coffee, food, decor, and people.

Twin also has Starbucks and Moxie Java locations to help part your eyelids in the morning.

Groceries

At the **Twin Falls Farmers Market** (N. College Rd., across from CSI's Herrett Center, 9 A.M.–1 P.M. Sat. May–Oct.) you can score farm-fresh offerings such as organic vegetables, eggs, and alfalfa honey as well as grab-and-go hot items and freshly baked pies. Also expect to see lots of locally made jewelry, pottery, and other artisanal crafts.

INFORMATION AND SERVICES
Information

The best spot to pick up visitor information is the **Buzz Langdon Visitors Center** (3591 Blue Lakes Blvd. N., 208/733-9458) on the southwest side of the Perrine Bridge. If you don't find an answer there, your next stop might be the **Twin Falls Chamber of Commerce** (858 Blue Lakes Blvd. N., 208/733-3974 or 800/255-8946, www.twinfallschamber.com).

For information on local recreation, contact the city **Parks and Recreation Department** (136 Maxwell Ave., 208/736-2265). For adventures farther afield, the **Sawtooth National Forest** office (2647 Kimberly Rd. E., 208/737-3200), east of downtown, also serves as the forest's Twin Falls Ranger District headquarters.

Services

Contact Twin Falls's main **post office** (253 2nd Ave. W., 208/733-0702) for general delivery inquiries. Twin Falls recently opened a beautiful new **public library** (201 4th Ave. E., 208/733-2964) across from the City Park. The periodicals section is a good place to escape the heat or the cold.

Just west of town you'll find emergency medical services at **St. Luke's Magic Valley Medical Center** (650 Addison Ave. W., 208/737-2000).

GETTING THERE AND AROUND
Getting There

Joslin Field–Magic Valley Regional Airport (TWF, 208/733-5215) is about four miles south of town on Blue Lakes Boulevard. Commercial air service is provided by **SkyWest** (435/634-3400, www.skywest.com), which makes several flights daily to and from its hub in Salt Lake City. Attention gamblers and revelers: **Allegiant Air** (702/505-8888, www.allegiantair.com) offers twice-weekly flights (Mon. and Fri.) to and from its hub in Las Vegas.

The **Greyhound Bus Station** is in the Snake River Chevron (1390 Blue Lakes Blvd. N., 208/733-3002).

Getting Around

At the airport, you can rent a car at **Budget** (208/735-8698, www.budget.com) and **Avis** (208/733-5527, www.avis.com).

Twin doesn't have a true city transit system, but the way the area is growing, don't be surprised to see one in the coming years. College of Southern Idaho operates **Trans IV Buses** (208/736-2133), a limited fixed-route service that runs twice daily between Twin and smaller towns in the outlying area.

North of the Snake River

West of Twin Falls on I-84 is Thousand Springs State Park's Malad Gorge unit, but first are two major routes that leave I-84 heading north. Highway 46 passes through Gooding on its way to the Camas Prairie and the town of Fairfield. U.S. 93 runs due north out of Twin Falls, passing near Jerome and continuing to Shoshone. There it veers northeast toward fly-fishing nirvana, the Little Wood River and the pristine trout-filled waters of Silver Creek. Highway 75 continues north out of Shoshone on its way to the Wood River Valley.

MALAD GORGE

The Big Wood and Little Wood Rivers meet near Gooding to form the Malad River. Today it would probably just be called the lower Big Wood if early fur trappers in the area hadn't experienced a culinary catastrophe. In 1819, Donald Mackenzie's expedition stopped at the river and dined on beaver steak. Many of the men subsequently fell ill, leading Mackenzie to christen the river with the French word for "sick." Subsequent expeditions in 1824 and 1830 reported similar fates. Before the fur trappers came along, Shoshone Indians had inhabited the area, hunting pronghorn and fishing for salmon; after the trappers, thousands of Oregon Trail pioneers passed by, many of whom were traveling the Kelton Road. The gorge was a major stop along that route.

When the Malad River reaches 2.5-mile-long Malad Gorge it gets a boost of springwater flowing into it at 1,200 cubic feet per second. The supercharged river froths and foams in tormented torrents down through the narrow lava-rock chasm. It reaches the height of its fury at Devil's Washbowl, where it plunges over a 60-foot waterfall into calmer waters. Below Devil's Washbowl, the canyon widens. Standing on the rim surveying the scene, you are 250 feet above the shimmering river below. Springs pour out from the rim in places, cascading down the cliffs in ribbon-like waterfalls. Rest assured, people cascading down the cliffs would not look nearly as beautiful: Signs warn visitors about getting too close to the edge of the precipice; deep fissures run parallel to the rim, indicating another layer of rock getting ready to slough off into the canyon. It could happen tomorrow, or it might take 1,000 years.

Although there is some disagreement among geologists, prevailing opinion seems to have it that the modestly sized Malad River on its own wouldn't have been powerful enough to carve such a deep canyon. Rather, the gorge is most likely another example of the work of the Bonneville Flood—the apocalyptic wall of water that crashed across the Snake River Plain almost 15,000 years ago, reconstructing the landscape dramatically as it went.

MAGIC VALLEY

Melon gravel seen in the area lends support to this theory.

Thousand Springs State Park's Malad Gorge Unit

The 652-acre Malad Gorge unit (office 1074 E. 2350 S., Hagerman, 208/837-4505) of Thousand Springs State Park is a day-use area ($5) on the south side of I-84 Exit 147. The center of activity is the **Devil's Washbowl** overlook and interpretive area. Here signs explain the human and geologic history of the site, and a footbridge allows visitors to take a breathtaking stroll out high above the gorge. It's definitely not for acrophobes. As you walk across the footbridge, which is within diesel-sniffing range of the highway, the rumbling of the big rigs roaring by on I-84 shakes the bridge and adds to the excitement. One odd feature—perhaps engendered by engineering requirements—is the placement of the overlook bridge directly above Devil's Washbowl; you can't actually see the falls well from the bridge. Continue across the decidedly ugly iron bridge and on down the trail for better views of the turbulent cascade.

Elsewhere in the park proper, a green picnic area with restrooms makes a good place to break out the lunch, while a loop road continues down to the Snake River rim, past a couple of "coves" or smaller gorges eroded out of the cliffs. Hiking trails let visitors get off the asphalt and see some of the park's wildlife, including lots of hawks and jackrabbits.

GOODING AND VICINITY

Today's Gooding was originally a railroad stop called To-po-nis, a Shoshone word meaning either "black cherries" or "trading post." Given the absence of orchards in the desert here, one might guess that the latter was the correct translation. The town's name was changed in 1896 to honor local sheep baron Frank Gooding, who went on to become a successful career politician. He was first elected mayor of the town bearing his name, then elected governor of Idaho, and then elected to the U.S.

Senate, where he served from 1921 until his death in 1928. In 1913, the town of Gooding was designated the Gooding County seat.

Cities of Rocks

North of town, Highway 46 climbs into the Bennett Hills, passing access roads to two different "cities of rocks"—areas of hoodoo formations carved by eons of erosion. The common mushroom-cap shapes are created because the layer of basalt (lava rock) on top is harder than the rhyolite (consolidated volcanic ash) underlying it and therefore less easily worn away by wind and water.

The first turnoff you'll come to heading north, 14 miles north of Gooding, is for **Little City of Rocks.** Four miles farther up the highway is the turnoff for **Gooding City of Rocks.** Their names seem to indicate the latter is the best area; actually, while both are worth exploring, Little City of Rocks is about a mile or less off the highway, allowing quick access to relatively tall, impressive formations. Gooding City of Rocks, on the other hand, lies at the end of a nine-mile dirt road, and the rocks—or those near the road, at least—are much more humble in size. But the Gooding City of Rocks area does offer great views of the Snake River Plain as well as opportunities for extended exploring; the Special Recreation Management Area here encompasses more than 20,000 acres where you might come upon Native American petroglyphs or a herd of desert-dwelling elk. Other residents in the area include deer, black bears, chukars, golden eagles, prairie falcons, red-tailed hawks, great horned owls, and an abundance of those stealthy beasts, range cattle. (Remember: If you hit a range animal in Idaho, you're responsible to pay for it, and you'll probably have to drop some money to fix your car too.)

Make sure to have water with you out here. Both areas are hot and dry, especially on lizard-sizzling summer afternoons. For more information, contact the **Bureau of Land Management Shoshone District** (400 W. F St., Shoshone, 208/732-7200).

Events

Gooding boasts a good-sized Basque community, which throws the annual **Basque Picnic** on the third Sunday in July at the Gooding County Fairgrounds. That same weekend is Gooding's **Summerfest,** a street fair with antique cars and hot rods, games and contests, arts and crafts, and lots of good eats. Call 208/934-4402 for information about both events.

The second week in August, the **Gooding County Fair and Rodeo** kicks up its heels at the fairgrounds on the northwest edge of town; the fair hosts the Miss Teen Rodeo Idaho contest. For a complete events calendar, call Gooding City Hall (208/934-5669).

Accommodations

The **Historic Gooding Hotel Bed & Breakfast** (112 Main St., Gooding, 208/934-4374, www.goodinghotelbandb.com, $75–95) is listed on the National Register of Historic Places. This beautiful B&B is actually run by Goodings, descendants of the town's founding family. It has two guest rooms with private baths and nine more with shared baths. Rates include a large country breakfast.

The **Get Inn** (301 University Dr., Gooding, 208/934-8579, www.getinnidaho.com, $55–70), in the old Gooding College Building just off U.S. 26, is another historic B&B in town. The Get Inn offers eight stylish rooms with shared baths and a continental breakfast. There's also an outdoor patio with a fire pit and a barbecue area.

Food

For big farm-style breakfasts, head to the **❤ Farmhouse Restaurant** (1955 Frontage Rd. S., Wendell, 208/536-6688, 7 A.M.–8 P.M. Sun.–Thurs., 6:30 A.M.–9 P.M. Fri.–Sat., under $10) right off I-84 Exit 157 in nearby Wendell. Besides homespun breakfast fare served with a smile, the restaurant also dishes up lunch and dinner. Try the Basque omelet—four fluffy eggs folded over spicy chorizo and roasted red bell pepper.

Grab a burger and a shake at **Stampede Burger** (2115 Main St., Gooding, 208/934-

4202, $3.50–8), a classic drive-in just south of town. You can also get chili dogs, finger steaks, and a pretty good hot pastrami sandwich.

Information

For information about the town, contact the **Gooding Visitor Center** (308 5th Ave. W., Gooding, 208/934-5669).

JEROME

This small town is the Jerome County seat, and it's primarily an agricultural service center. Businesses here include a cheese company, a milk transporter, a potato processor, and a PVC-pipe manufacturer. Jerome began in 1907 as a company town for the Twin Falls North Side Land and Water Company, which was developing the irrigation systems north of the Snake River. Like the neighboring dairy center of Wendell, Jerome was named for a son of W. H. Kuhn, one of the financiers of the Twin Falls North Side Irrigation Project. For more on the town's history, visit the **Jerome County Historical Museum** (220 N. Lincoln Ave., 208/324-5641, 1–5 P.M. Tues.–Sat. year-round, donation).

Minidoka Internment National Memorial

After the Japanese bombed Pearl Harbor in December 1941, the U.S. government decided that Americans of Japanese ancestry living along the Pacific coast were a threat to national security. Perhaps they would side with their former countrymen; perhaps they would radio secret military information to incoming squadrons of Zeroes, hell-bent on replacing apple pie with sushi on diner menus from Peoria to Pocatello. Some 110,000 Japanese Americans living on the West Coast were rounded up and herded into one of 10 internment camps across the West, beginning in August 1942. The U.S. Supreme Court later ruled this was unconstitutional, but it was a moot point by then. The *Enola Gay* dropped her lethal load over Hiroshima in August 1945, and eight days later the war in the Pacific was over. The U.S. government didn't bother to apologize for its internment atrocity until 1988, following years of tireless lobbying by Japanese Americans.

East of Jerome lies the site of one of these former camps, a place the government named Hunt. It was also called the Minidoka Relocation Center, which has an innocuous ring to it compared to "concentration camp." But that's what the 950-acre camp really was. Nearly 7,500 internees here lived a humiliating life in tarpaper barracks, surrounded by barbed wire and armed guards. Many of the young males were summoned out to serve in the U.S. armed forces. Go figure the logic in imprisoning people and at the same time asking the strongest among them to fight for your cause. Many young Japanese American men from Hunt died defending the United States from their ancestral cousins; their names are inscribed on one of the plaques here. In December 1944 the government allowed Japanese Americans to return to the West Coast; the camp closed in October 1945.

Other than the small memorial area, the rest of what was once the camp is now bucolic farmland betraying no evidence of its shameful history. But the site has been designated a national memorial, and planning is underway for some additional interpretation. To get to the site, take Highway 25 east from Jerome. The turnoff to the area is marked by a couple of the familiar roadside historical markers. You can also get more information by calling 208/837-4793.

Events

The second weekend in September, the locals come out for **Live History Days,** a celebration of pioneer life. Those old geezers knew a lot of skills. Maybe you'll learn something about farming, cooking, spinning, or weaving. The **Jerome Chamber of Commerce** (1731 S. Lincoln Ave., 208/324-2711) has the details.

Accommodations

The newish **Best Western Sawtooth Inn & Suites** (2653 S. Lincoln Ave., 208/324-9200, from $79 d) has 67 clean and comfortable rooms with cable TV and high-speed Internet.

Amenities include free breakfast and a 24-hour indoor pool and hot tub.

SHOSHONE AND VICINITY

Once a rowdy rail hub, Shoshone still seems to delight in its frisky heritage. The chamber of commerce pamphlets fairly gloat when relating the gory details surrounding the town's former brothels and speakeasies. Shoshone's layout also contributes to its Wild West ambience. Railroad tracks split the center of town, leaving the two main streets to face off across the tracks like a couple of gunfighters.

Architectural Highlights

The town's architecture is noteworthy for its extensive use of local lava rock. Construction with lava rock is a lost art. Somehow the pioneer masons learned how to fit the lightweight rocks together into solid foundations and walls—a feat modern-day builders have failed to duplicate. Adding to the architectural flavor are flaking signs for businesses long gone, painted on many exterior walls around town.

Right downtown on the north side of the tracks is the McFall Hotel (230 N. Rail St. W., Shoshone), an 1896 beauty that was recently restored. Now a private residence, the "haunted" hotel has a guest list that has included Teddy Roosevelt, Ernest Hemingway, and Erle Stanley Gardner. Maybe the ghost that roams the halls is really Papa Hemingway looking for some pickled herring and ale. Other fine original structures still standing include the Hotel Shoshone; the Nebraska Bar; the W. H. Baugh Building, now housing the Shoshone Showhouse movie theater; and the Doncaster, once a Prohibition-era speakeasy that later became an animal museum.

Events

Mannie's Jamboree, named after the late fiddler Mannie Shaw of Fairfield, is a 30-year fiddlers' tradition in Shoshone. So, rosin up the bow and git on down to the courthouse lawn during the second week of July. For more information on local events, contact **Shoshone**

historic downtown Shoshone

City Hall (207 S. Rail St. W., Shoshone, 208/886-2030).

Accommodations

The **Governor's Mansion Bed and Breakfast** (315 S. Greenwood St., Shoshone, 208/886-2858, $30–65) was originally owned by the brother of Frank R. Gooding, a sheep baron who served as governor of Idaho 1901–1905. The B&B has five nonsmoking guest rooms, and rates include full breakfast.

Food

The **Manhattan Cafe** (133 S. Rail St., Shoshone, 208/886-2142, breakfast, lunch, and dinner daily) is a small diner offering character in spades and a mean eggs-and-taters breakfast.

Just down the way, **Lacosta Mexican Restaurant** (115 S. Rail St., Shoshone, 208/886-9830, lunch and dinner Mon.–Sat., around $10) is a friendly place that serves traditional Mexican fare. Expect to see pork carnitas, tamales, enchiladas, chiles rellenos, and tacos galore. Most plates include rice and refried beans.

Information

Inquire about the highlights of the surrounding high desert at the **Bureau of Land Management Shoshone District** (400 W. F St., Shoshone, 208/732-7200). For information about area tourist attractions, stop by **2nd Time Around at the Whistle Stop** (102 S. Rail St., Shoshone, 208/886-7787), a wonderful antiques and collectibles shop that doubles as the **chamber of commerce.** Besides picking up some old Yellowstone National Park postcards and other cool stuff, you can get a historic walking tour brochure and insight about the town from the shop's owner, Claudia Reese.

NORTH OF SHOSHONE
Shoshone Indian Ice Caves

North of town on Highway 75 is the Shoshone Indian Ice Caves (1561 N. Hwy. 75, 208/886-2058, 10 A.M.–5:30 P.M. daily May 1–Sept. 30,

$8 adults, $7 seniors, $5 ages 4–12), which offers 40-minute guided tours through a lava tube with a fascinating history and geology. Water seeping into the tube from the Big Wood River as well as from percolating rainwater collects and freezes on the floor of the cave thanks to air currents that keep the cave perennially icy. The convenient, year-round source of ice was a boon for the early town of Shoshone—especially during the blazing summers. Outside the cave is a gift shop selling schlock as well as a museum boasting an impressive collection of gems and minerals.

Magic Reservoir

Continuing north on Highway 75 you'll pass two turnoffs to Magic Reservoir, which lies out of sight to the west. The first turnoff, right at the Big Wood River, leads to the west shore, while a turnoff farther north leads to the east shore. Boat ramps and laid-back fishing lodges are available at both areas.

The reservoir is five miles long, 1.5 miles wide, and about 120 feet deep at its deepest point. The fishing is good for rainbow trout and perch, and a few brown trout also lurk along the east side's rocky shore. Ice fishing is popular in winter, as is waterskiing in summer. Campers can pitch a tent anywhere around the shoreline (free). Lava Point, just north of West Magic, is the most heavily used primitive camping area. The reservoir is managed by the Bureau of Land Management Shoshone District (208/732-7200).

◖ Silver Creek

Silver Creek is born of crystal-pure alkaline springs in the high desert west of Picabo, and it meanders slowly down to the Little Wood River through wide-open meadows. The wild rainbow and brown trout here can see you coming a mile away and aren't easily fooled.

They're big and strong, and they lure fly-fishers from around the world. To avid fly casters, this is nirvana.

One of the prime fishing areas along the creek is the Nature Conservancy's **Silver Creek Preserve** (208/788-2203 or 208/788-7910). It's on the south side of U.S. 20, seven miles east of Highway 75 or four miles west of Picabo. The Nature Conservancy works constantly to keep the preserve and the surrounding lands in pristine shape, a difficult task given the ever-increasing usage of the area. At the heart of the 825-acre core area is a small visitors center with interpretive information and a store selling conservation-oriented items to support the preserve. The center is up on a small rise, offering sweeping views of the creek. It's also a trailhead for a 0.5-mile nature trail that loops down to and around the creek. Along the way is a boardwalk that takes you right out over the water, which is so clear you can see every grain of sand and piece of gravel on the bottom. Even if you're not a fishing fiend, this is a peaceful and pleasant place. If you *are* a fishing fiend, you can fish for free—catch-and-release fly-fishing only—but you'll have to sign in at the visitors center first. The preserve relies heavily on donations, so don't hesitate to leave a buck or five while you're here.

Fishing-guide service to Silver Creek is offered by a number of companies, including **Silver Creek Outfitters** (500 N. Main St., Ketchum, 208/726-5282, www.silver-creek. com).

To reach Silver Creek from Shoshone, either head north up Highway 75 and turn east on U.S. 20 or take U.S. 26/93 northeast through Richfield to Carey and turn west on U.S. 20. The latter route follows the Little Wood River, also known as a good brown-trout stream—one of Ernest Hemingway's favorite fishing holes.

South of the Snake River

ROCK CREEK STAGE STATION

Southeast of Twin Falls is Hansen and Rock Creek Road (County Road G3), which follows Rock Creek to its source in the heart of the South Hills, a remote mountain range that has get-away-from-it-all hiking, mountain biking, and skiing. For information about recreational opportunities, contact the **U.S. Forest Service Twin Falls Ranger District** (208/737-3200).

Rock Creek Stage Station dates back to the 1860s when the hardscrabble pit stop was one of southern Idaho's major transportation hubs and the first trading post west of Fort Hall. Oregon Trail wagon trains, stage lines, cowboys, and Indians all passed by here on their way to somewhere else. Gone are the horses whinnying in the stables and the rowdy pioneers downing whiskey and carrying on in the saloon. Now the only sounds breaking the pervasive stillness of the Snake River Plain are the babbling waters of the creek and the birds chirping in the willows.

Herman Stricker bought the property in 1875, and he and his wife, Lucy, scratched a life out of the expansive Snake River Plain. The old store—the oldest building in southern Idaho—still stands, alongside a couple of sod-roofed underground cellars. The dry cellar was used to store supplies and as protection from Native Americans, while the "wet" cellar housed booze for the saloon. Nearby is the turn-of-the-20th-century house Lucy had built after the Strickers' original home burned down in 1899, as well as a graveyard with the remains of a dozen or so pioneers. Among the graves are two identified only as "A Gypsy woman, 1893," and "Immigrant baby, 1897."

The site is a great spot for a picnic, and you'll come away with a feeling for what it must have been like on the Oregon Trail so long ago. Rock Creek Stage Station is five miles south of Hansen, a bit west of County Road G3 (watch for signs), and the buildings are open during summer for self-guided tours. Admission is free; donations are appreciated. For more

information, call the Friends of Stricker Ranch (208/423-4000).

U.S. 93 TO NEVADA

Between Twin Falls and Buhl, U.S. 93 turns south and makes a beeline for the Nevada border, carrying car- and busloads of gamblers through the high rangeland to casinos at Jackpot, just over the state line. Along the way are a couple of points of interest as well as the turnoff for the route west to Murphy Hot Springs and the old mining town of Jarbidge, Nevada. Keep your eyes peeled for birds of prey as you head south on the highway; they're abundant (and big) down here.

Rogerson

There's not much to Rogerson beyond a small store with gas and RV sites, the Salmon Dam Saloon, and a dog sleeping in the road. But that's all the town needs to supply the gamblers en route to Jackpot, or the anglers heading for either of the two reservoirs, Salmon Falls and Cedar Creek, west of town. The road to the reservoirs also continues past Three Creek to Murphy Hot Springs and Jarbidge, Nevada; it's paved all the way to the top of the downgrade into Murphy Hot Springs.

Murphy Hot Springs and Jarbidge

About 49 miles west of Rogerson via Three Creek Road, you get to Murphy Hot Springs. Native Americans from the Duck Valley Indian Reservation reportedly recognize this spot, where two forks of the Jarbidge River meet on their way down from the snow-covered Jarbidge Mountains, and where natural mineral water flows from the earth at 106°F, as a magic spot with healing powers. Those less metaphysically minded will appreciate Murphy Hot Springs simply as a remote and idyllic spot with rivers perfect for fishing or splashing, and picturesque canyon walls leading the eye ever upward toward the Jarbidge massif.

Past Murphy Hot Springs, the narrow gravel

MAGIC VALLEY

road continues 15 more miles to Jarbidge. It first descends one fork of the Jarbidge, past several shaded primitive campsites, before turning back on itself and climbing alongside a more westerly fork. At the U-turn in the road is the Bureau of Land Management's **Jarbidge River Recreation Site,** which, when the river is flowing just right, serves as the put-in point for white-water rafters and kayakers. Primitive campsites are found on both sides of the river around the put-in.

The Jarbidge River offers a Class IV whitewater run in its short spring season (May–June). The normal takeout is 29 miles downstream at the confluence of the West Fork Bruneau River at Indian Hot Springs. This is one of the remotest stretches of white water in the state, through steep-walled canyons filled with wildflowers, cacti, and junipers. Of course, the river is also full of rock gardens, and the shores are full of rattlesnakes. Those yearning for this kind of adventure can contact **Wilderness River Outfitters** (Lemhi, 208/756-3959 or 800/252-6581, www.wildernessriver.com) and sign up for a trip. The six-day trip ($2,150 pp) includes a run down the Bruneau River as well. It's expensive due to the difficult logistics and the fact that each raft carries just one guest plus the guide.

Up the road toward the Nevada state line you'll climb a canyon that's a veritable Rorschach test of phallic hoodoos. Numerous sandy beaches and swimming holes line the river for the next many miles. At the top of the hill, the canyon opens out into a broader valley, at the head of which sits Jarbidge, Nevada. Once a booming gold-mining town, today it's a remote mountain enclave supporting about 50 residents in summer, about 30 in winter. Here you'll find **Tsawhawbitt's Lodge B&B, The Outdoor Inn,** and the "world-famous" **Red Dog Saloon,** which boasts a portrait of Diamondtooth Lil, something of a "head madam" for the gaggles of working girls who once serviced the gold miners. Down at the Outdoor Inn, make sure to check out the wooden bar. It was hand-carved out of

Burmese mahogany in Massachusetts around 1865, shipped around the Horn, and used at the Golden Nugget in Las Vegas before being brought up here 25 years ago.

Jackpot, Nevada

Hard up against the border, Jackpot rises out of the Nevada desert like a neon oasis for parched Idaho gamblers. Taken together, the casinos are the second-largest employer in the greater Twin Falls area. And since most of the town's clientele comes from Idaho, not Nevada, the town runs on Idaho's mountain time, not Nevada's Pacific time.

Cactus Pete's Resort Casino (775/755-2321 or 800/821-1103) is the town's biggest gaming establishment. In addition to the slots and tables, the resort regularly books name entertainment, although Jackpot is not exactly Las Vegas. The acts here have usually long since vanished from the Letterman and Leno circuit, or the big arenas of their youth.

UP THE SNAKE RIVER
Murtaugh

The town of Murtaugh is a tiny farming hamlet set off from even the rural stretch of U.S. 30 that passes just to the south. Once a railroad town, Murtaugh retains some glimpses of its heritage. Check out the **Iron Rail Bar & Grill** (109 Archer St., 208/432-5657) down by the tracks. The 1908 building used to be the railroad depot, and later served as a Model T repair garage and a general store. Today it provides a character-infused stop for those who have come to partake of the numerous recreational opportunities nearby.

Murtaugh Reach

The bridge over the Snake River at Murtaugh is the put-in point for experienced rafters and kayakers attempting the Murtaugh Reach. At peak spring flows, this is one of the toughest stretches of white water in the state. The 15-mile section of river between Murtaugh and just above Twin Falls offers a number of Class III and IV rapids. Agricultural diversion in early summer makes for a short season, however. **Idaho Guide Service** (563 Trotter Dr., Twin Falls, 208/734-4998, www.idahoguideservice.com) and **White Otter Outdoor Adventures** (105 Mountain View Lane, Hailey, 208/788-5005, www.whiteotter.com) lead guided day trips on the Murtaugh Reach. Expect to pay about $125 pp with lunch.

Caldron Linn

Even the worst rapids on the Murtaugh Reach can't compare to what lies just upriver from the bridge: the man-eating falls at Caldron Linn, which early settlers nicknamed the Devil's Scuttle Hole. Linn is the Scottish word for waterfall, and this one's resemblance to a boiling, bubbling witch's caldron earned the cascade its sinister moniker. On October 28, 1811, Wilson Price Hunt's fur-trapping expedition attempted to navigate the rapids. One of the trappers, Antoine Clappine, drowned in the attempt. A year later, Robert Stuart's Astoria party passed this way and described the scene:

At the Caldron Linn the whole body of the River is confined between two ledges of Rock somewhat less than 40 feet apart, and here indeed its terrific appearance beggars all description – Hecate's caldron was never half so agitated when vomiting even the most diabolical spells as is this Linn in a low stage of water.

To get to the site, cross the Murtaugh bridge and turn east on the far side of the river, following signs down to the falls.

Murtaugh Lake

Those who prefer placid water underneath their boat can cross U.S. 30 to the south and head down to Murtaugh Lake, a haven for anglers, water-skiers, and white pelicans in the middle of the arid desert.

Camping is available at either of two areas on the west shore of the lake. **Dean's Cove** (free) has a small grassy area that's lined with a couple of docks, and you'll also find some tree-shaded picnic tables. The other area, **Murtaugh Lake Park** (free), is bigger, offering lots of grass, a baseball field, docks, picnic tables and shelters, restrooms, and boat ramps.

Milner Dam and Recreation Area

Milner Dam was completed in 1905, and the newly backed-up waters were diverted into canals that irrigated some 360,000 acres of cropland. Twin Falls, Jerome, and other towns to the west subsequently grew up along the river. Along the south side of Milner Reservoir, history and recreation share the spotlight at the Bureau of Land Management's Milner Historic Recreation Area ($3 day-use, $5 camping). The 2,055-acre site provides easy access to the water for anglers, boaters, and water-skiers. It also preserves a stretch of Oregon Trail ruts. At this point the westward-bound Oregon Trail pioneers had journeyed 1,315 miles from their starting point in Independence, Missouri. A small interpretive gazebo provides more details for trailophiles.

The character of the river changes here compared to points west. The volcanic basalt cliffs found farther downstream are replaced by low, verdant banks. Several free primitive campsites are along the reservoir's south bank.

Mini-Cassia Country

Before the Snake River was dammed and the volcanic soil of the central Snake River Plain irrigated, communities such as Oakley and Albion developed along rivers in the higher valleys to the south. After the advent of irrigation, communities developed on the Snake River Plain as well. Rupert and Burley, both founded in 1905, were the biggest in this region. Today Rupert is the seat of Minidoka County, which extends north from I-84 out into the lava fields. Burley is the seat of Cassia County, which encompasses the original high-valley settlements and several interspersed mountain ranges south of I-84. Together the two are known as Mini-Cassia Country, a combination of the two counties' names.

BURLEY

Burley lies near the crossroads of five pioneer trails. The Oregon Trail ran east–west about one mile south of town. The California Trail branched off the Oregon Trail and turned south up the Raft River Valley. The Salt Lake City–Oregon Trail route used after 1838 crossed the California Trail nearby. And the Salt Lake–California Trail route joined the California Trail just south of the City of Rocks. Finally, the Hudspeth Cutoff, first taken in 1849, came straight west from Soda Springs.

The town is named after David Burley, an Oregon Short Line Railroad agent who also helped foster the region's potato-farming industry.

Cassia County Historical Society Museum

One of the finer specimens on the historical museum circuit, the Cassia County Historical Society Museum (1142 Hiland Ave. at E. Main St., 208/678-7172, 10 A.M.–5 P.M. Tues.–Sat. Apr. 1–Oct. 1 or by appointment, donation), brings together an impressive collection of artifacts. You'll find a number of recreated rooms, including a doctor's office, a photo studio, and a saloon; collections of saddles, guns, hand

tools, sewing machines, dolls, toys, and more; and displays pertaining to the area's sheep, mining, and fur industries. Don't miss the collections of old newspapers and photographs. Among the newspaper articles are some detailing the trials and tribulations of Diamondfield Jack. A couple of other beautiful old photos show Shoshone Falls and Twin Falls before the dams were built.

Recreation

The city's 20 miles of river frontage make for easy access to Snake River recreation. Waterskiing is popular, with boat landings on the north side of Burley Bridge and adjacent to Burley Golf Course.

Burley Municipal Golf Course (131 E. Hwy. 81, 208/878-9807, $13–25) offers 18 holes over 6,500 yards. The scenic par-72 course lies astride the Snake River. Also here are a driving range, a pro shop, and a snack bar. Take I-84 Exit 208, to Main Street and turn left; the course is straight ahead on your left.

Events

On the last weekend of June, speedboats thunder down the Snake River during the **Idaho Regatta.** The event draws powerboat fans out of the woodwork, temporarily doubling the town's population. It's held at the riverfront marina.

The last weekend in July brings the **Spudman Triathlon,** an event that has been covered by ESPN and called one of "20 triathlons not to miss" by *Triathlete* magazine. Some 300 ironspuds compete. For more information on any of these events, call the **Mini-Cassia Chamber of Commerce** (208/679-4793).

Accommodations

Near I-84 Exit 208, **Budget Motel** (900 Overland Ave., 208/678-2200 or 800/635-4952, $50–89) has 139 nicer-than-average guest rooms along with a pool, a jetted tub, cable TV, and a kids' playground. Right next door, the 126-room **Best Western Burley Inn & Convention Center** (800 Overland Ave., 208/678-3501 or 800/599-1849, from $69 d) offers an outdoor heated pool, a guest laundry, and an on-site restaurant and lounge.

Food

Morey's Steakhouse (219 E. 3rd St. N., 208/679-1166, www.moreyssteakhouse.com, 4–9 P.M. Mon., 11:30 A.M.–9 P.M. Tues.–Fri., 4–9 P.M. Sat., dinner entrées $15–20) is the nicest place in this neck of the sagebrush. The restaurant's exterior is unattractive, but the dining room is elegant and the menu has lots of traditional steak, seafood, and pasta dishes. Expect to see prime rib, chicken-fried steak, shrimp scampi, and center-cut pork chops. The lunch offerings include burgers, finger steaks, hot sandwiches, and a noteworthy Cobb salad.

Garibaldi's Mexican Restaurant (610 Overland Ave., 208/678-2117, open lunch and dinner daily, $8–14) is where locals go for enchiladas, menudo (tripe soup), pork chili verde, and big burritos. Besides Mexican brews you can also get sangria and margaritas from the full bar.

Information

The **Mini-Cassia Chamber of Commerce** (1177 7th St., Heyburn, 208/679-4793) handles inquiries for both Burley and Rupert.

THE CITY OF ROCKS LOOP
Oakley and Vicinity

When the Saints go marching in, Oakley is one of the places they go marching in to—the Saints in this case being the Latter-day Saints, or members of the Mormon Church. Mormons settled the town between 1878 and 1880 and remain dominant here today.

The whole town has been designated a National Historic District, and a number of surviving turn-of-the-20th-century buildings are listed on the National Register of Historic Places. **Judge Benjamin Howells Mansion,** a Queen Anne–style home built by the judge in 1909, is today a private residence only rarely opened to the public. The nearby

1904 **Howells Opera House** was renovated in the 1980s to serve as an entertainment venue once again. And the Gothic Revival **Marcus Funk/Tanner Residence** was built in 1900 by a Mormon polygamist who intended one floor of the mansion for each of his three wives. The stone evident in much of the local construction—Oakley stone, a type of quartzite—is still quarried in the area and is shipped worldwide for use in construction and as flagstone.

Oakley's **City Park** (W. Main St.) provides a shady green with picnic tables, a playground, and the municipal pool (June 1–Labor Day). Also in the park is the memorial jail cell that once imprisoned, rightly or wrongly, the legendary Diamondfield Jack Davis. On West Main Street across from the park, the **Daughters of the Utah Pioneers Historical Museum** (208/862-7890, 2–5 P.M. Sat.–Sun. summer, donation) provides an artifact-filled peek at Oakley's past.

Seven miles southwest of town is **Goose Creek Reservoir,** where boating, fishing, and swimming help residents beat the summer heat.

City of Rocks National Reserve

Castles of eroded granite, some over 600 feet tall, create a mythic fairy-tale landscape at this out-of-the-way natural landmark. They also make City of Rocks (free entry) one of the country's top rock-climbing destinations. As at Yosemite, Joshua Tree, and Smith Rocks, you'll hear the clink of climbing gear from sunup until sundown and a host of foreign languages being spoken in the campgrounds that dot the preserve. Rock jocks have put up more than 600 routes, ranging in difficulty from 5.4 up to supposedly a 5.14a.

The 14,300-acre preserve also lies at a major intersection of pioneer trails. What a sight this must have been for those early adventurers. Some of them were moved to record their passage in axle grease on Signature Rock alongside the trail. Today the signatures of these California-bound settlers and miners can still be seen on the rock, between the preserve and

City of Rocks National Reserve

© IDAHO DIVISION OF TOURISM

Almo. Another bit of history here concerns a famous heist. In 1878, bandits held up the Overland Stage near Almo. Supposedly they buried their loot somewhere out in the City of Rocks, but the granite towers remain silent as to its whereabouts.

Among the most impressive rock formations at City of Rocks is Twin Sisters, on the west side of the preserve. The elder sister is composed of 2.5-billion-year-old granite, while the younger one was formed just 25–30 million years ago. The two look similar, however, because for millions of years they've been subjected to the same forces of erosion.

The reserve's 78 primitive campsites ($12 per vehicle) are administered from the reserve headquarters (3035 Elba-Almo Rd., Almo, 208/824-5519, www.nps.gov/ciro), four miles to the east.

Sawtooth Mountain Guides (208/774-3324, www.sawtoothguides.com) holds climbing classes and guided trips at City of Rocks several times a year and also plans instruction at Castle Rocks State Park.

Castle Rocks State Park

Rock climbers also flock to this newish state park next door to City of Rocks. Not only is it the first major new climbing area in the United States to open in the last 25 years, it was designed by climbers for climbers. Once a private ranch, Castle Rocks Ranch unit (day-use $5 per vehicle) includes many of the same sorts of challenging granite spires as its neighbor. Although crag climbing is the park's reason for being, it's not the only thing to do at the 1,240-acre preserve. Picnic grounds, horseback riding trails, and mountain biking are other activities, and the wildlife watching is superb: You may see mule deer, bighorn sheep, and even mountain lions. Castle Rocks Ranch unit is a day-use-only park.

The park has two other units near Almo: Smoky Mountain, with 38 serviced campsites ($22); and Administrative, a day-use area ($5) with a visitors center, a picnic area, an Oregon Trail wagon exhibit, and park offices (208/824-5519).

Almo

Almo was founded in 1881 as a stage stop on the Kelton-to-Boise route. Neither the stage route nor any other major thoroughfare passes through town today. Yet down at **Tracy's Merc** (3001 Elba-Almo Rd., 208/824-5570) you're liable to see license plates from all over the United States and to hear foreign languages from all over the world; that's because the town serves as the supply center for the City of Rocks. Tracy's, established in 1894, still uses a turn-of-the-20th-century National Cash Register to tally up the gallons of bottled water and other camping supplies it sells to climbers. You can hang your hat for the night at the frontier-themed **Almo Inn** (3020 Elba-Almo Rd., 208/824-5577, $100–170) next door to the **Almo Creek Outpost,** a rustic diner open morning, noon, and night.

On the south end of town you'll find the **City of Rocks National Reserve-Castle Rocks State Park Headquarters** (3035 Elba-Almo Rd., 208/824-5519), where you can pick up information about rock climbing or the area's rich human history.

Cache Peak Area

North of Almo, Highway 77 leads to the community of Elba, where you can turn west and head up into the highest reaches of the Albion Mountains. These are the state's highest mountains south of the Snake River. Here you'll find glacially carved high-alpine scenery—a rarity in southern Idaho.

The four **Independence Lakes** sit in a high cirque between Mount Independence (9,950 feet) and Cache Peak (10,339 feet). It's a three-mile hike up to the lakes, the lower two of which offer good trout fishing. To get to the trailhead, take Forest Road 548 east from Elba (or west from Oakley) up to the Basin-Elba Pass, and then take Forest Road 562 south to Forest Road 728 east. A small parking area is at the trailhead on Dry Creek.

Mountaineers looking to bag Cache Peak will find a Class 2 route up the northwest ridge—leave from Independence Lakes and head first to the saddle between Cache Peak and Mount Independence.

For more information, contact the U.S. Forest Service's **Burley Ranger District** (3650 Overland Ave., Burley, 208/678-0430).

Bureau of Land Management Recreation Areas

From Elba, a short jaunt north on Highway 77 brings you to Connor Junction. Here you can continue north to Burley or east to the Raft River Valley and beyond to I-84 on its southeasterly route to the Utah border. Three Bureau of Land Management (BLM) recreation areas are found in this general area.

The **Jim Sage Mountains** are on the right when you're heading north from Elba; they rise due south of Connor Junction. The mountains are public land and open for exploring but are entirely undeveloped.

East of Connor Junction on the way to Malta, you'll come to a signed turnoff on the left to the BLM's **McClendon Spring Recreation Site.** The gravel road climbs minimally and gradually before turning north and taking a level course to a beautiful cottonwood-shaded seasonal spring. The spot was used as a campsite by pioneers traveling the California Trail. Today, primitive campsites here offer panoramic views of the Raft River Valley and the Black Pine Mountains beyond. The Black Pine Range, with its distinctive bumpy top—high in the middle and low on both ends—looks like the back of a giant sleeping crocodile.

As you continue north from Connor Junction, a signed turnoff to the right leads to **Coe Creek BLM Picnic Area.** The BLM official responsible for designating this site must have been cruising around in the government-issue 4WD, contemplating what cruel joke he or she could inflict on the unsuspecting visitor. Not that there aren't some worthwhile reasons to check out this site, but the dirt road to get here climbs three long miles virtually straight up into the Cotterel Mountains—don't even consider bringing the Winnebago. You'll find a humble, overgrown, viewless picnic area next to a seasonal spring. The adjacent aspen grove is nice,

DIAMONDFIELD JACK: A STORY OF FRONTIER JUSTICE

In the late 1880s, great herds of both cattle and sheep grazed the rangelands of southern Idaho. Ranching was big business then, as it still is. Ranchers prospered, and ranching dynasties grew out of the high-desert chaparral. But cattle and sheep don't mix well on the range because of differences in their eating habits. Picture a lawnmower with an adjustable blade. If you set the blade high, you'll cut your grass at the level a grazing cow would. If you set it low, you'll cut your grass at sheep level. Sheep can graze where cattle have previously dined, but not vice versa; once sheep have grazed a meadow, cattle will find the cupboard bare.

For a while, the two ranching factions had a gentleman's agreement worked out whereby sheep would run the east side of the Goose Creek Divide, cattle the west. But as more and more sheepmen came to the area, they began to push over the divide into cattle country. Not surprisingly, this led first to animosity, then to confrontation. One of the biggest cattle dynasties in the region was the Sparks-Harrell Cattle Company. The company tired of sheepmen encroaching on its lands and decided to do something about it.

Jackson Lee Davis, a.k.a. Diamondfield Jack, showed up in Albion one day in 1895. No one knew where the mysterious stranger came from, but soon after his arrival he landed a job as a range rider with the Sparks-Harrell Company. His main duties, it seems, were not in the nature of fence-mending and cowpunching. Instead, he was employed at top dollar to keep shepherds off the ranch – a task he performed quite well by intimidation. He was only about 25 years old at the time, but he was a crack shot with a .45, talked a tough line, and tended to brag and boast loudly about his exploits, real or imagined. Soon he developed a reputation as a mean SOB.

In early February 1896, Jack and a man named Fred Gleason saddled up and rode out to tour the vast ranch. On February 17 two young shepherds were found dead in their sheep camp just east of Rogerson on Deep Creek, 80 miles southwest of Albion. Jack was immediately blamed but was nowhere to be found. A warrant went out for his arrest, and he was finally tracked down in Arizona and returned to Idaho to stand trial.

The sensational trial pitted cattlemen against sheepmen. The two dead sheepherders had been Mormons, and Albion was a Mormon town in sheep territory, so things didn't look good for Jack. Both sides hired high-powered attorneys: William Borah for the prosecution, James Hawley for the defense. Sparks-Harrell nearly went broke trying to save Jack from the gallows. Fred Gleason was tried and ac-

but the barbed wire and cow pies aren't. All in all, it's probably not worth the trip for anyone but the most curious adventurer or the duty-bound travel writer. The upside is in the views of Cache Peak, Mount Harrison, and Albion Valley that you'll get on the way back down.

For more information on the BLM lands in this area, contact the **BLM Burley District** (15 E. 200 S., Burley, 208/678-5514).

Howell Canyon Recreation Area

The popular Howell Canyon Recreation Area (free entry) in the Sawtooth National Forest above Albion offers year-round recreation opportunities ranging from camping, fishing, horseback riding, and hiking in summer to skiing and snowmobiling in winter. The road up the canyon leaves Highway 77 just south of Albion and winds its way up into the mountain heights. A good viewpoint pullout along the way puts the area's landscape into aerial perspective.

Heading up the mountain, you'll first encounter the short spur that leads down to **Bennett Springs Campground**, offering six free sites along an aspen-lined creek. Next up the hill comes the **Howell Canyon Snowmobile Area.** The trailhead parking area here serves

quitted in April 1897. Jack was convicted of first-degree murder, entirely on circumstantial evidence, and sentenced to hang on June 4, 1897. His lawyers appealed, and Jack received a stay of execution pending appeal. The appeals dragged on for four years, during which time Jack was jailed in Albion. There he became popular with the local townsfolk for his polite manners and jovial demeanor under the circumstances. Parents let their kids talk to Jack through his cell bars.

In November 1900, two cattlemen employed by Sparks-Harrell, Jeff Gray and J. E. Bower, confessed to the killing. They said they had gotten in a fight with the two sheepmen and killed them in self-defense, a story most subsequent researchers believe to be true. A corncob pipe found at the scene was identified as Bower's. The two men were tried and acquitted, the jury agreeing with the self-defense argument.

So Jack was set free, right? Wrong. Frontier justice wasn't bound by common sense. The case went all the way to the U.S. Supreme Court, which upheld the lower courts. The hanging would proceed, Jack's final days loomed, and his only hope now was a pardon from the state Board of Pardons.

The hanging was scheduled for July 3, 1901, anytime between sunrise and sunset, at the discretion of the sheriff. Thankfully, the sher-iff decided on sunset. Meanwhile, a couple of Jack's allies rode to the telegraph office in Minidoka to await word of a pardon from the Board. There was a telegraph line into Albion, but it would be too risky to rely on that – the sheepmen might cut it.

On the morning of July 3, the Board of Pardons met and commuted Jack's sentence from death to life imprisonment. He was to be transferred to Idaho Territorial Prison in Boise. The telegraph came through to Minidoka and the two riders grabbed it and rode off for Albion at breakneck speed, changing horses twice en route and arriving in Albion with just three hours to spare. When he got the news, the sheriff treated Jack to a sumptuous dinner, and the townspeople gave Jack gifts to send him on his way to Boise.

Jack spent 18 months at the Old Pen. During that time, his friends assembled enough proof of his innocence to convince the Board of Pardons to grant Jack an unconditional pardon and restoration of his good name. He was set free on December 18, 1902. On the day of his release, the state sent a buggy to take Jack from the prison into town. But first he stopped off at the old Natatorium resort on Warm Springs Boulevard and enjoyed drinks with James Hawley, his erstwhile lawyer, who had been elected mayor of Boise.

25–30 square miles of trails, mostly on snow-covered Forest Service roads.

A little higher is **Pomerelle Mountain Resort** (208/673-5599, snow report 208/673-5555, daily mid-Nov.–mid-Apr., full-day $35 adults, $25 seniors and ages 7–12, free under age 7 with an adult, night pass $15). The 8,000-foot elevation here makes for plenty of fluffy-dry powder on the area's 24 runs, all groomed; five runs are lit for night skiing (Tues.–Sat. late Dec.–mid-Mar.). A triple chair, a double chair, and a free rope tow serve 1,000 vertical feet. Snowboarders will like the half-pipe, while skinny-skiers can skate off down the small **cross-country ski** trail system on the far side of the parking lot. Rentals, lessons, and food are available at the base area, and a shuttle bus runs weekends and holidays from Jerome, Twin Falls, Burley, and Rupert. The resort is open for hiking in summer.

The ski area marks the end of the plowed road in winter. In summer, the road continues higher to **Thompson Flat Campground** (20 sites total, $8) situated near a high meadow filled with wildflowers and some cattle. The campground is in a neighboring lodgepole pine grove and is a fee area for either overnight camping or day-use picnicking, although cattle get in free.

A short distance past Thompson Flat, the road forks, the right fork descending to beautiful **Lake Cleveland.** The cirque lake is flanked on three sides by steep slopes, including some impressive granite walls. The high alpine feel makes the lake a favorite of Mini-Cassia anglers and campers. A small campground on the far (west) shore of the lake gets crowded in summer. A larger campground on the near side offers more room and fewer people, but it isn't right on the lake. Both sites are fee areas for either overnight camping or day-use picnicking. You're up at 8,300 feet—don't look for hookups. Fishing in the lake is good for rainbow trout.

Back at the fork in the road, bearing left will take you up a good graded road right to the summit of **Mount Harrison** (9,200 feet) and a Forest Service fire lookout. The irrigated farmlands down on the Snake River Plain stretch out to the northern horizon like a patchwork quilt. To the south, many of the mountains are across the state line in Utah. Mount Harrison is also known as a popular **hang gliding** area; international glider meets are occasionally held here.

Albion

Founded in 1868, Albion was a logging center for the timber cut in the Albion Mountains just outside town. The town enjoyed county-seat status until irrigation of the Snake River Plain drew most of the local populace down the hill. The county seat was moved to Burley in 1919. Albion gained particular notoriety in 1897 when Diamondfield Jack Davis was jailed, tried, and convicted for the murder of two sheepmen.

At the north end of town, a group of impressive old buildings stands abandoned on a hillock. They were constructed in 1893 for the campus of **Albion Normal School,** a state teacher's college that closed in 1951. The campus was taken over by Magic Valley Christian College, but that school also closed and moved to eastern Oregon. Eventually the state sold the 44-acre site and all the buildings to the

city of Albion. The city continues its efforts to attract some organization willing to spend the money to bring the buildings back to life. The buildings and the grounds are peaceful and beautiful; it's a shame to see them fade into oblivion.

For a good meal in Albion, visit **Sage Mountain Grill** (255 N. Main St., 208/673-6696, breakfast, lunch, and dinner daily, dinner entrées $10–29), a happening little place that dishes up homespun food with a global twist.

RUPERT AND VICINITY

Kitty-corner from Burley on the north side of I-84, Rupert is the Minidoka County seat. The U.S. Bureau of Reclamation laid out the town in 1905 when it was building Minidoka Dam. The downtown area surrounds a beautiful town square, a feature seldom seen in this part of the country.

The town might be named for a Bureau of Reclamation engineer, or it might be named for a pioneer-era mail carrier. To find out which is more likely, check in at the **Minidoka County Historical Museum** (99 E. Baseline Rd., Rupert, 208/436-0336, 1–5 P.M. Mon.–Sat., free), a mile east of town.

Rupert throws an **Independence Day Celebration** par excellence, with a rodeo, food, live music, and a big fireworks display. For more information, call the **Mini-Cassia Chamber of Commerce** (1177 7th St., Heyburn, 208/679-4793).

Minidoka Dam and Lake Walcott State Park

With the Reclamation Act of 1902, Congress authorized construction of dams along the Snake River and provided irrigated land to settlers to farm. The farmers would make annual payments to the government for a term, at the end of which they would receive title to the land along with water rights on it. Minidoka Dam was built in 1906, the first of the Reclamation Act projects on the Snake. After the dam was completed and irrigation began to turn the brown plains green, thousands of settlers disembarked at the Minidoka railroad station with hopes of sowing their dreams in southern Idaho's volcanic soil. Other dams on the Snake followed, eventually irrigating a total of 1 million acres of dry, high-desert chaparral.

A hydroelectric plant was soon added at Minidoka Dam; seven turbines weighing over five tons each were hauled in by horse-drawn wagon from the Minidoka rail station. Power from the plant—the first federal hydropower project in the Northwest—was used to pump water into the irrigation system, with the remainder delivered to surrounding towns. As a result, Rupert was one of the first towns in the country to be powered by electricity.

During construction of the 86-foot-high earth-filled dam, crews lived in an adjacent camp. When the dam was completed, their camp evolved into **Walcott Park** (208/436-1258), the focal point for recreation on the lake. The park was popular with the region's residents right from the start. On Fourth of July weekend in 1912, an estimated 500 revelers celebrated the holiday here. Today the 22-acre park is still popular with boaters, water-skiers, windsurfers, and anglers. The latter might come up with a trout, bass, or perch. Large expanses of grass and groves of mature shade trees make the park a picnickers' paradise, and beautiful walking or bike paths meander along the shoreline past cattails, cottonwoods, and willows. The campground offers tent sites ($12), RV sites with hookups ($22), and camping cabins ($50) that sleep up to five.

Minidoka National Wildlife Refuge

Lake Walcott is also the centerpiece of the Minidoka National Wildlife Refuge (208/436-3589), a 20,000-acre preserve established in 1909. Birdwatchers will have a field day; in fall, up to a 250,000 ducks and geese pass through. You might also spot whistling swans, snowy egrets, and great blue herons. Winter brings bald eagles, ospreys, Canada geese, and mallards. In spring, look for tundra swans, common loons, and lots of ducks, including buffleheads, common goldeneyes, and common mergansers. Summertime brings western and Clark's grebes and white pelicans. In addition to the abundant birdlife, the refuge also supports a healthy population of mule deer.

The U.S. Fish and Wildlife Service's refuge headquarters is next to Walcott State Park, where you'll find a campground with picnic areas and boat-launching facilities. Anglers heading out onto the water will find the fishing good for perch as well as rainbow and brown trout. Small populations of crappie and bass are also present.

Accommodations and Food

The **Uptown Motel** (102 S. Oneida St./Hwy. 24, Rupert, 208/436-8383, $35–55) is a relatively clean motor inn with 16 standard guest rooms. Amenities include cable TV and a complimentary breakfast.

If you're craving pizza and beer, go to **Doc's Pizza** (514 6th St., Rupert, 208/436-3300, lunch and dinner Mon.–Sat., $4–16). This family-friendly restaurant on the square dishes up big pizzas, nachos, and hot sandwiches. If that's not enough, take a little trip through the soup and salad bar.

EXPLORING THE WAPI FLOW AND GREAT RIFT

Confirmed desert rats, spelunkers, and lava lovers will find outstanding exploring opportunities in the barren desert northeast of Rupert. A vast sea of lava, the Wapi Flow, oozed out of a shield volcano at Pillar Butte only a relatively recent 2,100 years ago. The intense volcanic activity in this hot spot also created the Great Rift, a crack in the earth's crust over 800 feet deep in places and stretching northwest all the way to Craters of the Moon National Monument. The Great Rift has been designated a National Natural Landmark.

Note that all the sights in this area are found on unimproved dirt roads—impassable when wet, challenging when dry. As Sheldon Bluestein puts it in his book *Exploring Idaho's High Desert,* the roads require "either four-wheel-drive or maximum intestinal fortitude" to navigate. Make sure you have USGS

MAGIC VALLEY

topographic, Bureau of Land Management, or other good maps of the area. Top off your tank before you set out, and carry plenty of water with you. If ever a place called for carrying two spare tires, this is it. It's dry and desolate, and help is a long way off.

Area Highlights

The three **Baker Caves**—lava tubes, actually—were discovered in 1985 by local farmer Mark Baker and subsequently excavated by a team of archaeologists from Boise State University, the Idaho Archaeological Society, and the Bureau of Land Management (BLM). The caves held abundant evidence of human habitation dating to about 1,000 years ago. One contained the bones of some 17 bison butchered here. Also found at the site were a few stone pipes as well as evidence of cooking, bead-making, and reed arrow shafts.

The **Wood Road Kapuka** is an "island" of vegetation surrounded by pahoehoe lava. Here, pioneers cut a road in to get to the abundant junipers growing in the area, which they cut down for firewood.

Bear Trap Cave is an impressive gaping mouth in the ground suitable for a role in a Steven Spielberg movie. It's a lava tube created when an outer skin formed on a stream of lava, cooling and solidifying while the molten magma in the center of the tube flowed out. The entry to the cave is a spot where the tube's ceiling collapsed.

Crystal Ice Cave was once a commercial tourist attraction, but the site deteriorated and was closed to the public. The BLM doesn't really want people poking around the ice cave. Unlike the popular Shoshone Ice Cave, this one is not formed in a collapsed lava tube; rather, it is a part of the Great Rift, a massive fissure in the earth's crust plunging hundreds of feet deep in places. While falling in the wrong place in a lava tube might result in broken bones, a fall into the Great Rift could easily be fatal. As the sign at the site says: "Very dangerous—please stay out." The lava flows here make for excellent day hiking, however.

Other area points of interest include **Pillar**

Butte, source of the Wapi Flow; **Split Butte,** a prominent feature befitting its name; and **Higgins Blowout,** a craterlike depression in a butte near the Wood Road Kapuka.

If the foregoing descriptions have tempted you into further exploration of this unique and little-visited area, get directions and more information from the **BLM office** (15 E. 200 S., Burley, 208/678-5514).

EAST TOWARD AMERICAN FALLS
I-84 to Salt Lake City

East of the Rupert and Burley area, you'll soon come to a major interchange where I-84 splits off to the southeast heading toward Ogden, Utah, while I-86 continues westward toward American Falls and Pocatello.

I-84 crosses the Raft River Valley and climbs gradually up the Black Pine Valley through desolate undeveloped rangeland flanked most of the way by the Black Pine Range to the west and the Sublett Range to the east. Black Pine Valley (also called Juniper Valley) is home to few people but supports significant numbers of ferruginous hawks. These hawks—largest of the North American buteos—nest in the area's widespread stands of Utah juniper. They feast all summer on large local populations of jackrabbits and rodents, then head south to the southwestern United States and northern Mexico for the winter.

After cresting the pass, it's just a hop, skip, and a few gallons of gas to the Utah border.

One other note at this juncture: if time is not of the essence on your Utah-bound journey, you might consider continuing east on I-86 to the American Falls area, then turning south on one of the more rural and definitely scenic roads that eventually meet I-84 just over the Utah line at Snowville. Highway 37 leaves I-86 west of American Falls and drops through Rockland Valley, intersecting the Arbon Valley Highway outside Holbrook. The Arbon Valley Highway leaves I-86 east of American Falls and winds through beautiful wheat fields and through the Curlew National Grasslands on its way to the state line.

Eastbound on I-86

As you cruise east down I-86 bound for American Falls, you can spot a number of interesting topographical features on either side of the highway. **Horse Butte** is that big golden formation to the south just after the freeway splits. The butte is a fault scarp, relatively young in geologic age. Also to the south, you can make out three different mountain ranges along this stretch. The **Raft River Mountains** are the long, low range in the distance that seem to be running parallel to your direction of travel. They're located just across the border in Utah. The range that appears more like a single pyramid is the **Black Pine Range,** while farther east, the low, brown **Sublett Range** starts far to the south and runs north to almost directly in front of you.

On the north side of I-86, the vast black expanse of the Wapi Flow soon comes into view. The high point that you can see—a long butte with a little raised nipple toward its right edge—is **Pillar Butte,** the shield volcano that was the source of the flow.

SOUTHEAST IDAHO

Idaho is the number-one potato-producing state, and southeast Idaho is the number-one potato-producing region in the state. Across the region you'll see long A-frame potato sheds as well as miles of potato fields blooming in summer. Potatoes pervade not only the fields of southeastern Idaho but the culture as well: The mascot of the Shelley High School Russets is a gladiator potato, and the Idaho Potato Museum in Blackfoot—a kind of shrine to *Solanum tuberosum*—holds the world's largest potato chip and other spudobilia.

This corner of the state lays claim to the oldest nonnative settlement in Idaho. Franklin, near the Utah-Idaho border, was established by Mormon pioneers in 1860. These early immigrants thought they were still in Brigham Young's stronghold of Utah but ended up being Idaho's first settlers instead. The Mormons fanned out from Franklin, and today this ultraconservative bunch contributes an unmistakable character to the region. Southeast Idaho's nightlife is the state's tamest, and fine-dining opportunities are few and far between.

Pocatello and Idaho Falls are as cosmopolitan as it gets around here. Pocatello is the livelier of the two thanks to its rambunctious railroad heritage and college-town status. Idaho Falls—home to most of the employees of Idaho National Laboratory (INL), the state's single largest employer—supports a small urbane contingent that gathers at a handful of popular pubs and coffeehouses. Other noteworthy population centers include the Island Park vicinity, where folks live to snowmobile

HIGHLIGHTS

◖ Idaho State University: Idaho's second-largest university boasts beautifully landscaped grounds and the opulent Stephens Performing Arts Center. The campus is also home to the newly remodeled Idaho Museum of Natural History (page 176).

◖ Bear Lake State Park: This park doesn't offer much beyond basic campsites, but it has great access to gorgeous Bear Lake, which takes on a surrealistic turquoise hue thanks to the dissolved limestone deposits suspended in the water (page 195).

◖ Mormon Temple in Idaho Falls: It's hard to miss the golden angel Moroni perched atop this prominent temple on the Snake River. The wedding cake-like structure is the regional spiritual center for the Mormons (page 197).

◖ Harriman State Park: The fabled Henry's Fork runs through this state park, which used to be a cattle ranch for the Harriman family, who made their riches on the Union Pacific Railroad (page 215).

◖ Craters of the Moon National Monument: Take a hike among the bizarre lava-rock outcroppings and cinder cones at this barren wilderness preserve near Arco. You'll think you're on the moon (page 225).

LOOK FOR ◖ TO FIND RECOMMENDED SIGHTS, ACTIVITIES, DINING, AND LODGING.

in winter and fish the Henry's Fork in summer, and the Teton Valley, a rollicking fur-era rendezvous site that has retained a fun-loving spirit ever since.

Those looking to get away from civilization will find plenty of the big wide open. The landscape can be deceptive, especially in summer. Crossing the Snake River Plain on I-15 might lead you to think you're in low-altitude flatland, but both Pocatello and Idaho Falls lie at elevations of nearly 5,000 feet, and much of the lava-covered plain sleeps beneath a blanket of snow in winter. Not deceptive, however, are the mountains ringing southeast Idaho; they're unmistakably tall. The most prominent

of them, visible across much of the region, are the famed Tetons, rising just across the border in Wyoming. These lofty peaks provide superb slopes for downhill skiers; powder hounds flock to Grand Targhee, on the west side of the range near Driggs, as well as Jackson Hole, just a short drive to the east.

North of the Tetons, a token sliver of Yellowstone National Park slops over into Idaho. This Idaho-Wyoming border country harbors some of North America's biggest wild animals. More moose live in southeast Idaho's mountains than in any other part of the state, and grizzly bears can still be found in the area's remote highlands and valleys.

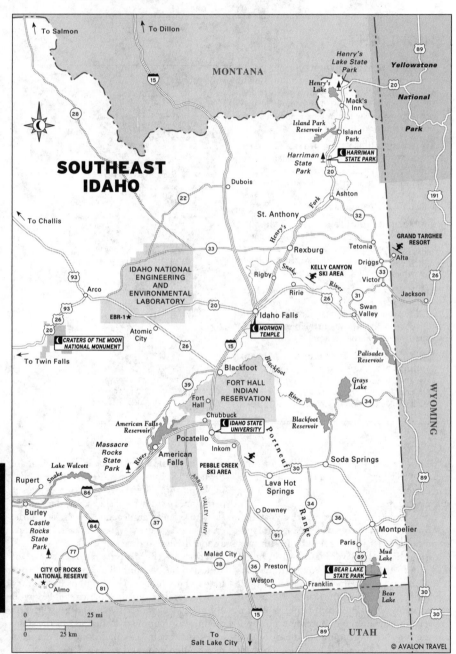

SOUTHEAST IDAHO

SOUTHEAST
IDAHO

MONTANA

To Salmon
To Dillon

Henry's
Lake State
Park

Yellowstone

Henry's
Lake

Mack's
Inn

National

Island Park
Reservoir

Island
Park

Park

Harriman
State
Park

HARRIMAN
STATE PARK

Dubois

Ashton

St. Anthony

Tetonia

GRAND TARGHEE
RESORT

To Challis

Rexburg

Driggs   Alta

IDAHO NATIONAL
ENGINEERING
AND
ENVIRONMENTAL
LABORATORY

Rigby

KELLY CANYON
SKI AREA

Victor

Ririe

Jackson

Arco

Swan
Valley

EBR-1 ★

Idaho Falls

CRATERS OF THE MOON
NATIONAL MONUMENT

Atomic
City

MORMON
TEMPLE

Palisades
Reservoir

To Twin Falls

Blackfoot

Grays
Lake

Fort
Hall

FORT HALL
INDIAN
RESERVATION

Blackfoot
Reservoir

American Falls
Reservoir

Chubbuck

IDAHO STATE
UNIVERSITY

Massacre
Rocks
State
Park

Pocatello

Inkom

Soda Springs

Lake Walcott

American
Falls

PEBBLE CREEK
SKI AREA

Rupert

Lava Hot
Springs

Burley

Castle
Rocks
State
Park

Downey

Montpelier

Paris

Mud
Lake

CITY OF ROCKS
NATIONAL RESERVE

Malad City

Preston

Almo

Weston

BEAR LAKE
STATE PARK

Franklin

Bear
Lake

0   25 mi

0   25 km

To
Salt Lake City

UTAH

WYOMING

To Challis

© AVALON TRAVEL

PLANNING YOUR TIME

You'll need the better part of a week to properly explore this expansive region. Island Park and Driggs are good base camps for year-round outdoor adventures, and you can access remote backcountry within a few minutes from either Idaho Falls or Pocatello, both along I-15.

Massacre Rocks to American Falls

MASSACRE ROCKS STATE PARK

In August 1862 three small wagon trains were plodding down the dusty Oregon Trail east of here when the first two trains in the line—the Smart and Adams parties—were attacked by a band of Shoshone. Six emigrants were killed and several more wounded. The next day, 36 men from the third wagon train in the line boldly rode out in pursuit of the Indians. They actually managed to find the Indian camp and were quickly forced to flee for their lives. Four more of their number died in the process. All told, 10 pioneers were killed. Whether that qualifies as a massacre is for you to decide.

The "massacre rocks" themselves—not actually where the skirmishes took place—straddle I-86 just north of Exit 28. The Oregon Trail passed between the rocks, just as I-86 does now. The pioneers on the trail called the narrow passage Gate of Death or Devil's Gate, reflecting their fear of Indian ambush. The name Massacre Rocks was coined long after the 1862 skirmishes by an enterprising entrepreneur who built a gas station and store here in the 1920s; the catchy name drew tourists in to find out more and perhaps buy a soda or two. The roadside stop also became a favorite gathering place for locals, but time eventually took its toll on the structures, which ended up being sold to the federal government and torn down.

Today Massacre Rocks State Park, set amid range grasses and junipers on a tranquil stretch of the Snake River, offers visitors a chance to study the area's Oregon Trail history as well as the much older history of the land itself. Evidence of the area's volcanic past abounds, as do telltale signs of the great Bonneville Flood, which roared down the river here some 14,500

years ago. Wildlife watchers and flora fans will also be enthralled; the park's 900 acres are home to more than 200 species of birds, including western grebes, white pelicans, and great blue herons, and almost 300 species of desert plants, among them locoweed, tumble mustard, and yarrow.

Geologic History

The Snake River Plain–Yellowstone geologic province, which includes the park, is a volcanic swath that began to erupt 15 million years ago. At Massacre Rocks the eruptions took place some 6.5 million years ago. The volcanoes weren't the towering, exploding type like Vesuvius, Krakatoa, or Mount St. Helens. Rather they were shield volcanoes, cracks in the earth's skin through which molten lava flowed out like blood from a wound. At Massacre Rocks, as the 2,000°F molten lava rose toward the earth's surface, it came in contact with the water in the Snake River Plain Aquifer. The water instantly turned to steam and created lava geysers, spattering yellow-brown volcanic tuff in all directions. Subsequent flows covered the older ones. The lava rock you see across the river to the north is much younger than that on the south side—only 75,000 years old. By comparison, the youngest flows in Idaho were along the Great Rift, north of Massacre Rocks, where the lava oozed out of the earth just 2,100 years ago.

Long after the lava flows ceased, another cataclysmic event further altered the landscape. Utah's Great Salt Lake is still fairly large today, but it's just a small remnant of enormous Lake Bonneville, which once covered some 20,000 square miles of Utah, eastern Nevada, and southern Idaho. About 14,500

SOUTHEAST IDAHO

years ago, the lake overflowed its natural rock dam, which soon collapsed under the force of the rushing water. Some 1,000 cubic miles of water burst through Red Rock Pass, smashing down through today's Marsh Valley, Portneuf Narrows, and Pocatello. The flood lasted about eight weeks and was the second-largest known flood in history. It held more water than the total annual flow of all the major rivers in North America combined. The floodwaters carved out the Snake River channel, carrying boulders along with it. When the waters finally receded, these boulders were dropped downstream as "melon gravel." The flood also carved out secondary channels that today appear like hanging valleys along the Snake River rim.

Visitors Center

Start off at the park visitors center, where you pay the standard state park $5-per-vehicle entrance fee. The small center overlooks the Massacre Rocks and provides a multipanel route map of the entire Oregon Trail from Independence, Missouri, to the Pacific Ocean, showing highlights and major stops along the way. The visitors center's other exhibits focus on the area's cultural and natural history. Many pioneer-era artifacts are on display. You'll find trailheads for the Geology Exhibit and Yahandeka Trails here as well.

Devil's Garden

A fenced-off area alongside the upper campground loop encloses Devil's Garden, a plot roughly 50 feet square holding numerous small pinnacles, each around six inches high. An interpretive sign theorizes that the pinnacles were formed when escaping gas vented through the volcanic ash, carrying silica up with it. The silica glued the ash together, creating hardened areas around each vent hole. The softer ash around the vents eventually eroded away, leaving the small pinnacles standing above the surrounding surface.

Register Rock

Along Rock Creek, a few miles west of the park proper, is a shady day-use area once popular with Oregon Trail wagon trains. Register Rock bears the carved-in signatures of dozens of emigrants who passed this way, including "H. Chestnut, Aug 20 1869." Now the rock is surrounded by a vandal-discouraging, seven-foot-high chain-link fence and sheltered by a gazebo. If you didn't pay the $5 entrance fee at the main park entrance, you'll have to pay it here. Mature shade trees and grassy lawns surround the rock, making the site eminently picnickable. To reach Register Rock, cross to the south side of the highway at the Massacre Rocks State Park exit and follow the signs.

Hiking Trails

Six different hiking trails thread their way through the park, one or another taking you down to the river, to high points overlooking the river, or to Oregon Trail ruts on the south side of the freeway. Start with the **Yahandeka Trail,** a 0.25-mile, self-guided interpretive trail that loops out from the visitors center. Interpretive signs along the way point out common vegetation in the area and explain some of the park's unique topography. Along any of the trails you're likely to surprise a cottontail bounding through the brush or see a white pelican or two cruising elegantly through the sky above your head. Also of note is the short **Geology Exhibit** trail starting at the visitors center. The trail climbs up to a great viewpoint of river and rocks, where signs detail the park's volcanic origins and explain how the Bonneville Flood reshaped a large part of southern Idaho.

Campground Facilities

The park's 52 campsites ($22–38) are divided into two loops. The upper loop is less crowded but a little closer to I-86 and therefore noisier. The lower loop is closer to the water, quieter, but more crowded and susceptible to swarms of bloodthirsty bugs. Both loops have some pull-through sites, some double sites, water, and restrooms with showers. All sites have water faucets and power outlets; site 23 is wheelchair-friendly. An RV dump station is available, and boaters can launch their watercraft at the ramp to the west of the interstate exit. The park is open for camping year-round, but facilities are limited in winter. Massacre Rocks also has two cabins ($50) that sleep up to five people.

To make campsite reservations, contact the Massacre Rocks State Park office (3592 N. Park Lane, American Falls, 208/548-2672).

AMERICAN FALLS AND VICINITY

Visitors coming to American Falls in search of a waterfall will be disappointed—they no longer exist. When American Falls Dam was built in 1925, it provided electricity to the city but obliterated the falls. The reservoir also inundated the original town site. The whole town was moved beforehand, but when the lake level drops in prime summer irrigation season, you can spy an old grain elevator and other evidence of southeast Idaho's Atlantis.

American Falls sits squarely in potato country, and farming drives its economy. Recreation on the reservoir provides the bulk of the local fun for the town's residents; it's especially popular with windsurfers, who take advantage of the strong winds that regularly rip across the Snake River Plain. Basic accommodations and food are available.

American Falls Dam and Reservoir

The largest reservoir on the Snake River and the second largest in the state, the American Falls impoundment offers recreation opportunities of all sorts, including fishing, waterskiing, sailing, and windsurfing. A Bureau of Reclamation **visitors center** (May–Oct.) on the dam's north side has historical photos and exhibits relating to the moving of the original town site and the dam's 1977 reconstruction as well as information on facilities around the reservoir. You'll also find a boat ramp and picnic areas.

Two marinas are on the reservoir near American Falls: **Willow Bay Recreation Area** is just north of town. It offers a boat-launch area, camping, bike paths, picnic areas, ball fields, horseshoe pits, and a burgers-and-fries café. Farther east—take I-86 Exit 44 and wind around some dirt roads down to the water, following the signs—is **Seagull Bay Yacht Club** (208/226-2086), a small private marina where nonmembers are welcome for a small fee.

Just below the dam on the river's south side is the Bureau of Reclamation's **Oregon Trail River Access,** offering boat ramps, docks, and restrooms but nothing in the way of grass or shade. To get here, take Lincoln Street to Falls Avenue to Valdez Street.

Pocatello and Vicinity

Pocatello (population 54,000) began in 1864 as a stage stop named after Chief Pocataro of the region's Shoshones. Pocataro (meaning unknown) and his warriors were a thorn in the side of encroaching settlers in this area until 1863, when the U.S. Army finally forced them into submission. Pocataro signed a peace treaty and ended up on the Fort Hall Reservation, where he died in 1884. His gravesite today can be seen only with scuba gear—it was flooded when American Falls Reservoir was created in 1925.

In 1879 the iron horse came to town, belching soot and putting Pocatello on the map when the Utah and Northern Railroad extended north from Salt Lake City and Franklin. It was followed five years later by the Oregon Short Line pushing west from Montana into Oregon. Pocatello became a regional division point and the biggest rail hub west of the Mississippi. By 1920 it had grown into a bustling city of 15,000, with a lively mix of people and commerce that enabled it to become a libertine oasis in the land of the Latter-day Saints.

Today, despite the continued presence of the railroad and the added presence of the university, Pocatello is relatively quiet. You can actually find bars and coffeehouses here—not

SOUTHEAST IDAHO

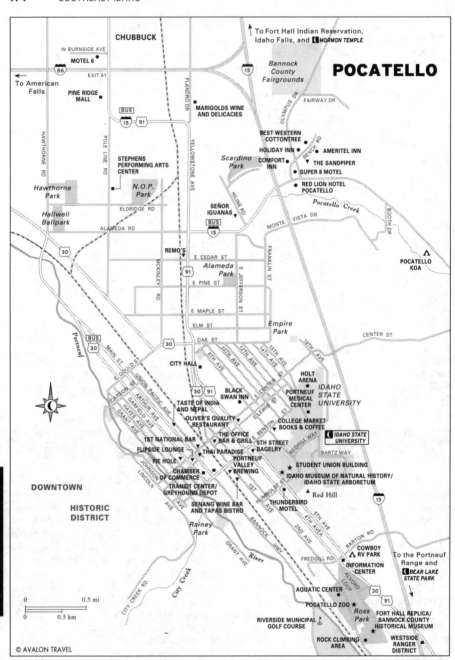

CHUBBUCK

W BURNSIDE AVE

MOTEL 6

86 EXIT 61

To American Falls

PINE RIDGE MALL

BUS 15 91

MARIGOLDS WINE AND DELICACIES

To Fort Hall Indian Reservation, Idaho Falls, and **MORMON TEMPLE**

15

Bannock County Fairgrounds

POCATELLO

OLYMPUS DR

FAIRWAY DR

BEST WESTERN COTTONTREE

HOLIDAY INN

Scardino Park

COMFORT INN

BENCH RD

AMERITEL INN

THE SANDPIPER

SUPER 8 MOTEL

RED LION HOTEL POCATELLO

STEPHENS PERFORMING ARTS CENTER

N.O.P. Park

Hawthorne Park

Halliwell Ballpark

HAWTHORNE RD

POLE LINE RD

ELDRIDGE RD

ALAMEDA RD

YELLOWSTONE AVE

FLANDRO DR

SEÑOR IGUANAS

BUS 15

Pocatello Creek

MONTE VISTA DR

HILINE RD

BOOTH DR

POCATELLO KOA

30

REMO'S

E CEDAR ST

Alameda Park

91

E PINE ST

E MAPLE ST

ELM ST

OAK ST

MCKINLEY RD

FRANKLIN ST

E JEFFERSON ST

Empire Park

CENTER ST

Portneuf

BUS 30

30

CITY HALL

MAIN ST

GOULD ST

UNION PACIFIC AVE

8TH AVE

10TH AVE

12TH AVE

14TH AVE

15TH AVE

18TH AVE

19TH AVE

30 91

BLACK SWAN INN

HOLT ARENA

PORTNEUF MEDICAL CENTER

IDAHO STATE UNIVERSITY

TASTE OF INDIA AND NEPAL

OLIVER'S QUALITY RESTAURANT

THE OFFICE BAR & GRILL

1ST NATIONAL BAR

FLIPSIDE LOUNGE

PIE HOLE

CHAMBER OF COMMERCE

THAI PARADISE

5TH STREET BAGELRY

PORTNEUF VALLEY BREWING

COLLEGE MARKET BOOKS & COFFEE

E CENTER ST

E LEWIS ST

E BENTON ST

REDHILL WAY

IDAHO STATE UNIVERSITY

BARTZ WAY

STUDENT UNION BUILDING

IDAHO MUSEUM OF NATURAL HISTORY/ IDAHO STATE ARBORETUM

Red Hill

CARSON ST

ARTHUR AVE

GARFIELD AVE

HAYES AVE

GRANT AVE

JOHNSON AVE

LINCOLN AVE

DOWNTOWN

HISTORIC DISTRICT

TRANSIT CENTER/ GREYHOUND DEPOT

SENANG WINE BAR AND TAPAS BISTRO

Rainey Park

THUNDERBIRD MOTEL

BANNOCK HWY

HUMBOLDT ST

1ST AVE

2ND AVE

4TH AVE

5TH AVE

6TH AVE

15

BARTON RD

COWBOY RV PARK

INFORMATION CENTER

To the Portneuf Range and **BEAR LAKE STATE PARK**

FREDGILL RD

ALVORD LOOP

30

91

AQUATIC CENTER

POCATELLO ZOO

RIVERSIDE MUNICIPAL GOLF COURSE

Ross Park

FORT HALL REPLICA/ BANNOCK COUNTY HISTORICAL MUSEUM

WESTSIDE RANGER DISTRICT

ROCK CLIMBING AREA

CITY CREEK RD

GRANT AVE

City Creek

River

Rainey Park

0   0.5 mi

0   0.5 km

© AVALON TRAVEL

always a given in Mormon country—but the street scene after dark is minimal, and the clubs are relatively tame.

One worthwhile activity in Pocatello is watching the summer sunsets. The late-afternoon light comes shooting in low and bright off the northwestern horizon, rolling down the Snake River Plain. You can head up to Red Hill on the Idaho State University campus for the best show.

SIGHTS
Historic Buildings
Downtown Pocatello's historic district, bounded roughly by Garfield Avenue and the railroad tracks and by Lander and Lewis Streets, holds a number of architectural delights dating back to the 19th century. Among the highlights: the 1898 **Trinity Episcopal Church** (248 N. Arthur Ave.); the 1916 **Valentine Building** and the 1919 **Carlson Building,** kitty-corner from each other at Arthur Avenue and Center Street; and the 1916 **Yellowstone Hotel** (230 W. Bonneville St.), down by the Old Oregon

Short Line–Union Pacific Depot at the east end of West Bonneville Street.

The most beautiful old building in town is the **Standrod Mansion** (648 N. Garfield Ave.), built in 1901. The gorgeous sandstone castle was designed by San Francisco architect Marcus Grundfor in a Classical Revival style; its interior is filled with oak, tile, and imported French marble.

Ross Park
Pocatello's biggest city park has a number of attractions worth a visit. On the lower level of the park is **Pocatello Zoo** (2900 S. 2nd Ave., 208/234-6264, www.pocatellozoo.org, 10 A.M.–6 P.M. daily June 16–Labor Day, limited hours Apr. 15–June 16 and Labor Day–Oct. 31, $4.50 ages 12–59, $3.25 over age 59, $2.50 ages 3–11, free under age 3), home to a humble menagerie of bears, badgers, bobcats, bison, mountain goats, mountain lions, and more. The new grizzly exhibit has been a big draw. Kids will surely like the petting barn.

Also on the lower level of the park you'll find

© IDAHO DIVISION OF TOURISM

Pocatello's Old Town

grassy and shaded picnic areas, horseshoe pits, volleyball courts, baseball fields, a playground, and the city's recently remodeled and expanded **Aquatic Center** (208/234-0472, $5.25 adults, $4.75 ages 10–17, $3.25 ages 4–9, $1.75 under age 4), which offers lap pools, waterslides, water volleyball, and even inner tubing on a "Lazy River." Lockers are available, but you'll need your own lock.

Upper Ross Park, accessed from Alvord Loop off South 5th Avenue, offers, among other things, the **Fort Hall Replica** (208/234-1795, 10 A.M.–2 P.M. Tues.–Sat. mid-Apr.–Memorial Day, 10 A.M.–6 P.M. daily June–Labor Day, 10 A.M.–2 P.M. daily Sept., $2.50 adults, $2 seniors, $1.50 ages 12–17, $1 ages 3–11), a reconstructed version of one of the most important trading posts on the Oregon Trail. Native Americans, fur trappers, and pioneers all congregated at the fort, which stood north of today's Pocatello on what is now the Fort Hall Indian Reservation. The reconstruction—recreated from the original plans—allows you a look at life here circa 1830–1850. Within the thick adobe walls are blacksmith and carpentry shops, a large Native American exhibit, and exhibits on the fort's history and the Oregon Trail. You can often see the zoo's hoofed animals better from the parking lot of the old fort than you can from the walkways inside the zoo itself. Kids can get a free look at the bison, deer, pronghorn, and other ungulates from behind the fence.

Next to the fort is the **Bannock County Historical Museum** (3000 Alvord Loop, 208/233-0434, 9 A.M.–6 P.M. daily Memorial Day–Labor Day, 10 A.M.–2 P.M. Tues.–Sat. Labor Day–Memorial Day, $4 adults, $3 seniors, $2 children).

The cliffs separating Upper and Lower Park are used for **rock climbing** practice. Some 75 recorded single-pitch routes vary in difficulty from 5.7 to 5.12c. About one-third of the climbs are bolted. Two different parking areas access opposite sides of the cliffs. To reach the "shady side," head for Lower Ross Park as if you were going to the zoo, but continue past it. Look for a big open parking area; the cliffs

are clearly visible. To get out to the sunny side, head south of town on 5th Street until it joins with 4th Street to form Old Bannock Highway, then look for the cliffs on the right.

Note that you'll have to leave Fido at home; no dogs are allowed in the park.

◖ Idaho State University

Idaho State University (ISU, 208/282-2700, University Relations 208/282-3620, www.isu.edu) began in 1901 as a two-year community and vocational college. By 1927 it had grown sufficiently large to warrant its designation as the southern branch of the University of Idaho. In 1947 it became Idaho State College, and in 1963 it gained its current status. Today, its enrollment is about 15,500. The 735-acre campus fronts South 5th Avenue, with its main entrance at South 5th Avenue and East Humbolt Street.

Several buildings on campus are worth a special mention. The recently renovated and expanded **Idaho Museum of Natural History** (S. 5th Ave. and E. Dillon St., 208/282-3317, 12:30–5 P.M. Wed.–Fri., 10 A.M.–5 P.M. Sat., $6 adults, $5 over age 55, $4 ISU students, $3 ages 4–11) offers displays focusing on important events in Idaho's natural history. This is the best place in the state to learn about dinosaurs and other prehistoric creatures that used to roam Idaho, including the remains of a Columbian mammoth found near Grangeville, which was excavated by ISU museum paleontologists in the mid-1990s.

At the museum you can also pick up a brochure detailing a guided walking tour to the **Idaho State Arboretum** (208/282-3317), a collection of labeled trees and shrubs spread around the museum grounds. Among the 51 botanical species you'll see are syringa, Idaho's fragrant state flower, and its cousin, the mock orange.

Also on campus are **Holt Arena** (208/282-2831), a large sports, concerts, and events venue, and the newly remodeled **Student Union Building,** which houses a movie theater (208/282-2701), a bowling alley (208/282-3335), a bookstore (208/282-3237), the ISU

© JAMES P. KELLY

Idaho Museum of Natural History, on the Idaho State University campus

Outdoor Program office (208/282-3912), and the Wilderness Rental Center (208/282-2945).

Fort Hall Indian Reservation

The Shoshone and Bannock of the Fort Hall Reservation were two separate peoples speaking two different languages yet sharing many cultural similarities. Both groups were hunters and gatherers who roamed the Great Basin region of Nevada, Utah, Wyoming, and Idaho in search of fish and game. When the nonnatives arrived, the two tribes were muscled onto the Fort Hall Reservation, established in 1867. The reservation originally encompassed 1.8 million acres, but 20 years later the allotment process of the Dawes Act reduced the size of the reservation to about 540,000 acres, where many of the 3,900 enrolled tribe members live today.

The reservation is just north of Pocatello on I-15. To learn more about its history and people, head for the **Shoshone-Bannock Tribal Museum** (208/237-9791, 9:30 A.M.–5 P.M. daily, $2.50 adults, $1 ages 6–18, free for tribe members with ID) just off I-15 Exit 80. You can view exhibits and historical photographs preserving their heritage and buy books, posters, and Native American art. You can also arrange tours of the Fort Hall Bottoms to view both the reservation's buffalo herd and the site of Nathaniel Wyeth's original 1834 Fort Hall trading post.

Across the street from the museum is the reservation's Trading Post complex, with a restaurant, a casino, and a gift shop selling Native American–made goods.

Some of the region's best fishing can be found on the reservation, on a stretch of the Snake River in the Fort Hall Bottoms, essentially the inlet waters of American Falls Reservoir. Few anglers compete for the plentiful 5–7-pound trout. To fish the Bottoms, you'll need to pick up a permit from the tribe, available at the TP Gas and Truck Stop at I-15 Exit 80. The fishing season usually runs April–October.

The spectacular **Shoshone-Bannock Indian Festival and Rodeo** (www.sbtribes.com/festival) draws Native Americans and nonnatives

SOUTHEAST IDAHO

from all over the United States and Canada. Traditional Indian dancing takes center stage—multitudes of dancers and drummers come attired in intricate dress and face paint. In addition, the event features a rodeo, an arts and crafts show, and a softball tourney. It all takes place the second week of August at the Fort Hall rodeo grounds.

RECREATION
Portneuf Greenway

This recreational path has been a work in progress since its inception in the mid-1990s. The idea for the Portneuf Greenway (208/234-4929, www.pgfweb.com), which gives bicyclists, joggers, and walkers a place to play along the Portneuf River, was spearheaded by a local nonprofit organization. There are 13 miles of connected paved trails, starting north of Poky at Swanson Reach and running south through the heart of Old Town, and then over to the university en route to the Edson Fichter Trail and Nature Area. All the dots have yet to be connected, but look for big developments along this scenic path in the coming years. You can pick up a trail map for $1 at the community recreation center (144 Wilson Ave., Pocatello, 208/232-3901) or at the chamber of commerce.

Hiking and Mountain Biking

The **Gibson Jack Trailhead,** at the top of Gibson Jack Road off Bannock Highway, offers access to one of the nicest hiking opportunities in the Pocatello area. The trail follows Gibson Jack Creek into a Research Natural Area, closed to motorized vehicles. It's about four miles from the trailhead to a gate at the area boundary. You won't find a single head of cattle on this spread, and as a result, the watercourse is in excellent shape. The creek is too small to offer much in the way of a swimming hole, but a couple of "dabbling holes" can cool the feet on a hot summer day.

City Creek is a local favorite for hiking and mountain biking. Following the trail up the creek will eventually take you to the top of **Kinport Peak** (7,222 feet), a quick fix for local mountaineers when time doesn't permit a trip to more rarefied realms. To get to the trail, take West Center Street west to Lincoln Avenue and turn left, and then right on City Creek Road. You can access this area from the Portneuf Greenway.

Mink Creek, south of town, provides a major focus for outdoor recreation in the area. The Bannock Highway, which originates on the southwest side of Pocatello, parallels the hills for several miles before veering right and climbing alongside Mink Creek. The road continues up and over Crystal Summit and down to the Arbon Valley on the other side of the range. Along the way it passes numerous trailheads offering gateways into the Bannock Range. The bottom of Mink Creek can also be accessed from the Portneuf Area exit of I-15 South (Exit 57).

Starting at the bottom of the hill, **Cherry Springs Nature Area** is the first turnout, where you'll find a beautiful nature trail winding through the creek-bed vegetation and breaking out onto the slopes on the far side. It's a day-use-only area. Continuing up Mink Creek, you'll pass trailheads to **Slate Mountain, West Mink Creek, Valve House Draw, Corral Creek-South Fork Mink Creek,** and **Porcelain Pot Gulch** before topping out at Crystal Summit—just under 6,000 feet in elevation. Some of these trailheads serve cross-country skiers and snowmobilers in winter.

Alpine Skiing

Pebble Creek Ski Area (3340 E. Green Canyon Rd., Inkom, 208/775-4452, snow report 208/775-4451, www.pebblecreekskiarea.com, Fri.–Sun. until Dec. 24, closed Dec. 25, daily Dec. 26–Feb., Wed.–Sun. Mar., Fri.–Sun. Apr., night skiing until 9:30 P.M. Fri.–Sat. Jan.–mid-Mar., full-day lift tickets $39 adults, $25 ages 6–12 and over age 69, $3 under age 6, beginner-lift-only tickets $12) is up East Green Canyon Road, just a short drive south of town on I-15 (follow signs from the Inkom exits). With 1,100 acres on Mount Bonneville, the small resort offers 2,200 vertical feet served by two double chairs and one triple chair. Head for Al's Drop to get your adrenaline pumping. Skiing, telemarking, and snowboarding lessons are offered, and rentals are available; day care is also available.

Portneuf Range Yurt System

On Pocatello's eastern flank lies a cross-country skier's nirvana. Wide-open snow-covered wheat fields gradually give way to the high ridges and backcountry bowls of the Portneuf Range—all just minutes from town. As a bonus, the area has a public yurt system. Several of the canvas-topped Mongolian-style shelters are spread across the area from just east of town to just north of Pebble Creek Ski Area. Some can be reached by novice skiers, and others require more skiing ability and backcountry savvy. Each is equipped with plywood bunk beds, a woodstove, a cook stove, a lantern, pots, a shovel, and an ax. You'll need to bring all your own winter-camping gear as well as mantles for the lantern and camping fuel for both the lantern and the stove. Most yurts sleep six.

Maintenance of the yurts is overseen by Idaho State University's Outdoor Program, but all users are expected to help keep the huts shoveled out and in good shape. The main office of the Outdoor Program (Student Union Building, S. 5th Ave. and E. Humboldt St., Pocatello, 208/282-3912) has maps and more information. Reservations are required and are made through the **ISU Wilderness Rental Center** (208/282-2945); call for information and current fees, which vary depending on the yurt and night of the week. Weekends tend to book up fast.

Don't let the fact that these yurts were built by public agencies lull you into a false sense of security in the backcountry. Avalanches aren't common but aren't unheard of; winter navigation is often problematic; and winter temperatures can bring hypothermia and even death to the unprepared. If you have any doubts about your backcountry skills, enjoy the yurts on an organized guided tour. Tours are offered periodically by the Outdoor Program and by the Pocatello Parks and Recreation Department (911 N. 7th Ave., Pocatello, 208/234-6232).

Other Cross-Country Ski Areas

The treks to the two lower yurts begin from **Rapid Creek Park N' Ski Area,** 11 miles north of Inkom on Rapid Creek Road at the junction with McKee Road. Trails are groomed regularly and include loops ranging from 1.2 miles to more than two miles in length.

Inman Canyon Park N' Ski, the trailhead to the Inman yurt, is four miles northeast of Inkom, up Rapid Creek and Inman Canyon Roads. The trailhead and some of the area's trail system are shared with snowmobilers, so be alert.

Five cross-country ski trailheads lie up Mink Creek, 15 miles south of Pocatello on the west side of the Bannock Range. Take Bannock Highway south and bear right at the Y just before Mink Creek; if you hit the town of Portneuf, you've gone too far. About 15 miles of beginner to intermediate trails are marked and groomed periodically; other ungroomed trails lace the area.

Heading up the creek, you'll first pass the turnoff up the East Fork. About a mile down this road is the **East Mink Creek** trailhead, shared with snowmobilers. Back on the main road and continuing up Mink Creek proper you'll pass several trails and trailheads, listed in order as you head up the canyon: **West Mink Creek** is a very popular, moderately difficult trail that leads through a Research Natural Area for four miles to a warming hut. **Valve House Draw** trail is well suited to beginner skiers. The **Corral Creek-South Fork Mink Creek** trail starts out as moderately difficult, then becomes steeper. It's little used and recommended for advanced skiers looking for solitude. The **Porcelain Pot** trail, up in the nosebleed zone at 6,000 feet, is a well-developed intermediate trail. Finally, the **Parity Trails** begin at Crystal Summit. One loops north to connect with the Corral Creek trail. A second, shorter loop connects with the Porcelain Pot trail; it's rated "More Difficult," entailing a challenging steep grade near Crystal Summit.

Outfitters

The on-campus **ISU Wilderness Rental Center** (Student Union Building, S. 5th Ave. and

E. Humboldt St., Pocatello, 208/282-2945, www.isu.edu/outdoor) rents a wide variety of gear for rafting, kayaking, skiing, snowboarding, camping, and hiking. It's also an excellent place to learn about recreational opportunities throughout Southeast Idaho.

ENTERTAINMENT AND EVENTS
Nightlife
Among other bars in Old Town, **1st National Bar** (232 W. Center St., Pocatello, 208/233-1516, until late nightly) is a venerable rock-and-roll and blues dance bar where a lot of local bands cut their teeth on the way to the small time. Don't be surprised to see some mullets and ripped jeans.

Nearby, college students and other younger folks go underground at the **Flipside Lounge** (117 S. Main St., Pocatello, 208/233-2116, until late Mon.–Sat.), a new club that brings to town alternative bands from around the Northwest. This intimate downstairs bar also has a funky dance floor, kept thumping late into the night by the in-house DJs.

Just across the tracks from downtown or through the tunnel, **The Office Bar & Grill** (251 E. Center St., Pocatello, 208/232-9816, until late nightly) is a popular weekend nightspot where middle-age types go on the lustful prowl. It's definitely a friendly place.

Performing Arts
Idaho State University's newish Stephens Performing Arts Center (1002 Sam Nixon Ave., Pocatello, 208/282-3595, www.isu.edu/stephens) is the beating heart of Poky's cultural scene. The impressive 123,000-square-foot building, perched on a hill above campus, boasts several venues, including the 1,200-seat Jensen Grand Concert Hall. Live theater, national touring acts and musical productions, and campus concertos—this place has it going on. The center is also home to the **Idaho State Civic Symphony** (208/234-1587, www.thesymphony.us), which presents about nine classical performances

September–April. In addition to the regular season, an annual pops concert features contemporary works.

Events
The **Dodge National Circuit Finals Rodeo** (208/233-1546, www.dncfr.org) comes to Holt Arena around the first week of April. It's a biggy—the country's second-largest points-qualifying rodeo. The top two cowboys from each of 12 circuits nationwide compete for glory and a goodly sum of cash. Out at Pebble Creek Ski Area the same time of year, the **Cowboy Classic Slalom and Barrel Race** (www.pebblecreekskiarea.com) features rodeo pros riding barrels down the mountain in a wild spectacle.

The **Revive at 5** summer concert series (Old Town Pavilion, 420 N. Main St., Pocatello, 5–8 P.M. Wed. late May–early Sept.) has a lineup of rock and jazz bands. For a complete events calendar, contact the **Greater Pocatello Chamber of Commerce** (324 S. Main St., Pocatello, 208/233-1525, www.pocatelloidaho.com).

ACCOMMODATIONS
Under $50
Several lodgings lie on either side of I-86 at the Chubbuck exit (Exit 61). This lodging area is closest to the airport. On the north side of I-86 is **Motel 6** (291 W. Burnside Ave., Pocatello, 208/237-7880 or 800/466-8356, under $40 s). This is one of the cheapest Motel 6s you'll find anywhere, and children 17 and under stay free with an adult family member. Amenities include a seasonal pool, cable TV, and a coin laundry.

The **Thunderbird Motel** (1415 S. 5th Ave., Pocatello, 208/232-6330 or 888/978-2473, www.thunderbirdmotelid.com, from $41) is just across the street from the ISU campus and close to Ross Park and downtown. It has an outdoor pool in summer and a guest laundry year-round, and some guest rooms have refrigerators and microwaves. Pets are welcome for a small extra charge.

$50-100

Clustered up against the hill on the east side of town (I-15 Exit 71) are most of the city's upscale chain motels. Among the cheapest in this category, but pretty ritzy for the money, is **Super 8** (1330 Bench Rd., Pocatello, 208/234-0888 or 866/378-7378, from $76 d), with 80 guest rooms. King rooms with in-room jetted tubs are available. Children under 13 stay free.

Red Lion Hotel Pocatello (1555 Pocatello Creek Rd., Pocatello, 208/233-2200 or 800/325-4000, from $79 d) offers a restaurant and lounge, an indoor pool, jetted tub, and sauna, and a small exercise room. Pets are allowed with a deposit; nonsmoking guest rooms and a coin laundry are available.

AmeriTel Inn (1440 Bench Rd., Pocatello, 208/234-7500 or 800/600-6001, from $79 d) has 148 guest rooms that include a number of suites, some with kitchenettes, some with king beds and in-room spas. All guest rooms have cable TV with free HBO, desks with phones, and Wi-Fi. Other amenities include an indoor pool, spa, and fitness center open 24 hours; complimentary continental breakfast and fresh-baked desserts in the evenings; and a free airport shuttle.

A little farther up the hill is **Best Western Cottontree Inn** (1415 Bench Rd., Pocatello, 208/237-7650 or 800/662-6886, from $89 d). King beds, kitchenettes, and family rates are available, and 60 percent of the guest rooms are nonsmoking. Amenities include a pool, a hot tub, cable TV, a guest laundry, and an on-site restaurant.

Holiday Inn (1399 Bench Rd., Pocatello, 208/237-1400 or 800/200-8944, from $79 d) has 196 guest rooms. With its Holidome indoor recreation area (including a pool complete with waterfall) and kids-eat-free restaurant policy, this is a good place for families. Other amenities include a guest laundry, a game room, and a fitness center.

$150-250

The **Black Swan Inn** (746 E. Center St., Pocatello, 208/233-3051, www.blackswaninn.

com, weekends $129–199, less weekdays) offers more than a dozen "Fantasy Theme Suites." Examples include the Caveman Suite, the Pirates Suite, the Jungle Falls Suite—check the website for pictures of the whole place. The Sea Cave Suite is home to a lovely mermaid. It's a fine line between "fantasy" and "cheese," and it's up to you to decide about this place.

CAMPING AND RVING

RV Parks

Pocatello KOA (9815 W. Pocatello Creek Rd., Pocatello, 208/233-6851, www.koa.com) is up Pocatello Creek Road past the cluster of motels and restaurants by I-15. The campground offers 48 RV sites with hookups ($30–37), four cabins ($43–47), and 18 tent sites ($18–28). A dump station is free to guests; nonguests can use it for a fee. Facilities include showers, a laundry, a game room, a playground, and a small grocery store that also sells gasoline and propane.

Cowboy RV Park (845 Barton Rd., Pocatello, 208/232-4587), on the south end of town near Ross Park, offers 41 RV sites with full hookups ($30–35) and four tent sites ($10–15). Facilities at this Good Sam park include showers and laundry.

U.S. Forest Service Campground

Caribou National Forest's Westside North Ranger District (4350 Cliffs Dr., Pocatello, 208/236-7500) supervises **Scout Mountain Campground** (24 sites, $10) perched at 6,500 feet on the shoulder of 8,700-foot Scout Mountain. Nearby is the East Mink trailhead, with trails that crisscross the mountains. To get to the campground, head south of town either on Bannock Highway or I-15 South (exit at the "Portneuf Area Recreation" sign, Exit 63). About five miles up the hill from the Bannock Highway–Portneuf Road junction, the East Fork road turns to the left. Follow the road to the campground at the end. Tightwads might prefer one of the free unofficial campsites found in several places along the East Fork, along the road to the campground.

FOOD

Upscale Fare

The Sandpiper (1400 Bench Rd., Pocatello, 208/233-1000, www.pocatellosandpiper.com, dinner from 4:30 P.M. Mon.–Sat., entrées $14–32) is part of a small regional chain that serves up reliably comfortable atmosphere and excellent food and drink. The menu emphasizes steak and seafood, but chicken, pork, and lamb dishes and first-rate salads are also available. An extensive list of microbrews and fine wines by the bottle or glass complements the dinner menu.

(Senang Wine Bar and Tapas Bistro (815 S. 1st Ave., Pocatello, 208/478-6732, www.senangtapas.com, 11:30 A.M.–11 P.M. Tues.–Sat., $8–26) is Pocatello's best restaurant in terms of contemporary cuisine. This elegant new bistro and wine bar, downtown in an old brick warehouse, serves a large menu of wine-friendly fare. Expect to see small plates like an artisanal cheeseboard, pan-seared prawns with chipotle-lime glaze, and roasted beets with goat cheese. Larger plates include creative versions of classic steak, seafood, and poultry dishes in accordance with the season. And, of course, there are more than 150 labels on the wine list, 50 of which are served by the glass.

Casual Dining

Remo's (160 W. Cedar St., Pocatello, 208/233-1710, www.remosrestaurant.com, lunch and dinner Mon.–Sat., entrées $12–32) is often cited as one of the city's best restaurants. Appetizers like roasted garlic on a baguette and carpaccio—thin slices of filet mignon with capers, sliced red onions, and Dijon sauce—start things off. Entrées feature steak and seafood with an Italian emphasis; pastas like garlic chicken fettuccine Alfredo; poultry dishes like chicken parmigiana; and lots of pizzas. The food is above average, and the wine list is among the best in town, including more than a dozen Italian reds. In summer you can dine alfresco on the casual front patio–bar, a pleasant spot on all but the hottest days.

For good pub grub and handcrafted ales, check out **Portneuf Valley Brewing** (615 S. 1st Ave., Pocatello, 208/232-1644, www.portneufvalleybrewing.com, 11 A.M.–10 P.M. Mon.–Thurs., 11 A.M.–midnight Fri.–Sat., $7–14). You'll find nachos, hot wings, big burgers, and pasta dishes washed down with Twisted Stick Amber Ale and Sunshine Pale Ale. The brewpub hosts live music four nights a week.

Ethnic Cuisine

Señor Iguanas (961 Hiline Rd., Pocatello, 208/233-4422, lunch and dinner Mon.–Sat.) doesn't drench its food in cheese the way many other Mexican restaurants do. The chiles rellenos, tamales, burritos, enchiladas, and shrimp dishes are consistent favorites. As an added bonus, you can also get a lime with your *cerveza*.

Fans of Thailand will surely enjoy **Thai Paradise** (140 S. Main St., Pocatello, 208/269-7313, lunch and dinner daily, $9–14) in Old Town. This friendly little joint serves stir-fried noodles, hotpot soups, spring rolls, and aromatic curries. Good picks are the fried tofu in peanut sauce and spicy beef salad—redolent of lime, chili paste, and garlic. The coconut ice cream is a great way to clean your palate afterward.

A few blocks away, you'll find **(Taste of India & Nepal** (330 N. Main St., Pocatello, 208/478-0172, www.tasteofindianepal.com, lunch 11 A.M.–2 P.M., dinner 5–9:30 P.M. Mon.–Sat., entrées $8–15), a new restaurant that turns to the Himalayas for inspiration. Besides standard Indian fare like samosas, chicken tikka, lamb vindaloo, and properly charred naan bread, the restaurant dishes up Nepali classics such as veggie momo dumplings and lamb kothay. Chase everything down with a delish mango lassi (yogurt drink).

Quick Bites

(Pie Hole (504 E. Center St., Pocatello, 208/232-3132, www.pieholeusa.com, 11 A.M.–2 A.M. Mon.–Wed., 11 A.M.–3 A.M. Thurs.–Sat., 11 A.M.–midnight Sun.) has been all the rage in downtown Poky since its 2010 debut. This Boise-based pizzeria specializes in hand-thrown New York–inspired pies, many offered by the slice (around $2). The interior is bright and open, and it has snowboards for backrests at some of the tables. The best thing about Pie Hole besides the great pizza is that it stays open really late.

College students flock to the **5th Street Bagelry** (559 S. 5th Ave., Pocatello, 208/235-1311, breakfast and lunch Mon.–Sat.) near campus. This little deli and coffeehouse serves bagel sandwiches, soups, and big salads. Try the huckleberry cream cheese slathered on a freshly baked blueberry bran bagel. The covered patio is a shady spot to beat the Pocatello heat. It's also a Wi-Fi hotspot.

Breakfast and Coffee

Oliver's Restaurant (130 S. 5th Ave., Pocatello, 208/234-0672, breakfast, lunch, and dinner daily, under $10) is a classic diner with a twist. The menu includes a full complement of vegetarian dishes, and a sign announces that the restaurant uses all-natural potatoes grown locally with no pesticides or herbicides. The service is excellent and the coffee endless. It's the place to go for a full breakfast of eggs-and-potatoes or pancakes.

◖ College Market Coffeehouse (604 S. 8th Ave., Pocatello, 208/232-3993, 7 A.M.–7:30 P.M. daily) occupies a handsome brick building in a quiet neighborhood near the university. An eclectic student scene makes for great people-watching. Pick up an espresso and one of the store's offbeat books or magazines and take them out to a table on the front porch. The house-baked goodies (muffins, scones, and biscotti) are pretty good.

Groceries

Marigolds Wine and Delicacies (1800 Flandro Dr., Pocatello, 208/237-9463, www.marigoldswine.com, 11 A.M.–9 P.M. Tues.–Thurs., 11 A.M.–10 P.M. Fri.–Sat.), in the Gold's Gym complex, is a new specialty store and café that stocks a large selection of wines from around the world. Besides bottles, Marigolds also sells

artisanal cheeses, bread, and lots of microbrews and imported beers. It also offers light lunch and dinner fare as well as a tea party menu.

Portneuf Valley Farmers Market (9 A.M.–1 P.M. Sat., 4–8 P.M. Wed. May–Oct.) sets up Old Town Pavilion (420 N. Main St., Pocatello). You can score a multitude of incredibly fresh vegetables and fruit, local beef, lamb, chicken, and sausages, kettle corn, fruit preserves, artisanal breads, and other freshly baked goodies. The market also has lots of locally produced crafts such as pottery, jewelry, and handmade soaps.

INFORMATION AND SERVICES

For more information about the city, contact the **Greater Pocatello Chamber of Commerce** (324 S. Main St., Pocatello, 208/233-1525, www.pocatelloidaho.com).

Recreation information is provided by the **City of Pocatello Parks and Recreation Department** (911 N. 7th Ave., Pocatello, 208/234-6232) and Caribou-Targhee National Forest's **Westside North Ranger District** (4350 Cliffs Dr., Pocatello, 208/236-7500).

The big mall in town is **Pine Ridge Mall** (4155 Yellowstone Ave., Chubbuck, 208/237-7160, 10 A.M.–9 P.M. Mon.–Sat., noon–5 P.M. Sun.), home to Sears, Dillard's, JCPenney, Foot Locker, and a dozen or so other stores to supply your every need.

For emergency medical services, go to **Portneuf Medical Center** (651 Memorial Dr., Pocatello, 208/239-1000) near the university.

GETTING THERE AND AROUND

Getting There

Greyhound Bus Lines (208/232-5365 or 800/231-2222) uses the city Transit Center (215 W. Bonneville St.) as its Pocatello terminal. Buses run south to Salt Lake City, northeast to Idaho Falls, and west to Burley.

Pocatello Regional Airport (PIH, 208/234-6154) is west of town off I-86, and

SkyWest (800/221-1212) provides daily flights to its hub in Salt Lake City. Car rental companies at the airport include **Avis** (208/232-3244, www.avis.com), **Budget** (208/233-0600, www.budget.com), and **Hertz** (208/233-2970, www.hertz.com).

Getting Around

Pocatello Regional Transit (215 W. Bonneville St., 208/234-2287, www.pocatellotransit.com) operates city bus service ($0.90 adults, $0.45 children and seniors). All the buses have bike racks.

South to Utah

HEADING DOWN I-15

Leaving Pocatello and heading south on I-15, you'll flow like lava past the basalt cliffs displaying the Snake River Plain's volcanic history. Mountains flank the highway to either side—the Portneuf Range on the left, the Bannock Range on the right. Straight ahead in the distance, the unique summit ridge of Oxford Peak reaches into the sky.

Those entering Idaho on I-15 from the south will find the **Gateway Southeast Idaho Visitor Center** (208/766-4788) at the Cherry Creek Rest Area, seven miles north of the Utah border. The center is well stocked with brochures covering all parts of the state.

Mormon Canyon

At I-15 Exit 47, U.S. 30 leads east toward Lava Hot Springs and Soda Springs, while the road to the west leads into the Bannock Range and the Bureau of Land Management's primitive **Mormon Canyon Campground.** To get to the campground, turn west at the Exit 47 off-ramp and follow the road to its T junction with Marsh Creek Road. Turn left, then right on Green Road almost immediately thereafter. Follow Green Road straight up to the campground on the eastern edge of the Caribou National Forest.

The site is actually in Goodenough Canyon, along Goodenough Creek. But Goodenough Canyon is a box canyon, while Mormon Canyon, just over a small ridge, provides access via a hiking and off-road vehicle trail up into the Bannocks—all the way to Scout Mountain, Mink Creek, and Pocatello if you so desire. The Mormon Canyon Trail crosses Goodenough Creek to the south. Alternately, a trail straight up Goodenough Creek leads past several primitive, secluded creek-side campsites. This dead-end trail makes a great day hike. To the north, a third trail leads to Bell Marsh Creek, and from there either up to Scout Mountain or back out to Marsh Creek Road. This latter trail in particular is great for relatively easy mountain biking; the Mormon Canyon trail is more difficult. A loop trip connects the two trails.

The campground here is quiet and idyllic. Shade abounds under a magnificent mix of trees, and Goodenough Creek babbles beautifully. Best of all, it's free.

Devil Creek Reservoir

Anglers fish for planted rainbow trout and kokanee salmon at this small impoundment seven miles north of Malad City. Primitive camping is available along one end of the west shore, and an RV park with a boat ramp is at the other end, nearest the exit from I-15.

MALAD CITY AND VICINITY

French trappers named the Malad River in the 1830s after eating some local beaver meat that didn't agree with them—*malade* is the French word for "sick." In 1843, a party led by John C. Frémont passed through the area and encountered a small band of emaciated Indians. Frémont noted that since the establishment of Fort Hall in 1834, trappers and buffalo hunters using the fort as a trading center and home base had devastated the Malad Valley's once-prolific buffalo herds, much to the dismay of local Native Americans.

THE LEGEND OF THE IRON DOOR

Thar's gold in them thar hills! Or at least there might be. One tale of treasure — in this case stolen, not mined — persists in the annals of Malad City folklore. Back when the stage-coach ran from Malad to Montana, holdups on the route were common. At some point during this era, three strangers showed up in a Utah town that had just been gutted by fire. The three men found a heavy iron door — off a bank vault, perhaps — among the ashes. They bought the door, loaded it on a wagon, and rode off to the north. It turns out the trio was a gang of stage-robbing desperados. They found a cave somewhere near Malad, installed the iron door over the mouth of the cave, and kept their considerable booty securely locked within.

As legend has it, the three of them had a falling out. Their disagreements led to a gun-fight that ended with all three wounded in the cave. One of them got out, locked the other two inside, and crawled to a nearby ranch for help. Alas, the grim reaper was closer than the nearest doctor. Knowing he was on his death-bed, with his dying breath the gunman told the rancher the tale of the iron door. But he died before he revealed the door's location. People have been looking for it ever since.

Supposedly the door was discovered one day by the late Glipsy Waldron, a rancher from Samaria. But he found it during a storm and couldn't relocate it when he returned. Others also found the door and tried to mark it for their return; one sheepherder supposedly tied a sheep to the door, in hopes that the animal's bleating would lead him back to it. No such luck.

In more recent times, Malad Valley miner Leo D. Williams and his partner, an Ogden doctor, found what looked like an old, abandoned mine shaft covered by rock and dirt. They had a hunch they might find the remains of the iron door inside, fallen to the bottom of the shaft. After digging a ways down, they found some humanlike bones; that jibed with the story of the two gang members who supposedly died inside the "cave." The doctor loaded the bones into his truck, intending to take them to Weber College for positive identification. But that same week he fell ill and died, and somewhere along the way the bones were lost. The mystery continues.

On his first sight of the Malad River Valley in 1854, Brigham Young didn't think much of the area, but in 1856 he sent 15 families here to try to add another settlement to the Mormon empire. They found good land with plentiful grass for livestock, numerous streams full of fish, and abundant game in the vicinity. They also found Chief Pocatello and his people camped in the area, so they built a fort, but growth escaped the settlement until Henry Peck came to town in 1864 with a plan to turn the valley's grasslands into a lucrative business. He planned to sell hay to the stage lines and freight wagons passing through the area as feed for their livestock. Peck began encouraging construction and growth in the valley and pushed for the county seat to be moved to Malad. In 1866 he went so far as to travel to Soda Springs, then the county seat, swipe the county records, and bring them back to Malad. History is unclear as to whether he had legislative authority to do so, but from that point on Malad took over as county seat.

Today, the sleepy little town has about 2,000 residents, and you can expect to find basic accommodations and restaurants along the downtown strip.

Recreation

Several reservoirs on the outskirts of town make good fishing holes. **Daniels Reservoir,** 18 miles northwest of town on Bannock Street, offers camping, a dock, and plenty of trout. **St. John Reservoir** is the local kids' pond three miles northwest of town. It's full of bluegill, bass, perch, and rainbow trout. **Crowther Reservoir,** on the edge of town to the north, is stocked with rainbows. **Pleasantview**

SOUTHEAST IDAHO

Reservoir, west of Malad on Lower St. John Road, offers two lakes and fishing for bass, rainbow trout, and tiger muskies.

U.S. 91
Oxford Peak

Hikers, off-roaders, and cow-pie collectors alike flock to tiny **Cherry Creek Campground,** located high on the slopes of 9,282-foot Oxford Peak. The trail to the top starts near here. As soon as you rumble over the cattle crossing at the National Forest entrance, you'll likely find yourself face to face with a herd of rangeland bovines, which tend to overrun the area around the small U.S. Forest Service campground (5 sites, free). To get here, take Malad Valley Road (Hwy. 191) southwest out of Downey and turn south on Aspen Creek Road, which soon turns into Cherry Creek Road (Forest Rd. 047). Follow the road straight up the creek for another six miles to the campground.

Downata Hot Springs

This popular full-service resort (25900 S. Downata Rd., Downey, 208/897-5736, www.downatahotsprings.com, noon–9 P.M. Mon.–Thurs., 11 A.M.–9 P.M. Fri.–Sat. Memorial Day–Labor Day, 11 A.M.–9 P.M. Fri.–Sat. Labor Day–Memorial Day, $9 age 3 and up, $1.50 under age 3), 3.5 miles south of Downey along U.S. 91, offers volleyball courts, horseshoe pits, picnic areas, wagon and sleigh rides, cabins, a restaurant, a campground, and more. The big draw in the arid reaches of Bannock County is the water. The resort's pure, 113°F natural hot springs feed a beautiful 300,000-gallon Olympic-size swimming pool, a whirlpool tub, and a couple of hydrotubes. Summer is prime time.

The resort has RV sites with hookups ($22–28) and tent sites ($15). Other accommodations include a ranch house ($250) that can sleep up to 12; a bunkhouse ($225) with room for eight; and some cabins and yurts ($75–150).

Bear River Massacre Site

Several times during the settling of the West, the U.S. Army annihilated whole bands of Native Americans in a single battle. In 1864 the Army killed 130 Cheyenne at Sand Creek, Colorado; 173 Piegan at Marias River, Montana, in 1870; and in the most infamous attack of all, 146 Lakota men, women, and children at Wounded Knee, South Dakota, in 1890. But here in Idaho, U.S. Army Colonel Patrick E. Connor assured his place in hell by leading the single biggest massacre of Native Americans in U.S. history. At dawn on January 29, 1863, Connor's California volunteers—assigned to suppress Native American resistance in the area—launched a surprise attack on a village of Northwestern Shoshone. An estimated 400 Shoshone were asleep that morning in Battle Creek Canyon when the thundering hooves of Connor's cavalry descended on the camp. A few people managed to escape by diving into the ice-choked Bear River and floating away; the rest—up to two-thirds of them women and children, even babies—were slaughtered. Only 14 bluecoats lost their lives in the one-sided battle.

Plans are afoot for a better memorial to the tragic event. At present, all you'll find at the site, on U.S. 91 a few miles north of Preston, are two historical signs.

PRESTON

The Franklin County seat, Preston was founded by Mormon pioneers in 1866. Originally called Worm Creek, it was later renamed for Mormon leader William B. Preston. Today, it's a hub of area farming; primary local crops include grains, hay, beans, and corn, and there are a number of dairy farms in the area.

Several beautiful examples of pioneer-era architecture still grace the town, among them the **Oneida Stake Academy** (151 E. 2nd St. S.), an early Mormon school, and the **Mathias Cowley home** (100 S. 100 E.), built for an early Mormon leader.

Napoleon Dynamite

Preston was pushed into the global spotlight in 2004 after the debut of the independent smash hit *Napoleon Dynamite,* filmed around town in 2003. Writer-director Jared Hess, who grew up in Preston, taps into the colloquialisms of this little Mormon burg as seen through the eyes of Napoleon Dynamite (Jon Heder), a quirky, alienated teenager with a dysfunctional home life. "Sweet"—Napoleon's language is indicative of the Mormon-influenced towns in the region, with a barrage of softened swear words such as "heck," "dang," and "frickin'." The film has grossed $44.5 million worldwide, not bad for a production that only cost $400,000 to make.

The **Preston Chamber of Commerce** (49 N. State St., 208/852-2703, www.prestonidaho.org) operates a small gift shop where you can buy Napoleon Dynamite paraphernalia that includes tote bags, postcards, hats, and T-shirts labeled "Vote for Pedro" and "If You Vote for Me Your Wildest Dreams Will Come True." You can also pick up a map of the sites around town where the movie was filmed. Grab some "tots" at Big J Burgers or play a round of tetherball at the school playground. Don't forget your "numchucks."

Entertainment and Events

The **Worm Creek Opera House** (70 S. State St., 208/852-0088) shows current-run flicks and hosts live community-theater productions. Summer is prime season for the local thespian troupe.

Two annual events make for fun times in town. The **Preston Night Rodeo** at the very end of July features Professional Rodeo Cowboys Association rodeo action and a carnival. The **Festival of Lights** opens on Veterans Day with a parade and then shines on through the end of the year with one of the state's best holiday lights displays. For more information or a complete events calendar, contact the Preston Chamber of Commerce (49 N. State St., 208/852-2703, www.prestonidaho.org).

Accommodations and Food

Plaza Motel (427 S. U.S. 91, 208/852-2020, from $52 d) is a well-kept motor inn on the edge of town with 31 nonsmoking guest rooms.

Amenities include cable TV and a laundry facility; pets are allowed.

Get your *Napoleon Dynamite* fix at ◖ **Big J Burgers** (196 N. Main St., 208/852-2800, lunch and dinner Mon.–Sat., under $10), a popular fast-food joint with some of the best burgers in the region. You can also get a thick milk shake and a side order of "tots." The restaurant has jumped on the *Napoleon Dynamite* bandwagon by offering its customers "Vote for Pedro" T-shirts and other souvenirs from the film.

On the way up to the Bear River Range, the **Deer Cliff Inn** (2016 N. Deer Cliff Rd., 208/852-0643, www.deercliffinnidaho.com, 5–9 P.M. Mon.–Sat. June–Aug., 5–9 P.M. Thurs.–Sat. May and Sept.–Oct., entrées $11–23) is right along the road at the base of impressively sheer Deer Cliff. The rustic restaurant offers gourmet dinners, and live entertainment ($3 cover) livens the place up at 7 P.M. Friday–Saturday nights. Cabins are also available.

Bear River Range Recreation

Two national forest fee campgrounds can be found in the area. Closest to Preston, at lowest elevation, is **Albert Moser Campground** (9 sites, $10–20), along the Cub River. Farther up the road is the turnoff to **Willow Flat Campground** (51 sites, $6–12), which occupies a beautiful spot in a steep-walled box canyon. Here the Cub River meanders over riffles and through pools, much to the delight of anglers. From the campground, a hiking trail leads to Willow Spring and Bloomington Lake, and a jeep trail crosses the range east to the Bear Lake region.

Just before the Willow Flat campground is Thomas Spring, once a popular stop on the Shoshone Indian trail between Cache Valley and Bear Lake. The Shoshone Trail was used as a mail route for many years. In summer it was probably a cushy route for the intrepid mail carriers, but in winter they must have cursed the glue right off their stamps as they slogged the mail over the mountains on snowshoes.

FRANKLIN

Thirteen Mormon pioneers arrived on the banks of the Cub River in April 1860 and immediately went to work establishing a town site. They had come north from Salt Lake City on the advice of Brigham Young and were under the mistaken impression that they were still in Utah. An official boundary survey in 1872 revealed that instead of founding just another Utah town, these pioneers had founded the very first town in Idaho. Later, Franklin enjoyed the first telephone and telegraph connections in Idaho and in 1874 the first railroad line into the state. Many buildings remain from the pioneer days, making for an interesting walking tour for students of history, especially that of the Mormons.

Historic Buildings

The log-cabin-style 1937 **Relic Hall** (113 E. Main St., 10 A.M.–noon and 1–5 P.M. daily May–Sept., donation) is what most towns would call a historical museum. Old portraits of the forefathers and mothers line the walls, most glaring down on visitors with dour expressions. Another interesting photo, for Mormon-history buffs, at least, shows the jail in Carthage, Illinois, where Mormon founders Joseph and Hyrum Smith were murdered by an angry mob. Old pioneer tools and artifacts fill the rest of the building.

Next door is a stone building dating from the 1860s that once housed the **FCMI store.** The FCMI (Franklin Cooperative Mercantile Institution) was one of the early branches of the Mormon ZCMI department store chain. Today, the FCMI building holds a collection of pioneer-era furniture.

Just down Main Street is the 1872 **Bishop Hatch House,** also constructed of locally quarried sandstone artfully carved by immigrant English stonemasons. Lorenzo Hill Hatch was the town's second Mormon bishop and its first mayor. Before settling in Franklin he served in the Utah legislature, and after his move to Idaho he became the first Mormon elected to the Idaho legislature. His house in Franklin was the largest in town when it was built to accommodate his three wives and 24 children. The Hatch home also became a popular guesthouse for visitors, including Brigham Young. Some say the house is the finest example of Greek Revival architecture in Idaho. It was purchased by the Idaho State Historical Society in 1979 but has not been fully restored and is not open to visitors.

For more information about the Relic Hall or Hatch House, contact the **Idaho Pioneer Association** (208/646-2437) in Franklin.

U.S. 30 to Bear Lake Country

LAVA HOT SPRINGS AND VICINITY

Today, the natural hot springs alongside the Portneuf River draw tourists to this small resort town, but long before the first nonnatives arrived, the Shoshone and Bannock people gathered here to partake of the waters. The Native American groups may have had their differences, but they considered the waters a gift of the Great Spirit and established a truce in the area so that all could benefit. The Hudspeth Cutoff on the Oregon Trail passed by here too. Perhaps that's one reason why the trail became so popular with trail-weary pioneers. Settlers moved into the area in the 1880s, and the present town was platted in 1911. It was incorporated as Lava Hot Springs in 1915.

Lava Recreation Complex

The biggest attraction in Lava Hot Springs is the state-owned Lava Recreation Complex (430 E. Main St., Lava Hot Springs, 208/776-5221 or 800/423-8597, www.lavahotsprings.com), which consists of two sites: On the west end of town is the 25-acre swimming facility (8 A.M.–11 P.M. daily

© IDAHO DIVISION OF TOURISM

Lava Recreation Complex

mid-May–Labor Day, $7.50 over age 11, $7 ages 3–11, $1.50 under age 3) featuring three 86°F pools, one of which is enormous and offers two Olympic-height diving platforms. Surrounding the pools is a large grassy expanse with volleyball courts and picnic tables. Down at the other end of town is the hot springs (9 A.M.–10 P.M. daily Oct.–Apr., 8 A.M.–11 P.M. daily May–Sept., closed Thanksgiving and Christmas, $7.50 ages 12–59, $7 ages 3–11 and over age 59), where several 110°F hot pools sit amid beautiful landscaping in a hollow between the highway and the Portneuf River. The hot pools are sulfur-free and thus have no odor.

Weekend and holiday passes as well as combined passes to both the Olympic pool and the hot springs are available, as are Monday–Thursday family specials. If you need a swimsuit or towel, you can rent 'em at either place.

Tubing the Portneuf River

In summer, kids love inner-tubing down the Portneuf River from one end of town to the other. The run is short—less than a mile—and takes about 10–15 minutes, depending on how fast the water is flowing. The put-in point is at Majestic Mart at the east end of town, and the takeout is at the Center Street Bridge just before the swimming pool facility. Some of the many tube-rental companies in town will pick you up at the bottom and shuttle you back to the top. But by the time you wait for the shuttle truck to arrive and load passengers, you'll probably find it nearly as fast just to walk back. Figure on making 3–4 runs in an hour. The crux of the run is the "rapids" near downtown. The water is shallow there and flows pretty quickly over a rocky riverbed—hang on tight or you might end up singing the black-and-blues. You also might want to consider renting one of the deluxe tubes with an added bottom.

Numerous tube companies hawk their wares right on the main drag through town. The going rate for a one-person tube is around $5 per hour; larger multiperson tubes are also available.

SOUTHEAST IDAHO

Historical Museum

The **South Bannock County Historical Center and Museum** (110 E. Main St., Lava Hot Springs, 208/776-5254, noon–5 P.M. daily year-round except Christmas and Thanksgiving, donation) offers interesting regional-history exhibits. One set of displays chronicles the history of each of the little communities in the area: Swan Lake, Virginia, Inkom, and McCammon, among others.

Accommodations

Lava Spa Motel & RV Park (359 E. Main St., Lava Hot Springs, 208/776-5589, from $79 d) is right across from the state hot springs. In addition to motel rooms, RV sites with full hookups ($30–40) are available. Tents are not permitted.

The elegant **Riverside Hot Springs Inn** (255 E. Portneuf Ave., Lava Hot Springs, 208/776-5504 or 800/733-5504, www.riversidehotspringsinn.com, $79–139) was built in 1914 and restored in 1991. Twelve guest rooms with private baths and four guest rooms with shared baths all include continental breakfast and use of the private indoor or common outdoor hot tubs. You'll find a television and phone in the lobby but not in the guest rooms. Out back is a beautiful patio overlooking the river. Smoking is restricted, and pets are allowed. **Greystone Manor B&B** (187 S. 2nd W., Lava Hot Springs, 208/776-5959, www.greystonelava.com, $85–115) offers three B&B rooms, including a honeymoon suite with its own jetted tub. Amenities include a billiard room and an upright piano. The old 1917 **Royal Hotel** (11 E. Main St., Lava Hot Springs, 208/776-5216, $79–99) has a few bed-and-breakfast rooms.

❖ Lava Hot Springs Inn (94 E. Portneuf Ave., Lava Hot Springs, 208/776-5830 or 800/527-5830, www.lavahotspringsinn.com, $69–129) occupies the old hospital-sanitorium just upriver from the Center Street Bridge. The inn's grounds feature five hot mineral pools, including an 80- by 20-foot pool for swimming. The pools are every bit as nice as anything at the state complex up the street, so if you stay here you can save the admission price you would've paid at the state's pools. A lap pool and 10 private hot mineral-water tubs are out front. Inside the inn, the decor is casually elegant. Several honeymoon suites—complete with in-room jetted tubs—make for an ultimate romantic getaway. A full breakfast is included in the rates. Some less-expensive rooms with shared bathrooms are available too, as are larger family suites, massage therapy, and complete spa services.

Camping

Ranch Inn Motel & Campground (9611 U.S. 30, Lava Hot Springs, 208/776-9917) offers 25 RV sites with full hookups ($30–50) and 100 tent sites ($20–30). Amenities at the campground include showers, restrooms, horseshoe pits, volleyball courts, picnic areas with tables and barbecue grills, and a nice stretch of riverfront for fishing.

River's Edge RV and Camping (101 W. Portneuf Ave., Lava Hot Springs, 208/776-5209) is down on the river near the swimming pool complex with RV sites ($25–35) and tent sites (around $20). Shower and laundry facilities are available, and pets are allowed.

Food

The restaurant at the old 1917 **Royal Hotel** (11 E. Main St., Lava Hot Springs, 208/776-5216, lunch and dinner daily) specializes in pizza and other light Italian fare. The food is outstanding; everything is made from scratch. Try the wonderful Royal calzone with pepper cheese, which you can accompany with one of the decent imported beers on the menu. A wall full of windows makes for bright and comfortable dining as well as good people-watching.

Watering holes in town include **Wagon Wheel Lounge** (225 E. Main St., Lava Hot Springs, 208/776-5224), which has a big sideyard beer garden with horseshoe pits and offers live music every Friday–Saturday night in summer; and **Blue Moon Bar & Grill** (89 S. 1st St. E., Lava Hot Springs, 208/776-5077), where you can shoot pool with the locals.

Information

For more information about the town, contact the **Lava Hot Springs Chamber of Commerce** (208/776-5500, www.lavahotsprings.org).

SODA SPRINGS

The Caribou County seat, Soda Springs is named for the numerous naturally carbonated springs that well up in the vicinity. The area was something of a novelty to pioneers, who named one of the water holes Beer Springs for its fizzy-salty taste and dubbed another Steamboat Springs because it sounded like a churning steam engine. Both these springs are now submerged under Alexander Reservoir. Also beneath the reservoir lies the original Soda Springs town site, which grew around the Army fort established in 1863 by Colonel Patrick Connor of Bear River Massacre infamy. The present town didn't take hold, however, until Brigham Young visited and supported the establishment of a new town site at the current location.

West of town along the highway you'll notice groves of **limber pine,** a species that usually grows at a much higher elevation. It's the weather in this particular spot that suits them; winter wind blows hard through the gap, making the spot even colder than the surrounding territory.

The Geyser

In November 1937, a drilling crew probing for hot water to supply a proposed municipal swimming pool inadvertently tapped into a pressurized underground chamber of geothermal water. They capped off the resulting geyser, and now it's on a timer, erupting every hour on the hour. The stream of hot carbonated water shoots 150 feet into the air and runs down over a small, mineralized mound at its base. Pathways lead to various viewpoints all around the site, which is on the west side of downtown, at the west end of 1st Street South.

Hooper Spring

One of the naturally effervescent springs that gave the town its name is Hooper Spring (3rd

St. E.). Oregon Trail pioneers stopped here to partake of the waters, and folks still come from all over to drink the water right out of the spring, claiming it helps their arthritis or other ailments. How does it taste? "I think it's gross," said one local. And looking out on the Monsanto slag pour and the nearby Kerr-McGee Chemical Corporation plant, you may lose all trace of thirst. The city built a gazebo over the spring itself and a park around it. The park has basketball courts, horseshoe pits, picnic sites, and a playground.

City Parks

Corrigan Park (Main St. and 1st St. S.) downtown is marked by a couple of old locomotives—the Dinky Engine and the Galloping Goose. The Dinky Engine was used to haul supplies during the construction of Alexander Dam. When the water began to back up into the reservoir, the little engine was trapped and drowned at the bottom of the lake. It remained there until 1976, when the reservoir was drained for repairs. Union Pacific Railroad retrieved and restored the Dinky and donated it to the city. The Galloping Goose carried mine workers and ore between Soda Springs and Conda from 1922 until 1936. The park also offers tennis and basketball courts and lots of grass.

Oregon Trail Public Park and Marina (8 A.M.–10 P.M. daily, free) west of town on Alexander Reservoir, offers a dock, a boat ramp, and picnic shelters. On the east edge of town, **Kelly Park** is a large open recreation area with baseball diamonds, tennis courts, a fishing pond, and jogging paths.

Recreation

Oregon Trail Country Club (2525 U.S. 30, 208/547-2204, closed winter, $11 for 9 holes, $18 for 18 holes), just west of town, offers a special thrill to golfers who also happen to be history buffs. The nine-hole, par-36 course surrounds the old Oregon Trail; wagon ruts can be seen on the course's south side between holes one, eight, and nine. The course managers don't mind if you walk from the clubhouse down between the fairways to take a look; just be careful you don't get in the way of a drive.

Trail Canyon Park N' Ski Area, 12 miles northeast of Soda Springs on Trail Canyon Road, offers 10 miles of trails in five loops as well as a warming hut. The trails are groomed periodically and are suitable for all ability levels.

Guest Ranch

The **Bar H Bar Ranch** (1501 Eight Mile Creek Rd., 208/547-3082, www.barhbar. com) was once cited in *National Geographic Traveler* magazine as one of the country's top 26 dude ranches. At this working 9,000-acre cattle ranch, you ride right alongside the ranch hands, roping, moving, and doctoring cattle, mending fences, and more. The no-frills ranch books only 4–6 guests per week for the typical one-week stay, so you'll receive personal attention and quickly become friends with the staff. It's not slave labor—any day you don't want to work, you're more than welcome to just saddle up and head for the hills. Those who find horseback riding to be a pain in the butt can explore the ranch on a four-wheel ATV instead. The summer rate here is $1,100 for a stay from Monday to Saturday noon, which includes all meals and activities. In winter, nightly rates are available, and you can rent snowmobiles or go cross-country skiing.

Forest Service Rentals

The Soda Springs ranger station (410 Hooper Ave., 208/547-4356) handles rentals for three guard stations (year-round, $35 per night) in the Caribou-Targhee National Forest. Northwest of Grays Lake National Wildlife Refuge, 45 miles northeast of Soda Springs, **Caribou Guard Station** lies along McCoy Creek in Caribou Basin. It sleeps up to eight people. **Johnson Guard Station** guards the Webster Range at the upper end of Upper Valley and sleeps six. And just two miles from the Wyoming border, **Stump Creek Guard Station** sleeps four and is reached most easily through Afton, Wyoming. All three are equipped with beds and mattresses as well as propane lights, heaters, and stoves.

HIGHWAY 34 TO WYOMING

Heading north out of Soda Springs, Highway 34 runs past Blackfoot Reservoir to Grays Lake, then makes a 90-degree turn east to Freedom, Wyoming. It's big open country. Blackfoot Reservoir has a small fishing-village scene, but Grays Lake can be all but deserted, even in the peak summer travel season.

Grays Lake National Wildlife Refuge

Iroquois trapper Ignace Hatchioraquasha discovered this valley around 1818 while out trapping beavers for the Northwest Company. Fortunately for cartographers, Ignace had an anglicized name: John Grey. How "Grey" became "Gray" is anyone's guess.

The remote 20,000-acre Grays Lake National Wildlife Refuge (74 Grays Lake Rd., Wayan, 208/237-6615)—actually a large marsh rather than a lake—has the world's largest concentration of nesting sandhill cranes as well as a few rare and endangered whooping cranes. The whooping crane is the tallest bird in North America, nearly five feet from head to toe. Its snow-white body is accented by a red-and-black head and jet-black wing tips, and its wingspan stretches some seven feet. The U.S. Fish and Wildlife Service has tried a number of strategies to bolster the population of whoopers but has met with little success. Only about 230 whooping cranes are left in the world.

The perimeter road encircling the refuge makes a scenic drive. In addition to the cranes, you'll likely see ducks, geese, white pelicans, herons, egrets, Franklin's gulls, grebes, bitterns, and phalaropes. Nonwinged species in the area include moose, elk, mule deer, muskrats, and badgers.

Refuge Headquarters along the southeast side of the refuge has a visitors center (daily Apr. 1–Nov. 15) with interpretive exhibits, including a mounted whooping crane. A short road leads from the headquarters up to a nearby hilltop, where you'll find an observation point equipped in summer with a free spotting scope. Hiking and cross-country skiing are permitted on the northern half of the refuge October 10–March 31.

Camping

Up the Blackfoot River at a point called the Narrows is the U.S. Forest Service's **Mill Canyon Campground** (10 sites, free). It's unremarkable except for its proximity to the river for fishing.

The out-of-the-way Forest Service **Gravel Creek Campground** (10 sites, $12) is definitely worth going out of your way for. After climbing into the Grays Range, you'll enter a lush forest filled with a veritable arboretum of tree species. Catch a trail to the top of Henry Peak (8,319 feet) or just nap alongside Gravel Creek. To get to the campground, take Wayan Loop off Highway 34 and turn south up Forest Road 191.

Pine Bar and Tincup Campgrounds, fronting Highway 34 near the Wyoming border, are more glorified rest stops than anything else. Both have five sites, and both are free.

MONTPELIER AND VICINITY
Butch Cassidy Robbed Here

According to local legend—which some locals question—famous desperado Butch Cassidy and his Wild Bunch gang rode into Montpelier on August 13, 1896, and relieved the local bank of some $16,500 in gold, silver, and currency. The deputy sheriff on duty couldn't find his horse, so he grabbed a nearby bicycle and rode off after the gang as they headed up Montpelier Canyon. Needless to say, his pursuit efforts were futile. One of the Hole-in-the-Wall Gang, Bob Meeks, was eventually caught and jailed for his part in the robbery, but Butch and Sundance escaped scot-free for this one. The bank building that the gang held up still stands, but it's now a print shop.

National Oregon Trail and California Trail Center

This interpretive center (320 N. 4th St., Montpelier, 208/847-3800, www.oregontrail-center.org, one-hour tours 9 A.M.–5 P.M. daily

May–Sept., $10 adults, $9 over age 59, $7 ages 6–11) houses interactive exhibits on life along the pioneer trails, among them a computer-controlled covered wagon. The center also offers regular living-history programs.

In the basement of the center is the **Bear Lake Rails and Trails Museum** (9 A.M.–5 P.M. Mon.–Sat. May–Sept., free) offering some great regional-history displays. Among the topics covered are the wild and woolly Bear Lake Rendezvous of 1827; nearby Big Hill, the toughest grade on the Oregon Trail up to this point; and the Native American history of Bear Lake Valley. Artifacts on display include many items brought across the plains on wagon trains by the area's early settlers.

Events

The fourth Saturday in July, Montpelier presents the **Oregon Trail Rendezvous Pageant** (www.bearlakechamber.com). Celebrations include a delectable Dutch-oven supper as well as pioneer-style music, drama, dancing, and more. For more information.

Accommodations

Budget Motel (240 N. 4th St., Montpelier, 208/847-1273, from $35 d) is an extremely affordable motor inn along the main drag. **Three Sisters Motel** (112 S. 6th St., Montpelier, 208/847-2324, $28–50) has eight guest rooms with refrigerators and microwaves. **Park Motel** (745 Washington St., Montpelier, 208/847-1911, from $45), a basic brick motor inn, has 25 nonsmoking guest rooms with cable TV.

Near downtown, you'll find **Super 8** (276 N. 4th St., Montpelier, 208/847-8888 or 800/800-8000, from $97 d), which offers 50 guest rooms, a hot tub, and an exercise room; continental breakfast is included.

Information

The **Bear Lake/Montpelier Chamber of Commerce** (925 Washington St., Montpelier, 208/847-0067, www.bearlakechamber.com) can provide you with more information about the area. For Caribou-Targhee National Forest recreation information, contact the **Montpelier**

Ranger District (322 N. 4th St., Montpelier, 208/847-0375).

On to Wyoming

Heading east out of Montpelier on U.S. 89 North, you'll soon come to the turnoff to Montpelier Reservoir. Anglers can try their luck either in the reservoir, which doesn't allow motorboats, or just downstream of the dam, where clean and clear Montpelier Creek meanders through verdant meadows, in and out of thickets, over riffles, and through cool pools—it looks like trout heaven. The U.S. Forest Service's primitive Elbow Campground (not signed) is just off the highway, right below the dam. Continuing east, you'll crest Geneva Summit (6,938 feet) and coast down the other side to the state line. From there it's another 30 miles to Afton, Wyoming.

U.S. 89 TO BEAR LAKE

Bear Lake was first seen by nonnatives in 1812, when a party of trappers passed this way on a return trip from Astoria, Oregon. Trappers played a leading role in the area's history, and two of the annual fur-trading rendezvous were held here in 1826 and 1827.

Half in Idaho, half in Utah, Bear Lake is 20 miles long and seven miles wide. Dissolved limestone particles suspended in the water give the lake a surreal turquoise-blue color, especially intense at sunrise. Rainbow and cutthroat trout tease anglers, while another fish, the sardine-like Bonneville cisco, is found nowhere else in the world. Besides fishing, popular summer pastimes on the lake include sailing and powerboating. The nearest boat rentals are at the Bear Lake State Recreation Area marina in Garden City, Utah, about three miles across the state line.

Ovid

On the way down to Bear Lake from Montpelier, you'll pass blink-and-you'll-miss-it Ovid, settled by Mormons in 1864. The town lies at the junction of Highway 36, which heads west to Preston, and U.S. 89, which continues south to Bear Lake and the Utah border. Twelve miles northwest of Ovid off Highway 36, the U.S. Forest Service Emigration Campground (19 sites, $12) occupies a delightful spot high on the east side of the Bear River Range at an elevation of 7,500 feet. It's surrounded by a beautiful mix of evergreen and deciduous trees, making it an especially nice location in fall. Wildflowers are abundant, and hiking trails lead to other parts of the range.

Paris

The little town of Paris, seat of Bear Lake County, was founded in 1863 by 30 Mormon families. As happened in Franklin, the settlers thought they were still in Utah.

Presiding majestically over Main Street downtown is the red sandstone Paris Stake Tabernacle, a Romanesque Mormon temple designed by one of Brigham Young's sons. It was built 1884–1889 with stone quarried 18 miles away and hauled by horse cart to the site, where immigrant Swiss stonemasons carved the stunning edifice. Tours of the tabernacle are offered daily in summer.

Paris Springs Campground (12 sites, $10–20) is six miles up into the mountains west of town in a quiet location a short hike from the namesake springs. No mere trickle, these springs gush profusely out of the ground at the head of a steep-walled box canyon. The campground isn't crowded; you may have it to yourself. Ice-cave diehards can take a fork lower down the canyon and continue 5–6 miles up a gravel road to the small Paris Ice Cave.

If you're hungry, try the Paris Grill (48 S. Main St., 208/945-1100), a friendly eatery serving everything from house-baked pies to burgers to calzones.

Bear Lake National Wildlife Refuge

This 18,000-acre reserve, most of it marsh, is one of the largest Canada goose nesting grounds in the western United States and home to the country's largest nesting population of white-faced ibis. Scads of ducks pass through in spring and fall, and deer and moose roam the refuge as well.

Spring is the best time to view the greatest numbers of species. Most migratory species begin arriving in April and begin leaving in August. Access restrictions apply for much of the year; contact the refuge headquarters (370 Webster St., Montpelier, 208/847-1757) for complete regulations. The best viewing area is in the refuge's Salt Meadow Unit at the northern end. To get here, take Paris-Dingle Road east out of Paris and turn south just after crossing the canal. The canal road leads to a boat-launching ramp and several parking areas.

◖ Bear Lake State Park

As Idaho's state parks go, Bear Lake State Park (208/945-2565) is pretty humble. You won't find interpretive information, campfire programs, or nature trails. The key attraction is Bear Lake itself. The park has two units: a day-use beach and boat ramp along the north shore, and a campground on the east shore. The normal state park motor vehicle entry fee of $5 applies. There are campsites at the 150-site **East Beach Campground** ($14, $18 with electricity hookup).

St. Charles and Vicinity

For what it's worth, Gutzon Borglum, the painter and sculptor who carved Mount Rushmore, was born in St. Charles in 1867. Recreation opportunities abound in St. Charles Canyon, which climbs into the Bear River Range west of town. A paved road (Forest Rd. 412) leads all the way up to **Minnetonka Cave** (435/245-4422, tours every half hour 10 A.M.–5:30 P.M. daily June–Labor Day, $7 adults, $5 ages 6–15, free under age 6, family rates available), one of only a few federal show caves in the country. Those who have traveled in southern Idaho and expect every "cave" site to be a lava tube are in for a surprise—this is a honest-to-goodness limestone cave, complete with stalagmites and stalactites. A half-mile guided tour takes you deep inside, up and down some 448 steps, and through nine rooms with formations with names like "the Seven Dwarfs" and "the Devil's Office." Bring a sweater; the cave is a constant 40°F.

On the way to the cave you'll pass a string of U.S. Forest Service campgrounds administered by the Montpelier Ranger District (322

© IDAHO DIVISION OF TOURISM

sailing at Bear Lake

SOUTHEAST IDAHO

N. 4th St., Montpelier, 208/847-0375). First, lowest, and least interesting is **St. Charles Campground** (6 sites, $23), followed by **Davis Canyon Campground** ($8), a primitive and unmarked site down on the creek where the main road climbs above the creek for a stretch. A spur leads down to the water. If you don't need a lot of amenities, this is an excellent place to spend a few nights. Next up is **Porcupine Campground** ($10–18), right on St. Charles Creek, where a newly added loop among lodgepole pines and aspens brings the total number of sites to 16. Continuing ever higher up the canyon, next is **Cloverleaf Campground** ($19), which offers 20 sites in three cloverleaf loops. It's not immediately on the creek, but it's convenient to a trail that climbs up to Minnetonka Cave.

Idaho Falls and Vicinity

Idaho Falls, the Bonneville County seat, owes a great deal of its economy to the Idaho National Laboratory (INL), the U.S. Department of Energy's top nuclear research facility deep in the desert about 30 miles from town. You'll see a regular stream of big yellow buses carrying the site's engineers and physicists to and from work and home.

Idaho Falls (population 57,000) was here long before INL, so it has an interesting mix of

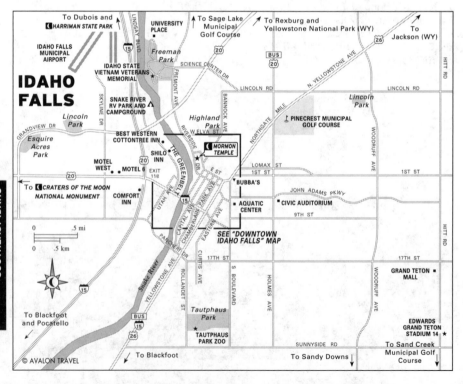

farmers and nuclear scientists. The two groups seem to coexist well enough. In any case, you'll find just enough culture—including the state's largest museum—to keep you entertained, along with plenty of that down-home charm that makes Idaho so great.

SIGHTS
The Falls
The falls at Idaho Falls were just rapids until 1910, when work began on the hydroelectric power plant just south of the Broadway Bridge. The diversion dam resulted in the cascade you see today. The falls may not be natural, but they're still a pleasant sight and sound. A greenbelt winds along the riverbank right by the falls, making for scenic jogging, strolling, or picnicking.

◖ Mormon Temple
The big Moroni-topped wedding-cake structure on the city's finest riverfront property is the Idaho Falls Temple of the Mormon Church (1000 Memorial Dr., Idaho Falls, 208/523-4504). The temple offers a place for non-Mormons to learn about the prevalent religion in southeast Idaho. A visitors center (9 A.M.–9 P.M. daily, free) has displays and videos about the church.

Museum of Idaho
Once a humble repository of local lore, this newly enlarged and renamed museum (200 N. Eastern Ave., Idaho Falls, 208/522-1400, www.museumofidaho.org, 9 A.M.–8 P.M. Mon.–Tues., 9 A.M.–5 P.M. Wed.–Sat., $7 adults, $5 ages 5–17, free under age 5, $20 family) has triple the space it did before, which reportedly makes it the state's largest museum. A full-size fleshed-out replica of a Columbian mammoth is the centerpiece attraction, but you'll also find a neat exhibit showing Eagle Rock (Idaho Falls's original name) as it may have looked on a typical day in 1891.

The Art Museum of Eastern Idaho
When you're out strolling the Greenbelt, be sure to stop by the relatively new Art Museum

Idaho Falls

© IDAHO DIVISION OF TOURISM

of Eastern Idaho (300 S. Capital Ave., Idaho Falls, 208/524-7777, www.theartmuseum.org, 11 A.M.–5 P.M. Tues.–Sat., $4 adults, $2 ages 6–17, free under age 6). In addition to traveling exhibits and works by local adult and child artists, the center hosts such special events as a holiday show the first weekend in December and a spring show in April.

Historic Architecture
Many 19th- to early-20th-century buildings still stand in Idaho Falls. An exploratory stroll through downtown yields views of the 1917 Hotel Idaho (482 Constitution Way), which was in use until 1979; the 1918 Underwood Hotel (347 Constitution Way), built for early Idaho Falls entrepreneur Jennie Underwood; and the 1915 Shane Building (381 Shoup Ave.), a Renaissance Revival retail space with terracotta accents.

Across the railroad tracks on the east side of Yellowstone Avenue is the Ridge Avenue Historic District, once the city's prime residential neighborhood, which has Queen Anne,

SOUTHEAST IDAHO

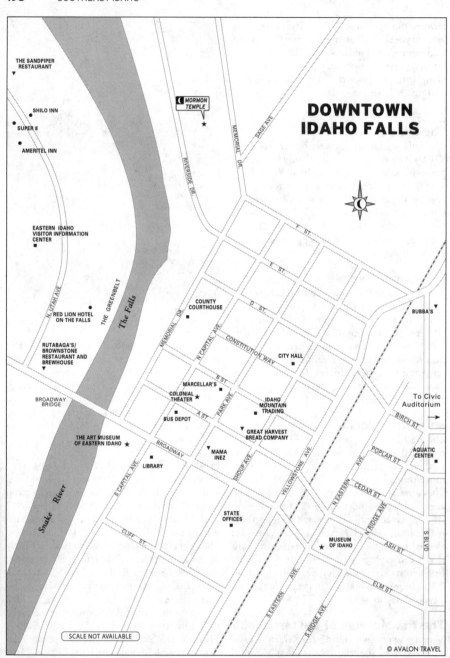

DOWNTOWN IDAHO FALLS

THE SANDPIPER RESTAURANT ▼

SHILO INN

SUPER 8

AMERITEL INN

MORMON TEMPLE ★

MEMORIAL DR.

SADE AVE.

RIVERSIDE DR.

EASTERN IDAHO VISITOR INFORMATION CENTER ■

N. UTAH AVE.

THE GREENBELT

The Falls

RED LION HOTEL ON THE FALLS

RUTABAGA'S/ BROWNSTONE RESTAURANT AND BREWHOUSE ▼

BROADWAY BRIDGE

THE ART MUSEUM OF EASTERN IDAHO ★

Snake River

F ST.

E ST.

D ST.

COUNTY COURTHOUSE ■

MEMORIAL DR.

N. CAPITAL AVE.

CONSTITUTION WAY

CITY HALL ■

BUBBA'S ▼

B ST.

MARCELLAR'S ■

COLONIAL THEATER ★

PARK AVE.

A ST.

BUS DEPOT ■

GREAT HARVEST BREAD COMPANY ▼

MAMA INEZ ▼

BROADWAY

S. CAPITAL AVE.

LIBRARY ■

SHOUP AVE.

IDAHO MOUNTAIN TRADING ▼

YELLOWSTONE AVE.

N. EASTERN AVE.

BIRCH ST

To Civic Auditorium →

POPLAR ST

AQUATIC CENTER ■

CEDAR ST

N. RIDGE AVE.

S. BLVD

STATE OFFICES ■

CLIFF ST.

MUSEUM OF IDAHO ★

ASH ST

ELM ST

S. EASTERN AVE.

S. RIDGE AVE.

SCALE NOT AVAILABLE

© AVALON TRAVEL

SOUTHEAST IDAHO

craftsman, and Colonial Revival houses surrounded by expansive lawns and venerable maple trees. Many are listed on the National Register of Historic Places. Among the most impressive: the 1896 A. D. Morrison house (258 Walnut St.); the 1916–1917 Tudor-Gothic Trinity Methodist Church (237 N. Water Ave.); and the 1910 Fuller House (101 N. Placer Ave.), which once did double duty as a home and a hospital.

The city publishes detailed walking-tour guides to both the downtown and Ridge Avenue districts. Pick up copies at the Eastern Idaho Visitor Information Center (630 W. Broadway, Idaho Falls, 208/523-1010).

RECREATION
Snake River Greenbelt
One of the best ways to spend an hour or more in Idaho Falls is a stroll along the city's greenbelt, a 29-acre park lining both sides of the Snake River. The most popular stretch lies between the Broadway Bridge and the U.S. 20 bridge; it's a 2.3-mile loop enjoyed by joggers, speed-walkers, and bicyclists as well as squadrons of ducks and Canada geese. In winter, the snow-covered landscape takes on a contemplative air, and the greenbelt becomes a whitebelt suitable for snowshoeing or cross-country skiing.

Tautphaus Park
The crown jewel of the city's 39-unit park system, Tautphaus Park (off Rollandet St., Idaho Falls) has acres and acres of grassy expanses, an abundance of trees and flowers, a fountain, baseball fields, tennis courts, and a playground.

In addition, **Tautphaus Park Zoo** (Rogers St. and Carnival Way, Idaho Falls, 208/612-8552, www.idahofallszoo.org, 9 A.M.–7 P.M. Mon., 9 A.M.–5 P.M. Tues.–Sun. Memorial Day–Labor Day, reduced hours Apr.–May and Sept., closed Oct.–Mar., $6 adults, $4.50 over age 61, $3 ages 4–12, free under age 4) houses more than 250 animals in recreated natural habitats simulating the respective creatures' home turf. Among the rare and endangered

species on display are snow leopards, red ruffed lemurs, Amur tigers, and cotton top tamarins. Across from the zoo is an ice-skating/hockey rink open in winter.

Other Parks and Recreation Facilities
At the west end of Science Center Drive at the river, 75-acre **Freeman Park** offers plenty of open space along with baseball diamonds, a disc golf course, picnic tables and shelters, a playground, and the **Idaho State Vietnam Veterans Memorial**—a stainless-steel sculpture engraved with the names of Idaho soldiers killed or missing in action in the Vietnam War.

The city's **Recreation Center** (520 Memorial Dr., Idaho Falls, 208/612-8480) offers racquetball courts, basketball courts, a weight room, showers, and lockers. The **Wes Deist Aquatic Center** (149 7th St., Idaho Falls, 208/612-8111) provides an indoor lap pool, hot tubs, and an outside wading pool open in summer. Call for hours and rates. You'll also find a municipal pool at **Reinhart Park** (1055 Washburn Ave., Idaho Falls).

For more information on the city's municipal parks and recreation facilities, call the **Idaho Falls Parks and Recreation Division** (208/612-8480).

Climbers in need of some good 5.11 can head to **Stonewalls** (751 S. Capital Ave., Idaho Falls, 208/528-8610, $10 per day), an indoor climbing gym with 6,500 square feet of climbing walls. Shoe and harness rentals are available. Call for current hours, which change monthly, but it's generally open afternoons and evenings.

Golf
Area golfers can choose from three city-maintained 18-hole courses to putt around on. In the heart of town, the 6,419-yard par-70 **Pinecrest Municipal Golf Course** (701 E. Elva St., Idaho Falls, 208/612-8485) is probably the toughest of the three, featuring small greens and lots of dastardly trees. On the southeast side of town, par-72 **Sand Creek Municipal Golf Course** (5200 S. Hackman Rd., Idaho Falls,

208/612-8115) is the longest of the batch. Its 18 holes stretch across 6,770 yards. On the city's north end you'll find **Sage Lakes Municipal Golf Course** (100 E. 65 N., Idaho Falls, 208/612-8535), which offers numerous water traps on a 6,566-yard par-70 course. All three courses are closed in winter, and 18 holes cost $20.50 nonresidents, $18 residents.

Spectator Sports

The **Idaho Falls Chukars** (tickets 208/522-8363, $6.50 adults, $5 seniors, box seats $9.50), a Pioneer League team affiliated with the Kansas City Royals, play summer evenings at the newish Melaleuca Field in Highland Park (Bannock Ave. and W. Elva St., Idaho Falls).

Outfitters

To buy or rent backpacking, climbing, skiing, and skating gear, check out **Idaho Mountain Trading** (474 Shoup Ave., Idaho Falls, 208/523-6679, www.idahomountaintrading.net).

ENTERTAINMENT AND EVENTS

Idaho Falls's big arts venue is the renovated **Colonial Theater/Willard Arts Center** complex (450 A St., Idaho Falls, 208/522-0471, www.idahofallsarts.org). There are typically several live shows here each week, including many touring acts. It's also the home of the excellent Idaho Falls Arts Council, which can fill you in on all the arts events around town.

Movies are big in Idaho Falls, with the **Edwards Grand Teton Stadium 14** (2707 S. 25th E., Idaho Falls, 208/552-0698) leading the pack among the multiplexes.

Mid-April brings the annual **Eastern Idaho Fly Tying and Fly Fishing Expo** (www. snakerivercutthroats.org), with demonstrations by more than 100 top tiers. The website is packed with info both on the event and the region's great angling opportunities.

The **Mountain Brewers Beer Festival** (www.northamericanbrewers.org) bubbles forth in early June at Sandy Downs, featuring more than 80 breweries in what has to be the Northern Rockies' biggest beer festival. It is ironic, given that Idaho Falls is strong Mormon country. Teetotalers will find plenty of hand-crafted root beers on tap too.

The Idaho Falls Arts Council (208/522-0471) sponsors free concerts at 7 P.M. Tuesday mid-June–August on Memorial Drive between D and E Streets. The arts council is also the sponsor of the annual **Snake River Roaring Youth Jam,** a kid-oriented arts festival in mid-August. Activities include a battle of the bands, family concerts, hands-on art tents, and the **Great Snake River Duck Race.**

SHOPPING

In Idaho Falls, 17th Street is the road to mall-ville. The long strip is encrusted with one fast-food emporium after another, all brightly lit and egging you on toward **Grand Teton Mall** (2300 E. 17th St., Idaho Falls, 208/525-8315, 10 A.M.–9 P.M. Mon.–Sat., noon–6 P.M. Sun.), the town's largest shopping center. JCPenney, Sears, Dillard's, Macy's, and Barnes & Noble are the mall's big guns.

ACCOMMODATIONS

Under $50

Out by I-15 Exit 118, you'll find two motels with rooms that dip below $50. **Motel 6** (1448 W. Broadway, Idaho Falls, 208/522-0112 or 800/466-8356, $43–56) offers 79 standard guest rooms with cable TV. **Motel West** (1540 W. Broadway, Idaho Falls, 208/522-1112, from $46) is another good budget choice, with an indoor pool and an on-site restaurant.

$50-100

Most of the city's chain lodgings cozy up to each other on Lindsay Boulevard, along the west side of the Snake River near the falls. From south to north on the riverbank side of Lindsay you'll find **Red Lion Hotel on the Falls** (475 River Parkway, Idaho Falls, 208/523-8000 or 800/733-5466, from $79 d); **Best Western Driftwood Inn** (575 River Parkway, Idaho Falls, 208/523-2242 or 800/939-2242, from $79 d); **Shilo Inn** (780 Lindsay Blvd., Idaho

Falls, 208/523-0088 or 800/222-2244, from $94 d), with rates at the top of this range; and **Best Western CottonTree Inn** (900 Lindsay Blvd., Idaho Falls, 208/523-6000 or 800/662-6886, from $79 d).

At all of these lodgings, you can get riverview guest rooms (worth the extra bucks, as the view in the opposite direction is less than exciting), and you'll be able to walk right out the door onto the greenbelt for your evening constitutional. The cylindrical-shaped Red Lion is the tallest and nearest the falls; the Shilo Inn probably has the best location and range of amenities.

Across Lindsay Boulevard, away from the river, is the spiffy, high-end **AmeriTel Inn** (645 Lindsay Blvd., Idaho Falls, 208/523-1400 or 800/600-6001, from $79 d), which offers a 24-hour indoor pool. Nearby is **Super 8** (705 Lindsay Blvd., Idaho Falls, 208/522-8880, from $69 d), with some rooms on the low end of this price category.

By I-15 Exit 118 near Motel 6 is **Comfort Inn** (195 S. Colorado Ave., Idaho Falls, 208/528-2804, from $60), also easy on the wallet.

CAMPING AND RVING
Snake River RV Park and Campground (1440 Lindsay Blvd., Idaho Falls, 208/523-3362) lies north of U.S. 20 in an industrial area dominated by a General Mills seed plant. But a long driveway and abundant trees provide a sufficient buffer against the sights and sounds out on the boulevard. Amenities, some seasonal, include a heated pool and jetted tub, a playground, and a camp store. The campground has 40 tent sites (around $25), 120 RV sites with full hookups ($28–35), and 10 camping cabins ($40–45).

FOOD
Upscale Yet Casual
In the Eagle Rock Station mini-mall near the falls is **(€ Rutabaga's** (415 River Pkwy., Idaho Falls, 208/529-3990, dinner 5–9:30 P.M. Tues.–Sat., brunch 10 A.M.–2 P.M. Sun., entrées $25–32), which features "semi-tough industrial

decor." It serves inventive appetizers and big salads as well as rotating dinner specials that might include fresh grilled swordfish, teriyaki duck, or herb-crusted rack of lamb.

The Sandpiper Restaurant (750 Lindsay Blvd., Idaho Falls, 208/524-3344, 4–10 P.M. Mon.–Sat., entrées $13–28) is part of the small southern Idaho chain that offers consistently good food and atmosphere in a traditional, casually elegant setting. Entrées include chicken, seafood, pasta, and prime rib as well as half a dozen different cuts of steak to suit your whim.

Ethnic Cuisine
Mexican food is big in Idaho Falls, and good choices include **Melina's** (187 E. 1st St., Idaho Falls, 208/524-5430, lunch and dinner daily, $6–12) and **Mama Inez** (344 Park Ave., Idaho Falls, 208/525-8968, lunch and dinner daily, $6–12). The best Mexican eats in town, however, may be what you get from the **Taco Truck**—a mobile taqueria that parks downtown behind Idaho Mountain Trading on certain nights of the week. Ask a local for the where and when, and don't miss it for super-cheap, super-authentic tacos, tamales, and the like. Or try the reader-recommended **Puerto Vallarta Mexican Restaurant** (1902 Jennie Lee Dr., Idaho Falls, 208/529-3267, 11 A.M.–9 P.M. Mon.–Thurs., 11 A.M.–10 P.M. Fri.–Sat.), reported to have very good salsa.

It's 20 miles north of town via I-15, but **BJ's Bayou** (655 N. 2880 E., Roberts, 208/228-2331, 4–10 P.M. daily, $12–20) offers downhome Cajun food to die for.

Barbecue and Brew
Without a doubt the place to go for barbecue is **Bubba's** (118 E. 1st St., Idaho Falls, 208/523-2822, lunch and dinner daily, $7–15). Brewpub duties in town are skillfully handled by **Brownstone Restaurant & Brewhouse** (455 River Pkwy., Idaho Falls, 208/535-0310, www.brownstonebrewpub.com, lunch and dinner daily, $8–17). It's a clean, spacious place with good handcrafted beer and a varied menu

ranging from pizza to pasta to burgers; vegetarians will also find plenty to eat.

Breakfast and Coffee

Idaho Falls is definitely a corporate-restaurant town, so most breakfast places are chains. One good pick for a big breakfast served all day is **Perkins Family Restaurant & Bakery** (2000 Channing Way, 208/529-9955, breakfast, lunch, and dinner daily), where you can get waffles, pancakes, omelets, and more.

With three Idaho Falls locations, **Java Espress** (1250 W. Broadway, 208/552-7664; 530 E. 17th St., 208/529-6699; 2139 E. 17th St., 208/552-5282) is the place to go for espresso drinks and breakfast pastries.

Groceries

The **Idaho Falls Farmers Market** (9 A.M.–1 P.M. Sat. May–Oct.) takes place downtown in the Key Bank parking lot (501 W. Broadway, Idaho Falls). You can pick up impeccably fresh produce, artisanal bread, local meats, and prepared food items.

It's worth a stop at **Great Harvest Bread Company** (360 A St., 208/522-7444, 6 A.M.–6 P.M. Mon.–Sat.) just to smell the heady, yeasty, and comforting aroma of the dozens of different flavors of freshly baked bread that permeates the place.

An imbiber's oasis in dry southeast Idaho, **MarCellar's Vintage Wines & Brews** (431 Park Ave., Idaho Falls, 208/523-0503) stocks a wide selection of premium wines and beers.

INFORMATION AND SERVICES

The all-in-one **Eastern Idaho Visitor Center** (630 W. Broadway, Idaho Falls, 208/523-1010 or 866/365-6943, www.visitidahofalls.com) is staffed by representatives from the Greater Idaho Falls Chamber of Commerce and other agencies. The center offers interpretive displays about the region, sells related books and maps, and stocks free literature on everything from accommodations to recreation opportunities.

The headquarters of the **Caribou-Targhee**

National Forest and the **Idaho Falls Bureau of Land Management** field office (both at 1405 Hollipark Dr., Idaho Falls, 208/524-7500) can provide additional recreational information about the area.

The **Idaho Falls Public Library** (457 Broadway, Idaho Falls, 208/612-8467) is one of the state's biggest and best.

GETTING THERE

Idaho Falls Regional Airport (IDA, 2140 N. Skyline Dr., 208/612-8224) is served by **Delta** (800/221-1212), with daily flights to Salt Lake City, and **United** (800/864-8331), which offers weekend flights to Denver. **Allegiant Air** (702/505-8888) has Monday and Friday flights to and from Las Vegas and Long Beach, California.

Car rental agencies at the airport include **Avis** (208/522-4225, www.avis.com), **Budget** (208/522-8800, www.budget.com), and **Hertz** (208/529-3101, www.hertz.com).

I-15 NORTH TO MONTANA

Waterfowl Sanctuaries

As I-15 beelines north to the Montana border, it passes three separate preserves that serve as aqueous stepping stones for migratory waterfowl on the Pacific Flyway. In spring and fall, the preserves draw vast numbers of snow geese and Canada geese; mallard, gadwall, and ring-necked ducks; green-winged and cinnamon teal; trumpeter swans; double-crested cormorants; herons; egrets; sandhill cranes; Franklin's gulls; white-faced ibises; and many other species. Numerous extras with important roles include shorebirds, songbirds, and raptors. All three refuges are open year-round. Camping, fishing, and boating are permitted subject to seasonal restrictions; inquire at the respective headquarters.

Twenty miles north of Idaho Falls is **Market Lake Wildlife Management Area** (806 N. 2900 E., Roberts, 208/228-3131), a 5,000-acre area surrounding 1,700 acres of spring-fed marsh. A map and birder's checklist are available at the Wildlife Management Area (WMA) headquarters. To reach the headquarters, take I-15 Exit 135 at Roberts and head east to Road 2880 East. Turn north on 2880 East and drive through the town of Roberts. At the fork in the road, bear right to Road 800 North and follow signs to the headquarters.

The huge **Camas National Wildlife Refuge** protects more than 10,000 acres of waterfowl-filled wetlands. The two largest lakes on the refuge cover 600 and 700 acres. In addition, Camas Creek winds through the area. During peak spring and fall migration periods, you might see up to 100,000 ducks. The birder's checklist for the refuge includes 177 species. Information and a map of the refuge are available from the headquarters (2150 E. 2350 N., Hamer, 208/662-5423). To get here, take the Hamer exit from I-15 into the town of Hamer, then turn north on the old highway. Go three miles north, then two miles west to the headquarters.

West of I-15 Exit 143, off Highway 33, **Mud Lake Wildlife Management Area** (1165 E. 1800 N., Terreton, 208/663-4664) centers around 7,000-acre Mud Lake. The lake is only about five feet deep and is ringed with bulrushes, cattails, sedges, and salt grass. This wetlands habitat is a prime staging area for some 50,000 snow geese that pass through in March–early April. The best place to view this extravaganza is the **Kaster Overlook Tower,** along the north shore of the lake in the heart of the 8,853-acre WMA. To reach the tower, turn off Highway 33 at Road 1100 East, 14 miles west of I-15. Take 1100 East north three miles to 1800 North and turn right. Follow this road 0.5 miles to the WMA headquarters, where you can pick up a map and get more information. From near the WMA headquarters, near the junction of 1100 East and 1800 North, a road leads northwest; follow it a couple of miles to the first intersection and turn right, then make the very next right in about 0.25 miles. The tower is a couple of miles down this road. If you picked up a map at the WMA headquarters, you'll have no trouble navigating around the preserve.

Dubois

Dubois lies in high-desert terrain at 5,149 feet. Some 20 miles to the north, the Centennial and Beaverhead Mountains form the Continental Divide. Northwest of Dubois, Medicine Lodge Road follows Medicine Lodge creek ever higher into the high peaks, eventually cresting at Medicine Lodge Pass (also called Bannock Pass) on the Montana border. Up Medicine Lodge Road, the U.S. Forest Service's **Webber Creek Campground** (4 sites, free) lies at a lofty altitude of 7,000 feet. The camp is on Webber Creek, but there's no improved water supply. The trail leaving from the trailhead here ascends alongside the creek up into the Beaverheads along the Continental Divide. Mountaineers can make their way over to the scenic Italian Peaks area for a Class 2 ascent of Scott Peak (11,393 feet), the highest of the Beaverheads. To reach the campground, turn west off Medicine Lodge Road on Forest Road 196 at Edie Creek Ranch and follow the road about five miles to the end. For more information, stop by the Caribou-Targhee National Forest's **Dubois Ranger District** (127 W. Main St., Dubois, 208/374-5422).

Spencer

As soon as you get off the interstate at the little outpost of Spencer, you'll be bombarded with signs for a number of different businesses, all imploring you to buy the town's claim-to-fame product: opal. The first opal was discovered in the area in 1948 by a couple of deer hunters. Precious gem-quality opal is rare because a unique combination of geological circumstances is required for its formation—it only forms at the bottom of still pools of underground water. The mineral's layers of microscopic silica spheres reflect light like millions of miniature prisms, brilliantly flashing the colors of the rainbow.

Spencer Opal Mines (27 Opal Ave., 208/374-5476, 9 A.M.–5 P.M. daily Memorial Day–Labor Day, $10 over age 12, $5 ages 4–12) sells permits to dig for opal at its commercial mine that entitle you to take up to one pound of rock; additional rock costs $10 per pound. You need to bring your own tools, including a rock hammer, sledgehammer, bucket, spray bottle, gloves, boots, and safety glasses; the safety glasses are obligatory.

A couple of U.S. Forest Service campgrounds are in the area. **Stoddard Creek Campground** (21 sites, $10–20) is three miles north of Spencer; take I-15 Exit 184, then turn west. The remote **Steel Creek Campground** (4 sites, free) is in the Centennial Mountains northeast of Spencer, midway between Spencer and Kilgore on Forest Road 006. To get to Forest Road 006, head north from Spencer to the Stoddard Creek Campground exit on I-15 (Exit 184), then turn east (right). The road climbs up Miner's Creek, crests Porcupine Pass, and drops down West Camas Creek about six miles to the campground.

U.S. 26 to Wyoming

A DETOUR TO NOWHERE

On the northeast edge of Idaho Falls, Lincoln Road (17th St. N.) turns east off U.S. 26. If you follow this road as far as it goes, you'll come to the boat ramp at **Ririe Lake,** a 1,500-acre impoundment popular with local anglers. If you turn southeast onto Bone Road instead, you'll be on the lonely way to Blackfoot Reservoir or Grays Lake National Wildlife Refuge. Along this route are the towns of **Ozone** and **Bone,** although "town" is perhaps too generous. Windbreaks, perhaps, or time posts—brief flashes of human habitation that will someday soon disappear off the land, then off the maps, and then out of the collective consciousness.

RIRIE AND VICINITY
Cress Creek Nature Trail

If you cross the Snake River headed toward Kelly Canyon but turn left instead of right just across the bridge, you'll soon come to a small parking area for the Bureau of Land Management's Cress Creek Nature Trail. The trail climbs steeply up a sage- and juniper-covered hillside and leads to sweeping views across southeast Idaho—from the lazy Snake River in the foreground all the way out to Big Southern Butte on the horizon. Cress Creek is a sparkling clear gem, and its incessant babbling provides the perfect soundtrack for your picnic.

Alpine Skiing
Kelly Canyon Ski Resort (5488 E. Kelly Canyon Rd., 208/538-6251, www.skikelly. com, day skiing 9:30 A.M.–4:30 P.M. Tues.–Sat., night skiing 5–9:30 P.M. Tues.–Sat., full-day lift tickets $36 adults, $28 seniors and ages 5–11, half-day $28 and $22, night-skiing $28 and $22) is about 25 miles from Idaho Falls. Take U.S. 26 toward Swan Valley, and watch for a signed turn to the left, a mile or so past the turnoff to Ririe. After crossing the Snake River, the road turns up the canyon and leads to the ski area. A shuttle bus is available from Idaho Falls on Saturdays and holidays; call for current schedule and route.

Call it a big small hill, or a small big hill—either way, it's a mellow family ski area with reasonable prices and enough varied terrain to satisfy everyone. Four double chairs serve 27 runs on 640 acres with a maximum vertical drop of 1,000 feet. The runs are 35 percent beginner, 45 percent intermediate, and 20 percent advanced; 70 percent of the area is groomed. There's a terrain park for boarders. A day lodge has a cafeteria and plenty of space to thaw out.

Cross-Country Skiing and Mountain Biking

Just past Kelly Canyon Ski Area, a network of cross-country ski trails laces the hills on Caribou-Targhee National Forest land administered by the Palisades Ranger District (3659 E. Ririe Hwy., Idaho Falls, 208/523-1412). Of the 20-some miles of trails, some are periodically groomed—others are marked but not machine-tracked. There are trails of all ability levels. Easiest is the one-mile Tyro Loop, beginning and ending at the Y junction just above the ski lodge. Most difficult are the five-mile Hawley Gulch Loop, which leads to a remote area and offers lots of big ups and downs along the way, and the Kelly Mountain Trail, which offers advanced skiers a chance for panoramic views of the Snake River Valley. In summer, these logging roads become prime mountain biking terrain.

SWAN VALLEY

Named for the whistling swans that once frequented the area, idyllic Swan Valley lies between the lofty Snake River Range to the northeast and the lower Caribou Range to the southwest. The south fork of the Snake River—a blue-ribbon cutthroat trout stream—flows gently through the valley from Palisades Reservoir back Idaho Falls. The reservoir and river provide water recreation, while hiking possibilities abound in the mountains to either side.

Fall Creek Falls

Fall Creek makes a beeline down out of the Caribou Range, plunging 60 feet into the Snake River at Fall Creek Falls. The falls are on the southwest side of the Snake River, west of the town of Swan Valley. Coming from town, turn left onto Snake River–Palisades Dam Road, just after the highway crosses the Snake River. Follow the road a short distance just across Fall Creek, then park. An overgrown trail leads to a view from the top of the falls. It's a beautiful cascade but is best viewed from a canoe or boat on the river.

Palisades Dam and Reservoir

At the time it was completed in 1959, Palisades Dam on the Snake River was the largest earthen dam ever built by the federal Bureau of Reclamation. An overlook at the outlet provides good views of the lake, dam, and spillway. The 16,100-acre lake has both wild and stocked cutthroat trout as well as smaller populations

of brown trout, kokanee, and mackinaw. Ice fishing is popular in winter. Five boat ramps dot the east shore, and two more are found at either end of the west shore.

Fishing

While Henry's Fork gets all the press, fly-fishing for trout on the South Fork of the Snake River between Palisades Dam and the Henry's Fork is also outstanding and less crowded. You'll be chasing primarily cutthroats and browns. Both South Fork Lodge and the Lodge at Palisades Creek specialize in helping anglers hook the big one, offering fishing-only trips and fishing-lodging packages.

Hiking

Trails lace the Caribou-Targhee National Forest units surrounding Swan Valley. The most noteworthy hike in the region is to **Palisades Lakes,** high in the Snake River Range northeast of the reservoir. To get to the trailhead, take the highway north from Palisades dam about four miles, then turn right onto Forest Road 255, and follow it three miles to the parking area. The trail climbs seven miles along Palisade Creek to the two lakes, both of which offer excellent fishing. Upper Palisades Lake, the larger of the two, sits at an elevation of 7,000 feet. It's the gem of the region—the only lake of appreciable size in the Snake River Range. The Palisades Peaks add a majestic background to the high alpine setting, and the lake is a good base camp for a couple of side trips. Another two miles up in **Waterfall Canyon** is a beautiful waterfall. Ambitious mountaineers can continue from here up the canyon trail to its T junction with the Little Elk Creek trail, then scramble straight ahead up the Class 3 north ridge of **Mount Baird** (10,025 feet), the range's highest peak.

Float Boating

The South Fork of the Snake River—from below Palisades Dam to its confluence with the Henry's Fork near Menan—is a beautiful, 64-mile-long, trout-filled watercourse perfect for those who eschew white-knuckle white water in favor of calm currents and placid pools. It's an easy eight-hour float in your raft, canoe, or kayak from below the dam to Heise. Along the way you'll pass 39 islands—some suitable for camping—and float through a magnificent canyon with 100-foot-high walls. Glorious stands of cottonwoods line the banks, holding in their uppermost branches the nests of bald and golden eagles. Ducks and geese are plentiful, and you might also spot great blue herons, grouse, deer, moose, otters, beavers, bobcats—maybe even a mountain lion or a mountain goat. All have been seen in the area. Side trails leading up Dry Canyon, Black Canyon, and Table Rock Canyon allow you to paddle ashore and explore terra firma if you so desire. The three canyons are linked by another trail that parallels the river's northern bank.

The river is floatable year-round, but some hazardous obstacles—notably canal diversions—do exist; be sure to pick up the *South Fork of the Snake River Boater's Guide* at the visitors center in Idaho Falls. The guide also describes the campsites available en route, some of which also have use restrictions.

Camping

Numerous U.S. Forest Service campgrounds are scattered between Fall Creek Falls and the south end of Palisades Reservoir. **Falls Campground** ($10) provides 24 sites just south of Fall Creek Falls on Snake River–Palisades Dam Road. **Palisades Creek Campground** (8 sites, $10) is at the Palisades Lakes Trailhead at the top of Forest Road 255. It offers restrooms, trailer parking, and good fishing in the creek. **Calamity Campground** ($12–24) is the valley's largest, with 41 sites on the northwest shore of the reservoir near the dam. A boat ramp makes this campground convenient for campers heading out on the water. Continuing around the west shore of the reservoir, next is the small and quiet **Bear Creek Campground** (free). Its eight sites are on Bear Creek about a mile from an arm of the lake. Past Bear Creek, you can continue to follow the road as it winds west through the mountains and

eventually circles back to the southern end of the lake and **McCoy Creek Campground** (18 sites, free), next to a boat ramp. This one is more easily reached, however, from the south off U.S. 89 in Wyoming.

Coming back up the east shore, **Alpine Campground** ($10–20) offers 19 sites by a lakeshore trail—a nice place to watch the summer sun go down over the lake. The 16 sites at **Blowout Ramp Campground** ($10–20) are adjacent to the Blowout boat ramp. **Big Elk Creek Campground** ($10) offers 21 sites at the mouth of Big Elk Creek. From the trailhead here you can hike up the creek into the heart of the Snake River Range.

All the Forest Service campgrounds open for the season around June 1; Alpine opens a little earlier, Palisades and Blowout Ramp a little later. Bear Creek and Blowout Ramp stay open through the end of October; the others all close for the season between Labor Day weekend and mid-September.

Fishing Lodges

Overlooking the Snake River, **South Fork Lodge** (40 Conant Valley Loop, Swan Valley, 208/483-2112, www.southforklodge.com, June–Oct., from $445) is one of the West's most plush angling lodges. It offers eight guest rooms in the main lodge plus two newish log buildings with five guest rooms each along with a restaurant and a tackle shop. Guided fishing is the specialty, and packages are available.

Just upstream from Swan Valley is the hamlet of Irwin and **The Lodge at Palisades Creek** (3720 U.S. 26, Irwin, 208/483-2222 or 866/393-1613, www.tlapc.com, cabins from $340). The lodge sits right along the highway, but also right along the Snake River at Palisades Creek. The log cabin–style accommodations are upscale rustic. You'll be exceedingly comfortable whether lounging on the porch of your cabin overlooking the Snake River or enjoying a gourmet meal served alfresco on the beautiful lodge deck. A minimum four-night stay is requested. Rates include meals and many activities; fishing guides during peak season cost $440 per day for 1–2 people.

Guest Ranch

A couple of the valley's working ranches let you experience the cowboy or cowgirl life up close and personal. **Granite Creek Guest Ranch** (Ririe, 208/538-7140, www.granitecreekranch.com) lies on a 4,000-acre spread up an idyllic valley on the south side of U.S. 26—look for the sign at mile marker 368. The ranch borders Caribou-Targhee National Forest land. Trail rides, cattle drives, fishing, hiking, canoeing on the ranch's lake, and evenings around the campfire are just some of the Old West activities you can enjoy at Granite Creek.

Accommodations are in rustic cabins, each with a private bath and shower. All-inclusive package stays cost about $1,050 per week for adults, $790 ages 6–12, $500 ages 3–5. Shorter stays are also possible. The cabins can also be rented without meals and ranch activities at lower rates. No smoking is permitted inside any of the ranch buildings, and no alcohol is permitted anywhere on the ranch. You can also come up for just a couple of hours or a day and enjoy some of the ranch's facilities and activities; call for rates.

Information

For more information about the area and recreation in the Caribou-Targhee National Forest, contact the **Palisades Ranger District** (3659 E. Ririe Hwy., Idaho Falls, 208/523-1412).

Teton Basin

Teton Basin was once known as Pierre's Hole after Iroquois trapper "Old Pierre" Tevanitagon. Old Pierre trapped here frequently until he was killed in Montana by Blackfoot Indians in 1827. In 1832, Pierre's Hole was the site of the annual rip-roarin' rendezvous of fur trappers, mountain men, and Native Americans—the original trade show.

The 6,000-foot-high valley is spectacularly situated between the Big Hole Mountains on the west and the Teton Mountains on the east. The Tetons are the youngest range in the Rockies; their steep granite faces tower over the landscape from just across the border in Wyoming. Beneath their western flanks lies Grand Targhee ski area, one of the West's best ski and summer resorts.

Both the Tetons and the Big Holes are laced with hiking and mountain-biking trails. For a complete hiking guide to the area, stop by the Caribou-Targhee National Forest's **Teton Basin Ranger Station** (515 S. Main St., Driggs, 208/354-2312).

VICTOR

At the south end of the valley, Victor is an important crossroads, especially for skiers. Coming in on Highway 31 from Swan Valley, turn right to get to Jackson Hole, left to get to Grand Targhee—what a wonderful decision to have to make.

Victor is named for mail carrier George Victor Sherwood, who courageously made his appointed run from here over to Jackson at a time when the local Indians were in a threatening and hostile mood.

Recreation

Among the almost endless hiking opportunities in the area, the **Moose Creek Trail** (Trail 038) follows Moose Creek up to the Teton Crest past a waterfall and alpine lakes. To get here, take Highway 33 southeast from Victor. Just before Mike Harris Campground, Forest Road 276 leads 1.5 miles east to the trailhead.

Across the valley in the Big Hole Mountains, the **Patterson Creek Trail** (Trail 054) climbs alongside Patterson Creek up to Mahogany Ridge and on to Red Mountain (8,715 feet) for panoramic views of the Tetons and the valley. To get to Patterson Creek, take Cedron Road west out of Victor. After several miles, the road bends north; continue north one mile and turn left out of the trailhead.

SOUTHEAST IDAHO

Entertainment

Old Pierre Tevanitagon would no doubt enjoy knowing that Victor remembers him to this day. **Pierre's Playhouse** (37 N. Main St., 208/787-7469, www.pierresplayhouse.com) is the venue for old-fashioned melodrama (8 P.M. Thurs.–Fri., 5:30 P.M. and 8 P.M. Sat. mid-June–late Aug.) presented by the Teton Valley Players. The playhouse also serves as a movie theater, showing current-run flicks, and it puts on an annual production of *A Christmas Carol* during the holidays.

Camping

Teton Valley Campground (128 W. Hwy. 31, 208/787-2647, www.tetonvalleycampground. com) is a tidy, pleasant, and friendly RV park just outside town. Amenities include a heated pool, a coin laundry, a rec room, large grassy sites, restrooms, and showers. It has RV sites ($31–41), cabins ($45), and tent sites ($22).

U.S. Forest Service campgrounds in the area include **Pine Creek Campground** (9 sites, $10–20), back down toward Swan Valley on Highway 31, just on the Victor side of Pine Creek Pass, and **Mike Harris Campground** (12 sites, $10), about the same distance southeast of Victor on Highway 33.

DRIGGS

Driggs is the "urban" hub of Teton Basin— the valley's largest town and a service and supply center for skiers, hikers, and horse-packers heading off into the Tetons or the Big Hole Mountains. Its atmosphere carries vague reminders of the valley's wild rendezvous heritage; Driggs still feels like a remote party town, full of independent outdoors enthusiasts.

Recreation

The road to the ski resort forks on the far side of Alta; the left fork takes you to Grand Targhee, the right fork to Teton Canyon. At the end of the road up Teton Canyon is the area's most popular trailhead. From here you can continue on foot up Trail 027 for 7.7 miles to the top of Teton Canyon and **Alaska Basin,** a scenic

alpine valley with a number of gem-like lakes. You're up in the high and wild here, surrounded by 10,000–12,000-foot peaks. The down side is that the area is heavily used. Another shorter trail offering an exceptionally scenic hike is the **South Darby Trail** (Trail 033). This 2.7-mile one-way hike begins at a trailhead at the end of Darby Canyon Road (Forest Rd. 012), which turns east off Highway 33 three miles south of Driggs. The trail climbs along the South Fork of Darby Creek, past waterfalls and beautiful wildflower-filled meadows.

If you think the Tetons and Teton Valley are impressive from the ground, wait till you see them from the air. **Teton Aviation** (208/354-3100 or 800/472-6382, www.tetonaviation. com) can take you aloft from Teton Peaks Centennial Airport in Driggs for a scenic airplane or glider flight. Flights in the single-passenger gliders cost about $250 for an hour. Airplane flightseeing costs $235 per hour for a planeload of up to three passengers.

OUTFITTERS

Your year-round recreational rental needs are deftly handled by **Yöstmark Mountain Equipment** (285 E. Little Ave., 208/354-2828, 9 A.M.–6 P.M. daily). Telemark packages and snowshoes are the hot rental items in winter. In summer, the store rents tents, backpacks, stoves, sleeping bags, duckies, fishing gear, and more. Yöstmark also manufactures the famous "Mountain Noodle" backcountry ski.

Entertainment and Events

Driggs enjoys the classic **Spud Drive-In Theatre** (231 S. Hwy. 33, 208/354-2727). Look for the big potato marquee.

Idaho offers no shortage of hot-air balloon rallies, but the **Teton Valley Summer Festival** (www.hotairballoon.com) has to be the tops. On Fourth of July weekend, some 30–40 balloons chase each other across the crystal-clear blue skies above the Tetons. If you can't drag yourself away when it's all over, stick around for the subsequent events up at Grand Targhee. In August, look for the **Teton County Fair.**

For more information and a complete events calendar, contact the **Teton Valley Chamber of Commerce** (208/354-2500, www.tetonvalleychamber.com).

Accommodations

Pines Motel Guest Haus (105 S. Main St., 208/354-2774 or 800/354-2778, $45–100) offers eight guest rooms, six with private baths, in a refurbished and expanded turn-of-the-20th-century log cabin. Breakfast is available for an extra charge. Amenities include cable TV, in-room phones, a jetted tub, a large lawn for summer picnics and barbecues, and an ice-skating rink in winter. Kids and pets are allowed.

Best Western Teton West (476 N. Main St., 208/354-2363 or 800/937-8376, from $98 d) offers a tidy and amenity-filled Best Western package. Luxuries include an indoor heated pool and hot tub.

Teton Valley Cabins (34 Ski Hill Rd., 208/354-8153, www.tetonvalleycabins.com, $79–99) are right on the road to the ski area. Here you'll find 20 cozy cabins that cost a little less in winter.

ALTA, WYOMING

Yes, technically both the little town of Alta and the Grand Targhee resort are in Wyoming, not Idaho, but unless you're Joe Mountaineer, the only way to get to either of them is through Idaho. How strange life must be for the residents of Alta—cut off from the rest of their state by the mighty Tetons. But I doubt they complain; this is one beautiful neck of the woods. A handful of lodgings options, a restaurant, and a golf course are all you'll find in Alta—most area services are in Driggs.

Golf

Targhee Village Golf Course (Stateline Rd. and Golf Course Rd., 208/354-8577, Apr.–Oct., $18 for 9 holes, $24 for 18 holes) is a nine-hole par-72 course stretching just over 6,000 yards. There is also a driving range and great views of the Tetons.

GRAND TARGHEE RESORT

The Tetons are some of the West's most magnificent mountains, and Grand Targhee (3300 E. Ski Hill Rd., Alta, WY, 307/353-2300 or 800/827-4433, www.grandtarghee.com) is certainly one of the West's most magnificent resorts. It's a little gem of a place—uncrowded, well designed, and reasonably priced. It's also just far enough off the beaten track to make you feel as if you've discovered your own personal Shangri-la, and that's a feeling the resort's friendly staff are pleased to encourage.

Alpine Skiing

Often overshadowed by the mega–ski resorts in Utah and by its Wyoming neighbor Jackson Hole, Grand Targhee (full-day lift tickets $69 adults, $44 seniors, $29 ages 6–12, free under age 6) is an awesome spot to ski and snowboard in its own right. And what nice powder this place has! The 3,000-acre, two-mountain ski heaven gets more than 500 inches of snow per year. In one recent year, the total topped 650 inches.

Grand Targhee is by no means unknown, but you have to work a little to get to it. That fact automatically keeps the dilettantes at bay, leaving the slopes wide open on most days. Fred's Mountain has 2,000 vertical feet and 1,500 acres of skiing, with the runs rated 10 percent beginner, 70 percent intermediate, and 20 percent expert. It is served by two quad chairs, one double, and an easy-on, easy-off "Magic Carpet" lift for the beginners area. The other mountain, Peaked, has 500 acres and 1,277 acres of lift-served terrain, but another 1,000 acres are reserved for powder skiing and riding. Snowboarders will find a terrain park as well as board rentals and lessons.

Half-day lift tickets are available; passes for the Shoshone Lift only, which serves the kids' area, are $44. Guided snowcat skiing over on Peaked Mountain is offered daily, weather permitting, and costs about $330 pp per day.

© IDAHO DIVISION OF TOURISM

skiing at Grand Targhee

Cross-Country Skiing

Twelve miles of immaculate cross-country tracks—both skating and traditional—leave from the resort's base area and head out into the surrounding glades. The tracks are groomed to perfection—it's the kind of place where you can work on your uphill glide. The farthest three-mile loop leads to a view of Grand Teton, and chances are good that you'll have the whole trail system to yourself. A warming hut on the far side would be a nice addition, as would trail names and marked junctions, but all in all, this is one of the state's finest tracked cross-country areas. A full-day trail pass costs around $15 for adults; lessons and rentals are available.

To find out all about the mountain's cross-country scene, check in at the Nordic Center (9 A.M.–4:30 P.M. daily winter) at the base of Shoshone lift.

Summer Recreation

Grand Targhee is a great place to be in summer too when the Tetons pierce the brilliant blue sky and wildflowers paint the alpine meadows of Targhee National Forest in a rainbow of brilliant colors. The resort offers **chairlift rides** (end of June–early Sept., $15 adults, $6 ages 6–12) up the mountain in summer for great views—including the back side of the Tetons—and a leisurely hike back down.

Mountain bikers will appreciate the resort's trail system. You can even load your bike onto the chairlift ($20 all day) and ride down from the summit. Bike rentals are available at the resort's Activity Center. If **rock climbing** is more your style, check out the climbing wall at the base of Shoshone lift; it costs $10 for a 15-minute session. Free activities include hiking and disc golf.

Horseback riding fans should gallop over to Crooked Canyon Stables at Grand Targhee, where they can sign up for a trail ride. One-hour ($39) and two-hour ($59) trail rides take in spectacular views of the Tetons, the Big Hole Mountains, the Teton Valley, and the Continental Divide.

Activity Center

The folks at the resort's Activity Center (307/353-2300, ext. 1355) in the base-area village can set you up with just about any activity that interests you, on or off the mountain, any time of year. In many cases they can handle all the arrangements for you right from the office.

Events

The second week of August brings the annual **Grand Targhee Bluegrass Festival,** packed with big-name pickers and fiddlers. To find out who's playing and when, call the resort (800/827-4433).

Accommodations

Three separate lodging options are available right at the resort's base area. **Targhee Lodge** ($125–139) offers standard guest rooms with two queens. The plush rooms of the exquisite **Teewinot Lodge** ($179–199) are furnished and decorated in Southwestern and Native American motifs. Each room has two queen beds, and amenities include a hot tub and a large lobby with a fireplace and ski racks. The

Sioux Lodge Condominiums come in various sizes that sleep anywhere from two ($199–219) to eight (over $250). The midrise Sioux Lodge building lacks architectural character, but you get great views from each of the fireplace- and kitchenette-equipped guest rooms. Rates vary depending on the date, and various discount packages are available. Pets are not allowed.

Food

The resort's main dining room, the **Branding Iron Grill** (breakfast, lunch, and dinner daily, dinner entrées $14–26), is itself a work of art; a high open-beam ceiling caps two-story-high windows and a massive fireplace. Casual elegance is the watchword. There is a distinctive gourmet menu, and the wine list offers a wide selection of California wines as well as a few from Idaho and Washington.

Other eateries include the **Trap Bar,** a favorite après-ski and evening spot, and **Snorkel's,** with espresso, deli sandwiches, and pastries.

U.S. 20 to West Yellowstone

RIGBY TO ST. ANTHONY
Rigby

Rigby's claim to fame is as the "Birthplace of Television." Inventor Philo T. Farnsworth (1906–1971), holder of more than 125 patents, first came up with the idea of the cathode ray tube while living in Rigby. You can find out more about Farnsworth and Rigby at the **Jefferson County Historical Society and Farnsworth TV & Pioneer Museum** (118 W. 1st S., 208/745-8423, 1–5 P.M. Tues.–Sat., $2 adults, $1 students, free under age 7).

Amid the teetotalers of the eastern Snake River Plain, potato vodka is now being produced by two distillers in Rigby; this will surely please martini fans.

For more information about Rigby, contact the **Rigby Chamber of Commerce** (208/745-8701).

Rexburg

The squeaky-clean lifestyle of the Latter-day Saints is much in evidence in Rexburg, home of the Mormon-owned Brigham Young University–Idaho. Established in 1888, the onetime junior college was originally named for Thomas Ricks, the Mormon leader who came north from Logan, Utah, in 1882 to found the town, but it got the Brigham Young University moniker and became a full-fledged university in 2001. Rexburg is also a favorite among "sunbirds," senior citizens who spend winters down south and summers in a cooler clime. Between the straitlaced Mormon collegians and the senior set, you might expect Rexburg to be one of Idaho's more sedate towns—and it is.

There's a pretty good arts and culture scene, though. The main event is the **Idaho International Dance & Music Festival** (www.rexcc.com/festival, single-event tickets $3–10), held end of July–first week of August. Folk dance groups from all over the world come here to share their fancy footwork and culture. A street dance, a parade, a rodeo, a country-western concert, and lots of food accompany the wide variety of dance styles presented.

Teton Dam Site

It seems amazing that a dam whose construction was opposed by the U.S. Environmental Protection Agency, the Idaho Fish and Game Department, and the Idaho Conservation League ever got built in the first place. Even the dam-crazy Army Corps of Engineers couldn't bring itself to endorse this turkey. The cost-benefit analysis on Teton Dam never made sense, no matter how you looked at it—not from an irrigation perspective, not from a flood-control perspective, not from a hydropower perspective. The dam wasn't needed or wanted by anyone other than the U.S. Bureau of Reclamation, presumably seeking to justify its own existence, and the Fremont Madison Irrigation District, seeking to save a little money on its water bill. What's even more amazing is that invincible Idaho engineering giant Morrison "No Task Is Impossible" Knudsen—prime contractor for the project—just plain screwed up.

Congress approved the dam in 1964 and construction began in 1972. The dam was completed in spring 1976, and the reservoir behind it began to fill up. On the morning of June 5, 1976, with the reservoir nearly full, crews noticed two leaks in the dam. Workers with bulldozers were dispatched to plug the leaks, but the porous volcanic earth beneath the dam was passing water like a sieve. The design had inadequately addressed the geologic features of the site.

IDAHO POTATO VODKA

The Gem State's prized potato crop gets turned into a multitude of products, like potato chips, French fries, instant mashed potatoes, potato soup, potatoes au gratin, hash browns, and even potato-based skin lotion. (OK, now I'm sounding like Bubba in *Forrest Gump*.) But did you know that potato vodka is also produced in Idaho? The little farming community of Rigby has turned into vodka central in recent years. Local russets are used to make **Teton Glacier Vodka.** Master distiller Pat Wernimont employs modern techniques to produce this crystal-clear spirit. Instead of using the typical pot-still process, he distills the vodka in a four-column continuous distillation system that raises the alcohol level and removes all impurities. The filtration process involves running the spirits through charcoal and garnet crystals. The end result is full-bodied potato vodka with a silky, smooth finish. **Silver Creek Distillers** (134 N. 3300 E., Rigby, 208/754-0042, www. glaciervodka.com) produces Teton Glacier,

and they have been known to give occasional tours of the facility.

Also in Rigby, two vodka-loving guys turn out flavored potato vodka on a smaller scale. Distillers Ken Wyatt and Ron Zier produce Mountain Huckleberry and Rainier Cherry vodkas under the **44° North** label (www.44northvodka.com). Besides these fruity yet dry vodkas, they also make grain vodka called Magic Valley Wheat.

Over on the western Snake River Plain, in the heart of Idaho's wine country at Sunny Slope, **Koenig Distillery** (20928 Grape Lane, Caldwell, 208/455-8386, www.koenigvineyards.com, tasting room noon-5 P.M. Fri.-Sun.) makes exceptionally smooth potato vodka in beautiful hand-hammered copper-pot stills. Distiller Andrew Koenig also makes delicious fruit brandies, while his brother, Greg, turns out award-winning varietal wines under the **Koenig Vineyards** label.

All these vodkas can be purchased at Idaho state liquor stores and at liquor stores throughout the country.

Imagine being one of those bulldozer operators and seeing the leaks get exponentially greater despite your best efforts. Imagine thinking about the frail, failed barrier that was keeping 80 billion gallons of water from washing you and that bulldozer as far as American Falls. When it became clear that the situation was out of control, the dozer operators fled for their lives, leaving the heavy equipment behind.

At 11:52 A.M. the entire dam burst, sending a wall of water downstream that destroyed everything in its path. It wiped the village of Wilford off the map—six people drowned and 150 homes were lost. Sugar City was hit at 1 P.M., and Rexburg at 2:30 P.M. The flood finally subsided in the Fort Hall bottoms of American Falls Reservoir three days later. When the destruction ended, the cost of the folly was estimated at between $800 million and $1 billion, not to mention the lives lost.

Today, you have to look for the site to find it. Drive out on Highway 33 east of Sugar City and look for a sign to the north, three miles east of Newdale. A short spur leads to an overlook of what was once the dam. It's an eerie site. Much of the dam infrastructure—ramps and concrete structures—remains in place, abandoned to the elements. Perhaps most fascinating, however, is the lack of any interpretive information at the site that owns up to culpability for the disaster.

Back in Rexburg, however, the **Teton Dam Flood Museum** (51 N. Center St., Rexburg, 208/359-3063, 10 A.M.–7 P.M. Mon., 10 A.M.–5 P.M. Tues.–Sat. May–Sept., reduced hours Oct.–Apr., $2 adults, $1 ages 12–18, $0.50 under age 12) has extensive displays on the event along with Rexburg-area pioneer memorabilia.

St. Anthony Sand Dunes

Prevailing wind patterns have created a 35-mile-long, five-mile-wide desert of sand dunes a few miles west of St. Anthony. The 10,000 acres of dunes—some hundreds of feet high—constitute a playground for the off-road-

vehicle set. Hiking and camping are possible in the area, but don't expect a wilderness experience; this is an area sacrificed to off-roading. The two hubs of dune-buggy and all-terrain vehicle activity are the scruffy **Sandhills Resort** (865 Red Rd., St. Anthony, 208/624-4127), on the east side of the dunes, which offers a bit of grass and RV sites ($18–60); and the **Egin Lakes Access Area** on the south side (off 500 N.), a free primitive camping area constantly abuzz with the sounds of internal combustion engines. For more information, contact the **Bureau of Land Management Idaho Falls District** (1405 Hollipark Dr., Idaho Falls, 208/524-7500).

St. Anthony

All the flies have been tied, the new rod has been purchased, the new waders are ready for that first splash of icy mountain water—now all Idaho's eager anglers can do is wait for the fishing season to open. One signal casting them off on their annual pursuit is St. Anthony's **Fisherman's Breakfast** (6 A.M.–2 P.M. last Sat. in May). It's free to one and all, but bring your best fish story to share. The **Fremont County Fair** comes to town for three days in early August; look for livestock shows, a rodeo, and a Dutch-oven dinner. To find out more, stop by the Greater St. Anthony Chamber of Commerce **visitors center** (420 N. Bridge St., 208/624-4870).

ASHTON AND VICINITY

Ashton was founded in 1906 and named after William Ashton, chief engineer for Oregon Short Line Railroad. As the world's largest seed-potato-producing area, Ashton's life revolves around the familiar tuber. Surrounding the city are some 11,000 acres planted in potatoes, which produce about 10 tons per acre. In addition to potatoes, the local fields grow wheat, barley, canola, hay, and peas.

Highway 47, designated by the state as the Mesa Falls Scenic Byway, is the scenic 25-mile back way between Ashton and Harriman State Park. Most of the sights listed below are on or near Highway 47.

Mesa Falls

Continuing north up Highway 47 past Warm River, you'll soon come to two impressive waterfalls on the Henry's Fork. At Lower Mesa Falls, the river squeezes through a narrow gorge and drops 65 feet. A turnout at the lower falls offers good but distant views of the cascade. Nearby is the U.S. Forest Service **Grandview Campground** (5 sites, free). Farther up the road, 114-foot Upper Mesa Falls offers a well-developed viewing area. Wheelchair-accessible walkways lead down to the top of the falls for close-up views. You'll also find the rustic old Big Falls Inn, which was a roadhouse back in the days before U.S. 20 was built. It's now a visitors center that's open seasonally.

Yellowstone National Park

Although nearly all of Yellowstone National Park—including its major tourist facilities—is found in Wyoming, a thin strip along the western border of the park extends into Idaho. Cave Falls Road leads about 25 miles northeast from Ashton into the southwestern corner of the park. It's a dead-end road, isolated from the rest of the park; you can't keep driving to Old Faithful without going back to Ashton and taking other highways through Montana or Wyoming. But this corner of the park, the "Cascade Corner," boasts an excellent backcountry trail system leading into the Bechler River drainage and more than half the park's waterfalls. From the end of the road at Cave Falls or from the nearby Bechler Ranger Station, you can hike to Dunanda Falls, Iris Falls, Ouzel Falls, Colonnade Falls, or Union Falls, among others. Pick up a map and a wilderness permit at the ranger station, which is up a spur road a few miles back toward Ashton from Cave Falls. The area didn't get torched in the 1988 firestorm that incinerated 36 percent of the Yellowstone's forests, so it remains heavily timbered. It's all grizzly country, so take appropriate precautions and check with the rangers for news of recent sightings and for trail-condition updates.

Cave Falls is a low, broad, and beautiful cascade on the Falls River. The nearby U.S. Forest Service **Cave Falls Campground** (23 sites, June 1–Oct. 1, $10–20), just outside the Yellowstone park boundary, gets filled up in summer; come after Labor Day for more breathing room.

Jedediah Smith and Winegar Hole Wildernesses

Yellowstone National Park is north of Cave Falls Campground, but the beautiful backcountry knows no boundaries. An area south of the park, extending all the way to Teton Pass, Wyoming, with only one small gap, has also been protected in the Winegar Hole and Jedediah Smith Wildernesses. Both of these pristine areas are grizzly bear heaven, and both are located entirely within the state of Wyoming.

Cross-Country Skiing

At the **Bear Gulch-Mesa Falls Park N' Ski Area,** about five miles past Warm River on Highway 47 North, you'll find a trailhead for cross-country ski tracks leading to Upper Mesa Falls. The trailhead is at the old Bear Gulch Ski Area. It's 8.8 miles from Bear Gulch to the falls and back; the trail climbs steeply at first, but then becomes more moderate as it traverses the rim of Henry's Fork Canyon. On the way back you'll get great views of the Tetons, 30 miles away. Other shorter loops are also marked and groomed. You won't have the area all to yourself; snowmobile trails parallel the cross-country trails.

Falls River Ridge Park N' Ski Area, 10 miles east of Ashton on Cave Falls Road (1400 N.), offers seven miles of beginner-intermediate trails that are periodically groomed. Loops of 2–6.1 miles are possible, and pieces of the trail system are shared with snowmobilers. Some of the trails wind through groves of lodgepole pines and aspens, but most of the trails cross open terrain. Watch for moose, coyote, and snowshoe hare tracks loping, scampering, or hop-skip-jumping, respectively, across the trail.

Forest Service Cabins

Caribou-Targhee National Forest's **Ashton-Island Park Ranger District** (46 U.S. 20, Ashton, 208/652-7442) offers three year-round rental cabins within a 30-mile radius of Ashton.

To the northwest, the one-room **Bishop Mountain Lookout** ($25) overlooks Island Park Reservoir from atop 7,810-foot Bishop Mountain. It sleeps four in two sets of bunk beds and has a woodstove and outhouse but no water or lights. In winter you'll need a snowmobile for access.

The two-bedroom **Warm River Hatchery** cabin ($45) lies 24 miles northeast of Ashton, about five miles east of Mesa Falls. It sleeps 10 in bunk beds and is furnished with a wood cookstove and a heater. Water must be taken from the creek and treated. You can cross-country ski to the cabin in winter.

Finally, 23 miles due east of Ashton on Forest Road 261 you'll find **Squirrel Meadows Guard Station** ($35), a two-room affair with a woodstove and bunk beds that sleep up to six.

Outside you'll find an outhouse and a hand pump for water. In winter you can ski in.

◖ HARRIMAN STATE PARK

Eighteen miles north of Ashton, Harriman State Park (3489 Green Canyon Rd., Island Park, 208/558-7368, day-use $5) was formerly a 10,700-acre cattle ranch and private retreat owned by several bigwigs of the Union Pacific and Oregon Short Line Railroads. Edward H. Harriman, father of Sun Valley founder Averell Harriman, bought into the ranch in 1908, and eventually the entire Railroad Ranch, as it was known, ended up in the Harriman family. The family donated the land to the state in 1977, stipulating that the property be used as a wildlife preserve. The park opened to the public in 1982.

The Henry's Fork flows right through the ranch, offering superb fly-fishing for cutthroat trout. Elk, beavers, muskrats, and sandhill cranes also call the park home, and some of the region's trumpeter swans winter on the park's lands.

© IDAHO DIVISION OF TOURISM

Harriman State Park

SOUTHEAST IDAHO

TRUMPETER SWANS

Harriman State Park is a prime wintering area for the Rocky Mountain trumpeter swan – a species that was close to extinction at the turn of the 20th century. Hunting and habitat changes brought about by human settlement had wiped out most of the swans. Only a few living in Alaska and the most remote areas of the Rockies survived. Those survivors wintered in this area, where hot springs feeding into the rivers keep the waters open and flowing even in the coldest times. Conservation efforts began in the 1930s. The wintering swans were fed grain at Red Rock Lakes National Wildlife Refuge 20 miles northwest of Harriman. The artificial feedings continued for almost 60 years until 1992. The feedings probably saved the swans from extinction – now the population of the species is about 3,000 – but they also created a problem of their own. The swans took to wintering only around the artificial-feeding areas and abandoned their migratory routes to points farther south. As a result, the southerly migratory routes were obliterated from the species' collective memory, and the Red Rock Lakes refuge and the area around the park are now overcrowded with the beautiful swans in winter. The park's aquatic vegetation is insufficient to support their numbers, so once again the species is faced with a threat to its survival. Game wardens now encourage the swans to keep moving south in winter by persistently hazing them so they don't get too comfortable.

The park is primarily a day-use-only area, and no camping is allowed, although there are several year-round yurts ($50) that sleep up to six, and cabin lodgings are available to larger groups by reservation. Many of the original Railroad Ranch buildings still stand; rangers lead regular free tours in summer.

Hiking, Biking, and Skiing

Twenty-one miles of trails are open to hikers, mountain bikers, and equestrians in summer and to cross-country skiers in winter. No motorized vehicles or pets are permitted on the trails. The trails are particularly noteworthy in winter as the park maintains one of the finest trail layouts in the state's Park N' Ski system. According to one survey of southeast Idaho cross-country skiers, it's also the most popular. About half the trails are groomed; the side closest to the highway is the groomed side and has the easiest trails, most traversing wide-open meadows. Both skating and traditional lanes are set up where the terrain permits; traditional tracks are set up through the trees. All trails start from the visitors parking area just off the highway.

ISLAND PARK

In 1939, geologists studying the Island Park area realized that the surrounding landscape was a giant caldera. When this area passed over the Yellowstone hot spot about 2 million years ago, a huge volcano erupted, blowing rhyolite tuff over a 6,000-square-mile area and creating a crater 23 miles in diameter. The crater subsequently collapsed, forming the caldera. Just north of Ashton, U.S. 20 crosses Big Bend Ridge, part of the rim of this ancient crater.

In winter, under a glaze of snow, the area is especially beautiful. Unfortunately it's also very popular with snowmobilers. The Big Springs snowmobiler parking lot is just up the road near Mack's Inn and serves a large trail system on National Forest land. As a result, the tranquility of winter in Island Park is spoiled by the constant two-stroke din and stench of hundreds of snow machines. If you're here to cross-country ski, go to the snowmobile-free Harriman State Park, where you'll have the best chance of getting a little peace and quiet.

Island Park Reservoir

Island Park Dam was built on the Henry's Fork in 1938, creating 7,000-acre Island Park Reservoir. The lake supports a population of landlocked kokanee salmon and whitefish as well as brook, cutthroat, and rainbow trout. Ice fishing is popular in winter. In summer, boaters enjoy the reservoir. You can rent personal watercraft at Sawtelle Mountain Resort, but be alert: The lake is known for unpredictable strong winds that have resulted in more than one unwary boater drowning in the chilly waters.

Hiking and Mountain Biking

The **Box Canyon Trail** makes an easy six-mile round-trip day hike. Start at Box Canyon Campground and follow the Henry's Fork south for three miles along the canyon rim. The trail provides access to the river's trout heaven for fly-fishing and delights wildflower watchers with bursts of summer color.

Across the highway to the east, the old **Union Pacific Railroad bed** has been converted into a recreation trail running north–south past Island Park. It's a multiuse trail, so you'll be sharing it with motorized vehicles. The closest access road to Island Park is Chick Creek Road (Forest Rd. 291), which leads east off the highway about three miles south of Island Park. From the highway it's four miles down Chick Creek Road to the trail.

Float Boating

The **Henry's Fork** between Island Park Dam and Last Chance makes a pleasant two-hour float suitable for beginners, and the **Buffalo River** from its headwaters to U.S. 20 is equally placid and popular. To reach the Buffalo River headwaters, take Forest Road 291 east off U.S. 20 about 2.5 miles south of Pond's Lodge. Follow Forest Road 291 about seven miles to Forest Road 292 and turn north, then in another two miles turn west on Forest Road 1219 to the put-in. The put-in can also be reached out of Mack's Inn; take the Big Springs Loop to Forest Roads 082, 292, and 1219. Be careful of fences spanning the river.

Ponds Lodge

Right on the west side of the highway, Ponds Lodge (3757 N. U.S. 20, Island Park, 208/558-7221, www.pondslodge.com, $85–295) may

not be the quintessential mountain resort, but it has a big restaurant serving homespun fare and a rustic saloon with a pool table, a jukebox, and a wood stove. The year-round lodge offers 14 cozy cabins; pets are allowed. The venerable Ponds is the bustling hub of Island Park activity, filled in summer with tourists en route to Yellowstone and in winter with boisterous snowmobilers. But the best part is that it's right next to the Brimstone Park N' Ski trailhead. The Brimstone trails are easy and flat, skirting the Buffalo River and the Henry's Fork, where trumpeter swans like to hang out in winter.

Henry's Fork Lodge

The most luxurious accommodations in town are at stunning Henry's Fork Lodge (2794 S. Pinehaven Dr., Island Park, 208/558-7953, www.henrysforklodge.com), off by itself on a secluded bend in the river. It has modern lodge architecture done right for a change, this time by architect Joseph Esherick. The stone-and-timber lodge and guest cabins are works of art in themselves yet fit in inconspicuously and harmoniously with the surroundings. The big back porch commands a sweeping 180-degree view of the river and comes complete with wooden rockers from which to take it all in. You have the river to yourself; the most ruckus you'll have to contend with is the splash of a trout rising on a mayfly or of swans landing on the crystal-clear water. Meals, in the gorgeous dining room that serves gourmet fare, are included in the rates and are also available to nonguests by reservation.

The lodge can arrange nature tours of the region and tours to Yellowstone and occasionally offers presentations on area topics by naturalists and historians. Fishing packages that include transportation from Idaho Falls or West Yellowstone, six days of accommodations and meals, and five days of guided fishing run about $3,360 pp based on double occupancy and two anglers per guide. Without the guide service, the cost drops to $2,160 pp. Superdeluxe suites are available for $30–50 pp per night extra. Three-night lodging packages are also available. Fishing-guide service for nonguests costs $480 per day for 1–2 anglers.

Other Area Accommodations

Off the east side of U.S. 20 about a mile north of Ponds Lodge is ◖ **Elk Creek Ranch** (Phillips Loop Rd., Island Park, 208/558-7404, www.elkcreekid.com, closed winter), a fishing lodge with a rustic but comfortable lodge and eight cabins. The lodge offers its own no-license private lake, and Elk Creek flows right past. Rates of $100 pp per day, $35 ages 7–14 include lodging, all meals, and fishing on the lake. The dining room is open to nonguests by reservation.

Across the loop road from Elk Creek Ranch, **The Pines at Island Park** (3907 Phillips Loop Rd., Island Park, 208/558-0192 or 888/455-9384, www.pinesislandpark.com, $189–389) offers large, fully equipped cabins with kitchens, hot tubs, and barbecue grills that sleep up to eight adults. The restaurant serves lunch and dinner, and the lodge building has a cozy lounge with a pool table. It's peaceful as the ranch is set off from the highway hubbub.

Camping

U.S. Forest Service campgrounds around Island Park Reservoir are administered by the **Ashton-Island Park Ranger District** (208/652-7442) and are accessed via Kilgore Road. They include the busy **McCrea Bridge Campground** (25 sites, $12), next to the boat ramp at the lake's inlet, and **Buttermilk Campground** (52 sites, $12–17), on the northeast shore of the lake next to a boat ramp. In the Ponds Lodge area are **Buffalo Campground** (105 sites, $12–24), on the Buffalo River on the east side of the highway, and **Box Canyon Campground** (17 sites, $12), also on the riverbank on the west side of the highway south of Ponds Lodge—from U.S. 20, take Forest Road 134 and then Forest Road 284. **West End Campground** (19 sites, free) is reached via a long drive west on Green Canyon Road (Forest Rd. 167), which turns west off U.S. 20

just south of Osborne Bridge near Harriman State Park. The campground offers a boat ramp and receives light use.

Information

The **Island Park Area Chamber of Commerce** (208/558-7755, www.islandparkchamber.org) can give you the lowdown on the area.

MACK'S INN AREA
Big Springs

One of the country's 40 largest springs, Big Springs pours 120 million gallons per day of superclear water into the Henry's Fork. The constant-temperature 52°F water emerges from underground at 186 cubic feet per second and makes ideal spawning habitat for fish. There are six different species: rainbow, cutthroat, and brook trout; coho and kokanee salmon; and mountain whitefish. You can feed the fish, but they can't feed you; the area is closed to fishing. Also at the springs, a mile-long interpretive trail heads downstream to the Big Springs boat-launch area, and another short trail crosses Big Springs bridge and leads to **Johnny Sack cabin** (July 4–Labor Day). The cute little cabin, on the National Register of Historic Places, was built by German immigrant Johnny Sack in the early 1930s. Sack also constructed a small waterwheel, using the flow of the springs to provide his cabin with electricity and water. The little waterwheel house is as artful as the cabin.

In summer, crowds of rafters, canoeists, and inner-tubers line up at the boat-launch area, 0.75 miles downstream from the springs, to put in on the **Big Springs National Recreation Water Trail**. It's a popular, placid, 2–4-hour float trip from here down the Henry's Fork to Mack's Inn. Both Big Springs and the boat launch are on Big Springs Loop Road (Forest Rd. 059), which leaves the highway at either Mack's Inn or Island Park village. At **Mack's Inn Resort** (4292 N. U.S. 20, Island Park, 208/558-7272) you can rent canoes and rafts, and they even provide a shuttle service.

Hiking

The **Coffee Pot Rapids Trail** offers an easy day hike on the west side of Mack's Inn. It begins from Upper Coffee Pot Campground and follows the Henry's Fork downstream for 2.5 miles, passing both placid pools and turbulent rapids. It's closed to motorized vehicles.

More difficult is the **Sawtell Peak-Rock Creek Basin Trail,** which starts near the top of 9,866-foot Sawtell Peak and crosses the Continental Divide on its way to Rock Creek Basin. It seems odd, but it's true—you'll first cross the Continental Divide heading west into Montana, then cross back to the east side into Idaho again. The trail is six miles round-trip, some of it steep, and outstanding views are the norm. To reach the trailhead, take Sawtell Peak Road (Forest Rd. 024) west off the highway, about 1.75 miles north of Mack's Inn. Follow the road 11.5 miles to the trailhead, or 13 miles to the summit of Sawtell Peak.

The **Continental Divide National Scenic Trail** passes near Mack's Inn on its meandering high-altitude route between Canada and Mexico. As the Continental Divide surrounds Mack's Inn on three sides, you've got a choice of segments and access points. To access the trail to the east, in the Henry's Fork Mountains, take Black Canyon Road (Forest Rd. 066) off the Big Springs Loop Road near its easternmost extension and follow it up to Reas Pass Creek. From here you can make your way north on foot to Reas Pass, then north to the east side of Targhee Pass. West of Mack's Inn, the divide runs "sideways," east to west across the Centennial Mountains. Access points are at the tops of Keg Springs Road (Forest Rd. 042) and East Dry Creek Road (Forest Rd. 327), both of which turn north off Forest Road 030 (Kilgore-Yale Rd. or County Rd. A2). Forest Road 030 turns west off U.S. 20 between Mack's Inn and Island Park. No matter which section of the Continental Divide Trail you choose, take plenty of water and good topo maps—the trail may be sketchy in places. And it's important to remember that many parts of the trail are in prime grizzly country.

For more information on any of these trails, contact the U.S. Forest Service's **Ashton-Island Park Ranger District** (208/652-7442).

Accommodations

Big, bustling **Mack's Inn Resort** (4292 N. U.S. 20, Island Park, 208/558-7272, www.macksinn.com) holds down the south bank of the Henry's Fork with accommodations and recreation options galore and hundreds of happy campers. Lodging options include an array of cabins ($59–180) and riverfront motel rooms ($100–150). RV spaces ($29.50) have full hookups; tent sites ($15) have no hookups. A rental shop offers rafts, canoes, and lots more stuff. Other amenities include a restaurant, a general store, and a shower facility. You won't run out of things to do, but you might feel like part of the herd.

One mile north of Mack's Inn, **Island Park Village Resort** (4153 N. Big Springs Loop Rd., Island Park, 208/558-7502, www.islandparkvillageresort.com) sprawls across a hillock on the east side of U.S. 20. The resort complex is full of upscale furnished 1–4-bedroom condos ($150–250), all with kitchens and fireplaces, and boasts amenities such as tennis courts, an indoor pool, and a nine-hole golf course.

On the west side of U.S. 20 across from Island Park Village is **Sawtelle Mountain Resort** (U.S. 20 milepost 395, 208/558-9366 or 866/558-9366, www.sawtellemountainresort.com), offering motel rooms ($50–100), a hot tub, and an RV park ($35–50) with full hookups. The resort also has some cabins and tent sites.

Camping

The Caribou-Targhee National Forest's **Big Springs Campground** (15 sites, $12–50) enjoys a prime location within walking distance of Big Springs and Johnny Sack cabin; sites are reservable. Across the highway to the west are **Flat Rock Campground** (38 sites, $12–17) and **Upper Coffee Pot Campground** (14 sites, $12–17). For more information, contact the U.S. Forest Service's **Ashton-Island Park Ranger District** (208/652-7442).

HENRY'S LAKE AND VICINITY

In a high mountain bowl at an elevation of 6,740 feet, surrounded on three sides by the Continental Divide, Henry's Lake has been a historically important campsite. Major Andrew Henry was the first nonnative to see the lake when he passed by in 1810. Jim Bridger camped on the lake's shores with trappers and Flathead Indians in 1835, and the Nez Perce camped here on their flight from General O. O. Howard during the Nez Perce War of 1877.

The lake is popular among anglers, who pursue rainbow-cutthroat hybrids, cutthroat and eastern brook trout, and mountain whitefish in the shallow waters.

Henry's Lake State Park

On the southeast shore of the lake, 586-acre Henry's Lake State Park (3917 E. 5100 N., Island Park, 208/558-7532, Thurs. before Memorial Day–end of Oct., weather permitting) provides anglers with a great base camp for fishing expeditions out on the water. The small park holds a reservable campground with 45 sites ($20–24), 25 with hookups, as well as showers, restrooms, a boat ramp, boat docks, a nature trail, and a picnic area. There also are two camping cabins ($50) that can sleep up to six.

Backpacking

The 14-mile **Targhee Creek Loop Trail** begins north of U.S. 20 near Targhee Pass and leads through dense forests, across wide-open ridgetops with panoramic views, and past five alpine lakes perfect for camping and fishing. The trailhead is at the end of Targhee Creek

Trail Road (Forest Rd. 057), midway between Targhee Pass and the junction of U.S. 20 and Highway 87. This is prime grizzly country, so be careful. Bear-proof food boxes are installed at many campsites. Use them if you can; otherwise hang your food well.

Trail Rides

Meadow Vue Ranch (3636 Red Rock Pass Rd., Island Park, 208/558-7411) lies west of U.S. 20 on the south side of the lake. The working ranch offers weeklong camps for youth and some daily activities for the public; call for info.

Jared's Wild Rose Ranch

Jared's Wild Rose Ranch (3778 Hwy. 87, 208/558-7201, www.wildroseranch.com), a resort on the lake's north shore, specializes in serving the needs of anglers. It has been around since the early 1800s; Zane Grey did some writing here. The resort has a café open early for breakfast and a well-stocked tackle shop. It also boasts boat rentals, boat slips, and boat ramps to get you in and out of the water with ease. Accommodations include cabins ($59–275), condos (from $300), motel rooms ($85–179), RV spaces ($30–35) with full hookups, and tent sites ($18).

Howard Springs

Travelers continuing on to Yellowstone on U.S. 20 will find the last best Idaho picnic stop along the east side of the highway at Howard Springs. General Oliver Howard passed these springs in hot pursuit of Chief Joseph and the Nez Perce in 1877; today, it's a day-use area.

Continuing north on U.S. 20, you'll cross **Targhee Pass** into Montana. Targhee, a Bannock chief, is remembered for his peace-making efforts during the turbulent 1860s.

Lava Land

North of Pocatello, I-15 stays close to the hills on one side and fronts the vast, wide-open Snake River Plain on the other. U.S. 26 and U.S. 20 head west from Blackfoot and Idaho Falls, respectively, forging bold straight paths out across the plain's lonely high-desert terrain. Not far from the lifeblood water of the Snake River, the plain doffs its irrigated mask of green to reveal the blacks, browns, grays, and reds of its volcanic origins.

BLACKFOOT AND VICINITY

The Bingham County seat, Blackfoot is a working-class agricultural hub ruled by King Spud; this is the number-one potato-producing county in the nation as well as Idaho's top grain producer. Founded in 1879, Blackfoot is the largest of the county's handful of small towns, most of which have declined in population in the last few decades.

Idaho Potato Museum

It really is worth getting off the highway and seeking out this shrine to Idaho's most famous vegetable, the Idaho Potato Museum (130 NW Main St., Blackfoot, 208/785-2517, www. idahopotatomuseum.com, 9:30 A.M.–5 P.M. Mon.–Sat. Apr.–Sept., 9:30 A.M.–3 P.M. Mon.–Fri. Oct.–Mar., $3 adults, $2.50 seniors, $1 ages 6–12). You'll find it in the old Oregon Short Line Railroad Depot. In addition to offering "Free Taters for Out-of-Staters," the museum houses endless potato anecdotes and trivia. Here you'll see the world's largest potato chip, made by Procter & Gamble's Pringles division; a picture of Marilyn Monroe dressed in a burlap potato sack; and a copy of the 1992 letter sent by Idaho governor Cecil Andrus to U.S. Vice President Dan Quayle following Quayle's well-publicized spelling-bee faux pas. The letter, which accompanied a gift box of

© JAMES P. KELLY

Blackfoot's Idaho Potato Museum, housed in an old railroad depot

SOUTHEAST IDAHO

Idaho bakers, reads: "As far as we're concerned you can spell potato any way you want as long as it's genuine Idaho. P.S. There is no 'e' in Idaho either." Next door to the museum is a gift shop selling T-shirts (not made from potatoes), potato fudge, potato hand lotion, and other potato products.

Recreation

Jensen Grove Park makes a nice place to get out of the car for a breather. A shady grove of cottonwoods gives the park its name and watches over an inviting picnic area. Waterskiers and summertime splashers make good use of the park's 55-acre lake. To get here, take I-15 Exit 93 east, then make the first left and follow it to the park. Golfers enjoy the adjacent 18-hole, 6,722-yard, par-72 **Blackfoot Municipal Golf Course** (3115 Teeples Dr., Blackfoot, 208/785-9960, Mar.–Oct., $21–23). Club and cart rentals are available.

Accommodations

The **Best Western Blackfoot Inn** (750 Jensen Grove Dr., Blackfoot, 208/785-4144 or 800/528-1234, from $74 d) is close to I-15 Exit 93. All guest rooms have two queens, and amenities include cable TV, an indoor pool, and free continental breakfast.

HELL'S HALF ACRE

Covering some 222 square miles, this geologically brand-spanking-new lava flow—about 2,000 years old—occupies almost the entire eastern half of the triangle formed by I-15, U.S. 20, and U.S. 26. You can get a pretty good look at the flow from the rest stop on I-15 just north of Blackfoot, but to really explore the flow, take U.S. 20 west of Idaho Falls for 20 miles, then turn south on a 0.25-mile gravel road to a parking area and trailhead. This is the Hell's Half Acre Wilderness Study Area, a 66,000-acre preserve managed by the Bureau of Land Management (BLM), Bonneville County, and the Idaho Alpine Club. From here you can head out across the lava on foot in any direction. A couple of suggested but unimproved trails are marked with colored poles. One of them is a

half-hour loop that takes you past several different volcanic features; the other is a 4.5-mile route that leads to the volcanic vent itself, the spot from which the molten goo oozed. From the vent, at an elevation of 5,350 feet, the lava flowed south down to a point near today's I-15, at an elevation of 4,600 feet.

The best time to visit is in late spring or early summer, when the wildflowers are blooming brightly and the summer sun has yet to turn the Snake River Plain's oven knob to "broil." For more information on the Hell's Half Acre area, contact the **BLM Idaho Falls District** (1405 Hollipark Dr., Idaho Falls, 208/524-7500).

BIG SOUTHERN BUTTE

You can't miss this landmark rising nearly 2,500 feet above the surrounding plain. It's visible on the horizon from nearly all of southeast Idaho. Like scores of other smaller buttes sprinkled across the Snake River Plain, Big Southern Butte was also created by the forces of volcanism, but unlike the other smaller buttes, the molten rock that spewed from the earth here was not basalt but much more viscous rhyolite. Think of it like an upwelling of Elmer's glue instead of water. The rhyolite cooled and solidified before it had the chance to spread and flatten out across the plain. Unlike the more common black basalt, rhyolite is light colored, which helps Big Southern Butte stand out in contrast to its surroundings.

You can hike to the top of the 7,560-foot butte or even drive up in a 4WD. To get to the road to the summit, start from Atomic City on U.S. 26, and take Cox's Well–Atomic City Road west. Continue across the railroad tracks, bearing right at the Cedar Butte Road intersection and left at the Cedar–Big Butte Road intersection. From here, the idea is to follow roads clockwise around the south and west sides of the butte, ending up at Frenchman's Cabin (and landing strip) on the butte's northwest corner. From the major intersection at Frenchman's Cabin, the road to the Butte leads off to the southeast. After 1.5 miles, you'll come to a gate. If it's locked, hike up the remaining 3.5 miles; if it's open and you have a 4WD vehicle, you have your choice of hoofing it or using the gas-guzzler. In either case, bring plenty of water. You'll pass through Douglas fir forest on the way up, and there are spectacular views from the summit. Backpackers can bivouac on top to catch sunrise over the Tetons.

IDAHO NATIONAL LABORATORY

The U.S. government established the Idaho National Laboratory (INL, 800/708-2680, www.inl.gov) in 1949 to build and test nuclear reactors for both civilian and military purposes. Today, Department of Energy contractor Bechtel BWXT conducts a broad spectrum of nuclear-related studies here, including research and development of electric vehicles, medical radiation cancer treatments, environmental cleanup technologies, and nuclear waste volume-reduction systems, among others.

You can't see much of INL from most roads in southeast Idaho. That's partially by design: The 890-square-mile site was selected for its remote location. The barren desert out on the sparsely populated Snake River Plain seemed the perfect place to toy with the newly uncorked nuclear genie. But even if you never see INL, it's hard not to think about it in your travels through the region. "The site," as many call it, has the nation's highest concentration of nuclear reactors; 52 have been built here over the years, and 13 continue to operate. That's a particularly interesting statistic given that the site is located in one of the nation's most geologically active areas and sits atop an aquifer that supplies drinking and irrigation water for much of southern Idaho. Many people see this as a nightmare in the making.

INL is also the federal government's current repository for nuclear waste shipments from all over the country. Spent reactor fuel from the nuclear Navy is shipped here by rail from Mare Island, California, and Newport News, Virginia. The U.S. Departments of Defense and Energy have no legal obligation to notify

states of these shipments—you wouldn't want terrorists sabotaging or stealing the radioactive cargo. But again, many people look at this process and see potential catastrophe. Storage of federal waste at INL is supposed to be temporary, but since no other plan to safely store nuclear waste is even close to being implemented, what that "temporary" label means is uncertain.

Isolated instances of small nuclear-waste spills have been reported over the years, and the INL is also a Superfund site, listed by the U.S. Environmental Protection Agency (EPA) for chronic contamination that took place over decades of use. Among the toxic substances detected in both monitoring and drinking-water wells on the Snake River Plain aquifer: hexavalent chromium, acetone, sodium hydroxide, and sulfuric acid. In addition, the EPA reports that

> carbon tetrachloride and trichloroethylene (TCE) have migrated from where they were buried to the Snake River Plain aquifer. Soils are contaminated with heavy metals such as lead and mercury, volatile organic compounds, and radionuclides.

You don't hear much protest about any of this in Pocatello or Idaho Falls, where most of INL's employees live. The site employs about 8,000 area residents and generates about $612 million in wages and more than $50 million in tax revenues annually.

EBR-1

Experimental Breeder Reactor-1, built in 1951, was the world's first atomic power plant. The reactor was decommissioned in 1964 and designated a National Historic Landmark in 1966, and it's open for guided or self-guided tours (8 A.M.–4 P.M. daily Memorial Day–Labor Day, free). The reactor is on U.S. 20/26, 18 miles southeast of Arco, 50 miles west of Idaho Falls, and 40 miles northwest of Blackfoot. For more information, call the EBR-1 office (208/526-0050) or the INL Public Affairs Office (800/708-2680).

ARCO

Arco was the first city in the world to be lit by atomic power. On July 17, 1955, scientists at the National Reactor Testing Station (now INL), 18 miles east of town, threw a switch and sent 2 million watts of electricity from Boiling Water Reactor No. 3 (BORAX-III) into the living rooms of Arco for a little more than an hour.

Number Hill

The graffiti-riddled hill behind town is a monument to adolescent fervor. Since 1920, every graduating senior class at the local high school has trudged up the hill to paint its class year on the rocks. The view of town from the cliffs is decidedly romantic. One can only imagine how many fond memories have been conceived up here each moonlit May for the past 80-odd years.

King Mountain

Consistent updrafts make the summit of King Mountain, north of town, a popular launching spot for hang gliders; the Idaho state distance record was set here. On the south flanks of the peak is one of the most impressive local destinations for hikers—a natural bridge spanning 80 feet. The massive limestone arch frames the rugged spruce-covered terrain. A map to the King Mountain area is available at the visitors center (132 W. Grand Ave., Arco, 208/527-8977).

Events

If you're gliding through town the third weekend in July, you'll be right on time for the **King Mountain Hang-Gliding Championships** (www.flykingmountain.com) up on King Mountain. If you ask around, you might even be able to get a tandem ride on one. Also in July, on the closest weekend to July 17, the anniversary date of the town's historic electrification, the whole town lightens up for **Atomic Days.** Featured are parades, a rodeo, a quilt show, sidewalk sales, nuclear exhibits, dancing, and other high-voltage festivities.

Accommodations and Food

For clean, comfortable lodging, head to **D-K Motel** (316 S. Front St., Arco, 208/527-8282,

atomic Arco

www.dkmotel.com, $38–80). This motor inn has 25 guest rooms, most at the low end of this price category. Amenities include cable TV, free Wi-Fi, and a laundry facility.

Nearby, grab some lunch at the aptly named ◖ **Number Hill Grill** (242 S. Front St., Arco, 208/527-8224, 10:30 A.M.–9 P.M. Mon.–Sat., under $10), a little fast-food shack with a red-and-white paint job. You can get tasty burgers, chicken sandwiches, wraps, salads, and breaded finger steaks. The super-thick milk shakes are delicious too.

Information

The **Lost River Visitors Center** (132 W. Grand Ave., Arco, 208/527-8977) can give you a map to the natural arch and answer your questions about the area.

◖ CRATERS OF THE MOON NATIONAL MONUMENT

Eighteen miles southwest of Arco, U.S. 20/26/93 enters Craters of the Moon National Monument (208/527-1300, www.nps.gov/crmo), an eerie, otherworldly landscape

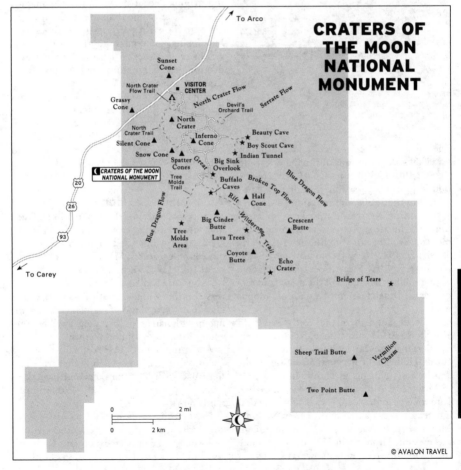

CRATERS OF THE MOON NATIONAL MONUMENT

© AVALON TRAVEL

© JAMES P. KELLY

hiking on the "moon"

the Moon National Monument and Preserve, managed jointly by the National Park Service and the Bureau of Land Management.

Lava fields cover much of southeastern Idaho, but what makes this area unique is the concentration of different volcanic features. Craters of the Moon lies along the Great Rift, a 60-mile-long perforation in the earth's crust along which eruptions have occurred as recently as about 110 B.C., practically yesterday on geologic time scales. The earth's crust is stretching apart, becoming thinner, and developing deep cracks and fissures above hot rising magma deeper down. When the magma reaches the crust and finds the cracks, it erupts out onto the earth's surface—sometimes placidly oozing, sometimes spouting forth in geysers of molten rock. Scientists say the area is due for another eruption any day now, sometime in the next 1,000 years.

From the air, the Great Rift looks like a giant dashed line of enormous cracks, dotted here and there with cinder cones marking the sites of volcanic vents. Craters of the Moon constitutes a summary of the Great Rift, where an entire textbook's worth of volcanic phenomena can be seen in one place.

A Lavaland Lexicon

Visitors to Craters of the Moon will be faced not only with an alien landscape but with an alien set of words used to describe the various volcanic features. Many of the words come from the Hawaiian language; those islands were built by similar volcanism, and the process continues today, so it's no surprise that Hawaiians were ahead of mainlanders in coming up with names for what they saw. These are a few of the more common terms:

A'a (pronounced "AH-ah" and meaning "hard on the feet") lava is full of sharp edges that slice open both sneakers and bare skin. You can't walk barefoot on *a'a*—and you certainly don't want to fall down on it.

Pahoehoe (pronounced "pa-HOY-hoy" and meaning "ropy") lava is smoother than *a'a* and won't make mincemeat of your Keds. It's also full of enclosed air pockets, so chunks of

pocked, cracked, contorted, and charred by lava flows and eruptions occurring at various times 2,100–15,000 years ago. When Oregon-bound pioneers passed by here on Goodale's Cutoff in the 1860s, they considered the area a forbidding wasteland and kept on moving, but the area soon caught the eye of geologists, who began studying it in the early 1900s. In 1921, U.S. Geological Survey geologist Harold T. Stearns described the area as resembling the craters of the moon and recommended the creation of a national monument at the site.

That idea, and the name, really took hold after Boise taxidermist-turned-explorer Robert Limbert made several long treks across the lava flows. He brought national attention to the area by describing his adventures in the March 1924 issue of *National Geographic* magazine. Later that year, President Calvin Coolidge designated the area Craters of the Moon National Monument. In August 2002 the monument was expanded from about 55,000 acres to more than 250,000 acres, now known as Craters of

pahoehoe are far lighter than equivalently sized *a'a* chunks.

Cinder cones form when an eruption sprays lava into the air. The lava droplets cool on the way down, and the resultant cinders accumulate as big ash heaps, generally with shallow-sloped sides that are highest right around the vent. Since the cinders are light, cinder cones are often elongated in the direction of the prevailing wind. **Spatter cones** form where steam vents disgorge denser globs of lava into the air. The heavier globs clot together like a hollow chimney around the vent, generally forming cones that are smaller than cinder cones and with steeper sides. Large globs of lava thrown skyward often solidify in midair and land as **lava bombs.** The bombs come in several different common shapes, including spindle, ribbon, and bread crust, the latter looking like a fine pumpernickel *bâtard.*

Kipukas are areas where a lava flow surrounded, but didn't cover, either an older flow or an area as yet untouched by lava. These "islands" of vegetation allow scientists a window on preflow vegetation in an area and allow them to compare that vegetation to postflow growth. Where lava flows into a tree, it makes a cast of the trunk, then cools around it. The trees themselves are long gone—burned to a crisp—but the impression of their scorched bark remains etched in the lava.

A **lava tube** is formed when the surface of a river of *pahoehoe* lava cools and hardens into a skin, while the interior of the stream stays molten and pours through. After the molten flow drains away, the hardened outer skin forms a hollow tube, often loosely called a cave. Sometimes these "caves" can even have "stalactites," which in this case aren't calcite deposits left by dripping water but lava that hardened in the act of dripping off the ceiling of the tube.

Flora

Looking at the dry, blackened landscape, you wouldn't expect much life to be found at Craters of the Moon. The area receives a limited amount of precipitation to begin with, about 15–20 inches per year. Arid conditions are compounded by wind-exacerbated evaporation, and rainfall and snowmelt sink through the porous lava before the plants have much of a chance to make use of it. Nevertheless, many plants have adapted to these harsh conditions.

Of primary importance to all the other plants in this land of abundant rock is the minute **lichen,** a symbiotic association of an alga and a fungus. It attaches itself to rocks and over time breaks down the rock into soil in which other plants can get a start. What an odd but heroic life form, the lichen.

Drought-tolerant desert dwellers such as **sagebrush, antelope bitterbrush,** and **prickly pear cactus** also inhabit the monument, but probably the most striking plant species here is the **dwarf buckwheat.** This tiny plant grows only a few inches tall, but its root system spreads out across an underground area up to three feet in diameter. As a result, dwarf buckwheat plants are spaced out across the lava fields, looking more like a gardener's plantings than nature's handiwork. In summer, the white-foliaged plants look like snowflakes against the black lava.

The most prevalent tree in the monument is the hardy **limber pine.** Its limber branches bend easily but don't break in the often heavy winds, and its very large seeds can germinate in cracks in the lava where other trees could never get started. In early summer, it's time for the wildflowers to show off; look for **monkeyflower, desert parsley, Indian paintbrush, bitterroot,** and **scabland penstemon,** among others.

Fauna

Small mammals can make a home in and among the cracks in the lava flows. Don't be surprised to see mice, voles, pikas, squirrels, and chipmunks darting about and keeping a close eye on your food. Of course, those little guys are food themselves for the local raptor population, which includes northern harriers, red-tailed and sharp-shinned hawks, and great horned and long-eared owls. Though you're unlikely to see them, gopher snakes, rubber boas, and rattlesnakes are also found here.

Besides *Homo sapiens,* the **mule deer** is the largest mammal inhabiting the monument. The park's healthy herd of these big-eared Bambis has made remarkable adaptations to life on the lava. In spring, the herd turns up in the wilderness area south of the monument, where they find high-quality forage, but since the area provides no pools of open water they get all their water from dew, condensed fog, and the vegetation they eat. When summer comes and the wilderness area dries out, the herd moves north into the smaller monument proper, congregating in larger-than-normal population densities around the few water sources. In fall, the rains return and the herd heads back south into the wilderness area. When snow falls, the deer leave the park entirely, off to their wintering grounds. It's a complicated schedule as mule deer migrations go, but it seems to be working well for this ingenious herd.

Visitors Center and Campground

After turning off the highway, on the left you'll find the monument's visitors center (208/527-1300, 8 A.M.–6 P.M. daily summer, 8 A.M.–4:30 P.M. daily in other seasons, closed federal holidays). Exhibits and videos explain the geology, flora and fauna, and history of the area, and National Park Service rangers answer questions and sell a variety of related science and history books.

Across the road from the visitors center is the monument's single campground (no reservations, $10). Its 52 sites are densely clustered in a relatively small area, but this is a blessing rather than a curse—it means the rest of the monument is less crowded. Water and restrooms are available at the campground, but showers, hookups, groceries, and other amenities are not. Rangers lead interpretive walks by day and present amphitheater programs in the evening. Check out those stars!

The day-use fee is $8 per vehicle or $4 pp for those entering by bicycle, motorcycle, or on foot. Day use and camping are free October–May, but there's no running water, and the campsites aren't plowed. When the loop road gets covered in snow, rangers turn it into a groomed cross-country ski trail.

Around the Loop Road

From the campground, a seven-mile road loops south into the heart of the monument, past many sight-filled stops. Among the highlights: the **Devil's Orchard,** where a short wheelchair-friendly interpretive trail loops through some bizarre formations; **Inferno Cone Viewpoint,** where you can hike up to the top of Inferno Cone for sweeping views across the lava flows and the Snake River Plain; the **Tree Molds** area, where a short hike leads to some prime examples of that phenomenon; and the **Cave Area,** where a trail leads to numerous lava tube "caves," most of which require a flashlight to explore. With multiple stops, a few short hikes, and a picnic lunch thrown in for good measure, plan a leisurely 3–4 hours to make your way around the loop.

Into the Wilderness

In 1970, Congress designated 43,000 acres south of the monument as Craters of the Moon Wilderness. You'll need a permit from a ranger at the visitors center to venture into this area, accessed past the end of the Tree Molds trail. Not surprisingly, the wilderness receives little use. In summer, temperatures are high and water is scarce. In addition, hiking on the lava chews up boots. In winter, it might seem tempting to head out into the snow-covered wilderness on cross-country skis, but unstable snow bridges can obscure deep cracks in the lava. A fall into the Great Rift would put an end to your cross-country ski vacation.

SAWTOOTH COUNTRY AND BEYOND

The upper reaches of the Snake River Plain finally relent to central Idaho's Rocky Mountains, a postcard-perfect panorama of craggy peaks and pastoral high-mountain valleys that in no way resembles the desert, apart from some patches of hardy sagebrush.

Wood River Valley is home to the mountain-chic resort towns of Hailey, Ketchum, and Sun Valley, a European-inspired ski destination with a celebrity guest book that has included Clark Gable, Marilyn Monroe, Ernest Hemingway, and Errol Flynn. Expect to find exceptional skiing and golfing, big-city boutiques, posh galleries, and upscale restaurants—the Wild West and Wilshire Boulevard come together in this isolated draw flanked by the Pioneer and Smoky Mountains.

North of Sun Valley, the softly contoured mountains give way to the more jagged and much larger Sawtooth, White Cloud, and Boulder Ranges, which stretch toward the sky like busted saw blades. These unspoiled mountains are a veritable playground for thrill-seekers wishing to get away from it all, an easy thing to do in the Frank Church–River of No Return Wilderness, the largest wilderness area in the lower 48. Outdoor enthusiasts flock to this unbridled high country for a serious dose of alpine fun—on Mother Nature's terms, of course. Year-round recreational fun abounds for the skilled and daring and for properly briefed novices. World-class white-water rafting and kayaking, hiking, mountain biking, and amazing backcountry skiing keeps the masses coming back.

The decidedly rustic and loveable Stanley, a

© DANA HOPPER-KELLY

HIGHLIGHTS

◖ Camas Prairie Centennial Marsh Wildlife Management Area: Springtime is the right time to see wildflowers and waterfowl strut their stuff in the verdant marshlands of this high prairie, framed by the looming Soldier and Trinity Mountains (page 237).

◖ Sun Valley Resort: Known as the country's first bona fide ski resort, this charming mountain getaway has been a popular destination for powder fanatics since it opened in 1936 (page 260).

◖ Redfish Lake: One of the most scenic lakes in Idaho, Redfish Lake is flanked by the massive granite faces of Mount Heyburn. Stay in the grand Redfish Lake Lodge or at one of the eight U.S. Forest Service campgrounds that surround the lake (page 268).

◖ Stanley: This frontier-themed town is situated in a high-mountain valley flanked by the imposing Sawtooth and White Cloud peaks. It's pure nirvana for outdoor recreationalists (page 270).

◖ Custer Motorway Adventure Road: Fans of ghost towns will get a kick out of this scenic drive that leads you to Custer and Bonanza, old mining towns in the Yankee Fork Historic Area (page 280).

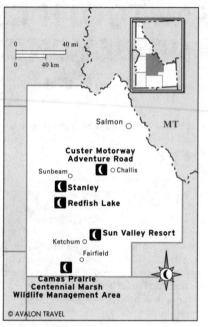

© AVALON TRAVEL

LOOK FOR ◖ TO FIND RECOMMENDED SIGHTS, ACTIVITIES, DINING, AND LODGING.

frontier-esque town crowned by massive peaks, is a wonderful place to kick back and relax after pushing your body to the limit. Grab a hotel room, some steaks and ale, and then plop into a hot tub with commanding views of Potato Mountain.

Mountaineers will find much to do on the steep faces around town, or you can head southeast to Mount Borah, Idaho's tallest peak, near Mackay.

The southwestern fringe of the Sawtooths is a land less traveled, meaning you can have a true Idaho experience. The Camas Prairie explodes with color each spring when its marshes

of blue camas lilies and other wild flowers sway in the gentle wind. The Soldier and Trinity Mountains offer quiet solitude, miles of remote trails, and a few nail-biting drives on primitive roads, like the Rocky Bar–Atlanta stretch.

PLANNING YOUR TIME

Since much of this mountainous region is extremely remote, backpacking and rafting trips generally take four days or more. But you'll want to allow yourself a few extra days to hang out in the Ketchum–Sun Valley area. Spring and fall are good times to visit; both the crowds and hotel rates go down.

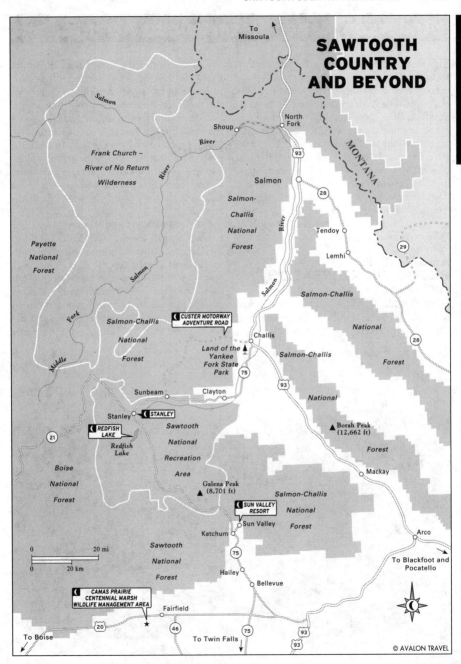

SAWTOOTH COUNTRY AND BEYOND

To Missoula

Salmon

Shoup

North Fork

River

Frank Church –
River of No Return
Wilderness

MONTANA

93

Salmon

Salmon-
Challis

National

Forest

River

Tendoy

28

Lemhi

Payette

National

Forest

29

Salmon

Salmon-Challis

National

28

Fork

Salmon-Challis

National

Forest

Middle

**CUSTER MOTORWAY
ADVENTURE ROAD**

Challis

Land of the
Yankee
Fork State
Park

75

Salmon-Challis

National

Forest

Sunbeam

Clayton

93

National

Stanley   **STANLEY**

Sawtooth

▲ Borah Peak
(12,662 ft)

21

**REDFISH
LAKE**

Redfish
Lake

National

Recreation

Forest

Boise

National

Area

Mackay

Forest

Galena Peak
(8,701 ft) ▲

Salmon-Challis

**SUN VALLEY
RESORT**

National

Ketchum

Sun Valley

Forest

Arco

0   20 mi

Sawtooth

75

National

To Blackfoot and
Pocatello

0   20 km

Forest

Hailey

Bellevue

**CAMAS PRAIRIE
CENTENNIAL MARSH
WILDLIFE MANAGEMENT AREA**

Fairfield

To Boise

20

★

46

75

93

To Twin Falls

93

© AVALON TRAVEL

Anderson Ranch Reservoir to Atlanta

This southwestern stretch of the Sawtooths is actually in the Boise National Forest district. Here you will discover Idaho without all the trappings of out-of-state tourism. To access this area from Boise, head east on I-84 to Mountain Home and take the exit for U.S. 20 northbound, after which the road leaves the flats of the Snake River Plain and rises dramatically past Bennett Mountain. Soon you will catch glimpses of the high country to come, as mountain peaks and undulating valleys suddenly appear to the left. The highway eventually straightens out on the Camas Prairie, leading to the Wood River Valley and beyond.

ANDERSON RANCH RESERVOIR RECREATION AREA

Southwest Idaho anglers come to this expansive reservoir year-round to fish for kokanee, chinook salmon, rainbow trout, yellow perch,

and smallmouth bass. In addition, the **South Fork Boise River** below the dam offers blue-ribbon trout fishing. Waterskiing is popular on the reservoir in summer—you'll find several boat-launching ramps around the lake—as is snowmobiling in winter. Two different roads traverse the east and west shores. To reach the west shore, turn off U.S. 20 on Forest Road 134 and you'll soon drop precipitously down to the dam. The road crosses the spillway and continues north up the west side of the reservoir.

Fall Creek Resort and Marina (2147 S. Fall Creek Rd., Fall Creek, 208/653-2242) lies at the Fall Creek inlet to the reservoir, eight miles up the west shore from the dam. This small resort is a beautiful spot to hang out for a few days. The spacious but smoky lounge and restaurant provide views of the cove and nearby mountains, and a downstairs fitness area has a sometimes-working sauna, spa, and exercise

Anderson Ranch Reservoir

© JAMES P. KELLY

equipment. The marina rents paddleboats, sells marine fuel, and maintains a small store for groceries, tackle, and marine supplies. Guest rooms (around $65) are available along with RV sites ($15–30) with water and electricity hookups; there's a dump station at the marina. There are some tent sites ($15) down by the creek. Other facilities include a small game room, a gift shop, a boat ramp and moorage, and shower rooms.

Continuing up Forest Road 113, it climbs to beautiful wooded tableland before descending to the lake's main inlet at the little town of **Pine.** Here Forest Road 113 joins the main road along the east shore. **Nester's Pine Resort** (12 N. Pine-Featherville Rd., Pine, 208/653-2210) offers RV sites ($25) with full hookups, 16 motel rooms ($60–81), and one cabin ($135). The resort also has a gift shop, a Laundromat, a bar, and a café open for three meals a day. Close by, the **Nitz Pine Store** (88 N. Pine-Featherville Rd., Pine, 208/653-2222) sells groceries, sundries, and fishing tackle.

To reach the east shore, continue east on U.S. 20 three miles past **Little Camas Reservoir** and turn left onto Forest Road 152; follow it down to Forest Highway 61 and make a left. This side of the reservoir is busier than the more remote Fall Creek Resort, but you probably won't see many Mercedes SUVs here either—primer spots and a few dents are totally acceptable in this microcosm of Idaho.

Deer Creek Lodge (730 S. Pine-Featherville Rd., Pine, 208/653-2454) offers a café, RV sites (around $30) with hookups, and a few tent sites (around $10). About two miles north of Deer Creek Lodge you'll meet the west shore road at Pine.

JOHNSON'S SPRINGS HOT SPRINGS

Forest Highway 61 crosses the South Fork Boise River at Johnson's Bridge, where you'll no doubt see many cars parked along the north side. On the east bank of the river, just downstream from the bridge, a hot spring sends toasty water flowing down into riverside pools suitable for soaking. It's a popular spot with area campers and is usually crowded.

TRINITY MOUNTAINS

An alpine gem in southern Idaho, the Trinity recreation area has craggy peaks and numerous small lakes that often remain snowbound into August. Trinity Mountain (9,451 feet) crowns the area, providing panoramic views of the Sawtooths and Smoky Mountains to the northeast, and the Snake River Plain and Owyhee Mountains to the southwest. If you make it all the way up to the Forest Service fire lookout on top, you'll be at the highest lookout in the Boise National Forest.

This is great mountain-biking country. Forest Roads weave through pine woods, aspen groves, and wildflower-filled meadows. One of the best hiking and backpacking trails in the area is the **Rainbow Basin Trail** (Trail 1174). It begins at Big Trinity Lake Campground and meanders south for about four miles past short spur trails to nine different alpine lakes that have rainbow and cutthroat trout. It's open to pedestrians only.

Big Trinity Campground (17 sites, $10) lies at the end of Forest Road 129E off Forest Road 129. Other U.S. Forest Service campgrounds in the vicinity include **Big Roaring Campground** (12 sites, $10) and **Little Roaring Campground** (4 sites, free). All the campgrounds are open July–September. For a bit more comfort, consider renting the Forest Service's **Big Trinity Guard Station** (reservations 877/444-6777, July 15–Sept. 30, $30), a cabin that sleeps six. For more information on the guard station or the campgrounds, contact the Boise National Forest's **Mountain Home Ranger District** (2180 American Legion Blvd., Mountain Home, 208/587-7961).

To reach Trinity Mountain and the Trinity Lakes, take Fall Creek Road (Forest Rd. 129) north from Fall Creek Resort on the west side of Anderson Ranch Reservoir, or take Trinity Creek Road (Forest Rd. 172) west off Featherville Road (Rte. 61) just south of Featherville.

FEATHERVILLE AND POINTS EAST

Featherville is a tiny Old West–style enclave at the confluence of the small Feather River and the big South Fork of the Boise River. Forest Road 227 heads east out of town and follows the South Fork of the Boise up to its headwaters. Along the way are numerous hot springs and U.S. Forest Service campgrounds, one of which will probably match your style. The following sites are listed from west (Featherville) to east (Big Smoky Creek).

Four small campgrounds (all $6) appear in rapid succession within the first seven miles east from Featherville. **Abbott Campground** (7 sites) comes first, followed closely by the like-sized **Chaparral Campground**, and 1.5 miles farther is five-site **Bird Creek Campground.** A couple of miles farther east is five-site **Willow Creek Campground.** The spur into Willow Creek Campground continues farther up to little-used **Willow Creek Hot Springs.**

Baumgartner Campground (reservations 877/444-6777, $10 single-vehicle site, $20 double-size), about 12 miles from Featherville, is the main destination for most of the campers headed up the South Fork. John Baumgartner was a local miner who died in 1941 and left his mining claims to the federal government for a park; this campground is the result. The big attraction here is the Forest Service–developed hot-springs pool—a deluxe, improved, concrete-lined number that can be crowded in summer. The large, 30-site campground lines the river amid groves of majestic ponderosa pines. A short nature trail starting near the hot pool loops across the hillside above the creek; signs explain aspects of the area's natural history along the way. There has been a lot of bear activity in the area in recent years, so keep a clean campsite, and don't smear kielbasa grease all over your shirt before crawling into your sleeping bag for the night.

Continuing east up the South Fork Boise, you'll pass swampy and unappealing Lightfoot Hot Springs along the shoulder of the road, and continue a while longer to **Bowns Campground** (12 sites, $6).

Just past Bowns, you'll come to the private cabins of the Big Smoky area, where you'll find a Forest Service guard station as well as Trapper's Inn (208/764-3104), a store with ice, bait, and other necessities of life in these parts. The business also has cabins and tent-cabins available ($50–70).

The road forks here; Forest Road 227 crosses Big Smoky Creek and heads out of the mountains down to Fairfield or Ketchum.

OVER TO ATLANTA

If you go straight at Featherville instead of veering east, you are headed for the mining town of Atlanta, and there is a choice of two routes. **Phifer Creek** is the easier and longer way, and if you're headed to Atlanta after coming down from the Trinities, this is the road you'll be on. **James Creek** (Forest Rd. 072) is a lot shorter, but it's steeper and more demanding; on this primitive route you'll be rewarded with incredible views and staircase waterfalls. The decision point—in other words, the road junction—is at the mining ghost town of **Rocky Bar.** The right fork is the James Creek route, the left goes via Phifer Creek. You can also get to Atlanta off Highway 21 near Idaho City.

ATLANTA

Although prospectors discovered precious metals around Atlanta in the 1860s, development of the area was hampered by its inaccessibility. Eventually the logistics problems were solved, and 1932–1936 the Atlanta Mining District ran the most productive gold mines in Idaho. Today, there's still some gold mining going on, especially during the summer months. The little village of about 50 people lies at the south end of the Sawtooths, which rise just north of town. Greylock Mountain (9,317 feet) dominates the skyline, summoning backpackers up into the high reaches of the Sawtooth Wilderness. The wilderness boundary is less than a mile from town.

Atlanta preserves its history in **Community Historic Park,** which has several pioneer-era buildings, among them the old jail. The town's biggest shindig is **Atlanta Days** in late July, which brings out all the local hermits for a dance, a community breakfast, and a horseshoes tournament.

Hot Springs

Atlanta is blessed with two hot springs near the center of town. **Atlanta Hot Springs** is up the hill on the right as you drive east from town toward Power Plant Campground. It's basically Atlanta's community bathtub—not a particularly private spot, but skinny-dipping is accepted. **Chattanooga Hot Springs** is one of the nicest in the state. It's in a much more secluded spot, unseen from the road, beneath bluffs lining the Middle Fork Boise River. The springs pour out of the bluff in a waterfall into riverside pools that have great views. When you start to get overheated, you're just steps from the cool water of the river. To get to Chattanooga, take the spur road heading north onto a grassy flat just west of Atlanta Hot Springs. Park on the bluff-top and descend the steep trail to the springs.

Accommodations

"Fancy" digs are available at the U.S. Forest Service's **Atlanta Guard Station** cabin (May 31–Sept. 30, $45) right in "downtown" Atlanta. It sleeps six in relative luxury, as guard stations go; this one has electricity, a living room, a woodstove, a kitchen with a propane stove and a refrigerator, an indoor toilet and shower, and indoor drinking water—a great deal for the price. In recent years, the cabin has been used for fire crew lodging, so it may not be available every summer. To reserve it, contact the Boise National Forest's **Idaho City Ranger District** (3833 Hwy. 21, Idaho City, 208/392-6681).

Although it is primarily a seasonal café and bar, **Beaver Lodge** (Main St., 208/864-2132, call for rates) also offers several rooms for rent; in summer the facility gets completely booked by miners, but you can probably score a room in other seasons.

Camping

Two free U.S. Forest Service campgrounds are in the area. **Riverside Campground** is closest to town and offers seven sites, while **Power Plant Campground** is down the road toward the trailhead and offers 25 sites.

Camas Prairie and the Soldier Mountains

Camas Prairie is sacred ground for the Shoshone-Bannock people, who once came to this idyllic prairie every spring to hunt elk and stock up on camas lily bulbs, a starchy staple of their diet. The ever-present Soldier and Smoky Mountains frame the marshlands and sprawling prairie to the north. Pioneer emigrants on Goodale's Cutoff, a popular spur of the Oregon Trail, traveled the entire length of the prairie in the shadow of these prominent mountains. Modern-day adventurers will discover many miles of backcountry solitude and a good ski area with short lift lines.

FAIRFIELD

This friendly little town provides travelers with basic services and a glimpse into the area's colorful history. In 1911 the Oregon Short Line Railroad completed its route across the Camas Prairie, giving birth to Fairfield. Trains no longer run, as they did for 70 years, but evidence of the railroad's existence is still present: An old caboose at the entrance to town serves as a visitors center, and the former depot has been turned into the **Camas County Historical Society Museum** (124 E. Camas Ave., Fairfield, 208/320-5994, 11 A.M.–4 P.M. Sat. Memorial Day–Labor Day, free). The museum is packed with telegraph machines, farm equipment, pioneer clothing, railroad photos, and other artifacts.

Fairfield is not much to look at today, but it has an honest farm-town feel. Alfalfa farming and cattle ranching floats the economy. Most

© JAMES P. KELLY

high above Fairfield in the Soldier Mountains

local kids are 4-H and FFA cardholders. But tourism is on the rise, and the town does have a handful of decent restaurants and lodging options for weary U.S. 20 sojourners.

Accommodations

The **Prairie Inn** (113 E. U.S. 20, Fairfield, 208/764-2247, from $59 d) is a big wood hotel that faces the highway. Don't let appearances fool you, though; the place is actually cleaner than it looks from the outside. Most guest rooms have queen beds, satellite TV, and free wireless Internet. You can get family suites and rooms with jetted tubs for a few extra bucks.

For a little more money, you can rent a cabin ($145–200) at **◖ Soldier Mountain Ranch** (Rte. 1, Corral, 208/764-2506, www.soldier-mountainranch.com). This Western-style resort also has guest suites in the main lodge ($50–100) and an 18-hole public golf course ($16–20) with incredible views of the prairie and nearby mountains. You can enjoy the resort's outdoor swimming pool and tennis court in the summer.

Food

◖ The Wrangler (105 W. U.S. 20, Fairfield, 208/764-2580, 11 A.M.–8 P.M. Thurs.–Mon., under $10) is the local burger joint. It's hard to miss; just look for the little red building skirted with river rock just off the highway on the left as you come into town. This old-school drive-in has tasty burgers, a large milk shake selection, and fries in all shapes and sizes. Try a "Road Kill" patty melt or a Powder Pig burger. The finger steaks are pretty good too.

Right on the main drag, you'll find **Jim Dandy's Pizza & Pasta** (505 Soldier Rd., Fairfield, 208/764-2030, 5–9 P.M. Wed.–Sun., $4.50–22) in a little storefront with an ornate copper awning. This dinner-only restaurant puts out decent pizza, standard pasta dishes, calzones, and big salads.

For basic breakfast and lunch offerings, head to the **Sawtooth Grill** (109 E. U.S. 20, Fairfield, 208/764-2256, breakfast and lunch daily) next to the Prairie Inn. Good picks are the flapjacks, omelets, and French toast, but the kitchen can be dreadfully slow, and your coffee cup may dry up like the Lake Idaho seabed.

Information

For more information about campgrounds and recreational opportunities in the Sawtooth National Forest, stop by the **Fairfield Ranger District** (102 1st St., Fairfield, 208/764-3202) just off the highway.

Head to the **yellow caboose** (Soldier Rd. and Poplar St., Fairfield, 208/764-2660) for visitor brochures and friendly advice from the volunteer employees.

◖ CAMAS PRAIRIE CENTENNIAL MARSH WILDLIFE MANAGEMENT AREA

A variety of waterfowl live in or visit this tranquil marsh southwest of Fairfield. Among the more interesting avian inhabitants on its 3,100 acres are sandhill cranes, great blue herons, and sharp-beaked curlews. Several species of raptors, including golden eagles, prairie falcons, peregrine falcons, and great horned owls, also frequent the area, as do mule deer and pronghorn. During the early spring, the marsh makes a great spot to enjoy the bright-blue camas blooms as well as Indian paintbrush and clusters of yellow yarrow. To get here, 10 miles west of Fairfield on U.S. 20, take Wolf Lane south. The turnoff is marked with a big wooden sign. Make sure to have extra batteries for the camera; you don't want to miss these gorgeous shots.

NORTH OF FAIRFIELD

The Soldier Mountains and Smoky Mountains immediately north of Fairfield are laced with a variety of trails and mostly open to off-road vehicles—it's something of a sacrifice area. Farther north, trails are open to hikers or off-road vehicles on existing roads only. Some hiking-only trails can be found, but many of them are not regularly maintained.

Next to Soldier Mountain Ski Resort, the U.S. Forest Service **Pioneer Campground** (May 20–Sept. 30, free) offers five sites. Just

south of the ski resort, Forest Road 094 splits off to the east. It winds up into the Soldier Mountains, over Couch Summit (7,008 feet), and down into the McHan Gulch drainage of Five Points Creek. Soon you'll come to the newly renovated Forest Service **Five Points Campground** (3 sites, free) and, a little farther down the road, the confluence of Five Points Creek and the larger Little Smoky Creek. This point is also the junction of Forest Road 094, which ends here, and Forest Road 227. Forest Road 227 (Little Smoky Rd.) follows the beautifully babbling Little Smoky east to a few dispersed campsites along the creek (or "crick," as true Idahoans call them). **Worswick Hot Springs** is an idyllic spot where Worswick Creek flows down to join Little Smoky. Several pools have clear, sulfur-free water of various temperatures ranging up to *really* hot. It's a reasonably popular spot, and you probably won't be alone, so use discretion before shedding your shorts. Past Worswick, the road splits, with Forest Road 227 continuing over Dollarhide Summit and on to Ketchum, and Forest Road 015 heading southeast to the **Little Smoky Winter Recreation Area,** a snowmobile trailhead.

Back at Little Smoky Campground, Forest Road 227 continues down the Little Smoky past **Preis Hot Springs,** an easy-to-miss (no sweat if you do) one-person tub along the right side of the road. Eventually the road takes you to the confluence of Little Smoky and Big Smoky Creeks, which in turn feeds the South Fork of the Boise River.

SOLDIER MOUNTAIN SKI RESORT

Twelve miles north of Fairfield up Soldier Creek Road, Soldier Mountain Ski Resort (208/764-2526, www.soldiermountain.com, 9 A.M.–4 P.M. Thurs.–Sun. Dec.–Apr., extended hours during Christmas break, full-day pass $33 adults, $23 ages 7–17 and 62–69, free under age 7 and over age 69) offers a friendly and inexpensive alternative to Sun Valley, some 60 miles to the east. The ski and snowboard area, owned by Hollywood star Bruce Willis, boasts a 1,400-foot vertical drop that's served by two double chairs and two surface lifts. All 36 runs are groomed, and they boast fun names like Wang Dang Doodle and Uh-Oh. Half-day passes, rentals, lessons, and a snowboard park are available. At the new base lodge—the old one burned down in 2009—you can chow down for breakfast and lunch, or grab a brew after cutting through the deep powder. A large sunny deck provides good views of the slopes.

If you've wanted to try **snowcat skiing,** this is a fairly affordable place to do it; the cost is $275 pp for a full day, including snacks, beverages, and lunch at a backcountry yurt. Call ahead for reservations. The resort recently started selling backcountry ski passes for $10, meaning you get a single-chair ride to the end of the line—you're on your own after that.

Bellevue and Hailey

At the junction of Highway 75 and U.S. 20, about 20 miles east of Fairfield, you can continue east on U.S. 20 to Craters of the Moon National Monument; or hang a right (south) at the junction to head to the Magic Valley and points south. If you take a left (north) on Highway 75, you'll soon enter the Wood River Valley, a slim draw flanked by the Smoky and Pioneer Mountains.

Coming into Bellevue, you can almost feel a buzz of excitement in the air. Anticipation, expectation—like a young Hollywood-bound starlet, you can't wait to see how closely the real thing matches the florid canvas of your imagination. The nation's first ski resort, playground of the rich and famous—what will it be like?

As it turns out, the analogy of coming into Los Angeles is apt. The relatively horrific traffic on Highway 75 on prime vacation weekends and 4–6 P.M. on weekdays makes it Idaho's equivalent of an LA freeway. And when you reach the airport at the south edge of Hailey, you'll see not only the expected Cessna 150s and crop dusters parked on the tarmac but also a formidable row of big gleaming turboprops and corporate Learjets.

BELLEVUE

It's hard to tell where Bellevue ends and Hailey begins. Bellevue's main drag (Hwy. 75), which moves at a snail's pace, is considerably shorter than Hailey's business district, yet it still has its charms. Bellevue was once called Biddyville,

but the name was changed to make the town sound more attractive. As with most upscale resort communities, people are either rich or they work for the rich. That said, many residents of Bellevue work in service-related jobs (landscaping, restaurants, housekeeping) in the Ketchum–Sun Valley area, but more and more vacation homes are popping up around this gateway town. With vacation homes come more restaurants and shops.

Accommodations
The **Silver Creek Cabins** (420 N. Main St., Bellevue, 208/280-1558, www.woodrivercabins.com, $85) are on the north end of the main drag. These cute but tiny log cabins have big beds and patios out front, a great spot to watch the sun drop over the Pioneer Mountains.

Bellevue's only other lodging option is the **Bell Mountain Inn** (1241 S. Main St., Bellevue, 208/788-0700, from $79 d), a two-story motel that's popular with construction workers and tourists alike. All guest rooms have small refrigerators, microwaves, coffeemakers, cable TV, and high-speed Internet.

Food and Drink
For upscale comfort food with a New American bent, check out the █ **Brick House Bar & Grill** (202 S. Main St., Bellevue, 208/788-4999, www.brickhouse-bar-and-grill.com, 5:30 P.M.–close Tues.–Sun., bar from 4 P.M., $15–21). You can't miss this new restaurant

because it's in a beautiful old brick building, formerly a bank, right on the downtown strip. The menu is sophisticated and down-home all at once. Starters might include Thai chicken wings, mushroom caps brimming with creamy seafood, and a remarkable tomato soup. Expect to see larger plates such as ultratender baby back ribs with honey-chipotle barbecue sauce, home-style fried chicken, braised lamb shank with a pinot noir reduction, and a sweet and spicy sesame noodle bowl. The expansive wine list plays well with the menu.

People come from all over the valley for the pizza at **South Valley Pizzeria** (108 Elm St., Bellevue, 208/788-1456, 4–9 P.M. daily, pizzas around $16, 2 for $23). This tucked-away pizza joint specializes in thin-crust pies. You can either pick your own toppings or choose one of the restaurant's specialty pizzas, including a Basque creation with chorizo, green chilies, garlic, and asiago cheese.

HAILEY

Hailey (population 7,800), 12 miles south of Ketchum and Sun Valley, is a small, relatively quiet town living in the shadow of its famous neighbors up the road. But as the Blaine County seat, Hailey boasts its own share of Idaho history. The town is named after John Hailey, who founded it in 1881 and served two terms as a territorial delegate to the U.S. Congress. Hailey flourished as a mining boomtown 1881–1889, and at one point had the largest Chinese population in the state; meticulous Chinese miners worked abandoned claims profitably long after other miners had left the area. Hailey was also the birthplace of 20th-century poet Ezra Pound.

Blaine County Historical Museum

To learn more about the town's history, visit the Blaine County Historical Museum (218 N. Main St., Hailey, 208/788-1801, 11 A.M.–5 P.M. Mon.–Sat., 1–5 P.M. Sun. Memorial Day–Oct. 31, free). The museum has a large political button collection, old mining and farming tools, a walk-through mine tunnel, Idaho's first telephone switchboard, and a display of Chinese dishes and artifacts.

Birthplace of Ezra Pound

One of the 20th century's most influential

© DANA HOPPER-KELLY

Hailey's main drag

poets, Ezra Loomis Pound was born in Hailey on October 30, 1885. His father was Registrar of the U.S. Land Office in Hailey's boomtown days. Ezra didn't have much of a chance to become an Idahoan—the family moved from Hailey to Philadelphia when he was barely a year old. Yet as a young man Ezra clung to a fascination with his birthplace. In his 1920 "Indiscretions" he described

the vastnesses of the Saw-Tooth Range, 5,000 feet above sea-level (and five million or five thousand miles from ANYwhere, let alone from civilization, New Yorkine or other)...the scenery, miles of it, miles of real estate, 'most of it up on end.'

Pound, something of a boy genius, also developed a taste for defying convention, authority, and social norms. He mastered nine languages, got fired as a college professor, and then exiled himself to Europe for 40 years. He befriended William Butler Yeats, fostered the careers of a number of literary greats—among them T. S. Eliot, Robert Frost, Ford Madox Ford, Ernest Hemingway, James Joyce, Amy Lowell, and Marianne Moore—and developed an attraction to the politics of fascist Italian dictator Benito Mussolini. His irascible anti-Semitic, anti-American radio broadcasts from Italy in the early 1940s got him arrested for treason after that country fell to the Allies in World War II. Pound was ruled mentally incompetent to stand trial, despite having written the award-winning *Pisan Cantos* while incarcerated, and was committed to a mental hospital in Washington, D.C. He was released after 12 years and moved back to Italy, where he died in 1971.

In later years, Pound's birthplace (314 2nd Ave. S., at Pine St., Hailey) was home to Roberta McKercher, a longtime Hailey journalist and community activist. The restored home now serves as the **Hailey Cultural Center** (208/726-9491, noon–5 P.M. Wed.–Fri.), a community gathering place. The public is welcome to stop by, but would-be visitors are asked to call ahead to be sure it's open.

Flightseeing

Glass Cockpit Aviation (2230 Aviation Dr., Hailey, 208/720-1537, www.glasscockpitaviation.com) is a flight school that offers scenic flights from the Sun Valley area to Galena Summit and back in a Cessna 172. This service costs $179 per hour for a maximum of three people.

Recreation

The onetime Union Pacific Railroad right-of-way between Hailey and Sun Valley is now part of **Wood River Trails** (year-round, free), a system of paved paths available for jogging, strolling, horseback riding, bicycling, rollerblading, or, in winter, cross-country skiing. The highway is within earshot along much of the route, but so is the Big Wood River.

The **Hailey Skate Park** (free) boasts a 16-foot full-radius concrete pipe, tall walls, and lots of other challenges for the board set. It's right across from the airport entrance on the south end of town.

When it warms up, head to the **Blaine County Aquatic Center** (1020 Fox Acres Rd., Hailey, 208/788-2144, daily Memorial Day–Labor Day, $5 adults, $4 seniors and ages 1–17), where you'll find a 25-yard, six-lane heated pool, a wading pool for kids, and a bathhouse with showers and locker rooms. Infants under a year old get in free but are prohibited from using the high diving board.

Entertainment

Company of Fools (208/788-6520, tickets 208/578-9122, www.companyoffools.org, $28 adults, $20 seniors, $10 students) is a Hailey-based theater company that presents about three productions a year. Its biggest claim to fame may be that both Bruce Willis and Demi Moore, onetime couple and still part-time locals, serve on its board of directors, and Willis even shows up in its productions from time to time. (A few years back, I saw him play a riveting version of Lee in Sam Shepard's *True West*.) But even without the celebrity cachet, this is one of the state's most important arts organizations. It performs at the nifty 1938 **Liberty**

Theatre (110 N. Main St., Hailey) and at various venues around Boise.

You can catch a flick at **Big Wood Cinemas** (801 N. Main St., Hailey, 208/578-0971, $8.50 adults, $6 seniors and ages 2–12) on the north end of town. This new four-theater complex shows first-run movies as well as matinees and weekly special deals.

Shopping

North & Co. (101 S. Main St., Hailey, 208/788-2783) is a stylish little boutique that will have you looking the Western-chic part lickety-split, with a large selection of fashionable clothing and footwear. Men will find duds by Carhartt, Quicksilver, and Billabong; women can pick up new designs by Lucky Brand, Roxy, and Level 99. Be prepared to drop some dough.

Accommodations

The 29-room **Airport Inn** (820 4th Ave. S., Hailey, 208/788-2477, from $80 d) is a stone's throw from the airport. Amenities include free Wi-Fi and a light breakfast. Suites and kitchenettes are available.

The **Wood River Inn** (603 N. Main St., Hailey, 208/578-0600 or 877/542-0600, www.woodriverinn.com, from $120 d) is a friendly hotel that offers all the amenities, including in-room refrigerators, microwave ovens, coffeemakers, and hair dryers. It also has an indoor pool. Rates include continental breakfast, and suites are available.

The **Spruce Inn** (416 1st Ave. N., Hailey, 208/720-8755, www.spruceinn.com, $110) is a clean and modern B&B in a renovated old house with four smartly designed guest rooms with separate but private baths. Amenities include a pool table, free Wi-Fi, and a big breakfast.

Food and Drink

It used to be that you had to go to Ketchum for an upscale dining experience, but now Hailey has some of the best fine dining in the valley.

One such place is **CK's Real Food** (320 N. Main St., Hailey, 208/788-1223, www.cksrealfood.com, lunch 11 A.M.–2 P.M. Mon.–Fri., dinner 5–10 P.M. daily, entrées $25), a deliciously funky restaurant in a gussied-up bungalow surrounded by plants you can eat. Chef-owner Chris Kastner is known in these parts to be a buy-local food guru. Sustainability is the name of the game: Used cooking oil is given to an area science teacher for biofuel projects; veggie scraps get composted for the garden; locally raised meat products and organic produce take precedence over well-traveled foodstuffs. The menu changes with the seasons and the whim of the globally influenced kitchen. One night you might see a beautifully braised Lava Lake lamb shank, and another time it could be braised Cuban-style pork shoulder with buttermilk polenta. How about a grilled gaucho steak in a pool of verdant chimichurri sauce? Smaller plates are all over the culinary map too. Thai-inspired seviche (with shrimp, finfish, and calamari) and a bright salad of broiled apricots, black figs, prosciutto, and hazelnuts also make appearances on the menu. The wine list boasts lots of Northwest labels.

Just down the street and also in a converted house is another excellent restaurant with a penchant for using local foodstuffs. **Three-Ten-Main** (310 N. Main St., Hailey, 208/788-4161, www.threetenmain.com, 5:30 P.M.–close Tues.–Sat., entrées $11–32) is owned and operated by Derek and Andrea Gallegos, who offer New American cuisine in a stylish yet comfortable dining room. Don't be surprised to find teasers like artichoke croquettes, tempura green beans with hot mustard-sesame dipping sauce, and a salumi plate with cured meats, goat cheese, and pickled red grapes. Main courses range from pan-roasted free-range chicken with potato gnocchi to grilled lamb chops and a ground rib eye–chuck steak burger on a house-baked cornmeal bun. Finish with a plate of crunchy beignets dusted with powdered sugar, which resemble the nearby mountains during ski season.

Across the street, it's hard not to notice **Wicked Spud Bar & Grill** (305 N. Main St., Hailey, 208/788-0009, 11 A.M.–9 P.M. daily), a fun little pub with a happening patio. There's even an oversized chessboard outside for cerebral types (the pieces are as tall as my six-year-old daughter). Expect to find lots of draft microbrews, burgers, and damn good fish tacos.

McClain's Pizza and Spirits (103 S. Main St., Hailey, 208/788-0960, 11 A.M.–9 P.M. daily, $7–25) is in the heart of downtown Hailey. This lively joint with a cocktail lounge serves hand-tossed pizzas as well as big salads, calzones, hot wings, and a mean meatball sandwich. The bar stays open late.

Next to the Liberty Theatre you can quell your craving for Thai food at the aptly named **A Taste of Thai** (106 N. Main St., Hailey, 208/578-2488, lunch and dinner daily, $7–14). The dining room is full of decorative imports from Thailand, but the quality of the food is hit or miss. Safe bets are usually the curry dishes, drunken noodles, fresh rolls, and the customary meat on a stick (satay). The waitstaff can be gruff at times.

The **Sun Valley Brewing Company** (202 N. Main St., Hailey, 208/788-0805, www.sunvalleybrewery.com, lunch and dinner daily) has a pub that offers 12 commendable handcrafted brews and a large menu of upscale bar food. Try an Asian-inspired appetizer (calamari tempura and lemongrass chicken) before committing to the pub's more substantial offerings: hot sandwiches, steaks, salads, and thin-crust pizzas. The Bianca is a good pick, topped with white sauce, artichoke hearts, asparagus, and three cheeses.

Open your tired eyes at the **Hailey Coffee Company** (219 S. Main St., Hailey, 208/788-8482, 6 A.M.–6 P.M. Mon.–Fri., 6 A.M.–4 P.M. Sat.–Sun.), a local roaster with a coffeehouse right on the main drag. Besides espresso drinks made from freshly roasted organic beans, you can also get in-house baked goodies such as flaky pastries, scones, and excellent banana bread.

Atkinsons' Market (93 E. Croy St., Hailey, 208/788-2294, 7 A.M.–9 P.M. daily), with other stores in Ketchum and Bellevue, is the place to go for wine, artisanal breads, and specialty cheeses as well as everyday grocery items. The deli puts out a rotating menu of fresh sandwiches, soups, and salads. The market is in Alturas Plaza, east of the main drag.

The **Hailey Farmers Market** (2:30–6:30 P.M. Thurs. June–Oct.) may be small, but it boasts a colorful profusion of seasonal produce and other foodstuffs. Besides oodles of organic produce, you'll also find freshly baked goods as well as locally produced meats, honey, eggs, and fresh-cut flowers. The market sets up in downtown's Bullion Square.

Information

Stop by the Hailey Chamber of Commerce's **Visitors Center** (309 S. Main St., Hailey, 208/788-3484, 8 A.M.–5 P.M. Mon.–Fri.) for brochures and information about the area. The **Blaine County Recreation District** (1050 Fox Acres Rd., Hailey, 208/578-2273) can give you the lowdown and brochures about recreational activities in the Wood River Valley.

Ketchum and Sun Valley

As Highway 75 slowly climbs alongside the Big Wood River from Bellevue to Ketchum, property values climb exponentially. Hailey, while by no means undeveloped, is positively rural compared to Ketchum, where you'll find yourself awash in a sea of multimillion-dollar homes. Clearly, the Ketchum–Sun Valley area is an aberrant element in the Idaho's modest economy. It's also unlike the rest of the state in its sociopolitical dynamics. Most of the residents weren't born in Idaho: The town is full of people who've made fortunes elsewhere and moved to Sun Valley because they can live anywhere they want, and this is a darn nice place.

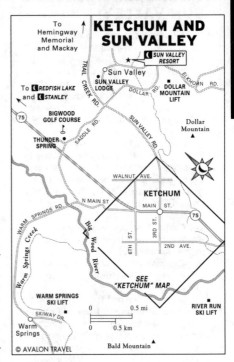

History

Among those impressed by the 1932 winter Olympics at Lake Placid, New York, was W. Averell Harriman, chairman of the board of Union Pacific Railroad. An avid skier, he soon came up with a grand plan to build a remote resort that the well-heeled would have to take the train to reach. This strategy had already proven enormously successful for the Canadian Pacific Railway, which started a luxury-lodging empire after its success building the Banff Springs Hotel. Harriman sent young Austrian Count Felix Schaffgotsch scouring the West in search of an ideal site for a destination ski resort that would draw the tourist throngs via the Union Pacific Railroad.

Schaffgotsch toured from the Cascades to Colorado, passing up many areas—including Aspen, Colorado—that would eventually be home to first-class ski resorts. When he saw the sleepy mining and sheep-ranching town of Ketchum, he wired Harriman with the news: "Among the many attractive spots I have visited, this combines more delightful features than any place I have seen in the United States, Switzerland, or Austria for a winter sports resort." Harriman was quickly on the scene to buy the 4,300-acre Brass Ranch. Construction of a no-expense-spared luxury lodge began

in May 1936, and now Harriman needed to tell the world about his new baby. He came up with a stroke of genius: draw Hollywood stars and other celebrities, and the lemminglike masses will follow. Shortly after the December 1936 opening of the lodge, Clark Gable and Errol Flynn swashbuckled their way through Ketchum to the delight of the paparazzi and the public, and the trend began that to this day marks the Wood River Valley as a Tinseltown playground.

When Harriman's Union Pacific mechanical engineers came up with the world's first chairlift, on Dollar Mountain—developed from the hoist systems used to load bananas into ships' holds—the resort's skiing legacy was firmly established.

STARGAZING IN SUN VALLEY

The night sky above Idaho's mountains is bright with constellations, but if you spend any time in the Sun Valley area you might see other kinds of stars too. Over the years, Sun Valley has had many famous part-time residents, including Gary Cooper, Lucille Ball, Marilyn Monroe, some of the Kennedys, and Ernest Hemingway. This valley of sun and snow continues to draw celebrities to its mountain charms. Rockers Steve Miller and Peter Cetera have been longtime homeowners. Folk superwoman Carole King lives just up the road on a big spread near Stanley. Hollywood luminaries who hold part-time addresses in Sun Valley include Jamie Lee Curtis, Clint Eastwood, Tom Hanks, Bruce Willis, Demi Moore (and her beau-in-tow Ashton Kutcher), Jean-Claude Van Damme, and Arnold Schwarzenegger, action star and former governor of California.

Most everyday residents here don't pay much attention to these big-name stars, who are occasionally seen hanging around town, so don't expect to find any maps to the stars' homes. These celebrities blend in well – just the way they like it. Sun Valley is a great place for people from all walks of life, including famous folks, to take a break from their hectic schedules.

Getting Oriented

The Ketchum–Sun Valley miniopolis consists of three separate areas, each virtually self-contained. **Ketchum,** right on the highway, is the biggest and the most like a real city, with the services—banks, lawyers, accountants—that keep life flowing smoothly for locals. Ketchum is the closest community to the ski resort's River Run lift.

The **Warm Springs** area lies a short distance northwest of downtown Ketchum at the base of the north side of Bald Mountain. It has a smaller, quieter feel than Ketchum proper,

although you'll still find hotels, condos, restaurants, and nightlife in abundance. The base area here features another plush day lodge and two detachable quads that practically come right down to the street to pick you up and whisk you mountain-ward.

In the opposite direction, northeast of Ketchum, is famous **Sun Valley,** essentially the resort's company town. Unlike Ketchum, Sun Valley—despite having more name recognition than its neighbors—is a small burg consisting primarily of the original Sun Valley Lodge and its sibling Sun Valley Inn, along with the company's restaurants and activity centers serving guests of those establishments. The rest of the area is residential, with condos and homes galore, but other than a small pedestrian mall with shops in the village, you won't find much in the way of basic services. Interestingly enough, Sun Valley is actually farther from Bald Mountain recreation than Ketchum. If staying at Sun Valley Lodge and skiing Bald Mountain is your plan, realize that you won't be skiing out the door of your room or even walking to the lifts, but rather taking a short free bus ride first. Sun Valley, however, is close to the less challenging and less expensive Dollar Mountain ski area, also part of Sun Valley Company's operation.

SIGHTS
Ketchum-Sun Valley Heritage and Ski Museum

Run by the Ketchum–Sun Valley Historical Society, the Heritage and Ski Museum (180 1st St. E., Ketchum, 208/726-8118, noon–4 P.M. Mon.–Fri., 1–4 P.M. Sat. year-round, free), in Forest Service Park, offers exhibits focusing on the town's rich history. Highlights span the days of the fur trappers and the Tukudeka people all the way to the arrival of Sun Valley Lodge and the Hollywood glitterati. A self-guided walking-tour pamphlet to town is available here.

Ore Wagon Museum

A bit of Ketchum's mining heritage is kept behind glass at the Ore Wagon Museum (East

Ave. and 5th St.), where you can see examples of the giant ore cars that once hauled supplies and mining booty up and down the valley. The heavily laden wagons were often towed in strings, pulled by teams of eight or more mules. This isn't a staffed museum, just a walk-by and peek-in point of interest.

Hemingway Memorial

After Averell Harriman completed his Sun Valley Lodge in 1936, he offered complimentary stays to some of the era's most glamorous people. One of the invitees was 40-year-old writer Ernest Hemingway. By the time he first visited Sun Valley in 1939, he had written *The Sun Also Rises* and *A Farewell to Arms* and had been featured on the cover of *Time* magazine. He stayed in Sun Valley Lodge that fall, working on *For Whom the Bell Tolls*. He returned in fall 1940 and again in 1941. During these visits, Hemingway found his niche in the rich Sun Valley social scene—duck hunting with Gary Cooper and partying at the Trail Creek cabin with Dorothy Parker and other luminaries.

© DANA HOPPER-KELLY

a tribute to Ernest Hemingway, topped with a bust sculpted by Robert Berks

Although Hemingway enjoyed these trips to Ketchum, after World War II he settled in Cuba with his fourth wife, Mary Welsh. In 1953 he won a Pulitzer Prize for *The Old Man and the Sea* and the following year he was honored with the Nobel Prize for Literature. The 1958 Cuban revolution along with Hemingway's deteriorating health led the couple to leave Cuba and become Ketchum homeowners in 1959. It was a short-lived residency: Plagued by depression and alcoholism, Hemingway slid into his final chapter. Ernest and Mary dined at Ketchum's Christiania Restaurant on July 1, 1961; early the next morning, Hemingway turned a shotgun on himself, ending his own life at the age of 61. When Mary Welsh Hemingway died in 1986, she left the couple's Ketchum home to the Nature Conservancy.

Meanwhile, Sun Valley's memorial to the great writer, a short distance up Trail Creek Road from the lodge, is as simple and eloquent as a Hemingway sentence. An obelisk topped with a bust sculpted by Robert Berks stands in a shady nook overlooking Trail Creek. It's inscribed with words written by Hemingway in 1939 as a eulogy for his friend Gene Van Guilder, who was killed in a hunting accident. Ironically enough, the words seem as though Hemingway could have written them for himself:

> *Best of all he loved the fall. The leaves yellow on the cottonwoods. Leaves floating on the trout streams. And above the hills the high blue windless skies...now he will be a part of them forever.*

Environmental Resource Center

Equal parts museum, store, classroom, and environmental-action clearinghouse, the Environmental Resource Center (471 Washington Ave. N., Ketchum, 208/726-4333, www.ercsv.org, call for hours) is a great place to refill your modern jaded soul with hope. You'll find great displays and human energy directed toward making the planet a healthier place. Regular video screenings and lectures are held, and the center's library houses books, magazines, videos, and CD-ROMs on local and global environmental issues.

Sawtooth Botanical Garden

South of town, the Sawtooth Botanical Garden (11 Gimlet Rd., Ketchum, 208/726-9358, www.sbgarden.org, dawn–dusk daily, free) is another nonprofit organization that teaches environmental stewardship. You can meander through beautiful gardens that delineate the region's five biomes, including a sagebrush xeriscape, a lava rock moonscape, and alpine, montane, and riparian gardens. It's a great spot for a picnic.

WINTER RECREATION
Alpine Skiing and Snowboarding

To the late Gretchen Fraser, the first U.S. Olympic skiing gold medalist (she won the slalom in 1948), Sun Valley's Bald Mountain was "the greatest mountain in the world." Following in her footsteps, local Olympic wunderkind Picabo Street (gold medalist in the Super G slalom in 1998) grew up schussing the chutes off the mountain's lofty summit. This is one Olympic-size mountain, all right, or rather one big mountain and one small mountain; you get a choice of two at **Sun Valley Resort** (800/894-9931, snow report 800/635-4150, tickets 208/622-6136, www.sunvalley.com, full-day lift tickets $82 adults, $55 seniors, $48 children). Bald Mountain—"Baldy" as it's called—is the big one, offering runs up to three miles long down some 3,400 vertical feet from its 9,150-foot summit. What's more, the 2,054 skiable acres are served by a decidedly decadent array of fast lifts and luxurious day lodges. The resort recently debuted its new Roundhouse Gondola system, featuring 56 eight-passenger cars that zoom up and down 2,000 vertical feet in less than 10 minutes. The express gondola starts at the River Run base and travels up to the Top Terminal Plaza, where the Roundhouse Restaurant is located. Seven high-speed detachable quads web the mountain along with four triple chairs and two double chairs. Lift lines? What lift lines?

In addition to all the quads, the resort boasts a state-of-the-art computer-controlled snowmaking system to ensure optimum snow conditions throughout the season.

And then there are the three lodges—one each at Warm Springs and River Run base areas, and one high on a mid-mountain ridgetop overlooking the valley. They're all spectacular multimillion-dollar affairs designed in a beautiful mountain mega-cabin theme—oversize logs, river rock, and sweeping expanses of glass. Their interiors are positively regal in their furnishings. Marble, chandeliers, and fine wines mix with trophy heads and fireplaces to give each lodge the air of the czar's dacha.

Luxury is the norm here, but if you come more for the skiing than the pampering, you might find a couple of chinks in the royal armor, depending on what you're after. Baldy might be the nation's ultimate mountain for cruisers. You'll find an incredible abundance of moderately steep, consistently pitched, and immaculately groomed intermediate runs, along with some excellent bowls, challenging tree skiing, and a new half-pipe on Lower Warm Springs. But extreme skiers looking for air time would be better off heading to Squaw Valley or Jackson Hole; the Limelight run off the Warm Springs quad is probably Sun Valley's biggest challenge. And while it's true that the lift system covers the entire mountain like a blanket and makes for short lift lines, that can have its own drawbacks. On a busy weekend the summit is like a circus: multiple quads continually dump out skiers in batches, while paragliders jump off the mountaintop, photographers photograph the skiers, and everyone stands around aimlessly admiring the world-class view. You'll also be hard-pressed to find those special, out-of-the-way, non–lift-served areas that reward a bit of a traverse or hike with relatively uncrowded and untracked terrain. Locals probably know a secret spot or two, but you may not be able to ferret them out. Finally, you have to pay top dollar for all those fancy quads, gondolas, and lodges. Half-day tickets and special deals are available.

The resort's other hill, Dollar Mountain, is on the Sun Valley side of Highway 75. It's a relatively uncrowded, wide-open beginner hill with three lifts and a handle tow on 628 vertical feet, great for floundering about on tele-skis or for kids still "making a pie." Tickets are about half the price of those on Baldy.

Heli-Skiing

Sun Valley Heli-Ski/EpicQuest (208/622-3108 or 800/872-3108, www.epicquest.com) offers a variety of chopper-drop packages that leave from the Sun Valley Gun Club across from Trail Creek Cabin. To go diving through the untracked fluff, all you'll need is intermediate or better skiing skills and a small trust fund. A full day with 5–6 runs for a total of around 10,000 vertical feet costs $1,100 pp. The company offers several other packages, topping out at around $9,000.

Cross-Country Skiing

Blaine County's cross-country ski trails rate among the country's best. The **Wood River Trails** system runs 19 miles from Hulen Meadows north of Ketchum all the way south to Bellevue along a former Union Pacific Railroad right-of-way. Three miles north of Ketchum, the **Lake Creek Trails** offer a 10-mile network of loops on the west side of the Big Wood River. The regularly groomed trails are part of the North Valley Trail System, which requires a $15 trail pass.

Sun Valley Resort's **Nordic Center** (208/622-2251), just past the lodge up Trail Creek, has 25 miles of groomed trails on the snow-covered golf course and surrounding hills and canyons. It is popular with the locals for lunch-hour or after-work exercise—you'll see them blasting by impossibly fast in high-powered skating form. The trails are meticulously groomed, including a set of narrow-spaced tracks provided especially for kids, and the area is beautiful enough, but you couldn't call it a wilderness ski experience; you practically stare into the living-room windows of the extravagant homes built astride the fairways. The best steeps are on the Diamondback Trail across the

road—it climbs to a ridgetop for a good view of Ketchum. Alas, the view is dominated by buildings, and the sounds of traffic rise up at you from three sides. Your only hope of finding winter tranquility here is to head out past Trail Creek Cabin to the distant Boundary and Proctor Loops. Somewhere out there, far from town, you'll start to hear the wind, the trees, the creek, and the birds. Rentals and lessons are available.

Backcountry Skiing

The joys of nearly unlimited skiable terrain in the mountains surrounding the Wood River Valley must be balanced against the backcountry's serious avalanche potential. If you know what you're doing, it could be heaven. If you don't, well, it could mean heaven in a different way. Before setting out, visiting backcountry skiers should at the very least call the Ketchum Ranger District's **24-hour avalanche and snow condition report** (208/622-8027). But there's no substitute for local experience—go with a guide if at all possible.

Sun Valley Trekking (Hailey, 208/788-1966, www.svtrek.com) offers guided tours to one or more of its five cozy and comfortable backcountry huts in the Smoky and Sawtooth Mountains. The huts have woodstoves with plenty of firewood, propane cookstoves, lanterns, toilets, wood-fired hot tubs or saunas, and bunk beds with sleeping pads. You can rent a hut and ski to it on your own, but first-time hut users are required to employ a guide for the first day. The company also offers classes in backcountry ski-touring, telemarking, and avalanche education. Full day guided tours and overnight packages range $160–200 pp per day. The company also offers guided day hikes in the summer, and one of its huts is open for summer use by hikers and mountain bikers.

Sleigh Rides

Dinner sleigh rides out to historic **Trail Creek Cabin** are offered through Sun Valley Resort's sports and recreation office (208/622-2135, call for prices). The 1937 log-and-stone cabin was a retreat popular with the Hollywood set—Clark Gable, Gary Cooper, Ava Gardner, and friends—and was Ernest Hemingway's favored New Year's Eve party venue. Sleighs depart from the Sun Valley Inn several times a night for dinner. The ride to the cabin along Trail Creek takes about a half hour. Dress warmly; blankets are provided.

SUMMER RECREATION

Although Sun Valley started as a ski resort, about a decade ago the Sun Valley Company and local civic leaders pushed to convert the area into a year-round destination resort. They succeeded, and now Sun Valley and Ketchum do even more business in summer than in winter. Summer is an undeniably magnificent time of year here. Hundreds of square miles of the surrounding mountains—accessible in winter only to experienced mountaineers—open up for everyone to enjoy.

Trail Systems

The 10 miles of paved pedestrian and bike paths in the **Sun Valley Trail System** loop around Dollar Mountain from Ketchum to Sun Valley to Elkhorn and out along Elkhorn Road back to the highway. A spur trail follows Trail Creek from Sun Valley Lodge out to Boundary Campground. The Sun Valley system connects with the 20-mile-long **Wood River Trails** system, which traces the old Union Pacific right-of-way from Lake Creek Road, north of Ketchum, down the valley to Bellevue. Ambitious long-term plans call for trails to eventually connect Stanley with Shoshone. For more information, contact the **Blaine County Recreation District** (1050 Fox Acres Rd., Hailey, 208/578-2273).

Hiking and Mountain Biking

You'll find no shortage of suitable ground for exercise; within a five-mile radius of Ketchum lie some 40 miles of unpaved hiking and mountain-biking trails, all of which get heavily used as workout terrain by area residents. West of downtown Ketchum, the **Bald Mountain Trail** (Trail 201) runs five miles up to the top

of Baldy itself. The trailhead for the five-mile hike is at the bottom of the River Run lift. Or be lazy and take your bike up the lift with you—Sun Valley ski area's detachable quads haul mountain bikers and their two-wheeled steeds in summer.

In the Sun Valley area, several trails leave from Trail Creek Cabin, two miles east of Sun Valley Village up Trail Creek Road. The **Trail Creek Trail** (Trail 305) follows the creek for 1.5 miles one-way and is barrier free. The **Proctor Mountain Trail** (Trail 119) climbs to the summit of that peak for panoramic views of the valley. The easy 1.75-mile **Aspen Loop Trail** (Trail 119A) and the more difficult 3.5-mile one-way **Corral Creek Trail** (Trail 119B) wind through aspen and evergreen forest. No bikes are allowed on the Aspen Loop or Proctor Mountain trails.

The Adams Gulch Trails are 1.5 miles north of Ketchum; follow Adams Gulch Road 0.75 miles off Highway 75 to the trailhead. The network of trails ranges from the **Shadyside Trail** (Trail 177A), an easy 1.5-mile stroll, to the demanding **Adams Gulch Trail** (Trails 177 and 142), a 14-mile loop. Intermediate-length hikes are also possible. Bikes are permitted on the Adams Gulch trails.

The **Fox Creek-Oregon Gulch Trails** lie a bit farther up the west side of Highway 75 and are accessed by two separate trailheads: the Lake Creek trailhead is right off Highway 75, four miles north of Ketchum; the Oregon Gulch trailhead is three miles farther north, off Highway 75 at Forest Road 143, just past the North Fork Store. These trails are more difficult than the Adams Gulch trails. Loops ranging 3–10 miles are possible, and bikes are allowed.

Hikers prepared to spend a long sweaty day on the dusty trail will want to check out the **Pioneer Cabin Trails.** The Union Pacific Railroad built the cabin in 1937 as a ski hut. It's still in use by hikers and skiers, and from its lofty 9,400-foot vantage you'll have sweeping views east to the crest of the Pioneer Range. The trailhead to the cabin starts at the end of Corral Creek Road, which branches off Trail

Creek Road a mile northeast of Boundary Campground. Take the Pioneer Cabin Trail (Trail 122) on the way up to the hut and descend via Long Gulch Trail (Trail 123) for an 8.5-mile loop. No bikes are allowed on the Pioneer Cabin Trails.

For more information on these hikes, pick up a trail brochure and map at the Ketchum Visitor Center (491 Sun Valley Rd., Ketchum, 208/726-3423) or at the Ketchum Ranger Station (206 Sun Valley Rd., Ketchum, 208/622-5371).

HIKING AND BIKING GUIDES

Sun Valley Trekking (208/788-1966, www. svtrek.com) offers half-day and full-day guided hikes anywhere in the Sawtooth National Recreation Area and the U.S. Forest Service's Ketchum Ranger District, except the Sawtooth Wilderness. Rates for 1–2 people are $200 pp half-day, $315 pp full day, not including lunch (which can be arranged at extra cost).

Venture Outdoors (800/528-5262, www.venout.com) offers bike tours ranging from three hours to six days. Several different day trips are offered for around $85 pp, including lunch.

Llama Trekking

Llamas are a lot cuter than horses, have a lot more personality, and love hiking around in the mountains as much or more than you do. They'll happily carry your gear, leaving you unencumbered to stop and smell the wildflowers along the trail. **Venture Outdoors** (800/528-5262, www.venout.com) is the area's llama-trekking specialist, offering hikes ranging 1–5 days in the Sawtooth National Recreation Area and Sawtooth National Forest. Day trips cost $75–95 pp including lunch.

Horseback Riding

Sun Valley Resort Horsemen's Center (208/622-2391) offers one-hour guided trail rides in the area for $40 pp or 90-minute rides for $52 pp. The rides leave the center on Sun Valley Road (between Ketchum and Sun Valley) starting at 9 A.M. daily in summer. Reservations are required; children must be at least eight years old and 52 inches tall. Spring and fall rides, group hayrides, winter sleigh rides, and stagecoach rides may also be available by appointment.

If you have your own horse, you can head out on one of the numerous trails that lace the Ketchum Ranger District. Stop in at the Ranger Station (206 Sun Valley Rd., Ketchum, 208/622-5371) for complete information on open trails and usage rules.

Golf

The **Sun Valley Resort Golf Course** (208/622-2251, $140–160 peak season) was designed by Robert Trent Jones Jr., and it's a beauty. The resort just added an extra nine on the north side of Trail Creek Road, stretching this par-72 course to 6,948 yards. Fairways on the main course follow Trail Creek, crossing it seven times on the front nine. Greens fees include mandatory rental of an electric cart. Reservations for tee times are required.

For less expensive golfing, check out the nine-hole **Bigwood Golf Course** (115 Thunder Trail Rd., Ketchum, 208/726-4024, $25 for nine holes, $50 for 18 holes), on the hill between Highway 75 and Sun Valley. This par-36 course, designed by Robert Muir Graves, has more than 3,200 yards of gorgeous greens. Cart rentals are available.

Tennis

Sun Valley Resort Tennis Club (208/622-2156, daily mid-May–mid-Oct., $15.50 pp per day, resort guests $12.25 pp per day) offers 17 courts, ball machines, lessons, and a pro shop. Free public courts are available at **Atkinson Park** (8th St. and 3rd Ave.) in downtown Ketchum.

Rafting

The local Big Wood River provides great fishing but no boating. However, several raft companies based in Ketchum–Sun Valley offer guided trips on nearby white water. **White Otter Outdoor Adventures** (105 Mountain View Lane, Hailey, 208/788-5005 or 877/788-5005, www.whiteotter.com) runs the Salmon

River day stretch out of Sunbeam as well as the Murtaugh and Hagerman reaches of the Snake River. Half-day Salmon River trips cost around $75 adults, $55 under age 13. Also running the Salmon day stretch is the Stanley-based **Sawtooth Adventure Company** (866/774-4644, www.sawtoothadventure.com).

Camping

Six U.S. Forest Service campgrounds south of the Sawtooth National Recreation Area boundary ring Ketchum and Sun Valley. Up Trail Creek Road about two miles past Sun Valley Village is **Boundary Campground** (8 sites, $10). Continuing out on Trail Creek Road over Trail Creek Summit in the direction of Mackay are **Park Creek Campground** (12 sites, $5), 26 miles from Ketchum, and **Phi Kappa Campground** (21 sites, $5), 23 miles out.

Up the East Fork Wood River (Forest Rd. 118 east of Hwy. 75 between Ketchum and Hailey) you'll find **Federal Gulch Campground** (15 sites, free) and **Sawmill Campground** (3 sites, free). Finally, west of Highway 75 out Deer Creek Road is **Deer Creek Campground** (3 sites, free), 20 miles from Ketchum.

For more information and campground maps, contact the **Ketchum Ranger District** (206 Sun Valley Rd., Ketchum, 208/622-5371).

YEAR-ROUND RECREATION
Fishing

The beautiful Big Wood River flows the length of the valley, offering good trout fishing around every bend. Anglers also enjoy success up Warm Springs Creek (which flows into the Big Wood from the west side of Ketchum), Trail Creek (which flows down from the east), and other tributaries. Throughout the valley, many sections of riverbank are privately owned. Access points for the public portions are marked by signs and noted in a fishing brochure published by the Blaine County Recreation District, available at the Ketchum visitors center and ranger station. One favorite

place to take the youngsters on a fish hunt is **Penny Lake,** along Warm Springs Road just on the edge of civilization.

Trout fishing is open year-round on the Big Wood River and Little Wood River, but restrictions apply on certain stretches of both tributaries. For details, contact the Idaho Department of Fish and Game (208/334-3700, www.fishandgame.idaho.gov), or hire a trusty river guide to take you out into the wilds. They'll know about all the particulars.

Local fishing guides include **Bill Mason Outfitters** (Sun Valley Village, 208/622-9305), which also offers outings for kids; **Silver Creek Outfitters** (500 N. Main St., Ketchum, 208/726-5282 or 800/732-5687, www.silver-creek.com), which features an extensive, full-service retail store; and **Ketchum on the Fly** (680 Sun Valley Rd., Ketchum, 208/726-7572, www.ketchumonthefly.com). Expect guide service to run $300–450 per day for 1–2 anglers.

Hot Springs

The closest hot springs to Ketchum is **Frenchman's Hot Springs,** 10.5 miles west of town via Warm Springs Road (Forest Rd. 227). **Warfield Hot Springs** is just 0.5 miles farther down the road. North of Ketchum you'll discover **Easley Hot Springs** and **Russian John Hot Springs** in the Sawtooth National Recreation Area.

Ice Skating

Sun Valley Lodge offers a pair of rinks, one indoors in a separate building behind the lodge, the other right outside the back door of the lodge (208/622-2194, $10.50 adults, $8.75 ages 6–17, free under age 5 with a paid adult, skate rental $4.25). Lessons are available. In winter, you can also skate for free on the pond at **Atkinson Park** (8th St. and 3rd Ave.).

Paragliding

Join a guide from **Fly Sun Valley** (160 W. 4th St., Ketchum, 208/726-3332, www.

flysunvalley.com) on a tandem flight off the top of Bald Mountain. Anyone, young or old, physically fit or physically challenged, can enjoy this thrilling experience, provided they can ante up around $225. The company also teaches the high-flying activity.

OUTFITTERS

Plenty of area shops rent the equipment you need to enjoy a variety of sports. Some of them are listed below.

Ski, Mountain Bike, and Skate Rentals

Area rental shops include **Sturtevants Ski & Sports** (314 N. Main St., Ketchum, 208/726-4512), **Formula Sports** (460 N. Main St., Ketchum, 208/726-3194), and **Pete Lane's** (River Run Plaza, Ketchum, 208/622-6123; Sun Valley Village, 208/622-2279). Pete Lane's does not rent skates.

Backcountry Shops

Mountaineering-oriented rental centers include **The Elephant's Perch** (280 East Ave., at Sun Valley Rd., Ketchum, 208/726-3497) and **Backwoods Mountain Sports** (711 N. Main St., at Warm Springs Rd., Ketchum, 208/726-8818). Both carry a full selection of cross-country ski gear, including touring, skating, and telemark skis, boots, and poles. They also carry climbing gear and rent a good selection of camping equipment—packs, tents, sleeping bags, and the like.

Snowboard Specialists

Snowboard-rental headquarters in town is the **Board Bin** (180 4th St. E., Ketchum, 208/726-1222), which has everything you'll need to rip it up. In summer, the store's passion turns to skateboards.

Also renting snowboards are **Sturtevants Ski & Sports** (314 N. Main St., Ketchum, 208/726-4512), **Pete Lane's** (Sun Valley Village, 208/622-2279; River Run Plaza, 208/622-6123), and **Ski Tek** (191 Sun Valley Rd. W., Ketchum, 208/726-7503).

Kayaks

Try **Backwoods Mountain Sports** (711 N. Main St., Ketchum, 208/726-8818) for kayaks; they also rent rafts and accessories. **Ski Tek** (191 Sun Valley Rd. W., Ketchum, 208/726-7503) has some boats to rent.

EVENTS

Ketchum–Sun Valley's events calendar is huge, and something's always going on. Some of the bigger bashes are listed below. For details and a complete list, contact the Sun Valley–Ketchum Chamber and Visitors Bureau (208/726-3423 or 866/305-0408, www.visitsunvalley.com).

Summer

The world-class **Sun Valley Ice Show** (208/622-2135, dusk Sat. late June–early Sept., show $32–62 adults, dinner and show $98) presents Olympic medalists and other world-champion skaters and features a lavish preshow outdoor buffet. It all takes place at the Sun Valley Lodge ice rink.

Music fills the upper Wood River Valley during numerous summertime events. The **Ketch'em Alive** music series (7–9 P.M. Tues. June–Aug.) presents bands from around the Northwest at Forest Service Park. The **Sun Valley Summer Symphony** (208/622-5607, www.svsummersymphony.com, July–Aug.) performs free outdoor concerts at Sun Valley Lodge. Also keep your eye peeled for occasional outdoor concerts put on by the Sun Valley Center for the Arts (schedule and tickets 208/726-9491, www.sunvalleycenter.org). Shows in the past have included the likes of Willie Nelson, Lyle Lovett, James Taylor, and Carole King. This organization is also responsible for the annual **Sun Valley Arts and Crafts Festival,** held in August at Sun Valley Resort.

Labor Day weekend brings the **Ketchum Wagon Days Celebration** (866/305-9899), a festival commemorating the town's mining history. Festivities include one of the West's largest nonmotorized parades, featuring those glassed-in ore wagons, along with pancake breakfasts, concerts, and street dances.

SAWTOOTH COUNTRY

© DANA HOPPER-KELLY

Trailing of the Sheep Festival in Ketchum

Fall

In mid-October, the saints come marchin' in to Sun Valley for the **Sun Valley Jazz Jamboree.** About 20 of the best Dixieland and ragtime jazz bands from the United States, Canada, and around the world recreate Bourbon Street and the Big Band era for the dancing crowds. The revelry takes place at Sun Valley Resort (www.sunvalley.com). If you'd rather see sheep marching than saints marching, look for the **Trailing of the Sheep Festival** (208/720-0585, www.trailingofthesheep.org), also in mid-October. This three-day shindig celebrates the Wood Rover Valley's sheepherding at various locations around the valley, with sheepdog trials, Basque and Peruvian music and dancing, arts and crafts, food, and a big parade where thousands of sheep get herded right down Ketchum's main drag.

Winter

Cross-country ski races fill the winter calendar. The biggest cross-country event in the valley comes in early February, when the huge **Sun Valley Nordic Festival** (http://svnordicfestival.com) draws upward of 700 cross-country ski racers from all over the world. They race right down the Harriman Trail from Galena Lodge to the Sawtooth National Recreation Area Headquarters—the very same 19-mile trail you can ski yourself on any other winter's day for about $15. In the world of cross-country skiing, this one's big—at least for an American event.

Early March brings a less serious race: the **Paw and Pole** fun race for dogs and their human associates, held at the Warm Springs Golf Course. The end of Galena Lodge's season brings **Ride, Stride, and Glide** (208/726-4010), a triathlon that features biking, snowshoeing, and running.

Spring

In late March, **SolFest** (www.visitsunvalley.com) celebrates the waning days of winter in the Sun Valley area with a three-day bash that showcases skiing and snowboarding exhibitions, live music, and more.

The **Mountain Wellness Festival** (www.sunvalleywellness.org), held over Memorial Day Weekend, features big-name speakers, intimate workshops, and a "Hands-on Hall" where you can try a variety of alternative and holistic health treatments.

KETCHUM

Ketchum (population 3,200) is the urban hub of the Wood River Valley, and contrary to what you might expect, it's closer to the main ski slopes on Baldy than Sun Valley Lodge itself. Although not large—the town core occupies perhaps 30 square blocks—every block is packed with restaurants, bars, galleries, outdoor outfitters, and boutiques. It's important to note that Ketchum, along with Hailey, has two distinct monthlong breaks—Spring Slack and Fall Slack—between the busy summer and winter seasons, when some businesses are closed and others offer great deals. This is a mellow time to visit the area,

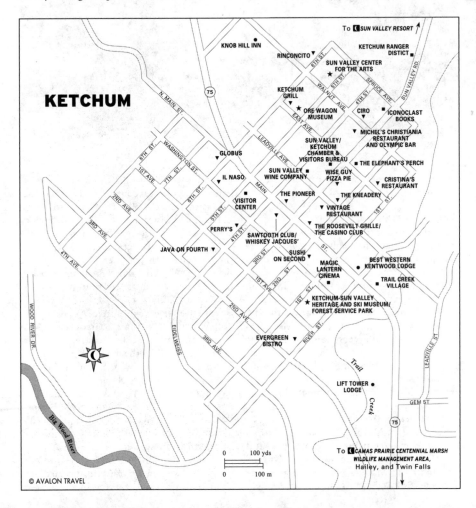

KETCHUM

To **C** SUN VALLEY RESORT

KNOB HILL INN
RINCONCITO
KETCHUM RANGER DISTRICT
SUN VALLEY CENTER FOR THE ARTS
KETCHUM GRILL
ORE WAGON MUSEUM
CIRO
ICONOCLAST BOOKS
MICHEL'S CHRISTIANIA RESTAURANT AND OLYMPIC BAR
SUN VALLEY/ KETCHUM CHAMBER & VISITORS BUREAU
GLOBUS
THE ELEPHANT'S PERCH
IL NASO
SUN VALLEY WINE COMPANY
WISE GUY PIZZA PIE
CRISTINA'S RESTAURANT
VISITOR CENTER
THE PIONEER
THE KNEADERY
VINTAGE RESTAURANT
PERRY'S
THE ROOSEVELT GRILLE/ THE CASINO CLUB
JAVA ON FOURTH
SAWTOOTH CLUB/ WHISKEY JACQUES'
SUSHI ON SECOND
MAGIC LANTERN CINEMA
BEST WESTERN KENTWOOD LODGE
TRAIL CREEK VILLAGE
KETCHUM-SUN VALLEY HERITAGE AND SKI MUSEUM/ FOREST SERVICE PARK
EVERGREEN BISTRO
LIFT TOWER LODGE
GEM ST.

To **C** CAMAS PRAIRIE CENTENNIAL MARSH WILDLIFE MANAGEMENT AREA, Hailey, and Twin Falls

0   100 yds
0   100 m

© AVALON TRAVEL

downtown Ketchum in winter

© IDAHO DIVISION OF TOURISM

and enough places stay open to make a trip worthwhile.

Art Galleries

Ketchum is gallery central. Whatever your taste in art, you'll probably find what you're looking for. All the galleries are within walking distance of each other, so you might want to make a walking-tour day of it, browsing from one to the next.

The nonprofit **Sun Valley Center for the Arts** (191 5th St. E., Ketchum, 208/726-9491, www.sunvalleycenter.org) has been the hub of the valley's art world for more than 20 years, presenting exhibits, lectures, films, and workshops. Pick up a schedule of local art happenings—something might be going on tonight.

Anne Reed Gallery (391 1st Ave N., Ketchum, 208/726-3036) is the place to go for contemporary paintings, sculpture, and photography, including works by Russell Chatham and Manuel Neri, among others. **Frederic Boloix Fine Arts** (320 1st Ave. N.,

Ketchum, 208/726-8810) is a posh upstairs gallery that features contemporary art and occasionally works by 20th century masters such as Picasso, Matisse, and Chagall. **Broschofsky Galleries** (360 East Ave., Ketchum, 208/726-4950) carries an eclectic mix of works from the 19th and 20th centuries, including Native American, Western, and contemporary paintings, jewelry, weavings, and pottery.

On the Baldy side of Main Street, **Gail Severn Gallery** (400 1st Ave. N., Ketchum, 208/726-5079) features a first-class collection of modern works by a distinguished list of artists, including the moody Morris Graves and photographer Edward S. Curtis; **Friesen Gallery** (320 1st Ave. N., at Sun Valley Rd., Ketchum, 208/726-4174) deals in contemporary paintings, sculpture, and glass. **Gallery OSCAR** (291 1st Ave. N., Ketchum, 208/725-5090) features original works of Idaho artists, and **Kneeland Gallery** (271 1st Ave. N., Ketchum, 800/338-0480) presents and sells works in a wide range of styles and mediums by artists living and working in the western

United States. The still life paintings of food are beautiful.

Entertainment

For nightlife involving libations and live music, head to the new and improved **Whiskey Jacques'** (251 N. Main St., Ketchum, 208/726-5297, 4 P.M.–2 A.M. daily). A fire in 2008 gutted the original structure, but the establishment was quickly rebuilt on the same spot. It still caterers predominantly to non-locals and over-30 divorced locals, with live bands and dancing, good hand-tossed pizzas, microbrews, and cocktails.

The **Casino Club** (220 N. Main St., Ketchum, 208/726-9901) has drawn its share of Ketchum characters over the years. It's a dark, unassuming, and somewhat mysterious place with nooks and crannies suitable for scandalous repartee with the object of your desire. The bar also has pool tables, darts, foosball, and plenty of stiff drinks.

For a more mellow night out, catch a film at **Magic Lantern Cinema** (100 2nd St. E., Ketchum, 208/726-4274), which features avant-garde indie films and foreign flicks that will stimulate your mind after you've challenged your body all day in the nearby mountains.

Shopping

Iconoclast Books (671 Sun Valley Rd., Ketchum, 208/726-1564, www.iconoclastbooks.com) recently moved into its new, more spacious digs. You'll find 4,500 square feet of new, used, rare, and out-of-print books as well as a small café serving espresso drinks and baked goodies.

For those afflicted with a shoe fetish, you must check out **Ozzie's Shoes** (407 Leadville Ave., Ketchum, 208/726-3604, www.ozziesshoes.com), a downtown shoe emporium that sells a large array of stylish footwear by Simple, Merrell, Tecnica, and the high-soled MBT line.

Sturtevants Ski & Sports (314 N. Main St., Ketchum, 208/726-4512) has lots of outdoor clothing, footwear, and cutting-edge accessories. Expect to find clothing lines by

North Face, Giro, and Prana. You can also pick up gear for skiing and snowboarding, fly-fishing, and biking.

Giacobbi Square (4th St. E. and Leadville Ave., Ketchum) is a small indoor mall with tourist gift shops, clothing stores, and **Atkinsons' Market** (208/726-2681), a boutique-style grocery store with a profusion of specialty foods along with wines and beers from around the globe. The **Ketchum Farmers Market** (2:30–6 P.M. Tues. early June–early Oct.) sets up nearby. You can please your body with impeccably fresh organic produce and other locally produced natural foodstuffs and aromatherapy products.

Accommodations

$50-100

You won't find many double-occupancy lodging choices for under $100 in the Sun Valley area. There's been talk of a youth hostel opening up, but nothing has happened so far. The **Lift Tower Lodge** (703 S. Main St., Ketchum, 208/726-5163 or 800/462-8646, from $85 d) may not look like much as you drive by, but the guest rooms are clean, comfortable, and extremely well priced. Out front is the restored 1939 Sun Valley lift tower that gives the lodge its name, but the best guest rooms are around back, where it's quiet and you'll find a hot tub and views of Baldy. The friendly and welcoming managers set out a complimentary continental breakfast in the lobby each morning. For those on a limited budget who don't need palatial quarters, this place is a steal. Attention bird hunters and other dog owners: The lodge offers two pet-friendly ($10 deposit) guest rooms.

$100-150

Best Western Kentwood Lodge (180 S. Main St., Ketchum, 208/726-4114 or 800/805-1001, from $120 d) lies along the highway at the south edge of downtown. Log and stone accents mark both the exterior and interior of the modern nonsmoking motel. Amenities include an indoor heated pool and spa, an on-site espresso bar, and microwaves and small refrigerators in each of the 57 guest rooms. Also available are guest rooms with full kitchens as well as spa suites.

The Austrian-styled **Best Western Tyrolean Lodge** (260 Cottonwood St., Ketchum, 208/726-5336 or 800/333-7912, from $130 d) is within easy walking distance of the River Run lift. Amenities include a heated pool, two indoor spas, and a fireplace in the lobby. All the beds are topped with thick comforters, and many different suites are available, some with kitchens or in-room jetted tubs. Rates include continental breakfast and après-ski cider. Pets are allowed.

Tamarack Lodge (291 Walnut Ave. N., at Sun Valley Rd., Ketchum, 208/726-3344 or 800/521-5379, www.tamaracksunvalley.com, $79–175) features an indoor heated pool, an outdoor jetted tub, cable TV, high-speed Internet, and free bike and snowshoe rentals. The nondescript yet modern **Clarion Inn** (600 N. Main St., Ketchum, 208/726-5900 or 800/262-4833, from $140 d) sits on the highway at the north end of town. It has a year-round outdoor heated pool and hot tub and offers free continental breakfast.

$150-250

Christophe Condominium Hotel (200 W. River St., Ketchum, 208/726-5601 or 800/521-2515, $90–330), near downtown, has around 15 nonsmoking condo-style guest rooms ranging from full suites with kitchens and laundry rooms to no-frills smaller units. It also has a year-round outdoor pool.

◖ **Bald Mountain Lodge** (100 Picabo St., Ketchum, 208/726-4776, www.baldmountainlodge.com) is the only hotel in town where you can nearly ski up to the front entrance. Located about 100 yards from the Challenger Lift at Warm Springs, this elegant lodge boasts amenities like ground-level ski lockers, an outdoor hot tub, a fitness room, and a roaring fireplace in the lobby. The lodge has some studio rooms for $90, but most of the larger suites here cost around $200.

OVER $250

◖ **Knob Hill Inn** (960 N. Main St., Ketchum,

208/726-8010 or 800/526-8010, www.knobhillinn.com, $275–525) is as plush as it gets in Ketchum. The foyer library and bar look out on a lushly landscaped garden with a fountain and a bright palette of flowers in spring and summer. The 26 guest rooms feature marble-appointed bathrooms with tubs and separate shower stalls. Each room has its own private balcony with great mountain views. Amenities include a jetted tub, a sauna, a year-round lap pool, and free breakfast. The on-site restaurant garners rave reviews for its contemporary Northwestern fare (expect to see huckleberries, morels, and locally raised meats on the seasonal menus). The only possible drawback here is the busy, if convenient, location. The inn is non-smoking, and pets are not allowed.

Thunder Spring (115 Thunder Trail Rd., Ketchum, 208/727-9635, call for rates) is a development of ultrahigh-end condominiums that sell for $1.2 million and up, but they're also available for rent by the night when the owners are away. It's extremely expensive but might provide a sample of how the very rich live.

Food
UPSCALE FARE
The old guard goes to the small and elegant **Michel's Christiania and Olympic Bar** (303 Walnut Ave. N., Ketchum, 208/726-3388, dinner daily, entrées $20 and up). This classy restaurant is reminiscent of an Old World ski chalet, with a cozy interior tastefully appointed in hardwoods and crisp white linen along with a flower-filled patio centered on a small fountain. On the decidedly Gallic menu are upscale delicacies like escargots bourguignon, lamb shank braised with wine, and various classic yet contemporary recipes featuring filet mignon, pheasant, Idaho trout, and halibut. The Olympic Bar, where the walls are adorned with photos of famous skiers, is the best place in town to enjoy a quiet cognac with a friend, and the tall windows beautifully frame Bald Mountain. You'll want to dress well.

If you desire local foodstuffs presented in a contemporary manner, check out ◖ **Ketchum**

Grill (520 East Ave., Ketchum, 208/726-4660, www.ketchumgrill.com from 5 P.M. daily, entrées $13–23) downtown in a 120-year-old converted house. The restaurant's patio, only open in the warmer months, is the place to be seen, and it's a wonderful spot to enjoy chef-owner Scott Mason's inventive Northwest-inspired cuisine and the excellent wine list. During the winter, giant icicles hang from the eaves of this dinner house, accentuating the elegantly lit dining room. The menu follows the seasons closely, using organic local food whenever possible. Late-summer starters might include almond-crusted goat cheese with apple slaw or shrimp cakes in a pool of roasted red pepper coulis. Main dishes like braised lamb shank with grilled tomato polenta, peppered duck breast with cherry chutney, and grilled elk loin with huckleberry-red wine reduction are typical summer offerings. Make sure to save room for the delish chocolate truffle cake or a wedge of silky goat cheese–lemon cheesecake. Prices run a little lower and the atmosphere is a bit more casual than at other top-tier places.

C **Vintage Restaurant** (231 Leadville Ave., Ketchum, 208/726-9595, dinner from 6 P.M. Mon.–Sat., entrées around $25) is another downtown fine-dining establishment that uses local ingredients on its seasonal New American menus. Chef-owner Jeff Keys even found time a few years back to pen a cookbook, aptly titled *Vintage Restaurant*. As in the pages of the book, the menu is globally influenced while at the same time rooted firmly in the Northwest. Expect to find dishes such as rock shrimp tamales, Cajun-style oysters with zesty orange aioli, pecan-crusted chicken breast with tomato chutney, and crispy skinned duck with brandied baked apples. Braised lamb shanks and various cuts of beef also make menu appearances on a consistent basis.

For upscale Italian fare, head to **Il Naso** (480 N. Washington Ave., Ketchum, 208/726-7776, 6 P.M.–close daily, entrées around $20), a comfortable yet luxurious restaurant that dishes up Tuscan-influenced cuisine such as

chilled melon-prosciutto soup, sautéed calamari, veal scaloppini, wild mushroom ravioli, and other seasonal pasta dishes. The wine list favors labels from Tuscany and Piedmont.

The Sawtooth Club (231 N. Main St., Ketchum, 208/726-5233, www.sawtoothclub.com, from 5:30 P.M. daily, entrées $17–26) is a venerable Ketchum restaurant owned by local restaurateur Tom Nickel that was recently rebuilt after a 2008 fire, the same blaze that also destroyed nearby Whiskey Jacques'. The dining room boasts spectacular mountain views, making it a great place to enjoy the restaurant's contemporary steakhouse offerings. Expect to find lots of mesquite-grilled steaks and seafood as well as inventive pasta and poultry dishes. Cocktails, microbrews, and a large wine list pair nicely with the menu.

CASUAL FINE DINING

There's a fine line between upscale dining and casual fine dining in Ketchum, considering most of these après-style establishments don't have strict dress codes (after all, it's a resort town where sporty attire is the norm). And many of the restaurants in this category also use the same sophisticated culinary concepts as the upscale places.

Globus (291 E. 6th St., Ketchum, 208/726-1301, dinner daily, entrées $14–33) prepares a pan-Asian menu in casually elegant surroundings. Look for dishes such as coconut milk–poached black cod, Wagyu beef tataki, sweet and spicy noodles, and smoked duck confit spring rolls with mango ketchup.

On the classy side of the pub-grub scene is the **Pioneer Saloon** (320 N. Main St., Ketchum, 208/726-3139, www.pioneersaloon.com, nightly), which produces a mean burger and excellent prime rib—both made from naturally raised beef. The bar is an old Ketchum landmark where trophy heads and pioneer artifacts line the walls, and locals can tell you stories about the town's glorious past. Entrées range from $10 for a burger to $31 for a full cut of prime rib. Expect to taste appetizers like Brie with smoked trout and a remarkable shrimp cocktail.

The Roosevelt Grille (280 N. Main St., Ketchum, 208/726-0051, www.therooseveltgrille.com, from 5 P.M. daily, entrées $16–27) is another popular spot offering a casual yet creative menu that features Idaho rainbow trout, small gourmet pizzas, salads, jambalaya, and grilled steaks—hand-cut from chemical-free grass-fed beef. Cozy up next to the fireplace and sip on hot-buttered rums, microbrews, and big glasses of Idaho merlot. The lively rooftop terrace is packed with pretty people during the warmer months.

Cornerstone Bar & Grill (211 N. Main St., Ketchum, 208/928-7777, 4:30–11 P.M. daily), in the historic Ketchum post office building, is a relative newcomer to the town's upscale pub scene. Chef Stephen Berks, formerly of Michel's Christiania, adds his impressive modern flair to classic steakhouse preparations. You'll find an espresso-crusted buffalo rib eye, braised Alaskan halibut with Parmesan polenta, upscale burgers, and extremely decadent macaroni and cheese. The bar mixes big-city cocktails and pours an expected array of microbrews and wines.

WINE BARS

It's no secret that wealthy people like expensive wine. This may help to explain why Ketchum has so many wine shops and wine bars. Two places worth checking out: **CIRO** (230 Walnut Ave., Ketchum, 208/727-1800, www.cirosunvalley.com), tucked away downtown just off Sun Valley Road, is more than just a wine bar; this hip place also has a full-service restaurant (lunch and dinner daily, entrées average $18–20), a specialty food market, and a wine shop with labels from around the globe. The modern mountain design boasts a limestone fireplace and pinewood accents juxtaposed with Ikea-looking furniture. An ornate wood-fired oven is the centerpiece of the exhibition kitchen, where cooks put out contemporary Italian fare like thin-crust pizzas, antipasto, cheese plates, Caesar salads, fresh pasta dishes, and a commendable flatiron steak in a puddle of mushroom-red wine reduction. Conclude with a dish of velvety panna cotta crowned with fresh raspberries. CIRO offers 38 wines by the glass and nearly 100 by the bottle as well as beers from around the world; finding the right wine shouldn't be an issue.

The Sun Valley Wine Company (360 N. Leadville Ave., Ketchum, 208/726-2442, www.sunvalleywineco.com, 10 A.M.–9 P.M. Mon.–Sat. and noon–6 P.M. Sun.), above the liquor store, is another spot to enjoy some stinky cheeses and a good glass of wine. In winter you can eat indoors by a crackling fire; in summer, go out on the deck. The wine-friendly menu has light offerings like panini sandwiches, soups, salads, small pizzas, and an artisanal cheeseboard with fresh fruit and baguette. This wine bar is really a wine shop at heart, housing the largest selection of labels in the valley as well as gourmet picnic baskets and gifts for wine fanciers.

ETHNIC CUISINE

Despo's (211 4th St., Ketchum, 208/726-3068, lunch and dinner Mon.–Sat.) dishes up Cali-Mex food in a festive Baja-influenced environment. Noteworthy menu picks include chiles rellenos, tortilla soup, fish tacos, and the ultratender pork carnitas. Wash everything down with an icy margarita or a *cerveza*.

《 Sushi on Second (260 2nd St., Ketchum, 208/726-5181, www.sushionsecond.com, from 5:30 P.M. daily, entrées around $20, sushi platters $30–85) has a chic Japanese interior with a long sushi bar and private tatami-mat rooms. Besides serving top-notch maki rolls, nigiri, and sashimi, the kitchen also has a flair for contemporary pan-Asian cuisine with dishes like ahi carpaccio, chili-rubbed mahimahi with coconut-curry risotto, and grilled Kobe-style beef with shiitake mushrooms. You know the seafood here is as fresh as it gets in Idaho because the restaurant has its own seafood import business, which keeps the jets coming in from various Pacific locales. Pay homage to this impeccably fresh fish by pairing it with a Japanese rice lager, some sake, or a glass of bubbly.

QUICK BITES

Wise Guy Pizza Pie (460 Sun Valley Rd., Ketchum, 208/726-0737, lunch and dinner daily), also with a shop in Hailey, sells New York–style pizza by the slice (around $3). Pizzas include pesto, Margherita (tomato, basil, fresh mozzarella), and a meaty creation called the Fat Guy, a pie with salami, pepperoni, sausage, ham, and bacon. (Could somebody please get me a stretcher?) The restaurant is really a sit-down kind of place that also sells whole pies, calzones, big salads, and hot sandwiches, and it delivers.

If you're into really good hot dogs, check out ◖ **Irving's Red-Hots** (Ketchum, 208/720-1664), a red-and-white sausage shack specializing in Chicago gut-bombs. Besides red-hots, you can also score other Windy City dogs of the beef variety. Ask them to "drag it through the garden," meaning they'll top your dog with marinated sport peppers, green relish, onions, and chopped tomato. But don't even think about asking for ketchup. This hot dog shack spends its summers downtown at the corner of Main and 4th Streets and its winters at the Warm Springs chair lift; hours change with the season.

VEGAN EATS

If the thought of a meaty hot dog offends your green sensibilities, Ketchum has got you covered with at least one good vegan place. ◖ **GLOW-Live Food Café** (380 Washington Ave., Ketchum, 208/725-0314, www.glowlivefood.com, 10 A.M.–5 P.M. Mon.–Sat., around $10) offers a completely raw vegan menu that favors local organic produce. You'll find lots of whole-grain dishes. A good choice is the Indian-inspired grain bowl with lightly steamed quinoa, kale, carrot, and a spicy cashew dressing. Also expect to see vegan sandwiches and wraps (with fillings such as almond hummus and a veggie terrine) made on "live" bread. The restaurant also makes desserts (no sugar, wheat, or dairy products) such as cookies, chocolates, and cakes that you can wash down with a spirulina-kicked fruit smoothie.

You can also pick up organic produce and other veggie-based treats at the **Ketchum Farmers Market** (4th St. and Main St., Ketchum, 2:30–6 P.M. Tues. early June–early Oct.).

BREAKFAST AND BRUNCH

The Kneadery (260 Leadville Ave., Ketchum, 208/726-9462, 8 A.M.–2 P.M. daily, around $10) serves standard American breakfast fare. You can get big plates of Belgian waffles, corned beef hash, omelets, pancakes, and several variations of eggs Benny. At lunch the menu is supplemented with burgers, sandwiches, and salads.

The best Sunday brunch in town is served at ◖ **Cristina's Restaurant and Bakery** (520 2nd St. E., Ketchum, 208/726-4499, www.cristinasofsunvalley.com, breakfast 7–11 A.M. Mon.–Sat., lunch 11 A.M.–5:30 P.M. Mon.–Sat., brunch 9 A.M.–4 P.M. Sun., $5–15), a Euro-inspired place on the south edge of downtown along a quiet side street. Its garden back patio feels far removed from the hustle and bustle—the perfect setting to enjoy a mimosa and a romantic tête-à-tête. Cristina's also serves lunch, and expect long lines on weekends.

Perry's (131 4th St. W., Ketchum, 208/726-7703, 7 A.M.–5 P.M. Mon.–Fri., 7 A.M.–4 P.M. Sat.–Sun., breakfast $4–10.50, lunch $6–13) is a longtime local favorite with lots of seating inside and out, a lively atmosphere, and plenty of good food.

COFFEEHOUSES

The flagship store of the small regional Java chain is Ketchum's **Java on Fourth** (191 4th St. E., Ketchum, 208/726-2882, 6 A.M.–6 P.M. Mon.–Fri., 7 A.M.–6 P.M. Sat.–Sun.). The floor plan is as funky as the crowd in this small but immensely popular caffeinery. You can't go wrong with either the food or the coffee, and the people-watching is outstanding.

The Ketchum Coffee Grinder (321 4th St. E., at Leadville Ave., Ketchum, 208/726-8048) is a coffeehouse–art gallery that specializes in Italian-roast espresso drinks. You can also get freshly baked goodies, sandwiches, and soups.

WARM SPRINGS AREA

On the north side of Baldy, with easy access to the mountain's Warm Springs lifts and day lodge, the Warm Springs area is a little too far from downtown Ketchum for convenient walking, but it does have a pleasant self-contained village feel, with lodgings (lots of condos), restaurants, and nightlife. Yes, there really are warm springs in the vicinity—occasionally your nose will pick up the alluring aroma of sulfur wafting around on the breeze.

SUN VALLEY

The incorporated city of Sun Valley starts just outside Ketchum, less than a mile up Sun Valley Road. Besides the ubiquitous ski condos and immodest eight-bedroom, nine-bath vacation homes, everything in Sun Valley proper centers around Sun Valley Company's operations. You'll find the famous Sun Valley Lodge, the slightly lower-crust Sun Valley Inn, and Sun Valley Village, with its various shops and restaurants that primarily serve guests of the resort. Nightlife is more sedate, favoring martinis and piano bars over Ketchum's beer and rock and roll.

◖ Sun Valley Resort

The grande dame of the Wood River Valley, **Sun Valley Lodge** (1 Sun Valley Rd., Sun Valley, 208/622-4111 or 800/786-8259, www.sunvalley.com, $229–529) opened in 1936, the realization of Union Pacific director Averell Harriman's pet project to build a world-class ski resort in the American West. Harriman's intended motif for the resort was "roughing it in luxury," but it's difficult to see where the "roughing it" part comes in, especially after renovations in 1986, 1992, and 2003. Old World elegance is the lodge hallmark, retained in the newly upgraded country-French decor. But new furnishings can't conceal the patina of history gracing these venerable halls. Harriman still presides over the oak-paneled foyer living room in the form of a portrait hanging above the fireplace, and the ghost of Ernest Hemingway still haunts Room 206, where the author holed up while working on *For Whom the Bell Tolls.*

Amenities at the lodge include a year-round glass-enclosed heated pool, an indoor and an outdoor ice-skating rink, and four restaurants, among them the stellar continental-cuisine Lodge Dining Room. A great many recreational facilities—in addition to world-class skiing—are available at the lodge or in the immediate

Sun Valley Village

© DANA HOPPER-KELLY

area. The bowling alley, golf course, stables, tennis courts, and a skeet- and trapshooting range are open to resort guests and nonguests alike. The resort's three swimming pools—including an Olympic-size pool adjacent to the tennis courts—and the sand volleyball courts are open to resort guests only.

In addition to the lodge, the resort offers a number of other accommodations options, including the **Sun Valley Inn** ($199–435); **condominium units** ($204–619); and for those who demand the most exclusive lodgings available, a number of **guest cottages** are scattered about the expansive resort grounds. The opulent cottages represent the ultimate in privacy—the View Cottage (over $1,000) lies near the shore of Sun Valley Lake. Various lodging specials are offered each year; call for more info.

Recreation Center

The resort's Recreation Center in Sun Valley Village (208/622-2135) can arrange whatever activity you're interested in, either on the resort grounds or anywhere in southern and central Idaho. Examples of off-resort activities the center frequently arranges for guests include white-water rafting trips, glider flights, guided fishing excursions, and wilderness pack trips.

Entertainment

The lodge's elegant **Duchin Lounge** (208/622-2145), just off the lobby, features excellent cocktails and the best live jazz for miles around. In Sun Valley Village, the **Opera** offers free shows of *Sun Valley Serenade,* the 1941 Hollywood classic starring Sonja Henie and John Payne and featuring music by the Glenn Miller Orchestra. This snowy musical screens at 5 P.M. daily year-round.

Food

The best Sunday brunch (10 A.M.–2 P.M. Sun., $27 adults, $19 ages 5–12) in the valley is served at the resort's **Lodge Dining Room** (208/622-2150).

Downstairs from the Lodge Dining Room is **Gretchen's** (208/622-2800, breakfast, lunch,

and dinner daily). In the morning, it's all about French toast, omelets, and eggs Benedict (I forgive the cooks for forgetting the hollandaise last time I ordered this dish). At lunch, the restaurant dishes up club sandwiches, burgers, and salads, and during dinner the lights get dimmed and the menu features dishes such as fennel seed–crusted halibut, grilled New York steak with ratatouille, and roasted free-range chicken on a bed of fingerling potatoes, asparagus, and locally foraged morels.

In Sun Valley Village, you can get good pizza and pasta at **Bald Mountain Pizza** (208/622-2143, from 5:30 P.M. daily, $9–15), which also serves calzones, salads, and an excellent chicken Parmesan. Around the corner, **The Ram Restaurant** (208/622-2800, 6–9:30 P.M. daily, entrées $23–30) is the place to go for European bistro fare. Settle into a big booth and enjoy a delicious caldron of cheese fondue, followed by crispy skinned duck confit and a braised lamb shank with fennel-leek polenta.

For a quintessential Sun Valley experience, sign up for a sleigh ride ($20 pp round-trip, not including food and beverage) out to dinner at the resort's historic **Trail Creek Cabin** (208/622-2135, entrées $17–28). After a brisk ride through the snow, you'll arrive to a cheery roaring fire and a menu of steaks, salmon, trout, and baby back ribs.

INFORMATION AND SERVICES
Information

The **Sun Valley-Ketchum Chamber and Visitors Bureau** (491 Sun Valley Rd., Ketchum, 208/726-3423 or 866/305-0408) has a well-stocked rack of brochures and area maps. The U.S. Forest Service **Ketchum Ranger District** (206 Sun Valley Rd., Ketchum, 208/622-5371) offers good advice for both local recreation and backcountry exploration.

Services

Ketchum has several property management companies that list rental units. **Resort Quest of Sun Valley** (200 W. River St., Ketchum,

208/726-5601 or 888/799-1393, www.re-sortquestsunvalley.com) and **Distinctive Properties** (Ketchum, 208/726-7664 or 877/978-2978) both handle higher-end condos and homes that you can rent by the day, week, or month.

If you want to mail a postcard or buy stamps, head to the Ketchum **post office** (300 Main St. N., Ketchum, 208/726-5161).

For emergency medical services, go to **St. Luke's Wood River Medical Center** (100 Hospital Dr., Ketchum, 208/727-8800), just off Highway 75 between Hailey and Ketchum.

GETTING THERE AND AROUND
Getting There
By air, you'll fly into Hailey's **Friedman Memorial Airport** (SUN, Hwy. 75, Hailey, 208/788-4956). **SkyWest** (800/221-1212) offers daily flights from Salt Lake City, and **Horizon Air** (800/547-9308) has nonstop flights from Seattle and Los Angeles.

If you're coming by car, figure on a 2.5-hour drive from Boise or Idaho Falls, 1.5 hours from Twin Falls, and five hours from Salt Lake City. **Sun Valley Express** (208/342-7750 or 877/622-8267) operates year-round shuttle bus service to and from Boise (one-way $54 adults).

Getting Around
Trying to walk across, or make a left turn across, one of the valley's main streets during the day can be a challenge. Unlike most of Idaho, you'll find traffic here. Fortunately, there is an excellent free bus service around town: **Mountain Rides** (208/788-7433, visit www.mountainrides.org) runs several bus routes connecting major Ketchum–Sun Valley destinations. It also offers bus service to Hailey and Bellevue (one-way $3 adults, $2 seniors and youth).

Rental car agencies at the airport include **Avis** (208/788-2382, www.avis.com) and **Hertz** (208/788-4548, www.hertz.com).

Sawtooth National Recreation Area

Driving north out of Ketchum on Highway 75, you don't need a sign to tell you when you've entered the 765,000-acre Sawtooth National Recreation Area (NRA). The houses suddenly disappear, and the grandeur of the mountains and the tranquility of the wooded river valley return. The dividing line between the two worlds is found at the Sawtooth NRA Headquarters and Visitor Information Center, seven miles north of Sun Valley on the east side of Highway 75. From here on up the valley, you'll see no more 4,000-square-foot "cabins," and traffic is much lighter.

The NRA, established in 1972, encompasses parts of four different mountain ranges. From the headquarters in the Wood River Valley, the Smoky Mountains are visible to the west, and the Boulder Mountains to the east. Across Galena Summit to the north, the famous Sawtooth Mountains dominate the western

skyline with a string of jagged summits, while the eastern horizon is shaped by the inscrutable White Cloud Peaks—more than 50 summits in the NRA stand over 10,000 feet.

Among these mountains are more than 300 alpine lakes, all suitable for fishing, some even big enough for boating and sailing (boat ramps are available on Alturas, Pettit, Redfish, and Stanley Lakes). And four major Idaho rivers—the Salmon, South Fork Payette, Boise, and Big Wood—start within the boundaries of the NRA.

Although the entire NRA is spectacular and wild, the centerpiece of the area is the 217,000-acre Sawtooth Wilderness, an alpine realm closed to motor vehicles and even mountain bikes. Hikers and horse-packers here can enjoy some of the country's most magnificent scenery. Unlike most mountain ranges, the Sawtooths rise suddenly. They're

not particularly tall, as peaks go—the tallest is under 11,000 feet—but their steep relief and abundant granite walls and spires are a mountaineer's paradise. Birders can watch for many of the 214 bird species found here either year-round or part-time; pick up a checklist at NRA headquarters. The area is so grand that from time to time someone pushes to see it recognized as a national park, but you won't hear many locals advocating that. Everything is working well at present, and no one wants to see the crowds, concessionaires,

and additional federal red tape that such status would inevitably bring.

NRA HEADQUARTERS TO GALENA SUMMIT
Sawtooth NRA Headquarters and Visitors Center
Although most of the Sawtooth NRA lies north of Galena Summit, the NRA headquarters is on the south side, nearer the Wood River Valley's major population base. You can't miss the visitors center (208/727-5013), on the east

springtime in the Sawtooths near Galena Summit

© DANA HOPPER-KELLY

side of Highway 75 just where all the fancy houses stop—the building is on the NRA's southern boundary. The visitors center sells a number of excellent natural-history books and offers copious exhibits and informational flyers. Here you can also pick up a free audio-disc interpretive tour of scenic Highway 75, which you return at the NRA's Stanley office up north. In winter, you'll find an ice-skating pond and groomed cross-country ski trails as well. The visitors center is open year-round; in winter you can buy ski permits here for the North Valley Trail System.

From the visitors center, you can continue north up the **North Fork Big Wood River.** The road ends after about five miles, and trails head up high into the Boulder Mountains from here. Mountaineers can follow Trail 115 up to West Pass, and from there scramble up to the summit of **Ryan Peak** (South Ridge, Class 2); at 11,714 feet, it's the highest peak in the range. From trailhead to summit, the six-mile hike climbs 5,000 vertical feet.

A less vertiginous day hike in the area is the **Amber Gulch Trail** (Trails 129–130), which leads about 4.5 miles one-way to Amber Lakes and views of the North Fork and the Pioneer Mountains.

North Valley Cross-Country Trails

You'll find many superb places to go cross-country skiing in Idaho, but in my book, the upper Wood River Valley is by far the best. The Blaine County Recreation District (208/788-2117) grooms some 60 miles of trails between Lake Creek and Galena Lodge. This is no penny ante snowmobile-set track system but a beautifully manicured skating and striding track set by Pisten Bully grooming machines—smaller versions of the LMC grooming cats you see at the big downhill ski resorts. You can ski anywhere you like on the trail system, as long as your legs and lungs will hold out, for $15 per day.

The **Boulder Mountain Trail** runs from Galena Summit down to the Sawtooth NRA visitors center. This is the route taken by the Boulder Mountain Tour, one of the country's largest cross-country ski events. The race draws upward of 700 participants annually, including world-class racers. If you can arrange a car shuttle, you can start at the top and ski all the way to the bottom, letting gravity do a lot of the work for you.

The Boulder Mountain Trail alone would be worth the trail fee, but there's more: Branching off the main trail are three separate side-trail systems on either side of the highway. At Prairie Creek, about halfway between Galena Lodge and the NRA headquarters (11 miles north of Ketchum), loops are set on both sides of the highway: On the east side, the **Billy's Bridge** system provides 4.3 miles of trails, while on the west side the **Prairie Creek** trails run another four miles up one side of the creek and down the other. Dogs are allowed on the Billy's Bridge trails but not on Prairie Creek. Both sides offer scenic views. At the NRA headquarters, the **North Fork Trail System** offers 2.5 miles of easy trails along the North Fork Big Wood; dogs are allowed. This trail is recommended for beginners.

In addition to all these trails, Galena Lodge is the hub of a fantastic 31-mile trail system that's also included in the $15 fee.

Day passes are sold at Galena Lodge, the NRA headquarters, and in Ketchum at the visitors center, Backwoods Mountain Sports, and the Elephant's Perch. For up-to-the-minute trail grooming information, call the Rec District's **North Valley Trails Hotline** (208/578-9754).

Hot Springs

Commercial or noncommercial—take your pick. **Easley Hot Springs Resort** (208/726-7522) offers a developed site with a pool and showers (daily in summer, closed in other seasons, $6.50 adults, $5 children 14 and under, $0.50 seniors) eight miles north of the NRA headquarters. **Russian John Hot Springs** is au naturel, 100 yards west of the highway near mile marker 146, just south of the turnoff to the 4-H camp.

Day Hikes

Recommended by the U.S. Forest Service are the **Lakes Trails,** a network accessing a half dozen or so named lakes in the Smoky Mountains on the west side of Highway 75. From a trailhead at the end of Baker Creek Road (Forest Rd. 162), it's a short two-mile hike up Trail 138 to the popular (and often crowded) fishing hole **Baker Lake.** A spur partway up Baker Creek Road takes you to a second trail from Trail 135, which leads two miles to **Norton Lakes.** The Forest Service recommends this trail for novice hikers; more athletic visitors might want to continue past Norton Lakes over Norton Saddle and down to **Miner Lake,** where you'll have great views of the Boulder Mountains.

Four miles farther up the highway, a third trailhead at the end of Prairie Creek Road (Forest Rd. 179) also provides access to the Lakes Trails. From here you can take Trail 136 up to shallow **Mill Lake,** a 2.5-mile one-way jaunt; or pick up Trail 134, which leads to a high-mountain loop that can take you to one or more of Miner, Norton, and **Prairie Lakes.** From this trailhead it's four miles and a steep climb to Miner Lake, and five moderate miles to Prairie Lakes. For a complete guide to the area, pick up *The Lakes Trails* brochure at the NRA visitors center.

At a hairpin turn on the south side of Galena Summit you'll find the trailhead for a short day hike up to **Titus Lake.** Since you're already at the top of the world, you won't have too much more "up" to go before you reach the lake—the trail climbs only about 500 vertical feet over the 2.5-mile trek.

Galena Lodge

Almost to Galena Summit, 24 miles upstream from Ketchum, you'll come to the region's cross-country ski nirvana: the incomparable **Galena Lodge** (15187 Hwy. 75, Ketchum, 208/726-4010, www.galenalodge.com), with the crown jewels of the Wood River Valley trails, a 31-mile network of loops winding through pristine high-mountain forests and glades, no snowmobiles to disrupt winter's subtle songs, all included in the standard $15 North Valley Trails user fee.

The lodge itself—just a day lodge, with

no accommodations—is intimate but not cramped, and the atmosphere is casual and friendly. A small restaurant serves a home-made gourmet lunch, a light après-ski spread, and brunch (10:30 A.M.–3:30 P.M. Sat.–Sun. summer only). The small bar keeps a variety of wines and a microbrew or two on tap, and a store with a rental and repair shop handles all your equipment needs. Lessons are available as well. After a morning on the trails, it isn't too difficult to spend most of an afternoon out on the sunny lodge deck, serenaded by the quiet rhythm of snowmelt dripping off the roof.

The lodge also maintains popular **backcountry yurts** ($100–155). Three yurts are available in winter and one in summer. They are popular, and reservations must be booked and paid for at least 30 days in advance. The lodge also hosts several events and special dinners throughout the year.

In summer, the trails are open free to hikers, equestrians, and mountain bikers. The store is open daily, offering mountain-bike rentals and trail maps. Wildflower walks and a range of other interpretive programs keep the lodge's events calendar full. Summer or winter, Galena Lodge is a fantastic place.

Galena Summit

Forgive your car its lack of performance as it struggles up the grade; Galena Summit, the crest of the hill, tops out at 8,701 feet. The summit marks the separation of two water-sheds: the Big Wood to the south, and the Salmon to the north.

Mountain bikers can ride the **Old Toll Road** down into the Sawtooth Valley from the sum-mit. The road was built in the 1880s and was the nightmare of early pioneers attempting to descend it with fully loaded wagons. The trail starts across the highway from the Galena Overlook, 0.25 miles north of the summit.

Camping

The **North Fork Campground** (28 sites, $14–28) lies across the highway and a bit farther up the road from the Sawtooth NRA head-quarters. Two miles farther up the valley is

Wood River Campground (30 sites, $14–28). At Easley Hot Springs, the reservable **Easley Campground** (reservations 877/444-6777, 10 sites, $10–18) has the advantage of being next to the hot-springs resort. All three of these U.S. Forest Service campgrounds are open approxi-mately Memorial Day–Labor Day.

SAWTOOTH VALLEY

After cresting Galena Summit, you'll be drop-ping down to the headwaters of the Salmon River—the famous watercourse that flows un-dammed for more than 400 miles to its con-fluence with the Snake River in Hells Canyon. **Galena Overlook** is a must-stop turnout just down the north side from the summit where you'll usually find a few poor souls trying to revive their cars—the altitude and steep grade put motors to the test—and many more gawk-ers enjoying a magnificent sweeping view of the Sawtooths. The road continues down into Sawtooth Valley, where history buffs will find several sights worth a look.

Historic Sites

Not far from the bottom of Galena grade, Forest Road 194 turns east to the 1909 **Pole Creek Ranger Station,** the first structure built by the Forest Service in the Sawtooth National Forest. It was constructed and occupied by Bill Horton, a district ranger in this area for more than 20 years. Today the site is listed on the National Register of Historic Places. Farther up Pole Creek is a trailhead for hiking and bik-ing into the Boulder Mountains and White Cloud Peaks.

A little farther north up the highway, a cou-ple of tributaries—Smiley Creek and Beaver Creek—flow into the Salmon River from the west. These two streams and their surround-ing lands supported a hive of early mining ef-forts in the Sawtooth Valley. Levi Smiley first found silver ore in this end of the valley in 1878, and other miners found gold on Beaver Creek in 1879. **Sawtooth City,** partway up Beaver Creek, boomed 1882–1886 and held on until the crumbs were exhausted around 1892. **Vienna** was the equivalent boomtown over on Smiley Creek that petered out around 1887. You can drive or mountain-bike to the former sites of both of these towns—Vienna is up Forest Road 077, and Sawtooth City is up Forest Road 204—and picnic with the ghosts among the occasional pieces of mining detritus.

Popular Lakes and Wilderness Trailheads

As Highway 75 continues north from Beaver Creek, it parallels the eastern boundary of the Sawtooth Wilderness, some three miles to the west. Between the highway and the wilderness lie several lakes popular with campers, anglers, hikers, bikers, and cross-country skiers. **Alturas Lake** (Forest Rd. 205) is the area's largest. Three **campgrounds** ($15–30) along its north shore—Smokey Bear, North Shore, and Alturas Inlet—have a total of 54 sites. In winter, **cross-country skiing** enthusiasts will find six miles of periodically groomed trails, rated easy to intermediate, that wind across open meadows and along a wooded creek.

Continuing north, **Petit Lake** (Forest Rd. 208) has a small free campground and is the site of the Tin Cup trailhead, a well-used access point into the Sawtooth Wilderness. Backpackers head out from here on the Petit-Toxaway Loop Trail, a two-day trip past several wilderness lakes. Undeveloped **Yellow Belly Lake** (Forest Rd. 365) is a favorite of anglers; no boat motors are allowed.

Off Forest Road 315 you'll find the trailhead to **Hell Roaring Lake.** The moderately difficult 10.4-mile round-trip trek to the lake makes a great day hike. Surrounded by the granite towers of Finger of Fate and the Arrowhead, Hell Roaring Lake lies in one of the most spectacular parts of the Sawtooth Wilderness.

Mountain Biking

On the south end of Sawtooth Valley, **Valley Road** (Forest Rd. 194) more or less parallels the highway on the east. It begins at Sawtooth City; to get here, follow the route to Pole Creek Ranger Station, but at the junction of Forest Roads 194 and 197 continue north on 194. Of course, you could always swing up the extra half-mile and back and check out the ranger station while you're in the area. The rest of the route north leads through pastures and ranchlands, and it rejoins Highway 75 about 0.5 miles south of Fourth of July Creek Road.

If you turn off Highway 75 on Forest Road 315, cross the Salmon River, and turn right, you'll find yourself on **Decker Flat Road** (Forest Rd. 210), an easy mountain-biking route that parallels the river for 14 miles north to Redfish Lake Road. The rangers recommend this scenic ride for families.

Just across the highway from Forest Road 315, **Fourth of July Creek Road** (Forest Rd. 209) leads east up into the White Cloud Peaks. This is the prime west-side access route into the White Clouds, a favored realm of mountain bikers.

Another popular trail begins 1.5 miles farther north on Highway 75. The 18-mile Fisher Creek–Williams Creek Loop starts at Fisher Creek Road (between mileposts 176 and 177 on Hwy. 75) and follows that road up to the old Aztec Mine, where it turns into single track. It then descends to the Warm Springs Creek drainage and turns back west, crossing a second saddle before descending Williams Creek to the highway. Hard-core bikers could instead follow Warm Springs Creek north, all the way down to the Salmon River at Robinson Bar east of Sunbeam.

Day Hikes

On the south end of the valley, **Horton Peak Lookout** provides a high vantage point overlooking the NRA. It's a strenuous eight-mile round-trip hike that gains 2,700 vertical feet. The trailhead is on Forest Road 459, which turns off Valley Road (Forest Rd. 194) about midway along its length.

In the Alturas Lake area, the **Cabin Creek Lakes** trail offers an easier trek. The eight-mile round-trip hike follows Cabin Creek up to a string of small lakes just inside the wilderness boundary. To reach the trailhead, take Cabin Creek Road (Forest Rd. 207) west from Highway 75, about 1.5 miles north of Alturas

Lake Road. Stay on Forest Road 207 at every road junction and find the trailhead about 0.25 miles north of Cabin Creek. You can also reach the trailhead from the south by taking Forest Road 207 north off Alturas Lake Road about one mile.

Farther north, across the highway from the Sawtooth Hatchery, a 0.75-mile spur road leads to the trailhead to **Casino Lakes.** It's a heart-pounding, five-mile one-way hike up 3,000 vertical feet to the cluster of small lakes at the head of Big Casino Creek.

Sawtooth Fish Hatchery

At the Sawtooth Fish Hatchery (Hwy 75, 208/774-3684), Idaho Department of Fish and Game fisheries biologists are trying to undo the devastating effects of the lower Snake River dams on the Salmon River's anadromous chinook salmon population. The small visitors center has plenty of information about the endangered salmon and explains the hatchery process. Perhaps the most fascinating exhibit is the simple dry-erase board at the entrance that lists the number of returning sockeye counted here—usually ranging from zero to a handful. Several 45-minute guided tours are given daily during summer and by appointment the rest of the year. Self-guided tours are possible too.

◖ REDFISH LAKE AREA

The largest lake in the Sawtooths is also the most developed and most popular. Venerable Redfish Lake Lodge—the region's social hub—as well as several campgrounds, trailheads, and water-sports opportunities are here, and the landscape couldn't be more sublime. Mount Heyburn's granite walls rise nearly 4,000 feet over the far end of the lake, and views up into the heart of the Sawtooth Wilderness will tempt you to don a backpack and hit the dusty trail.

The lake is named for the sockeye salmon that once spawned in Redfish Lake by the thousands; the fish turn a brilliant orange-red when they spawn. Thanks to human "progress" the numbers of this species are way down,

although they still exist here. There are also a few kokanee (landlocked sockeye) swimming around in the lake.

Redfish Rock Shelter

Near Highway 75 on the north side of Redfish Lake Road is a rock overhang that archaeologists believe was used by indigenous people for shelter as early as 9,500 years ago. Later, the Tukudeka band of Northern Shoshone—the sheep eaters—also camped here on their bighorn hunting forays into the area. A very short trail begins at a turnout between the north end of Little Redfish Lake and the highway and leads across the creek to the site.

Redfish Lake Visitors Center

The Forest Service's Redfish Lake Visitors Center (208/774-3376, summer only) provides interpretive information about Redfish Lake and the Sawtooth Wilderness and hosts guided hikes, campfire programs, slide shows, and children's activities. A short half-mile interpretive trail makes a great hike for the little ones. The visitors center is just a short distance from the lakeshore, just east of the lodge.

Day-Use Areas

The Sandy Beach boat ramp and day-use area ($5) on the lake's northeast shore attracts crowds of swimmers and sunbathers in summer. The North Shore Picnic Area near the visitors center also features a popular beach. Noncamping visitors are welcome to use the beaches at the Point and Outlet. All day-use areas are open 8 A.M.–10 P.M., and camping is not allowed.

Horseback Riding

Redfish Lake Corrals (208/774-3311), about halfway down the road to Redfish Lake, offers trail rides ranging in length from 1.5 hours ($45 pp) to a full day ($110 pp). The full-day rides head up to one or more of the Sawtooths' beautiful lakes and include a nice spread of food along the trail. Anglers are welcome. One special ride includes breakfast at the lodge, a boat ride across the lake, a trail ride to Alpine

Lake, a box lunch, and dinner back at the lodge that evening ($180 pp).

Day Hikes

Two popular hiking trails begin at the Redfish trailhead parking area, just past the turnoff to the lodge on Redfish Lake Road. The **Fishhook Creek Trail** (Trail 186) leads west several miles upstream along Fishhook Creek with minimal elevation gain. A short distance from the parking area it meets **Redfish Lake Creek Trail** (Trail 101), which heads south to the trailhead at the far end of the lake (5.2 miles) and continues into the Sawtooth Wilderness. Partway along this trail, a turnoff switchbacks up to **Bench Lakes,** four miles from the trailhead, where you'll have a bird's-eye view of Redfish Lake. All these are one-way trails—take them until your stomach growls like a grizzly bear, and then eat your picnic lunch and head back the way you came.

You also might consider taking the lodge shuttle across the lake and starting your hike from the trailhead at the other side. The 10.5-mile round-trip hike from the boat dock up Redfish Lake Creek to **Alpine Lake** (one of at least two lakes in the Sawtooth Wilderness with that unimaginative name) is particularly popular.

Out on the Water

Canoes, kayaks, fishing boats, sailboats, and ski boats ply Redfish Lake. **Boat rentals** of all sorts are available from the lodge; just wander down to the dock and find an attendant. Or sign up for one of the **Lady of the Lake Scenic Tours** ($15 adults, $5 children), one-hour lake cruises aboard a pontoon boat. Hikers can get a **boat shuttle** (208/774-3536, $15 round-trip, $8 one-way) ride to the trailhead at the far end of the lake.

Stanley Ranger Station

A couple of miles north of the Redfish Lake turnoff, you'll find Stanley Ranger Station (208/774-3000), the main ranger station serving the Sawtooths and White Clouds. Check in here before you venture into the wilderness.

The rangers have up-to-date information on backcountry conditions and can answer any questions about routes or campsites. In winter, a four-mile **cross-country ski trail** loop runs through lodgepole pine forest.

Redfish Lake Lodge

Although its widespread reputation might lead you to expect something along the lines of the Sun Valley resort, Redfish Lake Lodge (208/774-3536 summer, 208/644-9096 off-season, www.redfishlake.com, mid-May–early Oct.) is instead down-home Idaho all the way. You'll find nothing grand or imposing, which isn't to say it isn't nice—it is. But it's more rustic than regal, more folksy than aristocratic. It's like summer camp for the entire family. While Mom's out fishing on the lake, Dad can take the baby on a walk through the woods or a horseback ride along the creek. Meanwhile, the social scene around the lodge and its many neighboring campgrounds will excite even the most jaded and aloof teenager—this place is a natural incubator for adolescent romance.

Rather than one giant château-like lodge, this resort consists of a modest main lodge near the lakeshore and numerous outbuildings. Motel rooms ($70–175) in the lodge are available as well as private cabins ($150–500) that range from small cottages to larger lakeside gems. Facilities at the lodge include a dining room serving three meals a day, a cozy lounge where locals swap fish stories, a Laundromat, stables, a general store, a gas station, and a marina. Reservations are strongly recommended, and the sooner you make them (like January), the better, because this place books up months in advance.

Camping

Eight separate U.S. Forest Service campgrounds ($16–32) with a total of 119 sites dot the Redfish Lake area: **Sockeye, Mount Heyburn, Outlet, Glacier View** and **Point** ring the north end of the big lake; **Mountain View** and **Chinook Bay** are on Little Redfish Lake, closer to the highway; and **Sunny Gulch** is out on the far side of Highway 75. Reservable sites are offered in the Point, Outlet, and Glacier View campgrounds (reservations 877/444-6777); Sockeye and Mount Heyburn are first-come, first-served. For more information, call the NRA headquarters at 208/727-5013.

◖ STANLEY AND VICINITY

In 1864, Captain John Stanley led a party of miners into the Valley Creek area. The town that now bears his name started as a supply center for the gold-mining district that eventually dug in. The little town is the yin to Ketchum's yang: There are no fancy homes or cars; in fact, except for the two highways, the streets aren't even paved. Only about 90 people live here year-round, mostly because Stanley's harsh winters are among the coldest you'll encounter in the state. Recreation fuels the town's economy, which races in summer—when rafters, anglers, campers, and backpackers pass

A SLICE OF IDAHO HISTORY LOST TO POLITICS

Bethine Clark Church, wife of the late U.S. Senator Frank Church, spent much of her childhood in the White Cloud Mountains near Stanley. Her father, Chase Clark, who later became the 18th Governor of Idaho, acquired a chunk of prime Idaho wilderness in 1917 after a devastating car wreck left him in need of hydrotherapy. The Clark family purchased an abandoned stagecoach stop at the mouth of Warm Springs Creek, a tranquil spot where therapeutic steamy water bubbled up from deep within the earth. Chase, with the help of his entire family, homesteaded the 123-acre spread and turned it into a sublime mountain getaway, which they named Robinson Bar Ranch, although it was not a working ranch with livestock.

Over the years, the Clarks built a main lodge and several cabins on the property, and they even harnessed the natural spring water into two concrete-lined ponds the size of large swimming pools. Under the cobalt Sawtooth sky, the family spent many hours soaking away their pains. Chase enjoyed catching big salmon that were once prevalent in the nearby creek. The family eventually moved away from the ranch to Idaho Falls so Chase could pursue his law practice, and later to Boise after he won his Democratic gubernatorial bid in 1941. But the family always returned to Robinson Bar Ranch during the summer months to decompress in the steamy pools and enjoy each other's company in the unfettered wilderness.

As a young woman, Bethine became smitten by a gentleman caller by the name of Frank Church, a young man with a promising future in the Democratic Party. He had just earned his bachelor's degree at Stanford University, and the young couple felt that prenuptials were in order. Frank and Bethine were married in 1947 at Robinson Bar Ranch. Bethine's father, an ardent Democrat himself, was impressed by his son-in-law's intelligence, charm, and the fact that Frank was about to enter law school at Harvard University. Frank, however, went on to earn his law degree from Stanford University after spending only one year at Harvard. Later he became a four-term U.S. Senator from Idaho. Frank and Bethine had two sons, Frank Forrester and Chase, named after his grandfather.

During Frank's time in Washington, D.C., he earned a reputation for being an environmental watchdog. He cosponsored the Wilderness Act in 1964, which designated federally protected status to a large portion of central Idaho's pristine mountains that should be, in Frank's words, "Untrammeled by man; where man is a visitor who does not remain." This controversial Senate Act (Republicans were in favor of continued mining and logging in the area) gave birth to the River of No Return Wilderness, a 2.2-million-acre protected beauty enjoyed by many low-impact recreationalists today.

He was also involved in several other pieces of Senate legislation, like the 1968 Wild and Scenic Rivers Act and a 1972 Bill that created the 756,000-acre Sawtooth National Recreation Area (NRA), the first of its kind in the country. This is when things got tricky for the Churches, who now owned Robinson Bar Ranch

through town on their way into the surrounding wilds—and stays idling in winter, with the help of the few snowmobilers and skiers who venture up this way. Besides its decidedly down-home character, Stanley's biggest asset is its incredible view. The Sawtooths rise up like a giant picket fence just south of town; they're so dramatic that it's almost impossible to take your eyes off them.

Highway 75 intersects with Highway 21 near town. West on Highway 21 is the Ponderosa Pine Scenic Byway heading toward Lowman. Stanley is a wonderful place to hunker down for a few days, taking in the remarkable scenery and the frontier culture.

Stanley Museum

To find out more about the history of Stanley and the Sawtooths, stop by the Stanley Museum (208/774-3517, www.discoversawtooth.org,

© CHASE CHURCH

Frank and Bethine Church

on the fringe of what would soon be the Sawtooth NRA. Senate Republicans were calling the Churches' property a conflict of interest, stating that the Churches were simply trying to preserve the area around the ranch and not really looking out for the best interests of Idahoans. They couldn't have been more wrong, but the Churches made the heart-wrenching decision to let the ranch go – selling it for a mere $140,000 – in order to preserve the integrity of the upcoming Congress vote in 1972.

Just before Frank Church's death in 1984, the River of No Return Wilderness was renamed the Frank Church-River of No Return Wilderness, honoring a man who did so much to ensure that Idaho remains wild.

Carole King, the famous singer-songwriter, now owns Robinson Bar Ranch, but she currently has it up for sale for a whopping $16 million. Hopefully whoever buys the property, with all its buildings and hot springs pools, has the same vision as its previous owners, meaning not to commercialize this gorgeous slice of Idaho history.

11 A.M.–5 P.M. daily June–Sept., free) on the west side of Highway 75, a short distance north of the Highway 21 junction. The museum is housed in a 1933 Forest Service rangers cabin and offers exhibits focusing on pioneer life in the region.

Mountain Biking

Great views of the Sawtooths and White Clouds highlight the 6.5-mile ride down **Nip and Tuck Road.** The old wagon road (Forest Rd. 633) follows an easy grade west up Nip and Tuck Creek from Lower Stanley, then crests the hill and descends to Stanley Creek, ending at the intersection of Valley Creek Road and Highway 21.

Mountain biking is prohibited in the Sawtooth Wilderness, but east of town the White Cloud Peaks constitute the Holy Land for area mountain bikers.

Floating the Upper Main Salmon

The stretch of the Salmon River just downstream from Stanley is popular for white-water day trips; between Stanley and Basin Creek it's an easy float suitable even for inner tubes, while between Basin Creek and Torrey's Hole the river throws two Class III and two Class IV tantrums. The lower segment is usually runnable May–September. The upper stretch draws most floaters in May–June, as after that it usually gets a tad shallow.

Guide services on the Salmon River day stretch include **The River Company** (1150 Eva Falls Ave., Stanley, 208/788-5775 or 800/398-0346, www.therivercompany.com) and **White Otter Outdoor Adventures** (105 Mountain View Lane, Hailey, 208/788-5005 or 877/788-5005 www.whiteotter.com). Rates for a full-day guided trip on the river cost about $65 without lunch, $90 with lunch.

Outfitters

Next to the Mountain Village complex you'll find **Riverwear** (Hwy. 21, Stanley, 208/774-3592), a great outdoor store selling all the supplies you'll need for your raft or pack trip and renting a variety of gear as well. Sample

rentals: bikes for $25 per day, wetsuits for $8 per day, kayaks for $30 per day, rafts $65–125 per day.

Sawtooth Rentals (13 River Rd., Lower Stanley, 208/774-3409 or 877/774-3409) rents mountain bikes, rafts, kayaks, canoes, inner tubes, wetsuits, and other outdoor gear. They also run a motel. **White Otter Outdoor Adventures** (208/788-5005) rents rafts, kayaks, and related equipment for private trips from its office at the Sunbeam put-in.

Flightseeing and Air Taxi Service

Based at Stanley's little airport, **Stanley Air Taxi** (208/774-2276) can take you up to see the sights or fly you into the remote backcountry lodge of your choice. They also fly rafters to Indian Creek on the Middle Fork—the put-in of choice when the water starts to get too low at Boundary Creek.

Entertainment

Having a good time is the modus operandi at the **Rod-N-Gun Whitewater Saloon** (west end of Ace of Diamonds St., Stanley, no phone, spring–fall) in Stanley. This popular watering hole has live rock, country, and blues on weekends in the summer; expect to see some debauchery on the dance floor.

Accommodations

Mountain Village Resort (Hwy. 21 and Hwy. 75, Stanley, 208/774-3661 or 800/843-5475, www.mountainvillage.com, from $95 d) is the most obvious, well-established lodging in town. Guest rooms are modern rather than rustic, the adjacent dining room (serving breakfast, lunch, and dinner) is convenient but nothing to write home about, and the lounge often presents live entertainment. The motel's biggest plus is probably the natural hot springs spa on-site. Kitchenette suites are available.

Heading west on Highway 21 from the big junction, you'll pass a string of motels lining the highway. The motels on the north side front Valley Creek and have a nicer ambience than those on the south side.

Valley Creek Motel (1120 Eva Falls Ave.,

Stanley, 208/774-3606, $65–140) sits on high ground, resulting in some of the best views in town. All guest rooms have queen beds, private baths, Cable TV, and refrigerators. Valley Creek also offers basic RV sites ($26–30) with water, power, and sewer hookups.

Heading down Highway 75 to Lower Stanley, the delightful **Salmon River Lodge** (208/774-3422, cabins $85–95) sits off by itself on a spacious spread across the river from Highway 75. Turn in and cross the creaky old bridge over the Salmon. The cabins face the Sawtooths, and the river flows right past; anglers could drop a line practically off their cabin porch. The wide-open surroundings provide an expansive feel, in contrast to the sometimes densely packed and claustrophobic cabin complexes in some other parts of town. Cabins with kitchenettes are available.

Among the several accommodations in Lower Stanley, **Gunter's Salmon River Cabins** (208/774-2290 or 888/574-2290, closed winter, $65–112), about a mile and a half north of town on Highway 75, and **Redwood Cabins** (83 Hwy. 75, 208/774-3531, www.redwood-stanley.com, closed winter, $85–100) offer cabins right on the river.

Food

The **Kasino Club** (21 Ace of Diamonds St., Stanley, 208/774-3516, from 6 P.M. daily, from $12) is regarded as the finest of dining in Stanley proper. The kitchen specializes in prime rib and also offers a salad bar and a variety of meats, seafood, and pastas. Several microbrews are available.

Pizza is available downtown across from the post office at **Papa Brunee's** (37 Ace of Diamonds St., Stanley, 208/774-2536), where you can also get deli salads, sandwiches, and lots of beer to wash it all down.

In the morning, head to the **Stanley Baking Co. and Café** (250 Wall St., Stanley, 208/774-6573, www.stanleybakingco.com, 7 A.M.–2 P.M. daily May–Oct., breakfast $5–10) for biscuits and gravy, sourdough pancakes, breakfast burritos, house-made granola, and supreme vegetarian items. You can also get freshly baked scones, cinnamon rolls, coffee cake, and sticky buns to go with your espresso drink made from organic beans. The restaurant serves sandwiches and burgers at lunch. Try the delish veggie burger (patties made in-house with shiitake mushrooms, tofu, and toasted pecans) plopped on a crusty bun with provolone, fresh tomato, and mixed greens.

Information

The **Stanley-Sawtooth Chamber of Commerce** (208/774-3411, www.stanleycc.org, 10 A.M.–6 P.M. mid-May–Sept.), in the community building under a big flagpole, has all the information you'll need to know about the area. These friendly folks can also hook you up with backcountry outfitters and guides.

HIGHWAY 21 TO SAWTOOTH AND STANLEY LAKES

Spectacular mountain vistas and vast meadows awash in wildflowers combine to make this stretch of pavement, the Ponderosa Pine Scenic Byway, one of the most beautiful drives in Idaho. Several angler access roads branch off the highway and lead down to meandering Valley Creek, while other spur roads lead south off the highway to campgrounds at the foot of the Sawtooths.

Day Hike to Sawtooth Lake

A photographer's favorite, Sawtooth Lake enjoys the sheer granite face of 10,190-foot Mount Regan as a backdrop. The moderately strenuous five-mile trail takes you up past dramatic cliffs, a tall graceful waterfall, and gem-like Alpine Lake. Sawtooth Lake itself is one of the largest lakes in the Sawtooth Wilderness. Snow lingers in these heights until well into summer; don't be surprised to see miniature icebergs drifting across the lake even in July–August. On the hike back down, you'll get glimpses of Stanley on the valley floor below.

To reach the trailhead, take Iron Creek Road off Highway 21, three miles west of Stanley. The trailhead is at the end of the road. Also at the trailhead you'll find **Iron Creek Campground** (9 sites, $14).

Stanley Lake

Boating, fishing, and family camping are the prime pastimes at Stanley Lake, 2.5 miles off the highway on Stanley Lake Road (five miles west of Stanley). Three separate campgrounds line the lake's north shore: **Inlet** (14 sites, $15), **Lakeview** (6 sites, $15), and **Stanley Lake** (19 sites, $15). It's a beautiful spot offering access into the Sawtooth Wilderness along Stanley Creek, but it's also a dusty, relatively noisy, heavily used area best suited for those who don't like to be too far removed from their fellow human beings.

A challenging 12.5-mile **mountain-biking** trail loops from here north around Elk Mountain to Elk Meadows and back. Stay on Stanley Lake Road past the lake; turn off onto Trail 629, which leads to Elk Meadows and eventually intersects Forest Road 630; return to the lake on Forest Road 630. Elk Meadows is a good spot for watching wildlife.

Cross-Country Skiing

In winter, a short 2.5-mile loop is set at **Park Creek** turnout, about three miles northeast of Stanley Lake Road on Highway 21. The trail winds through open meadows and is rated easy to intermediate. It's groomed only periodically.

HIGHWAY 75 TOWARD SUNBEAM

Heading first north then east out of Stanley, Highway 75 hugs the Salmon River downstream. There are a string of hot springs along the riverbank; west to east, look for **Elkhorn Hot Springs,** 0.7 miles east of mile marker 192; **Mormon Bend Hot Spring,** 350 yards downstream from Elkhorn at mile marker 193, on the far side of the river; **Basin Creek Campground Hot Spring,** next to the campground, seven miles east of Stanley; and **Kem Hot Springs,** 0.7 miles east of mile marker 197.

For panoramic views of Salmon River Canyon and the Sawtooths, make the 12-mile round-trip **day hike** up to **Lookout Mountain.** You'll climb 2,600 vertical feet to

Stanley Lake

the lookout on the peak (9,954 feet). Bear left at each of the two forks along the way. The trailhead is at the end of Rough Creek Road (Forest Rd. 626), which turns off Highway 75, east 10 miles from Stanley.

Between Stanley and Sunbeam on Highway 75, U.S. Forest Service **campgrounds** on the Salmon River include **Salmon River** (30 sites, $14), **Riverside** (17 sites, $14), and **Mormon Bend** (16 sites, $12). All are open June 15– September 15.

SAWTOOTH WILDERNESS

Although it's nowhere near the largest wilderness area in Idaho, the 217,000-acre Sawtooth Wilderness is a prime contender for the grandest. Three major Idaho rivers start here in snowy tarns beneath granite spires: the South Fork Payette River drains the northwest third of the wilderness; the North and Middle Forks of the Boise River drain the southwest third; and the mighty Salmon is born of the waters flowing off the east side of the wilderness.

Rock climbers have a field day here on the big-wall granite faces of Warbonnet Peak, Elephant's Perch, and the Finger of Fate, among others. Mountaineers come to bag more than a dozen summits rising over 10,000 feet, the tallest being 10,751-foot Thompson Peak. Hikers and horse-packers are content to keep their feet on the 300 miles of trails lacing the preserve—trails that lead the backcountry adventurer through awesome glacier-carved valleys, past nearly 200 trout-filled alpine lakes and meadows lush with summer wildflowers.

Access Guide

A list of primary access points into the Sawtooth Wilderness, starting at the northern tip of the wilderness and proceeding clockwise:

- **Stanley Lake** trailhead, on Stanley Lake Road (Forest Rd. 455), six miles west of Stanley on Highway 21; access along the western edge of the wilderness into Sawtooth Lake and Baron Creek drainage
- **Iron Creek** trailhead, on Iron Creek Road

(Forest Rd. 619), three miles west of Stanley on Highway 21; access across the eastern boundary of the wilderness into Sawtooth Lake and Baron Creek drainage

- **Redfish Lake** trailheads, at the north or south sides of lake, on Redfish Lake Road, five miles south of Stanley on Highway 75; access into the heart of the wilderness up Redfish Lake Creek, and access to rock climbing on Mount Heyburn, Grand Mogul, and Elephant's Perch
- **Hell Roaring Creek** trailhead, on Forest Road 315 off Decker Flat Road (Forest Rd. 210), 17 miles south of Stanley off Highway 75; access to Hell Roaring Lake, Finger of Fate, the Arrowhead, Imogene Lake
- **Petit Lake** trailhead, on Petit Lake Road (Forest Rd. 208), 20 miles south of Stanley on Highway 75; access to the Petit-Toxaway Loop (a prime backpacking trail) and on into the South Fork Payette River drainage
- **Atlanta** trailhead, at the end of Middle Fork Boise River Road (Forest Rd. 268), about 60 miles northeast of Highway 21 (turn off Highway 21 at Lucky Peak Reservoir); access up Middle Fork Boise River drainage into the southern end of wilderness
- **Grandjean** trailhead, on Forest Road 524, about eight miles east of Highway 21 (turn off Highway 21 about 45 miles west of Stanley or 89 miles northeast of Boise); access up either Baron Creek drainage or South Fork Payette River drainage

Mountaineering Guides

The folks at **Sawtooth Mountain Guides** (Stanley, 208/774-3324, www.sawtoothguides. com) know every nook and cranny in the Sawtooths. Rock climbing and mountaineering in summer, hut-to-hut ski touring in winter—whatever your pleasure, they'll show you the way. The company has been in business for more than 30 years and regularly leads ascents of Mounts Heyburn, Thompson, Williams, and Warbonnet, the Finger of Fate, and the Elephant's Perch. Call for rates.

Information

To learn more about the Sawtooth Wilderness, contact the **Sawtooth NRA Headquarters** (208/727-5013) just north of Ketchum.

WHITE CLOUD PEAKS

From a distance, you might have to squint pretty hard to distinguish the white limestone peaks here from summer clouds; hence the name. Unlike the Sawtooths on the other side of Highway 75, the White Clouds aren't within a designated wilderness area, so mountain bikes are permitted. And while the Sawtooths top out at about 10,700 feet, the White Clouds' tallest peaks tower more than 1,000 feet higher. The highest in the range, 11,815-foot Castle Peak, is highly coveted by mountaineers; it offers no easy route to the top.

Before Congress established the NRA in 1972, mining companies were eyeing the molybdenum deposits in the White Clouds, and a large open-pit mine was proposed in the 1960s. Under the rules regulating the NRA, all lands within its boundaries are now closed to new mining claims. Pre-1972 claims can still be worked, however, provided they don't infringe on the area's prime mission as a recreational haven. Thankfully, all the old claims are currently dormant, and there's now a proposal to make Boulder–White Clouds a designated wilderness area.

The White Clouds receive less use than the Sawtooths. Those adventurers taking the time to seek out this pristine high country will find steep granite galore and water everywhere—more than 125 alpine lakes set the range aglitter in the summer sun. The lakes tend to be smaller than their Sawtooth counterparts but no less beautiful. Elk, deer, bighorn sheep, and mountain goats inhabit the lofty realm, keeping a sharp eye out for members of the area's small cougar population. Coyotes, foxes, beavers, badgers, and black bears add to the White Clouds' mix of resident wildlife.

Access Guide

Primary access routes are from the west, up Pole Creek–Germania Creek Road (Forest Rd.

197) and Fourth of July Creek Road (Forest Rd. 209); from the north, up Slate Creek Road (Forest Rd. 666), off Highway 75 about six miles west of Clayton Ranger Station; and from the northeast, up East Fork Salmon River Road (Forest Rd. 120), off Highway 75 about five miles east of Clayton.

Hiking

The west side's Fourth of July Road will take you from Highway 75 some 10 miles east into the heights before you'll have to park and continue on foot. From there, it's about 1.5 miles up Trail 109 to **Fourth of July Lake** and a mile farther to **Washington Lake.** The elevation gain is minimal. Both lakes are only a couple of crow-flapping miles to Castle Peak, the monarch of the White Clouds.

On the north side, six miles up Slate Creek Road, you'll come to a four-way intersection. Turn left and go a short distance to the trailhead for the **Crater Lake** trail. The trail follows Livingston Creek four miles and some 2,500 vertical feet up to the lake, from which you'll have views of the striking **Chinese Wall.**

The **Boulder Chain Lakes** attract a healthy share of the backpacking visitors to the range. The trail winds along the shores of eight lakes that lie at elevations averaging around 9,000 feet. Access is via the Little Boulder Creek trailhead, about 22 miles in on the East Fork Salmon Road. From there, Trail 682 ascends Little Boulder Creek about seven miles to the intersection of Trail 047. Turn right and continue another 1.5 miles to the first of the lakes.

Mountain Biking

Since all the trails in the area are open to mountain bikes, you can just get yourself a map and take off exploring. The prime access points for mountain bikers are **Fourth of July Creek Road** (Forest Rd. 209), which leads east up into the White Clouds from Highway 75; **Germania Creek Road** (Forest Rd. 197), which takes off from Pole Creek–Valley Road (Forest Rd. 194, off Hwy. 75 near Sawtooth City); and **East Fork Salmon River Road,** which heads south off Salmon River Road east of Clayton.

Mountaineering

The White Cloud Peaks aren't known for technical rock climbing; the predominant loose, friable limestone is a climber's nightmare. Still, many peak-baggers can't resist the allure of **Castle Peak** (11,815 feet), the highest in the range. All the routes to the summit are Class 3. Access is from Chamberlain Basin, reached via either Little Boulder Creek (Trails 682, 047, and 110) or Germania and Chamberlain Creeks (Trails 111 and 110). The approach to the north-side routes is via a cross-country trail from near the junction of the Wickiup Creek and Little Boulder Creek Trails (Trails 684 and 047).

Hot Springs

On the southeast side of the White Clouds, at the end of East Fork Salmon River Road, you'll find a couple of hot springs where you can soak in secluded privacy. **West Pass Hot Spring,** on a hillside above West Pass Creek, offers a pair of tubs with great views. Coming in on the East Fork Road, cross West Pass Creek (29 miles south of Hwy. 75) and almost immediately bear left on a road that climbs the hillside. Park on the flat and find the short trail past an old mine to the tubs. **Bowery Hot Spring** is in the same area. Continue straight up the East Fork at the West Pass Creek junction to the trailhead. Hike 100 yards up the road toward Bowery guard station, and at the bridge continue a short distance upstream to the spring.

FRANK CHURCH–RIVER OF NO RETURN WILDERNESS AREA

Access to this area, named for the late U.S. Senator from Idaho and lifelong champion of Idaho's wild lands, is relatively easy, which may or may not be a positive attribute, depending on your perspective. When Congress established the wilderness, rather than just drawing a big box for a boundary and letting all the pre-existing roads within it grow over, instead all

existing mining and logging roads were grandfathered out of the wilderness. As a result, even in the deepest heart of the Frank Church, you're never too far from one of these "cherry-stemmed" roads. Although purists consider this an unwanted intrusion, the roads do permit you to drive to a plethora of trailheads on all sides of the area.

For general information on the Frank Church wilderness, contact the **Salmon-Challis National Forests Supervisor's Office** (1206 S. Challis St., Salmon, 208/756-5100). Look for the big blue building right before you come into town.

Wilderness Trails

Backpackers with a map will be like kids in a candy store, with an astounding number of trails to explore. Backpackers entering the heart of the wilderness will be certain to encounter solitude; there's an awful lot of land to get lost in. Favorite destinations are the Bighorn Crags—a magnificent area of jagged spires and alpine lakes on the east side of the wilderness—and the two big rivers, each of which offers a trail running alongside much of its length. Hot springs abound alongside those rivers and elsewhere in the wilderness, allowing the enterprising backpacker to do a multiday spring-to-spring trip and have a hot soak every night. Horse-packers also enjoy the wilderness. Mountain bikes are not allowed. A compromise that aided passage of the bill creating the Frank Church makes one exception to the no-mechanized-vehicles rule; jetboats are permitted on the main Salmon.

White-Water Rafting

When the Lewis and Clark expedition came over Lemhi Pass looking for a route to the sea, they intended to follow the Lemhi River down to the **Salmon River,** then float the Salmon to the Columbia River. At camp in the Lemhi Valley, the local Shoshone told Captain Clark that the Salmon River Canyon was impassable, but Clark figured he'd go see for himself. Reaching a point 14 miles downstream from today's town of North Fork, Clark

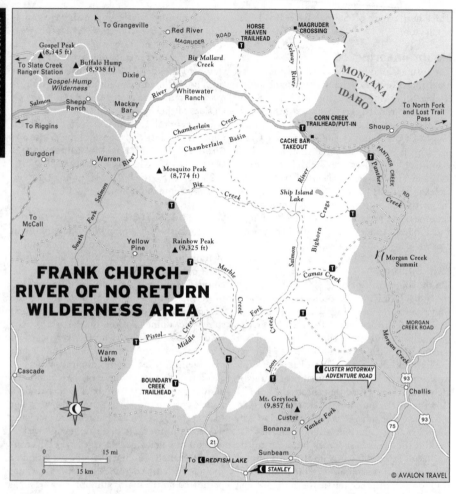

climbed high up the side of the canyon for a better view. From this high vantage point, he saw Pine Creek Rapids (Class III–IV) churning away downstream and nothing but a deep gorge with steep, rocky walls leading all the way to the horizon. Clark immediately opted for Plan B, and the expedition made a long detour to the north rather than attempt a descent of the Salmon. Later pioneers managed to float some sections of the upper Salmon, but paddling back upstream against the swift current was impossible; hence the river's nickname, the "river of no return."

The Salmon River drains some 14,000 square miles and flows undammed for its entire 420 miles, from its headwaters in the southern Sawtooth Valley to its confluence with the Snake River. For more than 180 miles of its length it flows through a deep gorge rising over a mile on either side of the river. From North Fork to the normal takeout at Riggins, the river drops 1,910 feet—an average of more than 12 feet per mile. Rapids on the river for the most part range Class II–III+, although a few Class IVs—Pine Creek, Big Mallard, Elkhorn, Vinegar—challenge even the experts, and many of the Class IIIs go Class IV in high water. Permits (www.recreation.gov) are required for this stretch of the river.

The **Middle Fork of the Salmon** is one of the world's greatest and most popular whitewater trips, drawing rafters and kayakers from around the globe. From the put-in at Boundary Creek, northwest of Stanley, the river flows 100 wet and wild miles through a wilderness little tarnished by human activity. Bighorn sheep, black bears, mountain goats, salmon and steelhead, bald eagles, and once again, wolves—the list of magnificent creatures inhabiting this land goes on and on.

The river itself puts up a premier challenge at any flow level. More than 30 significant rapids line the route, almost a third of them running Class IV. From Velvet Falls on Day 1 to the wild roller coaster of Rubber Rapids on Day 6, the Middle Fork rarely lets up. Another delight of the river is the abundance of hot springs along its banks, making great places for midday breaks or long, stargazing soaks at day's end.

Historical sites along the way include hermit cabins, Native American pictographs, and sites associated with the Sheepeater Campaign of 1879.

Permits (www.recreation.gov) are required year-round for boaters here.

Of the two, the Middle Fork is a more technical river, particularly in its narrow upper reaches. The Main Salmon has the big water—the biggest waves, the biggest holes, and the most adrenaline-inducing power. The Middle Fork is a wilderness river. Few roads lead to its banks, and only a handful of isolated ranches provide reminders of civilization. The Main Salmon also flows past just a few roads and ranches; however, its wilderness quality is sullied somewhat by the permitted presence of jetboats. You'll see more people on the Main

Salmon, more wildlife on the Middle Fork. The Middle Fork has the lion's share of hot springs, while the Main Salmon has most of the wide sandy beaches. Both rivers offer a lot of history: old mining claims, Indian camps, and pioneer cabins. Trips generally last 3–6 days on either river.

For specific details on boating the main Salmon River, contact the **North Fork Ranger District** (11 Casey Rd., North Fork, 208/865-2383). For information on Middle Fork float trips, contact the **Middle Fork Ranger District** (U.S. 93, Challis, 208/879-4101).

River Guides

If you go with an outfitter, which is recommended unless you've rafted these rivers before, you don't have to worry about getting a permit. Dozens of guide services offer trips on either or both rivers. Expect to pay $1,200–2,000 pp for an all-inclusive six-day trip. Several river outfitters and guides that can make it all possible:

- **Aggipah River Trips** (Salmon, 208/756-4167, www.aggipah.com)
- **Far and Away Adventures** (Sun Valley, 208/726-2288 or 800/232-8588, www.far-away.com)
- **Middle Fork River Tours** (Hailey, 208/788-6545 or 800/445-9738, www.middlefork.com)
- **North Fork Guides** (North Fork, 208/865-2534 or 800/259-6866, www.northforkguides.com)
- **Salmon River Outfitters** (McCall, 800/346-6204, www.salmonriveroutfitters.com)
- **Warren River Expeditions** (Salmon, 208/756-6387 or 800/765-0421, www.rafti-daho.com)
- **Wilderness River Outfitters** (Lemhi, 800/252-6581, www.wildernessriver.com)

For more listings of outfitters, see the Idaho Outfitters and Guides Association website (www.ioga.org).

Yankee Fork Country

The Yankee Fork River flows into the Salmon River between the Frank Church–River of No Return Wilderness on the north and Highway 75 on the south. Around the river lies one of Idaho's major historic mining districts, the Land of the Yankee Fork Historic Area. Prospectors first began exploring the area in the 1860s, and mining of one sort or another has been taking place ever since.

SUNBEAM
Sunbeam Hot Springs
These hot springs, emerging from the north bank of the Salmon River, first attracted tourists in 1824 when Alexander Ross's fur-trapping party soaked the fall chill out of their bones In 1937, the Civilian Conservation Corps built a bathhouse on the site. The tubs are long gone, but you can still make your way down the bank to crude pools along the river.

Sunbeam Village Resort
Up the hill from the river, at the bottom of Yankee Fork Road to Bonanza and Custer, you'll find Sunbeam Village Resort (100 Yankee Fork Rd., Sunbeam, 208/838-2211). The resort has a store, a motel, an RV park, and a café. Cabins ($75–125) are available as well as shaded RV sites ($20–25) with water, sewer, and electric hookups; weekly rates are available. Also here is the Sunbeam office of **White Otter Outdoor Adventures** (208/838-2406), where you can arrange a raft trip down the Salmon River.

◖ CUSTER MOTORWAY ADVENTURE ROAD
When gold was discovered on the Yankee Fork, the boomtowns of Bonanza and Custer sprang to life. The miners needed equipment and supplies to work their claims, and the nearest supply center was at Challis. Entrepreneur Alex Toponce saw a moneymaking opportunity. He won a charter from the Territorial Legislature to build a toll road between Challis and Bonanza. It was completed in 1879 and was the sole freight route into the Yankee Fork mines for a decade. In 1933, the road was restored by the Civilian Conservation Corps (CCC) and today is known as the Custer Motorway Adventure Road. It would be an unpleasant adventure to attempt the unpaved route with a trailer or a large RV. Also note that the road is subject to damage from spring runoff and is sometimes closed between Challis and Custer.

The organization of this chapter is from Stanley to Salmon, so the sights along the Custer Motorway are listed below from southwest (Sunbeam) to northeast (Challis).

Bonanza
Turning north off Highway 75 at Sunbeam—onto Yankee Fork Road (Forest Rd. 013)—you'll soon come to Bonanza, the first of the Yankee Fork boomtowns. It was founded in 1877 and by 1881 had a population of 600. Fires in 1889 and 1897 gutted much of the town, and most of the townsfolk moved to Custer as a result. Today, the site is a ghost town and less developed than Custer. A CCC-built Forest Service work camp presides over the slowly decaying miners' shacks, their tin roofs banging dirgelike in the wind. A short, dusty spur road (Forest Rd. 074) leads—appropriately enough—to two separate cemeteries. The first, **Bonanza Cemetery,** is the more typical of the two, with the graves of a town of souls who lived and died pursuing their glittering dreams. Among their causes of death: avalanche, black lung, blood poisoning, gunshot wound, heart attack, mining accident, pneumonia, scarlet fever, spinal meningitis, suicide, and typhoid fever.

Farther down the spur is **Boothill Cemetery,** where just three old wooden markers surrounded by a fence record the final resting places of Lizzie King and her two husbands. Husband number one, Richard King, came to

Bonanza with Lizzie in 1878. He was subsequently shot and killed in an argument. Lizzie moved to Butte, Montana, where she met prospector Bob Hawthorne. The two ended up back in Bonanza—running the Yankee Fork Dance Hall and Saloon—and got married in 1880. Hawthorne told everyone in town that he was filthy rich and had a large estate in England. When the truth came out that he was actually dirt poor, he apparently couldn't bear the humiliation; he shot and killed Lizzie and then turned the gun on himself. Both Lizzie and Bob were buried at Boothill next to Rich King, who no doubt would have killed Bob himself if they both weren't already dead.

Custer

Established two years after Bonanza, Custer went on to become the more important of the two gold-rush towns. It reached its peak population of 600 in 1896, at which time it was home to the huge General Custer stamp mill, the Nevada Hotel, the Miner's Union Hall, a cathouse, a brewery, and a sizeable Chinatown. It even had its own newspaper, *The Yankee Fork Herald,* which on April 28, 1880, reported: "There will be no religious services tomorrow; first, because there is no minister, and secondly, there is no church. But there will be several poker games running."

The mines all played out by 1911, and the town disappeared shortly thereafter. Today it's a resurrected boomtown full of Nikons and out-of-state license plates. A museum (summer only) tells the story of the town's heyday, and a self-guided walking tour leads visitors past mining-equipment detritus and other points of interest.

To Challis

Continuing northeast from Custer, the historic sites along the route get fewer and farther between. You'll pass the sites of several way stations where meals, refreshments, and fresh horses were available and see the remains of the toll station where Toponce & Co. collected the tolls. The rate for a wagon and team was $4. The station operated 1879–1889. A few miles

later, the road passes the U.S. Forest Service **Mill Creek Campground** (8 sites, June–Sept., $10), which has potable water.

A mile or so farther, Forest Road 080 turns off to the north and leads three miles to **Mosquito Flat Reservoir,** a popular fishing hole with primarily rainbow trout, a boat ramp, and drinking water. Just north of the reservoir is the **Mosquito Flat Campground** (9 sites, free).

Wilderness Lodge

Deep in the heart of the wilderness, accessible by plane or by car (20 miles past the Yankee Fork Gold Dredge up Loon Creek Rd., off Yankee Fork Rd.) is **Diamond D Ranch** (208/861-9206 or 800/222-1269, www.diamonddranch-idaho.com, June to mid-Oct.), which offers horseback riding, fishing in a private lake or in the nearby wilderness lakes, boating, a swimming pool, a hot tub, two saunas, and more. Modern cabins (weekly $1,475 adults, $1,275 ages 13–18, $945 ages 6–12, $645 ages 3–5) are available along with slightly cheaper lodge rooms. Rates include three meals a day and all activities. Stays of less than a week may be possible by advance arrangement.

CHALLIS

Alvah P. Challis surveyed and platted Challis as a mining and ranching supply town in 1876. Now it's the Custer County seat, but it's still a mining and ranching town. At the Forest Service office on U.S. 93, history buffs can pick up a guide to the town's historic structures, including pioneer houses, the old jail, and the old schoolhouse—all constructed between 1877 and 1914. The town claims to have the state's largest collection of pre-1900 log homes.

Land of the Yankee Fork Interpretive Center

Travelers heading from Salmon toward Stanley are best poised to take advantage of this modern and informative interpretive center (Hwy. 75 and U.S. 93, 208/879-5244, 9 A.M.–5 P.M. Thurs.–Sun. Apr. 1–Oct. 15, $5) before starting out on the Custer Motorway over to Sunbeam. Travelers coming from Sunbeam on the Custer Motorway will get here last and can at least get answers to any questions they came up with on the way over. The center commemorates the area's mining history in well-designed educational exhibits. You'll find out about the ghost towns of Custer and Bonanza along with other sights along the Custer Motorway.

Challis Hot Springs

The large, developed Challis Hot Springs resort (208/879-4442, year-round, call for rates) has been around since the mining days, although those old sourdoughs missed out on the big swimming pool and the RV sites with water and power hookups. Fishing the nearby Salmon River keeps some guests occupied, while horseshoes and volleyball are on the agenda for others. The resort offers RV sites, tent sites, and guest rooms. You'll find it east of Challis, 4.5 miles north of U.S. 93 at the end of Hot Springs Road.

Backcountry Roads

A long cherry stem probing 25 miles into the Frank Church–River of No Return Wilderness, Sleeping Deer Road (Forest Rd. 086) traverses a long, high ridgeline between Twin Peaks and Sleeping Deer Mountain. A spur road at Twin Peaks (not for the new Buick) leads to the West's second-highest staffed fire lookout. Farther on, the road is dotted with picnic areas offering great views of the Frank Church and several trailheads leading into the wilderness. At the end-of-the-road trailhead, you're within a long day's hike of the Middle Fork. Numerous little lakes also pepper the area.

A bit farther north up U.S. 93, **Morgan Creek Road** (Forest Rd. 055) ascends Morgan Creek, crosses a divide, and descends Panther Creek, joining the Salmon River Road west of Shoup. Along the way you'll pass the Bureau of Land Management's **Morgan Creek Campground** and a turnoff (Forest Rd. 057) to the U.S. Forest Service's **Little West Fork Campground.** Both are small, with no improved water source and no fees.

Outfitters

Challis is home to several outfitters that can guide you around the local backcountry, including up into the White Cloud Peaks. Try **Mile High Outfitters** (208/879-4500) or **White Cloud Outfitters** (208/879-4574, www.whitecloudoutfitters.com).

Information

For National Forest recreation information, contact the Salmon-Challis National Forest **Challis Ranger District** (208/879-4100) or the **Middle Fork Ranger District.** The two ranger districts share an office on U.S. 93 at Main Street in Challis. The **Challis Area Chamber of Commerce** (700 N. Main St., Challis, 208/879-2771) can provide additional information about the area.

Salmon and Vicinity

At the confluence of the Lemhi and Salmon Rivers, the town of Salmon is the Lemhi County seat and another contender for honors as the state's white-water capital. It's the staging center for the start of float trips down the main Salmon River and the end of trips down the Middle Fork. Although filled in summer with more river rats than you can shake a paddle at, the town has none of the boisterous buzz of Riggins or even Stanley—but it does have some visionary local officials who are helping Salmon make the transition from a resources-based economy better than many other similar Idaho towns. The newish Sacajawea Center and an ambitious plan for public spaces and trails are progressive moves. Yet Salmon is too remote ever to risk becoming another upscale resort town, and that's a good thing.

SIGHTS
Sacajawea Interpretive Cultural and Educational Center
This relatively new interpretive center (200 Main St., Salmon, 208/756-1188, www.sacajaweacenter.org, 9 A.M.–5 P.M. Mon.–Sat., 12:30–5 P.M. Sun., end of May–early Sept., $5 over age 5, $12 family), one mile east of Salmon on Highway 28, mainly serves to pay homage to the young Shoshone woman, a Lemhi Valley native, who accompanied the Lewis and Clark expedition. Its many facets are still coming together, but right now you'll find a small interpretive facility, an amphitheater, and a walking trail. You might even see living history demonstrations and reenactments too.

RECREATION
Rafting and Outfitters
In addition to the many weeklong raft trips that either begin or end in Salmon, the town is a base for several outfitters that offer shorter half-day to three-day Salmon River adventures. Salmon-based companies include **Kookaburra Rafting** (1115 U.S. 93, Salmon, 208/756-4386 or 888/654-4386, www.raft4fun.com) and **Idaho Adventures** (6 Adventure Lane,

© IDAHO DIVISION OF TOURISM

Sacajawea Interpretive Cultural and Educational Center

Salmon, 800/789-9283, www.idahoadventures.com). Idaho Adventures also offers gentle three-hour scenic trips on a traditional Salmon River scow.

Elk Bend Hot Springs

Those who prefer their hot springs undeveloped and au naturel will find a treat at Elk Bend (also called Goldbug Hot Springs), about 22 miles south of Salmon on U.S. 93. Look for a turnoff to the east near mile marker 282. Follow the road a short way down to a well-marked trailhead. The springs—a favorite among Middle Fork raft guides making the weekly commute between Salmon and Stanley—spring forth on a high bench overlooking the valley. It's a magical spot.

EVENTS

One of the strangest events in Idaho takes place near Salmon at the end of June. The **Salmon River Testicle Festival** (208/756-2815) is a one-day event that celebrates cattle ranching in the area, but deep-fried bull nuts take center stage at this homespun festival, put on by the Lemhi County Cattlewomen. The event is held on a private ranch just east of town on Highway 28. Besides Rocky Mountain oysters, there's plenty of other food, including finger steaks, salads, and desserts along with live music.

Salmon River Days, leading up to and including Fourth of July weekend, focuses on the twin themes of Old West traditions and river recreation. A free breakfast will give you the energy you'll need to take in the plethora of scheduled events, including kayak and raft races, an auction, a rodeo, and a parade. **Sacajawea/Heritage Days,** held the third weekend in August, is based at the Sacajawea Center. This festival focuses on history, but you can also expect arts and crafts, food, live music, and Dutch-oven cooking demonstrations. For a complete events calendar, contact the Salmon Valley Chamber of Commerce (200 Main St., Salmon, 208/756-2100).

ACCOMMODATIONS
$50-100

Sacajawea Inn (705 Challis St., Salmon, 208/756-2294, from $60 d) is a recently revamped old motor inn with 21 small but clean guest rooms. Amenities include cable TV and an outdoor fire pit where you can roast marshmallows and wieners. The motel also has a small dining room that serves breakfast daily. Pets are allowed, and the motel is nonsmoking.

The biggest motel in town is the 100-room **Stagecoach Inn** (201 Riverfront Dr., Salmon, 208/756-2919, from $65 d), right at the Salmon River bridge. Queen beds are standard; some guest rooms with king beds are available. Amenities include a heated pool, free continental breakfast, and a coin laundry; pets are not allowed. Get a room facing the river.

Wagons West Motel (503 Riverfront Dr., Salmon, 208/756-4281, from $55 d) boasts its own island park on the river. Two-bedroom kitchenette suites are available.

Twelve miles south of Salmon on U.S. 93 is the **C** Greyhouse Inn (1115 U.S. 93 S., Salmon, 208/756-3968 or 800/348-8097, www.greyhouseinn.com, $65–129), a beautifully restored 1894 Victorian farmhouse turned into a B&B with four guest rooms (two with shared bath) plus two cabins and a carriage house. Rates include full breakfast.

Forest Service Cabins

The **Salmon-Challis National Forest** (1206 S. Challis St., Salmon, 208/756-5100) offers four cabins for rent. In the Salmon River Mountains, south of Salmon and west of U.S. 93, are the **Williams Creek, Peel Tree,** and **Iron Lake** A-frame cabins (June 30–Oct. 31, $20); all three sleep up to six people. Across the Salmon River on the western slopes of the Lemhi Range is the **North Basin** cabin (June 30–Oct. 31, $20). It's 19 miles south of Salmon as the crow flies. The forest office can help with reservations and directions to the cabins as well as information on other recreational opportunities in the area, and ask about additional rental cabins that may have become available.

FOOD

◖ **Bertram's Brewery & Restaurant** (101 S. Andrews St., Salmon, 208/756-3391, www.bertramsbrewery.com, 11 A.M.–9 P.M. Mon.–Fri., 6 A.M.–9 P.M. Sat.–Sun.) serves handcrafted microbrews and sodas in the grand old 1898 Redwine Building in downtown Salmon. Expect to find beer-friendly appetizers and burgers (around $8) as well as big steaks, seafood, and pasta dishes ($16–22) in the evening. The restaurant is smoke-free, and kids are welcome.

Junkyard Bistro (405 Main St., Salmon, 208/756-2466, 11 A.M.–11 P.M. Mon.–Sat., 11 A.M.–9 P.M. Sun.) is a funky little beer and wine bar that dishes up tasty appetizers, sandwiches, and burgers.

NORTH TO MONTANA

Heading north of Salmon on U.S. 93, you'll soon pass through the small towns of North Fork and Gibbonsville before summiting Lost Trail Pass (7,014 feet), at which point you'll be in Montana.

LEWIS AND CLARK NATIONAL BACKCOUNTRY BYWAY

About 20 miles southeast of Salmon on Highway 28, you'll come to a turnoff near Tendoy that leads to this well-marked loop road that lets you follow in the footsteps of Lewis and Clark. The unpaved but well-graded route first passes an interpretive display that fills you in on the history of the Corps of Discovery in this area. The road then climbs up and across a heavily logged plateau before dropping down to historic **Lemhi Pass,** where an advance party led by Meriwether Lewis first set eyes on the land that would eventually become the state of Idaho. Lewis planted the U.S. flag on the west side of the pass, claiming the land for the United States. When the expedition crossed the Continental Divide here in 1805, they were no longer in territory covered by the Louisiana Purchase, and Britain and the United States would jockey for control of the Pacific Northwest for many years to come.

The pass offers sweeping views into both Idaho and Montana. The total 39-mile loop takes about half a day to negotiate, including stops for a picnic lunch (bring your own; there are no services along the way) and frequent oohs and aahs.

Lemhi Pass is usually accessible June–September, but check with the Bureau of Land Management's **Salmon Field Office** (1206 S. Challis St., Salmon, 208/756-5400).

Basin and Range Country

Southeast of the Challis-Salmon stretch of U.S. 93, three parallel mountain ranges separated by road-bearing valleys provide a great example of what geologists call a basin-and-range formation. As the earth's crust stretches apart at the rate of 0.5 inches per year, the ground breaks into blocks formed of peaks and valleys. The Lost River, Lemhi, and Beaverhead Ranges and the valleys between them are aligned as neatly as F to B-flat on a piano. The Beaverhead Range forms part of the Continental Divide, while the Lost River Range is home to Idaho's highest mountain, 12,662-foot Borah Peak.

UP WARM SPRINGS CREEK

Turning southeast out of Challis down U.S. 93, you'll head up Warm Springs Creek and eventually enter **Grandview Canyon,** a narrow slot perfect for an ambush by desperadoes. Fortunately for you, you're not in an old Glenn Ford western. Geologists will tell you that this odd little canyon was formed by the creek eroding down through a once-buried knob of Devonian dolomite. Past the impressive canyon you'll climb up to **Willow Creek Summit** (7,160 feet), a favored winter grazing area for elk. When you crest the pass the road heads down into the **Big Lost River Valley.**

IT'S ALL YOUR FAULT

At 8:06 A.M. on Friday, October 28, 1983, the **Lost River Fault** ripped open with explosive force, releasing 10,000 years of pent-up energy in a devastating 40-second shift. At the earthquake's epicenter here in the valley, the west side of the fault instantly dropped while the Lost River Range was shoved even higher, creating a 21-mile-long fault scarp up to 14 feet high in places. The quake's energy ran northward up the fault line, scissoring apart the valley floor at a speed of 5,000 mph and sending 400 billion gallons of displaced groundwater gushing forth in springs and geysers. When the quake hit Challis, 20 miles to the north, a masonry wall collapsed, killing two children on their way to school. Within minutes, the temblor rocked Salt Lake City, Portland, Seattle, and parts of western Canada. Measured at 7.3 on the Richter scale, the earthquake caused some $15 million in property damage. It was the worst quake ever in Idaho and one of the worst in the history of the West. A well-marked turnoff from U.S. 93 leads a short way to an interpretive site explaining the cause of the quake.

BORAH PEAK

As you head southeast down the Big Lost River Valley, the massive wall of the Lost River Range rises abruptly on the left. From along the highway, this range is nowhere nearly as exciting a sight as, say, the snowy Sawtooth Range. The terrain here is dry and relatively barren in comparison, and the mountains look not so much like high alpine spires as big hulking blocks of rock. Look for the turnoff marked "Borah Peak Access" and look to the left. This mountain monarch rises abruptly from the valley floor and leads the eye right to the summit, which, unlike many high peaks, isn't hidden behind lower interlopers.

Climbing the peak takes 8–12 hours round-trip, depending on your speed and physical condition. While the route isn't technical, it is very steep and strenuous, gaining almost a vertical mile in less than 3.5 miles. One short stretch involves third-class climbing (use of hands and feet) across "Chicken-out Ridge," a knife-edge ridge with serious exposure—if you fall, you'll fall a long, long way. Snow often lingers on a steep saddle near the summit well into midsummer. Use of an ice ax for insurance makes the necessary traverse across that saddle less scary. While the Forest Service brochure might lead you to think it's an easy walk to the summit, never underestimate the risks associated with climbing high peaks. If you're out of shape or don't have the proper equipment or clothing, don't attempt the hike. If you do attempt it, make sure to check in at the ranger station in Mackay first. Those who are prepared will find the climb exceedingly enjoyable.

A little south of Borah down U.S. 93 you'll get a glimpse of another Idaho giant. A roadside sign indicates the Matterhorn-like **Leatherman Peak** (12,230 feet), visible through a slot in the nearer ridgeline. Leatherman is the state's second-highest peak and a far more impressive sight than Borah.

MACKAY

Copper discoveries in the area led to the founding of Mackay (MACK-ee) in 1901. Ranching and recreation have since replaced mining as the mainstay of the local economy. The laid-back little town is the primary supply point for hikers heading up Borah Peak and for anglers trolling for trout in Mackay Reservoir and the Big Lost River. Basic accommodations and food are available.

RVing golfers will appreciate **River Park Golf Course and RV Campground** (717 Capitol Ave., Mackay, 208/588-2296, greens fees $13–18, RV sites $25). The RV sites lie right between the sixth and eighth tees. The course has nine holes, and the RV park has full hookups.

West of town, the White Knob Mountains rise to over 10,000 feet. They are home to rugged old mining roads that will surely chew up your wheel bearings, but it's a beautiful drive if you have a high-clearance vehicle, preferably with 4WD.

For more information on the town, contact the **City of Mackay** (208/588-2274). For recreation information, contact the U.S. Forest Service's **Lost River Ranger District** (716 W. Custer St., Mackay, 208/588-2224).

NORTH-CENTRAL IDAHO

North-central Idaho quickly goes from rugged peaks to rolling meadows as U.S. 95 unravels like a teased ribbon. This varied topography is what geologists and archeologists dream about. It's easy to get night sweats pondering all those massive mountains, myriad lakes, and dinosaur bone–filled prairies. Let's not forget the long mountain valleys that look like the set of *Bonanza*.

The western skirt of Idaho borders with Oregon and Washington, but Hells Canyon, the deepest river gorge in North America, even deeper than the Grand Canyon, makes crossing the border impossible for more than 70 miles. This is where the Snake River gets furiously funneled through an abysmal chasm en route to its confluence with the Columbia River in Washington. The high-walled gorge may look

hellish, but it's pure heaven for white-water fanatics who come in droves for the unrelenting rapids. The Seven Devils, the most underrated mountain range in Idaho, hems the gorge to the east like a broken spine. Backpackers and mountain bikers will find miles of extreme backcountry untouched by human development. Remote trailheads lead to dramatic vantage points overlooking the gorge. Along the way, don't be surprised to see elk, bighorn sheep, cougars, black bears, and birds of prey; some say grizzlies roam these parts too.

A few miles southeast of Hells Canyon, the West-Central Mountains run parallel with the Oregon border, creating two distinct Idaho valleys. Long Valley is a remote spread along Highway 55 fringed by high mountains to the west and east. The area is home to more than

HIGHLIGHTS

(Ponderosa State Park: Considered to be the crown jewel of Idaho's park system, the 1,000-acre state park is on a peninsula protruding into Payette Lake. Visitors enjoy hiking, biking, fishing, swimming, camping, and cross-country skiing in this densely forested wonderland (page 296).

(The Seven Devils: This unfettered mountain range skirts the east side of Hells Canyon. Seven devilishly named peaks offer outdoor enthusiasts unlimited wilderness opportunities (page 308).

(River Trips in Riggins: People in Riggins like to think of their small town as Idaho's white-water capital. This is where the main Salmon and Little Salmon Rivers smash together in a spectacle of wild rapids (page 311).

(Nez Perce National Historic Park: This park system has 38 historic sites in Idaho, Washington, Oregon, and Montana, but the park's headquarters near Lewiston serves as the nerve center for it all. Here you'll find an interpretive center and a wonderful picnic area next to the Spalding Mission site (page 327).

(Following the Lochsa River: Follow the trail of the Lewis and Clark expedition along the steep grades of the Lochsa Face. This scenic river stretch along U.S. 12 is pure nirvana for anglers and white-water fanatics (page 336).

(University of Idaho: Located in Moscow, University of Idaho is the most beautiful college campus in the state. The 320-acre campus boasts a variety of architectural styles and plenty of green space for picnicking (page 339).

LOOK FOR **(** TO FIND RECOMMENDED SIGHTS, ACTIVITIES, DINING, AND LODGING.

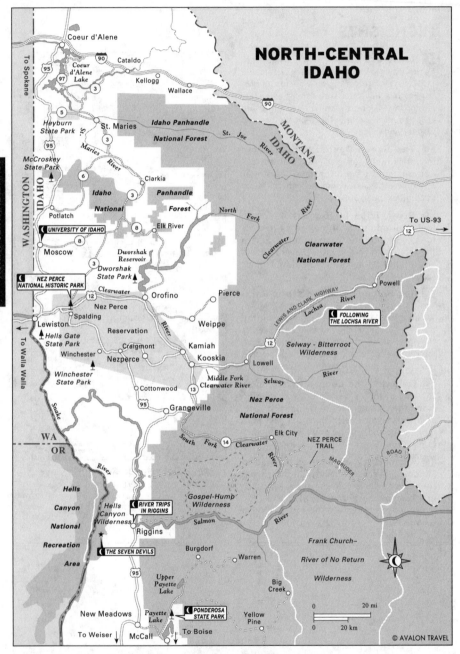

NORTH-CENTRAL IDAHO

130 lakes, including Payette Lake, a scenic waterway that's popular with boaters and anglers in summer. The burgeoning resort town of McCall lies on the lake's southern shores. Often outshone by the Ketchum–Sun Valley area to the east, McCall is hardly an ugly cousin. The spectacular high-country here offers outdoor enthusiasts a long list of mountain fun: skiing and snowboarding at Brundage Mountain, backcountry hot springs, hiking, and mountain biking.

Just north of McCall is Riggins, a little hamlet where the main Salmon and Little Salmon Rivers come together in a wild exhibition of rapids. The town teems with activity in the spring and summer months when thousands of anglers and rafters show up for a piece of the action. Thirty-pound steelhead salmon run the rivers just a few feet from the downtown strip.

Traveling north on U.S. 95, western Idaho's primary north–south arterial, the rough landscape starts to soften as it unfolds into the Camas Prairie near Grangeville. The landscape rolls on to the west, while more impressive mountains and wild rivers dictate the scenery on the east side of the vast prairie.

Lewis and Clark buffs will find much to do in this region, where the Corps of Discovery endured some of its harshest setbacks, namely at the Lochsa River and its alpine hinterlands. These early explorers probably would never have made it to the mouth of the Columbia River had it not been for the help of the Nez Perce people, who still thrive here today.

The Clearwater and Snake Rivers meet near Lewiston, a city that boasts the only inland seaport in the West. Above the Clearwater River Valley lies the Palouse, a colorful quilt of fertile farms and undulating hills. Moscow is home to the University of Idaho. This friendly college town is a great place to chill for a few days, and possibly take an excursion to see ancient cedars and hemlocks, which stand majestic in the nearby forests.

PLANNING YOUR TIME

North-central Idaho encompasses a large portion of the state, from the McCall area all the way to the southern shores of Coeur d'Alene Lake. Much of it is wilderness, which requires travelers to clear their calendars in order to fully enjoy what the region has to offer. You should plan on spending at least a week to 10 days.

Cascade and Vicinity

North of Smiths Ferry, the steep canyons of the Payette River open up into Long Valley, a beautiful dell of scenic mountain vistas and lakes. Cascade is the first settlement you'll come to heading north on Highway 55. The town was named for some waterfalls on the North Fork Payette River that lost their thunder in 1948 to Cascade Dam. The resulting 30,000-acre Cascade Reservoir (now referred to as Lake Cascade) is one of the state's busiest fishing holes. Perch are the most numerous fish in the lake and are sought by both boating anglers in summer and ice-fishers in winter. But the lake also holds healthy populations of rainbow trout, Coho salmon, and smallmouth bass.

Cascade, the Valley County seat, has taken an economic double hit in recent years. First, Boise Cascade closed its lumber mill, leaving hundreds of folks out of work. Things were looking up for a while when Tamarack Resort was being built northwest of town; many locals landed construction and service-related jobs at the all-season resort. But Tamarack went belly up in 2008, during the second phase of its construction, after only being open for about four years. Now the Tyrolean-style lodge, fancy ski lifts, and championship golf course sit empty near the west shore of Lake Cascade—an eerie reminder of the recent worldwide economic downturn. The Village, which would have been a self-contained little city with shops, restaurants, and bars, is in an incomplete state on a knoll exposed to the elements. All is not lost, though; other tourism has bolstered the economy. Boating, fishing, hunting, mountain biking, camping, cross-country skiing, and a new white-water park keep people flowing into town, especially on weekends (Cascade is only about an hour and a half drive from Boise).

RECREATION
Lake Cascade State Park
The relatively new Lake Cascade State Park (office 970 Dam Rd., at Lakeshore Dr., near Crown Point, Cascade, 208/382-6544) has 12 units around Lake Cascade's 86 miles of shoreline, including the Crown Point, Ridgeview, Sugarloaf, Buttercup, and Blue Heron units. Crown Point, the closest unit to town, is on the east shore of the lake just north of the dam's spillway. You'll find 29 campsites ($14–16), some right on the lake, with nearby central water and vault toilets. These first come, first served sites (other park unit campgrounds are reservation-only) are adjacent to sandy alcoves and wave-smoothened rocks that make for great swimming holes, and the **Crown Point**

Railroad Grade Trail runs right behind the campground. This 2.7-mile recreational trail, on a stretch of the old Oregon Short Line Railroad, is a mellow spot for a stroll or bike ride along the shore of the lake. Boaters will like the fact that the park system operates six boat ramps around the lake.

Biking
About eight miles south of town, Clear Creek Road (Forest Rd. 409) intersects Highway 55 and climbs a gentle grade to the northeast. The narrow road winds through tall pine forest and alongside babbling Clear Creek. Add occasional vistas and potential wildlife sightings and you've got an easy and ideal bicycling adventure. Bring a picnic lunch. Those looking for a little more challenge can continue up the road, over Clear Creek Summit and Railroad Pass, and down Curtis Creek to Warm Lake Road for a pleasant loop trip.

Golf
The nine-hole **Cascade Golf Course** (117 Lakeshore Dr., 208/382-4835, Apr.–Oct.,

Lake Cascade

© IDAHO DIVISION OF TOURISM

$15–27) lines the east shore of Lake Cascade. Lessons, cart rentals, and a small pro shop are offered. There's also a restaurant and lounge with spectacular views of the lake and looming West-Central Mountains.

Cross-Country Skiing

Just north of town, Warm Lake Road turns east off Highway 55. Five miles up Warm Lake Road is the **Crawford Park N' Ski Area,** and three miles farther on you'll find the **Scott Valley Park N' Ski Area.** The latter is the better of the two, with seven miles of well-marked trails. The north-side trail heads into the woods and follows the ridge north, climbing slightly and providing open views of the valley. The south side of the loop crosses a wide-open treeless field where you'll feel like Diane Keaton skiing across Finland in the movie *Reds.* If you can't find your glide here, it's hopeless.

In its frozen state, Lake Cascade offers cross-country gliders miles of ungroomed skiing possibilities.

Kelly's White-Water Park

The new three-acre Kelly's White-Water Park (208/315-2363, www.kwpid.com, daily late spring–early fall, free) is a white-water playground on the North Fork Payette River that boasts several water features that will delight kayakers of all skill levels. Boaters can hone their rolling skills and work on other technical kayaking maneuvers. The park has a visitors center with kayaking exhibits, restrooms, and a changing area. There's even an amphitheater where the park hosts live music (the band Blues Traveler played a fund-raising show here in 2010). It's just south of Cascade at mile marker 114 on the east side of Highway 55. You can just show up with your boat, and on-site river rangers will help you out.

ACCOMMODATIONS AND FOOD

Accommodations

Dutch Oven Bed & Breakfast (507 S. Main St., Cascade, 208/286-1401, www. dutchovenbedandbreakfast.com, $79–104) is a new inn in a log home downtown that cares just as much about food as it does about comfy lodging. Besides having several guest suites, the rustic inn serves made-to-order meals in the morning, including inventive omelets and eggs Benny.

The **Ashley Inn** (500 N. Main St., Cascade, 208/382-5621 or 866/382-5621, www.theashleyinn.com, from $129) looks a bit out of place along the highway north of downtown Cascade. You can bet the owners wish they had a piece of lakeside property. Still, it's by far the nicest place in town, with lots of art, an indoor pool, and fireplaces in each of the 67 guest rooms. Rates include a breakfast buffet featuring fresh fruit, eggs, biscuits and gravy, and pastries.

Camping and RVing

The beautiful ◖ **Water's Edge RV Resort** (620 N. Main St., Cascade, 208/382-3120 or 800/574-2038, www.watersedgervpark.com, spring–fall), at the north end of town along Highway 55, lies on the banks of the Payette River. Amenities include bathroom and laundry facilities, beach volleyball courts, horseshoes, free kayaks and canoes for guest use, and evening campfires. The resort has 120 RV sites with full hookups ($25–36), 20 tent sites ($21–23), and two camping cabins ($65–99).

Food

For homespun diner fare, head to **Grandma's Homestead Restaurant** (224 N. Main St., Cascade, 208/382-4602, breakfast, lunch, and dinner daily, breakfast about $8) right on the main drag. The dining room looks like Granny's living room with lots of knick-knacks and cutesy artwork. Sit in a large booth and enjoy a chicken-fried steak with all the trimmings. Expect to find standard breakfast dishes in the morning, while later in the day it's all about sandwiches, burgers, and finger steaks.

Load up the cooler for your outdoor excursion at **D-9 Grocer** (102 S. Main St., 208/382-4215, 8 A.M.–7 P.M. Mon.–Sat., 9 A.M.–6 P.M.

Sun.). This small-town store has the campsite basics, like cold cuts, hot dogs, buns, condiments, doughnuts, fruit, sundries, and most importantly, cold beer—domestic and imported. You can also buy bundles of firewood for grilling those franks. The friendly folks who work here know the area well and will gladly point you in the right direction.

INFORMATION

You can get updated information about the area at **Cascade Chamber of Commerce** (500 N. Main St., Cascade, 208/382-3833). For recreation information, stop by the **Cascade Ranger District** (540 N. Main St., Cascade, 208/382-7400).

WARM LAKE

East of the highway, Warm Lake Road leads up into the mountains to the South Fork of the Salmon River and the community of Warm Lake. This is wild country, near the west edge of the Frank Church–River of No Return Wilderness. The owner of Warm Lake Lodge once saw a wolf investigating his dumpster, and the Forest Service has recorded wolf sightings in this area since the early 1980s, well before their reintroduction.

Hot Springs

Hot springs lovers could spend a whole weekend exploring the many hot pools in the Warm Lake area, among them **Molly's Tubs, Vulcan Hot Springs, Penny Hot Spring,** and **Trail Creek Hot Spring.** Molly's Tubs and Vulcan lie along or just off Forest Road 474, south of Warm Lake Road 1.3 and 6.5 miles, respectively. Penny Hot Spring is 4.5 miles north of Warm Springs Road off Forest Road 474, across from the former Penny Campground. Trail Creek is west of Warm Lake, 0.5 miles east of mile marker 61 on Warm Lake Road. For more information, check out Evie Litton's *The Hiker's Guide to Hot Springs in the Pacific Northwest* or consult the rangers at the **Cascade Ranger District** (540 N. Main St., Cascade, 208/382-7400).

Accommodations

Warm Lake's two mountain lodges are both open year-round. In winter, either would make a good base camp for cross-country skiing in Boise National Forest. **Warm Lake Lodge** (15 Lodge Rd., Cascade, 208/632-3553, www.warmlakelodge.com, $59–120) has been around since 1911. Its rustic cabins line the shore of Warm Lake and range in size from a small unit with one double bed to a hot tub–equipped unit that sleeps 10. Some units have kitchenettes. Campsites ($15) are available, and other facilities at the resort include a restaurant and lounge, a store, a post office, and a boat dock. Pets are discouraged.

North Shore Lodge (175 N. Shoreline Dr., Cascade, 208/632-2000, www.northshorelodgeidaho.com, $75–135) offers cabins of various sizes, all with kitchenettes. Other facilities include a restaurant and lounge, a store, gas and oil sales, canoe and boat rentals, horseshoe pits, volleyball courts, and docks. Pets are allowed but must be leashed.

Forest Service Campgrounds and Cabins

Boise National Forest campgrounds in the Warm Lake area include **South Fork Salmon River** (14 sites, $15), **Shoreline** (25 sites, $15), and **Warm Lake** (12 sites, $15). In addition, the **Stolle Meadows Guard Station** (May–Mar., $50), which sleeps up to five, is available for rent; winter access is by cross-country skis or snowmobiles only. For reservations, call 877/444-6777.

YELLOW PINE

Out past Warm Lake, past Landmark, past Halfway Station, and past Johnson Creek, you'll finally come to Yellow Pine, one of the state's most remote communities. The tenacious outpost once supplied the Big Creek mining district; today, it's home to the **Yellow Pine Harmonica Festival** in early August, an annual blow that draws reasonably large crowds, considering the effort it takes to get out here.

Camping

North of Yellow Pine and north of Wapiti Meadows on Forest Road 340, the U.S. Forest Service **Big Creek Campground** (4 sites, $10) lies between two trailheads providing access into the Frank Church–River of No Return Wilderness.

DONNELLY

This little hamlet along Highway 55, near the north shore of Lake Cascade, had high hopes when nearby Tamarack Resort was open and continuing to grow. Now, with the resort closed indefinitely, many new buildings around town—meant for restaurants and retail shops—are vacant. But the downtown strip (Hwy. 55) does have some mainstay restaurants and bars that still thrive on a seasonal basis.

Gold Fork Hot Springs

Getting to hot springs in the Cascade-McCall area usually requires a short hike, but you can drive right up to Gold Fork Hot Springs (1026 Gold Fork Rd., Donnelly, 208/890-8730, noon–9 p.m. Sun.–Mon. and Wed.–Fri., noon–11 p.m. Sat. year-round, $8 adults, $6 children, cash or check only), a commercial operation that offers soakers a variety of manmade pools and tubs fed by mineral-rich springs that bubble up from deep within the earth. And you'll need to relax after driving the sometimes bumpy six-mile dirt road that leads to the pools. The turnoff, Davis Creek Lane, is about three miles south of Donnelly on Highway 55; look for a blue-and-white sign.

Accommodations

Boulder Creek Inn & Suites (629 Hwy. 55, Donnelly, 208/325-8638, www.bouldercreek-inn.com, from $69 d), on the west side of the highway right before you come into town, is a newish hotel that offers 43 clean and cozy guest rooms. It'll cost you a little more for suite with a hot tub. Amenities include cable TV, Wi-Fi, guest laundry rooms, and free continental breakfast.

Food

Buffalo Gal (319 N. Main St., Donnelly, 208/325-8258, 5–9 p.m. Wed.–Sun.) is a culinary oasis in this land of overcooked steaks and domestic longneck brews. The dinner-only restaurant serves contemporary fare with global flair as well as sushi. Sushi in the mountains? Why the hell not. The beverage list includes sake, regional wines, and microbrews. Look for the beige building emblazoned with red trim downtown on the west side of the highway.

Across the way, you'll find **Flight of Fancy** (282 N. Main St., Donnelly, 208/325-4432, 7 a.m.–4 p.m. Mon.–Sat., 8 a.m.–2 p.m. Sun.), a funky little bakery and espresso bar in an old house. The kitchen here puts out a multitude of yummy baked goods such as scones, pastries, cookies, and lemon bars.

McCall and Vicinity

With an ideal location on the shore of beautiful Payette Lake surrounded by millions of acres of national forest land, it's not surprising that McCall (population 3,000) is a recreation center. More than that, however, it's one of the state's most unabashedly fun towns and knows how to have a good time. Its young, outdoor-oriented populace enjoys practically out-the-back-door skiing at Brundage Mountain, boating on the lake, and hiking in expansive backcountry. When the locals aren't outdoors, you'll find them having a good time with friends at the bars and restaurants downtown. Tourism drives the economy—vacation homes dot the lakeshore, and thousands of visitors pour in on summer weekends and for Winter Carnival, the town's biggest annual event. Yet McCall seldom feels too crowded; if you come

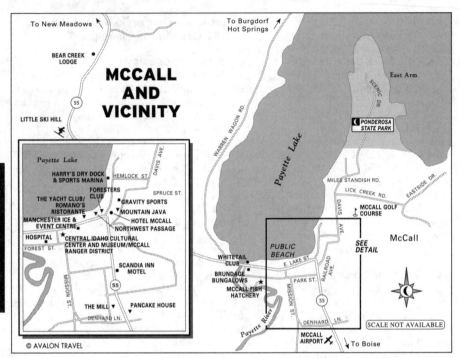

To New Meadows

To Burgdorf
Hot Springs

BEAR CREEK
LODGE

**MCCALL
AND
VICINITY**

East Arm

55

LITTLE SKI HILL

PONDEROSA
STATE PARK

Payette Lake

HARRY'S DRY DOCK
& SPORTS MARINA   HEMLOCK ST.

FORESTERS
CLUB   SPRUCE ST.

THE YACHT CLUB/
ROMANO'S
RISTORANTE

GRAVITY SPORTS
MOUNTAIN JAVA
HOTEL MCCALL

MANCHESTER ICE &
EVENT CENTRE

NORTHWEST PASSAGE

HOSPITAL   CENTRAL IDAHO CULTURAL
CENTER AND MUSEUM/MCCALL
RANGER DISTRICT

FOREST ST.

SCANDIA INN
MOTEL

55

THE MILL   PANCAKE HOUSE

DENHARD LN.

DAVIS AVE.

MISSION ST.

Payette Lake

WARREN WAGON RD.

SCENIC DR.

MILES STANDISH RD.

LICK CREEK RD.

DAVIS
AVE.

MCCALL GOLF
COURSE

EASTSIDE DR.

PUBLIC
BEACH

SEE
DETAIL

McCall

WHITETAIL
CLUB

E. LAKE ST.

BRUNDAGE
BUNGALOWS

MCCALL FISH
HATCHERY

PARK ST.

RAILROAD
AVE.

MISSION ST.

55

DENHARD LN.

Payette River

MCCALL
AIRPORT   To Boise

SCALE NOT AVAILABLE

© AVALON TRAVEL

in the off-season, you'll think you've discovered your own private paradise.

☾ PONDEROSA STATE PARK

Considered by many the crown jewel of Idaho's state park system, Ponderosa State Park occupies a 1,000-acre peninsula jutting into Payette Lake, two miles northeast of downtown McCall. The peninsula was never logged in the early days, so the old-growth ponderosa pines—up to 400 years old and 150 feet tall—are big and abundant. Lodgepole pine, Douglas fir, and grand fir tower over the park, and wildflowers brighten the meadows and forest floor. Besides conifer forest, marshes and arid sagebrush flats provide habitat for a wide variety of species, including woodpeckers, muskrats, ducks, foxes, ospreys, and in summer, big hungry mosquitoes. Summer visitors can hike or bike through the park, or head for the park's beaches to play in the waters of Payette Lake.

In winter, the park becomes especially quiet and serene under a blanket of snow. Cross-country ski trails lead to views overlooking frosty Payette Lake and the mountains beyond. Summer or winter, it's possible to get far enough away from civilization to feel alone in the wilderness—an impressive achievement for Idaho's most popular state park.

Visitors Center

Most of the visitor facilities (208/634-2164) are on the south and west sides of the peninsula. Immediately upon entering the park and paying the usual $5 per vehicle state park entry fee, you'll come to the visitors center. Rangers are on hand to answer your questions, provide you with a park map, and fill you in on the park's schedule of interpretive programs. Something takes place at the park amphitheater just about every night all summer long, and rangers lead guided hikes many mornings. Also ask about the junior ranger program, designed to keep youngsters happy and maybe expand their minds a bit too.

Hiking, Biking, and Skiing

Pick up a park trail map from a ranger at the visitors center. Road bicyclists will enjoy the scenic paved loop road down the peninsula to Osprey Cliff, which affords great views of Payette Lake and McCall. Hikers and mountain bikers will find a seven-mile system of dirt trails more to their liking. The off-pavement trails also lead from the visitors center out to the tip of the peninsula, offering loops of several different lengths. All the trails are open to hikers, and two are open to mountain bikers as well.

In winter the trails lie beneath a blanket of snow, over which easy- to intermediate-level cross-country ski trails ($2 pp per day, annual pass $35) are set. Most of the trails are groomed and include skating lanes where trail width allows. **Lighted night skiing** (6–11 P.M. daily) is available on the wide and relatively flat Northern Lights trail. Skiing at the park costs $2 per person per day. are available for. Snowshoeing ($2 pp per day) is permissible at the park, but you must stay on the fringe of the cross-country ski trails.

Camping and Cabins

The park proper has 137 campsites in three loops just west of the visitors center. Each loop includes restrooms and showers, and in the vicinity you'll find a volleyball court, beaches, boat docks, and a day-use picnic area with a boat ramp.

Single-vehicle tent sites ($12) and RV and camper sites ($22–44) with electricity all have water. Northwest Passage Campground is first come, first served; The Peninsula and RV Campgrounds (888/922-6743) are reservation-only end of May–Labor Day.

The park has four new cabins (888/922-6743, year-round, $135–150) available to rent that are especially nice for ski-in overnights in winter. All cabins have heating and air-conditioning, full kitchens, and sleep up to six. A nonrefundable $10 reservation fee is required.

OTHER SIGHTS AND RECREATION
Central Idaho Historical Museum

The Central Idaho Historical Museum (1001 State St., at Lake St., McCall, 208/634-4497, 11 A.M.–3 P.M. Wed.–Sat. June–Aug., donation) comprises several restored Civilian Conservation Corps buildings that house local logging history exhibits and offices of community organizations.

Fish Hatchery

The kings of their genus, chinook salmon can grow to be five feet long and weigh well over 100 pounds. The Columbia, Snake, and Salmon Rivers were once honeymoon highways leading from the Pacific Ocean over 700 miles inland to the royal spawning grounds on the Salmon River's South Fork and other high-mountain tributaries. But then came the dams, and logging-induced siltation, and the number of chinooks returning to spawn dwindled to disastrously low levels. To help compensate for declining chinook populations, the Idaho Department of Fish and Game raises chinooks at the **McCall Fish Hatchery** (300 Mather Rd., McCall, 208/634-2690, self-guided tours 8 A.M.–5 P.M. daily year-round). Hatchery personnel trap spawning fish near Warm Lake on the South Fork and then perform massive artificial insemination at the hatchery. More than 2 million juvenile salmon are raised and released annually, hopefully to make their way downriver to the sea. With luck, maybe one-tenth of 1 percent will someday return to the spawning grounds.

Brundage Mountain

McCall owes much of its high fun factor to the fantastic Brundage Mountain (208/634-4151 or 800/888-7544, snow report 208/634-7669, www.brundage.com, lifts 9:30 A.M.–4:30 P.M. daily, full-day lift tickets $55 adults, $37 ages 12–17 and seniors, $23 ages 7–11, free under age 7), a first-rate ski and summer resort just outside town. In winter, the resort's 1,300 acres and 1,800-foot vertical drop are served by a high-speed quad chair, two triple chairs, and two surface lifts. From the top of the mountain at 7,640 feet, you'll enjoy sweeping views of the Payette Lakes, Salmon River Mountains, and the impressive Seven Devils Range.

Powder hounds will want to avail themselves of the resort's snowcat skiing as well, which will take them to untracked runs far from the crowds. And parents will appreciate Brundage's Kids' Center, which offers the finest kids' programs and facilities of any ski resort in Idaho; your little Picabo-in-training will feel special at the separate, well-designed children's lodge opening right out onto the bunny slope. Day care is available.

Reduced-price lift tickets are offered after 1 P.M., and both ski and snowboard rentals and lessons are available.

Snowcat skiing ($239 pp per day) includes off-piste skis, lunch, and snacks. Die-hards will opt for the overnight cat-ski adventure ($689 pp), which includes a stay in a backcountry yurt. Reservations are required for all snowcat skiing (800/888-7544).

In summer, the resort runs a chairlift (Fri.–Sun. late June–Labor Day, full-day pass $30 adults, single-ride $10 adults, $5 ages 7–14 and over age 69) to the top of the mountain for mountain bikers and sightseers. From the top, bikers can access a 15-mile single-track trail system built especially for mountain bikes. Mountain-bike rentals are available; an introductory package ($45) includes a bike, a helmet (required), and a single-ride lift pass.

Also in summer, the resort's amphitheater becomes an alpine concert venue extraordinaire. Look for shows throughout the season. Bring a lawn chair and your picnic basket.

To reach the resort, take Highway 55 east toward New Meadows, and watch for the signed turnoff to your right about eight miles outside town.

Little Ski Hill

This dual alpine and cross-country area (208/634-5691, www.littleskihill.org, 3:30–8:30 P.M. Tues.–Thurs., lifts 3:30–9:30 P.M. Fri., 12:30–9:30 P.M. Sat., extended hours during Christmas holidays, $11 adults, $9 ages 5–17) is about three miles northwest of town on Highway 55. A nonprofit operation run by Payette Lakes Ski Club, it began in 1937, making it the second-oldest ski hill in Idaho after Sun Valley. Although the alpine area—one T-bar serving one hill—is humble, it's also cheap. The grooming is excellent, and the slope facing the highway is just steep enough to entertain an intermediate skier.

The cross-country area (dawn–dusk daily, full-day $10 adults, $5 ages 5–17) is one of the best in the state. The longest loop in the 31-mile system passes several side trails, some climbing a ridge to offer speedy-turny descents on the way back. The main trail meanders south through a string of valleys far from the highway. If you have the energy, go all the way to the end—it gets better as you go. Both skating and traditional tracks are set, and you don't have to share them with snowmobiles. No rentals are available, but lessons are available by appointment. Combined cross-country and alpine season passes are $90 adults, $35 ages 5–17.

A small day lodge along the highway includes a snack bar and some picnic tables for sack lunches. Friday-night telemark races are common, as are cheap BYOB feeds accompanied by live acoustic music.

Ice Skating

McCall's pride and joy is the year-round **Manchester Ice & Event Centre** (200 E. Lake St., McCall, 208/634-3570, www.manchester-icecenter.com). The indoor facility is a great place to skate ($6.50 adults, $5 under age 13, skate rental $2), with huge windows that look out on Payette Lake. Public skating sessions are held at least once daily; call for current hours. The Idaho Steelheads pro hockey team occasionally trains here, and many hockey clinics and camps are held throughout the year. A snack bar (from 10 A.M. daily) is available for both skaters and spectators.

Day Hikes near McCall

The Payette National Forest surrounding McCall is full of trails, allowing you to plan hikes of just about any length you want, from a couple of hours to a couple of weeks. Stop in at the **McCall Ranger District** (102 W. Lake St., McCall, 208/634-0400) for trail suggestions and a list of the topographic maps you'll need for the hike you choose.

Duck Lake Trail begins up Lick Creek Road (Forest Hwy. 48), just past Lick Creek Summit. An overlook at the summit provides panoramic views of the glacier-carved landscape. The trail climbs ever so slightly for about a mile to Duck Lake, making for a pleasant two-mile round-trip jaunt. Those looking for a slightly longer hike can try Trail 083 from Duck Lake up and over a steep ridge to Hum Lake. From Hum Lake the trail loops back to Lick Creek Road; then it's about a two-mile walk down the road back to the car.

Closer to McCall, don't forget the beautiful trails at Ponderosa State Park.

Fishing

Between the Payette Lakes and the numerous streams around McCall, the intrepid angler can catch cutthroat, rainbow, lake, and brook trout, as well as kokanee, kamloops, and bass. Anglers who are also backpackers should know that the Payette National Forest surrounding McCall contains some 300 mountain lakes and 1,400 miles of streams.

Golf

At **McCall Golf Club** (925 Fairway Dr., McCall, 208/634-7200, May–Oct., $16–39), on the east side of town, you can choose between three different nine-hole courses or combine them as you wish. The scenic course also has a pro shop and a restaurant.

The 18-hole, par-72 **Whitetail Club Golf Course** (501 W. Lake St., McCall, 800/657-6464) was designed by Roger Packard and two-time U.S. Open winner Andy North. The lovely course is semiprivate, but you can play here if you stay at the Shore Lodge. Call for greens fees and information about package deals.

Outdoor Outfitters

Gravity Sports (503 Pine St., McCall, 208/634-8530, www.gravitysportsidaho.com) rents canoes, kayaks, and mountain bikes in summer and cross-country touring skis, telemark skis, skating skis, snowboards, and snowshoes in winter. You also can rent similar winter and summer gear at **Pro Peak Sports** (309 E. Lake St., McCall, 208/634-7400, www.propeaksports.com).

Harry's Dry Dock & Sports Marina (1300 E. Lake St., McCall, 208/634-8605) rents ski boats, pontoon boats, fishing boats, canoes, and jet skis in summer as well as snowmobiles in winter.

ENTERTAINMENT AND EVENTS

Nightlife

Rock-and-rollers usually wind up at **The Yacht Club** (203 E. Lake St., McCall, 208/634-5649, until late daily) for loud live music and dancing. It's basic—a bar, a pool table, and a dance floor—but bands from Boise often make it up here to help patrons boogie the night away. Expect a few bucks' cover charge when bands are playing. It's now nonsmoking. Across the street is the **Foresters Club** (304 E. Lake St., 208/634-8529, 4:30 P.M.–late Tues.–Sun.), a longtime bar that was recently cleaned up. It used to be a smoky old dive palace where fighting was a nightly occurrence but is now gentler, kinder, and nonsmoking. Plus it has 11 Northwest microbrews on tap and live music on weekends.

Events

McCall's **Winter Carnival** (www.mccallwintercarnival.com) is the biggest and best winter fest in the state, and it's not uncommon for more than 20,000 people to pack in on opening day. Motel rooms are booked a year in advance for this party. Fanciful snow sculptures line the streets, and an ice-carving contest brings out world-class artists. Sled dog races, a sledding hill, and an ice-skating rink draw devotees, while everyone enjoys the Mardi Gras–themed parade, fireworks, food, and fun. It runs for 10 days at the end of January and beginning of February.

For its size, McCall boasts a rich and diverse music scene. All summer long, Brundage Mountain hosts concerts and other events. In mid-July the **Summer Music Festival** (www.thesummermusicfestival.com), formerly the McCall Folk Music Festival, takes place at nearby Roseberry, with three evenings of live jazz, blues, country, swing, and traditional music.

For a complete events calendar, contact the **McCall Chamber of Commerce** (802 N. 3rd St., McCall, 208/634-7631, www.mccallchamber.org).

ACCOMMODATIONS
$50-100
Scandia Inn (401 N. 3rd St., McCall, 208/634-7394, www.thescandiainn.com, from $75 d) has some of the best rates in town. This mountain-style motor inn (it's made out of pine logs) is within walking distance of downtown and the lake. It has 16 nonsmoking guest rooms with cable TV and high-speed Internet. Pets are not allowed. Speaking of made-from-logs motor inns, there's another one right across the way. The **Rustic Inn** (402 N. 3rd St., McCall, 208/634-7671, www.thewoodsmanmotel.com, $55–70 d) also has budget rates for its alpine-inspired guest rooms. Amenities include in-room refrigerators and microwaves, Wi-Fi, and cable TV.

Just west of town, on the way to Brundage Mountain, **Brundage Inn** (1005 W. Lake St., McCall, 208/634-2344 or 800/643-2009, www.brundagevacations.com, from $89 d) is a two-story hotel with 22 standard guest rooms. It's owned and operated by Brundage Vacations, a property management company that also rents out cabins around town. **Brundage Bungalows** (308 W. Lake St., McCall, 208/634-2344 or 800/643-2009,

from $89) features cute separate bungalow cabins with microwaves, refrigerators, and cable TV. Pets are allowed; smoking is not allowed indoors. The front desk at the Brundage Inn handles check-in for the bungalows and for the company's more expensive cabins (from $495) right on the lake.

$100-150
❰ Hotel McCall (1101 N. 3rd St., McCall, 208/634-8105 or 866/800-1183, www.hotelmccall.com, $135–150, suites $350) has been in operation since 1904. This beautiful hotel recently underwent a major renovation, adding more guest rooms and large suites, many of which boast spectacular views of Payette Lake and Brundage Mountain. Amenities include a lake-view garden patio, an infinity indoor pool, and milk and cookies at night. The hotel also houses Rupert's, one of the finest restaurants in town.

The Hunt Lodge (210 N. 3rd St., McCall, 208/634-4700, www.thehuntlodge.com, from $149 d) is a Holiday Inn property just south of town. This stylish mountain inn has 85 guest rooms along with an indoor pool, self-laundry, a fitness center, and free continental breakfast.

Bear Creek Lodge (3492 Hwy. 55, McCall, 208/634-3551, www.bearcreeklodgemccall.com, $120–200) lies a few miles northwest of town at mile marker 149 on Highway 55. While this makes it slightly less convenient than in-town lodgings for enjoying McCall's lively social scene, the location also has its advantages—it's closer to Brundage Mountain and the Little Ski Hill and farther from McCall's noise and bustle. The beautiful modern lodge lies alongside Bear Creek on a scenic 65-acre spread. Accommodations include 13 guest rooms equipped with fireplaces and refrigerators as well as separate duplex cabins featuring king beds and in-room hot tubs. In the gorgeous dining room you'll be served a complimentary gourmet breakfast spread. In the evening you can hang out in the comfy wine bar area.

$150-250

On the south shore of Payette Lake, **(Shore Lodge** (501 W. Lake St., McCall, 800/657-6464, www.shorelodgemccall.com) is a family-friendly lakeside resort with lots of charming amenities. Built in 1948 but extensively remodeled in recent years, this grand lodge has something for everyone, including a fine-dining restaurant, a game room, a movie theater, an outdoor swimming pool, a marina, and a private golf course. Expect to find standard guest rooms as low as $129, the most extravagant suites topping out at $750, and everything in between. The lodge offers special rates during the fall and spring months.

For more lodging options in this price range, contact **Mountain Lakes Realty** (805 N. 3rd St., McCall, 208/634-2728 or 800/799-3881, www.mountainlakesrealty.com), which lists short-term condo and cabin rentals in the McCall area.

FOOD

McCall is known for its mountain cuisine, so don't be surprised to find lots of local elk, trout, huckleberries, and hand-foraged morels on menus around town.

Upscale Fare

The Northwest and Southwest tastefully come together at **(Rupert's** (Hotel McCall, 1101 N. 3rd St., McCall, 208/634-8105, www.hotelmccall.com, lunch 11:30 A.M.–3 P.M., dinner at 5 P.M. Thurs.–Mon., dinner entrées $16–28), within view of picturesque Payette Lake. Chef Gary Kucy, formerly of Tamarack Resort, changes his fusion menu with the season, usually featuring local wild mushrooms and huckleberries in summer. The restaurant has the best wine list in town, pairing well with dinner entrées such as pan-roasted duck breast served with zesty yam puree and huckleberry gastrique. You might also see broiled golden trout with sweet pepper hash or a juniper-marinated elk strip loin with sweet onion jam. The lunch menu has white cheddar macaroni and cheese, sandwiches,

burgers, and an excellent chimichurri shrimp and avocado salad.

Across the street, **Northwest Passage** (317 E. Lake St., McCall, 208/634-8781, dinner daily, entrées $13–26) is another restaurant where the chef has his eyes on the forest floor. Christopher Bradbeer uses local morels and cèpes in creative ways, like in crispy phyllo triangles with smoked Gouda or stuffed in Berkshire pork loin. The lakeside deck overlooks the bustling marina, and you can enjoy a bevy of global offerings, like pork tonkatsu with gingery plum sauce, coq au vin, and American Kobe beef with sophisticated sauces. End the night with a crock of bubbling huckleberry bread pudding.

The Narrows Restaurant (501 W. Lake St., McCall, 800/657-6464, dinner daily, $16–49) at Shore Lodge also serves creative Northwestern cuisine in its beautiful dining room. Expect to see starters like goat cheese fondue and Dungeness crab cakes with green apple–fennel slaw. Larger plates include Moroccan-style pork shank tajine, steamed Alaskan halibut in a fragrant miso broth, bouillabaisse, and big cuts of American Kobe beef. The extensive wine list plays well with the menu.

For traditional steakhouse fare, try **The Mill** (326 N. 3rd St., McCall, 208/634-7683, from 5:30 P.M. daily, cocktail lounge from 5 P.M. daily), on the west side of Highway 55 up the hill from the lake, where you can get steaks, seafood, and a variety of other meat and poultry dinners, most priced in the $20 range, although the lobster tail is around $50. The restaurant recently celebrated its 40th anniversary.

Casual Dining

Fans of funky mountain brewpubs will surely like **(Salmon River Brewery** (300 Colorado St., McCall, 208/634-4772, www.salmonriverbrewery.com, 4–10 P.M. Wed.–Thurs., 4–11 P.M. Fri.–Sat. winter, entrées around $8), a new establishment just south of town. The small brewery and restaurant handcrafts about

ON THE LOOKOUT FOR MOREL MUSHROOMS

Soon after the snow melts away in Idaho's mountains, morels pop up on the forest floor. These coveted edible mushrooms are a tasty harbinger that summer is on its way. Morels grow in great numbers in the McCall area, but you must know where to look.

First off, morels have a distinct conical cap with a honeycomb design. Most morels that grow in Idaho are western blonds from the yellow morel family (*Morchella esculenta*). The color changes from white to beige to darker brown as the mushroom ages.

Morels love that perfection combination of moist and hot, so a spring rainfall in the mountains followed by a warm spell usually yields a harvestable crop. Morels have a symbiotic relationship with trees, especially broadleaf trees like aspen and ash. They don't typically thrive in acidy soils around cedars and other conifers, but morels seem to do all right in north-central Idaho's ponderosa pine and tamarack forests, as long as a few deciduous trees are there to help balance the soil. Around old stumps and fallen trees are great places to look for these wild mushrooms. It's OK to forage for morels on Forest Service land, unless you're doing it for commercial purposes; in that case you need a permit.

If you do encounter some morels, don't be a little piggy and take them all, and never pull the mushroom (stem and all) out of the ground, because that kills the fungi – the mycelium lives underground; the cap is the fruit. Just cut off the mushroom cap at mid-stem with a sharp knife, allowing another cap to take its place in a few days.

Most locals aren't willing to give up their prized morel spots, or their favorite fishing holes, but they will generally offer you some advice at the pub, especially if you buy them a pint. There are several wild mushroom guidebooks on the market. Try David Arora's *All That the Rain Promises and More: A Hip Pocket Guide to Western Mushrooms*, which offers identification tips, great photos, and a healthy dose of humor.

Morels have a deliciously nutty, creamy taste with a meaty texture. If you don't feel like combing the forest on your hands and knees, just head to Rupert's or Northwest Passage, two restaurants in McCall that use morels in creative ways in springtime.

---

eight seasonal brews, including Salmon River Quiver IPA and Sweep Boat Stout. Kick back in the rustic dining room or on the amusing back patio and quaff ale while enjoying a black and blue elk burger or a big plate of smoked pork spareribs. Other noteworthy picks are the stout-soaked bratwurst, smoked salmon tacos, and macaroni and cheese studded with grilled veggies. Oddly, the brewery has a small sushi bar in the corner that puts out fusion maki rolls and other Japanese offerings.

Bistro 45 (1101 N. 3rd St., McCall, 208/634-4515, www.bistro45mccall.com, 8 A.M.–10 P.M. daily, small plates $8–11) is a venerable downtown wine bar and café next to Hotel McCall, with a great patio and boccie ball courts. This place pours a large array of wines by the glass to go with small bites like goat cheese tapenade, steamer clams and mussels, and baked Brie. You can also get panini sandwiches, salads, and quiche, and the small retail wine shop is packed with good labels from around the globe.

For burgers and barbecue and beer, check out **Woody's** (501 3rd St., McCall, 208/634-3722, daily), a new family-friendly restaurant south of town where you'll find slow-smoked brisket, pulled pork, and beef ribs with the expected sides. Burgers, sandwiches, and fries round out the menu. The drive-thru here can be painfully slow, though.

Ethnic Cuisine

Downtown, you can score raw fish at **The Sushi Bar** (415 Railroad Ave., McCall, 208/634-7874, dinner from 4 P.M. Tues.–Fri., lunch and dinner from 11 A.M. Sat.–Sun., $5–13.50). Besides fusion rolls, nigiri, and sashimi, the upstairs restaurant also serves hot Japanese items like miso soup, tataki, inari pockets, and noodle dishes from various parts of Asia. Of course there's plenty of sake and rice lager on hand to wash everything down.

Across the way, **Chapala** (403 Lenora St., McCall, 208/634-3905, lunch and dinner daily, $8–12) turns out standard Mexican fare in a festive dining room. Noteworthy dishes include carne asada, pork carnitas, chicken mole, and enchiladas suiza, splashed with zesty tomatillo sauce.

Romano's Ristorante (203 E. Lake St., McCall, 208/634-4396, from 5:30 P.M. Tues.–Sun., entrées $12–18), in the Yacht Club Building, is the place for spaghetti and meatballs, garlic bread, seafood pasta, and chianti.

Breakfast and Coffee

The Pancake House (209 N. 3rd St., McCall, 208/634-5849, 6 A.M.–2 P.M. daily, breakfast $5–9) is a local dining institution dating to 1949, but the restaurant moved into its new, much larger digs south of town in 2002. As the name suggests, this breakfast-and-lunch hotspot focuses on pancakes, but also expect to find Belgian waffles, omelets, eggs Benedict, and "Those Potatoes," a pile of crispy spuds with gooey cheese and bacon. The lunch menu has everything from burgers to entrée salads and club sandwiches.

◖ **Mountain Java** (501 Pine St., McCall, 208/634-2027, daily), next to Gravity Sports, is a fun little coffeehouse that also sells cookbooks (my favorite reading material). Sit on the patio with your steamy espresso drink and watch boats buzz by on the lake, or cross-country skiers in winter.

INFORMATION

McCall Chamber of Commerce (802 N. 3rd St., McCall, 208/634-7631, www.mccallchamber.org) is the place to go for more information about the town. For Payette National Forest recreation information, try the **McCall Ranger District** (800 W. Lakeside Ave., McCall, 208/634-0700).

GETTING THERE AND AROUND

Getting There

Salmon Air (208/756-6211 or 800/448-3413, $155 one-way, $310 round-trip) flies daily between Boise and McCall Municipal Airport (MYL, Hwy. 55 and Dienhard Lane, McCall). You can get reduced fares with 14-day advance purchase.

Northwestern Trailways (bus stop 147 3rd St., McCall, www.northwesterntrailways.com) offers daily bus service to and from Boise.

Getting Around

McCall Air (300 Deinhard Lane, 208/634-7137 or 800/992-6559, www.mccallaviation.com) flies rafters, backpackers, anglers, and guest-ranch customers into the backcountry just about anywhere in Idaho. It's at the airport south of town along Highway 55.

EXPLORING THE BACKCOUNTRY

McCall is surrounded on three sides by the Payette National Forest, which offers some 2,000 square miles of prime hiking, biking, and horseback-riding country. Pick up a map at the McCall Ranger District, and the friendly rangers will mark it up for you with a highlighter pen.

Burgdorf Hot Springs

Burgdorf Hot Springs (208/636-3036, $5 adults, $3 ages 5–13), a natural hot springs resort, makes a scenic and relaxing day trip from McCall. Take Warren Wagon Road off Highway 55 at the west end of McCall and follow it north, past Payette Lake and past Upper Payette Lake. The U.S. Forest Service **Upper Payette Lake Campground** (20 sites, $10–15) is on the shore of the lake and offers a boat-launching ramp. Continuing up the highway, you'll pass thousands of acres of lodgepole pines charred in the fires of 1994. Eventually you'll come to the end of the pavement at the junction with Forest Road 246, the road in to the hot springs. In winter, the snowplows clear no farther, so you'll have to ski or snowmobile the rest of the way. Turn left on Forest Road 246 and follow it two miles to the hot springs.

The resort has been around since 1865, and the current owners and managers are in the process of restoring an old hotel and several creaky dilapidated cabins on the property. The restored cabins ($35 for one person plus $25 each additional person) are very rustic—no electricity but lots of character. The large, beautiful 50- by 75-foot hot-springs pool has rustic log sides and a sand bottom. It's about five feet deep and fed by a constant flow of 104°F spring water. A bonus for wildlife watchers: Across the road from the resort is a big open meadow where a large herd of elk comes to browse in the early evening in summer. If you're lucky, you might spy a moose here as well. It's a popular show; you'll find the dirt road to the hot springs lined with parked cars and folks peering through binoculars at the numerous animals.

Camping is available right next door at the U.S. Forest Service's **Burgdorf Campground** (6 sites, free).

Warren

Dedicated explorers can continue farther east on Forest Highway 21 to the old gold-mining town of Warren, which in the boom days supported more than 2,000 people. According to the Payette National Forest's walking-tour guide to the historic town, "except for occasional bar fights, Chinese tong wars, highway robberies, and a huge 1904 business-district fire, Warren was considered a relatively calm mining camp." Today a handful of century-old buildings still stand, including a former hotel, saloon, and assay office.

If time gets away from you in your explorations of the town, and you don't want to drive back to McCall in the dark, call **Backcountry Bed & Breakfast** (Warren, 208/636-6000, $60–75). Inside you'll find a rec room with a pool table and TV, and outside you'll find

miles of wide-open country for snowmobiling, cross-country skiing, hiking, fishing, or whatever else you might fancy. The B&B is open year-round, but the roads aren't plowed this far, so you might have to fly or snowmobile in.

East of Warren on Forest Road 340 is the remote U.S. Forest Service **Shiefer Campground** (4 sites, free), a great place for isolated fishing on the South Fork Salmon River. At this point you are 77 road miles from McCall.

Camping

In addition to the Payette National Forest campgrounds already listed, several others lie to the east and northwest of McCall. **Kennally Creek Campground** (12 sites, $10–15) offers a horse-unloading ramp and hitching rails at the Kennally Lakes trailhead. Take Highway 55 south from McCall a little over 10 miles, then turn east on Forest Road 388 and follow it 19 miles to the campground.

Three more campgrounds are accessed via Lick Creek Road (Forest Hwy. 48), which begins east of Ponderosa State Park. **Lake Fork Campground** (9 sites, $10) is nine miles east of McCall, **Ponderosa Campground** (14 sites, $10) lies along the Secesh River 31 miles from McCall, and **Buckhorn Bar Campground** (10 sites, $10) is on the South Fork Salmon River beneath Sixmile Ridge—continue past Ponderosa Campground and bear right at two forks, first following Forest Highway 48, then turning off onto Forest Road 674.

Northwest of McCall, take Highway 55 past the turnoff to Brundage and turn right on Forest Road 453 to reach **Last Chance Campground** (23 sites, $10–15). Alternately, turn up toward Brundage and continue past it to **Grouse Campground** (21 sites, $10–15) on Goose Lake, or a dozen miles farther to **Hazard Lake Campground** (12 sites, $10–15), which is near good hiking on the Lava Ridge National Recreation Trail.

The Hells Canyon Corridor

HELLS CANYON NATIONAL RECREATION AREA

Between Pinehurst and White Bird, U.S. 95 parallels the eastern edge of Hells Canyon National Recreation Area (NRA), a 652,488-acre preserve straddling the Snake River in Idaho and Oregon. For some 71 Wild and Scenic miles, the Snake carves its way northward through Hells Canyon, the deepest river gorge in North America. This is one mother canyon. A few roads lead down to it in places, but none dare run through it.

Below Hells Canyon Dam, the Snake's raging rapids and placid pools create a recreational haven for rafters and jetboaters. Hikers can follow trails along the water's edge, beneath towering walls of crumbling black basalt, or climb out of the canyon to explore the high country along its rim—most notably the Seven Devils Mountains. This range of high peaks has some of the state's most magnificent alpine scenery and offers great views of the canyon floor more than a vertical mile below.

The 215,000-acre **Hells Canyon Wilderness** makes up a large portion of the National Recreation Area; motor vehicles and mountain bikes are prohibited. Although the majority of this wilderness lies across the river in Oregon, Idaho's share includes most of the Seven Devils range as well as 18 river miles between Hells Canyon Creek and Willow Creek.

© DANA HOPPER-KELLY

NORTH-CENTRAL IDAHO

The Snake River cuts through Hells Canyon.

History

The canyon has long been popular with people, thanks to its mild winters, abundant game, and fish-filled river. Some 1,500 Native American archaeological sites have been found in the canyon, including evidence of human habitation going back 7,100 years. At **Upper Pittsburg Landing** you can look at petroglyphs (rock etchings) and pictographs (rock paintings) created by the canyon's first residents.

Before nonnatives came to the area, Chief Joseph's band of Nez Perce made an annual migration from their summer home in Oregon's Wallowa Mountains to warmer winter quarters here in the canyon. Shoshone, Northern Paiute, and Cayuse people also inhabited the region from time to time. The first nonnatives to enter the canyon—John Ordway, Peter Weiser, and Robert Frazier, led by several Nez Perce guides—came over from Kamiah in 1806, pronouncing the path down to the Snake "the worst hills we ever saw a road made down." Wilson Price Hunt's fur expedition of 1811 explored the upper reaches above today's Hells Canyon Dam but turned back before seeing the heart of the gorge.

The first population influx occurred in the 1860s, when the West's mining frenzy reached the area. Some placer mining took place along the river, and hard-rock mines soon riddled the southern Seven Devils. Copper was the big find; today you can drive to what's left of **Cuprum,** an aptly named copper-mining center. Later, homesteading farmers and

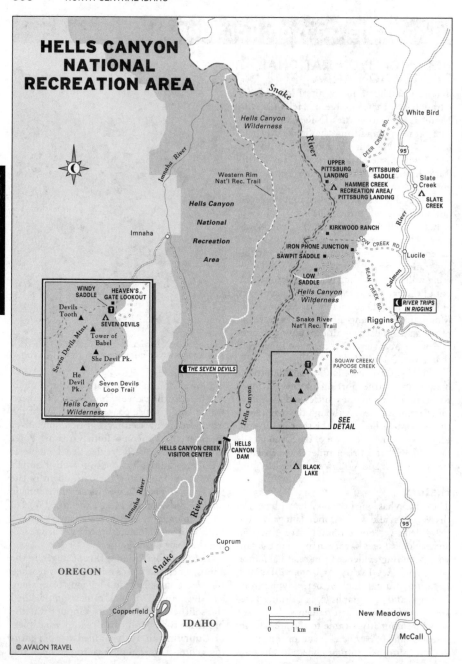

HELLS CANYON NATIONAL RECREATION AREA

Snake River

Hells Canyon Wilderness

DEER CREEK RD.

White Bird

95

UPPER PITTSBURG LANDING

PITTSBURG SADDLE

Slate Creek

SLATE CREEK

HAMMER CREEK RECREATION AREA/ PITTSBURG LANDING

Western Rim Nat'l Rec. Trail

Hells Canyon National Recreation Area

Imnaha River

Imnaha

KIRKWOOD RANCH

COW CREEK RD.

River

IRON PHONE JUNCTION

SAWPIT SADDLE

Lucile

LOW SADDLE

BEAN CREEK RD.

Salmon

Hells Canyon Wilderness

RIVER TRIPS IN RIGGINS

Snake River Nat'l Rec. Trail

Riggins

WINDY SADDLE

HEAVEN'S GATE LOOKOUT

Devils Tooth

SEVEN DEVILS

Tower of Babel

She Devil Pk.

Seven Devils Mtns.

He Devil Pk.

Seven Devils Loop Trail

Hells Canyon Wilderness

SQUAW CREEK/ PAPOOSE CREEK RD.

THE SEVEN DEVILS

SEE DETAIL

Hells Canyon

HELLS CANYON CREEK VISITOR CENTER

HELLS CANYON DAM

BLACK LAKE

Imnaha River

Snake River

95

OREGON

Cuprum

Copperfield

IDAHO

0   1 mi
0   1 km

New Meadows

McCall

© AVALON TRAVEL

ranchers made their way into the area. The farmers planted orchards and row crops on the fertile alluvial terraces, supplying both themselves and local miners with high-quality fresh produce. Ranchers grazed cattle and sheep on whatever relatively level areas they could find. A good example of an early sheep ranch is preserved today at **Kirkwood Ranch,** as interpretive site along the river accessible on foot, bicycle, or boat.

After World War II the Army Corps of Engineers suddenly found itself with nothing to do and latched onto dams as its new raison d'être. The Corps dammed its way inexorably up the Columbia River before casting eyes on the Snake. Hells Canyon, with its narrow width and steep gradient, looked like a prime target. In 1964 the Federal Power Commission gave the green light for development of a dam in the canyon. The proposal drew protest from canyon conservationists and eventually ended up before the U.S. Supreme Court. After years of legal wrangling, Congress created the Hells Canyon National Recreation Area in 1975, ensuring that no more dams would be built. The Snake is now undammed from Hells Canyon Dam at the south end of the canyon to Lower Granite Dam just beyond Lewiston, a distance of more than 100 miles.

Flora and Fauna

Hells Canyon is a unique biome thanks to the extreme elevation changes that occur within its narrow boundaries. The land rises from 1,500 feet along the river to above 9,000 feet in the Seven Devils, all within about 10 miles as the crow flies. Each altitude zone supports a particular plant and animal community—from cacti and rattlesnakes on the canyon floor to lupines and marmots up high. And since those zones are horizontally compressed, you'll find many species living in abnormally close proximity.

The Snake River is one of the few remaining strongholds of the **white sturgeon,** a huge, primeval-looking monster that can reach lengths of 10 feet or more. If you catch one, the law requires you to put it back. Other fish in the river include steelhead, salmon, rainbow trout,

bass, crappie, and catfish—quite a mix. On land, you'll find deer, black bears, elk, mountain goats, and hopefully still some **bighorn sheep,** which have been devastated by recurring plagues that rapidly sweep through the population. Finally, the skies over the NRA are home to more than 100 species of birds, among them hawks, owls, and even bald and golden eagles.

The canyon's unique flora includes rare flowers such as Snake River phlox, rough harebell, the endangered MacFarlane's four-o'clock, and the bartonberry, found only in Hells Canyon. Once-thick stands of ponderosa pine have been extensively logged; logging is permitted in the NRA outside Hells Canyon Wilderness. Other common trees in the NRA include hackberry, cottonwood, and alder.

Pittsburg Landing

Just south of White Bird on U.S. 95, signs mark a turnoff to Hammer Creek Recreation Area and Pittsburg Landing. Cross the Salmon River and make a quick left onto Deer Creek Road (Forest Rd. 493). Deer Creek Road winds up to Pittsburg Saddle and drops steeply down the other side to Pittsburg Landing, a total distance of 17 miles.

This important Native American archaeological site is also the only place south of Hells Canyon Dam on the Idaho side where you can drive right down to the river. Naturally, that makes it a popular launch and takeout point for rafters. At the end of the road you'll find an NRA campground (28 sites, $8), a boat-launching ramp, a dock, and a small ranger information booth. Nearby, a short spur road leads to another boat-launch area at Upper Pittsburg Landing, passing a gallery of Native American rock art on the way. The numerous pictographs and petroglyphs here mark the site as a favored studio for ancient Picassos. Upper Pittsburg Landing also marks the trailhead for the Hells Canyon National Recreation Trail. It can be extremely hot and dry in summer, and there's little shade. Campers will want to bring big floppy hats, plenty of sunscreen, and ice chests full of cold beverages.

The Seven Devils

Second only to the Sawtooths for spectacular alpine scenery, the Seven Devils Range rises steep and crag-like between the Salmon River on the east and the Snake River on the west. From the lofty summit of He Devil Peak (9,393 feet)—highest point in the NRA—it's a dizzying drop of nearly 8,000 feet in just over five miles down to the Snake at the bottom of Hells Canyon.

You can access the heart of this spectacular mountain range via Squaw Creek–Papoose Creek Road (Forest Rd. 517), which turns west off U.S. 95 on the south side of Riggins at the Hells Canyon NRA headquarters. A 19-mile drive up the gravel road leads you to **Heaven's Gate Lookout** (8,429 feet), where you'll be treated to possibly the most magnificent view in all of Idaho. The 360-degree panorama takes in four states: Idaho, Oregon, Washington, and Montana. To the northeast, the Camas Prairie spreads out all the way to the Clearwater River. To the southwest, Hells Canyon frames the foreground for the snowcapped Wallowa Mountains of Oregon, Chief Joseph's homeland. To the southeast, the Salmon River Mountains roll across the horizon. And practically right in front of you, the Devils' own cathedrals of granite tower over Seven Devils Lake and the U.S. Forest Service **Seven Devils Campground** (7 sites, free). A notice posted here warns visitors not to get too close to the mountain goats that occasionally wander into camp.

A number of trails open to hikers and horsepackers start from Windy Saddle trailhead, between the lookout and the campground. The most popular, the Seven Devils Loop Trail, encircles the range's highest peaks while leading past sapphire-blue lakes and verdant wildflower-painted meadows.

Unlike the low country of Riggins or Hells Canyon, up here it's relatively cool and comfortable even in the scorching days of August. Snowfields linger right through summer in places.

Sawpit Saddle

Another off-pavement route leads to two canyon viewpoints but does not descend to the river. The three-hour loop follows **Bean Creek Road** (Forest Rd. 241) from its junction with U.S. 95, north of Riggins 0.25 miles, west to Iron Phone Junction. A loop farther west from Iron Phone Junction on rougher roads—Forest Road 2060 and Forest Road 1819—leads to views at Sawpit Saddle, Low Saddle, and Cold Springs. From Sawpit Saddle you can glimpse the Snake River, glimmering in the sun far below. The route returns to Iron Phone Junction, then back the way you came.

Boating

In 1865 a Portland riverboat company tried to run the first steamboat up through Hells Canyon as a route to the south Idaho goldfields. After 4.5 days of slowly chugging up the canyon, the vessel reached the mouth of Oregon's Imnaha River. There the captain discovered an eight-foot-long gash in the bow and decided to beat a hasty retreat. The swift current carried the boat back out of the canyon in less than four hours. Four years later, the steamboat *Shoshone*—built in southern Idaho for a venture that subsequently failed—successfully ran the Snake River downstream through Hells Canyon. It was followed in 1891 by another steamboat, the *Norma*. It's unclear how much was left of those boats when they reached Lewiston. In 1925, Amos Burg became the first bold adventurer—or the first dang fool, depending on your perspective—to canoe down the Snake River through Hells Canyon. He was accompanied by perhaps the first river guide, a man named John Mullins. Before the trip, Mullins told Burg "he knew every rock in the river." After the trip, Burg added, "he ought to, since he hit them all."

The Snake is a big river. Its dam-controlled flow rates range anywhere from 5,000 cubic feet per second in low water to an incredible 80,000 cubic feet per second or more during spring runoff. Both jetboats and rafts are allowed on the river, but certain nonmotorized periods have been reserved for rafters who want to paddle in peace and quiet.

The **Hells Canyon Creek Visitors Center,** on the Oregon side of the river just below

Hells Canyon Dam, is the most common put-in point for commercial raft trips. Pushing off from here, you don't have much time to prepare yourself for **Wild Sheep Rapids,** just 5.8 miles downstream. Wild Sheep, the river's longest rapids, is Class IV most of the time, Class V at high flows. Once you make it through that one, you'll barely have time to catch your breath before **Granite Creek Rapids** comes into view. This one's another Class IV–V monster with huge waves and a raft-eating hole at river center. Depending on whether you enjoy or abhor an adrenaline rush, the good (or bad) news is that the hardest part of the river is at the top. More Class II–IV rapids lie ahead, but the trip gets gradually less terrifying as you continue downstream.

Besides rapids, you'll find a few nice beaches (although the silt that would ordinarily keep the beaches alive and replenished is now backed up behind the upstream dams), a few bits of shade, a slew of campsites, and a few historic sites. It's a 2–3-day trip from the put-in at Hells Canyon Creek to the takeout at Pittsburg Landing, a distance of 32 miles. Add another 2–3 days to continue down to the confluence with the Grand Ronde at Heller Bar, 79 miles from the put-in.

While some jetboat tours also leave from Hells Canyon Creek, more of them leave from Lewiston and head upriver.

Among the commercial guide services (south of Lewiston) offering guided raft and jetboat trips down the Snake are **Hells Canyon Adventures** (Oxbow, OR, 541/785-3352 or 800/422-3568, www.hellscanyonadventures.com) and **Exodus Wilderness Adventures** (Riggins, 800/992-3484, www.riverescape.com).

For just rafting, contact **Mountain River Outfitters** (Riggins, 888/547-4837, www.mtnriveroutfitters.com); **Hughes River Expeditions** (Cambridge, 208/257-3477 or 800/262-1882, www.hughesriver.com); and **Idaho Afloat** (Grangeville, 800/700-2414, www.idahoafloat.com). For a complete list, see www.fs.fed.us/hellscanyon.

Private parties planning a float or powerboat trip through Hells Canyon must obtain a **permit** from the U.S. Forest Service. For information, contact the **Hells Canyon NRA Riggins Office** (1339 U.S. 95, 208/628-3916) just south of town across the highway from the Little Salmon River.

For daily **river flow levels,** you must call **Idaho Power Company** (800/422-3143) to find out how much water they intend to let out of Hells Canyon Dam during your trip.

Hiking and Horse-Packing

The U.S. Forest Service maintains some 900 miles of hiking-equestrian trails in the NRA, most on the Oregon side of the river. Some of the lower-altitude trails remain open year-round; in winter, snow closes the mountain trails up on the rim. Water sources at lower elevations are few and far between, and it gets hot down there; carry plenty of water with you. Also be alert for three common pests in the area: rattlesnakes, ticks, and poison ivy.

The **Hells Canyon National Recreation Trail,** a 31-mile footpath along the banks of the river, leads from Pittsburg Landing south right into the river. Sheer walls of rock block the last two-mile stretch just above Hells Canyon Dam; as a consequence, hikers generally take this trail south to north, paying one of the jetboat operators at the Hells Canyon Creek boat launch to drop them at the beginning of the trail on their way downriver. Note that portions of this trail may be submerged when the river rises above 40,000 cubic feet per second.

Up in the high country, the **Seven Devils Loop Trail** forms a 27-mile circle around the range's highest peaks, passing by or near some 30 alpine lakes along the way. This popular multiday backpack trip offers spectacular vistas looking down into Hells Canyon and up to the summits of He Devil, She Devil, Devils Tooth, and the Tower of Babel, among others. Main access to the loop is at Windy Saddle, but you can also hike in on Trail 214 from Black Lake, to the south, accessed through the small town of Council. This nine-mile trail follows upper Granite Creek north for a time, eventually meeting the Seven Devils Loop at

Horse Heaven Junction, the loop's southernmost point.

For those looking to hike from rim to river, four different trails follow the snowmelt down to the Snake. From south to north, trails descend from the Seven Devils along Devils Farm Creek–Granite Creek, Little Granite Creek, Bernard Creek, and Sheep Creek. You can get the appropriate maps at the NRA office in Riggins. Don't forget that down in the canyon it's usually 15–20 degrees warmer than up on the rim.

Access Points

In addition to the eastern access points (Pittsburg Landing, Seven Devils, and Sawpit Saddle), there are several southern access points, listed below. Paved Highway 71 (to Hells Canyon Dam) and gravel Deer Creek Road (to Pittsburg Landing) are usually open year-round. The other routes are unpaved and generally open mid-July–October. For current conditions and more information about these access points, call the Riggins NRA office (208/628-3916). A summary of all access routes covered in this guide:

- **Hells Canyon Dam:** The approach from the south is via Highway 71, off U.S. 95 at Cambridge. If your vehicle is too wimpy for one of the other routes, don't despair—views of the canyon from along the pavement here are outstanding.

- **Kleinschmidt Grade:** An alternative off-pavement route to Hells Canyon Dam from Council.

- **Black Lake:** An off-pavement route from Council to a southern Seven Devils trailhead.

- **Windy Saddle:** A road from Riggins leads to a viewpoint and trailhead high in the Seven Devils.

- **Bean Creek Road:** Rough off-pavement loop to good views of the canyon; begins 0.25 miles north of Riggins.

- **Kirkwood Ranch:** From Lucile, Cow Creek Road (Forest Rd. 242) climbs toward

Kirkwood Bar, but it's a rough road and ends prematurely. You'll need an all-terrain vehicle, horse, or backpack and sturdy boots to make it down to the ranch. You can also hike in to the ranch from Pittsburg Landing.

- **Pittsburg Landing:** A road from just south of White Bird leads to the Snake River, a boat ramp, a campground, a trailhead, and Native American rock art.

NEW MEADOWS

At New Meadows, U.S. 95 meets Highway 55. Go north on U.S. 95 for Riggins; head east on Highway 55 to reach McCall. The original town of Meadows was a thriving burg west of the present town, but when the Pacific & Idaho Northern Railroad arrived from Weiser in 1911, the company pulled a typical railroad shenanigan. Rather than bring the tracks into town, they brought the town to the tracks. The company bought a large tract of land outside town, built a lavish $30,000 depot, and then sold lots around it. The population made the shift. New Meadows grew, very profitably for the railroad, and old Meadows faded away. The railroad hauled Meadows Valley cattle and lumber to market until 1979.

Today, the railroad grade has been turned into the Weiser River Trail (www.weiserrivertrail.org), a meandering 84-mile recreational path that runs south of town along U.S. 95. Mountain bikers, hikers, and horseback riders will enjoy this newly developed trail, which goes from pine tree–studded mountains to wide-open canyon lands at its starting point in Weiser. Along the way, you'll pass through the small burgs of Council, Cambridge, and Midvale. You can download a map of the trail at the website.

Zim's Hot Springs

The biggest attraction in the New Meadows area is Zim's Hot Springs (2995 Zims Rd., New Meadows, 208/347-2686, 9 A.M.–11 P.M. daily Memorial Day–Labor Day, 10 A.M.–10 P.M. Tues.–Sun. Labor Day–Memorial Day, $7 adults, $6 seniors and ages 3–17), which draws a sizable crowd of regulars up from

McCall for nighttime après-ski soaks. The developed hot springs resort lies west of U.S. 95 in Meadows Valley, four miles north of town; watch for signs along the highway. An artesian well pumps sulfur-free hot water continuously through the 90–96°F swimming pool and 105°F soaking pool. You can also camp at Zim's, which has RV sites ($20) with water and electricity hookups as well as tent sites ($10) with no hookups.

Golf

North of town is **Meadow Creek Golf Resort** (1 Meadow Creek Ct., New Meadows, 208/347-2555, $36–56), a scenic 18-hole par-72 course that stretches across 6,696 yards. The resort also has a restaurant and lounge.

Accommodations

The **◖ Hartland Inn and Motel** (U.S. 95 and Hwy. 55, New Meadows, 208/347-2114, www. thehartlandinn.com, $52–105) offers 11 motel units and five B&B guest rooms in a beautiful 1911 mansion. The Inn also has a small wine and beer bar, **Stein & Stirrup,** where you can grab a libation and a light snack before bedding down.

Camping and RVing

Meadows RV Park (3278 Hwy. 55, New Meadows, 208/347-2325, spring–fall), 2.5 miles east of town on Highway 55, features 37 RV sites ($12–24) with full hookups as well as tent sites ($12). The quiet, tidy park includes showers and a laundry.

Information

For information about the area, check in at the Payette National Forest's **New Meadows Ranger District** (3674 U.S. 95, New Meadows, 208/347-0300) just west of downtown.

RIGGINS

While Salmon and even Banks also compete for the title of "Idaho's white-water capital," Riggins takes the prize. The Salmon River flows right through town on the last legs of its run down from Redfish Lake. The Little Salmon River joins it here, and the Salmon flows another 60 miles through Lower Salmon Gorge to the Snake River. The Snake River's Hells Canyon stretch lies just over the Seven Devils to the west. In short, Riggins is surrounded by a lot of big water. You can feel a buzz of excitement as soon as you enter town. Guide shops and outfitters line both sides of the highway, and packs of river rats—chronically young, tan, and buff—linger insouciantly outside local delis and coffeehouses, planning the next trip.

Get out on the water as soon as the area's short spring begins to wilt away. Riggins sits at the narrow bottom of Salmon River Gorge, whose walls trap the heat like an oven. It bakes in summer; shade is at a premium, and local ice-cream vendors dish out the sundaes nonstop.

Entertainment and Events

The best entertainment in town is the after-dark people-watching at the **Seven Devils Steakhouse and Saloon** (312 N. Main St., Riggins, 208/628-3351), which hosts live music on weekends. Like the nearby river, the dance floor is pretty wild.

On the Riggins events calendar, the town's annual **Salmon River Jet Boat Races** are held in mid-April; the boats roar up the main Salmon River between White Bird and Riggins in an international competition, the first leg of the U.S. Championships. The first weekend in May, the venerable **Riggins Rodeo** kicks up its heels, bringing Western fun and the obligatory parade. For more information on these and other events, call the Salmon River Chamber of Commerce (208/628-3778, www. rigginsidaho.com).

◖ River Trips

Riggins is considered by many to be the best place for white water in Idaho; it's home to several guide services offering float trips on either or both the main Salmon run above town and the Salmon River Gorge stretch downstream from Riggins. Among the many are **Epley's Whitewater Adventures** (Riggins, 208/628-3586 or 800/233-1813, www.epleys.com);

NORTH-CENTRAL IDAHO

white-water fun in Riggins

© DANA HOPPER-KELLY

Exodus Wilderness Adventures (Riggins, 800/992-3484, www.riverescape.com); **Brundage Whitewater Adventures** (Riggins, 888/889-8320, www.raftbrundage.com); and **Wapiti River Guides** (Riggins, 208/628-3523 or 800/488-9872, www.wapitiriverguides.com), which uses gorgeous wooden dories on its trips.

Rates for float trips generally range $55–65 for a half-day trip, $75–95 for a full day, and $300–350 for two-day trips. Exodus and Wapiti run the priciest, most upscale trips; Wapiti emphasizes natural history, while Exodus makes use of jetboats on some of its excursions.

Fishing

If you'd rather float and fish than paddle white water, call **Mountain River Outfitters** (Riggins, 888/547-4837, www.mtnriver-outfitters.com), which leads fishing trips on the Salmon River near Riggins. **Exodus Wilderness Adventures** (Riggins, 800/992-3484, www.riverescape.com) and **Wapiti River Guides** (Riggins, 208/628-3523 or 800/488-9872, www.wapitiriverguides.com) also offer guided fishing.

If you want to go fishing on your own, remember that steelhead season is in the spring and fall, and you'll need a special permit in addition to a fishing license. Stop by **Hook, Line, & Sinker** (112 N. Main St., Riggins, 208/628-3578) to pick up a steelhead fishing permit ($12.75 residents, $31.50 nonresidents) and a little advice, to which you'll reply, "A cork, some yarn, and a what?" For more information about steelhead fishing, contact the Idaho Department of Fish and Game (208/334-3700).

Hiking

Riggins is surrounded by great backcountry full of hiking trails. To the west lies Hells Canyon National Recreation Area. About 20 miles east is the Gospel-Hump Wilderness. Access the Gospel-Hump at the Wind River Pack Bridge trailhead, on Salmon River Road (Forest Rd. 1614) east of town.

Accommodations

Around half a dozen mom-and-pop places line either side of the highway through town, most with rates near the middle of this category. The friendly **◖ Riggins Motel** (615 S. Main St., Riggins, 208/628-3001 or 800/669-6739, from $69 d) has good shade along with a hot tub, cable TV with HBO, a barbecue, and picnic tables. The motel is in the middle of town on the west side of the highway. On the south side of Riggins is **Salmon River Motel** (1203 S. Main St., Riggins, 208/628-3231, $39–85), a clean little road motel with cable TV and coin laundry; pets are allowed.

The **Best Western Salmon Rapids Lodge** (1010 S. Main St., Riggins, 208/628-2743 or 877/957-2743, from $112 d) enjoys prime real estate at the confluence of the Salmon and Little Salmon Rivers. All 55 guest rooms have refrigerators, hair dryers, cable TV, and high-speed Internet. Amenities include an indoor pool and a fitness room, an outdoor patio and a hot tub, and complimentary breakfast.

Camping

River Village RV Park (1434 N. Main St., Riggins, 208/628-3443, year-round) has 20 RV sites ($20) with full hookups and eight tent sites ($15). It has cable TV and laundry facilities.

Salmon River Road (Forest Rd. 1614) follows the river 28 miles east from town to Vinegar Creek, a popular boat-launch site. Along the way, you'll pass Ruby Rapids, a good place to look for garnets along the shore, as well as **Allison Creek Picnic Area,** the U.S. Forest Service **Spring Bar Campground** (14 sites, $10), and the **Van Creek Picnic Area and Campground** (2 sites, free).

Backcountry Guest Ranch

Shepp Ranch (208/866-4268, www.sheppranch.com, $300 pp per day) is 45 miles east of Riggins on the north bank of the Salmon River at the mouth of Crooked Creek. The ranch's backyard is the 206,000-acre Gospel-Hump Wilderness, and outdoor recreation in the midst of this wild solitude is the main attraction. Available activities include jetboating, rafting, trail riding, fishing, hiking, and soaking your cares away in the hot tub. The family-style meals are made with fresh garden vegetables, local berries, and trout from the river. No roads lead into the ranch, so you have to come by trail, boat, or plane; call for more information and to make arrangements.

Food

◖ Shelly's Back Eddy Grill & Alehouse (533 N. Main St., Riggins, 208/628-9233, 11 A.M.–10 P.M. Sun.–Thurs., 11 A.M.–11 P.M. Fri.–Sat., around $8) is a new establishment on the north end of town with 11 microbrews on tap. The back patio is a good spot to hang out at night and quaff ale as wild river stories become more and more epic with each downed pint. The pub-inspired menu has burgers (beef, elk, bison), nachos, panini sandwiches, pizza, and fried ravioli.

The menu at **River Rock Café** (1149 S. Main St., Riggins, 208/628-3434, breakfast, lunch, and dinner daily, dinner entrées $11–23) literally has something for everyone, with delish omelets in the morning, focaccia sandwiches and calzones for lunch, and big steaks and baby back ribs at night. The restaurant also sells boxed lunches to go (around $9)—good for your outdoor adventures.

Information

Contact the **Salmon River Chamber of Commerce** (208/628-3778, www.rigginsidaho.com), which has a visitor information booth in the center of town on the west side of the highway. For recreation information, contact the **Hells Canyon NRA Riggins Office** (1339 U.S. 95, 208/628-3916) just south of town.

NORTH OF RIGGINS
Slate Creek

Ten miles south of White Bird on the highway is the U.S. Forest Service's Slate Creek Ranger Station, home of the Nez Perce National Forest's **Salmon River Ranger District** (304 Slate Creek Rd., White Bird, 208/839-2211). Out front, a small 1909 log cabin that once

THE BATTLE OF WHITE BIRD HILL

In 1855, the Nez Perce swallowed their pride and agreed to the government's treaty creating a 5,000-square-mile reservation for the Indians. Not long thereafter, gold was discovered on the reservation, and miners came pouring in, so in 1863 the government drew up a new treaty, reducing the original size of the reservation to 500 square miles. The Nez Perce bands whose lands were not affected by the treaty signed it; the others did not. The government originally took no action against these "nontreaty" Nez Perce, but in January 1877 the government's Indian Agent for the Nez Perce ordered all nontreaty Nez Perce onto the reservation by June 14. On June 2, the nontreaty bands of Chiefs Joseph and White Bird gathered at Tolo Lake, just north of White Bird, preparing to enter the reservation, but a trio of angry young braves rode out of that camp and killed four whites in the area. The rebel braves were soon joined by 17 others and went on to kill a dozen more whites over the next couple of days. Word reached Army general Oliver O. Howard at Fort Lapwai, who sent two companies of troops under the command of Captain David Perry to put down the uprising. Howard sent off a message to General McDowell in San Francisco, describing the situation and saying, "Think we will make short work of it."

Knowing that troops were on the way, Joseph and White Bird realized there would be trouble. Despite having resigned themselves to entering the reservation and living in peace, it now seemed that their only alternative was to fight or flee. They moved their camp to the bottom of White Bird hill and planned their defense for the anticipated attack. As it turned out, their plan was a good one. Early on the morning of June 17, about a year after Custer's annihilation at the Battle of the Little Bighorn – Perry and about 100 cavalrymen rode confidently south from Fort Lapwai, reached the top of this hill, and started down it in search of the Indian camp. For most of the way the soldiers had no view of the camp. The Nez Perce used the topography to their advantage, taking positions hidden from

© DANA HOPPER-KELLY

fabled White Bird Hill

Perry, but ready to spring into action if the need arose.

Some authorities say the Nez Perce sent three warriors riding toward Perry carrying a flag of truce, and that they were fired on by the soldiers. Other authorities say there was no such effort, and the Nez Perce attack took the Army completely by surprise. In any case, Perry was suddenly faced with a barrage of gunfire from the Nez Perce. One of the first Indian gunshots picked off Perry's bugler, which was particularly troublesome for the bluecoats: Perry had spread his men out in three different groups and now had no way to communicate commands. Each of the other two groups had a bugler also, but both had dropped their horns at some point in the panic. Perry's cavalry found itself in chaos, not knowing how to respond to the well-planned attack. Though the Indians were significantly outnumbered, the Army troops fled back up White Bird Hill as best they could, with the Nez Perce in hot pursuit.

When the battle was over, the Nez Perce had killed 34 of Perry's men and sustained not a single loss themselves. But they knew General Howard, like the hydra, would come after them with far more troops, hungry for revenge. The Nez Perce packed up their camp and began their now legendary flight, which ended in surrender three and a half months and 1,500 miles later at Bear's Paw, Montana.

housed the head ranger now serves as a Forest Service museum.

Slate Creek, now a ghost town, formerly supplied the booming mining camp of Florence. Heading east, Slate Creek Road (Forest Rd. 354) runs up past the Bureau of Land Management (BLM) **North Fork Campground** (5 sites, free) and up to the boundary of the Gospel-Hump Wilderness, where you'll find the Forest Service's **Rocky Bluff Campground** (4 sites, free). Just south of Slate Creek Road on the river is the BLM's **Slate Creek Campground** (6 sites, $10), which has good wheelchair accessibility.

Hammer Creek

The BLM's **Hammer Creek Recreation Area** is a popular put-in point for rafters heading down the Lower Salmon Gorge. Here you'll also find a campground (8 sites, $10) with good wheelchair accessibility. To get to the area, turn off U.S. 95 at a well-marked turnoff just before the White Bird exit. The sign is marked Hammer Creek–Pittsburg Landing. Cross the Salmon River, turn right, and follow the road to the campground. For more information, contact the **BLM Cottonwood Field Office** (1 Butte Dr., Cottonwood, 208/962-3245).

White Bird

Just past the turnoff to the little town of White Bird, U.S. 95 climbs White Bird Grade. This hill was long a major stumbling block in the effort to link the north and south halves of the state. Road construction began here in 1915 using convict labor and wasn't completed for regular traffic until 1921. That old road is east of today's U.S. 95, the White Bird Grade portion of which wasn't completed until 1975.

As you drive up the highway today from White Bird onto the Camas Prairie, you'll pass one of the most important battlefields in the history of the West, **White Bird Battlefield,** on the expansive hillside to the right, where the opening battle of the Nez Perce War took place in 1877. A turnout along the highway toward the top of the hill describes the battle in detail, but to get the best feel for the history of the event, continue to the top of the hill and take the drive down the old road, where there are several trailheads leading into the battlefield area. An excellent National Park Service pamphlet, *White Bird Battlefield Walking Tour,* brings the battle to life, moment by moment, as you hike through the canyon. For a copy of the pamphlet or more information about the site, contact **Nez Perce National Historical Park** (208/843-7001).

Grangeville and Vicinity

After climbing out of White Bird Canyon, you'll top out onto the Camas Prairie, where Native Americans once harvested the roots of the camas plant that grew profusely here. There's another Camas Prairie in the southern part of the state near Fairfield. Anyway, Grangeville began in the mid-1800s as the site of a grange hall and gristmill built by local farmers and ranchers. Later it became a major supply center for miners working in the nearby mines. Today, the town of about 3,500 is the seat of enormous Idaho County, an area bigger than New Jersey. The county spans the width of Idaho from Oregon to Montana.

Grangeville is still a hub for Camas Prairie agriculture; the prairie's fertile volcanic soil produces bumper crops of wheat, barley, canola, peas, clover, and hay. The town also serves as a base camp for recreation trips to Hells Canyon National Recreation Area; the Frank Church–River of No Return and Gospel-Hump Wilderness Areas; and the Clearwater, Lochsa, Salmon, Selway, and Snake Rivers. It's a hospitable place with basic services, albeit not overly exciting.

the Camas Prairie surrounding Grangeville

SIGHTS
Tolo Lake Mammoth Replica
In 1994 an excavating crew working on an Idaho Department of Fish and Game project at nearby Tolo Lake unearthed a large fossil bone and tusk. The subsequent archaeological dig, conducted by Idaho State University, yielded more than 400 specimens, many of which were complete mammoth skeletons from the Pleistocene era. To commemorate this massive find, a group of citizens in Grangeville purchased a life-sized plastic replica of a mammoth and had it housed in a glass-walled structure for all to see. The exhibit (free) is especially impressive at night when it's all lit up. The replica is in Eimers Park (U.S. 95 and Pine St., Grangeville), just north of town next to the chamber of commerce visitors center (208/983-0460).

Bicentennial Historical Museum
Catch a glimpse of local history at the small Bicentennial Historical Museum (305 N. College St., Grangeville, 208/983-2573,

1–5 P.M. Wed.–Fri. June–Sept., donation) near downtown, which has old toys, flapper dresses, early mining exhibits, and Nez Perce artifacts. Most impressive is the displayed mammoth tusk from Tolo Lake.

RECREATION
Alpine Skiing
Snowhaven Ski & Tubing Area (208/983-3866, 10 A.M.–4 P.M. Sat.–Sun. and holidays mid-Dec.–mid-Mar., full-day $17 over age 6, $15 seniors, free under age 7) is seven miles south of Grangeville on the Grangeville-Salmon Road (Forest Rd. 221). The road starts on the east end of town opposite the National Forest headquarters; follow it straight up the hill and don't turn left at a junction just outside town. Snowhaven is a small area with one T-bar and one rope tow serving a 40-acre hill with a 400-foot vertical drop. Half-day passes are available, and lessons are offered for all levels as well as for telemarkers, snowboarders, and cross-country skiers. There's also a lift-serviced tubing hill (one hour $7, two hours

$11, full-day $20) that blasts riders down an 850-foot-long stretch of the mountain. Ski and tubing combination passes cost $22.

The small day lodge offers light food—burgers, nachos, and the like, but no booze—and the south-facing deck, complete with picnic tables, is sunny and pleasant. Snowhaven's peak elevation of just 5,600 feet means the season here is short.

Cross-Country Skiing

Two miles farther up the road is the **Fish Creek Meadows Park N' Ski Area.** The 10 miles of cross-country trails are groomed only once a week, and the surrounding area is used heavily by snowmobilers. The area offers a small ski-in cabin with a woodstove, picture windows, and views toward the Gospel-Hump Wilderness. If you've had enough of Fish Creek and want to practice your tele-turns, you can take an ungroomed but marked seven-mile ski trail over to Snowhaven. For more information, contact the **Grangeville Chamber of Commerce** (U.S. 95 at Pine St., Grangeville, 208/983-0460, www. grangevilleidaho.com).

Summer and Fall at Fish Creek Meadows

The ski trails here become **mountain biking, horseback riding,** or **hiking** trails after the snow melts. In late summer the area abounds with ripe huckleberries. Near the trailhead you'll find a U.S. Forest Service campground ($6) and a day-use area with a picnic shelter. Much effort has gone into making the area wheelchair-accessible.

Recreation information is available from **Nez Perce National Forest Headquarters** (104 Airport Rd., Grangeville, 208/983-1950) on Highway 13 at the east end of town.

ACCOMMODATIONS AND FOOD
Accommodations

Gateway Inn (700 W. Main St., Grangeville, 208/983-2500, $49–70) is a locally owned hotel with 23 recently remodeled guest rooms. Amenities include an outdoor pool, cable TV,

and a free breakfast spread. For no-frills lodging, head to the **Downtowner Inn** (113 E. North St., Grangeville, 208/983-1110, from $65 d), a small motel with 16 relatively clean guest rooms.

◀ **Whitebird Summit Lodge** (2141 Old White Bird Hill Rd., Grangeville, 208/983-1802 or 866/562-5398, www.whitebirdsummit.com, around $120) is a comfy guest ranch at the top of the White Bird Grade. Room rates include a great view, a big breakfast, and easy access to the area's recreational activities. The lodge, owned by Frank and Terri Schmitz, doubles as an outfitter, offering package deals on rafting and fishing trips.

Food

Bishop's Bistro (123 W. Main St., Grangeville, 208/983-1153, breakfast, lunch, and dinner daily, dinner entrées cost around $10) is a friendly little restaurant where you can expect to find chicken-fried steaks, panini sandwiches, and traditional Italian pasta dishes.

Get a little history with your dinner at **Oscar's** (101 E. Main St., Grangeville, 208/983-2106, breakfast, lunch, and dinner daily), a venerable downtown restaurant on the property of the city's first grange hall, thus the name "Grangeville." This place really shines at night with a large selection of hand-cut steaks and seafood, and let's not forget big baked potatoes.

ACROSS THE CAMAS PRAIRIE
Cottonwood

Cottonwood began in 1862 when a Mr. Allen, first name unknown, lopped down a couple of cottonwood trees and used them to build a way station. The outpost eventually included a hotel, saloon, a store, and a stage station. Today, Cottonwood still offers services to sojourners, especially along the charming downtown strip.

North of town, **Dog Bark Park Inn** (2421 U.S. 95, Cottonwood, 208/962-3647, www. dogbarkparkinn.com, $92 d, $8 per additional person) is one of the strangest places to call it a night in Idaho. "Sweet Willy," a 30-foot-high beagle, disguises a studio apartment that can sleep up to four—two in the main room in the beagle's belly and two in a loft in the mutt's muzzle. Rates include a refrigerator and pantry stocked with all the makings for a hearty continental breakfast.

For more information about the town, contact **Cottonwood Chamber of Commerce** (506 King St., Cottonwood, 208/962-3231). Also in town is the **Bureau of Land Management Cottonwood Field Office** (1 Butte Dr., Cottonwood, 208/962-3245).

You can tune in **National Public Radio** in the area at station KNWO (90.1 FM).

Keuterville

Keuterville Road separates the tourist from the gypsy. The "big" towns of the Camas Prairie—Grangeville and Cottonwood—aren't big by anything other than rural Idaho standards, but a highway runs through them and you'll find them on your map. Keuterville Road, on the other hand, doesn't go anywhere you need to be. It makes a long lazy loop out around the back of Cottonwood Butte, connecting farms and wooded ranches and eventually entering a maze of lonely gravel roads between the butte and Winchester. Drive slowly: Speeders annoy the white-tailed deer, which outnumber people back here. And make sure your gas tank's full; road signs are minimal, road forks are frequent, and many of the forks dead-end. You may get lost, which is exactly why you drive out Keuterville Road in the first place.

Near the turnoff from U.S. 95 and visible from the highway, **St. Gertrude's Monastery** is impressive enough to pull even pagans in for a gander. The twin-towered Romanesque priory was built of locally quarried stone and has been home to the Benedictine Sisters since 1920. It's now on the National Register of Historic Places. Adjacent to the monastery, the **Historical Museum at St. Gertrude** (465 Keuterville Rd., Keuterville, 208/962-2050, 9:30 A.M.–4:30 P.M. Tues.–Sat., $5 adults, $2 ages 7–17) has a potpourri of historical artifacts, including pioneer and mining gear, a mineral collection, and utensils handcrafted by legendary Salmon River mountain man Sylvan Hart.

Continuing down the road, you'll enjoy distant views of the Seven Devils mountains; a roadside collection of antique tractors; and finally Keuterville itself. The town, such as it is, was founded around a sawmill in 1883 and named after settler Henry Kuther. Unfortunately for Henry, the Post Office Department needed glasses back then, and what should have been "Kutherville" came out Keuterville instead. Rafters have been known to float Grave Creek, a tributary of a tributary of the Salmon River, which starts just south of town.

Winchester

Winchester Lake State Park (1698 Forest Rd., Winchester, 208/924-7563, day-use $5) occupies a woodsy area at the foot of the Craig Mountains. Its centerpiece is 103-acre Winchester Lake, a **fishing** hole popular with warm-weather anglers in summer and ice-fishers in winter. The lake is stocked with rainbow trout and also has largemouth bass and bullhead catfish. A boat ramp is available (electric motors only), and there are some canoes and kayaks available for rent. When enough snow falls, a small **cross-country skiing** trail system is set up. Two beginner–intermediate groomed trails skirt the lake and loop around Craig Mountain. Another 0.75-mile trail is more difficult and is ungroomed. The elevation is only about 4,000 feet, so the snowpack is vulnerable to rain and warm spells. Call for conditions before coming to ski. The park's campground offers the usual state-park amenities: clean restrooms and showers, campsites with hookups, and picnic tables and grills. There are also three yurts ($50–65) available year-round, each heated and able to sleep up to six.

Winchester Lake is named for the adjacent small town of Winchester, which in turn is named for the rifle that won the West. You can see a giant one suspended above one of the town's main streets.

About a mile past the park (follow signs) is the **Wolf Center** (1721 Forest Rd., Winchester, 888/422-1110, www.wolfcenter.org, 9 A.M.–5 P.M. daily summer, $5 adults, $2 ages 6–13, free under age 6), a joint project of the Nez Perce tribe and the Wolf Education and Research Center. It's the home of the Sawtooth Pack, a wolf pack that was once studied and photographed by Jim Dutcher in a large compound near Ketchum. Inside the visitors center you'll find exhibits on wolves and their place in the ecosystem as well as information on Nez Perce culture. Interpretive trails and an observation platform surround the visitors center. The center is open for self-guided tours, and guided tours are available—call for cost, dates, and times.

Lewiston and Vicinity

Lewiston (population 32,000) lies at the confluence of the Snake and Clearwater Rivers, in the traditional homeland of the Nez Perce and a pivotal point for Lewis and Clark on their journey west in 1805. At an elevation of just 736 feet above sea level, it's also Idaho's lowest city. The resulting mild winters allow golfers to enjoy the sport year-round and make for a lovely spring season that turns the city into a riot of blooming trees.

Amazing as it may seem considering it is 470 miles from the Pacific Ocean, Lewiston

NORTH-CENTRAL IDAHO

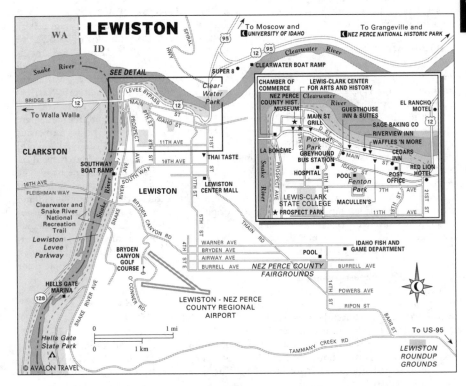

© AVALON TRAVEL

is Idaho's only seaport. Barge traffic comes up the Columbia and Snake Rivers to serve the Port of Lewiston, at the upper limit of commercial navigation on the Snake. River, rail, and road connections make Lewiston an important packing and shipping center. The city's largest employer is the big Potlatch mill perched on the south bank of the Clearwater River. The town also likes its jetboats, those nimble aluminum speedsters that hammer up through the rapids on the Snake and Salmon Rivers. Several manufacturers in town make Lewiston the jetboat capital of the West.

Like Pocatello in southeast Idaho, Lewiston feels blue-collar to the core, which isn't to say it lacks in culture—Lewis-Clark State College regularly brings the arts to town, a venerable community-theater troupe draws audiences for live drama, and the historic downtown has made some modest attempts at a facelift. But on a day-to-day basis, when the sun goes down, it takes the town with it.

Early History

When gold was discovered up the Clearwater River in 1860, the site of today's Lewiston was transformed from a Nez Perce horse pasture into a port and mining supply camp. Steamboats cruised up the Columbia and Snake Rivers, dropping off thousands of hopeful prospectors. The community that soon sprouted around the steamboat docks was squatting illegally on the Nez Perce reservation, but the cooperative Nez Perce agreed to give nonnative merchants one square mile where they could sell their goods to the miners. The earliest buildings were simple wood frames covered with canvas, which gave the settlement its early nickname, "Ragtown." Lewiston was formally founded on the site in May 1861.

The miners were just passing through, not looking to acquire land and settle down, but soon farmers showed up to grow crops to supply the mines. The farmers did need land, and lots of it. As the early mining strikes up the Clearwater River turned into a full-fledged boom, Lewiston grew exponentially. When Congress created Idaho Territory in 1863,

Lewiston was named territorial capital, but the city was still trespassing on the Nez Perce reservation. In typical fashion, the U.S. government "renegotiated" the original treaty, vastly reducing the reservation's size and moving its boundaries well outside of Lewiston.

The city's capital status lasted just a year and a half. By the end of 1864 the Clearwater mines were in decline. Down south, however, the Boise Basin mines were booming, and Boise sought the coveted capital crown. In April 1865, Territorial Secretary and Boise supporter C. DeWitt Smith rode into Lewiston with a contingent of federal troops from Fort Lapwai, stealing away the Territorial seal and archives under threat of force. Smith delivered the purloined goods to Boise, and Lewiston's governmental glory days came to an end.

SIGHTS
Lewis-Clark State College

Founded in 1893, this four-year state college (500 8th Ave., Lewiston, 208/792-5272 or 800/933-5272, www.lcsc.edu) offers undergraduate degrees in about 20 fields as well as two-year associate degrees in a variety of vocational programs. The school's Warriors men's baseball team is legendary, having won the National Association of Intercollegiate Athletics (NAIA) World Series numerous times. As a matter of fact, the NAIA World Series is held in late May at Harris Field on campus. Home field advantage, perhaps? The school's 3,000 students attend classes in one of the most beautiful parts of Lewiston—a hilltop neighborhood full of stately homes and towering trees overlooking the city and rivers below. Even if you're not a student, the small campus—covered with green lawns and tidy brick buildings—makes a nice place for a picnic or an impromptu round of disc golf.

Lewis-Clark Center for Arts and History

Affiliated with Lewis-Clark State College, this downtown museum and gallery (415 Main St., Lewiston, 208/792-2243, 11 A.M.–4 P.M. Tues.–Sat., free) presents rotating shows of local and regional artists as well as other exhibits of artistic or historical interest. A permanent historical display remembers Lewiston's early Chinese community. The gift shop sells jewelry, crafts, books, and assorted CDs by past performers in the center's concert series.

Nez Perce County Historical Museum

The little Nez Perce County Historical Museum (0306 3rd St., at C St., Lewiston, 208/743-2535, 10 A.M.–4 P.M. Tues.–Sat. Mar.–mid-Dec., donation) once housed the Luna House Hotel. In its early days the hotel was a primitive timber-and-canvas affair, matching Lewiston's wild and woolly character. Territorial governor Caleb C. Lyon spent the night at the hotel once, reluctantly accepting the sandbags placed around his bed after he was told they were there to protect him from stray gunshots in the streets.

The museum's exhibits cover all aspects of the area's history, both its Nez Perce and Euro-American heritage. Among the highlights is a fantastic collection of old photographs and a huge, stunning triptych of Chief Joseph in three stages of his life, painted by Dan Piel, a former art professor at Washington State University.

Spiral Highway

Call it the Lombard Street of Lewiston: This "old road" to Moscow snakes back and forth up some 64 switchbacks to the top of Lewiston Hill, nearly 3,000 feet above the city. Up on the canyon rim you'll get impressive views of Lewiston, Clarkston, and the two rivers. The old road joins the new U.S. 95 at the top. From town, turn left at the second exit north of Clearwater Memorial Bridge, and then soon make a right onto the old road, following the signs.

Champion Trees

When Lewis and Clark came through in 1805, the only trees they noted were the humble redstem willow and hackberry. But over the years, Lewiston residents have planted trees of every

description all over town, turning the city into something of a giant arboretum. You'll see variegated box elder, blue ash, red maple, umbrella black locust, American chestnut, flowering ash, flowering pink dogwood, and numerous others, many of which are Idaho "champion trees"—the biggest specimens of their respective species in the state. A free map to the champion trees is available at the **Lewiston Chamber of Commerce** (111 Main St., Lewiston, 208/743-3531, www.lewistonchamber.org).

RECREATION
Hells Gate State Park

Tenters and RVers passing through town will find Hells Gate State Park (5100 Hells Gate Rd., Lewiston, 208/799-5015, $5 per vehicle) unbeatable. The 200-acre park, just four miles south of downtown, is right on the river; swimming, boating, and fishing are steps from your campsite. It offers fun and informative interpretive programs, plenty of green grass and trees, picnic tables and barbecue grills, and clean restrooms with showers. Here you'll also find boat-launch ramps and trails for hiking, biking, or horseback riding. Thanks to Lewiston's mild, low-elevation winters, the park and marina are both open year-round.

The park's newish **Lewis and Clark Discovery Center** (208/799-5015) contains a wealth of information on Lewiston's natural history and the exploration and settlement of Hells Canyon, including a 32-minute film about the Lewis and Clark expedition.

Of the park's 93 campsites ($16–24), 64 have water and power hookups. Eight camping cabins ($50) can each sleep up to five.

Clearwater and Snake River National Recreation Trail

Urban hikers and bicyclists will appreciate this 25-mile-long trail system, which runs along both the Idaho and Washington riverbanks. On the Idaho side, the trail begins at Lewiston's Clearwater Park. It crosses Memorial Bridge, turns west past Locomotive Park, Clearwater Landing, West Pond, and the Lewis and Clark

Interpretive Center, then continues south down the popular **Lewiston Levee Parkway** to Hells Gate State Park. On the Washington side of the Snake, the trail connects Looking Glass Park on the south with Swallows Park and the Clarkston Greenbelt on the north. Southway Bridge (the "new" bridge) provides the connection for the two halves of the trail system. The trail is wheelchair accessible.

Hells Canyon Jetboat Tours

Several companies run jetboat tours up the Snake River through Hells Canyon. Unlike propeller-driven craft, jetboats move forward by shooting a jet of water out the back. Their inboard automobile engines turn powerful turbine pumps. The advantage of this design is its shallow draft; jetboats can navigate shallow rocky rapids that would destroy a standard inboard or outboard motor.

Unlike rafts, jetboats can go both up and down the river. Also unlike rafts, they pound through the rapids with a deafening roar, beating Mother Nature over the head with huge amounts of raw horsepower. In Hells Canyon—much of it surrounded by wilderness—the jetboats seem out of place to many people.

The marina at Hells Gate State Park serves as the departure point for two commercial jetboat operators: **Snake River Adventures** (800/262-8874, www.snakeriveradventures. com) and **Riverquest Excursions** (800/589-1129, www.riverquestexcursions.com). Half-day trips typically cost around $100 adults, $50 children.

Steelhead Fishing

In fall, the Clearwater River comes alive when the steelhead season opens. The river draws anglers from all over the country for a chance to hook one of these brawny fighters. Many angling guides lead trips on the Clearwater during fly-fishing season (late Aug.–Nov.) and drift-tackle season (Nov.–Apr.). Plan on spending about $500 per day for two people. Contact **FishHawk Guides** (888/548-8896, www.fish-hawkguides.com) to arrange a trip.

Golf

Bryden Canyon Golf Course (445 O'Connor Rd., Lewiston, 208/746-0863, www.brydencanyongolf.net, $17–26), south of the airport, offers a public 18-hole course, a driving range, a pro shop, lessons, a putting green, and a restaurant serving breakfast and lunch as well as beer and wine.

ENTERTAINMENT AND EVENTS

Entertainment

Lewiston Civic Theatre (805 6th Ave., Lewiston, 208/746-3401, www.lctheatre.org, Sept.–June) has presented community theater in Lewiston since 1961. Productions take place at the company's Anne Bollinger Performing Arts Center, and the performance season runs concurrently with the academic year. The **Lewis-Clark State College Artist Series** regularly brings touring opera, ballet, concert music, and drama productions to the city. For more information, call the Lewis-Clark Center for Arts and History (415 Main St., Lewiston, 208/792-2243).

Events

Lewiston's **Dogwood Festival** (www.lcsc.edu/dogwood) blooms for the entire month of April at various locations around town. Garden tours take center stage, while a sailboat race, crafts fair, concerts, and wine tastings add to the fun.

The **Lewiston Roundup** (www.lewiston-roundup.org) is the highlight of the year for rodeo fans; you'll find cowboys and cowgirls struttin' their stuff the first full weekend in September at the rodeo grounds (2100 Tammany Creek Rd., Lewiston). The third week of September, the **Nez Perce County Fair** comes to town.

ACCOMMODATIONS

Under $50

El Rancho Motel (2240 3rd Ave. N., Lewiston, 208/743-8517, $42–50) has some of the least expensive rooms in town. Amenities include an outdoor pool, cable TV, and high-speed Internet, but that's about it.

$50-100

The recently revamped 【 **Cedars Inn** (1716 Main St., Lewiston, 208/743-9526 or 877/848-8526, www.cedarsinnlewiston.com, from $59 d) is a friendly, clean, and affordable hotel— the trifecta for those traveling with kids—on the east side of town. Plus there's an outdoor pool, a laundry facility, and free continental breakfast.

For a few more bucks, you can check into the **GuestHouse Inn & Suites** (1325 Main St., Lewiston, 208/746-3311 or 800/806-7666, from $62 d). Here you will find 75 guest rooms, some with balconies and views of the river. Amenities include an outdoor pool and hot tub, a fitness room, high-speed Internet, and an on-site restaurant and lounge.

For a little more money, **Comfort Inn** (2128 8th Ave., Lewiston, 208/798-8090 or 800/228-5150, www.comfortinn.com, from $99 d) can put you up in one of its 52 guest rooms, all of which have cable TV, refrigerators, and microwaves. Other amenities include an indoor pool, a business center, a free morning newspaper, and breakfast. Pets are allowed.

$100-150

The nicest place in town, with guest rooms often available in a lower price range, is the **Red Lion Hotel** (621 21st St., Lewiston, 208/799-1000 or 800/232-6730, www.redlionlewiston.com, from $109 d). The bright and modern inn offers 130 guest rooms, including 43 suites. Expect amenities like two heated pools (one indoor, one outdoor), a jetted tub, a full-size health club, and some of Lewiston's most agreeable dining options.

FOOD
Upscale Fare

Macullen's (1516 Main St., Lewiston, 208/746-3438, www.macullens.com, 11 A.M.–10 P.M. Mon.–Fri., 4–10 P.M. Sat., entrées $12–35) is a fine-dining restaurant near downtown that has earned a loyal following for its steak and seafood menu. You'll find lots of classic dishes prepared with a contemporary twist. Appetizers include steamer clams, chilled prawns with mango cocktail sauce, fried squid, and a delicious little pizza with red grapes, Gorgonzola, and Gouda. The salmon bisque and French onion soup are good picks too. The entrée menu is all about hand-cut steaks, grilled finfish, Alaskan crab (market price), and pasta. Pair a glass of Columbia Valley chardonnay to the grilled herbed salmon with caper beurre blanc sauce. Or go big with a porterhouse steak, cut from dry-aged local beef. The cocktail lounge stays open late.

Over at the Red Lion Hotel, **Meriwether's American Grill** (621 21st St., Lewiston, 208/748-1151, breakfast, lunch, and dinner daily, brunch Sun., dinner entrées $15–29) offers a full menu of appetizers, gourmet salads, pastas, poultry dishes, steaks, and seafood. The dining room looks out over the valley through huge picture windows.

Casual Dining

Also at the Red Lion, **M. J. Barleyhoppers Sports Bar and Brew Pub** (208/799-1000, daily) brews up half a dozen microbrews right on the premises and also carries a variety of other microbrews and imports on tap and in bottles—about 60 different beers in all. Don't try them all in one night. The bar offers pub grub, but you can also order anything on the menus of the Red Lion's other restaurants.

Main St. Grill (625 Main St., Lewiston, 208/746-2440, 10:30 A.M.–9 P.M. Mon.–Fri., 7:30 A.M.–9 P.M. Sat., 7:30 A.M.–8 P.M. Sun., sandwiches around $8, dinner entrées $10–15) is a lively place downtown with a sidewalk patio and retro lunch counter. The walls in the dining room chronicle the successes of Lewis-Clark State College's baseball team with a profusion of newspaper articles and photos. The expansive menu has everything from burgers to wraps to big salads and hot sandwiches. Especially tasty are the Philly cheese steak and Reuben. At night, you can get grilled steaks, pork ribs, and inventive pasta dishes, and breakfast is served on weekends.

【 **La Bohème** (301 Main St., Lewiston, 208/798-1647, www.laboheme.com, breakfast and lunch 7 A.M.–2 P.M., dinner 4–9 P.M.

NORTH-CENTRAL IDAHO

Mon.–Sat., $6–13) is a classy bistro downtown in an old brick building. The menu features Euro-inspired sandwiches, soups, salads, antipasto, and a tasty fruit and cheese board. Noteworthy sandwiches include the caprese (tomato, pesto, mozzarella) and muffaletta with provolone, salami, and green olive tapenade. And yes, there's a wine list.

Ethnic Cuisine

When you need your fix of pad Thai, garlic prawns, or eggplant tofu, head to **Thai Taste** (1410 21st St., Lewiston, 208/746-6192, lunch and dinner Tues.–Sun.). Dishes can be prepared as spicy as you'd like, from "For Those Who Hesitate" to "Dragon Fire."

For Mexican eats, check out **El Sombrero** (629 Bryden Ave., Lewiston, 208/746-0658, lunch and dinner daily, entrées around $10), a popular chips-and-salsa place that serves pozole (hominy soup), chiles rellenos, tamales, enchiladas, and tacos. The restaurant has a good selection of Mexican beers and sodas.

Breakfast and Coffee

Waffles 'N More (1421 Main St., Lewiston, 208/743-5189, 6:30 A.M.–2:30 P.M. daily, under $10) is the spot to go for, you guessed it, waffles and more. Besides waffles served in about every conceivable form, you also can get omelets, biscuits and gravy, and other traditional breakfast fare. The small restaurant can get extremely busy on weekends.

For freshly baked pastries and good espresso drinks, try **(Sage Baking Company** (1303 Main St., Lewiston, 208/743-4009, 7 A.M.–5:30 P.M. Mon.–Fri., 7 A.M.–4 P.M. Sat.). This stylish bakery and coffeehouse near downtown makes scones, muffins, Danishes, and savory artisanal bread, which it uses on its sandwiches, or you can buy whole loaves for the road.

Groceries

The **Lewiston Farmers Market** (3–7 P.M. Wed. early June–mid-Oct.) sets up in the D Street parking lot across from Brackenbury Square. You can pick up locally grown produce (some organic), meat products, eggs, honey, baked goodies, and seasonal preserves. The market offers cooking demonstrations as well.

INFORMATION AND SERVICES
Information

Stop by the **Lewiston Chamber of Commerce** (111 Main St., Lewiston, 208/743-3531, www.lewistonchamber.org) for more information about the area. The **Lewiston Morning Tribune** (505 Capital St., Lewiston, 208/743-9411, www.lmtribune.com) is one of the state's best daily newspapers.

Services

Emergency medical services are available at **St. Joseph Regional Medical Center** (415 6th St., Lewiston, 208/743-2511).

GETTING THERE

Lewiston-Nez Perce County Regional Airport (LWS, 406 Burrell Ave., Lewiston, 208/746-7962) offers commercial air service. **Horizon Air** (800/547-9308) and **SkyWest** (800/221-1212) provide regularly scheduled flights. Car-rental companies at the airport include **Budget** (208/746-0488, www.budget.com) and **Hertz** (208/746-0411, www.hertz.com).

Clearwater Country

U.S. 12 heads east from Lewiston, winding along the banks of the Clearwater River on its way to Montana. Traditionally this was part of the homeland of the Nez Perce people, who fished for the Clearwater's then-abundant salmon; hunted deer, elk, and other wild game in the Clearwater Mountains; and regularly crossed Lolo Pass into Montana on buffalo-hunting trips.

In September 1805 the Nez Perce encountered nonnatives for the first time when members of the Lewis and Clark expedition—cold, weak, and hungry—staggered into Nez Perce Chief Twisted Hair's camp on the Weippe Prairie. The Nez Perce nursed the explorers back to health, sent them off downriver, and tended their horses until the expedition's return trip the following spring.

The Nez Perce and the Lewis and Clark expedition form the historical foundation for the area. Interesting are the roadside markers along U.S. 12—known as the Lewis and Clark Highway—that point out one historical site after another. A portion of the route from Lewiston to Kooskia has also been designated

by the state as the **Clearwater Canyons Scenic Byway.** As it climbs slowly up the steep-walled gorge, the vegetation gradually changes—from arid grass- and brush-covered hills near Lewiston to lush green pine forests around Kooskia and points east.

NEZ PERCE RESERVATION

Thirteen miles east of Lewiston you'll enter the Nez Perce Indian Reservation, home to many of the 3,300 or so enrolled Nez Perce tribe members. The Nez Perce homeland once spanned from eastern Oregon all the way across Idaho into Montana. In 1855, enough white settlers had moved into the area to cause Washington Territory's governor to clamor for a treaty. The "deal" he negotiated, to which the peaceable Nez Perce reluctantly agreed, established the Nez Perce Reservation across a 5,000-square-mile area. But just five years later, white prospectors discovered gold on the reservation, and the deal was off. In 1863 a new treaty reducing the size of the reservation to just 500 square miles was drawn up. Some bands of the Nez Perce signed the treaty; others

NORTH-CENTRAL IDAHO

© DANA HOPPER-KELLY

rising above the Clearwater River Valley

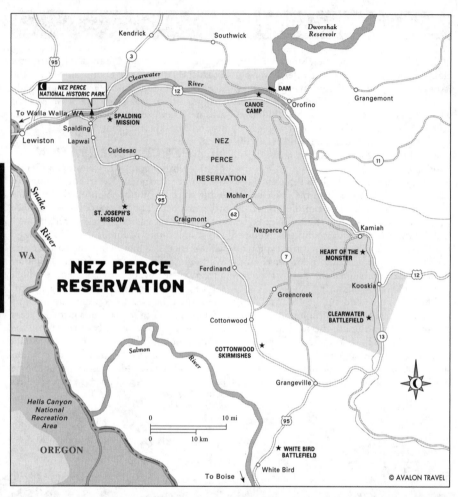

refused. The nontreaty Indians kept to their traditional lands, and the government looked the other way until 1867, when it demanded with threats of force that the nontreaty Nez Perce move onto the pocket-size reservation. Seeing no choice but to comply, most of the nontreaty Nez Perce resigned themselves to this restricted way of life. But on June 13, 1877, three disgruntled Nez Perce braves took revenge on nonnatives in the Salmon River canyon. General Oliver O. Howard was called on

to put down the Nez Perce once and for all, and the Nez Perce War began.

After holding off the Army on a 1,500-mile, 3.5-month flight, the Nez Perce finally surrendered at Bear's Paw, Montana, just 42 miles from the Canadian border and freedom. After the war, the nontreaty Nez Perce were exiled first to Kansas, then to Oklahoma, and the remaining Nez Perce were subjected to the "allotment" of their lands. In the process, the size of the Nez Perce Reservation was further reduced. Today it encompasses 88,000 acres (137.5 square miles), less than 3 percent of its original size under the 1855 treaty and a microscopic fraction of the land the Nez Perce once roamed. Lapwai, just down U.S. 95 from the park visitors center, is the seat of the Nez Perce government.

◖ Nez Perce National Historic Park
VISITORS CENTER
A brief detour from U.S. 12 onto U.S. 95 leads to the headquarters of Nez Perce National Historic Park (39063 U.S. 95, Lapwai, 208/843-7001, www.nps.gov/nep, free). Call it a "concept" park: It consists of 38 separate historic sites in Idaho, Washington, Oregon, and Montana. Taken together, the sites tell the story of 11,000 years of Nez Perce culture, from their pre–Lewis and Clark days to the present. To visit them all entails a 400-mile drive.

The park's visitors center (daily year-round, call for hours, free) is a large facility on the hill next to the site of Henry and Eliza Spalding's old Lapwai Mission. Inside you'll find an auditorium screening a film on Nez Perce history and a bookstore selling books about the Nez Perce and Northwest history. In the exhibit room you'll find a copy of the 1855 Nez Perce Treaty signed by President James Buchanan as well as the Spalding-Allen collection of Nez Perce artifacts, recently purchased from the Ohio Historical Society. It seems the good Reverend Spalding—as much as he tried to get the Nez Perce to adopt the white man's ways—also admired and collected Nez Perce handiwork. In 1846 he sent his collection to a friend in Ohio, and in the mid-1990s the Nez Perce tribe succeeded in raising the $600,000 acquisition price to reacquire the exquisite collection, which includes gorgeous beaded hide clothing, ornate cradleboards, porcupine quillwork, elk-tooth accessories, and more.

The park headquarters is the nerve center for the other sites composing Nez Perce National Historic Park. Of the 38 sites, 29 are in Idaho, described below.

SPALDING MISSION
The mission—within walking distance of the visitors center—was originally called the Lapwai Mission. Established by Presbyterian missionaries Henry and Eliza Spalding in 1836 and originally located a bit farther south, it was moved to this site at the mouth of Lapwai Creek in 1838. The Spaldings were the first nonnative family to reside in Idaho and produced a number of "firsts" during their tenure, including the first gristmill, first sawmill, first printed literature, and first nonnative child born in the state. A sense of history pervades this grassy, tree-shaded flat along the riverbank. You can easily imagine how wonderful it must have been for the Spaldings when they first arrived more than 160 years ago. The alluvial bar provided fertile ground for the mission gardens, and salmon filled the Clearwater River then.

Wander over to the Lapwai Cemetery and spend a reflective moment at the gravesite of Henry and Eliza. Imagine how they must have felt as a two-person minority among the indigenous Nez Perce, and how they felt in 1847 when they learned that the Cayuse had killed Marcus and Narcissa Whitman and might be headed their way. Imagine how they felt fleeing their home of 11 years, in fear for their lives, and how much Henry must have loved this place to have returned later in life to die here among the Nez Perce in 1874.

The site is well aligned along the beaten path but nevertheless an amazingly peaceful spot with lots of grass, picnic tables, and big shade trees. Bring a lunch and soak it in.

WEST OF SPALDING
West of the visitors center, at mile point 306.7 along U.S. 95, is **Coyote's Fishnet.** According to Nez Perce legend, Coyote was happily fishing here one day when Black Bear came along and began to tease him. Coyote lost his temper. He tossed his fishnet onto the hill on the south side of the river, and tossed Black Bear onto the hill on the north side, turning them both to stone in the process. With some

imagination, you can see the net and the unfortunate bear today.

Lewiston's Hells Gate State Park was once the **Hasotino Village Site,** a long-used Native American fishing village. **Buffalo Eddy** archaeological site, upstream on the Snake River from Hells Gate, has a number of Native American petroglyphs. Just north of Lewiston on U.S. 95 is the former site of **Donald Mackenzie's Post.** Mackenzie was a fur trader who had early contact with the Nez Perce. His trading post here lasted less than a year, however.

SOUTH ON U.S. 95

Continuing south from the visitors center on U.S. 95, you'll see a marker pointing out the general vicinity where the Spaldings' first home once stood, built soon after their arrival in the area in November 1836. At today's town of Lapwai, you'll find the site of **Fort Lapwai,** the first military fort in Idaho, built in 1862 to keep the Indians from messing with the miners who were flooding into the area. Also here is the site of the **Northern Idaho Indian Agency,** created by the government to monitor compliance with the Indian treaties. Continuing south, you'll come to a sign marking the **Craig Donation Land Claim.** Mountain man William Craig was a friend of the Nez Perce; he served as an interpreter for them and married a Nez Perce woman. His 1846 claim was the first by a nonnative settler in what is now Idaho. A little farther on is the turnoff to **St. Joseph's Mission.** It was the first Roman Catholic mission among the Nez Perce, built by Father Joseph Cataldo of Old Mission fame and dedicated in 1874.

Much farther south, outside the reservation, U.S. 95 passes five more park sites. Just south of Cottonwood, a sign marks the site of the **Cottonwood Skirmishes,** a couple of early engagements in the Nez Perce War. Small parties of Chief Joseph's band attacked various Army detachments and volunteers in this area on July 3 and 5, 1877. The diversionary attacks allowed the main band of Nez Perce to cross the Camas Prairie unnoticed and link up with Chief Looking Glass's band on the Clearwater

River. A turnoff here leads seven miles to **Weis Rock Shelter,** a habitation site used by indigenous people for more than 8,000 years. West of Grangeville is **Tolo Lake,** where the Nez Perce bands of Chiefs Joseph and White Bird were camped when a few angry braves touched off the Nez Perce War.

EAST OF SPALDING ON U.S. 12

Ant and Yellowjacket, just east of the U.S. 95 turnoff on U.S. 12, is another case of Coyote turning something to stone. The two insects were fighting over the right to eat salmon. Coyote tried to settle the dispute, but they paid no attention to him. To make an example of them, Coyote turned Ant and Yellowjacket to stone. Look up on the hill and you'll see the two creatures—backs arched and jaws locked in combat—now frozen there for all eternity.

Farther east, at the **Lenore Archaeological Site,** evidence indicates that this good fishing hole along the Clearwater was used by the ancestors of the Nez Perce some 10,000 years ago. Continuing east, you'll come to **Canoe Camp** near Orofino. On their westward journey in 1805, the Lewis and Clark expedition stayed here for 10 days, recuperating from a harrowing crossing of the Bitterroots. Up until this point, they had traveled by horseback; here they left their horses with the Nez Perce and continued downriver by canoe. The dugout canoe you'll see is an example of the sort of vessels the expedition fashioned.

Several sites are found around Kamiah. At mile point 67.6, two signs mark the sites of Lewis and Clark's **Long Camp** and the **Asa Smith Mission.** On their return trip from Astoria to St. Louis in spring 1806, Lewis and Clark camped here for a month while waiting for the snows to melt out of the Bitterroots. By all accounts it was an idyllic time, spent in the good company of the Nez Perce. In 1839, missionary Asa Smith tried to start a mission here among the Nez Perce, but the pioneer life proved too much for him, so in 1841 he moved to a mission in Hawaii. At mile point 75.9, a sign memorializes **Looking Glass's 1877 Campsite,** up near Clear Creek. The great Nez

Perce war chief Looking Glass tried to remain neutral in the conflict between the U.S. Army and the nontreaty Nez Perce. He told the Army, "Leave us alone. We are living here peacefully and want no trouble," but the Army nevertheless destroyed his village and stole his horses. He then joined Chiefs Joseph and White Bird in the fight and flight for freedom.

According to their legend, the Nez Perce people originated at the **East Kamiah-Heart of the Monster** site. Once again Coyote plays the leading role in the story. Before human beings inhabited the earth, a monster went on a feeding frenzy here, devouring all the creatures in his path. Coyote saw this and came to the rescue. He tricked the monster into devouring him too, but little did the monster know, Coyote had a stone knife with him. Once inside, Coyote slashed the monster open, cut it into little pieces, and flung the pieces far and wide. Each piece became a different Native American tribe. Coyote then wrung the blood from the monster's heart, and the Nez Perce people sprang from the drops. What was left of the monster's heart is still visible here today.

OTHER SITES

South of Kooskia on Highway 13 is the **Clearwater Battlefield**, scene of one of the hardest-fought battles of the Nez Perce War. On July 11, 1877, Army general Oliver O. Howard tried a surprise attack on the Nez Perce encampment, but his plan failed. Twenty-four Nez Perce warriors managed to hold off Howard's 600 troops until 100 more warriors could get into position to keep Howard pinned down. Behind the fighting, the rest of the Nez Perce withdrew northward toward Kamiah.

North of Kamiah, up on the **Weippe Prairie**, just west of Weippe on Highway 11, a marker commemorates the first meeting of the Nez Perce with Lewis and Clark. The explorers must have been a scraggly, scrawny bunch at that point. They were near starvation when they stumbled upon the Nez Perce encampment; the Native Americans revived them and sent them on their way. A historical marker at **Musselshell Meadow,** due east of Weippe

on the unimproved Lolo Trail, marks the last active camas-gathering grounds of the Nez Perce. Northeast of Weippe on Highway 11 in **Pierce** is a monument marking the beginning of the end of the Nez Perce's glory days. Now Pierce lies outside the reservation, but it was squarely on the reservation in September 1860 when W. F. Bassett, a member of E. D. Pierce's prospecting expedition, found the first gold in Idaho. Miners came running, and soon a treaty was drafted to take the land away from the Nez Perce.

East of Kamiah on U.S. 12, the **Lolo Trail** marker shows the spot where Lewis and Clark crossed the highway and picked up their old trail on their return trip in 1806. The Nez Perce also came this way in 1877, with General Howard hot on their heels. The sign at **Lolo Pass** also commemorates the Nez Perce trail. It was here in 1805 that Lewis and Clark reentered Idaho after an aborted attempt to negotiate the Salmon River Canyon far to the south.

Reservation Recreation

The Idaho Department of Fish and Game's **Myrtle Beach Campground** offers 16 free sites with no developed water. It's along U.S. 12 east of the Juliaetta turnoff. To fish on the waters of the Nez Perce Reservation, you need a permit from the tribe, available, among other places, at Valley Foods in Lapwai (208/843-2070). Nonresident permits run $12.75 for the first day, $6 for each additional consecutive day.

OROFINO AND VICINITY

The seat of Clearwater County, Orofino's name means "pure gold" or "fine gold" in Spanish, a tribute to the first gold strike in Idaho at nearby Pierce in 1860. The town straddles the banks of the Clearwater River. Logging is the linchpin of the economy; a small park on the north bank of the river has an infomercial for the industry. Recreation also brings in the dollars. In summer, anglers fish the Clearwater, boaters and campers flock to Dworshak Reservoir, and backcountry explorers head up the North Fork of the Clearwater to the Mallard-Larkins

Pioneer Area. In winter, popular pursuits include snowmobiling and both alpine and cross-country skiing.

Dworshak Dam and Reservoir

The North Fork of the Clearwater River was dammed in 1971 by the Army Corps of Engineers, who built Dworshak Dam, the largest straight-axis dam in North America. That's a fancy way of saying it's a straight line across the dam from one end to the other. At 717 feet high, only two dams in the country are higher.

Before the dam was built, the North Fork was used for log drives out of the forests upriver. The dam put an end to the log drives but allowed water access for loggers into previously inaccessible areas. Logs are still towed across the river and hauled out at several locations. In summer, 90-minute tours of the dam are available at the visitors center on the dam's north end (208/476-1255).

Dworshak Reservoir is a favorite spot for boaters, anglers, and water-skiers, many of whom whine profusely when the reservoir is drawn down to help speed salmon smolts to the sea, implying that a muddy shoreline is more of a problem than the extinction of a species. Anglers probe the lake in search of introduced kokanee salmon, stocked rainbow trout, and obese smallmouth bass; a state-record 117.6-ounce smallmouth was caught here in 1982. Idaho Fish and Game's fishing guide to the lake suggests that nymphs and poppers can add a thrill to your fishing experience. Sounds like fun, eh?

The lake spreads its long skinny tendrils 54 miles back upriver—from the air it looks like a giant neuron. Boat ramps are available at Bruce's Eddy on the dam's east side, at Big Eddy marina and day-use area on the west side, and at several other locations. Big Eddy marina offers the only fuel dock on the lake. Boaters can also take advantage of more than 120 "minicamps" scattered around the lake's 184 miles of shoreline. Each of these primitive campsites has a tent pad, an outhouse, a picnic table, and a grill. The sites are free, and most are accessible only by boat.

The Bureau of Reclamation operates **Dent Recreation Area** on the shore of the lake just over Dent Bridge off Elk River Road (Wells Bench Rd.). Here you'll find a boat-launch area, restrooms, and a fish-cleaning station as well as the large **Dent Acres Campground** (208/476-3294, reservations 877/444-6777, fee). The campground features 50 grassy sites on a slope overlooking the lake and offers picnic shelters with tables and grills and a playground. RV sites with full hookups are also available.

Dworshak State Park

Although, the small Dworshak State Park (reservations 208/476-5994, $5 day-use fee) lies just four miles from Dworshak Dam as the osprey flies, humans have to make a 45-minute drive around the west of the lake to get here. The park is 26 miles northwest of Orofino; head downriver from downtown to Ahsahka and follow the signs: up County Road P1 through Cavendish, then east on Freeman Creek Road to the park. You'll find 105 campsites ($14–22)—each with a picnic table and a grill, 46 with hookups—surrounded by trees and open meadows. Swimming, waterskiing, boating, and fishing for kokanee and rainbow trout are the most popular pastimes; others enjoy playing volleyball and horseshoes. Amenities include a shower house and restrooms, a boat ramp, a fish-cleaning station, and a sandy beach. There also are four cabins ($50) available that can sleep up to five.

The Bridges of Clearwater County

Two spectacular bridges cross Dworshak Reservoir far out along its eastern reaches. You'll cross **Dent Bridge** to get to Dent Recreation Area or Elk River. The 1,050-foot-long suspension-span bridge is a smaller version of San Francisco's Golden Gate Bridge, though lacking the Day-Glo orange paint. **Grandad Bridge** is way up the North Fork and connects the town of Headquarters with Elk River. It's a three-span cantilever-deck design; you'll need a Forest Service map to find it.

Swimming and Floating

Travelers looking to beat the summer heat can head to the **community swimming pool** on H Street, just up the hill from the main drag to Grangemont. On the other hand, who needs a pool when the Clearwater River is right down the street? Tubing and raft floating are popular on the river in late spring–summer.

Accommodations

White Pine Motel (222 Brown Ave., Orofino, 208/476-7093 or 800/874-2083, $42–75) offers 18 guest rooms with queen beds and cable TV. Pets are permitted for a small fee.

Helgeson Place Hotel Suites (125 Johnson Ave., Orofino, 208/476-5729 or 800/404-5729, www.helgesonhotel.com, from $75 d) is downtown in a century-old brick building. Its 20 suites (1–2 bedrooms) feature kitchenettes and either king or queen beds. Amenities include tanning booths and a private outdoor jetted tub.

Food

For a good meal downtown, try the local favorite **Ponderosa Restaurant and Lounge** (220 Michigan Ave., Orofino, 208/476-4818, breakfast, lunch, and dinner daily). This family restaurant serves prime rib on weekend evenings.

Information and Services

The **Orofino Chamber of Commerce** (217 1st St., Orofino, 208/476-4335, www.orofino.com) can field your questions about the area. The U.S. Forest Service **Clearwater National Forest Supervisor's Office** (12730 U.S. 12, Orofino, 208/476-8267), just west of town, has lots of brochures, maps, and advice for exploring the nearby backcountry.

NORTH FORK CLEARWATER RIVER
North Fork-Superior Adventure Road

Here is one of the most beautiful backcountry drives in Idaho—a cruise of some 160 miles up the North Fork Clearwater River and over

Hoodoo Pass to Superior, Montana. The Civilian Conservation Corps built the primitive but well-graded road in 1935, and today it's used by loggers, fly-fishers, campers, and those just looking for a relaxing drive through the great outdoors. Wildlife abounds back here—watch out for moose on the road. Bring your camera and binoculars, and don't forget to fill your gas tank and load up the emergency gear before you go; no services are available along the way.

From Orofino, take Grangemont Road to its intersection with Highway 11 and turn left. Soon the highway becomes a narrow corridor through dense forest, leading to the old Potlatch company town of **Headquarters.** During its logging heyday, some 170 million board feet of cut timber was transported here via the Beaver Creek flume. Logging is still going strong in these parts; watch for trucks. Active logging roads are usually flagged with bright ribbons every few miles.

Past Headquarters, Highway 11 becomes Forest Road 247. The road crests a small saddle and then follows babbling Beaver Creek down to its confluence with the North Fork Clearwater River. A few miles east up the North Fork, the pavement ends. From here, the dirt road is narrow and occasionally washboard. At **Bungalow Ranger Station,** Forest Road 247 splits off across the river and winds its way up Orogrande Creek, over French Mountain Pass, and down French Creek to Pierce. This allows you to make a nice loop trip from Orofino.

Beyond Bungalow, Forest Road 250 continues east to Kelly Forks Ranger Station. You can continue straight up Forest Road 250 through Black Canyon, a scenic but rough stretch through old-growth cedar groves beneath steep canyon walls; or turn right and take the longer loop on Forest Road 255 through the old Moose City mining area. This road, the better choice for RVs, joins up with Forest Road 250 again at Deception Gulch, farther east. East of Deception Gulch, Forest Road 250 climbs to the headwaters of the North Fork on Long Creek and hops the Continental Divide over to Superior, Montana, and I-90.

Recreation

The North Fork and its tributaries are popular with anglers hoping to catch west slope cutthroat trout, rainbow trout, and whitefish. One of the tributaries, **Kelly Creek,** is classified a blue-ribbon trout stream. Kelly Creek and the waters that feed it are restricted to catch-and-release fishing. The North Fork is also a favorite for easy **rafting and kayaking** trips. The water level isn't very high; the most fun and challenging floating trips usually take place in May–June.

Many hiking trails leave from Forest Road 250 and wind through thick forests up into the mountains. Of particular interest is the **Mallard-Larkins Pioneer Area,** a 30,500-acre roadless area on the high divide between the North Fork and St. Joe watersheds. Inhabiting the Mallard-Larkins is one of the state's largest mountain goat populations. You might also spy some of the region's resident moose, elk, deer, black bears, or cougars. Access to the Mallard-Larkins is gained via Isabella Creek (Forest Rd. 700, at the Beaver Creek–Clearwater confluence) or Avalanche Ridge; the trailhead is on Forest Road 250 three miles east of Canyon Ranger Station.

Camping

A number of U.S. Forest Service campgrounds line the North Fork. From west to east: **Aquarius** (7 sites, $7), at the Beaver Creek–Clearwater confluence; **Washington Creek** (23 sites, $7); **Weitas** (6 sites, free); **Noe Creek** (6 sites, $7); **Kelly Forks** (14 sites, $7); **Hidden Creek** (13 sites, $7); and **Cedars** (5 sites, free).

WEIPPE

To get to the historic Weippe (WEE-ipe) prairie from Orofino, head south on U.S. 12 for eight miles, and then go east on Highway 11 for about another 12 miles. The story goes that Captain William Clark first saw the Weippe Prairie from high up on the east.

The Lewis and Clark expedition had been picking its way along the Lolo Trail's steep terrain, and the sight of this relatively level prairie must have given Clark renewed hope. He pulled together an advance party and rode ahead to check it out. Arriving on the prairie on September 20, 1805, he surprised three young Nez Perce boys, who tried to hide in the grass. Clark managed to corral two of the boys and convince them he wasn't a danger. Soon Clark and his men were enjoying salmon steaks and camas roots at the Nez Perce village; the expedition was saved.

The prairie today isn't too terribly different than it was back then. The wide-open vistas remain, and at nearby Musselshell Meadows, the camas bulbs still bloom profusely in spring. In summer, Weippe makes a good base camp for hiking or horseback riding along the Lolo Trail. In winter, this rolling prairie makes for great cross-country skiing.

THE LOLO MOTORWAY

Although U.S. 12 roughly follows the route of the Lewis and Clark expedition—at least closely enough to be labeled the Lewis and Clark Highway—the expedition's actual route followed the Nez Perce's Lolo Trail, up on the highlands north of the river.

The Lolo Trail marked the most difficult conditions the expedition had yet faced on their trip west. Crossing the trail in September 1805, they encountered an early fall snowstorm that not only left them wet and cold but drove the wild game down to lower elevations. The expedition's hunters found little or nothing to kill, and the explorers were forced to eat their own horses to survive.

In the 1930s the Civilian Conservation Corps built the 150-mile-long Lolo Motorway (Forest Rd. 500) on or near the original Lolo Trail. The route runs from Lolo Creek south of Pierce over Lolo Pass into Montana. It's a primitive road not suitable for trailers and RVs and is usually covered by snow from sometime in October until early July. The usual off-road precautions apply: bring warm clothing, extra water, and extra food. Unlike Lewis and Clark, you can't eat your ride. If you're traveling west to east, you'll be retracing the Corps of Discovery's 1806 return trip.

Access Guide

From Weippe, head east where Highway 11 makes a 90-degree turn. After about 10 miles is a T intersection and Forest Road 100. Turn right and follow that road about nine miles farther to the junction with Forest Road 500.

From Kamiah, take Forest Road 100 east out of town through Glenwood and follow it another 10 miles to the intersection with Forest Road 500. Heading east to west, the most commonly used access to the trail corridor is Parachute Hill Road (Forest Rd. 569), which turns north off U.S. 12 just east of Powell.

Campground and Cabin

At the junction of Forest Roads 100 and 500 is the primitive **Lolo Creek Campsite** (5 sites, free). Heading farther east on Forest Road 500, you'll pass the **Castle Butte Lookout** (mid-July–mid-Sept., $30), a cabin that sleeps two with a two-night minimum stay; maximum stays may also apply. For reservations, contact the **Lochsa Ranger District Kooskia Office** (502 Lowry St., Kooskia, 208/926-4274).

KAMIAH

Kamiah (KAM-ee-eye) was a favorite winter camp of the Nez Perce, who came here to fish for steelhead in the Clearwater River. Lewis and Clark hung out here for a month on their way back east in spring 1806 while waiting for Lolo Pass to open up. In modern times, the town became dependent on the timber industry. When that industry suffered a downturn, Kamiah attempted to bolster tourism by refurbishing a three-block strip of downtown in a Victorian Western theme. It doesn't really work, but the great outdoors around here is so beautiful, it hardly matters what the town

looks like. Expect to find typical services in this gussied-up little burg.

KOOSKIA

Kooskia (KOO-skee) got its name from the Nez Perce word *kooskooskia,* which Lewis and Clark translated as "clear water." Historians now believe the explorers didn't get it quite right, that it should have been "where the waters join." Either translation proves appropriate for the town, which lies at the confluence of the Middle and South Forks of the Clearwater River. History buffs will want to check out the renovated 1912 **Old Opera House Theatre** (208/926-0094) on the downtown strip. The performance hall has year-round productions and a throwback sarsaparilla bar.

Accommodations

Western Motor Inn (6 Main St., Kooskia, 208/926-0166, www.westernmotorinn.com, $49–89) is a recently remodeled motel in downtown Kooskia with 20 nonsmoking rooms. All rooms have microwaves, refrigerators, and coffeemakers. Other amenities include cable TV and wireless Internet. The motel has a giant white elk on the roof, meaning that hunters are welcome.

Reflections Inn (6873 U.S. 12, Kooskia, 208/926-0855 or 888/926-0855, www.reflectionsinn.com, $79–108) is 11 miles east of Kooskia on 10 acres off U.S. 12, between mile markers 84 and 85. It offers seven guest rooms, each with a queen bed, a private bath, and a private entrance, and there is a hot tub out under the starry skies. There's a common room outfitted with a full kitchen and a lounge area. Rates include a full breakfast and afternoon refreshments.

Information

The U.S. Forest Service **Lochsa Ranger District Kooskia Office** (502 Lowry St., Kooskia, 208/926-4274) can provide local recreation information.

Lewis and Clark Highway

LOWELL

At the small town of Lowell, the Lochsa and Selway Rivers meet to form the Middle Fork of the Clearwater River. The name Lochsa (LOCK-saw) is a Native American word meaning "rough water." The Selway, also far from smooth, was likely named after Montana sheepman Thomas Selway, who ran his herds here around the turn of the 20th century and had a cabin along the river. Lowell is supported almost entirely by recreation. In summer, its motels and campgrounds fill up with rafters, kayakers, anglers, bicyclists, and backpackers.

Accommodations and Camping

Three Rivers Resort (115 Selway Rd., Lowell, 208/926-4430 or 888/926-4430, www.idaho3rivers.com) is the happening spot in little Lowell and has been a mainstay for more than 35 years, owned by the Smith family for all of them. Enjoying prime real estate right where the Lochsa and Selway come together to form the Clearwater River, the resort gets jampacked with river rats in summer. It even runs a busy guide service. Rafters aren't the only ones who enjoy this place, though: Three Rivers has something for every kind of camper, including 40 RV sites ($22.50–25) with hookups, tent sites ($10 pp adults, $5 pp children), a variety of cabins ($125–155), some on the river, and several small motel rooms ($59–69). There's also a pool, three jetted tubs, a restaurant and grocery store, and Lochsa Louie's Bar. In addition, the resort offers a couples-only cabin ($155) up in the woods. Old No. 1 has a fireplace, a jetted tub on the deck, a full bath and kitchen, and great views of the rivers.

Just a few miles west of Lowell, back down U.S. 12, the U.S. Forest Service **Wild Goose Campground** (4 sites, $8) is right on the north bank of the Clearwater.

UP THE SELWAY RIVER

Forest Road 223 (Selway Rd.) crosses the Lochsa River at Lowell and follows the Selway

Three Rivers Resort in Lowell

© DANA HOPPER-KELLY

River southeast. It dead-ends at a trailhead about 25 miles later, just past the 1912 Selway Falls Guard Station. The road is paved as far as the O'Hara Creek Bridge; after that it can turn washboard.

Amazingly enough, the road up the Selway seems *under* used. The river can be jammed down at Three Rivers Resort, but in a few minutes' drive up here you might find a great spot all to yourself. Deer feed in the grasslands along the riverbank, adding to the idyllic landscape.

Fenn Historic Ranger Station and Forest Service Cabins

Four miles down Forest Road 223 (Selway Rd.) you'll find this trim green-and-white building housing the Nez Perce National Forest's **Moose Creek Ranger District** Fenn Ranger Station (208/926-4258), which handles reservations for two Forest Service rental cabins in the area;

you can also reserve them through the National Recreation Reservation Service (877/444-6777, www.recreation.gov). The **Meadow Creek Cabin** (mid-May–mid-Sept., $40) is 15 miles up the Meadow Creek National Recreation Trail and sleeps eight. **Lookout Butte** (mid-June–late Sept., $40) is a 60-foot-high tower south of the Selway River above Goddard Creek that sleeps four. Small children are discouraged because of the tower's height.

Across the road from Fenn Ranger Station, **Selway Pond** (also called Fenn Pond) is a stocked trout pond with fishing piers, a picnic area, and an encircling wooden plank walkway—all wheelchair friendly.

Selway Falls

Twenty-one miles up the road from Lowell you'll come upon awesome Selway Falls. It's not a high graceful waterfall but a low, wide, awesomely powerful man-eater. Here the Selway River pounds down in a thundering drop between house-size granite blocks. Woe to the unfortunate paddler who misses the warning signs strung across the river upstream;

this white water would undoubtedly be his or her last.

Hiking

The Forest Service has laid out a one-mile **interpretive trail** at O'Hara Creek Campground, explaining the agency's efforts to rehabilitate the salmon-spawning grounds. Road-building and logging at one time clogged O'Hara Creek with silt, and the fish populations declined. The interpretive sites are situated along the road, so you could even drive to them. Along the way you might spot one of the area's resident ospreys, beavers, or belted kingfishers.

Two National Recreation Trails make for longer, more strenuous day jaunts or casual overnighters. The **East Boyd-Glover-Roundtop National Recreation Trail**, a U-shaped 14.5-mile trail, climbs the east side of Boyd Creek up to Roundtop Mountain, then descends the east side of Glover Creek farther east. You can loop back to the car along the main Selway Road, a scenic little stroll. The **Meadow Creek National Recreation**

© DANA HOPPER-KELLY

Selway Falls

Trail is part of the Idaho State Centennial Trail. It leaves from Slim's Camp and follows Meadow Creek south. The first four miles are relatively level, winding through lush cedar and fir forest along the creek bottom. The trail then begins to climb and continues south as far as you want to go—be it to the Sawtooths or Murphy Hot Springs, near the Nevada border.

Trailheads in the area—**Big Fog Saddle** (at the end of Forest Rd. 319), **Race Creek** (at the end of the main Selway Road Forest Rd. 223), and **Indian Hill** (at the end of Forest Rd. 290)—provide hiker access into the Selway-Bitterroot Wilderness.

Camping

A string of U.S. Forest Service campgrounds line the Selway up as far as Selway Falls. From northwest (Lowell) to southeast (Selway Falls), these include **Johnson Bar** (9 sites, $6); **O'Hara Bar** (32 sites, $10), with good wheelchair access; **Rackliff** (6 sites, $5); **Twenty-Mile Bar** (2 sites, free); **Boyd Creek** (6 sites, $5); **Glover Creek** (7 sites, $5); **Selway Falls** (7 sites, $5); **Race Creek** (3 sites, free); and south up Forest Road 443, **Slim's Camp** (2 sites, free).

For more information, contact the Forest Service **Moose Creek Ranger District** Fenn Ranger Station (208/926-4258).

◪ FOLLOWING THE LOCHSA RIVER

From Lowell, U.S. 12 follows the Lochsa River northeast to its headwaters, then continues over Lolo Pass into Montana. Keep in mind it's 64 miles up the highway to the next services at Powell.

The Lochsa Face, a steep 73,000-acre strip of land between the river and the Selway-Bitterroot Wilderness, runs parallel to the Lochsa's south bank. Elk, moose, and mountain lions inhabit this wild paradise of stark cliffs, steaming hot springs, and crystalline trout streams.

Lochsa Historical Ranger Station

Spring 1934 was wet, cool, and green in Central Idaho, but a long heat wave began in June that turned the lush vegetation into a tinderbox. On August 10 a dry lightning storm hit the Clearwater River area, sparking a number of blazes, including the disastrous Pete King fire just downstream from the ranger station. Thanks to abundant ladder fuels, the Pete King blaze turned into a crown fire that rapidly spread and burned out of control for 44 days before a heavy, prolonged rain arrived and extinguished the flames. At one point, fire surrounded the ranger station and threatened to incinerate it, but the 200 firefighters who had gathered here valiantly fought it off. Two were killed by falling trees, but the ranger station and the rest of the firefighters were saved. In the end, the fire charred some 375 square miles.

Today the Lochsa Ranger Station (208/926-4274, 9 A.M.–5 P.M. daily summer, free) serves as tribute to both the Pete King crews and all of Idaho's forest firefighters. A self-guided tour leads from a museum building, full of historical photos, around the grounds to several outbuildings that contain old tools of the firefighting trade as well as the humble 1930s-era furnishings once used by the fire crews. The site is 48 miles east of Kooskia on U.S. 12.

Colgate Licks and Vicinity

A large turnout on the north side of the highway marks this one-mile loop nature trail to a natural salt lick. It's a nice place to stop and stretch your legs, and wildlife photographers will find this an excellent spot to try to bag a trophy portrait. A bit farther east is Jerry Johnson Campground, and a bit farther east of that the trail to **Jerry Johnson Hot Springs** begins. Look for the pack bridge crossing the river and the cars parked along the road nearby—Jerry Johnson is one of the best-known hike-in hot springs in Idaho. The trail leads across the bridge and up Warm Springs Creek for about a mile to an area dotted with hot pools. In winter, the hot springs make a great ski or snowshoe excursion. You may never get the place to yourself, but you can bet the people you share a hot soak with will be cool.

Powell

Lochsa Lodge (115 Powell Rd., Lolo, MT, 208/942-3405, www.lochsalodge.com, year-round, $45–105), at milepost 163 on U.S. 12, is a high-mountain retreat alongside the upper Lochsa River just a short distance from the Selway-Bitterroot Wilderness boundary. Although it has been here since 1929, it burned to the ground in 2001 and has been entirely rebuilt. The lodge offers both motel rooms and private log cabins along with a store with gas and a restaurant. Favorite winter activities include cross-country skiing and soaking in the nearby hot springs.

Just a little farther down the road past the lodge you'll find the U.S. Forest Service **Powell Ranger Station** (208/942-3113).

Elk Summit Road (Forest Rd. 360) leaves U.S. 12 just east of Powell and leads south to a trailhead into the Selway-Bitterroot Wilderness. At the trailhead is the Forest Service's primitive **Elk Summit Campground** (15 sites, free). It's not hard to tell where the official wilderness area begins: It's the part that's not clearcut by loggers.

DeVoto Memorial Cedar Grove

Students of Idaho history remember Bernard DeVoto as a statesmen and editor of the annotated *Journals of Lewis & Clark*. A sign here explains:

> This majestic cedar grove is dedicated to the memory of Bernard DeVoto (1897-1955), conservationist, author, and historian. He often camped here while studying the journals of Lewis and Clark. At his request his ashes were scattered over this area.

The grove is truly magnificent. Towering cedars on either side of the highway shade the cool forest floor covered with bracken ferns, foam flowers, maidenhair ferns, sword ferns, and dogwoods. Short loop trails wind through the woods; the one on the south side of the highway offers interpretive signs and leads to picnic tables by the rushing river.

Lolo Pass

Atop the Continental Divide on the Idaho-Montana state line is Lolo Pass (5,233 feet). A spiffy new visitors center tells the tales of the Nez Perce and of the Lewis and Clark expedition. Outside, a 0.25-mile interpretive trail circles a restored wetlands area in warm weather. In winter, snowmobilers and cross-country skiers will find a warming hut.

Running the Lochsa River

White-water enthusiasts from around the world seek out the Lochsa River, considered one of the country's most difficult. Lewis and Clark took one look at it and decided to struggle along the steep canyon walls rather than attempt to float downstream. The Lochsa tumbles furiously off Lolo Pass in a swirling, crashing torrent. Among its more than 60 rapids are nine rated either Class IV+ or V-, including Ten Pin Alley, Bloody Mary, the Grim Reaper, and Lochsa Falls. Although U.S. 12 runs right alongside the river, wide-eyed rafters will be far too panicked trying to read the water ahead to care about or even notice the cars going by.

Three Rivers Rafting (208/926-4430, www.idaho3rivers.com) charges around $100 for a one-day white-water run on the Lochsa, which includes lunch, a wetsuit, a paddle jacket, a helmet, a life jacket, shuttle service, and hot tubs and showers after the trip.

Fishing

As with the Selway River, chinook salmon, steelhead trout, and Pacific lamprey come up the Lochsa River to spawn. Cutthroat trout, mountain whitefish, and bull trout are also resident. Bull trout fishing is prohibited along the entire river. All waters of the main Lochsa, and Lower Crooked Fork Creek from White Sand Creek to Brushy Fork Creek, are restricted to artificial flies and lures, single barbless hooks, no bait. All other tributaries have no bait restrictions. The main Lochsa above Wilderness Gateway Campground is catch-and-release only, as is the section of Crooked Fork Creek from

White Sand Creek to Brushy Fork Creek. For opening dates and other information, contact **Idaho Department of Fish and Game** (208/334-3700).

Camping

Numerous U.S. Forest Service campgrounds line the Lochsa. From Lowell heading east are **Apgar Creek** (7 sites, $8); **Knife Edge** (5 sites, free); the humongous **Wilderness Gateway** (89 sites, $8), with wheelchair access; **Jerry Johnson** (19 sites, $8), which also has wheelchair access; **Wendover** (26 sights, $8); and **Lewis & Clark** (17 sites, $8).

Moscow and Vicinity

Leaving Lewiston and heading north, U.S. 95 climbs steeply out of the Clearwater River Valley and onto a vast tableland of mostly treeless rolling hills called the Palouse. This is rich agricultural land planted with wheat, barley, chickpeas, and lentils. Each spring when the dryland crops sprout from the furrowed hills, the landscape becomes a sea of green stretching as far as the eye can see.

The Palouse extends north from Lewiston virtually all the way to Coeur d'Alene, spreading west across the border into Washington and east of U.S. 95 about 30 miles before giving way to mountains. Plopped down in

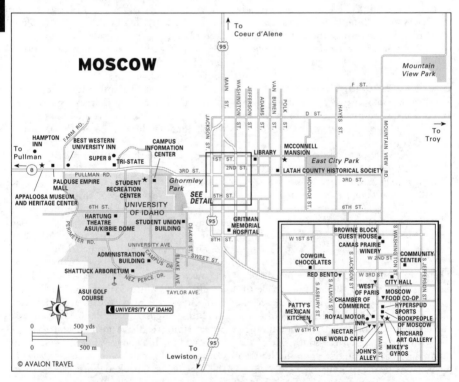

© DANA HOPPER-KELLY

University of Idaho

the middle of the Palouse as if set down by a twister, Moscow (population 23,000) is a cultural oasis in this wide-open sparsely populated area. It's the home of the University of Idaho and has coffeehouses, brewpubs, used-book stores, nightlife, and some fine dining—all in a small town with a decidedly friendly, laid-back atmosphere.

Early on, the town was called Hog Heaven thanks to the abundance of hog food (camas roots) covering the prairie. When the town took on a more permanent character, the self-respecting townsfolk sought a name with a bit more panache. They tried Paradise for a while but ended up with Moscow (MOS-coe) when an early postmaster decided the area reminded him of a northeastern Pennsylvania town by that name.

SIGHTS
◖ University of Idaho
As a bone thrown to north Idaho to convince it not to become part of Washington, the Idaho Territorial Legislature established

the University of Idaho (208/885-6111, www. uidaho.edu) here in 1889. Idaho's oldest university, the school has about 12,000 students in 10 colleges. The main 320-acre campus, on the west side of downtown, climbs a small hill overlooking the Palouse. The buildings reflect a variety of architectural styles—from the centerpiece Gothic administration building complete with carillon to the **Kibbie Dome,** a big bloated bubble hosting indoor sporting events, concerts, and conventions. The school also boasts the state's largest **library**—housing 1.6 million volumes and government documents—and the **University of Idaho Press,** a superb resource publishing an extensive catalog of books on the history, natural history, geography, art, and literature of Idaho and the Northwest.

Concerts, lectures, stage productions, and other events take place at the school's modern and acoustically superior **Hartung Theater.** Gardeners and outdoor lovers will enjoy a walk through both the **Shattuck Arboretum,** a 14-acre forest plot planted with evergreens and hardwoods, and the **University of Idaho Arboretum and Botanical Garden,** a 63-acre living laboratory featuring trees and shrubs from around the world. Spring is an especially beautiful time for a visit, when the lilacs, crabapples, and cherry trees come into bloom.

Campus tours are available at the **Student Union Building** (709 Deakin Ave., Moscow). Visitors may park on campus at metered spaces any time, subject to the restrictions posted on each meter. Visitors may obtain free short-term parking permits at the Campus Information Center (Pullman Rd. at W. 3rd St., Moscow). The permits are required for nonmetered parking year-round, including all vacation periods.

Appaloosa Museum and Heritage Center

The Dalmatian of the horse world, the spotted Appaloosa was prized by northern Idaho's Nez Perce people as a rugged and hardy breed. Early pioneers called this horse "a Palousey" due to its prevalence on the Palouse Prairie. That slang moniker became corrupted to "Appaloosa" over the years—at least, that's how the story goes. The Appaloosa Horse Club celebrates the historic breed at the Appaloosa Museum and Heritage Center (2720 W. Pullman Rd., Moscow, 208/882-5578, 10 A.M.–5 P.M. Mon.–Fri., 10 A.M.–4 P.M. Sat. year-round, suggested donation $2 pp, $4 family) right at the Washington state line. Inside you'll find Appy-related historical artifacts, photos, and paintings as well as the Appaloosa Hall of Fame. In summer you'll likely find a corral of the critters out back.

McConnell Mansion

On the east side of downtown Moscow lies the Fort Russell Historic District—a jewel box of gorgeous 19th-century homes presiding over quiet tree-lined streets. One of these gems, the 1886 McConnell Mansion (110 S. Adams St., 208/882-1004, 1–4 P.M. Tues.–Sat., donation) was once the home of William "Poker Bill" McConnell, Idaho's third governor. Now the Victorian Gothic houses a museum

offering period-furnished rooms and changing historical exhibits. It is operated by the Latah County Historical Society, which also publishes two walking-tour guides, one to other historical residences in the Fort Russell district and the other to historical buildings downtown. You can pick up copies of those guides at the McConnell Mansion or at the chamber of commerce office (411 S. Main St., Moscow, 208/882-1800, www.moscowchamber.com) downtown.

Prichard Art Gallery

The university's downtown art gallery, Prichard Art Gallery (414 S. Main St., Moscow, 208/885-3586, Mon.–Sat., call for hours) showcases student, faculty, and regional art and hosts lectures, readings, and workshops.

Camas Prairie Winery

Camas Prairie Winery (110 S. Main St., Moscow, 208/882-0214 or 800/616-0214, www.camasprairiewinery.com, noon–6:30 P.M. Mon.–Sat.) is north Idaho's oldest winery, in business since 1983. It produces and sells a number of varietals, including five sparkling wines, along with unusual items such as honey mead, herbed wine vinegar, and wine jellies.

RECREATION
Parks

Moscow boasts nearly a dozen city parks—some appropriate for a quiet picnic, others for a rousing game of one-on-one. **Ghormley Park** (W. 3rd St. and Home St., Moscow), adjacent to the University of Idaho campus, includes a municipal swimming pool, softball fields, tennis courts, barbecues, and horseshoe pits. **East City Park** (E. 3rd St. and S. Hayes St., Moscow) provides a basketball court, a sand volleyball court, horseshoe pits, playgrounds, and picnic areas. **Mountain View Park,** a big, open space clear out on the east edge of town (take F St. east to Mountain View Rd.), offers plenty of space for you and your pooch to get some exercise. In addition to the usual park facilities, you'll find a bike path along Paradise Creek.

Latah County's **Robinson Park** (2094 Robinson Park Rd., Moscow) encompasses almost 55 acres of open space, including picnic areas, two softball diamonds, a sand volleyball court, horseshoe pits, a nature trail, and an ice skating rink.

For a complete list of parks or more information, contact the **Moscow Parks and Recreation Department** (208/883-7085, www.moscow.id.us).

Recreation Center

The University of Idaho's newish **Student Recreation Center** (1000 Paradise Creek St., Moscow, 208/885-7529, daily year-round) has a 55-foot freestanding climbing pinnacle, the largest of its kind on any college campus in the United States. Other amenities include a running track, free weights, circuit training, and locker rooms with saunas. Nonstudents can use the center for $6 per visit. The rec center is on the north side of campus, not far from the campus information center.

The **Outdoor Program Office** (208/885-6170, 10 A.M.–4:30 P.M. Mon.–Fri.) is also in the rec center. Stop by to rent a wide range of equipment or to learn about upcoming classes and trips, which are usually open to nonstudents.

Bill Chipman Trail

This paved seven-mile trail links Moscow with Pullman, Washington. Built on a former railroad bed, it has a nice gentle grade, and it's well-used by cyclists, strollers, joggers, and in-line skaters. Find it on the north edge of the University of Idaho campus or anywhere south of Pullman Road, which it parallels.

Mountain Biking

The city's fat-tire fanatics consider **Moscow Mountain,** five miles north of Moscow, the premier mountain-biking destination. To get here, you can take either U.S. 95 north to Lewis Road then Lewis east to Foothill Road, or take D Street east to Mountain View Road, and Mountain View north to Moscow Mountain Road. Most of the Moscow Mountain trails

are on private land, so camping is verboten and you should be on your best behavior.

Other worthwhile biking areas in the region include McCroskey State Park and Palouse Divide Adventure Road.

Golf

The **University of Idaho Golf Course** (1215 Nez Perce Dr., Moscow, 208/885-6171, Apr.–Nov., $17–25), on the west side of campus, is open to the public. The hilly, often windy 18-hole, par-72 course offers a pro shop, refreshments, a driving range, cart rentals, and lessons.

Outfitters

For specialized outdoor gear beyond what Tri-State can provide, check out **Hyperspud Sports** (402 S. Main St., Moscow, 208/883-1150, 10 A.M.–6 P.M. Mon.–Fri., 9 A.M.–6 P.M. Sat., noon–4 P.M. Sun.), which carries a great selection of mountaineering and climbing equipment, tents, backpacks, and extreme sports gear.

ENTERTAINMENT AND EVENTS
Nightlife

If you want to throw back some beers and listen to live music, head to **John's Alley** (114 E. 6th St., Moscow, 208/883-7662, www.alleyvault.com), a popular bar that hosts a bevy of touring bands and local musicians such as Tony Furtado, Luau Cinder, and Clumsy Lovers. Burgeoning indie superstar Josh Ritter hails from these parts, so don't be surprised to see him jam here.

The Garden Lounge (313 S. Main St., Moscow, 208/882-8513, until late daily) is an intellectual dive bar downtown. Average joes, college professors, and other cerebral types come for stiff drinks and stimulating conversation, like whether or not Bukowski was a misogynist or just a true admirer of women.

Performing Arts

The **Idaho Repertory Theater** (tickets 208/885-7212) has presented summer stock productions in Moscow for half a century. Affiliated with the University of Idaho's Department of Theater Arts, the troupe's home stage is the E. W. Hartung Theater on campus.

Lionel Hampton Jazz Festival

Los Angeles Times jazz critic Leonard Feather has called this event "the number-one jazz festival in the world." Hosted by the University of Idaho's Lionel Hampton School of Music in late February, the festival (208/885-7212 or 888/884-3246, www.uidaho.edu/jazzfest) draws many of the biggest names in jazz to a four-day blowout of concerts, clinics, and student competitions. It's a rare opportunity to see lots of the masters all in one place— jazz buffs shouldn't miss it. Headliner concerts are presented in Kibbie Dome on the university campus. Tickets go on sale in early December.

Off-Campus Events

Spring is in the air when the **Renaissance Fair** (www.moscowrenfair.org) comes to town; on the first weekend in May, bold knights, fair maidens, and tankards of grog take thee back to the days before silverware and indoor plumbing. Music fills Moscow's East City Park during **Rendezvous in the Park,** the second and third weekends in July. The festival features various styles of music, from blues to bluegrass, and plenty of kids' activities to keep the little dudes happy. In September, the **Latah County Fair** comes to town beginning the second weekend after Labor Day. For information on any of these events, call the Moscow Chamber of Commerce (411 S. Main St., Moscow, 208/882-1800, www.moscowchamber.com).

SHOPPING

Bookpeople of Moscow (521 S. Main St., Moscow, 208/882-7957, www.bookpeople.net, 9 A.M.–8 P.M. daily) provides the perfect place to hunt for that old copy of Richard Brautigan's *Rommel Drives on Deep into Egypt.* There's a coffee bar here too.

Cowgirl Chocolates (428 3rd St., Moscow, 888/882-4098, www.cowgirlchocolates.com) is a fun little chocolate shop with a bent on merchandising. Besides dark chocolate truffles, assorted seasoned bars, and caramels, the place has T-shirts, hats, and shoulder bags emblazoned with a cowgirl silhouette. Cowgirls and chocolate: pretty cool.

Highway 8 westbound to Pullman is also called Pullman Road, and it is where you'll find **Tri-State** (1104 Pullman Rd., Moscow, 208/882-4555, www.t-state.com), which bills itself as "Idaho's Most Interesting Store." That claim is debatable, but the large venue does sell all things outdoors, including gear for camping, backpacking, kayaking, fishing, and snowshoeing. Also expect to see name-brand shoes and clothing alongside shelves filled with gardening, hardware, and kitchen supplies.

If that isn't enough, head to the **Palouse Mall** (1850 W. Pullman Rd., Moscow, 208/882-8893, 10 A.M.–9 P.M. Mon.–Sat., 11 A.M.–6 P.M. Sun.), a big modern supermall with about 60 stores.

ACCOMMODATIONS

Most of Moscow's motels cluster along one of two strips. The older, established motels are along Main Street (U.S. 95), in or close to downtown, while the newer budget chains and a few fancier places are 5–10 blocks from downtown along Pullman Road (Hwy. 8), which runs west from downtown to Pullman, Washington. The Pullman Road lodgings are convenient to the University of Idaho campus, the big shopping mall, and a gauntlet of fast-food establishments. In addition to the motels, there are a couple of nice B&Bs in the country just outside town.

It's a good idea to reserve ahead for a stay in Moscow; there aren't many motels, and everything gets booked up well in advance anytime a major event happens at either the University of Idaho or nearby Washington State University. If you can't find a room through the usual channels, contact **Moscow/Pullman Bedfinders** (208/882-9716, www.moscowpullmanbedfinders.com), which helps locate overflow bed-and-breakfast accommodations (from $75) during big college weekends when the motels are full.

$50-100

At the low end of this category, you'll find the 60-room **Super 8** (175 Peterson Dr., Moscow, 208/883-1503, from $71 d). It's four blocks from campus, so rates will be higher during special events at the university.

Downtown, the no-frills **Royal Motor Inn** (120 W. 6th St., Moscow, 208/882-2581, $40–115) has 38 guest rooms with cable TV and high-speed Internet. Pets are allowed.

Best Western University Inn (1516 W. Pullman Rd., Moscow, 208/882-0550 or 800/325-8765, www.uinnmoscow.com, from $85 d) offers 173 guest rooms, an indoor pool, a jetted tub, a sauna, a fitness area, a restaurant, and a lounge.

Behind the Palouse Mall, the **La Quinta Inn** (185 Warbonnet Dr., Moscow, 208/882-5365, from $89 d) is a pleasant place to stay, with an indoor pool and hot tub, a fitness center, and a big breakfast bar.

$100-150

For those who prefer quieter, more private lodging, why not rent an entire house? It may not be big, but the **Little Green Guesthouse** (1020 S. Adams St., Moscow, 208/669-1654, www.littlegreenguesthouse.com, $100–130) has its charms. This one-bedroom cottage is in a mellow neighborhood within walking distance of downtown. Amenities include a full kitchen, a queen bed, satellite TV, free Wi-Fi, and a hammock in the shade. Pets are not allowed.

Equally cool is the 【 **Browne Block Guest House** (112 S. Main St., Moscow, 208/883-3661, www.browneblockguesthouse.com, $110 first night, $85 second night), a private downtown apartment above **Camas Prairie Winery** in an 1890 brick building. This one-bedroom suite is decked out with antique furniture and a full kitchen. Other amenities include a queen bed, free Wi-Fi, cable TV, a laundry room, and a parking permit.

FOOD
Upscale Fare

Serving excellent contemporary Northwest cuisine is the modus operandi at the 【 **Red Door** (215 S. Main St., Moscow, 208/882-7830, www.red-door-restaurant.com, dinner 5:30–9:30 P.M. Mon.–Sat., brunch 9 A.M.–1 P.M. Sat.–Sun., lounge 4 P.M.–late daily, entrées $11–33), a farm-to-fork restaurant downtown. A multitude of local foodstuffs end up on the seasonal menus, and the dining room and lounge area are as swanky as it gets in this little college town. Grab a booth and dig into small plates such as seared polenta with romesco (red pepper and almond sauce) and a delightful beet salad with spinach, hazelnut vinaigrette, and sheep's milk feta. Order a bottle of Northwestern wine, which should play well with larger plates like Thai coconut shrimp, pan-seared wild sockeye salmon, and filet mignon crowned with house-made bacon and blue cheese.

In Friendship Square, you can take a little trip to France at **West of Paris** (403 S. Main St., Moscow, 208/596-8189, www.westofparis.com, from 5 P.M. Tues.–Sat., entrées $21–38), where chef Francis Foucachon dishes up classic Lyonnaise fare with contemporary upgrades. The dining room is classic too, with crisp white tablecloths and elegant glass chandeliers. Enjoy the lobster bisque, trout amandine, baked escargot in parsley butter, and a terrine layered with duck, pork, truffle mushrooms, and pistachios. Multi-course fixed price menus also are available. As expected, the wine list favors French labels, yet some Walla Walla Valley wines are offered as well.

Also downtown, you'll find 【 **Nectar** (105 W. 6th St., Moscow, 208/882-5914, from 4 P.M. Mon.–Sat., entrées $9–24), a hip newcomer to Moscow's restaurant scene. This stylish little place, with exposed brick walls and a long wood bar, serves food designed with wine in mind. Order a bottle of Washington wine and some artisanal cheeses with honeycomb while perusing the main menu, which has upscale dishes like white truffle pasta, grilled lamb chops with preserved lemon couscous,

NORTH-CENTRAL IDAHO

MOSCOW'S ORGANIC FARMING REVOLUTION

The Palouse has long been a bastion of traditional farming. Dryland (with no irrigation) farmers here produce some of the largest lentil and chickpea crops in the United States. But in recent years, an unparalleled organic farming scene has taken hold in the Palouse, anchored by the vibrant Moscow Farmers Market (8 A.M.–1 P.M. Sat. May–Oct.). Organic farmers set up booths at this popular public market held downtown in Friendship Square. Moscovites come in droves for spring onions, garlic, asparagus, raspberries, pattypan squash, heirloom tomatoes, eggplant, and other impeccably fresh organic produce. And when they're not shopping at the farmers market, many folks around here connect with local community-supported agriculture (CSA) farmers, who provide a weekly larder of organic produce and eggs for their consumer members.

Another exciting development is the Moscow Community Garden, spearheaded by the Palouse-Clearwater Environmental Institute (PCEI, 208/882-1444, www.pcei.org), a nonprofit group with a focus on sustainable agriculture and other earth-friendly educational programs. The community garden has become a social hub for like-minded people who want to grow their own organic food. If you would like to tour the Moscow Community Garden, contact the PCEI, or just stop by garden at 1050 West C Street – people are friendly and would gladly show you around.

fresh garlic at Moscow Farmers Market

© DANA HOPPER-KELLY

and a beef tenderloin burger with sun-dried tomato ketchup.

Ethnic Cuisine

◖ **Patty's Mexican Kitchen** (450 W. 6th St., Moscow, 208/883-3984, www.pattysmexican-kitchen.com, 9 A.M.–8 P.M. Tues.–Sat., around $8) near the university is the spot to go for Mexican grub. Sit on the deck next to the *barbacoa* pit and devour a big burrito and a cold *cerveza*. The menu also has torta sandwiches, tamales, fish tacos, and enchiladas. The freshly made salsa is particularly good.

If you're craving Japanese and Korean food, head to **Red Bento** (215 W. 3rd St., Moscow, 208/596-4041, lunch and dinner daily) near downtown. Expect to find everything from chicken katsu to sushi rolls to beef bulgogi, a spicy Korean-style stir-fry served with aromatic rice. The teriyaki (chicken, beef, salmon, and pork) is what keeps the masses coming back.

Gambino's Italian Restaurant (308 W. 6th St., Moscow, 208/882-4545, lunch and dinner daily, entrées $8–11) offers pizza, spaghetti and meatballs, and chicken cacciatora del padrone. The atmosphere alone is worth the price: red-and-white checkered tablecloths you can really put your elbows on. Just don't let Mama Gambino catch you.

Cheap Eats

It's imperative that a college town have cheap eats, but oddly enough, Moscow doesn't have any pizza-by-the-slice joints. Here are two good places where you can eat on the fly: Locals have filed into **Mikey's Gyros** (527 S. Main St., Moscow, 208/882-0780, under $5) for more than 30 years. Tucked away in an old mall downtown, this restaurant counter puts out various gyro sandwiches, falafel, hummus platters, spinach pie, and tabbouleh, a bulgur wheat salad with lemon, scallions, and parsley.

For steamed bagel sandwiches, try **Moscow Bagel** (310 S. Main St., Moscow, 208/882-5242, 7 A.M.–3 A.M. daily), a little deli that opens early and stays open late, where you can score deli sandwiches and chewy bagels with traditional fillings like lox and cream cheese and garlicky hummus.

Breakfast and Coffee

The Breakfast Club (501 S. Main St., Moscow, 208/882-6481, 6 A.M.–2 P.M. Mon.–Fri., 7 A.M.–2 P.M. Sat.–Sun., under $10) serves traditional morning fare with a twist. Try the huckleberry zucchini bread, French toast Benedict, or a chicken-fried steak biscuit. You also can get omelets, flapjacks, and inventive egg scrambles. The restaurant serves lunch to boot.

For coffee and conversation, check out ◖ **One World Café** (S. Main St. and E. 6th St., Moscow, 208/883-3537, www.one-world-cafe. biz, 6:30 A.M.–11 P.M. Mon.–Fri., 7 A.M.–11 P.M. Sat.–Sun.). Relax in one of the comfy chairs and sip an espresso drink made from locally roasted organic beans, or a cup of loose-leaf tea. The small kitchen turns out freshly baked scones, cinnamon rolls, brownies, biscotti, and quiche. Expect live acoustic music and other performances at night.

Groceries

For organic veggies, fresh juices, ginseng ginger ale, whole-grain breads, and the like, head for **Moscow Food Co-op** (121 E. 5th St., Moscow, 208/882-8537, 7:30 A.M.–9 P.M. daily). The store also has a great beer and wine selection. Almost everyone in town shops at **Moscow Farmers Market** (8 A.M.–1 P.M. Sat.), held in Friendship Square (403 S. Main St., Moscow).

INFORMATION

You can learn more about the town at **Moscow Chamber of Commerce** (411 S. Main St., Moscow, 208/882-1800, www.moscowchamber.com). Moscow has a **National Public Radio** affiliate station, KRFA (91.7 FM).

GETTING THERE

Pullman-Moscow Regional Airport (PUW, 3200 Airport Complex N., Pullman, WA, 509/334-4555), just across the state line, is served by **Horizon Air** (800/547-9308). Rental cars are available at the airport, and most motels offer free shuttle service to guests.

Across the Palouse

Outside Moscow in every direction, two-lane roads wind through pastoral countryside, making lazy curves over and around the scenic, gently rolling hills of the Palouse. It's great for road biking. Dotting the farmland are tidy villages and hamlets, many left over from the logging days. They're commonly tucked away in the draws between the hills, which helps give most of them a pleasant, cozy feel. Time seems to slow down out here, measured not so much by the ticking of the clock as by the turning of the leaves, the first snowfall of winter, foals in the pasture, or laughter at the swimming hole.

U.S. 95 TO COEUR D'ALENE
McCroskey State Park

Moscow mountain bikers probably make the most use of this odd little state park (day-use $5). The reserve was the brainchild and labor of love of eastern Washington resident Virgil McCroskey, son of homesteaders who came west from Tennessee after the Civil War. He wanted to create a park dedicated to his mother, Mary Minerva McCroskey, and indirectly dedicated to all the Northwest's pioneer women. He bought 4,500 acres, built the roads, cleared viewpoints, and put in picnic areas and campsites, envisioning an end result similar to the Skyline Drive route through Great Smoky Mountains park in his native Tennessee. He attempted to donate the park to the state, only to have the state refuse it because there was no money for maintenance. In 1955 a deal was worked out where the state would accept the park if McCroskey would maintain it for 15 years. In 1970 his obligation came to an end and McCroskey promptly died. Since then, the state has taken responsibility for the area but has kept it minimally developed. You'll never run into crowds, even in midsummer.

The park is about 20 miles north of Moscow along a tall wooded ridgetop with great views of the Palouse. Coming up U.S. 95, watch for the turn onto Skyline Drive—the street sign is the only sign you'll see—at the crest of the hill

on the west (left) side of the highway. It's a terrible blind turn across the highway; be careful, although there's not much you can do except make the turn as fast as possible and hope for the best.

Skyline Drive makes a long run down the ridge past viewpoints, a trailhead, and a nice picnic area, then swings north, giving you a choice of either dropping west into Washington or north and east to DeSmet.

If you're coming from Coeur d'Alene instead of Moscow, turn in at DeSmet, continue for about six miles, and turn left on King Valley Road, just past the cemetery. Follow that road through the valley and up the mountain, eventually reaching signs marking Skyline Drive. For more information, contact the Idaho Parks Department's North Region headquarters (2885 Kathleen Ave., Coeur d'Alene, 208/769-1511).

DeSmet and Tensed

Heading north on U.S. 95, just before you come to DeSmet you enter the Coeur d'Alene Indian Reservation. DeSmet, Tensed, Plummer, and Worley are all reservation towns. Other than the route to McCroskey State Park, there's nothing in DeSmet for the casual visitor, although photographers might appreciate the rolling farmland and open vistas.

The town was named after an early Jesuit missionary, Father Pierre Jean de Smet. The Belgian-born de Smet arrived in north Idaho in 1842 and began a mission near today's town of St. Maries. He became a good friend to the Coeur d'Alene people and succeeded in converting many of them to Christianity. The original mission was built on the St. Joe River floodplain. After being inundated on several occasions, the mission was moved to Cataldo and again in 1876 to present-day DeSmet to keep the Indians out of the way of the Silver Valley miners. A new mission was built, and the town that grew around it was named in the missionary's honor. The mission is no longer standing.

Tensed was originally a "suburb" of DeSmet, but when it grew big enough to get its own post office, it needed its own name. The residents applied for the name Temsed, which is DeSmet spelled backwards. The postal service misprinted it, and the town became Tensed.

Plummer and Worley

Plummer is the commercial center of the Coeur d'Alene Reservation. Although small, it offers sufficient visitor services to make it a good base camp for exploring Heyburn State Park—six miles east on Highway 5—and the northern Palouse country. Farming and logging are two important mainstays of the area's economy, and Plummer supplies those industries and their workers.

Worley, named for a onetime superintendent of the reservation, is home to the tribe's major cash cow, the **Coeur d'Alene Casino** (27068 S. U.S. 95, Worley, 800/523-2464, www.cdacasino.com). The glitzy venture entices passersby with high-stakes bingo, video pull-tab machines, and virtual card tables. The casino also has a hotel, restaurants, and a golf course.

After passing through Worley, the highway bends around Lake Coeur d'Alene (out of sight to the east) through more beautiful rolling farmland interspersed with wooded hillocks. You won't see the lake until just before you drop down across the Spokane River and into the city of Coeur d'Alene.

ELK RIVER AND VICINITY

If you take Highway 8 east from Moscow, it eventually ends at Elk River, a remote town founded in 1909 by the Potlatch Timber company. Potlatch built the world's largest electrically powered sawmill, and the Milwaukee Railroad soon arrived to haul out the lumber. Elk River thrived until 1927, when Potlatch built a bigger and better mill in Lewiston. Elk River's decline was exacerbated by the Great Depression, and Potlatch abandoned the town in 1936. The town's population, which peaked at around 1,200, today remains under 200.

The little town bills itself as the gateway to Dworshak country—Dworshak Reservoir

lies about 10 miles south, or 23 miles east near Orofino. The much smaller but much closer **Elk Creek Reservoir,** a popular fishing hole, lies just south of town; plumb its depths for rainbow and brook trout, largemouth bass, and bullhead catfish. Elk River is also a great huckleberry-picking area; fresh huckleberries find their way onto local seasonal menus.

Elk Creek Falls Recreation Area

Hidden in 960 acres of dense forest three miles south of Elk River, the Elk Creek Falls Recreation Area (free) is named for its outstanding physical feature—Elk Creek cuts through a narrow gorge, plunging 300 feet in three falls on its way to the north fork of the Clearwater River. In winter, access to the falls is theoretically available to cross-country skiers from two **Elk River Park N' Ski** trailheads—one a couple of miles west of town where the summer road to the falls joins Highway 8, the other on the southeast corner of town; but plowing and grooming at these areas can be hit-and-miss. If you buy a Park N' Ski permit from Huckleberry Lodge, they'll give you a photocopied map of the 24-mile trail system. The east trailhead is within walking distance of the lodge, but it's probably easier (and definitely shorter) to find your way to the falls starting from the access road west of town. From there you follow the snow-covered but well-signed road for 2.5 miles, right to the falls trail. In summer, drive down this road to the falls trailhead.

Winter or summer, the hike to the falls from the falls trailhead is worth the effort. It's 1.25 miles to the lower falls viewpoint, and about a mile to either of the middle or upper falls viewpoints. The trail to the lower falls descends through a lush forest of elegant cedars. At the lower falls viewpoint you'll have a great view of a 50-foot cascade dropping over a black basalt cliff. The middle trail, with a drier exposure, leads primarily through fir. The upper falls trail takes you closest to the water before looping back past two leviathan ponderosa pines. All three trails connect with one another. Wildlife in the vicinity includes black bears, moose, elk, deer, and maybe even a mountain lion or two.

King Cedar

The reigning monarch of Idaho's trees—the state's largest—is a giant Western red cedar north of Elk River on Forest Road 382. Its hulking trunk measures more than 18 feet in diameter, while its crown looms 177 feet above the forest floor. The tree is estimated to be more than 3,000 years old. The area has been developed with a boardwalk providing wheelchair access to the magnificent tree and its beefy old-growth brethren.

Half the fun of checking out the Big Tree is the drive. The road follows Elk Creek about 10 miles north from town up into Upper Elk Creek Basin, a secluded and quiet area with wildflower-filled meadows and mountain vistas. Informal campsites here make excellent places to kick back and relax for a few days— drop a line in the creek, perhaps, and see if anything fishy happens.

Morris Creek Cedar Grove

High up on the shoulder of Elk Creek basin, along the Morris Creek tributary, you'll find another 80-acre grove of 500-year-old cedars surrounds a short loop trail. It's a nice place, accessible by a long and winding road. Take Forest Road 1969 off Elk Creek Road (Forest Rd. 382) and follow it up, up, up to the grove. If you find yourself in the upper basin, you missed the turn.

Accommodations

Grab a room at **Elk River Lodge & General Store** (201 S. Main St., Elk River, 208/826-3299, www.elkriverlodge.net, $59–99). Nine lodge rooms are conveniently located above the store, where there's also a common area and a big deck. Wake up to fresh coffee and a continental breakfast.

Food

For three meals a day of fine family fare, including huckleberry hotcakes, huckleberry milk shakes, and huckleberry pie, try the **Elk**

River Country Cafe (101 S. 1st St., Elk River, 208/826-3398).

HIGHWAY 6: THE WHITE PINE SCENIC BYWAY

Seventeen miles north of Moscow up U.S. 95 you'll come to the turnoff for Highway 6, which leads east 35 miles to its junction with north-south Highway 3. This stretch of Highway 6 is part of the state-designated White Pine Scenic Byway and passes most of the white pines that gave the route its name. You'll go through a string of small towns along this stretch, including Potlatch, Princeton, and Harvard.

Palouse Divide Park N' Ski Area

The hardcore cross-country skier can tour the entire Palouse Divide Adventure Road, a 31-mile semicircle ending at Laird Park. For less of an epic trek, stay on one of two other marked and periodically groomed loops that keep you closer to the downhill ski area. Grooming here is sporadic. The forest roads are skiable when ungroomed, but the narrow loop trails really aren't. Views of the surrounding mountains are panoramic, taking in clear-cuts in every direction. Park in one of two lots: One is along Highway 6, the other at the North-South Ski Bowl.

Palouse Divide Adventure Road

This off-pavement route leaves Highway 6 at the North-South Ski Bowl and follows Forest Road 377 down the Palouse Divide. Along the way you'll get great views of the Palouse, particularly from the Forest Service's **Bald Mountain Lookout Tower** (5,334 feet). After 17 miles, the road reaches a T intersection with Forest Road 447. Turn right (west) and loop back to Highway 6 (14 miles farther), or turn east and follow the Emerald Creek drainage 14 miles over to Clarkia and Highway 3. From late spring to late fall, a sturdy car or truck can negotiate the dirt roads; keep an eye out for both ripe huckleberries and rumbling logging trucks. The rest of the year, you'll need a snowmobile or cross-country skis.

Emida

Unless you live in town, **Drifters Western Bar & Grill** (Hwy. 6, Emida, 208/245-1301, daily) *is* Emida. Drifters may look like just another backwater roadhouse, but this place is something special. As you trudge up to the porch, don't be surprised if the door is opened for you from the inside by one of the waitresses, who might offer a cheery "Hi, come on in!" This is a genuinely friendly place.

Seven miles past Emida you'll come to the junction with Highway 3, which heads south to Clarkia and north to St. Maries.

HIGHWAY 3: CLARKIA TO ST. MARIES

Clarkia

About 20 million years ago during the Miocene period, the site of today's town of Clarkia was the bottom of a lake. Plants and insects that floated to the bottom of the lake were buried in sediments. More recently, Clarkia flourishes as a timber town. Passing through today, you'll be amazed by the unbelievably long string of railroad cars, each loaded to the brim with what used to be a forest. The town is a hub for the Bureau of Land Management's Grandmother Mountain Recreation Area—full of hiking trails—and the Marble Creek Recreation Area, offering camping and hiking across Hobo Divide in the St. Joe River drainage.

Emerald Creek Garnet Area

The Idaho state gemstone, the star garnet, is found only two places in the world: Idaho and India. Here you can dig the 12-sided crystals from the earth at a U.S. Forest Service–managed dig site (9 A.M.–5 P.M. Fri.–Tues. summer). The gems are normally found at a depth of 1–10 feet in alluvial sand and gravel deposits just above bedrock, and range from BB- to golf ball–size.

You need a permit ($10 adults, $5 ages 6–12) to become a garnet miner for a day. Permits are available at the site, about one mile's hike from the parking area. Each permit is good for five pounds of garnets. If you want more than that, you'll have to buy an additional permit.

Digging is permitted in designated areas only. The Forest Service recommends you budget at least four hours at the site, and bring with you grubby boots, a shovel, a bucket, a coffee can, and a screen box for washing gravel.

It's in a gorgeous area, surrounded by woods, meadows, creeks, and wildlife, including black bears. Four miles east of the dig site, **Emerald Creek Campground** ($6) makes an outstanding place to camp during your rockhounding endeavors.

For more information on the garnet area or the campground, contact the Forest Service's **St. Joe Ranger District** office (222 S. 7th St., St. Maries, 208/245-2531).

Grandmother Mountain Recreation Area

The Bureau of Land Management (BLM) manages this beautiful 12,140-acre recreation area (free) about 10 miles east of Clarkia on Forest Road 301. The trailheads are well marked. Four moderately easy trails loop through peaceful meadows and old-growth hemlock forests en route to a string of high-mountain fishing holes, including Fish Lake and Lost Lake. The only downside to hiking here is that most of the trails are mixed-use, meaning you'll probably encounter all-terrain vehicles along the way. Regardless of all that noise, wildlife is abundant in the Lund Creek drainage, home to elk, moose, deer, and black bears.

Primitive campsites (free) are available at **Crater Lake Saddle, Crater Peak,** and **Orphan Point Saddle.** For maps and more information about Grandmother Mountain, contact the BLM **Coeur d'Alene Field Office** (3815 Schreiber Way, Coeur d'Alene, 208/769-5000).

Hobo Cedar Grove Botanical Area

If you can visit only one of the several old-growth cedar groves sprinkled through northern Idaho, try to make it this one. The 500-year-old cedars here escaped the saws, axes, and forest fires of the early 20th century. Today they are protected as a National Natural Landmark. The 240-acre grove lies on a gentle slope traversed by a half-mile interpretive nature trail and a longer one-mile loop trail. The easy trails wind through the cool, shady forest, past brooks and lacy beds of lady ferns. Sunlight filters through the dense canopy, casting heavenly spotlights now and again on the fairy-tale landscape. If you stop and wait long enough, perhaps you'll catch sight of one of the gnomes or trolls that must inhabit this mystical realm. In addition to the western red cedars, botanists will note grand fir, western larch, Pacific yew, and Engelmann spruce. Chances are good you'll have the area all to yourself, particularly on weekdays.

To get to the grove, take Forest Road 321 northeast from Clarkia for 10 miles. Along the way you'll pass Potlatch's Merry Creek clear-cut. According to the Potlatch sign, this 46-acre plot was cut in 1988–1989, yielding 730 million board feet (MBF) of lumber. It will be harvested again in 2050 to produce 1.8 MBF. This is sustained yield? And hang on to your hats—thanks to this clear-cut, "More than nine jobs were produced." Presumably that means 10.

Continuing up the road, you'll crest Hobo Pass (4,525 feet) and almost immediately bear right onto Forest Road 3357. Find trailhead parking about two miles down the road.

For more information, contact the Forest Service's **St. Joe Ranger District** (208/245-2531).

St. Maries River

From Santa to St. Maries, the highway follows the St. Maries River, a placid watercourse that was once used as a log-drive highway. Floaters will find it a slow, relaxing paddle. Anglers can drop a line for a cutthroat or rainbow trout; note that the river is stocked between Clarkia and Santa, and that Alder Creek, which joins the St. Maries at the Lotus railroad crossing, is closed to all fishing.

St. Maries

A timber town clinging to life in the wake of the forest-products slowdown and the devastating floods of 1996, St. Maries (pronounced "St. Mary's"), the Benewah County seat, has a gritty blue-collar feel. The city enjoys a beautiful setting: It's surrounded by big mountains, and the lush cottonwoods along the St. Joe River turn a glowing gold in fall. Boating and floating are favorite pastimes, and camping, fishing, and hunting opportunities abound.

For more information, visit the **St. Maries Chamber of Commerce** (906 Main Ave., St. Maries, 208/245-3563, www.stmarieschamber.org). A small visitors center and museum occupy the historic log-cabin **Hughes House** (S. 6th St. and Main Ave., St. Maries, 208/245-3212), toward the east end of town.

HEYBURN STATE PARK

Heyburn is the largest of Idaho's state parks, encompassing more than 5,500 acres of land and 2,300 acres of water and offering 132 campsites ($14–24). Boating and fishing are major draws, and hiking and biking trails wind along the forested lakeshore. The park is home to one of the largest concentrations of nesting ospreys in North America, and deer, elk, bears, and wild turkeys wander through. Another odd twist: Wild rice is grown and harvested in the shallows of the lake.

The park's several segments are strung one after the other along Highway 5. The biggest segment and the park's "main entrance" is located on Chatcolet Road, six miles east of Plummer or 12 miles west of St. Maries on Highway 5. Here you'll find the large **Hawley's Landing Campground** as well as the park headquarters (there is no visitors center) and hiking trails. The **Lakeshore Loop Trail** is an easy 0.5-mile-plus trail connecting Hawley's Landing Campground and the Plummer Creek Bridge. Along the way, amateur botanists can spot larch, grand fir, and western red cedar trees as well as bunchberry, oceanspray, and thimbleberry. Look for ospreys, wood ducks, and great blue herons out on the marsh. The **Plummer Creek Trail,** about 0.5 miles, is also easy and passes through groves of cedars, grand firs, ponderosa pines, western hemlocks, and cottonwoods. Here you might spy a rubber boa slithering through the underbrush or hear songbirds merrily chirping away. The **Indian Cliffs Trail** forms a three-mile loop lined by wildflowers like syringa, heartleaf arnica, and buttercup. The trail takes you up out of the forest to panoramic ridgetop views.

A mile east of the main park entrance along the highway is the park's **Rocky Point** area, where you'll find a park-managed **marina** with a small store, a gas dock, and restrooms as well as an interpretive center with exhibits on local natural history and Native American arts and artifacts.

Continuing east another mile, you'll find a picnic area and public docks at **Cottonwood Point.** Just east of Cottonwood Point on the highway is a turnout offering views of **a river flowing through a lake.** Before Post Falls Dam backed up the Spokane River in 1904, the water level of Coeur d'Alene Lake was significantly lower. The St. Joe River flowed down through the lowlands now underwater in Heyburn State Park and was flanked on either side by natural tree-lined levees. The dam raised the lake's water level enough to flood these southern lowlands, but not enough to crest the levees along the river. As a result, the levees now appear as island strips separating the water of the river from the water of the lake. Eventually, the down-sloping topography of the riverbed reaches the surface elevation of the lake, and the phenomenon disappears. Before the dam was built, the four lakes at Heyburn State Park—Chatcolet Lake, Hidden Lake, Round Lake, and Benewah Lake—were four separate bodies of water. Today they're separate in name only; the waters flow together to make up the southern reaches of Coeur d'Alene Lake.

At the park's eastern end is a turnoff to the **Benewah Use Area** (day-use $5), where you'll find another campground, more docks, and some of the best sunsets in Idaho.

Out on the Water
Fishing at the park is excellent. That tug on the end of your line will most likely turn out to be a bass, kokanee, cutthroat trout, perch, or submerged log. Note that at the east end of the lake, **Benewah Creek** is closed to all fishing; the bull trout need their privacy while they're doing their spawning. Just about any other water-based form of recreation is a sure bet at the park as well; **waterskiing, swimming, kayaking, sailing,** and **canoeing** are all popular pastimes.

Rental Cabins
Three cottages ($115) and two camper cabins ($50) are available year-round for overnighters in the park.

Information
For campground or cabin reservations, marina rates, or other information, contact Heyburn State Park (57 Chatcolet Rd., Plummer, 208/686-1308).

NORTH-CENTRAL IDAHO

THE PANHANDLE

Idaho's Panhandle is shimmed like a log wedge between Montana, Washington, and British Columbia. This stovepipe-shaped section of the Gem State is a mere 45 miles wide at its skinniest swath, but what the Panhandle lacks in landmass, it more than makes up for with a multitude of large glacial lakes and densely forested mountains.

The booming resort towns of Coeur d'Alene and Sandpoint bring in the lion's share of local tourism thanks to their prime real estate on Idaho's two largest lakes: Coeur d'Alene and Pend Oreille. But much of the region is remote and unpopulated, just a few miles on either side of the busy I-90 and U.S. 95 corridors.

Outdoor recreation abounds in north Idaho. White-water rafting near Bonners Ferry; hiking and mountain biking in the Selway-Bitterroot Wilderness; shredding morning powder at Silver Mountain; and cruising the sky-blue waterways in old wooden boats keep locals busy year-round, and they don't mind sharing their wondrous playground with others.

People in the Panhandle are unabashedly independent, and friendly to boot. The state capital in Boise seems like a world away, and many folks here don't think that secession is such a bad idea. Why do you think they call it "north Idaho" instead of northern Idaho? Independent sovereignty probably won't happen anytime soon, but the Panhandle is definitely far removed from other parts of the state.

Historic sights are intertwined along the trodden pathways. The old mission in Cataldo, just east of Coeur d'Alene in Silver Valley, offers glimpses into Idaho's early Catholic

HIGHLIGHTS

◖ Tubbs Hill: This gorgeous 120-acre nature preserve on Coeur d'Alene Lake is a Frisbee fling away from downtown Coeur d'Alene (page 357).

◖ Old Mission State Park: It may be small, but this state park in Cataldo boasts a beautiful Greek Revival–style mission, the oldest existing building in Idaho (page 372).

◖ Wallace: Old mining towns don't get any funkier than Wallace, which is so historic that the entire town is on the National Register of Historic Places (page 377).

◖ Silverwood Theme Park: People from across the Northwest flock here for wild amusement park rides, like the 55-mph wooden roller coaster aptly named Timber Terror (page 381).

◖ Schweitzer Mountain Resort: This all-season resort near Sandpoint has the most stunning views in the Panhandle. The skiing and snowboarding is remarkable too (page 393).

◖ Priest Lake State Park: Idaho's northernmost state park has three units, two of which are on Priest Lake's pristine east shore (page 397).

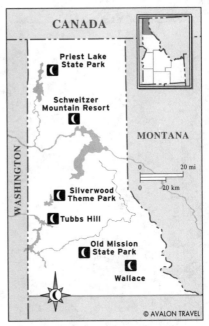

LOOK FOR ◖ TO FIND RECOMMENDED SIGHTS, ACTIVITIES, DINING, AND LODGING.

culture, which sought to bring Coeur d'Alene Indians into its fold in the mid-1900s. Nearby, travelers will marvel at the Victorian architecture and sheer funkiness of Wallace, a lovingly restored mining town with a taste for debauchery. A profusion of antiques shops, old saloons, and strange museums make this place one of the most interesting stops in the Panhandle, or in Idaho, for that matter.

To the far north, Priest Lake shimmers like a bright diamond below sharp mountain peaks. Ancient cedar and hemlock forests line the shore, and huckleberry bushes are just about everywhere you look, including on local menus in late summer.

PLANNING YOUR TIME

The Panhandle is the state's smallest region in terms of square miles, but it offers some of the best resorts and recreational opportunities in Idaho, most of which are easily accessible from I-90 and U.S. 95. Allow yourself at least a week to explore the area. Coeur d'Alene and Sandpoint are good base camps.

THE PANHANDLE

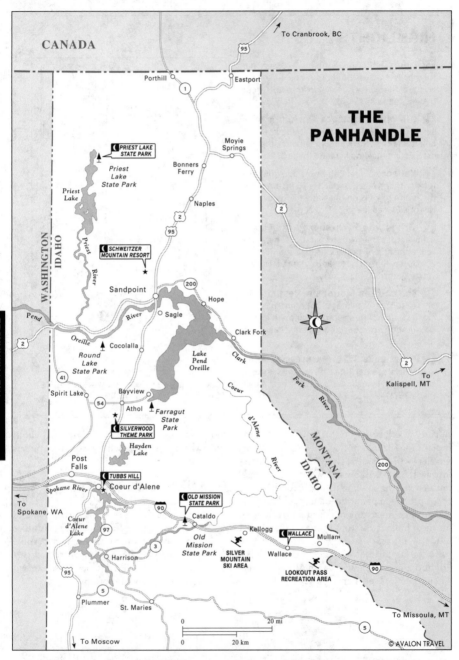

Coeur d'Alene and Vicinity

Shortly after the Mullan Road opened the Panhandle to miners and settlers, U.S. Army general William Tecumseh Sherman came through scouting locations for a new fort. The Army wanted a north Idaho base to protect the burgeoning white populace from Native American attack and to make sure the Brits didn't push their way south of the 49th parallel. In 1878, construction of Fort Coeur d'Alene began.

The fort, and the town that grew around it, were named for the local Native Americans. Although they called themselves *Schitsu'umsh,* meaning "The Ones That Were Found Here," the French trappers called them the *coeur d'alène*—"heart like an awl." Authorities agree the name arose from the Native Americans' shrewd trading abilities but argue whether the trappers coined the phrase first or adopted it after hearing the Native Americans use it to describe the French. In any case, the name stuck. After

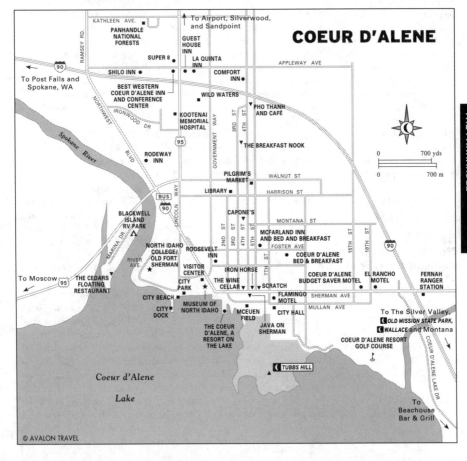

COEUR D'ALENE

THE PANHANDLE

© AVALON TRAVEL

Sherman died, the fort's name was changed to honor him, but the town that grew around the fort kept the moniker Coeur d'Alene. In the 1880s the town became the lake's biggest steamship port; ships carried passengers and supplies to and from the booming Coeur d'Alene Mining District and communities around the lake.

Today, Coeur d'Alene (population 44,000) ranks as the top resort town in the inland Northwest. In summer, the long lakefront boardwalk bustles with bikini-clad sun worshippers, Frisbee-fetching dogs, ice cream–licking youngsters, and busloads of camera-toting tourists. Out on the lake, Jet Skis buzz and flit like hopped-up waterborne mosquitoes while water-skiers race the wakes of the cruise boats, and parasailers brighten the skies overhead. No question—this city is alive and exciting in summer.

In winter the crowds disappear, and a quiet, intense beauty descends with the first snowfall. Skiers make the morning commute out to one of the region's three downhill resorts, while bald eagles—intent on fattening up on the lake's abundant kokanee salmon—make their annual pilgrimage to Wolf Lodge Bay. It's a great season to relax at one of the town's numerous bed-and-breakfasts—to sit by a crackling fire, pick up a good book, and drift off to dreams of spring.

SIGHTS
North Idaho College and Old Fort Sherman

The campus of this two-year junior college (1000 W. Garden Ave., 208/769-3300, www. nic.edu) occupies the grounds of old Fort Sherman, one of the major military installations in the Northwest from 1878 to 1901. It was from here that troops were dispatched up the Silver Valley to quell the mining wars of 1892. Today only a few structures from the fort remain, scattered among modern school buildings. The campus is a nice place to just poke around on, thanks to its prime lakefront real estate, expansive lawns, and big evergreens.

Museum of North Idaho

Kootenai County's history is featured at the Museum of North Idaho (115 Northwest Blvd., Coeur d'Alene, 208/664-3448, www. museumni.org, 11 A.M.–5 P.M. Tues.–Sat. Apr.–Oct.), in front of City Park. Exhibit topics include the Mullan Road, Fort Sherman, early transportation—including railroads and steamboats—and local industry, especially logging and mining.

An annex, the **Fort Sherman Museum,** on the North Idaho College campus (W. Garden Ave. and N. College Dr., Coeur d'Alene, 1–4:45 P.M. Tues.–Sat. May–Sept.), has exhibits including a 1924 smoke-chaser's cabin, a model of old Fort Sherman, and a lifeboat from the *Miss Spokane*—a passenger boat that plied Coeur d'Alene Lake in the 1920s. The museum provides a walking-tour brochure to the several Fort Sherman structures that have been preserved.

A single admission of $3 adults, $1 ages 6–16, $7 family is valid for both museums.

Sightseeing Tours
SIGHTSEEING CRUISES
Lake Coeur d'Alene Cruises (208/765-4000, www.cdalakecruises.com) offers 90-minute tours of the lake (daily late Apr.–late Oct., $19.75 adults, $17.75 seniors, $11.75 ages 6–12). Also available are Sunday brunch cruises, Pirates of the Coeur d'Alene cruises, and a Fourth of July fireworks cruise. All public cruises leave from City Dock at Independence Point, next to the Coeur d'Alene Resort.

Another motorized way to tour the lake is offered by **Bobby D's Custom Tours** (208/667-0807 or 208/699-7206, www.lake-coeurdalenecruise.com), a year-round charter service offering private trips aboard its 26-foot Alumaweld cabin cruiser, *The Joanna*. Especially awesome are the bald eagle viewing cruises (Nov.–Feb.), where you'll see dozens of these majestic birds hanging out in old snags along the shoreline. For $100 per hour with a two-hour minimum, you can charter the boat helmed by an experienced captain.

ON GUARD FOR HUMAN RIGHTS

Idaho – especially the state's Panhandle region – has long had a reputation as a haven for racists, but events in recent years show that perceptions and reality may both be turning.

From 1973, Richard Butler ruled the white-supremacist Aryan Nations organization from a compound in Hayden, Idaho, a few miles north of Coeur d'Alene. The ultraright-wing racist and his followers were an unending source of embarrassment to the vast majority of north Idahoans. Groups including the Kootenai County Task Force on Human Relations and the Human Rights Education Institute spoke out strongly against the Aryan Nations' presence in their backyard.

Finally, in 2000, Butler was forced into bankruptcy by a $6.3 million civil judgment resulting from a suit filed by the Southern Poverty Law Center on behalf of an Idaho woman and her son who said Butler's group shot at them in 1998. Philanthropist Greg Carr, an Idaho native, purchased Butler's compound and donated it to the North Idaho College Foundation, which now operates the Hayden Lake site as a **peace park.** Groups wishing to visit can make an appointment by calling 208/769-5978. Meanwhile, the Human Rights Education Institute, again aided by a donation from Carr, opened a human rights interpretive center (414 Mullan Ave., Coeur d'Alene, 208/292-2359, www.hrei.org) in a historic building in downtown Coeur d'Alene's City Park. The center features permanent and traveling human rights' exhibits, educational programs, and community outreach.

A small fuel charge applies. All cruises leave from City Dock.

FLIGHTSEEING
Brooks Sea Plane (208/664-2842 or 208/659-1511, www.brooks-seaplane.com) takes passengers aloft on 20-minute sightseeing flights around the lake ($60 adults, $30 under age 12). You'll fly aboard either a float-equipped Cessna 206 or a gorgeous seven-passenger De Havilland Beaver, the bush pilot's workhorse. The planes leave from City Dock on Independence Point, next to the Coeur d'Alene Resort. Longer flights are also available. **Big Country Helicopters** (208/765-0620, www.bigcountryhelicopters.com) offers chopper hops (from $130 pp) of a half-hour or longer around the area.

RECREATION
◖ Tubbs Hill
One of the city's highlights, this beautiful 120-acre wooded preserve (free) juts out into the lake right next to the Coeur d'Alene Resort. Trails loop around the peninsula through groves of Douglas fir and century-old ponderosa pine. Some paths climb up the hill for panoramic views; others drop down to hidden coves and beaches. It's all a city park, open to foot traffic only and within easy walking distance of anywhere downtown. The best time to enjoy Tubbs Hill is during an after-dinner stroll, when you can walk off your meal and enjoy a gorgeous sunset at the same time. For more information, contact the Coeur d'Alene Parks Department (710 E. Mullan Ave., Coeur d'Alene, 208/769-2252).

Biking and Skating
The **North Idaho Centennial Trail,** a 23-mile hiking, biking, and skating trail, stretches west from Higgins Point on Coeur d'Alene Lake's northeast shore through the cities of Coeur d'Alene and Post Falls to the Washington state line. Ambitious folks can continue west on the abutting Spokane River Centennial Trail; it's another 22 miles to Spokane. For most of its length, the trail is either completely separated from traffic or off on a big, wide shoulder. Animals on leashes are allowed, and interpretive signs mark many points of interest along the way. You can pick

up the trail at City Park, downtown, or on Coeur d'Alene Lake Drive.

Swimming and Sunbathing

When those sunny summer days roll around, **City Beach** is the place to be. The water warms up enough for swimming and splashing, and the beach, boardwalk, and adjacent **City Park** fill with skaters, Frisbee-throwers, joggers, swimmers, gawkers, and gawkees—the people-watching can't be beat.

If the tame lakeshore bores you, head to **Wild Waters** (2119 N. Government Way, Coeur d'Alene, 208/667-6491, www.wildwaterswaterpark.com, $25 over 48 inches, $20 under 48 inches, $13 seniors and disabled, free under age 3) near I-90. This recently renovated waterslide theme park also has a grassy area for sunning, hot pools for soaking, a video arcade, and a snack bar. The park is open the last two weekends in May (including Memorial Day Monday), then daily the first weekend in June–early September. Hours are 11 A.M.–6 P.M., 11 A.M.–7 P.M. in midsummer. Parents can get a viewing-only pass for $13, which allows them to keep an eye on Junior without getting wet themselves.

Parasailing

On sunny summer afternoons, the blue skies over Lake Coeur d'Alene are complemented by the brightly colored chutes of **Coeur d'Alene Parasail** (208/765-2999, www.cdaparasail.net, 10 A.M.–7 P.M. Sun.–Fri., solo $60, tandem $90). You'll be towed 400 or more feet in the air behind a speedboat for an 8–10-minute ride over the lake. And thanks to the specially designed boat and hydraulic winch system, you won't even get wet.

Boat Rentals

Boardwalk Marina at the Coeur d'Alene Resort (208/765-4000) rents 20-foot speedboats for $125 per hour with a two-hour minimum. Tax and fuel are additional, and you'll have to leave a credit card for a deposit.

On the other side of the dock, **Island Rentals** (208/666-1626) rents out Jet Skis

during the summer months. Expect to pay around $85 per hour (fuel and lifejacket included) for one of these little zippers.

You'll also find more humble people-powered canoes, paddleboats, and such available for rent at City Dock in summer.

Fishing

Coeur d'Alene Lake has hungry populations of kokanee, chinook salmon, and northern pike. **Fins & Feathers** (1816 Sherman Ave., Coeur d'Alene, 208/667-9304), a tackle shop and guide service, can help you find the biggest ones and provide the boat and all equipment as well. The going rate for a party of two is $325 for a half-day trip, $495 for a full day.

While the big lake is the obvious centerpiece of the area, don't forget 300-acre **Fernan Lake,** east of I-90 at the Sherman exit, where you can fish for wild cutthroat trout and stocked rainbows as well as warm-water species like largemouth bass, crappie, perch, and catfish. In winter you can probe beneath the frozen crust, primarily for perch. Boat ramps and docks are found at either end of the lake.

Golf

The star attraction for Coeur d'Alene linksters is **Coeur d'Alene Resort Golf Course** (900 Floating Green Dr., Coeur d'Alene, 208/667-4653, www.cdaresort.com, nonguests from $175). The beautiful lakeside course boasts a great gimmick: The 14th hole features a moveable floating green. A cute little putt-putt boat ferries you out to it, assuming your ball actually made it to the green and isn't on its way to Davey Jones's locker. Aim carefully.

All the golf magazines rave about the 6,804-yard, par-71 course, designed by Scott Miller in 2003 with extensively renovated in 2003 with 500 new yards to play. Guests of the resort get a major price break and a free water-taxi ride from the hotel to the course. Rates include a cart and caddie. Clubs and golf shoes can be rented. No plebes, please: "Proper attire is required at all times," reads the rule, "Men—slacks or suitable length shorts and shirts with sleeves and collars.

Women—dresses, skirts and blouses, slacks, culottes, or proper length shorts."

Humbler courses in town include **Coeur d'Alene Golf Club** (2201 S. Fairway Dr., Coeur d'Alene, 208/765-0218, about $28), a 6,274-yard, par-72 course, and **Ponderosa Springs Golf Course** (1291 N. Galena Dr., Coeur d'Alene, 208/664-1101, about $12), a nine-hole course.

White-Water Rafting

You won't find any white-water rivers in the Coeur d'Alene area, but you will find **ROW Adventures** (202 Sherman Ave., Coeur d'Alene, 208/765-0841 or 800/451-6034, www.rowadventures.com), one of Idaho's biggest and best rafting companies. The company runs all the Idaho standards—the Snake River through Hells Canyon, the Salmon, the Middle Fork Salmon, the Lochsa, and the Selway Rivers—plus lesser-known white water like the Moyie, Clark Fork, St. Joe, and Owyhee Rivers. ROW is an acronym for both River Odysseys West and Remote Odysseys Worldwide; in addition to domestic rivers, the company runs raft trips in Ecuador, barge trips on French canals, yacht trips along the Turkish coast, trekking trips in Nepal, and more.

Backcountry Hiking and Mountain Biking

The U.S. Forest Service's **Coeur d'Alene River Ranger District** Fernan Ranger Station (2502 E. Sherman Ave., Coeur d'Alene, 208/769-3000) is on the east side of I-90. Stop by for information on nearby backcountry hiking and biking opportunities. The Forest Service publishes descriptive flyers on several hiking trails, primarily found deep in the Coeur d'Alene Mountains between Hayden Lake, Lake Pend Oreille, and the upper North Fork of the Coeur d'Alene River. A couple of trails to the east begin closer to town, around the Wolf Lodge District. In addition, logging roads lace the nearby mountains; just continue east from the Fernan Ranger Station on Fernan Lake Road, which skirts the north shore of the lake and then climbs up toward Huckleberry

Mountain. Past that point, dirt roads suitable for hiking or mountain biking spin off in every direction. Inquire at the ranger station to find out which, if any, of these roads are being actively logged.

CANFIELD MOUNTAIN TRAIL SYSTEM

The Canfield Mountain Trail System is part of the web of logging roads mentioned above. Its 32 miles of single- and double-track trails are open to hikers, equestrians, motorcycles, and mountain bikes; fat-tire bicyclists currently make best use of the area. Several access points are available along Forest Road 1562, which links Nettleton Gulch Road with Fernan Lake Road in a meandering, roundabout fashion. Nettleton Gulch Road intersects 15th Street 1.1 miles north of I-90 Exit 14, becoming Forest Road 1562 farther east. On the east side, Forest Road 1562 intersects Fernan Lake Road 5.5 miles east of I-90 Exit 15. Pick up a map to the trail system at the Fernan Ranger Station.

Skiing

Although Coeur d'Alene has no downhill ski areas to call its own, several are close enough for a day trip. North up U.S. 95 about 50 miles is **Schweitzer Mountain,** high in the Selkirks overlooking Sandpoint and Lake Pend Oreille. To the east on I-90 are **Silver Mountain**—40 miles from town at Kellogg and home of the world's longest gondola—and **Lookout Pass,** 20 miles beyond that at the Montana border. Popular cross-country areas in the vicinity include **Fourth of July Pass Park N' Ski Area,** 18 miles east of Coeur d'Alene at Fourth of July Pass, and Farragut and Round Lake State Parks to the north.

Outfitters

Vertical Earth (2175 N. Main St., Coeur d'Alene, 208/667-5503, www.verticalearth.com, daily) rents out mountain bikes, snowboards, snowshoes, and cross-country skis, including telemark demo gear. And you're not too far from mega-outfitter **REI** (1125 N. Monroe St., Spokane, WA, 509/328-9900, www.rei.com), just over the border in Washington.

THE PANHANDLE

ENTERTAINMENT AND EVENTS
Nightlife

The **Iron Horse** (407 E. Sherman Ave., Coeur d'Alene, 208/667-7314) in downtown Coeur d'Alene is the place to go for drinks and dancing. This venerable nightspot features live music (usually rock and country) on weekends. The Iron Horse also has a full-service restaurant serving breakfast, lunch, and dinner daily.

Performing Arts

North Idaho College sponsors the bulk of the area's concerts and dramatic performances, like the Coeur d'Alene Summer Theatre. For current listings, call the college's **Boswell Hall Schuler Performing Arts Center** (208/769-7780). The **Citizens' Council for the Arts** (208/667-9346, www.artonthegreen.org) has lots of information on the region's fine and performing arts scene.

Events

Highlights of the town's events calendar include **Fred Murphy Days,** the last weekend in May, honoring a locally legendary steamboat captain with good food and drink, contests of strength and skill, street dances, a parade, and a good deal of giddiness; **Fourth of July,** which brings an Independence Day parade to beat the band; **Art on the Green** (www.artonthegreen.org) at North Idaho College in early August; and the **Coeur d'Alene Wooden Boat Festival** (www.coeurdalene.org/woodenboatshow.htm), which beautifies the lake the third weekend in August. From the weekend following Thanksgiving until after New Year's Day, the Coeur d'Alene Resort area and lakeside boardwalks glow with more than 1 million **holiday lights.** For more information about area events, call Coeur d'Alene Chamber of Commerce (208/664-3194, www.cdachamber.com).

SHOPPING

For an excellent selection of regional art, check out **Art Spirit Gallery** (415 Sherman Ave., Coeur d'Alene, 208/765-6006, www. theartspiritgallery.com, 11 A.M.–6 P.M. daily summer) downtown, which offers great stuff from about 30 established and emerging artists from the Idaho Panhandle, Washington, and Montana. Featured artists include George Carlson, nationally known for his monumental sculptures, and Russell Chatham.

Fans of antiques and collectibles will have a field day here. The phone book is chock-full of dealers and antiques malls. Check out the lovably funky **Wiggett's Antiques Marketplace** (115 S. 4th Ave., Coeur d'Alene, 208/664-1524) next to Coeur d'Alene Resort.

Also downtown, you'll find a handful of cool stores in Coeur d'Alene Resort's **Plaza Shops** (210 E. Sherman Ave., Coeur d'Alene), including **Papillon Paper Emporium** (208/664-0736) and **Bruttles** (208/664-6586), which sells truffles and other chocolate treats.

The biggest shopping mall in town is **Silver Lake Mall** (200 W. Hanley Ave., Coeur d'Alene, 208/762-2112, 10 A.M.–9 P.M. Mon.–Sat., 11 A.M.–6 P.M. Sun.), north of I-90 on either U.S. 95 or Government Way, with 50 stores that include Sears, JC Penney, and Macy's.

ACCOMMODATIONS

Sherman Avenue runs between Coeur d'Alene Resort and I-90 on the east side of town. A number of mostly inexpensive–moderate older independent motels are along this strip. The area has the advantage of being surrounded by quiet old residential areas and being near funky, character-filled shops and restaurants. On the west end, the lodgings are within easy walking distance of downtown; on the east end, you'll be near I-90.

The other motel district is along Appleway Avenue, which parallels I-90 to the north. This area has the advantages of being close to I-90 and being surrounded by modern shopping malls and fast-food emporiums, which are also the disadvantages. Most of the major chain motels are here.

$50-100

The **Budget Saver Motel Coeur d'Alene** (1519 Sherman Ave., Coeur d'Alene, 208/667-9505,

THE PANHANDLE

$50–120) doesn't look like much from the outside, but it's well worth the low prices—among the cheapest in town. The rooms are decent, and some have two bedrooms—a nice touch for added privacy. In the same area, you'll find **El Rancho Motel** (1915 Sherman Ave., Coeur d'Alene, 208/664-8794, $39–75), which has 14 standard rooms.

If you want to be a few blocks from the lake, try the **◖ Flamingo Motel** (718 Sherman Ave., Coeur d'Alene, 208/664-2159 or 800/955-2159, www.flamingomotelidaho.com, from $90 d), a gussied-up motor inn with a pool and some kitchenettes.

Over on Appleway Avenue, you'll find **Super 8** (505 W. Appleway Ave., Coeur d'Alene, 208/765-8880 or 800/800-8000, from $66 d); **La Quinta Inn** (280 W. Appleway Ave., Coeur d'Alene, 208/765-5500, from $74 d); and **GuestHouse Inn** (330 W. Appleway Ave., Coeur d'Alene, 208/765-3011, from $89 d).

A few miles north of town on U.S. 95 is **Silver Lake Motel** (6160 Sunshine St., Coeur d'Alene, 208/772-8595 or 800/732-8094, www.silverlakemotel.com, from $56), with amenities like an outdoor pool, a lounge, and free continental breakfast.

$100-150

Among the plushest places in town are the **Shilo Inn** (702 W. Appleway Ave., Coeur d'Alene, 208/664-2300 or 800/222-2244, from $139 d), which offers all minisuites with kitchenettes, and the **Best Western Coeur d'Alene Inn and Conference Center** (506 W. Appleway Ave., Coeur d'Alene, 208/765-3200 or 800/251-7829, from $129 d), a full-service hotel with an indoor pool and spa. Both hotels sometimes have guest rooms for under $100.

Coeur d'Alene is the bed-and-breakfast capital of Idaho; about a dozen are sprinkled throughout town, with a half-dozen more in the outlying areas. Unless specified, the B&Bs below serve a full breakfast, don't permit children under 12 or pets, and don't allow smoking indoors. Note that B&B prices vary widely with the particular guest room rented, and some places have guest rooms that exceed this price category. For more listings of area B&Bs, visit the North Idaho Bed and Breakfast Association's website (www.nibba.com).

East of town, off the lake's north shore, **◖ Katie's Wild Rose Inn** (7974 E. Coeur d'Alene Lake Dr., Coeur d'Alene, 208/765-9474 or 800/371-4345, www.katieswildroseinn.com, $89–200) sits high on a promontory overlooking Bennett Bay. Wild roses grace the grounds, and a rose motif runs throughout the interior. The inn sits alongside the Centennial Trail bike path. Of the four guest rooms, two have private baths and two share a bath. One has an in-room jetted tub.

◖ The Roosevelt Inn Bed & Breakfast (105 E. Wallace Ave., Coeur d'Alene, 208/765-5200 or 800/290-3358, www.therooseveltinn.com, $119–279) occupies the redbrick 1906 Roosevelt School, which was converted in 1994. All guest rooms have private baths and are furnished with antiques; some guest rooms have a lake view. Common areas include a small exercise center and two parlors—one with a TV and Internet access, the other a quiet room for reading or writing. Rates include a gourmet full breakfast.

The McFarland Inn Bed & Breakfast (601 E. Foster Ave., Coeur d'Alene, 208/667-1232 or 800/335-1232, www.mcfarlandinn.com, $135–165) offers five guest rooms in a graceful turn-of-the-20th-century home furnished with both elegant antiques and modern amenities. A gourmet breakfast and afternoon tea are served daily, and fresh coffee and goodies are always available. Each guest room has a private bath with a claw-foot tub and a shower. Children over 14 are welcome.

Just west of town in a tranquil country setting is **American Country Bed & Breakfast** (705 Zircon Lane, Coeur d'Alene, 877/664-9650, www.americancountrybedandbreakfast.com, $125–215). This Americana-inspired inn offers a big deck, a big breakfast, and big smiles from its hosts Brian and Shar Scott. The B&B has three guest rooms and a cottage made to look like a tree house. Children and pets are not allowed, and smoking is permitted outside.

Over $250

By many people's standards, **The Coeur d'Alene, a Resort on the Lake** (115 S. 2nd St., Coeur d'Alene, 208/765-4000 or 800/688-5253, www.cdaresort.com), owned by publishing magnate Duane Hagadone, is *the* hotel in Idaho. It seems to be a pet of travel writers; the resort gets a lot of press and has been included more than once on *Condé Nast Traveler* magazine's "Gold List" of the world's best hotels. It definitely ranks high in terms of location, rising into the sky over the shores of exquisitely beautiful Coeur d'Alene Lake, and it offers a mind-boggling array of extravagant amenities. With all that in mind, is there any room for disagreement with the glowing reviews? Does anyone dare not like this place? Yes, and yes. One wonders what architect R. G. Nelson was thinking, putting a skyscraper on a beautiful lakeshore. Unlike, say, Yosemite's Ahwahnee Hotel, this big tan monster doesn't complement the environment, it competes with it, resembling nothing so much as a giant tower of Legos. In addition, although codeveloper Jerry Jaeger was once quoted as saying, "This will be a place to come and play; nobody's going to wear a tie," the self-conscious "informality" here is cloaked in Gucci and Chanel, and you'll feel out of place in jeans. Standard guest rooms usually run $250 or more in summer; pay much less and you risk getting a depressing "economy" room that'll make you wish you stayed at Motel 6 for half the price. The high-end guest rooms can fetch as much as $499 in summer. Lower prices are offered in the off-season. Spa, ski, golf, and other packages are available.

Vacation Rental Companies

Coeur d'Alene Vacation (509/954-6111, www.cdavacation.com) lists year-round vacation home rentals, some on the lake. **Resort Property Management** (2120 N. 3rd St., Coeur d'Alene, 208/667-6035, www.resort-propertiesidaho.com) has listings for more than 75 summer cabins in the $100–500 per night range.

CAMPING AND RVING

Blackwell Island RV Park (800 S. Marina Dr., Coeur d'Alene, 208/665-1300 or 888/571-2900, $35–46 with full hookups) is a large park with boat docks and grassy pull-throughs just across the Spokane River from town: Take U.S. 95 south one mile from I-90 and turn left on Marina Drive.

River Walk RV Park (1214 Mill Ave., at Northwest Blvd., Coeur d'Alene, 208/765-5943 or 888/567-8700, $22–36) offers 42 sites with full hookups. The park has showers, restrooms, and a laundry room.

FOOD
Upscale Fare

Beverly's (115 S. 2nd St., Coeur d'Alene, 208/765-4000, www.cdaresort.com, lunch and dinner daily, entrées $24–55) is the Coeur d'Alene Resort's premier dining room, on the hotel's seventh floor overlooking the lake. On the menu you'll find entrées that make optimum use of fresh Northwestern ingredients in high-cuisine fashion. The restaurant maintains a huge wine cellar; chances are they'll have exactly what you're looking for.

The Cedars Floating Restaurant (208/664-2922, www.cedarsfloatingrestaurant.com, dinner from 4 P.M. daily, $22–39) is also affiliated with Coeur d'Alene Resort. This is the place to go for fresh fish and romantic atmosphere. To get here, head south on U.S. 95 toward Moscow. On the edge of town, turn left onto Marina Drive immediately after crossing the Spokane River. This takes you out onto Blackwell Island, an area of working boat shops and boat storage yards. The restaurant is all the way out at the tip of the island, moored where the Spokane River flows out of Coeur d'Alene Lake. Fish entrées vary, depending on availability, but might include wild salmon, swordfish, halibut, or ahi; some are grilled, others cooked on a cedar plank. Poultry, pasta, steaks, and rack of lamb are also available.

For fine Italian dining, make a reservation at **Angelo's Ristorante** (846 N. 4th St., Coeur d'Alene, 208/765-2850, www.angelosristorante.net, lunch 11 A.M.–4 P.M.

Mon.–Fri., dinner 5–10 P.M. daily, $14–25). Here you'll find a classic Mediterranean dining room and upscale preparations of antipasto, pasta, risotto, scampi, steaks, and rack of lamb. Expect to see a big wine list of Italian and Washington labels.

◖ **Scratch** (501 E. Sherman Ave., Coeur d'Alene, 208/930-4762, lunch 11 A.M.–3 P.M. Mon.–Fri., dinner 3–10 P.M. Mon.–Thurs., 3–11 P.M. Fri.–Sat., dinner entrées $16–38) is a global fusion restaurant and lounge downtown that uses local foodstuffs in a creative manner. The menu changes with the season and availability of products. The dinner menu leans toward Asia and the Mediterranean for inspiration.

Casual Dining

Capone's Pub & Grill (751 N. 4th St., Coeur d'Alene, 208/667-4843, www.caponespub. com, lunch and dinner daily) entices beer drinkers with some two dozen Northwestern microbrews on tap. The decor is vintage sports, with old baseball mitts, skis, golf clubs, and ice skates hanging from the ceiling and historical sports photos lining the walls, including one of…Jerry Garcia? Seems there's a Deadhead subplot in the bullpen. Whatever game you're looking for, you'll probably find it on one of the five TVs connected to two satellite dishes. The friendly and comfortable place also serves an extensive menu of first-class pub grub, including burgers, subs, and creative, made-from-scratch gourmet pizzas (try the Thai chicken variation). Live entertainment several nights a week draws a fun crowd. Capone's is well worth the short hop up from downtown.

The **Beachouse Bar & Grill** (3204 Coeur d'Alene Lake Dr., Coeur d'Alene, 208/664-6464, dinner daily, $12–22), at the north shore's Silver Bay Marina, serves steaks, seafood, barbecued ribs, and pasta. You're paying a lot for atmosphere—this is one of only two places in town right on the water—and for the restaurant's association with the Hagadone Corporation. The resort's guests are chauffeured here by boat, which no doubt adds to

the overhead. Still, this is a good place for a lakeside dinner, preferably out on the deck.

◖ **Bistro on Spruce** (1710 N. 4th St., Coeur d'Alene, 208/664-1774, www.bistroonspruce.com, lunch 11 A.M.–2:30 P.M. Mon.–Fri., dinner 5–9 P.M. Mon.–Thurs., 5–10 P.M. Fri.–Sat., entrées $13–23) is a casual new restaurant with a decidedly Mediterranean menu. Expect to find Guinness onion soup, mushroom risotto, paella (saffron rice with sausage and seafood), and pan-roasted duck breast with Marsala reduction. Oh, yeah, there are lots of microbrews and wines by the glass.

Wine Bars

◖ **The Wine Cellar** (313 Sherman Ave., Coeur d'Alene, 208/664-9463, 4:30–10 P.M. Mon.–Thurs., 4:30 P.M.–midnight Fri.–Sat.) is a venerable downtown wine bar that features live jazz nightly. The wine list has more than 250 worldwide labels, which play well with the Mediterranean menu. The sidewalk patio is a great place to people-watch while sipping syrah and noshing on tapas.

Just down the street, you'll find **Barrel Room No. 6** (503 E. Sherman Ave., Coeur d'Alene, 208/664-9632, 4 P.M.–late Wed.–Fri., 2 P.M.–late Sat.), which is Coeur d'Alene Cellars' wine bar. You can taste the winery's vintages in a stylish space with big sofas and wine-barrel furniture. This happening little place supplements its wine list with microbrews and a light menu of appetizers and desserts. Coeur d'Alene Cellars (3890 N. Schreiber Way, Coeur d'Alene, 208/664-2336, www. cdacellars.com, tasting room 11 A.M.–5 P.M. Tues.–Sat.) also has a tasting room at the winery, where it produces several remarkable varietal wines and blends made from Columbia Valley grapes.

Ethnic Cuisine

Sushi fans will surely like **Takara Japanese Restaurant & Sushi Bar** (309 Lakeside Ave., Coeur d'Alene, 208/765-8014, www.cda-sushi. com, lunch and dinner daily). This downtown restaurant puts out a large selection of maki rolls, nigiri, and sashimi. You also can get hot

THE PANHANDLE

a sampling of produce at the Kootenai County Farmers Market in Coeur d'Alene

© DANA HOPPER-KELLY

offerings like tempura, sukiyaki, and teriyaki. Don't worry, there's plenty of sake and Japanese rice lager to wash everything down.

If you're craving a bowl of pho (Vietnamese beef noodle soup), head to **Pho Thanh & Café** (2108 N. 4th St., Coeur d'Alene, 208/665-9903, lunch and dinner daily, around $10), a little Vietnamese restaurant near I-90. The servers can be rude at times, but the kitchen pumps out decent Southeast Asian standards such as pho, crispy spring rolls, steamed rice plates, and vermicelli noodle dishes.

For standard Mexican fare, check out **Toro Viejo** (117 N. 2nd St., Coeur d'Alene, 208/667-7676, lunch and dinner daily, around $10). This festive downtown eatery dishes up enchiladas, tacos, burritos, and fajitas. The restaurant also serves margaritas and Mexican beers.

Breakfast and Coffee

The Breakfast Nook (1719 N. 4th St., Coeur d'Alene, 208/667-1699, 6 A.M.–2 P.M. Mon.–Sat., 7 A.M.–2 P.M. Sun., under $10) is the place for big American-style breakfasts. The menu has steak and eggs, French toast, eggs Benny, pancakes, and omelets galore.

Downtown, **C Java on Sherman** (324 Sherman Ave., Coeur d'Alene, 208/667-0010, 6 A.M.–8 P.M. Sun.–Wed., 6 A.M.–9 P.M. Fri.–Sat.) is a clean, well-lighted place to enjoy great joe while reading Hemingway or writing the great American novel. Big front windows command the best people-watching corner in north Idaho, and many caffeine-laced concoctions are available; go for the trademark Bowl of Soul (espresso in steamed milk topped with chocolate and cinnamon). The pastries are baked on the premises. Bigger breakfasts are available too. Both the atmosphere and the help are young, hip, and friendly.

Groceries

Pilgrim's Market (1316 N. 4th St., Coeur d'Alene, 208/676-9730, www.pilgrimsmarket.com, 9 A.M.–8 P.M. daily) is a natural food store that specializes in organic local produce, meats, and bread. The market also has bulk foods, dietary supplements, and earthy beauty products.

Head to the bustling downtown **Kootenai County Farmers Market** (5th St. and Sherman Ave., Coeur d'Alene, 4–7 P.M. Wed. May–Sept.) for impeccably fresh local produce and meats, honey, salsa, eggs, and artisanal bread. You also can get hot food like wood-fired pizzas and lamb burgers, plus there's live music.

INFORMATION AND SERVICES

Coeur d'Alene Chamber of Commerce's **Visitors Bureau** (105 N. 1st St., Coeur d'Alene, 208/664-3194, www.coeurdalene.org) is conveniently located downtown across from City Park. It's well stocked with maps and brochures on lodging, restaurants, and recreation.

Recreation information for most of north Idaho is available from the Supervisor's Office of the **Idaho Panhandle National Forests** (3815 Schreiber Way, Coeur d'Alene, 208/765-7223). The **Idaho Department of Parks and Recreation** (2885 Kathleen Ave., Coeur d'Alene, 208/769-1511) maintains its north region headquarters in Coeur d'Alene. The **Coeur d'Alene Parks Department** (710 E. Mullan Ave., Coeur d'Alene, 208/769-2252) has additional information about area recreation.

National Public Radio listeners can pick up Spokane's **KPBX** (91.1 FM). Another station, featuring a great jazz repertoire, is **KEWU** (89.5 FM), the radio station of Eastern Washington University in Cheney.

If you need emergency medical services, head to **Kootenai Medical Center** (2003 Kootenai Health Way, Coeur d'Alene, 208/666-2000) just off Lincoln Way near I-90.

GETTING THERE AND AROUND
Getting There

Spokane International Airport (GEG, 9000 W. Airport Dr., Spokane, WA, 509/455-6455) is about 35 miles away. It's served by several major airlines, including Alaska Airlines, Southwest, United, and Delta. The airport has a typical gamut of rental car agencies inside the main terminal.

Shuttle service to and from Coeur d'Alene and the surrounding area is provided by **Payless Airport Shuttle** (208/762-7433 or 888/870-7433, $45 one-way for 1–2 people) by appointment only.

Getting Around

Parking in downtown Coeur d'Alene can be challenging, especially during the peak summer months. If you don't feel like riding a bike, jump on one of the free **Citylink** (www.idahocitylink.com) buses, which have three urban routes and service to the Coeur d'Alene Casino in Worley. See the website for schedule and route information.

POST FALLS

Frederick Post planted the seed for the city of Post Falls when he built a sawmill along the Spokane River in 1800. He needed permission from the locals to take advantage of the falls for his mill, so he negotiated a land-use deal with Coeur d'Alene Chief Seltice. Today the riverfront city between Coeur d'Alene and Spokane is one of Idaho's fastest-growing towns, with a population that has more than tripled since 1980 to over 26,000.

Parks

Legend has it that Post and Chief Seltice signed their deal on **Treaty Rock,** today preserved as part of a small four-acre park near the corner of Seltice and Compton Streets, two blocks west of Spokane Street. Short trails wind through the park and lead to the historic granite outcropping. Post's name is indeed carved on the rock, and below it are some Native American pictographs. But as the interpretive information at the site notes, no concrete evidence exists that this rock is actually the "contract" between Post and Seltice.

At **Falls Park,** visitors can walk to overviews of Post's famous falls and the narrow Spokane River gorge. Interpretive signs illuminate early area history; picnic tables, a playground, and a small fishpond make the 22-acre park a pleasant place for a lunch break. To get to the park, head south on Spokane Street from I-90 and watch for a posted right turn at 4th Street.

Q'emiln Riverside Park was once the site of a Coeur d'Alene Indian village. Q'emiln (ka-MEE-lin) means "throat of the river" in the Coeur d'Alene language. This 90-acre park on the south side of the Spokane River has five miles of beautiful hiking trails through steep, rocky gorges. Also here are boat ramps, horseshoe pits, playground areas, and picnic shelters. A parking fee ($3.50 cars/$6 boats) is charged Memorial Day–Labor Day. To get to the park, take I-90 Exit 5 for Spokane Street, follow Spokane Street south across the river, and turn right on Park Way Drive just on the other side.

Corbin Park is named for early Post Falls railroad developer D. C. Corbin. The 24-acre park lies on the riverbank on the west side of town and offers a softball diamond, a volleyball court, a boat ramp, and picnic areas. To get here, take I-90 Exit 2 for Pleasant View Avenue and head south to Riverbend Avenue; take Riverbend east (left) to Corbin Park Road, and follow it into the park.

For more information on the city's parks, contact **Post Falls Parks and Recreation** (408 Spokane St., Post Falls, 208/773-0539).

Centennial Trail

From Post Falls, you can follow the Centennial Trail bike and hiking path all the way to Higgins Point on Coeur d'Alene Lake, or west to Spokane and beyond. The 63-mile-long interstate trail system is a favorite of hikers, cyclists, and skaters in summer and cross-country skiers in winter. Access the trail at Falls Park.

Cruises

The *Red Lion River Queen* (208/773-1611) sternwheeler cruises up the Spokane River on sightseeing excursions in summer. The 90-minute cruises ($16.75 ages 13–54, $12 ages 4–12, $15.75 over age 54) depart Red Lion Templin's Hotel on the river at 2 P.M. Tuesday–Friday and at 11 A.M. Saturday. They also offer Sunday brunch cruises, wine-tasting cruises, and various seasonal cruises.

Boating

Rent a boat for fishing or cruising the Spokane River or Coeur d'Alene Lake at **Red Lion**

Templin's Hotel on the River (414 E. 1st Ave., Post Falls, 208/773-1611). The hotel's marina rents out gas-powered pontoon boats for $75–95 an hour, with a two-hour minimum.

Rock Climbing

The city's **Q'emiln Riverside Park** offers dozens of single-pitch bolted climbs on reasonably solid river-canyon granite. It's a beautiful spot and seldom gets crowded. If you drive into the park, you'll have to pay a parking fee. Climbers being climbers, most park just outside the gate on Park Way Drive and walk in; from the entrance gate it's just a short hike to the climbing areas.

Accommodations

Sleep Inn (157 Pleasant View Rd., Post Falls, off I-90 Exit 2, 208/777-9394 or 800/851-3178, from $99 d) and **Howard Johnson Express Inn** (3647 W. 5th Ave., Post Falls, 208/773-4541 or 800/829-3124, from $60) each offer an indoor pool, a hot tub, and free continental breakfast. On the east side of town, **Comfort Inn** (3175 E. Seltice Way, Post Falls, 208/773-8900 or 800/424-6423, from $92 d) offers 47 guest rooms and a complimentary continental breakfast bar.

Red Lion Templin's Hotel on the River (414 E. 1st Ave., Post Falls, 208/773-1611 or 800/283-6754, www.redlion.com, from $149 d) sits on the banks of the Spokane River and is the state's only hotel listed in *Idaho Wildlife Viewing Guide* as an outstanding critter-watching site. Ospreys and mallard ducks are among the hotel's neighbors. Amenities include an indoor pool, a sauna, a spa, a fitness center, tennis courts, a marina with boat rentals, guest laundry, and a restaurant overlooking the river. Nonsmoking and wheelchair-accessible rooms are available, as are suites with jetted tubs, family suites, and parlor suites.

The River Cove B&B (212 Parkwood Pl., Post Falls, 208/773-1014, www.therivercove.com, from $129) bills itself as "a scenic waterfront retreat." From the back deck you can look past the pines to the water's edge below. Each of the guest rooms has a private bath, and rates include a gourmet breakfast. In winter, you can enjoy cross-country skiing right on the premises. Smoking is allowed outside only, and small children are not allowed.

RV Parks

RVers in the area have two good options to park their rigs for the night. **Coeur d'Alene RV Resort** (2652 E. Mullan Ave., Post Falls, 208/773-3527, around $35) is an upscale park offering 191 spotless sites with full hookups. Amenities include a beautiful clubhouse with a fireplace; a heated pool, spa, and fitness center; a playground; tennis and volleyball courts; horseshoe pits; and a nine-hole putting green.

Suntree RV Park (350 N. Idahline Rd., Post Falls, 208/777-8888, www.suntreervpark. com, $34–38) offers 111 sites with full hookups. Amenities include a pool, a hot tub, and shower and laundry facilities.

Food

One of the region's best restaurants lies outside Post Falls in sleepy little Hauser Lake, a short and scenic drive away. At **Chef in the Forest** (12008 N. Woodland Beach Dr., Post Falls, 208/773-3654, www.chefintheforest.net, from 5:30 P.M. Wed.–Thurs. and Sat., from 5 P.M. Fri. and Sun., entrées $21–36) the dinner-only menu features appetizers like warm Brie with fresh fruit and entrées such as roast duckling with fresh brandied raspberry sauce and filet mignon forestière covered with sautéed mushrooms. Great food, wine, and atmosphere make this a favorite excursion for area residents. Reservations are strongly recommended. From Post Falls, take Seltice west to McGuire Road, McGuire north to Highway 53, then west to Hauser Lake Road, and go east on North Woodland Beach Drive around the lake to the restaurant.

In town, the **White House Grill** (712 N. Spokane St., Post Falls, 208/777-9672, www. whitehousegrill.com, lunch and dinner Mon.–Sat., $8–16) dishes up Greek food with a whole lot of attitude. The employees are zany at this little restaurant, which serves everything from deep-fried feta and hummus to gyro sandwiches and lamb kebobs. Let's not forget flaky baklava and retsina wine.

WOLF LODGE DISTRICT
Eagle-Watching

A short distance east of Coeur d'Alene on I-90, Exit 22 is marked "Wolf Lodge District," where Wolf Lodge Creek empties into Wolf Lodge Bay. Wolves are no longer in evidence, but the bay's kokanee salmon population attracts a sizable population of bald eagles each winter. The eagles migrate down from the Canadian northlands to escape the harsh arctic winter. Here they find a relatively mild climate and easy food—the kokanee congregate to spawn and die at just about the same time the eagles begin arriving in late November. The eagle population peaks in late December—about 40 birds on average—and by March most of them have moved on. The best viewing time is in early morning, when the eagles do most of their feeding. The best viewing locations are at the Mineral Ridge Boat Ramp on the south side of the bay and at the Mineral Ridge trailhead, a little farther down the road on Beauty Bay.

Hiking

The **Mineral Ridge National Recreation Trail** leaves from the Mineral Ridge Recreation Area, which you'll come to just after rounding the corner from Wolf Lodge Bay into Beauty Bay on Highway 97. The 3.3-mile nature trail loops past an abandoned mine and cabin. The **Caribou Ridge National Recreation Trail** makes a nice day hike, running 4.6 miles from Beauty Creek Campground up to the Mount Coeur d'Alene Picnic Area. You'll find huckleberries in season along the way, and there are great views of the lake. The trail is moderately difficult, climbing 1,800 vertical feet in four switchbacks up onto the ridge. Beauty Creek Campground is less than a mile down Forest Road 438, which turns off Highway 97 along the east shore of Beauty Bay.

Horseback Riding

Rider Ranch (6219 S. Wolf Lodge Creek Rd., Coeur d'Alene, 208/667-3373, www.riderranch.com) offers guided trail rides, hayrides,

THE PANHANDLE

and parties for kids on a family-owned and operated working ranch in Wolf Lodge Creek Valley. Basic 90-minute trail rides ($40 pp) have a two-person minimum. Chuck wagon dinner rides ($55 pp) have a six-person minimum. All activities are scheduled by advance reservation only. Wolf Lodge Creek Road turns off the frontage road on the north side of I-90, a little less than a mile east of Exit 22.

Accommodations

You'll find the ultimate in solitude at **Wolf Lodge Creek B&B** (515 S. Wolf Lodge Creek Rd., Coeur d'Alene, 208/667-5902 or 800/919-9653, www.wolflodge.com, $125–250). Deer graze alongside the horses in this tranquil valley. You can hear yourself think out here, yet you're less than a half-hour's drive from the city. The big and modern wooden bed-and-breakfast sits on 27 acres and has five guest rooms, all with private baths. A separate cabin is also available. Hiking opportunities are right outside the door—the inn adjoins national forest lands—and a hot tub and sauna provide great evening relaxation. Rates include a full country breakfast.

Camping

Lake Coeur d'Alene Camping Resort (10588 E. Wolf Lodge Bay Rd., Coeur d'Alene, 208/664-4471 or 888/664-4471, www.campcda.com) is on the south side of I-90. Among the plethora of amenities: lake access with free small-boat moorage for guests; a heated pool and spa; a playground; hiking and bike trails; laundry and shower facilities; and boat and canoe rentals. The resort has 47 RV sites ($32–43) with hookups, 48 tent sites ($27), and 19 cabins ($56–135).

Along the I-90 frontage road 1.7 miles east of the Wolf Lodge exit (north side of I-90) is **Wolf Lodge Campground** (12329 E. Frontage Rd., Coeur d'Alene, 208/664-2812). The RV park offers 55 grassy sites ($30–35) with hookups on a large pleasant flat along Wolf Lodge Creek. Tent sites ($22) and cabins ($50–115) are also available.

Also in the area is the U.S. Forest Service

Beauty Creek Campground (20 sites, $18), just up Road 438 from Beauty Bay.

Food

Folks come from miles around for the steaks at **Wolf Lodge Inn** (11741 E. Frontage Rd., Coeur d'Alene, 208/664-6665, dinner daily). Here you can get darn near half a steer served up in front of you; the Rancher cut weighs in at 42 ounces. All steaks are flame-broiled over an open-pit cherrywood and tamarack fire and served with salad, bread, and buckaroo beans. Also on the menu are shrimp, salmon, trout, lamb chops, scallops, and, yes, Rocky Mountain oysters. Reservations are recommended.

LAKE COEUR D'ALENE SCENIC BYWAY

If you continue south from the Wolf Lodge exit around the east shore of the lake, you'll be traveling on the state's designated Lake Coeur d'Alene Scenic Byway. Keep your eyes peeled for ospreys; this area has the largest concentration of them in the western United States. The beautiful birds love the wetlands around the lake's east shore. You won't have to look so hard to spot the sunsets around here—the showy spectacles light up the sky and lake on a regular basis.

Arrow Point

About nine miles south of Beauty Bay en route to Harrison is the **Arrow Point Resort** (4502 S. Arrow Point Rd., Harrison, 877/525-3232, www.arrowpointresort.com, around $200), which occupies a finger of land jutting into the lake. The secluded, upscale resort offers furnished 2–3-bedroom condo units, a marina, beaches, and an indoor pool.

Bell Bay

At the south end of Powderhorn Bay, Highway 97 turns inland briefly before crossing the Coeur d'Alene River and rolling into Harrison. This inland stretch cuts off the nose of a peninsula sticking out into the lake. Here Road 314 (E. Point Rd.) turns off the highway and leads west some three miles across wide-open private

BOUNTIFUL BIKE TRAILS

Over the past few years, north Idaho has become one of the best bicycling destinations anywhere, thanks to the Route of the Hiawatha and the Trail of the Coeur d'Alenes, two unforgettable biking experiences.

The 15-mile **Route of the Hiawatha** is a rails-to-trails conversion on the old Milwaukee Road. The main trailhead (accessible via I-90 Exit 5 at Taft, Montana) begins just outside the 8,771-foot St. Paul Pass Tunnel, which means you start and end your ride by cycling through the 1.8-mile tunnel – in the dark, with only a bike light or headlamp to guide you. The packed gravel trail includes eight other tunnels and seven railway trestles, the highest 230 feet off the valley floor. Guardrails and a gentle downhill grade make the Route of the Hiawatha an easy and enjoyable ride for nearly everyone. A shuttle ($9 adults, $6 ages 6-13) runs from the end of the trail back to the first tunnel several times each day late May-early October.

Bike rentals, including lights and a rack, and trail passes ($9 adults, $6 ages 6-13) are available at the trailhead and at Lookout Pass ski area (I-90 Exit 0 on the Montana-Idaho border east of Wallace, 208/744-1301, www.skilookout.com).

The **Trail of the Coeur d'Alenes,** now an Idaho state park, spans 72 miles across the Idaho Panhandle from Mullan in the east to Plummer in the west. The fully paved trail sits on the old Union Pacific rail bed and

marks the railroad's efforts – in conjunction with the state of Idaho and the Coeur d'Alene Tribe, which comanages the trail – to seal over the mine waste and tailings that contaminated the area in its mining heyday. Signs along the way warn users to stay on the trail and eat at designated waysides, which may make some cyclists feel squeamish about riding the trail at all, but state and tribal officials say casual users need not worry about contamination.

The best and most scenic part of the mostly flat, free-access trail lies between Pinehurst (milepost 48.7), where it leaves the I-90 corridor, and the old Chatcolet Bridge south of Harrison (near milepost 8). Avid cyclists may want to tackle this section in a long day, but most riders will want to savor shorter out-and-back rides that can be done along any stretch of it. Be sure to carry your own water and snacks, since services are limited in most areas. Remember, though, that you can get a filling meal at the Enaville Resort near milepost 47, and an enormous ice cream cone at The Creamery in Harrison (milepost 15).

Bike rentals and shuttle service are available at **Excelsior Cycle & Sport Shop** (21 Railroad Ave., Kellogg, 208/786-3751) and **Pedal Fushers** (101 N. Coeur d'Alene Ave., Harrison, 208/689-3436). Maps and brochures are available at all trailheads, or contact the trail office at **Old Mission State Park** (31732 S. Mission Rd., Cataldo, 208/682-3814).

property to the U.S. Forest Service **Bell Bay Campground** (26 sites, $14–16) on the lakeshore. You'll feel isolated out here—it's a nice place to kick back.

Harrison

Until 1889 the southeast shore of Coeur d'Alene Lake was part of the Coeur d'Alene Indian Reservation, but then timber companies cruising the area decided that the shore would be a perfect spot for a sawmill, so they planted a

bug in then-president Benjamin Harrison's ear. Harrison "withdrew" a narrow strip of land from the reservation to accommodate the loggers.

The town was founded in 1891 and named after the president to ensure greasy wheels for the future. By the turn of the century, Harrison was home to 2,000 people, 11 lumber mills, a dozen saloons, and a thriving red-light district. Steamboats plying Coeur d'Alene Lake made Harrison a major port of call, and at one point it was the largest population center on the

THE PANHANDLE

lake. But fire devastated the town in 1917, and shortly thereafter the arrival of railroads rendered the steamboats obsolete. The local timber industry dwindled, and Harrison's glory days were over.

Today the town's 270-some residents rely on tourism to feed the coffers. Fishing and boating were long the primary draws, but increasing numbers of cyclists are using Harrison as a base camp for the Trail of the Coeur d'Alenes. Sunsets are stupendous here too. If you're looking for a refuge from the hectic tourist scene on the north shore of the lake, Harrison offers it.

If you're here to ride, **Pedal Pushers** (101 N. Coeur d'Alene Ave., Harrison, 208/689-3436, www.bikenorthidaho.com) is the place to get bike gear and other information. The shop rents bikes (road bikes $9 per hour, 2-hour minimum) and related equipment like car racks and helmets. It also offers repairs and runs seasonal shuttle service for the Trail of the Coeur d'Alenes.

Cyclists and other travelers congregate at the **Osprey Inn** (134 Frederick Ave., Harrison, 208/689-9502, www.ospreyinn.com, $66–120). Built in 1915, the inn was originally a boardinghouse for lumberjacks. Each of the five newly reconstructed guest rooms has a private bath with a shower. Rates include full breakfast. Harrison also offers RV and tent camping at its waterfront, with a small swimming beach and playground nearby.

Harrison's big annual event is the **Old Time Picnic,** held on the last weekend in July. In addition to potato salad and hot dogs, look for live entertainment and a parade along the lake. For more information, visit the **Harrison Chamber of Commerce** (www.harrisonidaho.org).

Chain of Lakes Route

South of Harrison, Highway 97 runs into a T intersection with Highway 3. If you turn right, you'll end up in St. Maries. Turn left to stay on the designated scenic byway, which takes you up the South Fork Coeur d'Alene River past 10 major lakes. Most of the wetlands in this Chain of Lakes area are included in the **Coeur d'Alene River Wildlife Management Area,** a favorite stopover for migratory waterfowl.

This beautiful area harbors a dirty little secret. Each spring, tundra swans stop at the Chain of Lakes on their way south; many never make it out. The area lies downstream from the Kellogg Superfund site, and the aquatic plants here contain deadly concentrations of lead. The swans eat the contaminated plants and die of starvation as the lead and other heavy metals inhibit nutrient absorption. Local environmentalists morbidly dub the annual event "The Rite of Spring." As you drive up this scenic highway, eventually rejoining I-90 near Cataldo, it's hard to imagine environmental problems lurking unseen. For more information, call the Idaho Department of Fish and Game's Coeur d'Alene office (208/769-1414).

The Silver Valley

East of Coeur d'Alene, I-90 climbs Fourth of July Pass and drops down the other side into the valley of the South Fork Coeur d'Alene River. In 1859, Jesuit missionary Pierre Jean de Smet described this valley as a verdant paradise: "Imagine thick, untrodden forest, strewn with thousands of trees thrown down by age and storms in every direction, where the path is scarcely visible." But this almost primeval scene was not to last. In 1885, prospector Noah Kellogg discovered a huge vein of a lead-silver-zinc ore called galena near the present-day town of Wardner. The find brought miners and mining companies flooding into the area, burrowing into the hills like mad, money-hungry moles. Over the next 100 years, more than $5 billion in precious metals would be taken from the earth, making "The Silver Valley" one of the most lucrative mining districts in world history while at the same time turning it into a lifeless toxic waste dump. The once verdant forests of the South

Fork were cut down for houses, mine timbers, and railroad ties. But that was just the beginning. In 1917 the first lead smelter was built near the Bunker Hill mine so that ore could be processed on-site. The U.S. Environmental Protection Agency's Superfund site description tersely outlines the consequences:

> During the majority of time the smelters were operating, few environmental protection procedures or controls were used. As a result, there is widespread contamination of soil, water, and air from lead and other heavy metals.

The smelters belched toxic plumes into the air, and the sulfur dioxide fallout killed what vegetation was left on the hillside. Water pollution was an even greater problem. Until 1938, all residues from the Bunker Hill's mine tailings were discharged directly into the Coeur d'Alene River. Thereafter, the wastes were diverted into an unlined settling pond that leaked toxic effluent into the groundwater. In addition, spring floods routinely washed heavy metals from tailings piles into the river and on downstream. Between the 1880s and the 1960s, an estimated 72 million tons of contaminated tailings ended up in the Coeur d'Alene River system; today scientists debate the potential health threat of the heavy-metal sludge coating the bottom of Coeur d'Alene Lake.

Meanwhile, in the mid-1970s, it was discovered that lead had found its way into the blood of the valley's children in alarming concentrations. A class-action suit brought by a number of parents against Gulf Resources and Chemical Corporation, then-owner of the Bunker Hill mine, ended in an out-of-court settlement, but the lead problem persists, as evidenced by the Panhandle Health District's publication *Coeur d'Alene River System and Heavy Metal Exposure, A Public Awareness Message*. Among other precautions, the pamphlet advises local residents:

> Clean shoes and change soil-stained clothes before going home. Keep soiled clothing in a plastic bag and launder it separate from the rest of your wash. Don't can whole fish caught from the lower Coeur d'Alene River system. Don't eat large amounts of fish, water fowl, or aquatic plants.

The Bunker Hill smelters shut down in 1981, pulling the rug out from under the local economy and leaving behind one of the country's largest Superfund toxic-cleanup sites. A 1992 report by the U.S. Geological Survey called the Coeur d'Alene River drainage the worst example of heavy-metal pollution in the world. Gulf conveniently declared bankruptcy, sticking taxpayers with the cleanup tab.

The towering smokestacks of the Bunker Hill smelters—built in 1977 in an attempt to disperse toxic clouds away from the local citizenry—were demolished in May 1996, and the blood-lead levels of valley residents today have declined to just above normal. The ongoing Superfund cleanup is making progress on a 21-square-mile area around Kellogg, and the hillsides are recovering their natural blanket of green. But heavy metals continue to leach into the river from upstream mine sites, flowing down to Coeur d'Alene Lake and into Washington.

Small-scale mining still takes place in the Kellogg area today, but the valley has turned to tourism as a long-term solution for generating revenue. In 1988, Kellogg's citizens voted to tax themselves in order to spruce up the local ski hill and install the world's longest gondola to get people here. Today, Silver Mountain Resort is the town's biggest draw in both winter and summer.

FOURTH OF JULY PASS

East of Wolf Lodge Bay, I-90 ascends and crests Fourth of July Pass (3,070 feet). The pass gets its name from an Independence Day weekend celebrated in 1861 by U.S. Army engineer Lieutenant John Mullan (1830–1909) and his crew of road builders. They were working on what later became known as the **Mullan Road,** a historic route connecting Fort

THE PANHANDLE

Benton, Montana, with Fort Walla Walla, Washington.

Originally intended as a military road and an alternative to south Idaho's Oregon Trail, the route came to be used by railroad builders and miners in the Coeur d'Alene River valley. Today, I-90 overlays much of Mullan's old road.

I-90 Exit 28, atop the pass, leads to two sites of interest. On the north side of the highway is **Mullan Road Historical Park,** where a 0.5-mile interpretive trail leads to the Mullan Tree, or rather the place where the Mullan Tree once grew. It had been engraved with the words "M. R., July 4, 1861." The "M. R." probably stood for "Military Road," not "Mullan Road." But consensus has it that John Mullan was an intelligent and resourceful man, so what the heck, Mullan Road it is. In any case, the western white pine blew down in 1962, and Mullan's inscription was removed for preservation and is on display at the Museum of North Idaho in Coeur d'Alene. The site is a little anticlimactic as a result, but the path through the woods is delightful. In the parking lot is a monumental bust of Mullan whose face, unfortunately, has fallen off.

On the south side of the highway is **Fourth of July Pass Park N' Ski Area.** A large parking area provides access to two five-mile loop trails and a third nonlooping trail that continues through the woods for just under two miles. Some steep grades on the loops make those trails best suited to intermediate or better skiers. The third trail is gentle enough for beginners.

CATALDO AND VICINITY
◖ Old Mission State Park

Old Mission State Park (31732 S. Mission Rd., Cataldo, 208/682-3814, 8 A.M.–6 P.M. daily summer, 9 A.M.–5 P.M. daily in other seasons, parking $5) is at I-90 Exit 39. Even from a distance the old Cataldo mission, visible from I-90, is powerful and striking. At once monumental and simple, the Greek Revival–style structure sits atop a grassy hill that slopes down to the placid waters of the

the old Cataldo mission

South Fork of the Coeur d'Alene River. It fits naturally into its surroundings, a tribute to the man who designed and helped build the mission and served as its first spiritual leader, Father Antonio Ravalli, born May 16, 1812, in Ferrara, Italy. Ravalli was ordained as a Jesuit priest in 1843 and sent to work with the Coeur d'Alene Indians alongside Father Pierre Jean de Smet. When Ravalli arrived, de Smet's mission was located on the St. Joe River near present-day St. Maries, but the regular floods (a phenomenon that persists today) caused de Smet to look for a higher and drier spot. Ravalli was assigned the task of supervising the relocation.

The park's literature calls Ravalli a Renaissance man; while that might be a cliché, it fits him perfectly. By the time he reached Idaho at the age of 31, Ravalli had studied literature, philosophy, theology, mathematics, science, medicine, art, and architecture. The Native Americans and missionaries began building the mission in 1847, following Ravalli's plans, out of hand-hewn timbers held together with wooden pegs. The foot-thick walls were made of woven straw and river mud. The result, formally called the Mission of the Sacred Heart, is the oldest building still standing in Idaho.

The exterior is beautiful, but Ravalli's artistic handiwork and creativity really shine inside. Out on the wild frontier, with no budget to speak of, Ravalli became a master at decorating on the cheap. See that marble altar? It's actually made of wood, carefully painted by Ravalli to simulate marble. And those cast iron chandeliers? They're tin, cut into elegant patterns by the artistic priest. Ravalli also painted the side altars with scenes depicting heaven and hell and carved the statues of the Virgin Mary and Saint John the Evangelist standing on either side of the altar.

The mission opened for worship in 1853 and operated for 23 years. During that time it served as a welcome resting place for Native Americans, pioneers, John Mullan's road-building crew, and military contingents. Father Joseph Cataldo, a strong and popular leader of Idaho's Roman Catholics, took the reins in 1865; the nearby town is named in his honor. In 1876, mission activities were relocated to DeSmet in a political move that was heartbreaking for the mission's Native American congregation.

Today, the mission serves as the centerpiece of an outstanding state historic park. A modern interpretive center screens a short film illustrating the mission's history and offers exhibits about the Coeur d'Alene Indians and the Jesuits. Self-guided interpretive trails lead across the grounds to natural features and points of historical interest.

The park hosts a few events each year. On the second Sunday in July is the **Historic Skills Fair,** where you can watch spinning, quilting, black powder shooting, and other anachronisms done just the way the old-timers used to do. On August 15 is the annual **Coeur d'Alene Indian Pilgrimage** and its associated "Coming of the Black Robes Pageant." Traditional Native American foods are featured.

Snowcat Skiing
Peak Adventures (208/818-9408, www.peak-snowcats.com, Dec.–Apr.), at I-90 Exit 40 in Cataldo, offers snowcat ski trips high into the St. Joe Mountains south of town. The cost for full-day trips is $225, including guides and lunch; reservations are required.

UP THE NORTH FORK OF THE COEUR D'ALENE RIVER
The next town you come to as you head east from Cataldo on I-90 is Kingston, near the confluence of the two major forks of the Coeur d'Alene River. I-90 follows the South Fork, while Forest Highway 9 leaves I-90 and follows the North Fork up to the old gold-mining towns of Prichard and Murray. Besides its considerable history, the North Fork area is rife with recreation opportunities.

Note: On older Forest Service maps, the North Fork of the Coeur d'Alene is labeled as the main Coeur d'Alene River, while the Little North Fork—the first major tributary of the North Fork—is labeled the North Fork of the Coeur d'Alene. The Forest Service has changed this to reflect standard local usage on its newer maps.

Enaville Resort
Off I-90 Exit 43 and 1.5 miles north on Coeur d'Alene River Road (Forest Hwy. 9) is Enaville Resort (208/682-3453, www.enavilleresort.com, breakfast, lunch, and dinner daily). It's not a resort like the Coeur d'Alene Resort; it's more like a last resort. Enaville was established in 1880 and over the years within its log walls has been a gold rush–era bar, a railroad way station, a boardinghouse, and a whorehouse. Today it's a family restaurant and tavern specializing in such delectables as buffalo burgers and Rocky Mountain oysters. Kitschy Western art and memorabilia—including old swords and a blunderbuss—fill the walls, floors, and ceilings. It's all a bit of living history and definitely worth a stop for a meal.

The Little North Fork
Little North Fork Road leads up to the U.S.

Forest Service **Bumblebee Campground** (25 sites, $16) and, after another 20 miles or so to **Honeysuckle Campground** (8 sites, $16). Between the two campgrounds is Laverne Creek, which marks a boundary for anglers. From here on upriver, fishing is catch-and-release only with single barbless hooks, flies and lures only, and no bait. The Little North Fork is stocked with rainbows above Bumblebee Campground.

Prichard

Twenty-three miles from Kingston is Prichard, a town named after the first prospector to strike gold in the Coeur d'Alenes. Today there's not a whole lot here, but Silver Valley residents come from miles around for the prime rib dinners at **Gloria's Steak House & Lodge** (21428 Coeur d'Alene River Rd., 208/682-3031, daily year-round). Gloria's also rents motel rooms ($50–100; rates include prime rib dinner for two) and has a hot tub.

To Murray

At Prichard, you can turn off the North Fork and head east up Prichard Creek. At the confluence of Prichard and Eagle Creeks, turning up Forest Road 152, then Forest Road 805, leads up the west fork of Eagle Creek to **Settlers Grove of Ancient Cedars.** A trail winds through the grove, which has many trees 6–8 feet in diameter.

Continuing east on Prichard Creek Road, you'll soon come to the gold-rush boomtown of Murray. As many as 25,000 people lived in the area between Murray and neighboring Eagle City in its heyday. Wyatt Earp ran a saloon in Eagle in the 1880s, and Murray was the Shoshone County seat for 14 years. You'd never guess it looking at the sleepy little town today. You can thank the Coeur d'Alene Mining Company, which dredged Prichard Creek 1917–1924, for the ugly tailings piles along the creek-side.

More area history can be gleaned at **The Sprag Pole** (6353 Prichard Creek Rd., Murray, 208/682-3901), which consists of a friendly bar and grill on one side and Walt's Museum, a

veritable warehouse full of great old stuff, on the other. A sprag pole was the old-time equivalent of a parking brake—a long pole strategically planted to keep wagons from rolling. The other bar in town is the **Bedroom Goldmine Bar** (6273 Prichard Creek Rd., Murray, 208/682-4394), site of the Bedroom Mine. A former owner sunk a shaft right in his bedroom. It's no longer being used.

From Murray, you can head back to Kingston the way you came, or take Forest Road 456 over King's and Dobson Passes 20 miles to Wallace. The old **Murray Cemetery,** at the bottom of King's Pass grade on the way out of town toward Wallace, has the graves of such famous locals as Andrew Prichard and Maggie Hall, a kindly madam better known as Molly B'Damn.

KELLOGG AND VICINITY

In attempting to rise anew from the ashes of its mining industry, Kellogg took two major steps: It replaced the narrow winding road up to the local ski hill with the world's longest gondola, which now whisks skiers up some 3,400 vertical feet in 3.1 miles to the snowy slopes; and it gave the town a partial face-lift, turning it into a Bavarian-themed village. The gondola might be called a success—it's certainly a unique attraction and makes it easier for visitors to enjoy the mountain. The Alpine Village, however, seems a little out of place. Other than snowy peaks, nothing about this gritty mining town or the surrounding area is even vaguely reminiscent of the Alps. Uptown Kellogg is a charming historic district, but many of the storefronts sit vacant as all the attention is given to the area surrounding the burgeoning Silver Mountain Resort.

Silver Mountain

There has been a ski area on the slopes of Kellogg and Wardner Peaks since the late 1960s. First called Jackass (for Noah Kellogg's famous donkey), then Silverhorn, the resort struggled with one main drawback: the steep, circuitous road skiers needed to negotiate to reach the base area from Kellogg. When the

© IDAHO DIVISION OF TOURISM

skiing at Silver Mountain near Kellogg

up to the four-lane tubing hill (Sat.–Sun. and holidays, $20 adults, $18 youth and seniors) for two-hour sessions. Scenic gondola rides (17 adults, $13 youth and seniors) are possible year-round.

In summer, the resort is open weekends and holidays only and hosts barbecues and entertainment in its mountaintop amphitheater. Other summertime draws include gondola-served hiking and mountain biking on an extensive, newly expanded trail system. A single ride up the gondola in summer costs $17 adults, $13 juniors; family rates are available. Full-day mountain-bike passes also are available.

The resort recently unveiled an indoor water park connected to its fancy new lodge. **Silver Rapids Water Park** is an expansive year-round aqua playground featuring a continuous surf wave, a flowing river, waterslides, private cabanas, and a small restaurant with hot tubs, but you must be a guest of the resort's Morning Star Lodge. Packages start at $199 for four people, which includes a studio suite in the lodge and a two-day pass to the water park. Day-use for nonguests can be arranged for parties of 15 or more.

Bunker Hill Staff House Museum

Otherwise known as the Shoshone County Mining and Smelting Museum, this museum (820 McKinley Ave., Kellogg, 208/786-4141, 10 A.M.–6 P.M. daily late May–Sept., small entrance fee) occupies the former staff house for resident and visiting bigwigs of the Bunker Hill & Sullivan Mine Co. The house was built in 1906 for a manager of the Bunker Hill mine. Exhibits cover the town's mining history, with an emphasis on Bunker Hill itself. A great collection of old photos includes one of a burro, supposedly Noah Kellogg's famous sidekick. Another display lists the Bunker Hill's staggering statistics: 1,900 tons of ore mined daily; 400 tons of waste rock removed daily; 3,500 gallons of water expelled per minute; 160,000 cubic feet of air circulated each minute. During the mine's 96-year life span, 37 million tons of ore were excavated, yielding more than 165 million ounces of silver, as well as copious

mines shut down in the early 1980s, Silver Mountain represented the city's best hope for economic recovery—a chance to fill the void with tourist dollars. The late city councilman Wayne Ross envisioned an aerial tramway that would bypass the road and take visitors directly from town to the mountaintop. He successfully negotiated funding, and in 1990 the new, improved **Silver Mountain Ski Resort** (610 Bunker Ave., Kellogg, at I-90 Exit 49, 208/783-1111 or 866/344-2675, www.silvermt. com, 9 A.M.–4 P.M. daily, lift tickets $50 ages 18–61, $35 ages 7–17, $40 over age 61, free under age 7) with the world's longest single-stage gondola (3.1 miles) opened.

The area gets plenty of snow—some 300 inches per year on average. The resort has 1,500 acres with a 2,200-foot vertical drop and a longest run of 2.5 miles. Intermediate runs are most prevalent, but 40 percent of the runs are either advanced or expert. Besides the gondola, the area is served by one fixed-grip quad, two triple chairs, two double chairs, and a surface lift. The gondolas also take people

amounts of lead and zinc. Don't miss the display in the basement—an ingenious 3-D model of the Bunker Hill mine's enormous underground labyrinth.

Wardner

To see where it all began, take Kellogg's Division Street up the hill into Milo Gulch to the town of Wardner (population 230). Just 1,000 yards up the gulch from today's Wardner City Hall, Noah Kellogg found the gleaming rock that sparked the Silver Valley's mining boom. In "downtown" Wardner, locals keep the memories of the mining days alive at **Wardner Gift Shop and Museum** (652 Main St., 208/786-2641). The free museum has a fascinating collection of photographs and memorabilia.

Noah Kellogg's Grave

On the way up Division Street heading toward Wardner, you'll spot signs directing you east (left) up the flanks of the mountain to the local cemetery. Here you'll find the grave of Noah Kellogg, marked by a fence and a tasteless modern monument that steals all dignity from the site. It's a poignant place to ponder the dead miners who couldn't take their wealth with them, and the costs of their obsession on the scarred valley below.

Sunshine Mine Memorial

The Sunshine Mine is recognized as the world's all-time greatest silver producer. But on May 2, 1972, extraction of that bounty exacted a horrific price. Some time after 11 A.M. a fire broke out more than 3,000 feet down in the mine's depths. Warnings spread as soon as the first smoke was noticed. Those among the 173 miners at work that day who got word of the blaze bolted for the hoists that would take them toward the surface. Failure of a mine-wide alarm system prevented others from getting the warning until it was too late. Smoke and carbon monoxide soon asphyxiated the hoist operators, trapping the miners left beneath them. Despite the valiant efforts of local, national, and even international rescue workers, 91 miners died in the tragedy. Just east of Kellogg, off I-90 Exit 54, is the Sunshine Mine Memorial, a huge sculpture of a miner at work dedicated to those who died in the disaster.

Accommodations

On the low-priced end of the spectrum are **Sunshine Inn** (301 W. Cameron Ave., Kellogg, 208/784-1186), with a small restaurant and a big lounge with pool tables, and the **Trail Motel** (206 W. Cameron Ave., Kellogg, 208/784-1161, from $45 d). Both are on the north side of I-90.

GuestHouse Inn & Suites (601 Bunker Ave., Kellogg, 208/783-1234 or 800/214-8378, from $89 d) is especially noteworthy for its convenient location adjacent to the Silver Mountain gondola. Amenities at the newish 61-room hotel include an indoor pool and spa, free continental breakfast, cable TV with HBO, a guest laundry, and ski and bike storage.

One of the bigger, fancier motels in town is (**Silverhorn Motor Inn** (699 W. Cameron Ave., Kellogg, 208/783-1151 or 800/437-6437, www.silverhornmotorinn.com, from $89 d). It offers queen beds and an on-site restaurant, guest laundry, and a jetted tub. Pets are allowed.

Silver Mountain Resort's new **Morning Star Lodge** (610 Bunker Ave., Kellogg, 208/783-1111 or 866/344-2675, www.silvermt.com, from $199 peak season) offers plush condo-style suites ranging from studio units to lavish loft suites. The resort has several skiing and water-park packages as well as cheaper off-season rates. Amenities include kitchens, decks, and preferential treatment at the resort's facilities.

Food and Drink

Down at the gondola base, **Noah's Canteen** (610 Bunker Ave., Kellogg, 208/783-2440, lunch and dinner daily, entrées $10–27) serves upscale pub fare in a casual dining room with a roaring fireplace. Expect to find steaks, seafood, burgers, wraps, and pizza. The adjacent lounge area has more than 10 microbrews on tap.

(Silver Spoon Restaurant (699 W. Cameron Ave., Kellogg, 208/783-1151, 6 A.M.–9 P.M. daily, under $10), at the Silverhorn Motor Inn, offers freshly baked goods, huckleberry pancakes, and other homespun fare.

In Uptown Kellogg, you'll find **Moose Creek Grill** (12 Emerson Lane, Kellogg, 208/783-2625, www.moosecreekgrill.com, lunch Wed.–Fri. summer, dinner Tues.–Sat. year-round, $9–25) in an old blue house. This casual new restaurant serves burgers, steaks, salads, pork chops, fish tacos, and inventive pasta dishes. Try the delish dark chocolate turtle cake for dessert. Lots of Northwestern microbrews and wines by the glass are available.

Information

The **Historic Silver Valley Chamber of Commerce** operates a visitors center (10 Station Ave., Kellogg, 208/784-0821, www.silvervalleychamber.com), which has lots of brochures and general information about the area.

(WALLACE

East of Kellogg, I-90 climbs through Osburn to Wallace. Of all the towns in the Silver Valley, Wallace feels most like the quintessential mining town. It is a compact place—the valley narrows into a tight canyon, forcing the town to creep off the canyon floor and up the steep wooded slopes. In the small downtown, you'll still find a mining supply store along with many well-preserved 19th-century buildings; the entire town is listed on the National Register of Historic Places. You'll discover a treasure trove of antiques shops, old saloons, funky restaurants, and museums.

Up on the hill—hidden in the trees up steep, narrow, switchbacking lanes—are old miners' cabins and newer facsimiles. This is where Hollywood starlet Lana Turner spent her early years, in a house overlooking the rough-and-tumble town.

Sometimes after a storm, when mists hang over the hillsides and raindrops drip off the rooftops and pines, the town takes on an

© IDAHO DIVISION OF TOURISM

THE PANHANDLE

Wallace has a checkered past.

almost tangible tranquility. Walk up the hill—up the rickety wooden stairs, past the small clapboard houses—and you'll half expect to find a grizzled old prospector sitting on his front porch, plucking the melancholy strains of "My Darling Clementine" on a banjo. It's almost enough to make you want to trade in the minivan for a pickax and mule.

Museums

A trio of museums commemorate Wallace's three greatest industries. The **Wallace District Mining Museum** (509 Bank St., Wallace, 208/556-1592, 10 A.M.–5 P.M. daily May–Labor Day weekend, 10 A.M.–5 P.M. Mon.–Sat., 10 A.M.–3 P.M. Sun. Apr. and Sept.–Oct., 10 A.M.–5 P.M. Mon.–Fri., 10 A.M.–3 P.M. Sat.–Sun. Nov.–Mar., $3 adults, $1 ages 6–17, $7 family) offers exhibits about mining, miners, and the hard-rock life they led during the valley's boom days. You can ponder historic photos and artifacts and watch two different videos on the valley's mining history. More than 1 billion ounces of silver were mined in the region over the course of a century. That's 62.5 million pounds, or 31,250 tons.

The **Northern Pacific Depot Railroad Museum** (6th and Pine St., Wallace, 208/752-0111, 9 A.M.–7 P.M. daily summer, reduced hours spring and fall, closed Oct. 31–Mar. 15, $2 adults, $1.50 over age 59, $1 ages 6–16, $6 family) occupies the beautiful château-style 1901 Northern Pacific Depot. Bricks used in the building's construction were imported from China and destined for a fancy Tacoma hotel; the hotel never got off the ground, and the bricks ended up here. Until 1980, the Northern Pacific's Yellowstone Park Line stopped at this depot on its run between Chicago and Seattle. In 1986 the depot was carefully moved to its present site after the new I-90 threatened to run right over it. Old railroad photos and paraphernalia fill the museum. One of the most interesting exhibits is a huge glass route map that once hung in another Northern Pacific depot.

Perhaps the most interesting of the three museums is the **Oasis Bordello Museum** (605 Cedar St., Wallace, 208/753-0801, 9:30 A.M.–6:30 P.M. Mon.–Sat., 10 A.M.–5 P.M. Sun. May–early Oct., tour $5). Mining towns have historically been populated with a far higher percentage of men than women, and this imbalance created numerous business opportunities for enterprising women of questionable virtue. The Oasis was just one of several brothels that once lined this end of town. Interestingly enough, the Oasis remained in business until 1988, which was 15 years after Idaho's governor officially proclaimed prostitution illegal in the state and 93 years after the first brothel opened. The workers apparently left in a hurry, and the rooms have been preserved as they were when abandoned.

The 20-minute upstairs tour offers many interesting anecdotes, such as the fact that in 1982 the Oasis women bought the town a new police car with money saved from their earnings. Their relatively recent departure takes this museum out of the realm of a charming Western anachronism and into the somewhat seedier reality of the modern world. Nothing on the tour is particularly graphic or offensive, but it's nevertheless more jeans and G-strings than petticoats and lace. Entry is free to the ground-floor store, which sells assorted scents and frillies, and to the basement museum, which offers glimpses of a still and other artifacts from Wallace's rowdy days gone by.

Sierra Silver Mine Tour

Rarely can someone not drawing a paycheck from a mining company go down the shafts for a look around. The 75-minute Sierra Silver Mine Tour (420 5th St., Wallace, 208/752-5151, www.silverminetour.org, every 30 minutes 10 A.M.–4 P.M. daily May–early Oct., $12.50 adults, $11 seniors, $8.50 ages 4–16, $41 family of 2 adults with 2 or more kids) allows you to do just that. The mine you'll explore was once an operating silver mine. From Wallace, you'll board a trolley for the short ride to the mine, then don hard hats and make your way down into the cool, dark depths. Guides explain the mining process, history, and various techniques.

Recreation

The Route of the Hiawatha mountain bike trail goes right through Wallace along its 15-mile run to the Montana border. In summer, this brings to town an endless flow of Lycra-clad bicyclists who mingle with leather-clad Harley riders at the sidewalk cafés.

For information on the local backcountry and trail maps for the areas on both the North and South Forks of the Coeur d'Alene River, contact the U.S. Forest Service **Coeur d'Alene River Ranger District Silver Valley Office** (Smelterville, 208/783-2363).

Entertainment

Sixth Street Melodrama (212 6th St., Wallace, 208/752-8871 or 877/749-8478, www.sixthstreetmelodrama.com, $13–15) is a long-running local thespian troupe. In summer, the players present old-fashioned melodrama with plenty of audience participation. In winter and spring, the company offers more serious performances, often musicals. Check the website for a current playbill and schedule.

Events

The second Saturday in May, Wallace celebrates **Depot Days** with a street fair, a car show, food, and live music. For more information call the Northern Pacific Depot Railroad Museum (208/752-0111). The **Huckleberry/Heritage Festival** in mid-August brings a 5K run and walk, a pancake breakfast, crafts booths, and more. The chamber of commerce (208/753-7151) can fill you in on the details.

Accommodations

The Brooks Hotel (500 Cedar St., Wallace, 208/556-1571, www.thebrookshotel.com, from $70 d) is the grande dame of the old Wallace hotels, but she's a little scruffy behind the ears. Off the lobby is a good family restaurant serving three meals a day. **Stardust Motel** (410 Pine St., Wallace, 208/752-1213, $40–80) is a retro motor inn that is hit or miss in the cleanliness department, but the place is affordable, and you could easily stumble back to your room from the saloons thanks to the motel's close proximity to downtown.

Wallace Inn (100 Front St., Wallace, 208/752-1252 or 800/643-2386, from $129 d) is the most modern and upscale place in town. Amenities include a heated indoor pool and jetted tub, a sauna and steam rooms, and a restaurant. The inn offers a free shuttle to Lookout Pass Recreation Area.

If you're into privacy, why not rent an entire house? **The Bungalow at 214 Cedar** (214 Cedar St., Wallace, 208/512-7686) is a Victorian-era home near downtown with three bedrooms and a full kitchen. You can rent the house for $85 per night per couple, $15 for each additional person up to eight guests. You'll have to leave a $500 deposit, all of which is refundable except for a $50 cleaning fee.

The **Beale House B&B** (107 Cedar St., Wallace, 208/752-7151 or 888/752-7151, from $170) occupies a 1904 Victorian residence in a quiet residential neighborhood. The house has a long and distinguished history, well documented in a collection of old photographs available for perusal. A crackling fireplace inside and a bubbling hot tub outside combine to take the chill off those après-ski evenings. Four of the five guest rooms share baths (which often turns out to be private, depending on how full the place is). Rates include full breakfast. Children and pets are not allowed.

Camping and RVing

Down by the Depot RV Park (108 Nine Mile Rd., Wallace, 208/753-7121), just across the I-90 from downtown, offers 45 sites with hookups ($25) and for tents ($18). Amenities include showers, restrooms, a laundry room, a game room, and a saloon.

Food and Drink

The **1313 Club Historic Saloon & Grill** (608 Bank St., Wallace, 208/752-9391, www.1313club.com, lunch and dinner Mon.–Sat., dinner entrées $11–22) has several sidewalk tables perfect for people-watching. The efficient service and selection of microbrews in bottles and on tap are among the best in town.

The menu is all about burgers, hot sandwiches, and deep-fried finger steaks. At night, you can get big steaks and pork chops served with garlicky mashed potatoes and grilled baguette.

Nearby is **Smoke House Barbecue & Saloon** (424 6th St., Wallace, 208/659-7539, 11 A.M.–9 P.M. daily, entrées $7–27), a historic bar that dishes up apple wood–smoked pork ribs, pulled pork sandwiches, bison, wild Alaskan salmon, and brisket. Sides include red beans and rice, coleslaw, and macaroni and cheese. Service here can be spotty, but the beer is cold and the food is good enough to make up for a little forgetfulness.

Locals call Wallace the "Center of the Universe," which might help to explain why the **Red Light Garage** (5th St. and Pine St., 208/556-0575, breakfast, lunch, and dinner daily, breakfast under $10) has a spaceship in its parking lot. This funky little restaurant and junk store, in a former service station, serves burgers, burritos, wraps, and a damn good huckleberry milk shake. You can also get breakfast items in the morning, like one big huckleberry pancake, egg-filled burritos, and freshly baked cinnamon rolls, but the coffee could peel the chrome off your Harley's tailpipe. If you're in a hurry, this might not be the place for you—the servers and cooks appear to have lead in their pants. Regardless, it's a fun place, and there's live music out on the patio on weekends during the warmer months.

Wallace Brewing Company (610 Bank St., Wallace, 208/660-3430, www.wallace-brewing.com, 1–6 P.M. Tues.–Thurs., 1–8 P.M. Fri.–Sat.) is the place to go for locally hand-crafted beers. The delicious array includes Jack Leg Stout, Vindicator IPA, and Red Light, a honey wheat lager that pays homage to the town's former ladies of the evening.

Information

Historic Wallace Chamber of Commerce

The **Historic Wallace Chamber of Commerce** (10 River St., Wallace, 208/753-7151, www.wallaceidahochamber.com) operates a visitors center right off I-90 Exit 61. Next door is the **Mining Heritage Exhibition,** a free park with an array of brightly painted old mining equipment and some picnic tables.

LOOKOUT PASS

Lookout Pass Ski and Recreation Area (208/744-1301, www.skilookout.com, 9 A.M.–4 P.M. daily mid-Dec.–New Year, 9 A.M.–4 P.M. Thurs.–Sun. the rest of the season, closed Christmas Day), at I-90 Exit 0, right on the state line, may be small in stature, but it's big in heart. The state's second-oldest ski area, Lookout has been faithfully serving Silver Valley since 1938. Over much of its life, the area owed its existence to the volunteer efforts of the Idaho Ski Club and others. It is famous for its family-friendly atmosphere and offers skiing, snowmobiling, and other winter activities as well as summer fun like mountain biking. It's the main outfitting point for the Route of the Hiawatha cycling trail.

Alpine Skiing

Although this is a humble mountain in some ways, the snow quality and quantity—a whopping 387 inches per year average—are excellent, and the sweeping views into two states provide a real "high mountain" feeling, despite a peak elevation under 6,000 feet. Lookout Pass recently expanded a bit and now has about 18 runs (the longest is 1.2 miles) and 1,150 feet of vertical drop served by a rope tow and two double chairs. The mountain's back side sports a snowboard and ski terrain park.

Lift tickets (weekend $35 adults, $25 juniors and seniors) won't break your budget, and midweek rates are a few bucks less. Half-day tickets and various special promotional tickets are available too. You can also find ski and snowboard rentals, lessons, and day care services.

The day lodge is cozy and well-kept, offering both food and drink. The bar's lively social scene is especially friendly and intimate, since most of the patrons are locals who know one another. The season here generally runs mid-November–late March or early April.

Cross-Country Skiing

A 16-mile system of cross-country ski trails, ranging in difficulty from beginner to advanced, is accessible from the resort's base area. Some are shared with snowmobiles. Cross-country skiers can purchase a single-ride lift ticket ($7) and ski their way back down to the base area on the trails.

U.S. 95 to Lake Pend Oreille

HAYDEN LAKE

Heading north on U.S. 95 from Coeur d'Alene, you'll soon come to the turnoff to the town of Hayden Lake, a wealthy bedroom community of Coeur d'Alene. The lakeshore is ringed with expensive homes but not much public lakefront, giving the whole area the appearance of an upper-crust country club.

Recreation

In Hayden Lake, babies are born with silver putters in hand. Golf is as natural as breathing here, and you half expect electric golf carts to replace automobiles on the city streets. The chichi Hayden Lake Country Club is private, but the semichichi, semiprivate **Avondale Golf Course** (10745 Avondale Loop Rd., Hayden Lake, 208/772-5963, year-round, $32–53) has been known to accommodate plebeian passers-through on its 6,525-yard, par-72 course.

Hikers in summer and cross-country skiers in winter enjoy the trails at **English Point** (free), a bit of national forest preserved along the lake's north shore. To get here, turn east off U.S. 95 onto Lancaster Road and drive about 3.5 miles to English Point Road.

Accommodations

On the lake's north side, reached by turning east off U.S. 95 at Lancaster Road (the first major intersection north of Hayden junction), is **Bridle Path Manor** (1155 E. Lancaster Rd., Hayden, 208/762-3126, $90–150), a large Tudor–style house on an expansive horse ranch. Horse fanciers can take trail rides through the woods; others can stay in and play billiards or relax by the fireplace. Rates for the five guest rooms include a full breakfast. Kids are welcome.

One of the biggest old mansions on Hayden Lake is now a gloriously refurbished bed-and-breakfast. The **Clark House** (5250 E. Hayden Lake Rd., Hayden, 208/772-3470 or 800/765-4593, www.clarkhouse.com, $149–179) was built in 1910 as a summer home for millionaire F. Lewis Clark and his wife, Winifred. At the time of its completion, the 15,000-square-foot manse was the most expensive residence in Idaho. After extensive reconstruction, it once again recalls its glory days, although the sprawling estate it reigned over has shrunk over the years from 1,400 acres to 12. Rates at the house include a full gourmet breakfast, all guest rooms have private baths, and you'll enjoy king or queen feather beds, fireplaces, Roman tubs built for two, and great views of the lake. Smoking, pets, and children under 12 are not allowed. The B&B's dining room also has a good reputation; it serves three-course dinners (Tues.–Sat., from $29 pp) to both guests and nonguests by reservation.

Camping

Way around the lake's east side is the U.S. Forest Service's **Mokins Bay Campground** (16 sites, $16) on a six-acre lakeshore plot. Take Forest Road 3090, which circles the lake; it's a long dozen or so miles from town to the campground along either the north or south shores—the northern route is probably the best bet.

ATHOL AND VICINITY
◖ Silverwood Theme Park

Silverwood Theme Park (27843 N. U.S. 95, Athol, 208/683-3400, www.silverwood-themepark.com, Sat.–Sun. early and late in the season, daily in peak season, early

THE PANHANDLE

Silverwood Theme Park

© IDAHO DIVISION OF TOURISM

May–Oct., $42 adults, $22 ages 3–7 and over age 65), a 700-acre amusement park, is literally a scream—let's see you keep your mouth shut on that upside-down corkscrew roller coaster, or on Tremors, a coaster that plummets into the bowels of the earth, or on the Timber Terror, a 55-mph wooden coaster sure to please even the most obsessed roller-meister. Monster, Roundup, Scrambler, Skydiver, and other "high-intensity" rides will scare the living daylights out of you, and the park recently added Aftershock, a new coaster that drops 177 feet at 65 mph into three upside-down loops. Don't miss the magic show or the ice spectacular. In 2003, Silverwood debuted its new **Boulder Beach** water park, with water-slides, a wave pool, lazy river, and tree house–themed kids area. Admission is included in the Silverwood rates.

Those wanting to make a week or weekend of it will find the park's own 126-site RV park ($36) right across the street. Amenities include full hookups, shaded sites, showers, picnic tables, volleyball courts, horseshoe pits, barbecue grills, a laundry, and a small store with propane. Tenters are welcome, with a maximum of two tents per site ($30). Guests receive discounted admission to the amusement park.

Farragut State Park

During World War II the 4,000-acre Farragut State Park (13550 E. Hwy. 54, Athol, 208/683-2425, day-use $5), on the southern shores of Lake Pend Oreille, had a large U.S. Naval Training Center. The site was supposedly "discovered" by Eleanor Roosevelt on a flight from Washington, D.C., to Seattle. FDR was looking for an inland body of water to train submariners in safety, away from the eyes and ears of the enemies. Eleanor saw Lake Pend Oreille and described it to her husband, who deemed it perfect for the task. Construction of the base began in 1942. By the fall of that year, the base's population of 55,000 military personnel made it the second-largest naval training facility in the country and the largest "city" in Idaho. At war's end the base was decommissioned, and in 1964 Farragut State

Park was established, named after Civil War hero Admiral David Farragut (1801–1870), whose important victories on the Gulf Coast and Mississippi River allowed the Union Army to capture and control the region.

Today, the sprawling park, with its many long loop roads and open areas, still retains a military-base ambience. Four separate campgrounds have a total of 135 sites ($14–40) plus several camping cabins ($50–55) that can sleep up to five; the Whitetail campground ($16–18) is closest to the lake, the park's prime recreational attraction. Sunbathing and splashing are favorite activities, and a concessionaire rents pedal boats, rafts, and beach chairs. A boat-launching area is available for those hauling their own vessels. Those who prefer terra firma fun can explore the park's hiking, biking, and horseback-riding trails, and you can rent horses at the Thimbleberry Group Area, off Highway 54 toward the west end of the park. The north-side trails wind through beautiful woods, while the south-side trails skirt the lakeshore. In winter, the park sets and grooms 10 miles of mostly flat cross-country ski trails. Unusual offerings here include a model-airplane flying field and a shooting range often used by black-powder enthusiasts (watch for the occasional cannon shot). To get to the park, take Highway 54 four miles east from U.S. 95 at Athol.

Bayview

The little fishing village of Bayview is an uncrowded hideaway. Docks, boats, and fishing resorts ring the calm waters of Scenic Bay, and the views across the lake are superb. Front and center on the water is friendly **Boileau's Resort** (208/683-2213), where you can walk out the dock to the marina bar and grill for a sandwich, a can of beer, and an earful of fish stories.

Although the Naval Training Center has disappeared, the Navy still makes good use of Lake Pend Oreille for submarine research and development. On the south edge of Bayview is the **Naval Surface Warfare Center, Acoustic Research Detachment,** where the Navy develops stealth technology for submarines. Lake Pend Oreille is the ideal spot for such work for a number of reasons, including its deep, still water; flat bottom contour; isothermal temperature profile; low ambient noise; low echo interference; and large, unobstructed operating areas.

To get to Bayview, continue on Highway 54 from Athol through Farragut State Park. Coming from the north, turn east off U.S. 95 at Careywood.

COCOLALLA, SAGLE, AND VICINITY
Cocolalla Lake

Stretching between the towns of Cocolalla and Westmond, this 800-acre lake attracts anglers all year. They come to round up the usual suspects: rainbow, cutthroat, brown, and brook trout; channel catfish; largemouth bass; crappie; and perch. In winter, you'll see the diehards out on the lake bundled up in their snowsuits, drilling holes through the ice to sink a line. In summer, you can launch a boat onto the lake from a ramp at the northeast end.

Round Lake State Park

This small park (208/263-3489, day-use $5) is two miles down Dufort Road, which turns west off U.S. 95 four miles north of Cocolalla. You'll find 53 wooded campsites ($16) ringing beautiful, 58-acre Round Lake. The shallow lake warms up in summer, making for pleasant swimming. Drop a line for brook and rainbow trout, largemouth bass, sunfish, perch, bullhead, and crappie; ice fishing is popular in winter. Hikers and cross-country skiers enjoy seven miles of trails, groomed in winter, that follow the lakeshore or head off into the forest through lush stands of western red cedar, western hemlock, ponderosa pine, Douglas fir, and western larch. Keep your eyes peeled for some of the park's abundant resident wildlife. Winter also brings out ice skaters and sledders; areas are specifically maintained for both activities.

Sagle and Garfield Bay

Another goofy postal story explains Sagle's name. Back in 1900, the first resident to apply

THE PANHANDLE

for a post office applied for the name Eagle. That name was already taken, so he changed it to Sagle. The town marks the turnoff to Garfield Bay, a great out-of-the-way spot with a couple of character-laden bar-restaurants, a couple of campgrounds, and a small golf course.

Just as you come into Garfield Bay from Sagle, a road branches left and climbs the hill to the north. A short distance down that road, Forest Road 532 branches off to the right and leads to the **Mineral Point Interpretive Trail** (Trail 82), a short and pleasant nature trail winding through groves of Douglas fir, ponderosa pine, Pacific yew, and western red cedar. Along the way you'll find benches where you can sit and enjoy superb views of the lake. This peaceful spot is perfect for a picnic, and chances are good you'll have it all to yourself. The trail connects with another that leads down to the water at the U.S. Forest Service **Green Bay Campground** (3 sites, free). Pick up an interpretive brochure or get more information at the office of the Forest Service **Sandpoint Ranger District** (1500 U.S. 2, Sandpoint, 208/263-5111).

Bottle Bay

This major bay opening onto the northern arm of Lake Pend Oreille is a favorite stop-off of cruise boats and anglers. **Bottle Bay Resort & Marina** (115 Resort Rd., Sagle, 208/263-5916) has a restaurant and a collection of vacation cabins (from $129). The resort also rents out canoes, kayaks, and paddleboats.

Bottle Bay can be reached via Bottle Bay Road—accessed from Sagle or from just across the long bridge from Sandpoint—or via a cut-off from Garfield Bay Road. Bottle Bay Road leads around the lakeshore, approaching Bottle Bay from the north; Garfield Bay Road winds around Gold Mountain and finds its way up to Bottle Bay from the south.

Sandpoint and Vicinity

Sandpoint and Lake Pend Oreille sneak up on the driver heading north up U.S. 95 thanks to dense woods on either side of the highway. When the road rounds the last bend and the view opens up, it's hard to stifle the oohs and aahs. The huge, brilliant-blue lake is ringed by high mountains, and you have to drive right across the water on a very long bridge to enter Sandpoint. What a grand entrance.

The town perches on the lake's northwest shore, on a "sandy point" first noted by Canadian fur trapper and geographer David Thompson in 1808, the same year that the first nonnative settlement was established. When the railroads and timber companies found their way here, the town took root. It's still a mill town, but a couple of other elements add to the economic and cultural mix.

Back in the 1970s, the town's cheap rents and stunning surroundings were discovered by artists. Then recreation-minded visitors latched on to the area's great skiing, fishing, and other outdoor activities. Today, the logger, artist, and outdoor recreationist are all part of a pleasantly diverse cultural tapestry.

Sandpoint is full of outstanding restaurants and lively nightclubs, and it offers a full calendar of performing-arts events.

SIGHTS
Bonner County Historical Museum

A good place to start your study of Sandpoint is the Bonner County Historical Museum (Lakeview Park, 611 S. Ella Ave., Sandpoint, 208/263-2344, 10 A.M.–4 P.M. Tues.–Sat., reduced hours in winter, $3 adults, $1 ages 6–18, free under age 6). Exhibits explain the region's history, beginning with the indigenous Kootenai peoples and continuing through the days of steamboats and railroads. You also can ask the friendly volunteers about the supposed lake creature, called Pend Oreille Paddler.

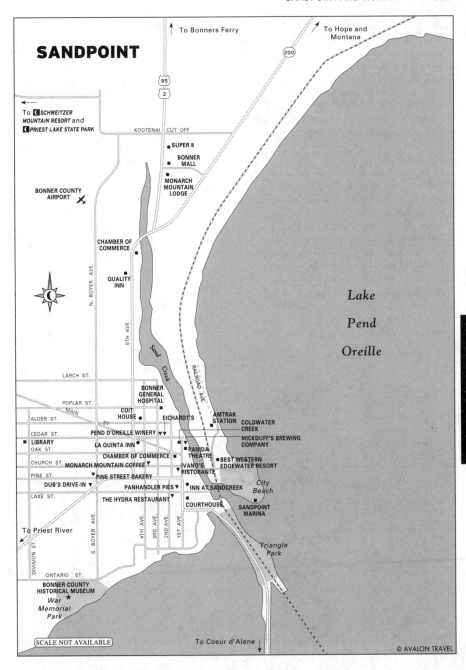

THE PANHANDLE

SANDPOINT

To Bonners Ferry

To Hope and Montana

200

95
2

To ☪SCHWEITZER
MOUNTAIN RESORT and
☪PRIEST LAKE STATE PARK

KOOTENAI CUT OFF

• SUPER 8

■ BONNER
MALL

BONNER COUNTY
AIRPORT ✈

■ MONARCH
MOUNTAIN
LODGE

CHAMBER OF
COMMERCE ■

• QUALITY
INN

N. BOYER AVE.

5TH AVE.

Sand Creek

RAILROAD AVE.

Lake
Pend
Oreille

LARCH ST.

■ BONNER
GENERAL
HOSPITAL

POPLAR ST.

MAIN ST.

ALDER ST.

• COIT
HOUSE

■ EICHARDT'S

■ AMTRAK
STATION

COLDWATER
CREEK

CEDAR ST.

PEND D'OREILLE WINERY ▼ ▼

LIBRARY ■
OAK ST.

LA QUINTA INN •

MICKDUFF'S BREWING
COMPANY

CHURCH ST.

CHAMBER OF COMMERCE ■

■ PANIDA
THEATRE

MONARCH MOUNTAIN COFFEE ▼

PINE ST.

IVANO'S ▼
RISTORANTE

• BEST WESTERN
EDGEWATER RESORT

▼ PINE STREET BAKERY

DUB'S DRIVE-IN ▼

PANHANDLER PIES ▼

• INN AT SANDCREEK

LAKE ST.

THE HYDRA RESTAURANT ▼

COURTHOUSE ■

City
Beach

■ SANDPOINT
MARINA

S. BOYER AVE.

4TH AVE.

3RD AVE.

2ND AVE.

1ST AVE.

To Priest River

Triangle
Park

DIVISION ST.

ONTARIO ST.

BONNER COUNTY
HISTORICAL MUSEUM

War
Memorial
Park ★

SCALE NOT AVAILABLE

To Coeur d'Alene

© AVALON TRAVEL

LAKE PEND OREILLE RECREATION

Largest of the state's lakes, Pend Oreille is 43 miles long and more than 1,100 feet deep in places. In summer, swimmers splash along the shores, sailors glide silently across the clear waters, water-skiers skim over the surface, and anglers troll the depths searching for some of the 14 species of resident game fish.

City Beach

As soon as the hot summer sun arrives, it seems the whole town heads for City Beach. On a July weekend you'll find blankets covering nearly every square inch of this relatively small spit of sand extending out into Lake Pend Oreille. Besides the beach itself, the recreation area includes a playground; areas for basketball, volleyball, and picnicking; and docks from where the lake cruise ships depart. In winter, City Beach takes on a quieter, more contemplative air, but it's still a great place to watch the whitecaps on the water and let the chill wind cleanse your spirit. The beach is at the foot of Bridge Street, off U.S. 95 downtown.

Boat Rentals

Sandpoint Marina (120 E. Lake St., Sandpoint, 208/263-1535) at Dover Bay rents ski boats and pontoon boats ($350–650 per day). Hourly rentals with a two-hour minimum are available too. The marina also rents kayaks, canoes, and water-ski equipment.

Scenic Boat Cruises

To get a duck's-eye view of Sandpoint, hook up with **Lake Pend Oreille Cruises** (208/255-5253, www.lakependoreillecruises.com) for 1.5-hour sightseeing cruises (2:30 P.M. daily mid-June–mid-Sept., $19 adults, $18 seniors, and $14 under age 12) aboard the custom-designed *Shawnodese* from the dock at City Beach. Also offered are dinner cruises, eagle-watching cruises, and other seasonal trips; call for a full schedule.

Fishing

Kamloops, kokanee, whitefish, perch, crappie, bluegill, largemouth bass, rainbow, brown, brook trout—whatever your piscatory pleasure, it's waiting for you here. World-record rainbows

Lake Pend Oreille

and bull trout have been pulled from the lake's depths. You can rent a boat and head out on your own, but it probably makes more sense to avail yourself of local expertise. Fishing guides in the area include **Pend Oreille Charters** (208/265-6781, www.pocharters.com) and **Diamond Charters** (208/265-2565, www.diamondcharters.com).

Kayak Tours

Lake Pend Oreille's many bays and islands make for prime exploring by kayak. **Full Spectrum Tours** (208/263-5975, www.kayaking.net) can teach you kayaking or take you on a tour. Rates range from about $70 for a half-day trip with no food to $450 for a three-day, two-night adventure. The season runs June–September. They also rent kayaks and canoes ($25–40 for 2 hours).

OTHER RECREATION
Golf

The Lower Pack River meanders through the golf links at **The Idaho Club** (151 Clubhouse Way, Sandpoint, 208/265-8600 or 800/323-7020, $80–145), creating periodic water hazards on 15 of the course's 18 holes. This semiprivate golf resort gives first dibs to its members, who have vacation homes on the property, but the 6,923-yard, par-71 course is open to the public. Greens fees for nonmembers vary by season and include a cart. Your tee shots might be critiqued by some of the area's abundant wildlife, including elk, deer, bald eagles, and ospreys. The moose play through. Traversing the fairways of the scenic course, you'll play past stands of cedar and birch, the latter glimmering gold in fall. To get to The Idaho Club, take Highway 200 east from Sandpoint about seven miles and turn left just past milepost 37.

For a quick nine holes, head to **Elks Golf Course** (30196 Hwy. 200 E., Sandpoint, 208/263-4321, around $16). The par-35 course plays a little under 3,000 yards.

Hiking and Biking

One of the best places for a hike, run, or bike ride in town is also one of the easiest to get to. The **Long Bridge** that you drove into town

© IDAHO DIVISION OF TOURISM

City Beach in Sandpoint

THE PANHANDLE

on has a pedestrian and bike path along the east side of it. To access the trail from downtown, follow signs from the foot of Lake Street. **Outdoor Experience** (314 N. 1st Ave., Sandpoint, 208/263-6028) rents cruiser bikes ($35 per day, $20 for 2 hours).

Sandpoint Ranger District (1500 U.S. 2, Sandpoint, 208/263-5111) has pamphlets about the area's hiking and mountain biking trails, some of which are described in this guide.

South of town across the lake, the 3.7-mile one-way **Gold Hill Trail** (Trail 3) climbs the northern flanks of Gold Hill, providing panoramic views of the city and the lake. The lower trailhead is on Bottle Bay Road, about five miles north of Sagle. To get to the upper trailhead, take Sagle Road six miles to Contest Mountain Road (Forest Rd. 2642) and follow that road six more miles to the trailhead.

North of town, the easy 0.5-mile one-way **Caribou Lake Trail** (Trail 58) leads to a small lake in the Selkirks north of Schweitzer Mountain Resort. Take U.S. 95 north from town 13 miles to Pack River Road. Follow that road five miles to Caribou Creek Road (Forest Rd. 2684), and continue down that rough road seven miles to the trailhead.

East of town, the long **Round Top-Bee Top Trail** (Trail 120) is especially popular among mountain bikers. The route traverses a long, high divide linking Trestle Peak, Round Top, Cougar Peak, and Bee Top. It's about 20 miles long and provides many great views from its 6,000-foot heights. The northwest trailhead is on Forest Road 275, which leaves Highway 200 at Trestle Creek between Sandpoint and Hope. Look for the trailhead at a hairpin turn in the road about 15 miles in. The southeast trailhead is off Lightning Creek Road (Forest Rd. 419), about five miles north from Clark Fork.

Outfitters

For backcountry gear, head to **Outdoor Experience** (314 N. 1st Ave., Sandpoint, 208/263-6028). The full-line adventure-gear store sells packs, mountain bikes, and backcountry duds, and also rents cross-country skis, snowshoes, telemark skis, and kayaks. Bike mechanics are on duty here seven days a week. **Sports Plus** (819 U.S. 2, Sandpoint, 208/263-5174) is a local favorite selling water-skis, skateboards, and mountain bikes. Bike mechanics are on duty. Schweitzer Mountain Resort (10000 Schweitzer Mountain Rd., Sandpoint, 208/255-3081) is the best place to rent alpine skis and snowboards.

ENTERTAINMENT AND EVENTS
Entertainment

The **Panida Theatre** (300 N. 1st Ave., Sandpoint, 208/263-9191, www.panida.org) is the focus of Sandpoint's flourishing entertainment scene. The beautiful Spanish Mission–style theater hosted vaudeville and movies after its construction in 1927. Age took its toll over the years, but in 1985 the city purchased the theater and is in the process of restoring it to its former glory. Today, the Panida is on the National Register of Historic Places and stages local drama productions, a foreign- and art-film series, concerts by touring and local musicians, and many other special events. The theater's name is a combination of *pan* from Panhandle and *ida* from Idaho, but nevertheless it's pronounced "PAN-idda."

Eichardt's (212 Cedar St., Sandpoint, 208/263-4005, nightly) is the most reliable place to hear live music, especially if you like blues.

Events

In early August, the big 10-day **Festival at Sandpoint** (208/265-4554 or 888/265-4554, www.festivalatsandpoint.com) concert series takes place at Memorial Field. The 2010 lineup included Brandi Carlile, Big Bad Voodoo Daddy, and Michael Franti and Spearhead. The **Pend Oreille Arts and Crafts Fair** brightens City Beach the first weekend in August with a bevy of locally produced paintings, photography, jewelry, and pottery.

On the cold side of the calendar, Sandpoint's five-day **Winter Carnival** celebrates snow season with snow sculptures, snowshoe softball, and a torchlight parade. It all takes place at the tail end of January.

For a complete calendar of events, contact the **Greater Sandpoint Chamber of Commerce** (208/263-2161 or 800/800-2106, www.sandpointchamber.org).

SHOPPING

Wolf sweatshirts, moose clocks, Native American jewelry, and much, much more—**Coldwater Creek** (311 N. 1st Ave., Sandpoint, 208/263-2265, www.coldwatercreek.com) carries nature-inspired goods of every description, but it's probably best known for its line of women's apparel and fashion accessories. One of Sandpoint's biggest employers, this mail-order and national mall retailer has its flagship store in a two-story brick building downtown. There's even a wine bar, where you can unwind after a frenzied shopping spree.

Zany Zebra (317 N. Main St., Sandpoint, 208/263-2178) sells tie-dye, hemp Hacky Sacks, funky art postcards, cool clothing, and more.

Named after one of the great Northwest trappers, **Finan McDonald Clothing Company** (301 N. 1st Ave., Sandpoint, 208/263-3622) is an upscale store carrying stylish outdoor clothing and accessories for men and women.

The Corner Book Store (106 Main St., Sandpoint, 208/265-2886) sells new and used books of all genres. This is a great place to hang out and peruse the shelves for those hard-to-find titles.

Art Galleries

Sandpoint enjoys a reputation as an art colony, and some 15 galleries are scattered through the downtown area. A couple of favorites are **First Light Gallerie** (302 N. 1st Ave., Sandpoint, 208/263-7148), which spotlights the remarkable acrylic and watercolor paintings of Scott Kirby and photography by Do Verdier, and **Art Works** (214 N. 1st Ave., Sandpoint, 208/263-2642), a local artists' co-op gallery offering an eclectic collection of paintings, sculpture, pottery, jewelry, wood and glass works, and more.

Many local galleries, restaurants, and shops participate in **Artwalk** (208/263-6139, www.artinsandpoint.org) a self-guided art tour of the town. You can pick up a list of the featured artists, their respective media, and the locations of their works at the chamber of commerce or many of the galleries around town.

ACCOMMODATIONS

Summer is peak season in Sandpoint, and summer rates are listed; winter rates are significantly lower.

$50-100

Quality Inn (807 N. 5th Ave., Sandpoint, 208/263-2111 or 800/635-2534, from $69 d) is in a hectic location right on U.S. 2/95. It's got an indoor pool, a decent restaurant, and 62 guest rooms. **Super 8 Motel** (476841 U.S. 95 N., Sandpoint, 208/263-2210, $49–99) has 60 guest rooms and a hot tub. Children 12 and under stay free when accompanied by an adult.

In the Bonner Mall area on the way to Schweitzer, you'll find **Monarch Mountain Lodge** (363 Bonner Mall Way, Sandpoint, 208/263-1222 or 866/756-1222, www.monarchmountainsandpoint.com, $69–105), offering 48 guest rooms, two spas, a sauna, and a free continental breakfast. Some guest rooms have fireplaces.

$100-150

The 1907 **Coit House** (502 N. 4th Ave., Sandpoint, 208/265-4035, www.coithouse.com, $89–150) is a B&B within easy walking distance of downtown. The creaky, character-filled Victorian is full of antiques, and each guest room has its own bath, cable TV, and phone. Rates include a full breakfast featuring fresh-baked breads. Children under 12 are discouraged, and discounts are offered for longer stays. Smoking is allowed outside only.

The **Inn at Sand Creek** (105 S. 1st Ave., Sandpoint, 208/255-2821, www.innatsandcreek.com, from $99) offers three guest rooms, two with Victorian decor and one with Western decor, and a condo. Two of the guest rooms have a fireplace, and all have cable TV. Amenities include a hot tub, a sun deck, and a picnic-barbecue area. Smoking is not allowed.

Best Western Edgewater Resort (56 Bridge St., Sandpoint, 208/263-3194 or 800/635-2534, from $107 d) enjoys a prime piece of lakefront real estate overlooking City Beach, just a block from downtown. All 54 guest rooms face the water and offer either a private balcony or a private patio; for a luxurious splurge, try one of the suites with a jetted tub or a fireplace. The resort has an indoor pool, and rates include continental breakfast. The inn's Trinity restaurant is a great place for dinner or a sunset cocktail.

$150-250

La Quinta Inn (415 Cedar St., Sandpoint, 208/263-9581 or 800/282-0660, from $189 d) is right in the heart of downtown. Amenities include a heated pool, a whirlpool tub, and an adjacent restaurant open for breakfast, lunch, and dinner daily.

Western Pleasure Guest Ranch (1413 Upper Gold Creek Rd., Sandpoint, 208/263-9066, www.westernpleasureranch.com, call for rates) sits on a 960-acre spread about 16 miles northeast of town. The working cattle ranch has been around since 1940. Summer trail rides through forest inhabited by deer, elk, bears, moose, and wild turkeys lead to views of Lake Pend Oreille and the Selkirks. Winter sleigh rides are provided courtesy of a beautiful team of Percherons; the horses pull guests through whitewashed woods on a 45-minute ride culminating in hot drinks and popcorn. Cross-country ski trails are also set up and groomed in winter.

Accommodations are in either modern log cabins or a new lodge building. Each of the cabins has a full kitchen and woodstove and can accommodate up to six people. The 10,000-square-foot lodge sports a massive river-rock fireplace and has six guest rooms. In summer season, late June–mid-September, package stays are offered that include daily rides, evening entertainment, lodging, and all meals with a three-night minimum. Packages

without the trail rides and packages with breakfast only are also available.

Vacation Rentals

North Idaho Property Solutions (877/223-0345, www.nivacationrentals.com) lists rentals of float homes, cottages, and condos in a variety of price ranges.

CAMPING AND RVING

On the south side of the long bridge, Lakeshore Drive leads west around Murphy Bay to the Corps of Engineers' **Springy Point Recreation Area** and its campground (reservations 877/444-6777, 38 sites, mid-May–Labor Day, $18, no hookups).

FOOD AND DRINK
Upscale Fare

Walk into **The Hydra Steakhouse** (115 Lake St., Sandpoint, 208/263-7123, lunch Tues.–Fri., dinner daily, entrées $12–32) and you'll think you're in a plant-filled grotto. The rambling interior is done up in green with lots of wood, and subdued lighting adds to the aura of cool tranquility. The menu offers steak, chicken, seafood, and pasta entrées plus a large salad bar. A good wine list offers several selections by the glass, and a half-dozen microbrews are on tap in the lounge.

Trinity at City Beach (58 Bridge St., Sandpoint, 208/255-7558, www.trinityatcitybeach.com, breakfast, lunch, and dinner daily, dinner entrées $15–26), in the Best Western Edgewater Resort, has a stylish dining room with killer views of the lake. During the day, the menu focuses on breakfast and typical lunch fare. At night, the restaurant gets serious with high-end entrées like langostino ravioli, hazelnut-crusted trout, and prime rib with Parmesan mashed potatoes. The wine list boasts lots of European and Northwestern labels.

❰ The Bistro/Inn at Sand Creek (105 S. 1st Ave., Sandpoint, 208/265-2277, 4–9:30 P.M. Wed., 1–9:30 P.M. Thurs.–Sat., brunch 10 A.M.–3:30 P.M. Sun., entrées $17–30) puts out contemporary Northwestern fare. The menu emphasizes locally grown produce and other regional foodstuffs. In summer you might find dishes like wild salmon tartar, pan-seared chicken breast with cornbread panzanella, and an Idaho Wagyu (Kobe) New York steak crowned with blue cheese butter.

Casual Dining

It's hard to beat **Eichardt's** (212 Cedar St., Sandpoint, 208/263-4005, from 11:30 A.M. daily, under $15), a pub and grill suitable for all but the fanciest night out. The restaurant pours a dozen great microbrews, including pale ales, IPAs, ESBs, and thick cream stouts. The wide-ranging menu includes burgers, sandwiches, steaks, and seafood. The atmosphere is warm and casual, and Eichardt's regularly hosts live music on weekend nights.

MickDuff's Brewing Company (312 N. 1st Ave., Sandpoint, 208/255-4351, www.mickduffs.com, lunch and dinner daily, $7–15) is a great spot for a burger and a handcrafted beer. This downtown brewpub serves lots of burgers, hot sandwiches, finger food, steaks, and grilled salmon with onion rings. The brewmasters here make a rotating selection of ales, porters, and stouts.

Wine Bars

One of the best boutique wineries in Idaho happens to be in Sandpoint. (**Pend d'Oreille Winery** (220 Cedar St., Sandpoint, 208/265-8545, www.powine.com, 10 A.M.–6:30 P.M. Mon.–Thurs., 10 A.M.–8 P.M. Fri.–Sat., 11 A.M.–6 P.M. Sun.) has a comfy tasting room and wine bar downtown. You can sample the offerings of winemaker Steve Meyer, who produces an array of varietal red and white wines, blends, and a few sweet wines, like an extremely drinkable Huckleberry Blush. Most of his wines are made from Columbia Valley grapes. The place even serves a light menu of wine-friendly food.

As promised, there's a small wine bar at Coldwater Creek (311 N. 1st Ave., Sandpoint, 208/255-1293) that pours a wide variety of wines by the glass, including many vintages from the Northwest. You also can get appetizers and panini sandwiches.

Ethnic Cuisine

Ivano's Ristorante (102 S. 1st Ave., Sandpoint, 208/263-0211, lunch Mon.–Fri., dinner daily, $12–26) is an excellent Italian joint with an elegant but comfortable atmosphere. The upscale menu offers appetizers, various pasta dishes, and entrées of chicken, veal, seafood, and steak.

Jalapeño's (314 N. 2nd Ave., Sandpoint, 208/263-2995, lunch and dinner daily, dinner entrées $8–12) is the local favorite for Mexican food. It's geared toward the Yanqui palate, perhaps, but offers large portions and reasonable prices.

Get your Thai fix at **Bangkok Cuisine** (202 N. 2nd Ave., Sandpoint, 208/265-4149, lunch Mon.–Fri., dinner Mon.–Sat., dinner entrées $8–14), where you can find MSG-free dishes with or without meat, either spicy or mild. Beer and wine are available.

Pizza

Second Avenue Pizza (215 S. 2nd Ave., Sandpoint, 208/263-9321, lunch and dinner daily) serves decent pizza pies and cold beer. Here you can get creative veggie concoctions like the Schweitzer Mountain Ski Flakes Special, which includes "fresh spinach, tomatoes avalanched with feta cheese, garlic, moguls of mushrooms, black olives, and at the peak—knee deep in asiago cheese." Seven or so microbrews on tap help wash it down in style. The restaurant is nonsmoking.

Burgers and Sandwiches

Dub's Drive-In (U.S. 2 W. and Boyer St., Sandpoint, 208/263-4300, daily) is a Sandpoint institution offering traditional artery-clogging burgers in sizes suitable for big and little tykes alike. For dessert or a summer cooler, try a soft ice-cream cone.

You can also clog your arteries downtown at (**Joe's Authentic Philly Cheesesteaks** (102 Church St., Sandpoint, 208/263-1444, 10 A.M.–8 P.M. daily, under $10). This little shop puts out several variations of the City of Brotherly Love's most famous sandwich, as well as hoagies, burgers, and Reubens.

MCMANUS MUSES ABOUT THE SELKIRK MOUNTAINS

Outdoor humorist Patrick McManus, who hails from Sandpoint in Idaho's Panhandle, has made a living out of adding levity and wit to potentially fatal situations associated with outdoor fun. He has written 13 books about the lighter side of the great outdoors, including *Never Sniff A Gift Fish, How I Got This Way,* and *They Shoot Canoes, Don't They?* Besides penning nonfiction books (he admits to some fictional embellishment), McManus has also been an editor at *Field & Stream* magazine and a longtime columnist for *Outdoor Life* magazine, in which he wrote the hilarious kicker "The Last Laugh." In recent years, he has tried his hand at writing mystery novels and even a children's book. McManus, who now lives in nearby Spokane, Washington, offers this humorous recollection about the mountains near his hometown:

When I was a boy camping in the Selkirk Mountains, the range contained at least one grizzly bear. I know this because our rural postman was once treed by it. He was a large and flabby man, so it was hard for me to imagine him scurrying up a tree, but he explained that the sight of a grizzly headed your way can virtually flood you with such energy and enthusiasm for climbing that you could zip up a dozen such trees, if any of them proved unsatisfactory. I explored the Selkirks from the time I was 12 until I went off to college and can report there was not a single dark night our postman's grizzly did not populate my thoughts.

Breakfast and Coffee

The best bet for a full breakfast is **Panhandler Pies** (120 S. 1st Ave., Sandpoint, 208/263-2912, 6:30 A.M.–10 P.M. Mon.–Sat., under $10), which offers a full menu for breakfast, lunch, and dinner and bakes 23 different kinds of pie for dessert.

On the edge of downtown, one step removed from the beaten path, is **Monarch Mountain Coffee** (208 N. 4th Ave., Sandpoint, 208/265-9382, daily). It's a spacious, bright, and shiny place great for writing that postcard to the folks back home. Plus the coffeehouse roasts its own beans and serves freshly baked goods and light breakfast items.

Speaking of yummy baked treats, **Pine Street Bakery** (710 Pine St., Sandpoint, 208/263-9012) keeps its ovens full with fresh croissants, sweet pastries, cookies, tarts, and loaves of rustic bread. The bakery also serves espresso drinks and Tazzina teas.

Groceries

The **Farmers Market at Sandpoint** (9 A.M.–1 P.M. Sat. and 3–5:30 P.M. Wed. May–Oct.) fills Farmin Park (3rd Ave. and Oak St., Sandpoint) with fresh produce, eggs, prepared foodstuffs, fresh-cut flowers, and crafts.

Foodies definitely need to check out **Pend Oreille Pasta & Wine** (476534 U.S. 95, Sandpoint, 208/263-1352, www.pendoreillepasta.com, 9 A.M.–6 P.M. Mon.–Sat.). This specialty food store and wine shop carries sausages, artisanal cheeses, freshly baked breads, cured olives, and prepared pasta dinners. Finding that perfect bottle of vino is not a problem here.

For natural foods, bulk foods, vitamins, juices, and organic health products, try **Winter Ridge Natural Foods** (703 W. Lake St., Sandpoint, 208/265-8135).

INFORMATION

The **Greater Sandpoint Chamber of Commerce** (231 N. 3rd Ave., Sandpoint, 208/263-2161 or 800/800-2106, www.sandpointchamber.org) keeps a small visitors center across from Farmin Park. Recreation information is available from the U.S. Forest Service

Sandpoint Ranger District (1500 U.S. 2, Sandpoint, 208/263-5111). Sandpoint's gorgeous **public library** (1407 Cedar St., Sandpoint, 208/263-6930) offers free Internet access and a relaxing space to peruse periodicals (a ski magazine, perhaps?).

GETTING THERE

To reach the **Amtrak** station (450 Railroad Ave., Sandpoint, 800/872-7245), turn left off Bridge Street, which is just across Sand Creek on your way toward City Beach. Amtrak's *Empire Builder* stops on its run from Chicago to Seattle or Portland. Eastbound trains arrive at 2:32 A.M. daily, westbound trains arrive at 11:49 P.M. daily. The closest lodging to the train station—within bleary-eyed, suitcase-lugging stumbling distance—is the Best Western Edgewater Resort.

◖ SCHWEITZER MOUNTAIN RESORT

High in the Selkirk Mountains, a short 11-mile drive north of town, is Schweitzer Mountain Resort (10000 Schweitzer Mountain Rd., Sandpoint, 208/263-9555, snow report 208/265-9562, www.schweitzer.com). One of Idaho's top ski areas, Schweitzer offers a vertical drop of 2,400 feet, two massive bowls, and outstanding base-area lodging and dining. After the snow melts, you can come up the hill for hiking, horseback riding, and even lift-served mountain biking.

Alpine Skiing and Snowboarding

Seemingly underused, Schweitzer's lifts seldom have any appreciable lines. The resort's new high-speed "six-pack" chair (the first in Idaho, nicknamed "Stella") plus a single detachable quad, four double chairs, and two handle tows serve 2,500 acres of terrain and 59 named runs rated at 20 percent beginner, 40 percent intermediate, 35 percent advanced, and 5 percent expert. More than half the runs are groomed, including some of the steep upper slopes, by means of winch cats. The longest run measures a quad-burning 2.7 miles. Racing enthusiasts can try out the NASTAR

Schweitzer Mountain Resort, playing host to a music festival

course, while snowboarders enjoy the resort's terrain park.

Full-day lift tickets cost around $65 adults, $55 seniors and college students with ID, $49 ages 7–17, free under age 7. Two lifts are lighted for night skiing Friday–Saturday and holiday evenings until 9 P.M. Lessons and a wide range of rental equipment such as skis, snowboards, tele-gear, and snowshoes are available at the base area. The resort offers day-care services (208/255-3038) and discounted beginner packages including rentals, lessons, and lift tickets.

Cross-Country Skiing

Schweitzer sets and grooms 19 miles of cross-country trails just to the north of the base area. The trails are better groomed than any Park N' Ski area and offer great views and pleasant, rolling terrain. The well-marked trails leave the busy lodge area and climb around the ridge to the north. Both a wide skating lane and traditional tracks are set up. An all-day trail pass costs $12 adults, $10 seniors and ages 7–17; rental gear is available.

THE PANHANDLE

Mountain Biking

Schweitzer maintains 20 miles of mountain-bike trails on the resort property, and those trails connect with many more miles of logging roads that wind through the Selkirks. You can rent top-notch bikes at Schweitzer for about $50 per half day, $85 per full day. Those who love the downhill but loathe the uphill can load their fat-tire friend onto the resort's quad chair-lift and get a ride to the top ($20 for an all-day pass). For more information, call the activity center at 208/255-3081.

Horseback Riding

Mountain Horse Adventures (208/263-8768, www.mountainhorseadventures.com) offers guided horse treks around the mountains here in summer. Three-hour rides cost $60.

Hiking

In summer, the hills around Schweitzer are bursting with berries and wildflowers. Add panoramic views of Lake Pend Oreille and you've got ideal hiking country. Ten miles of trails meander through the hills. Those who want the mountaintop views without the toil can ride the resort's quad chair to the summit for around $10, then enjoy a downhill stroll.

Free trail maps are available at the base area, and guided hikes are sometimes offered on Saturday mornings in July–August.

Accommodations

Schweitzer Mountain Bed & Breakfast (110 Crystal Court, Sandpoint, 208/263-7117, $110–280) is up Crystal Springs Road from the main Schweitzer parking lot. This mountaintop B&B has five guest rooms, each with a private bath. Amenities include a hot tub, a TV room, and ski-in, ski-out access. Rates include breakfast, as well as tea, coffee, and beverages throughout the day. Smoking, children, and pets are not allowed.

The resort has two slope-side lodges and condos in the base area. The **Selkirk Lodge** (10000 Schweitzer Mountain Rd., Sandpoint, 877/487-4643, $210–293 peak season) sits right at the base of the lifts, its tall gabled roof giving it the air of a Bavarian château. Some guest rooms have jetted tubs, and there's an outdoor heated pool and hot tub complex. The newer **White Pine Lodge** (10000 Schweitzer Mountain Rd., Sandpoint, 877/487-4643, $330–578 peak season) has 1–3-bedroom accommodations, plus outdoor hot tubs and a shopping and dining village.

Highway 200: Pend Oreille Scenic Byway

HOPE AND VICINITY

East of Sandpoint, Highway 200 skirts the north shore of Lake Pend Oreille, soon coming to Hope, East Hope, and even Beyond Hope. On a warm summer's day, this area of big trees and big water is sublime. Perhaps that's why famed Canadian geographer and explorer David Thompson built the very first fur-trading outpost in Idaho, Kullyspell House, on the Hope peninsula way back in 1809. Today, Thompson is commemorated here with the David Thompson Game Preserve. Also on the peninsula are posh homes hidden away in the woods, a superb national forest campground, and great views of the lake at every turn.

Accommodations

◖ **Red Fir Resort** (1147 Red Fir Rd., Hope, 208/264-5287, www.redfirresort.com, Apr.–Nov., $95–165) is a little gem tucked away on the secluded northwest side of the Hope Peninsula, facing Ellisport Bay and the Cabinet Mountains beyond. Twelve cabins perch on a quiet and gentle tree-covered slope overlooking the lake. The cabins vary in size, with some sleeping up to eight; a few are below and above this price range. Each cabin has a private deck, a barbecue, a full kitchen, and a bath. The resort also has its own dock and swimming area.

Right next to the Floating Restaurant, **Pend**

Oreille Shores Resort (47390 Hwy. 200, Hope, 208/264-5828, www.posresort.com, $155–230) is a plush condo development on the lake. Each of the 51 units has a kitchen, a washer and dryer, a stereo, cable TV, and a fireplace. An on-site athletic club features an indoor pool, hot tubs, racquetball and tennis courts, a sauna, and a weight room.

Camping and RVing

Out on the Hope peninsula, you'll find an RV park and a superbly located National Forest campground. To get to the peninsula, continue east two miles past Hope and watch for the Sam Owen Road turnoff on the right. Especially appealing here is the area's status as a game refuge. In the early morning and evening hours, large numbers of nearly tame deer feed on the grassy hills, very near to the Winnebagos and awestruck, clucking campers. Keep your camera ready.

Island View RV Resort (1767 Peninsula Rd., Hope, 208/264-5509, year-round) has 60 sites ($35–40) with full hookups. The resort also has a marina, gas, boat rentals, a rec room, a small store, a laundry, and hot showers.

Also on the Hope peninsula, the Forest Service's **Sam Owen Campground** ($16–20) offers million-dollar lakefront property. This is without a doubt the Ritz of the state's Forest Service campgrounds. Locals love it, so it fills up in summer, but it's a big area and the sites are large. Head straight for the Skipping Stone Loop; units 32, 33, and 35 are among the choicest, just steps from the water. The area also makes a great day-use ($5) destination. For more information call the USFS **Sandpoint Ranger District** (208/263-5111, reservations 877/444-6777 or www.recreation.gov).

Houseboat Rentals

You could spend a far worse one-week vacation than lazily cruising Lake Pend Oreille with some friends on a houseboat. **North Idaho Boat & Home Vacations** (1245 Hwy. 200, Hope, 208/755-0970, www.sandpointhouse-boats.com), at Hope Marine Services, rents small (15-foot, sleeps 8) and large (32-foot, sleeps 10) houseboats. In peak summer season, houseboats cost around $400 per day; multi-day packages are available, which brings the price down slightly. A refundable $500 damage deposit is required. All boats have a propane barbecue, a swim ladder and water slide, an AM/FM radio and CD player, a VHF radio, charts, a fishfinder, and all safety equipment. The layout includes a full kitchen, a bathroom, a stateroom, a living room, and a full-length sundeck up top. You may never want to come home. The company also has rental properties on terra firma.

Food

Known all over the Panhandle as "the Floater," the **Ⓒ Floating Restaurant** (Hwy. 200, East Hope, 208/264-5311, lunch and dinner daily, brunch Sun. Apr.–Oct., dinner entrées $15–22), at Hope Marine Services, is a local landmark. You walk out on a creaky-tippy dock to it, past sailboats and motorboats and rowboats, and then sit either inside or out on the big marina-side deck. The seafood seems appropriate—try the scrumptious Copper River salmon with orange-ginger sauce or a Caesar salad with grilled prawns. The food is good, but ah, the atmosphere. Kick back with a good microbrew or glass of wine; watch the sun set over the boats bobbing in the harbor; listen to the cry of the seagulls so far from Pacific shores.

CLARK FORK AND VICINITY

Clark Fork is the last outpost of civilization you'll pass through before crossing into Montana. The town enjoys a scenic location in the shadow of the Cabinet Mountains, at the confluence of the Clark Fork River and picturesque Lightning Creek. "Downtown" has a couple of stores and taverns but not much else. A couple of RV parks are in the vicinity.

Cabinet Gorge Dam

Virtually at the Idaho-Montana border, this is the last point of interest along Highway 200 before you leave the state behind and venture into Montana. The dam is 208 feet high and 600 feet long and backs up the 20-mile-long Clark

THE PANHANDLE

Fork Reservoir, almost entirely in Montana. The spectacle of the water surging through narrow Cabinet Gorge is powerful indeed. Imagine what it must have looked like when ancient glacial Lake Missoula broke through to carve out the gorge in the first place.

Hiking

A popular and strenuous trail starts outside Clark Fork and leads to the top of **Scotchman Peak,** a 7,000-foot sentry watching over Lake Pend Oreille to the west and the lofty Montana skyline to the east. The views from the summit can't be beat. The trail is only seven miles round-trip but climbs some 3,700 vertical feet in less than four miles. To reach the trailhead, follow Clark Fork's Main Street north. It soon turns into Forest Road 276. Continue past the turnoff to the University of Idaho's Forestry Field Campus. When the road forks about a mile farther down the road, bear right, following signs to Trail 65. One mile farther, turn left on Forest Road 2294A, then turn left again 0.5 miles down that road. After a little over two miles, make one last left and proceed 220 yards to the trailhead. If all that seems too confusing, ask the rangers at the Sandpoint Ranger District Office in Sandpoint to draw you a map.

Huckleberry Tent and Breakfast

You read it right: This business (180 Thunderbolt Dr., Clark Fork, 208/266-0155, www.huckleberrytentandbreakfast.com, Apr. 15–Nov. 15) specializes in tents and breakfast among the huckleberry bushes. Stay the night in a decked-out canvas tent ($125

d) with nearby fire rings, wonderful mountain views, and no TVs or other modern devices to distract you from the great outdoors. Wake up to a big homespun breakfast, which will probably include huckleberries in late summer.

U.S. 2 WEST

West of Sandpoint, U.S. 2 follows the lazy and scenic Pend Oreille River down to the town of Priest River and on to the Washington state line. In the town of **Laclede,** named after a French engineer on the Great Northern Railway, is the Corps of Engineers–built **Riley Creek Recreation Area,** where you'll find a campground (reservations 877/444-6777, 67 sites, mid-May–Labor Day, $24 with hookups). Laclede is also well known to **rock climbing** enthusiasts for Laclede Rocks, right off the highway two miles west of Laclede. The area has a couple of easy routes, but most are in the 5.8–5.10 range. One 5.12 top-rope problem challenges the very skilled. Come in summer when it's hot and you can end your climb by jumping into the nearby Pend Oreille River.

Like Priest Lake, the town of **Priest River** was named in honor of Jesuit priest and early area missionary Father John Roothaan. Logging has long been its lifeblood; great log drives down the Priest River once fed the big mills here. Today the town is in the process of sprucing itself up for a tourist economy.

West of Priest River is **Albeni Falls Dam,** another Corps of Engineers project built in 1951. As the dam was built right at the falls, the falls themselves are now gone. In summer, free tours of the dam are offered daily at the powerhouse (208/437-3133).

Priest Lake

Surrounded by the dense forests and lofty, snowcapped peaks of the Selkirks, Priest Lake is a secluded, off-the-beaten-path gem. There are no cities along the lakeshore, and the biggest towns on the lake, Coolin and Nordman, are not much more than small supply stations for anglers, campers, and the few hardy souls who live up here.

The area is a haven for wildlife. Black bears are common at the lake, and a few grizzlies roam the high country around the periphery. Deer and moose are plentiful, mountain goats inhabit rocky crags near the east shore, and a small herd of endangered woodland caribou survives tenuously in the wildest reaches of this northern realm; wildlife photographers will love it.

The lake is also a favorite of anglers, who fish for lunker mackinaw in forest-shaded coves along the lake's edge. Campers looking for solitude camp on one of several islands in the lake, or they boat or hike north to Upper Priest Lake. The upper lake—connected to the much larger lower lake by a two-mile-long narrow and shallow channel called the Thorofare—is preserved for the wilderness experience. Waterskiing and jet skiing are prohibited on the upper lake, where canoes are the vessels of choice. Trails through cool, dense forest lead between the lower and upper lakes to campgrounds reached only by boat or on foot.

Around the shore of the lower lake you'll find numerous resorts, lodgings, and campgrounds of varying degrees of luxury as well as several marinas and a couple of villages offering convivial contact with members of your own species. Many of the restaurants feature huckleberry dishes of every description. Priest Lake is huckleberry heaven—people come from all over the region in mid–late summer to pick the delectable fruit.

◖ PRIEST LAKE STATE PARK

Historical sites, natural-history interpretive information, and abundant recreation opportunities make Priest Lake State Park (day-use

© IDAHO DIVISION OF TOURISM

Priest Lake

$5) an outstanding destination. Two of the three units of the park are found along the lake's east shore.

Park headquarters is at the **Indian Creek Unit,** 11 miles north of Coolin on East Shore Road. Once a logging camp for the Diamond Match Company, the site displays a remnant of the logging operation—a section of the old flume, built in 1946, that once floated logs into the lake from up to three miles away.

The campground's broad sandy beach attracts swimmers and sunbathers; others prefer to hike one of the two easy hiking trails meandering through the woods or play volleyball or basketball on the campground's courts. A boat-launching ramp lets you float your boat. Throughout summer, the interpretive center presents a full slate of events, including educational campfire programs, guided walks and bike rides, and junior ranger activities. In winter, the park offers easy access to more than 300 miles of groomed and marked snowmobile and cross-country ski trails.

Some of the Indian Creek Unit's 93 campsites ($18–26) have hookups. Two cabins ($50–55) are also available. Other on-site facilities include a camp store, showers, toilets, and an RV dump station. The campgrounds are popular and fill up in summer. Make reservations by contacting the Priest Lake State Park office (314 Indian Creek Park Rd., Coolin, 208/443-2200).

Twelve miles farther north along the east shore, at the mouth of Lion Creek on the lake's northern tip, is the park's **Lionhead Unit** (open summer–fall only). Canadian-born silent-film actor and filmmaker **Nell Shipman** operated a movie studio on this site 1922–1925, producing wildlife and outdoor-adventure films and maintaining a veritable menagerie of 70 animal actors used in the films. Although several of the shorts and features filmed here were successful, the studio's high-overhead operation eventually drove it into bankruptcy. The animals were shipped off to the San Diego Zoo, and Shipman returned to Los Angeles to continue to work in the film industry, though no longer as a star; she died there in 1970. Most

of her films have been rediscovered, restored, and assembled in a collection at Boise State University.

Also at the Lionhead Unit is the sunken shell of the *Tyee II* lying in the shallow waters of Mosquito Bay just offshore. The vessel was a steamer tug used to haul large booms of logs from the Diamond Match flume site to the lake's outlet, where the logs were ferried down the Priest River to the sawmill. Towing a full load of logs, the tug managed just 0.5 mph and took some 60 hours to reach the end of the lake. On such a trip, the tug would typically burn 10 cords of wood. The operation lasted until 1959, when the *Tyee* was stripped of its iron and scuttled where you see it today.

The Lionhead Unit campground (47 sites, $16) is smaller than the one at the Indian Creek Unit and less developed; the sites don't have hookups. Hiking trails wind through the woods, across Lion Creek, and out to the beach, where you just might find moose tracks in the sand. The park is also an excellent launching place for boaters heading to Upper Priest Lake.

The **Dickensheet Unit** is the most primitive of the state park's three units, on Priest River south of the lake between Coolin and the road junction with Highway 57. The campground (11 sites, $12) has minimal facilities. It's a great place to kick back with a fishing pole, away from the crowds up on the lake.

OTHER SIGHTS AND RECREATION
Priest Lake Museum and Visitors Center

The informative Priest Lake Museum and Visitors Center (208/443-2676, 10 A.M.–4 P.M. Tues.–Sun. Memorial Day–Labor Day, free), just north of Hill's Resort on Luby Bay, is a good place to begin your exploration of the area. The museum occupies a log cabin built by the Civilian Conservation Corps in 1935. It was originally a residence and office for the Kaniksu National Forest's first ranger. Inside you'll find exhibits on the threatened grizzly bear and woodland caribou—including sand castings of their tracks—and on rare area plants such as the northern beechfern, deerfern, black snakeroot, and salmonberry.

The most entertaining fact you'll learn here is how the name of the local national forest came to be changed from Priest River National Forest to Kaniksu National Forest. It seems the Forest Service wanted a fresh start after the antics of Priest River National Forest's first supervisor, Benjamin McConnell, gained public attention. McConnell was dismissed for "public drunkenness, habitating with a newly divorced woman, and shooting his pistol in the middle of town." The new name, Kaniksu, was the local Native American term for the Jesuit missionaries in the area. Friendly volunteer docents at the museum are on staff to answer your questions.

Vinther-Nelson Cabin

You'll need a boat to get to this historic log cabin (10 A.M.–3 P.M. Wed.–Sun. summer, free) on Eightmile Island. The cabin was built in 1897 by the Crenshaw brothers, who tried their hand at mining on the island. After a year with no luck, the Crenshaws gave up and sold the cabin to W. J. Anders and family. Anders cleared the land and planted crops but couldn't make a go of it. In 1900 he sold out to two cousins—Sam Vinther and Nels Nelson, who intended to revive the mine and make a fortune; they never struck pay dirt. Nevertheless, the two men and their families continued to live on the island. In 1967 the U.S. Department of Agriculture ordered that all private buildings on Priest Lake's federally owned islands be demolished. The descendants of Vinther and Nelson negotiated an agreement to allow the cabin to remain standing as a historic site open to the public. Inside the cabin you'll find a restored kitchen and a small museum. Outside, trails lead to great views and the old mine site, long since caved in.

Hanna Flats Cedar Grove

This small area just south of the Priest Lake Ranger District office in Nordman (look for signs marking the turnoff to the west) offers a short nature trail in summer, cross-country ski trails in winter, and a soggy, mosquito-infested bog in spring. Pick up the interpretive trail brochure at the ranger station; it explains that one reason these cedars survived is because they weren't considered valuable by early loggers. An interesting subplot dates from the settler days when a man named Gumpp built a cabin here. He moved away for the winter, and when he returned found Jim Hanna and family living in his house. They had come upon the cabin, assumed it was abandoned, and moved in. Gumpp didn't raise a stink; he just moved on.

Beaver Creek Recreation Site

This is the main jumping-off point for hiking, mountain biking, and canoeing to Upper Priest Lake Scenic Area. Once the site of the Beaver Creek Ranger Station, the area offers a campground ($18), a picnic area (day-use $7), a boat launch into the main lake, trailhead parking for the hiker-biker Navigation and Lakeshore Trails, and a 1,600-foot canoe-portage trail directly to the Thorofare. The site is on the lake's northwest shore; turn east on Forest Road 2512 at Nordman and follow it north 12 miles.

Granite Falls and Roosevelt Grove

Actually just over the border in Washington, but reached only via Idaho, the short Granite Falls Trail (Trail 301) leads to views of upper and lower Granite Falls and continues to the Roosevelt Grove of Ancient Cedars. To get to the trailhead, continue north on Highway 57 past Nordman; the road eventually becomes Forest Road 302. Most of the old-growth cedar grove went up in flames in 1926, but about 22 acres are left. The cedars—estimated average age 800 years—are impressive, but it's lower Granite Falls that steals the show. The roaring water rounds a corner at the top of the falls and plummets down a huge granite dihedral. Clever Forest Service engineers have constructed a truly scary viewpoint right out over the cliff edge.

Also at the trailhead is **Stagger Inn Picnic**

THE PANHANDLE

Area (free). The area was named by firefighters who used it back in the 1920s as a base camp. At that time, the road up the east shore ended at Nordman, and the firefighters had to hike in from there—a distance of about 14 miles. By the time they got here, they were exhausted, and many had to "stagger in."

On the way back to Priest Lake, don't miss the wacky **Shoe Tree.** You won't believe your eyes. In a gnomish scene right out of a fairy tale, old pairs of shoes completely cover the trunk of a huge cedar just off the highway. The local tradition started decades ago, but no one seems to remember why. If there's a Priest Lake local out there who knows the whole story, please fill me in. The tree is at the short spur to Trails 261 and 264, south of Granite Falls on the west side of the road.

Hiking and Biking

A favorite for hikers and mountain bikers alike is **Navigation Trail** (Trail 291). It begins at Beaver Creek Recreation Site and first enters a dense, fern-filled cedar forest. The trail can be mucky in places, but it's always beautiful. You'll pass an abandoned trapper's cabin before arriving at Plowboy Campground on the south-west shore of Upper Priest Lake. It's an easy three-mile hike to this point. You can picnic and head back from here, or continue north another three miles to Navigation Campground at the upper end of the lake. Between the two campgrounds the trail traverses a wooded lakeside slope, offering great views of the water and mountains at many points along the way. This portion of the trail is also easy. Fit hikers will have no problem hoofing it all the way from Beaver Creek to Navigation Campground and back—a round-trip distance of 12 miles—in half a day.

Beaver Creek is also the trailhead for **Lakeshore Trail** (Trail 294), which heads south along the western edge of the lake for 7.6 miles. It's an easy and popular trail open to both hikers and bikers. Along the way you'll cross five streams, pass numerous campsites, and get great views of the lake.

Probably the most popular and heavily used trail at Priest Lake is the nine-mile **Beach Trail** (Trail 48), which runs right by Hill's Resort, Luby Bay Campground, and several summer cabins. It's open to hikers only—no mountain bikes—and runs between Kalispell Bay boat launch on the north and Outlet Bay on the south. Along the way it meanders through woods and along the beach, jumping back to Lakeshore Road for two short stretches.

Mountain bikers can make best use of the east side of the lake, particularly the northeast shore north of Priest Lake State Park's Lionhead Unit, where numerous gravel roads have been closed to motor vehicles, making ideal mountain-biking country. For starters, try Caribou Creek Road, right out of the Lionhead campground.

For a map of the area and a longer list of trails, stop by the Priest Lake Ranger District office (32203 Hwy. 57, Priest River, 208/443-2512) south of Nordman. You can rent a mountain bike ($25 per hour, $45 half-day, $75 full day) on the west shore at Hill's Resort on Luby Bay (208/443-2551).

Rock Climbing

How can you resist the looming block of **Chimney Rock** on the skyline of the Selkirks above the east shore of the lake? To anyone who has ever strapped on sticky shoes and a harness, this granite monument cries out to be climbed. The 350-foot-high west face is split by several flake and crack systems, offering routes ranging from 5.3 to 5.11b. Access is via Horton Creek Road, which turns east off the lake's east shore road about 2.5 miles south of Priest Lake State Park's Indian Creek Unit. Follow the road all the way to the end and park. It's a one-to two-hour hike up to the base of the rock from there. And as long as you're up there, you might want to check out neighboring **Mount Roothan,** which offers several other good routes. For more information, consult Randall Green's excellent book, *Idaho Rock,* now out of print but available via used book sources.

Floating the Priest River

The 44-mile stretch of the Priest River between Priest Lake and the town of Priest River makes a relatively easy float trip, taken either in segments or one long 14-hour day. The toughest rapids, Binarch and Eight Mile, are rated Class III. You'll also encounter three other Class II rapids along the way. In periods of high water—spring and early summer—the Class III rapids are unsuitable for novices. Later in the summer, the river's average depth decreases to three feet or less, and the slow, lazy stretches dominate; after mid-July, plan on dragging the bottom in places. For more information, contact the U.S. Forest Service Priest Lake Ranger District (32203 Hwy. 57, Priest River, 208/443-2512).

Fishing

Kokanee, cutthroat trout, rainbow trout, mackinaw—Priest Lake is full of scaly dinners-in-waiting. The Idaho Parks and Recreation Department suggests trying the following not-so-secret fishing spots: off East Shore Road about 5–6 miles south of Indian Creek; off the end of Pinto Point; and, for deep trolling, off the Kalispell-Papoose-Bartoe Island group (try a chartreuse crocodile as a trolling lure).

Boating

The west shore resorts all have marinas with boat rentals. In and around Coolin you'll find **Coolin Marine** (2148 Cavanaugh Bay Rd., Coolin, 208/443-2469) and **Blue Diamond Marina** (958 Blue Diamond Rd., Coolin, 208/443-2240) about five miles from town, both of which rent boats.

Free **boat-launching ramps** are available at Coolin and at the Forest Service Luby Bay Campground on the west shore. Ramps that charge a fee can be found on the east shore at Cavanaugh Bay Marina and on the west shore at Priest Lake Marina (Kalispell Bay), Elkins Resort (Reeder Bay), and Grandview Resort (Reeder Bay).

Note: The Thorofare is a no-wake zone, and waterskiing and jet skiing are prohibited in Upper Priest Lake.

Huckleberry Picking

The Priest Lake area is loaded with huckleberries, and the menus of many local restaurants boast huckleberry pies, milk shakes, pancakes, cocktails—you name it. Berry-picking season runs mid-July–October. The berries like the sun, so the best places to find them are in open areas along logging roads and trails, mostly west of the lake. You can pick up a berry-picking map from the U.S. Forest Service's Priest Lake Ranger Station, on Highway 57 just south of Nordman. Remember, bears love huckleberries too. If you hear something big thrashing around in the bushes nearby, it's best to yield dibs on the area.

Cross-Country Skiing

In winter, cross-country skiers and snowmobilers take advantage of the hundreds of miles of groomed and marked trails in the area. About five miles of mostly easy ski trails wind through the Indian Creek Unit of **Priest Lake State Park** on the lake's east shore. Across the lake, **Hanna Flats Cedar Grove** just south of Nordman tracks about four miles of easy loops as well. Heading south toward Priest River, the **Chipmunk Rapids Trail System** offers another 10.5 miles of trails.

ACCOMMODATIONS
Resorts

Several resorts dot the lake's west side. The biggest, plushest, and most popular with the tourist set is the venerable **Hill's Resort** (4777 W. Lakeshore Rd., Priest Lake, 208/443-2551, www.hillsresort.com, year-round, $1,450–3,060 weekly summer) on beautiful Luby Bay. Both *Better Homes and Gardens* and *Family Circle* magazines have named Hill's as one of their favorite family resorts in the country. The Hill family has run the resort since 1946 and offer accommodations in either private cabins or condo-like housekeeping units, most with fireplaces. Amenities include a marina;

THE PANHANDLE

Hill's Resort

©IDAHO DIVISION OF TOURISM

swimming areas; tennis and volleyball courts; hiking, biking, cross-country skiing, and snowmobiling trails; a gourmet restaurant; and a lounge with live entertainment in season. In summer, bookings are taken only for stays of a week or longer. Summer rates are in effect from the last Saturday in June until the Tuesday after Labor Day weekend. The rest of the year, rates are about 15 percent lower, and nightly rates are available. Units vary in size, sleeping 2–12 people.

 Elkins on Priest Lake (404 Elkins Rd., Nordman, 208/443-2432, www.elkinsresort. com, year-round) is another full-service resort. Accommodations are in individual log cabins, most with fireplace and all with kitchens, full baths, and separate bedrooms; you need to bring your own soap and towels. The lodge restaurant, overlooking the lake and nicely landscaped grounds, serves top-notch Pacific Rim–inspired cuisine daily in summer and between Christmas and New Year's, with a limited schedule the rest of the year. The Trapper Creek Lounge is one of the west shore's social hubs, often presenting live music that draws in the locals. Other amenities include a marina, beaches, volleyball, and recreation trails. You must book for a week or longer in peak summer season (early July–late Aug.). Peak season weekly rates range $1,498 for a creek-side cabin that sleeps four to $4,529 for a lakefront cabin that sleeps 14. The rest of the year, rates are about 15 percent lower and a two-night minimum (three nights on holiday weekends) is in effect.

Grandview Resort (3492 Reeder Bay Rd., Priest Lake, 208/443-2433) offers cottages, lodge rooms, and suites with, yes, grand views of Reeder Bay. Amenities include a small swimming pool, a marina with boat rentals, and a bright dining room overlooking the lake. It's open year-round. Peak season rates range from around $90 for a lodge room with one queen bed up to $297 for a private lake-view cottage that sleeps 10. Weekly rates are available, and pets are not allowed.

Inns

The **Inn at Priest Lake** (5310 Dickensheet Rd., Coolin, 208/443-2447, $69–135) is a short distance from the lake and offers little in the way of views. The big hexagonal structure looks something like a stone fort dropped incongruously into the woods. But the inn's modern amenities are welcome and include a year-round heated pool and spa, a restaurant, and a lounge. Spa suites and kitchenettes are available. The inn has a nicely landscaped backyard and is within walking distance of Coolin culture. Pets are allowed for a few extra bucks. The inn's year-round RV park offers 12 nice pull-through sites ($25) with full hookups, including TV. Restroom and shower facilities are available.

In Coolin, the **Old Northern Inn** (220 Bay View Dr., Coolin, 208/443-2426, www. oldnortherninn.com, $105–165) occupies the former Northern Hotel, a turn-of-the-20th-century haven for travelers to the secluded shores of Priest Lake. The restored two-story wooden structure has antique furnishings and first-class modern amenities. The atmosphere is one of rustic elegance. The beautiful cedar-paneled living room features a stone fireplace and picture windows looking out on the lake. Old photographs and newspaper clippings provide a historical accent. The lake is practically at your doorstep—just a short walk down a wooded slope to the private dock and beach. The four standard guest rooms and two suites all have private baths. Rates include a full breakfast (look for huckleberry pancakes) and afternoon wine and cheese. Children over age 12 are welcome, but pets aren't. Smoking is permitted outdoors only. The inn is on your left just before you come to the Leonard Paul Store and Coolin Marina.

CAMPING

Priest Lake State Park offers 151 campsites at its three units. For information and reservations, contact the state park office (314 Indian Creek Park Rd., Coolin, 208/443-2200).

Forest Service Campgrounds

Forest Service campgrounds ring both lower and upper Priest Lake. Many more are found on two islands out in the lake. All campsites are open mid-May–end of September, weather permitting. Camping is limited to 14 days.

From south to north on the west shore, the campgrounds (about $18) are: **Outlet** (31 sites); **Osprey** (18 sites); **Lower Luby Bay** on the lakefront, and **Upper Luby Bay,** across the road in the woods (54 sites total), with an RV dump station; **Reeder Bay** (24 sites); **Beaver Creek** (41 sites). Reeder Bay, Beaver Creek, and the two Luby Bay campgrounds accept reservations (877/444-6777). For more information, call the Priest Lake Ranger District (208/443-2200).

Four more campgrounds (free) on Upper Priest Lake are accessible only by boat or on foot. On the west side of the upper lake are **Plowboy Campground** (4 sites) at the south end of the lake and **Navigation Campground** (5 sites) on the lake's north end. Along the east shore of the upper lake are **Geisinger's Campground** (2 sites) and **Trapper Creek** (5 sites).

Island Camping

In addition to the mainland campgrounds, the Forest Service maintains extremely popular boat-in campgrounds on Kalispell Island (12 campgrounds and two day-use areas), Bartoo Island (five campgrounds and two day-use areas), and Fourmile Island (one campsite). All are first-come, first-served ($10).

Some of the campgrounds have vault toilets; others don't. Because of the heavy summer use, the Forest Service now requires campers staying at campgrounds without vault toilets to carry and use their own portable toilets while on the island. When they return to the Kalispell boat launch—the most commonly used public boat launch for trips to the islands—a free SCAT (Sanitizing Containers with Alternative Technologies) machine there will clean their portable toilets. The machine works like a giant coin-operated dishwasher, flushing the waste into the mainland sewage system and sterilizing the container.

Island campers are permitted to stay 14 days maximum. Pick up a map to island campgrounds at the Priest Lake Ranger District office (32203 Hwy. 57, Priest River, 208/443-2512).

A Safety Reminder

This is bear country, so keep a clean camp. Dispose of all trash properly and promptly, and don't leave food out on picnic tables.

FOOD

The resort restaurants are safe bets for good grub around Priest Lake. On the west shore, **Hill's Resort** and **Elkins Resort** both have excellent reputations for fine cuisine.

In downtown Priest Lake, locals flock to **Millie's Restaurant and Lounge** (28441 Hwy. 57, Priest Lake, 208/443-2365, lunch and dinner daily) for wood-fired pizzas, hot wings, fish tacos, burgers, and cold beer.

For good comfort food, go to **Ardy's Café** (205 Cavanaugh Bay Rd., Coolin, 208/443-4086, breakfast, lunch, and dinner daily), on the east side of the lake in Coolin. In late summer, this classic diner makes good use of local

THE PANHANDLE

huckleberries, putting the plump little buggers in pies, pancakes, milk shakes, and more.

INFORMATION

For more information, contact the **Priest Lake Chamber of Commerce** (208/443-3191, www. priestlake.org). For national forest recreation information, contact the U.S. Forest Service's **Priest Lake Ranger District** (32203 Hwy. 57, Priest River, 208/443-2512). The ranger station is just south of Nordman on the east side of the highway.

North to Canada

NAPLES

From Sandpoint, U.S. 95 continues north toward the Canadian border. Ten miles south of Bonners Ferry is the tiny farming and logging community of Naples. Other than an occasional rowdy night of darts at the Northwoods Tavern, the tiny hamlet is usually quiet as can be. Its setting is magnificent. Just west of town, forested ridges climb in ever-higher waves up into the lofty Selkirk Mountains. The rugged peak of Roman Nose—usually snowcapped well into summer—dominates the skyline, sending several creeks rushing down toward Naples from the alpine snowfields. Heading north from town on the scenic old road, you'll cross one beautiful creek after another. One of these, Ruby Creek, flows past Ruby Ridge just outside town.

Spend some time pulled up to the bar at the Northwoods and you'll quickly get a neatly distilled view of what draws a certain independent breed to northern Idaho. At the very heart of it, there just aren't many other people here. The state's visitors guide dutifully lists population figures for almost every town in Idaho, but not Naples. One suspects the local residents probably like that. And since the economy lives and dies by the logging industry, just about every residence prominently displays a green sign reading "This Family Supported by Timber Dollars." Depending on your point of view, logging might be a topic of conversation to avoid down at the Northwoods Tavern, but there's a lesson to be learned. Even if you're diametrically opposed to the loggers' environmental stance, you can't make the disagreement personal; the people you meet at the

Northwoods—and places like it in little logging towns across the state—are by and large some of the finest, most honest and upfront people you'll ever meet.

Entertainment

Right downtown is the **Northwoods Tavern** (Old U.S. 95, Naples, 208/267-1094, until late daily), the area's social hub. Inside you'll find a couple of pool tables, dartboards, a jukebox, good conversation, and plenty of standard domestic beer.

Camping and RVing

Just north of town on U.S. 95 is **Blue Lake RV Resort** (242 Blue Lake Rd., Naples, 208/946-3361, www.bluelakervresort.com), a large and clean full-facility park surrounding a nice fishing pond. Sites with hookups ($31–45), camping cabins ($49), pole tents ($45), and tent sites ($10) are available. Amenities include a shower facility and a clubhouse with a full kitchen.

BONNERS FERRY AND VICINITY

In 1834, 24-year-old New Yorker Edwin Bonner came west, intent on using his already considerable experience in the retail trade to establish himself as a successful frontier businessman. After opening a department store in Walla Walla, Washington, he passed through Idaho's northernmost reaches and noted that the well-traveled ford of the Kootenai River—used by miners stampeding north to British Columbia's goldfields—needed a ferry. By 1864 he had built his ferry and begun to operate it successfully. Eventually Bonner left the area and settled in Missoula, Montana, where he became a wealthy and powerful merchant and political leader. Despite his departure, the town that grew up here stuck with its original name.

Boundary County Historical Museum

A repository of regional history, the small Boundary County Historical Museum (7229 Main St., Bonners Ferry, 208/267-7720, 10 A.M.–4 P.M. Tues.–Sat. summer, donation), across from City Hall, holds a wealth of historical photos and artifacts. Check out the proud portraits of the Bonners Ferry High School class of 1925—all 20 graduating seniors.

Kootenai National Wildlife Refuge

Before the building of dikes and Montana's Libby Dam tamed the Kootenai River, annual spring floods washed over the valley floor, creating prime wetlands for migratory waterfowl. The dikes made for flood-free farming but took away the wildlife habitat. The 2,774-acre Kootenai National Wildlife Refuge (Riverside Rd., 5 miles west of Bonners Ferry, 208/267-3888, sunrise–sunset daily, office 8 A.M.–4:30 P.M. Mon.–Fri.) was created to mitigate that loss. The refuge is kept flooded with water diverted from the Kootenai River and two local creeks. Today, tens of thousands of waterfowl pass through the refuge every year. A 4.5-mile loop road circles the refuge, and several hiking trails (one is wheelchair accessible) lead to good photo vantage points.

In spring, look for mallards, northern pintails, American wigeon, and tundra swans on their way north. In late summer and early fall, the refuge attracts large numbers of Canada geese. Birdwatchers might also catch sight of bald eagles and ospreys. Among other wildlife occasionally seen: black bears, white-tailed deer, moose, and elk. In all, 230 bird species and 45 mammal species have been observed here.

Lookout

Up in the Selkirks about four miles south of the Canadian border is the rentable U.S. Forest Service **Shorty Peak** lookout (July 1–Sept. 30, $25). It's a 2.5-mile hike to the 15- by 15-foot cabin, perched at an elevation of 6,515 feet. The tower sleeps two and offers panoramic views of Creston Valley and the surrounding peaks. This lookout is in grizzly country, so take all appropriate precautions. For reservations, directions, and more information, contact the **Bonners Ferry Ranger District** (6286 Main St., Bonners Ferry, 208/267-5561, reservations 877/444-6777 or www.recreation.gov).

Rafting

Northeast of Bonners Ferry, the **Moyie River** provides Panhandle rafters with a one-day white-water stretch during its high-water season (Apr.–June). Lots of rock gardens among the Class II–III rapids can make it an interesting ride. **ROW Adventures** (Coeur d'Alene, 208/765-0841 or 800/451-6034, www.rowadventures.com) runs guided Moyie day trips ($90–115) that begin and end in Moyie Springs.

The lazy **Kootenai River** isn't in a hurry to do much of anything. It eases out of Montana into Idaho, wanders aimlessly back and forth up the Purcell Trench, and then crosses the border into British Columbia to feed Kootenay Lake. The Class I float is perfect for leisurely canoeing and wildlife watching, particularly west of town where the river flows past Kootenai National Wildlife Refuge.

Golf

Mirror Lake Golf Course (U.S. 95, 208/267-5314, about $16 for 9 holes) is just south of Bonners Ferry. The popular nine-hole course offers broad, unimpeded views of the Purcell Trench looking out toward Kootenai National Wildlife Refuge. Cart and club rentals are available, and ask about local "Stay and Play" packages.

Cross-Country Skiing

The northernmost of the state's Park N' Ski areas, **Snow Creek Park N' Ski** lies 14 miles west of Bonners Ferry. Turn west off U.S. 95 south of town just before the golf course. The

THE PANHANDLE

turnoff is marked with a sign for the Park N' Ski area. Follow the road west for a short distance, and watch for Snow Creek Road 402 on the right. Snow Creek Road heads north up the valley a couple of miles before branching west once again and beginning its climb into the Selkirks. You'll probably need chains to make it to the trailhead; the road is steep and very icy in places. Parking at the trailhead may consist of no more than one small plowed slot, depending on the good graces of the plow driver.

The well-marked trail system provides a variety of interesting routes. On the Hemlock trail, you'll see numerous examples of the trail's namesake, the delicate mountain hemlock. It was John Muir's favorite tree, easily recognizable by its graceful drooping crown. Another trail, the Toboggan Run, should be avoided by all but expert skiers—it's a long, steep climb on a narrow trail through many trees. If you have climbing skins with you, use them. Otherwise, prepare for herringbone hell. The only thing worse than going up Toboggan Run would be going *down* Toboggan Run. Unless you have a death wish, don't try to descend this trail unless plenty of soft, fresh snow is on the ground to cushion your inevitable face-plant.

Although these trails are high in the mountains, they're not high enough to offer any panoramic views. The trail system here is not extensive: The longest loop will take you just over an hour, about the time it takes to drive to the trailhead from Bonners Ferry in all but the best conditions. Grooming is minimal, and on weekends, snowmobilers will be buzzing about the vicinity.

Accommodations

On the south approach to town is **Bear Creek Lodge** (5952 Main St., Bonners Ferry, 208/267-7268, $60–110), which offers 12 guest rooms, a hot tub, a full-service restaurant, and complimentary continental breakfast.

On the north end of town, two miles north of the Kootenai River on the west side of U.S. 95, is the **Bonners Ferry Log Inn** (43 Tobe Way, Bonners Ferry, 208/267-3986, www.bonnersferryloginn.com, $50–94). Even though the inn is right along the highway, it's farther away from the hustle and bustle than the motels on the south side of town. The beautifully landscaped grounds, warm, comfortable guest rooms, and toasty hot tub will combine to drop your blood pressure off the bottom end of the sphygmomanometer.

The largest and swankiest lodging in town is the **Best Western Kootenai River Inn and Casino** (7169 Plaza St., Bonners Ferry, 208/267-8511 or 800/346-5668, from $139 d). The inn is owned by the local Kootenai tribe, and for better or worse, Indian gaming is here to stay. Slot machines and bingo in north Idaho may seem tacky, but the money the gambling operation sucks in helps keep the tribe alive. In any case, the inn boasts the best location in town and offers all the finest amenities. Some rooms under $100 are available. The inn's restaurant overlooks the river and offers upscale fare and outstanding ambience.

Paradise Valley Inn (621 Treetop Bluff Lane, Bonners Ferry, 208/267-4180 or 888/447-4180, www.paradisevalleyinn.com, year-round, from $89) offers elegant and comfortable B&B accommodations on a secluded 64-acre spread 10 minutes southeast of town. Views from the modern ranch house are impressive, and all five guest rooms have private baths. Rates include a big breakfast served inside or out on the log porch. To reach the inn, take Paradise Valley Road east off U.S. 95 at the stoplight in Bonners Ferry and follow the signs for 3.5 miles.

Food

A rare treat awaits discriminating diners in Bonners Ferry. **Alberto's** (6536 S. Main St., Bonners Ferry, 208/267-3410, 8 A.M.–9 P.M. daily, entrées $10–16) is a superb gourmet-caliber Mexican restaurant, among the very best in Idaho. Alberto hails from Mexico City, bringing with him his favorite recipes from central Mexico. Everything on the small but artful menu is made from scratch. Try the heavenly Azteca, a baked concoction consisting of layered corn tortillas, shredded chicken, cheese, and an out-of-this-world homemade mole. Carne asada and camarones (shrimp), separately or together, are other specialties of the house. Entrées come with excellent tortilla chips, salsa, and soup. Choose from six Mexican *cervezas,* all served in chilled mugs.

At the Kootenai River Inn, **The Springs Restaurant** (7169 Plaza St., Bonners Ferry, 208/267-8511, breakfast, lunch, and dinner daily, dinner entrées $12–20) offers upscale atmosphere, an eclectic menu of steaks, seafood, poultry, and pastas, and great views of the Kootenai River.

When the need for caffeine calls, **The Creamery Café** (6426 Kootenai St., Bonners Ferry, 208/267-2690, 8 A.M.–4 P.M. Mon.–Fri.) answers with a gamut of espresso drinks. In addition to great high-octane joe, you can also get sandwiches, frozen yogurt, and other goodies. The smell of fresh-made waffle cones beckons halfway down the block.

Information

The **Bonners Ferry Chamber of Commerce Visitors Center** (U.S. 95, 208/267-5922, www.bonnersferrychamber.com) is in the parking lot across the highway from the Kootenai River Inn. It's usually closed in winter, although if you drive by, you might find someone there. The U.S. Forest Service **Bonners Ferry Ranger District** office (6286 Main St., 208/267-5561) is on the south edge of town. They can hook you up with recreation information.

U.S. 95 TO EASTPORT

U.S. 95 leaves Bonners Ferry heading north, following the Kootenai River for a time. Then it branches east, winding its way through the Purcell Mountains to the Canadian border crossing at Eastport. For much of the way you drive through a veritable tunnel of trees. Several nice lakes line the route, but they're all sheltered from view.

Camping

At **Smith Lake,** anglers will find a boat ramp and a small lake full of rainbow trout, bass,

BORDER CROSSING REGULATIONS

As of 2009, U.S. citizens must have a passport or similar document to enter Canada and to reenter the United States after their visit. The U.S. Department of Homeland Security's Western Hemisphere Travel Initiative requires all American citizens returning from Canada, Mexico, and the Caribbean to present one of the following documents: a valid passport, a passport card, an enhanced driver's license, or a Trusted Traveler Program Card (NEXUS, SENTRI, or FAST). To apply for these documents, contact the U.S. Department of State (877/487-2778, www.travel.state.gov). Canadian citizens now need a passport or similar documentation to enter the United States. Citizens of all other countries need passports and appropriate visas to enter Canada and the United States.

Customs regulations for both countries are extensive. Generally, you can transport a limited dollar amount of foreign-bought goods across the border duty-free. Above that limit, you must declare your purchases and pay duty on them.

Some items may require a permit to transport them between the two countries. Red flags immediately rise with firearms and other weapons, pets, agricultural products, and drugs – prescription or otherwise. For customs regulations and information pertaining to the Idaho border crossings, contact the U.S. Customs office in Eastport (208/267-3966, www.cbp.gov), or the Canadian Customs offices at the Idaho border: Kings Gate (250/424-5391) for Eastport and Rykerts (250/428-2575) for Porthill.

and catfish as well as the Forest Service's **Smith Lake Campground** (7 sites, free). To get here, take Smith Lake Road (Forest Rd. 36) off U.S. 95, seven miles north of Bonners Ferry. Another 12 miles down U.S. 95 is Brush Lake

Road (Forest Rd. 1004), which leads to **Brush Lake** and a campground (4 sites, free).

Nineteen miles from Bonners Ferry is Robinson Lake Campground Road (Forest Rd. 449), which leads into large **Robinson Lake** and a campground (10 sites, $8). A two-mile interpretive trail points out the intricate interactions within the forest ecosystem. Boaters note: The boat-launching ramp at Robinson Lake is on the lake's north side, accessed a little farther down the highway. No gasoline motors are permitted on Robinson Lake.

Copper Falls

Take time to stretch your legs at this exquisite spot just a short distance off the highway. Turn east at the Copper Creek campground sign and head down Forest Road 2517 a couple of miles past the campground (16 sites, $6). Be careful of logging trucks. A pullout on the right and a sign on the left mark the trailhead. The easy trail climbs briefly, then traverses a beautiful slope of mixed conifers before descending slightly to the falls. An interpretive brochure, hopefully available at the trailhead, explains the biological points of interest along the way. The falls make a beautiful 80-foot cascade, perfectly proportioned to allow you an up-close look without getting soaked. After crossing the creek, the trail loops back to the trailhead a little lower down Copper Creek—a total distance of less than a mile. Benches are well placed at particularly

tranquil spots. Bring a picnic lunch and enjoy an alfresco repast in the cool clean air by the rushing waters.

Eastport

The Eastport border station marks the international boundary between the United States and Canada. It's open 24 hours. Those interested in cultural differences will note that canary-yellow Union Pacific locomotives rub elbows with their cherry-red Canadian Pacific cousins, while the Yankee-sharp U.S. Customs and Immigration building contrasts nicely with its older, more civilized Canuck counterpart. The Moyie River knows no border, however. It flows past unimpeded on the way to its confluence with the Kootenai, some 20 miles to the south as the Canada goose flies.

HIGHWAY 1 TO PORTHILL

From its junction with U.S. 95, Highway 1 continues up the Purcell Trench, past fertile farmland and the Kootenai River on the west and the abruptly steep Purcell Range on the east. The Purcells continue on into British Columbia, Canada. They don't have to stop at the border—but you do. The Porthill border crossing is open 7 A.M.–11 P.M. daily. At Porthill, you might notice the tall trellises of the Elk Mountain Farms hops plantation on the valley floor to the west. The plantation cultivates about 2,000 acres of aromatic hops for use in Anheuser-Busch beers.

BACKGROUND

The Land

Idaho has more than 83,000 square miles of land within its borders, making it the 11th largest state in the nation in land area. Most of the state's population is concentrated along the Snake River Plain in the south and along the state's western fringe, leaving vast amounts of land either sparsely settled or uninhabited.

MOUNTAINS

Virtually the entire state is covered with mountains. Even on the wide grin of the Snake River Plain, which arcs across the width of southern Idaho, mountains rim the horizon in most directions.

Southern Ranges

The mountains rising up right behind Idaho's capital city of Boise are, appropriately enough, the **Boise Mountains.** Their lower slopes mirror the brown desert that spreads out along the Snake River Plain, while the upper slopes are home to Boise's backyard ski resort, Bogus Basin. Across the Snake River, in the state's southwest corner, are the **Owyhee Mountains.** Silver City, high in the Owyhees, was once one of the West's richest little towns, thanks to the vast seams of silver and gold found nearby.

East of the Owyhees, still on the south side of the Snake River, a string of north–south-trending ranges leads, one after the next, to the

AN IDAHO ALMANAC

- **Birthday:** The 43rd state, Idaho joined the Union on July 3, 1890.

- **Capital:** Boise

- **Dimensions:** 483.5 miles long at its tallest point, varies from 45 miles wide at the tip of the Panhandle to 310 miles along the southern border. Area is 83,557 square miles, making it the 13th largest state in area.

- **Population:** 1,567,582, according to the 2010 census

- **High point:** Borah Peak (12,662 feet), in the Lost River Range near Mackay

- **Low point:** Lewiston (738 feet), where the Snake River flows into Washington

- **State motto:** *Esto Perpetua,* meaning "It Is Forever." The motto adorns the state seal, which was designed in 1891 by Emma Edwards Green. It's the only state seal in the country designed by a woman.

- **State song:** "Here We Have Idaho," written in 1931 by Albert J. Tompkins, McKinley Helm, and Sallie Hume Douglas

- **State flower:** the syringa, which explodes into bloom like delicate white fireworks

- **State tree:** the western white pine, once abundant north of the Clearwater River. You can still see specimens of the hulking trees along the White Pine Scenic Byway (Hwy. 6 between Potlatch and St. Maries), but logging and disease have taken a severe toll on the once mighty stands.

- **State bird:** the mountain bluebird, found throughout the West

- **State fruit:** the huckleberry

- **State gemstone:** the star garnet, which is found only in Idaho and India. The "star" is the rays within the garnet – normally four, sometimes six.

- **State horse:** the Appaloosa, proud horse of the Nez Perce. Horse lovers will want to visit the Appaloosa Museum in Moscow.

- **State folk dance:** the square dance

- **State insect:** the monarch butterfly

- **State fish:** the cutthroat trout, named for a red or orange slash on the bottom of its lower jaw

- **State fossil:** the Hagerman horse, discovered in the 1920s near Hagerman

Wyoming border. This incredible procession of peaks is a prime example of basin-and-range topography, caused by the slow stretching apart of the earth's crust. Just across the Wyoming border rise the impressive granite spires of the Teton Range.

Central Ranges

The Wood River Valley is the most common gateway to the lofty ranges of central Idaho: the **Smoky Mountains** (home of Sun Valley's famous ski hill), **Pioneer Mountains,** the **Sawtooth Range,** and the **White Cloud Peaks.**

All of these ranges are high and wild, but the state's highest point, the 12,662-foot summit of

Borah Peak, is farther east in the **Lost River Range.** Experienced mountaineers who make it to the top of Borah will also have a great view to the east of the lofty **Lemhi Range.**

In the very center of the state, the **Salmon River Mountains** make up most of the Frank Church–River of No Return Wilderness, south of the Salmon River. Farther west, the **Seven Devils Mountains** tower over Hells Canyon, providing spectacular views to hikers and horseback riders.

On the other side of the state, running north-south along most of Idaho's eastern border, is the **Bitterroot Range,** the towering rugged peaks that helped make Idaho the last of the Lower 48 states to be explored by

Sawtooth Mountains

nonnatives. The **Beaverhead** and **Centennial Ranges** are subranges of the Bitterroots on the Idaho-Montana border.

Northern Ranges

North of the Salmon River, the **Clearwater Mountains** extend north all the way to the St. Joe River. Across the St. Joe are the **St. Joe Mountains.** North of I-90, the **Coeur d'Alene Range** extends north to Lake Pend Oreille. Finally, way up in the Panhandle are the **Selkirk, Cabinet,** and **Purcell Ranges.** The Selkirks are home to small numbers of rare woodland caribou, and both the Selkirks and Cabinets remain grizzly bear country.

RIVERS AND LAKES
Along the Snake and Salmon

From its abundance of famous white-water rivers to its more than 2,000 lakes, Idaho is rich in water resources. Start with the mighty **Snake River,** which begins in Wyoming and then traverses the entire southern width of Idaho. The Snake enters Idaho at **Palisades Reservoir,** a popular lake with boating anglers; below Palisades Dam, it's commonly called the **South Fork of the Snake** to differentiate it from the Snake's **Henry's Fork** tributary, which begins in a massive spring near Island Park. Both rivers are revered for fly-fishing.

As the Snake makes its way west across southern Idaho, it is dammed in many places—major turn-of-the-20th-century irrigation projects made Idaho the breadbasket it is today—forming reservoirs used for both water storage and recreation. Evel Knievel once tried to leap a rocket-powered cycle across the famous **Snake River Canyon** at Twin Falls, about 500 feet deep.

After passing through rapids-ridden Hells Canyon along the state's western border, the Snake rolls into Lewiston—an inland seaport—then on into Washington, eventually linking up with the Columbia River and the Pacific Ocean near Portland, Oregon.

The state's other famous river is the **Salmon River,** one of the country's longest free-flowing watercourses. It begins high in the

Sawtooth Valley and flows through the Frank Church–River of No Return Wilderness before joining the Snake River in Hells Canyon. The Salmon was nicknamed the River of No Return early in the history of Euro-American exploration; because of its powerful rapids, explorers could float down the river but they could never boat back up. Today, jetboats defy this rule on parts of the main Salmon. The Salmon's largest tributary, the **Middle Fork Salmon River,** is another prime white-water run, even more remote and wild than the main Salmon.

South Idaho Waters

Other rivers beginning in and around the high peaks of the Sawtooths flow into southwest Idaho. The **Boise River** and **Payette River** both offer water recreation very near Boise, making them chock-full of boaters in summer. On the South Fork Payette you'll find some of the most spectacular white water in the state— a kayaker's heaven. Farther west, the **Weiser River** irrigates the farmlands of Hells Canyon rim country.

In the far southwestern corner of the state, the **Bruneau, Jarbidge,** and **Owyhee Rivers** cut deep, rugged canyons into the desert far from civilization. The rivers draw rafters and kayakers to their remote reaches in spring along with a few hardy canyon hikers year-round.

In south-central Idaho, the **Big Wood River** flows down from the heights north of Sun Valley to rendezvous with the Snake at the bottom of Malad Gorge. Along the way it's joined by the **Little Wood River,** which is fed by **Silver Creek.** All three draw anglers; Silver Creek is among the state's three most famous trout streams. East of the Little Wood, the **Big and Little Lost Rivers,** and **Birch Creek** flow down from high valleys and disappear into the lava of the Snake River Plain, later to emerge at **Thousand Springs** along the Snake River in Hagerman Valley.

Down in the state's southeastern corner, **Bear Lake** boasts surreal turquoise-blue waters well used by water-skiers and anglers.

North Idaho Waters

Two of the finest white-water rivers in the

Middle Fork Salmon River

© IDAHO DIVISION OF TOURISM

country, the **Lochsa** and **Selway,** begin high along the Continental Divide and race their way down in furious rapids, coming together to form the more placid **Clearwater River,** an important spawning ground for anadromous salmon and steelhead. Farther north, through the southern reaches of Idaho's Panhandle, the **St. Joe River** and **St. Maries River** flow through big-timber country into the south end of **Coeur d'Alene Lake,** also fed by the **Coeur d'Alene River,** a historic waterway through the heart of Silver Valley mining country. It is drained by the **Spokane River,** which flows west into Washington state.

Sandpoint, farther north up the Panhandle, lies on the shores of **Lake Pend Oreille,** the state's largest body of water. The lake is so deep that the U.S. Navy uses it to test submarines. Others prefer to boat on the surface of the water, and marinas dot the shoreline. The lake is fed by the **Clark Fork River** and drained by the **Pend Oreille River.** A tributary of the Pend Oreille, **Priest River** flows south out of **Priest Lake,** the state's most northerly major lake and one of its most beautiful. Tall mountains ring the shore, and wildlife is abundant in the area.

The **Kootenai River** and **Moyie River** drain the northernmost reaches of the state along the Canadian border.

CLIMATE

Idaho's varied topography, ranging in elevation 738–12,662 feet, and large size—the state spans seven degrees of latitude and six degrees of longitude—make for a complicated climate. Generally speaking, the state enjoys a relatively temperate, maritime-influenced climate that is drier than Washington and Oregon and milder than Montana and Wyoming. Also generally speaking, the north half of the state is lower, warmer, cloudier, and wetter than the south half.

Humidity is not much of a problem anywhere in the state. In the hottest months, humidity is generally a comfortable 25 percent or lower. Other weather woes you'll seldom see in Idaho include dense fog, tornadoes, and hailstorms—although high winds are common on the Snake River Plain.

Boise

Boise's climate is warm and dry in summer, cold and dry in winter. In July, highs average around 90°F, and overnight lows drop to around 59°F. Hot spells with temperatures over 100°F usually occur every summer but are short-lived. About 90 percent of July days are sunny, and the city usually gets only about 0.25 inches of rain that month. Fall in Boise offers stable, pleasant weather. Average high temperatures are around 78°F in September, 65°F in October, and 50°F in November, with average overnight lows of 50°F, 40°F, and 30°F, respectively.

In winter, temperatures remain relatively mild. January is the coldest month, with an average high temperature of around 37°F and an average overnight low around 22°F. Extended cold spells with high temperatures of 10°F or lower are not uncommon. Sunny days drop to around 40 percent in December–January. January is also the city's wettest month, although Boise is a dry place; average January precipitation is around 1.5 inches. Winds are relatively calm in winter, keeping windchill problems low.

Winds pick up a bit in spring in time for the city's kite festival. Spring has the most changeable weather and the biggest temperature swings. Daytime high temperatures average around 50°F in March, rising to 61°F in April and 71°F in May. Spring is also a relatively wet season in Boise and in southwest Idaho in general, with precipitation averaging more than one inch per month all season.

Southwest Idaho

Most of this region's sizable population lives in the relatively low-lying areas along the Snake River Plain and the valleys of the Boise, Payette, and Weiser Rivers. As in the southwest Idaho city of Boise, summers are toasty and winters are mild. Winter brings freezing temperatures only a couple of months of the year, in December–January. The state's reporting station at Swan Falls, on the floor of the Snake River Canyon south of Boise, records the highest annual mean temperature in Idaho, 55°F.

At **Parma,** along the Boise River, at an elevation of 2,215 feet (about 600 feet lower than Boise), July days run around 93°F on average, while January days come in around 38°F.

Magic Valley

This part of the state also shows a wide range in elevation. Its lowest stretches along the Snake River are the warmest year-round. In **Twin Falls** (3,690 feet), July daytime highs average around 90°F, while overnight lows drop to around 55°F. January in Twin Falls brings daytime highs around 40°F and lows around 20°F.

From Twin Falls east up the Snake River Plain, freezing temperatures generally last December–February. Daytime high temperatures in **Burley,** about 500 feet higher than Twin Falls, average 88°F in July and just 36°F in January. Precipitation in south-central Idaho is heaviest in May, followed in no particular order by December, January, April, and June.

Southeast Idaho

Eastern Idaho may have the most complex weather in the state. Farthest from the reaches of the Pacific maritime storms, this region is influenced partially by pooped-out westerlies, partially by southerly storms pushing north from the Gulf of Mexico, and partially by disturbances from every other direction as the surrounding mountains swirl and break storms into any number of tracks. Precipitation patterns are the opposite of what you'd expect in the west and north parts of the state. Rainfall is heaviest in spring and summer, when thunderstorms are common. The region also has the widest temperature variations from season to season. Winter storms are among the coldest in the state, so it's no surprise that Grand Targhee Ski Area, in the Tetons just outside of Driggs, offers the state's lightest powder.

Pocatello (4,454 feet), on the Snake River Plain, sees July highs averaging 89°F

and January highs around freezing, 32°F. In July, **Idaho Falls** (4,730 feet) stays just a couple of degrees cooler than Pocatello, but its January highs average a frigid 28°F. Both cities are wettest in May–June. The **Island Park** area (6,300 feet) can see brutal cold: On December 17, 1964, the mercury dipped to -51°F. Temperatures aren't usually that severe, however; January highs average 25°F and July highs a pleasant 79°F.

Sawtooth Country and Beyond

High altitudes mean lower temperatures, which makes the high country a great place to be in summer and a bitterly cold spot in winter. The National Weather Service reporting station near **Stanley,** at an elevation of 6,780 feet, holds the record for the state's lowest annual average temperature: a nippy 35.4°F. Much of the high country's precipitation comes as snow, a great boon to Sun Valley's reputation as a premier ski destination. December and January are the wettest months in Sun Valley, with high temperatures right around freezing. Spring comes late to the mountains; snow covers the high peaks and meadows until well past summer solstice. Look for wildflowers in June at the earliest, and not till July in many places. In summer, Sun Valley enjoys high temperatures in the 70s and low 80s with minimal precipitation.

East of Sun Valley in the rain shadow of the high peaks, the Lost River, Pahsimeroi, and Lemhi Valleys are among the state's driest regions, receiving an average of just over eight inches of precipitation annually.

North-Central Idaho

North-central Idaho is unique for its deep canyons—Hells Canyon of the Snake River, Salmon River Gorge, and the canyons of the Clearwater River and its tributaries. Towns on the floors of these canyons have the lowest elevations in the state and are sheltered from the wind, giving them the state's warmest temperatures. In summer, you'll definitely want air-conditioning in places like **Lewiston, Riggins,** and **Orofino,** where average temperatures hover around 90°F and periods of 100°F temperatures are not uncommon. On the plus side, in winter, none of these cities has a mean temperature below freezing. Lewiston golfers play year-round, and a lush spring comes to town in March–April, when blossoms explode into color.

Up out of the canyons, on the prairies of north-central Idaho, higher elevations and increased wind make for cooler temperatures year-round in places like Moscow and Grangeville. Daytime high temperatures in **Moscow** (2,660 feet) average 84°F in July and 35°F in January. Precipitation in Moscow averages 23 inches annually, with winter the wettest season.

The Panhandle

North Idaho's maritime-influenced climate derives from prevailing westerlies that carry warm, wet storms from the Pacific and Gulf of Alaska across the Northwest. The Washington Cascades wring some of the moisture from these storms, but the Columbia River Gorge ushers other storms right on through to drop rain and snow on the Panhandle's mountains. Consistent with maritime weather patterns, winters here are cloudy and wet, while summers are clear and relatively dry. July is the prime travel month in the Panhandle, with precipitation reliably lower than in other months. Temperatures are more moderate year-round than at corresponding latitudes on the east side of the Continental Divide.

In the Silver Valley town of **Kellogg** (2,290 feet), look for July highs in the mid-80s, January highs in the mid-30s, and about 30 inches of rainfall per year. Farther north in **Sandpoint** (2,100 feet), July highs generally average 80°F, and January brings highs right down to freezing. Sandpoint receives an average of 34 inches of precipitation per year.

Flora

DESERT AND SHRUBLAND
Sagebrush Country

Before the arrival of settlers and their irrigation practices, southern Idaho was largely an arid desert covered in heat- and drought-tolerant grasses and shrubs. Dominant among them is **sagebrush**—genus *Artemisia*—which comes in at least 23 different species in Idaho. One of the most common is big sage *(Artemisia tridentata)*. In addition to the pleasant, pungent aroma characteristic of all sages, big sage can be readily identified by its silvery sheen and the three rounded teeth on its leaf tips. Most sage species are small shrubs, but one variety, basin big sage, can grow to the size of a small tree.

In sage-dominated areas, you'll likely also encounter **antelope bitterbrush,** a favorite browse of antelope, deer, elk, and domestic livestock. Occasional particularly alkaline soils in the sagebrush zone support a number of salt-loving shrubs—botanists call them halophytes—including **greasewood, winterfat,** and **shadscale.**

Alongside the streams and rivers that slice benevolently through this barren landscape, larger, lusher vegetation flourishes. The *bois* that gave the Boise River its name were magnificent stands of **black cottonwood.** These impressive trees can grow to more than 100 feet tall and eight feet in diameter, and they light up bright yellow in fall. Black cottonwood is the state's largest native broadleaf tree, found along every major river in the state. Another native species, **narrowleaf cottonwood,** grows principally in southeast Idaho; look for it along the South Fork of the Snake River, downstream from Palisades Reservoir.

Another common plant along Idaho riverbanks is **willow.** About 30 species inhabit the state, making *Salix* the largest genus in Idaho. Willows range in size from shrubs to large trees. Their bitter bark is the source of salicylic acid, a proven headache remedy. Perhaps this explains why the bark is a favorite food of the perennially busy beaver. In winter, the yellows and oranges of the plant's leafless stems brighten drainages across the state. While shrub-size willows are most common in the wild, the large **golden weeping willow** (*Salix alba* Tristis) is a popular tree-size ornamental.

Juniper Highlands

In the high-desert areas of southern Idaho, you'll find occasional tracts of juniper. These evergreens are too small for commercial lumber production but are widely used across southern Idaho for fence posts and firewood. The tiny, spherical, pale-blue cones are frequently called "berries," and they're responsible for giving your gin its just-so flavor. The berries, along with the tree's scaly leaves, make the juniper easy to identify.

Near the Utah border on I-84 you'll pass through a large area of **Utah juniper** that supports a population of ferruginous hawks. To the east are occasional woodlands of **Rocky Mountain juniper,** the most common species in the state, while to the west stretch vast areas dominated by **western juniper,** the largest of the three species found in Idaho. The Owyhee County Backcountry Byway passes through a particularly large and absolutely stunning forest of western juniper.

A couple of pines are commonly found growing in and around juniper woodlands, primarily in the southern reaches of the state. The hardy **limber pine** ordinarily prefers higher elevations but has established a community among the juniper woodlands around Soda Springs as well as atop the lava fields of Craters of the Moon National Monument. **Singleleaf piñon** also enjoys the company of junipers, in and around south-central Idaho's City of Rocks. The piñon is an anomaly in many ways. It is a Great Basin species most commonly found farther south in Nevada—the City of Rocks community is the northernmost tip of its range and its only foothold in Idaho. It's also the world's only species of pine growing single needles akin to a fir; all other pines grow needles in bundles of 2 to 5. And unlike other pines, the piñon bears extra-

large seeds called pine nuts, a food enjoyed and often relied on by Native Americans.

Mountain Shrub Zone

As you head up into Idaho's southern hills, the sagebrush-dominated desert vegetation gives way to a habitat of predominantly broadleaf shrubs. The most common species of this zone is **curlleaf mountain-mahogany.** It's no relation to the exotic Southeast Asian mahogany prized for fine woodworking, but its dark wood is similar. Deer and elk love the stuff and tend to keep it trimmed down to shrub size. You can identify mountain-mahogany by its narrow and leathery one-inch-long green leaves, and by the unique 2–3-inch-long feathery tails emerging from its seed pods. Other common shrubs in this zone include **black chokecherry,** found throughout the state in warm, relatively low-altitude locations; **antelope bitterbrush,** whose range extends down into the sagebrush zone; and **western serviceberry,** one of Idaho's most ubiquitous plants.

A number of relatively small native trees also inhabit this zone, including **interior box-elder** and **bigtooth maple.** The latter lights up like a blowtorch in fall, all dark reds and oranges. It's the state's largest color-changing tree.

FORESTS

Botanists classify Idaho's forests under the umbrella heading of **Rocky Mountain montane,** a biome that includes most of the forest lands of the Rockies, extending from British Columbia in the north, through Idaho, and on down to New Mexico in the south. Several different specific forest types make up this biome.

Ponderosa Pine Forest

On sunny slopes at lower elevations (1,000–3,500 feet), the ponderosa pine is king. It's the widest-ranging and most common pine in North America and one of the grandest as well. A large ponderosa can reach over seven feet in diameter and be as tall as an 18-story building.

Mature ponderosas have thick, platelike bark that provides protection from forest fires; the bark is colored so intensely golden-orange it seems to glow in the sunshine. As a result, many foresters call them "pumpkins." The tree's thirsty root system sucks up nutrients to such a degree that no other trees or even shrubs of consequence can grow within a wide radius of the trunk. This makes the ponderosa look like a solitary loner and accentuates its magnificence.

Ponderosa pine needles are 4–8 inches long and grow three to a bundle, but unless you're looking at a young tree that hasn't developed its characteristic bark or size, you probably won't need to get up so close for identification. The best place in Idaho to see these beautiful trees is, not surprisingly, along the state's **Ponderosa Pine Scenic Byway,** Highway 21 between Boise and Stanley.

Douglas Fir Forest

Above the ponderosas at a cooler and wetter altitude is the Douglas fir zone. Douglas fir is named after David Douglas, a 19th-century naturalist who named and catalogued many of the trees found in the Pacific Northwest. This tree is a little harder than ponderosa pine to identify from a distance. No particular distinguishing features are apparent until you get up close and personal. Look at the cones. Odd paper-thin bracts—each forked like the hind end of a horseshoe crab—protrude from behind the normal woody cone scales. Most of central Idaho—millions of acres—is covered with Douglas fir. It's the most important fodder for Idaho's timber industry, and you can find it across the state. The biggest one, a 209-foot-tall skyscraper nearly six feet in diameter, rules the woods southeast of Clarkia.

Cedar-Hemlock Forest

Given an even cooler, wetter environment than the Douglas fir zone, things start to get interesting. Where the ponderosa pine rules essentially alone, and the Douglas firs have but one or two interlopers keeping them company, the cedar-hemlock zone is shared by three climax species and several other prominent hangers-on. Here the woods can take on the dark, wet, fecund feel of a rain forest.

© IDAHO DIVISION OF TOURISM

Hobo Cedar Grove in north-central Idaho

The three climax species in this zone are **grand fir, western red cedar,** and **western hemlock.** Southern Idaho is too dry to support these trees, so this zone is found primarily in maritime-influenced west-central and northern Idaho.

Grand fir prefers the zone's drier ranges, usually equating with either lower altitudes or lower latitudes. Like all true firs, its cones stand upright on the branches and its needles grow singly from the twigs.

Western red cedar is generally a little thirstier, growing higher within the zone or by hunkering down near streambeds. Western red cedars have a different family tree, so to speak, than pines and firs. They're in the juniper family *(Cupressaceae)* and, like junipers, their leaves are scalelike rather than needlelike. Their foliage looks distinctly ferny from a distance. They're the giants of this zone, not so much in height—all three climax species in this zone top out around 170 feet—but in bulk. The biggest western hemlock is about six feet in diameter, the biggest grand fir a foot wider, but the biggest western red cedar measures over 18 feet in diameter. This goliath can be found in Giant Cedar Grove, north of the hamlet of Elk River in Clearwater County.

The western hemlock thrives in the wet and stormy high-altitude end of the zone. Forests dominated by this tree have an enchanted, primeval quality, giving the impression that if you took a short nap on the forest floor, you might awaken covered by a blanket of lush ferns and mosses. Head for Priest Lake State Park to see what the western hemlock forests are all about.

Another prominent inhabitant of this zone is **western white pine,** Idaho's **state tree** and the battleship of the state's arboreal fleet. Its hulking gray trunk rises straight as an arrow off the forest floor, reaching heights of nearly 200 feet. The biggest white pine in Idaho is nearly seven feet in diameter. The species is very valuable to the timber industry. Between the chainsaws and the dreaded white pine blister rust—a fungus lethal to these leviathans—it's lucky Idaho has any specimens of its state tree left standing. At least one narrow corridor is preserved for visitors; check out the **White Pine Scenic Byway,** Highway 6 north of Potlatch in north-central Idaho.

One more resident of the cedar-hemlock zone is worth mention. Scattered throughout the wetter areas of the Panhandle and densely concentrated in the mountains around Elk City is the **Pacific yew.** This tree has attracted a lot of attention in recent years since the discovery that its bark contains taxol, a compound that slows the growth of cancerous tumors. The yew is a relatively small tree with flat, one-inch-long leaves and thin, reddish bark.

Subalpine Forests

The highest forests of Idaho—ranging in elevation from around 5,000 feet right up to the timberline—are the airy realm of **Engelmann spruce, subalpine fir,** and **mountain hemlock.** Both Engelmann spruce and subalpine fir have steeply peaked crowns; the latter is especially pointy on top, looking almost surreally cartoonish. The two trees are usually found growing together as neighbors. If you can't tell them apart by their shape, look at the cones: the fir's stand up on the branches, while the spruce's hang down.

The third climax species of the subalpine forests is the exquisitely elegant mountain hemlock, John Muir's favorite tree. You'll have no trouble recognizing this one—just look for the graceful, droopy crown. These trees require a cool, wet climate, and as a result are found only in the high mountains of Idaho's Panhandle, and then usually on the wettest north-facing slopes.

Several other trees also prefer life in the subalpine zone. **Limber pine** is found at subalpine heights in the sunny east-central and southeast portions of the state, and it has been known to grow occasionally at lower elevations. Look for it in the lava fields at Craters of the Moon National Monument. **Whitebark pine** is a gnarly denizen of the craggy timberline reaches, ranging from the high country of central Idaho north to the Panhandle. It's almost never found lower than the subalpine zone. Grizzly bears like to chow down on whitebark pine nuts in fall, so it's not a bad idea to know what the tree looks like if you're hiking in bear country. Both the limber and whitebark pines have short needles that come five to a bundle. Male whitebark cones are easy to identify—they're purple. **Subalpine larch** is another high-altitude habitué. It requires a cold but sunny climate and is found above 8,000 feet in the Sawtooths, above 7,000 feet in the Selkirks. Like all larches, its needles turn brilliant gold in fall.

Two More Ubiquitous Trees

A prolific deciduous tree counts as one of the regulars in Idaho's forests. The splendid **quaking aspen** provides a delicate counterpoint to the deep green of surrounding conifers. Its albino bark and shimmering leaves—light green in spring, brilliant gold in fall—light up the woods across much of the state. The South Hills' Rock Creek Canyon is a veritable Jackson Pollock of aspens and cottonwoods in autumn.

Unfortunately, the bark of this beautiful tree is often defaced. Aspen bark is a favorite food of beavers, so stream-bank aspens are frequently chewed up. Less justifiable are the initials, hearts, four-letter words, and other symbols carved into aspen trunks in the high country by thoughtless humans. This tradition probably started with bored Basque sheepherders and was picked up by modern-day campers and 4WD explorers. The scars last the life of the tree, a sad reminder of the inability of our species to just leave the earth alone.

Another tree found widely across Idaho is the **lodgepole pine.** It's easy to identify: its long, straight trunks, once used by Native Americans as lodge poles, are covered with a thin, pale, distinctively pebbly bark. The lodgepole's clever reproductive strategy has led to its ubiquity. The tree produces two types of cones. Some of the cones open and drop normally, allowing the tree a chance to reproduce in any openings in the understory. Others remain closed and tightly sealed with resin until fire sweeps through. The flames melt the resin, freeing the seeds and allowing them to get started on the open, sunlight- and nutrient-rich burned-out slopes. Thanks to this unique trait and a fast-growing nature, lodgepoles tend to come back first and dominate forests charred by fire. The lodgepole isn't too picky about its habitat. It'll grow anywhere from the Douglas fir zone to the subalpine zone, but it does prefer cold temperatures. You'll find good examples of lodgepole forest at Harriman State Park near Island Park, a very cold place in winter that was burned out many summers ago.

Fauna

THREATENED AND ENDANGERED SPECIES
Wolves

Largest of the wild dogs, the wolf stands close to three feet tall at the shoulder, stretching as long as six feet from nose to tail tip. An average adult male weighs around 100 pounds. Wolves are intelligent, playful, social animals with one unfortunate character trait that has made them pariahs in their homeland. Although wild deer and elk form the mainstay of their diet, they've also been known to eat livestock. The wolves' taste for steak tartare has caused some of the most heated debate in the Northwest and probably more than a few fistfights over the years in saloons across rural Montana, Wyoming, and Idaho.

For many years, ranchers killed the animals with abandon. Once the most numerous large predator in the United States, wolves were virtually exterminated from the American Rockies by the 1930s—trapped, shot, and poisoned by ranchers and bounty hunters. In 1988 the gray wolf population in Boise National Forest was estimated at between four and nine.

In 1973, Congress passed the Endangered Species Act, designed to identify and protect endangered species and nurse their populations back to self-sustaining levels. As originally written, the act required the U.S. Fish and Wildlife Service to take positive action to reintroduce endangered species to their former habitat, at the same time placing severe penalties on anyone attempting to harm those species in any way. When it came the wolves' turn for protection under the law, it set off a major political battle in the West, pitting ranchers against the government and environmentalists, who pushed for the act's full implementation on behalf of the beleaguered wolf.

More than a decade of political wrangling ensued, as powerful Western ranching interests and their allied representatives in Washington—both elected and nonelected—attempted to overthrow the Endangered Species Act. At last a deal was reached that seemed to please no one—probably the sign of a good compromise. The act was not overturned, and the U.S. Fish and Wildlife Service proceeded with efforts to reintroduce wolves to the West. But the Act was amended to allow reintroduction of the wolves as "nonessential,

wolves, reintroduced in central Idaho in the mid-1990s

© IDAHO DIVISION OF TOURISM

experimental" populations south of I-90, which removes the strictest protective measures of the federal government from such populations. (North of I-90, where there isn't much ranching, the wolves received regular endangered species status.)

The compromise appears to have worked. Fifteen gray wolves were released into central Idaho in 1995, and by 2002 the state's wolf population had climbed to more than 250 in an estimated 19 packs. In the broader Northern Rockies region—including Idaho, Montana, and Wyoming's Yellowstone National Park, where wolves were reintroduced in the mid-1990s—there were an estimated 664 wolves in 44 packs by 2003. These numbers helped lead the Fish and Wildlife Service in March 2003 to reclassify gray wolves as a "threatened" species.

The controversy and contention about wolves rages on in Idaho. In 2008, to the dismay of environmentalists and the delight of ranchers and hunters, the Federal Government delisted wolves from endangered species protection.

This action paved the way for wolf hunting in Idaho and Montana. The Idaho Department of Fish and Game allocated a quota of 220 wolves to be taken during the 2009 hunting season; approximately 134 wolves were killed legally in Idaho, and 72 were taken in Montana.

In 2010, the 9th U.S. Circuit Court of Appeals overturned the ruling, which once again gave wolves protection under the Endangered Species Act, to the consternation of Idaho's top elected officials.

Grizzly Bears

At one time this biggest and most powerful of North American mammals was widespread across the West, but that was before Lewis and Clark set the stage for human encroachment on grizzly habitat. In the Lower 48, a population once estimated at tens of thousands of animals was reduced by humans—either directly by hunting or indirectly by habitat loss—to about 1,200 today. In 1975, grizzlies were given threatened status under the Endangered Species Act, and today Idaho is one of only four states where *Ursus arctos* still lives (the others are Washington, Montana, and Wyoming).

Not that Idaho harbors vast numbers of them: Chris Servheen, grizzly bear recovery coordinator for the U.S. Fish and Wildlife Service, estimates there may be 100 in Idaho at any given time. Unless you go backpacking in a few specific areas of the state and get extremely lucky, you'll never see a grizzly. They roam the northern tip of the Panhandle north of Sandpoint, particularly in the Selkirk Mountains; the Bitterroot Range from Clark Fork south to the headwaters of the St. Joe River; and along the Wyoming border from near Henry's Lake south to Alpine.

The grizzly is immense. A full-grown adult male averages 450 pounds and can weigh up to 500 pounds. Just coming across a fresh grizzly print in the mud is enough to set the adrenaline flowing as the scale of this beautiful beast becomes apparent. No matter how big and bad you think you are, you're a wimp compared to the griz.

Grizzlies are far larger than black bears, but at a distance, it might be difficult to gauge an animal's size. You can't tell a black bear from a grizzly by color alone—grizzlies can appear black and black bears can be brown. Look for the dish-shaped head profile and the telltale Quasimodo shoulder hump.

Salmon

Idaho was once home to literally millions of anadromous fish—fish that are born in freshwater, migrate downstream to the sea, grow into adults there, then return upriver to their birthplace to spawn. Idaho is at the headwaters of the great Columbia River Drainage; historically, the total run of adult fish to the Columbia River has been estimated at 8–16 million fish, of which the Snake River may have produced 1.5–3 million. Salmon and steelhead once made their way annually from the Pacific up the Columbia to the Snake River, and up the Snake River to prime spawning grounds on the Salmon and Clearwater Rivers and their tributaries, a journey of up to 900 miles. Redfish Lake in Idaho's Sawtooth Mountains gained its name from the first settlers to the area, who found the lake colored red with the bodies of thousands of sockeye salmon each spawning season. Idaho's Native Americans relied on the salmon as a staple in their diet for centuries.

Then the dams came—humans harnessed the waters of the Columbia for cheap electricity. Twelve dams were constructed on the Columbia, Snake, and Clearwater Rivers between 1938 and 1973. The main-stem dams were equipped with fish ladders to help adults get upstream to spawn but provided no help for offspring making their way back to the sea. The fish were sucked into dam turbines and killed, died of disease exacerbated by the warmer temperature of the slower-moving water, or succumbed to increased predation during the journey. Before the dams, the young smolts made it to the Pacific in 7–10 days. After the dams, it took two months or more for those who made it at all.

Three species of salmon—the coho, chinook, and sockeye—once spawned in Idaho waters, along with the steelhead, an anadromous rainbow trout. The coho was officially declared extinct on the Snake River in 1986. The sockeye may be next; from 1991 to 2003 only 16 wild sockeye have returned from the ocean. All sockeye that return are captured and placed in a captive-breeding program in an effort to save the species. Wild chinook salmon were declared a threatened species when returns declined to a few thousand adults in the early 1990s, and wild steelhead were listed as threatened under the Endangered Species Act in 1997. Although artificial production (hatchery) programs produce millions of smolts every year and provide some surplus fish for fishing, the once-abundant wild and natural runs remain at a tiny fraction of the historical numbers. None of the mitigation measures attempted, including capturing smolts above the dams and barging or trucking them to the sea, has worked to restore natural spawning and wild salmon runs.

Environmentalists have urged the breaching of four dams on the Lower Snake River, but the idea hasn't gained political traction, and the salmon issue remains mired in legal maneuvering. Dams *are* a primary culprit in the salmon's fate, but the issue is more complex than simply "dams versus salmon." Water withdrawals for 3 million acres of irrigated Idaho cropland, the Northwest's continuing population boom, highway and home construction that fragment salmon habitat, and insatiable demand for cheap electricity—all are contributing to the salmon's decline. When it comes down to it, we can have our modern ultraconsumptive lifestyle, or we can have wild salmon, but we probably can't have both.

Bull Trout
Back in 1949, a world-record 32-pound bull trout was pulled from Lake Pend Oreille. But the bull trout—actually not a trout at all, but a char—hasn't been doing so well in recent years, and it's now listed as threatened. A predator fish that prefers the coldest waters, bull trout are also sometimes called Dolly Varden.

Woodland Caribou
Two small herds of Selkirk Mountains woodland caribou cling to a precarious existence in the Panhandle's Selkirk Range and neighboring eastern Washington and British Columbia. Populations had declined to around 25 animals in the early 1980s. Today, after extensive management efforts to strengthen populations, there are still only around 35–40 animals left. Habitat loss and low birthrates have inhibited their comeback. Wildlife biologists have proposed establishing a third herd, hoping to keep the gene pool strong and avoid catastrophic loss of animals from disease. The caribou, a medium-size member of the deer family, has a broad muzzle, large hooves, and impressive antlers with shovel-like brow tines.

OTHER FAUNA
Mammals
BLACK BEARS
Common and numerous throughout Idaho and the West, the black bear *(Ursus americanus)* is much more likely to be encountered by Idaho hikers and backpackers than its larger cousin,

the grizzly. The black bear was once a shy, nervous creature of little threat, but continued human-bear encounters have left it less afraid of humans and more likely to be trouble. Black bears are smaller than grizzlies, have straight (as opposed to dished) head profiles, and lack the grizzly's trademark shoulder hump. Also note that unlike grizzlies, many black bears are adept at climbing trees.

WILD DOGS AND CATS
The wolf's little cousin, the **coyote** *(Canis latrans),* is alive and well in Idaho. This survivor plays a leading role in many Nez Perce legends; he's a cagey prankster who always seems to have a lesson to teach. **Mountain lions** inhabit remote parts of Idaho but are so shy and elusive they are seldom seen by humans. Other cool cats found in Idaho include the **bobcat** and the **Canada lynx.**

HORNS AND HOOVES
Elk were found across the country when European explorers first arrived. By 1900 the New World's new residents had killed off 99 percent of them. The rest were found almost entirely in Yellowstone National Park. Today Idaho supports several herds. Don't miss the wintertime elk-viewing Hap and Florence Points Memorial Sleigh Rides in Donnelly, or the summertime evening browsing at Burgdorf Hot Springs near McCall.

White-tailed deer and **mule deer** are plentiful, as is the largest member of the deer family, the **moose.** Priest Lake in the Panhandle is a possible spot to spot a moose, as are the Caribou National Forest of southeast Idaho and along the North Fork of the Payette River near McCall.

Mountain goats can often be seen on the high cliffs of central Idaho, while **bighorn sheep** share the arid southwestern deserts and highlands with **pronghorn.** Owyhee County is also home to small herds of **wild horses.**

SMALL MAMMALS
Beavers have become popular helpers in restoring rangelands eroded by cattle. Dams

bighorn sheep

built by the 50-pound, paddle-tailed rodents create wetlands, slow fast-moving storm water before it can do erosion damage, and catch eroded topsoil before it's washed downstream. **River otters** inhabit many of the state's waterways. I've seen them right by the falls in Idaho Falls and on the South Fork of the Snake near Ririe. **Marmots** and **pikas** inhabit rocky areas, usually above the timberline. The pika's sharp whistle is familiar to high-country backpackers.

Life isn't so good these days for the **Northern Idaho ground squirrel,** a species found only in a 20- by 61-mile area in Adams and Valley Counties. In the mid-1980s there were about 5,000 such squirrels; today there are fewer than 500, and they're listed as threatened. Ground squirrel populations have declined mainly due to habitat loss and fragmentation.

Birds
RAPTORS
Southwest Idaho provides the focal point of human efforts to preserve raptors, or birds of prey. On the outskirts of Boise you'll find the World Center for Birds of Prey, and, farther south, the Birds of Prey National Conservation Area. The latter preserve protects a stretch of the Snake River and the surrounding cliff tops where, in spring, the world's densest concentration of nesting raptors can be found—more than 700 pairs of 14 different species.

A cruise down just about any rural road in the region will provide close-up looks at big birds of prey perched on power lines or soaring on thermals. One day while I was getting lost near Eden in the south-central part of the state, I happened on a farmer's plowed field where I had to stop and rub my eyes in disbelief. Scattered across the field—perhaps the size of a couple of football fields put together—were literally scores of hawks, looking like so many crows in a wheat field.

But Idaho's incredible cast of raptors—including red-tailed hawks, Swainson's hawks, ferruginous hawks, goshawks, northern harriers, peregrine falcons, prairie falcons, bald eagles, golden eagles, short-eared owls, great horned owls, ospreys, and others—aren't just found in southern Idaho. For example, **bald eagles,** whose populations have recovered from near extinction and have been down-listed from endangered to threatened status under the Endangered Species Act, can be found in winter across the state, from Boise to Coeur d'Alene, fishing in open waters. **Ospreys** seem to particularly like the southeast shores of Coeur d'Alene Lake around Harrison, while **ferruginous hawks** congregate in the Juniper Valley near the Utah border. And the ubiquitous **vulture** will carry on wherever there's carrion.

WATERFOWL
Eastern Idaho lies along a major avian migratory route, and its lakes and wetlands become mass staging areas for hundreds of thousands of **ducks** and **geese** in spring and fall. **Sandhill cranes** flock to Gray's Lake National Wildlife Refuge in some numbers; if you're lucky, you might catch a glimpse of the endangered **whooping crane** there as well. The largest of all North American waterfowl is the rare **trumpeter swan,** which weighs 30–40 pounds and has a wingspan of up to eight feet. Hunting and habitat loss had reduced their numbers to as few as 200 at the turn of the 20th century. Though they are still rare, the trumpeter population is now about 3,000. Trumpeters migrate through the Henry's Fork area; look for them at Harriman State Park in winter.

Fish
TROUT
Many consider the anadromous steelhead trout to be the state's premier game fish. Adult steelhead weigh 10–15 pounds and are found in the Snake, Salmon, and Clearwater Rivers and their tributaries.

True trout species in Idaho include **rainbow, cutthroat, brook, brown,** and **lake trout,** this last also known as mackinaw. Also in the trout family are Idaho's **kamloops** and **kokanee.**

STURGEON
For sheer size, the king of Idaho's piscine population is the bottom-feeding white sturgeon. These giants live about as long as people—100-year-old individuals have been reported, although the oldest fish officially documented by state biologists was 65. Today, these fish grow to lengths of over 11 feet and weigh upward of 300 pounds. In the old days, before commercial fishing and the construction of the Snake River dams, individuals up to 20 feet long and weighing more than 1,000 pounds were reported (and yes, photographed for posterity). But populations have declined steadily since the turn of the 20th century. Commercial sturgeon fishing has been banned since 1943, and today all sport sturgeon fishing is catch-and-release only. In 1995, sturgeon fishing on the Kootenai River was closed completely. The strongest remaining sturgeon populations are found today on two stretches of the Snake River: between Bliss Dam and C. J. Strike Dam, and between Hells Canyon Dam and Lewiston.

WARM-WATER FISH
Idaho's lakes harbor a number of species prized by anglers, including largemouth and smallmouth **bass,** three different species of **catfish,** and **perch, crappie,** and **tiger muskie.** The **Bonneville cisco** is a rare sardine-like fish living only in the waters of Bear Lake, in Idaho's southeastern corner.

History

THE EARLIEST INHABITANTS

The earliest people to roam the state on a more-or-less continuous basis probably came into the area some 14,000 years ago. Luckily not yet clear on the concept of no-trace camping, these nomadic hunters left remnants of their existence behind. At the bottom of Wilson Butte Cave near Dietrich in south-central Idaho, archaeologists have discovered bones of a prehistoric horse, camel, and sloth dating from 13,000 B.C. and a spear point dated to 12,500 B.C.—one of the oldest conclusive bits of evidence of human habitation in the country.

Native Americans

Before the arrival of the Lewis and Clark expedition in 1805, the Northwest, including the future Idaho, was inhabited by numerous tribes of indigenous peoples. The **Kootenai** tribe roamed the territory now comprising southern British Columbia, northeastern Washington,

the Idaho Panhandle, and northwestern Montana. They fished for salmon and sturgeon in the rivers; hunted deer, elk, and caribou; and gathered wild vegetables, roots, and berries. The **Coeur d'Alene** tribe lived around Coeur d'Alene Lake. They too hunted deer and fished in the lake and its feeder rivers. To catch salmon, they trekked to Spokane Falls, which blocked salmon migration to Coeur d'Alene Lake and the upstream rivers.

Eastern Oregon's Wallowa Valley, parts of southeastern Washington, and Idaho's Clearwater River Valley were once the home territory of the **Nez Perce** tribe. They fished for salmon in the Clearwater River, hunted deer, elk, moose, bighorn sheep, and bears, and gathered camas roots from the vast field on the Camas Prairie around Grangeville.

Southwestern Idaho was part of the territory wandered by the **Shoshone** and **Paiute** tribes of the Great Basin, a vast area spanning

© IDAHO DIVISION OF TOURISM

Native American pictographs along the Middle Fork Salmon River

parts of southeastern Oregon, northeastern California, southwestern Idaho, and northern Nevada. Tribal cooks in this desert landscape had an entirely different list of ingredients to choose from; hunters brought in pronghorn, sage grouse, squirrels, rabbits, and prairie dogs as well as deer. Some bands found pine nuts; some searched for seeds and berries. Bands were small, and the people were peaceful.

The Shoshone people coexisted in south-central and southeastern Idaho with the **Bannock** people; the two tribes had distinct languages but shared similar hunter-gatherer lifestyles.

The Spanish introduced horses to North America in their forays into Mexico and today's southwestern United States, and by around 1700 the horse reached the Native Americans of Idaho. It was seized on by the various tribes, whose migratory lifestyles suddenly got much easier. Soon many tribes made forays across the Continental Divide into what is now Montana and Wyoming. There they found great herds of buffalo that would sustain them until the nonnatives came and wiped out the herds. The trails blazed by the Idaho tribes crossing east to the buffalo-hunting grounds were the same trails later used in the opposite direction by explorers, fur trappers, and pioneers.

THE ADVENTURES OF LEWIS AND CLARK
The Corps of Discovery

Even before the April 1803 brokering of the Louisiana Purchase gave the U.S. title to most of the West, President Thomas Jefferson secretly began planning an exploratory expedition to find a viable northern route between the Mississippi River and the Pacific Ocean. Jefferson looked to his personal secretary, a young Virginian named Meriwether Lewis, to lead the mission. Lewis had been a captain in the Virginia state militia. Much of his duty had been west of the Alleghenies, and he had considerable experience dealing with indigenous Native Americans.

Lewis chose fellow Virginian William Clark as his cocommander. Clark also had considerable military experience. He was known as a skilled negotiator with Native Americans as well as a qualified mapmaker. He also recruited many members for the expedition. By the winter of 1803–1804, Lewis and Clark and their party of about 40 men were camped at the confluence of the Missouri and Mississippi Rivers near St. Louis. Lewis was 29; Clark, 33.

In May 1804, the expedition, known as the Corps of Discovery, set out west. Their mission: to follow the Missouri River to its headwaters in the Rocky Mountains, cross the Rockies, and find the nearest navigable waterway to the Pacific Ocean. The first summer was marked by several meetings with Indian nations and by Lewis and Clark's careful recording—via their journals and sketches—of many plants and animals unknown in the Eastern United States.

By October 1804, the expedition had reached North Dakota. They wintered there near a village of Minnetaree (Hidatsa), Mandan, and Amahami people and picked up their famous guide, a teenage Shoshone woman named Sacagawea. As a girl, Sacagawea had lived with her people in the Lemhi Valley near present-day Salmon, Idaho. But on a hunting expedition into Montana, her band had been attacked by the Minnetarees. Sacagawea, about age 12, was captured and taken east to be traded among the Indians like legal tender. She ended up as the property and wife of French trapper Toussaint Charbonneau. When Lewis and Clark reached the Minnetaree village, they hired Charbonneau as an interpreter, at least in part with the hope that Sacagawea might be able to help them find her people and negotiate for horses to cross the Rocky Mountains. When the Corps of Discovery resumed its westward journey in May 1805, Sacagawea, Charbonneau, and the couple's two-month-old baby joined the expedition.

Scouting the Bitterroots

A small advance party led by Lewis crossed the Continental Divide on August 12, becoming the first nonnatives to lay eyes on the land that would become Idaho. It was the last piece of the American jigsaw puzzle to be filled in and the beginning of the end for the region's Native American inhabitants. The explorers' route across the Continental Divide is today commemorated by the **Lewis and Clark National Backcountry Byway**, which connects Montana's Highway 324 with Idaho Highway 28 at Tendoy. It can be negotiated in summer by a sturdy passenger vehicle or a trusty Appaloosa.

The party continued down the western side of the pass and soon surprised a small group of Shoshone women. After being assured of the party's peaceful intentions, the women led the group back to their main encampment, where they were received with open arms. In a twist of fate, Sacagawea and a Shoshone woman saw each other and gleefully embraced. It seems Sacagawea had found her people at last—the Shoshone woman was a childhood friend. Later that night, the two groups celebrated with a reunion feast. But it was a bittersweet reunion for Sacagawea, who learned that most of her family was dead.

Lewis told the Shoshone chief, Cameahwait, of his plan to navigate the Lemhi River downstream, eventually to the Columbia. The chief advised against it, telling Lewis that not far to the north, past a major confluence (with the Salmon River), the river cascaded through steep, impassable canyons. Lewis suspected the chief was exaggerating and decided to forge ahead with the plan.

Continuing West

On the morning of August 17 Clark and a small party began to scout a route down the Lemhi River. Not far past the confluence of the Lemhi and Salmon Rivers, the steep route along the Salmon was judged impassable, exactly as Chief Cameahwait had told Lewis. Clark dispatched a messenger relaying the word to Lewis, who agreed that the expedition should abandon the Lemhi-Salmon Rivers route and instead attempt the Nez Perce route—the Lolo Trail—that crossed the Bitterroot Mountains far to the north. Lewis and the rest of the expedition set out immediately, crossing Lemhi Pass and catching up

with Clark once again. Sacagawea bade a sad farewell to her people and, along with the rest of the corps, headed north.

They doggedly worked their way up the Continental Divide, first along the west side via the North Fork of the Salmon, then across to the Montana side near **Lost Trail Pass** (U.S. 93 today) and down into the Bitterroot River Valley, where they camped with a party of 400 Salish people.

Over the Bitterroots, Barely

After camping for a few days at the junction of the Bitterroot and Lolo Creek, the party proceeded west up the creek along a traditional Nez Perce hunting trail. On September 13 they crested **Lolo Pass** and dropped back into Idaho. They camped in present-day Packer Meadows near Lolo Pass and along the Lochsa River near what's now the Powell Ranger Station. Game was scarce, and they had to kill a horse for meat. On September 15, the party set off up Wendover Ridge to gain the Nez Perce trail to the north. It began to snow, obscuring the trail and slowing progress even further. Clark was "as wet and as cold in every part as I ever was in my life, indeed I was at one time fearful my feet would freeze in the thin moccasins which I wore." It's a wonder they didn't lose anyone to hypothermia. The early-season storm had driven the game out of the mountains to lower, warmer elevations, making food scarce for the expedition. They shot another horse for dinner and huddled around campfires trying to get warm.

By September 18, the expedition had run out of spare horses to fricassee. (Picture yourself on a remote mountain trail in 1805, in stormy weather, with no Gore-Tex, no road, no car, no ready-made food, and no idea what lay ahead. It's safe to say that the expedition was running on hope at this point.) Clark and a party of six hunters went on ahead to find, kill, and bring back food. Two days out, they sighted the Weippe Prairie—a welcome, easily traversable bench unlike the steep canyons they'd been crossing, and also where they met the Nez Perce. Although some discussed killing the strangers, Nez Perce oral history says they were stopped by a woman named Watkuweis who—like Sacagawea—was kidnapped when she was younger and had been helped by white people. The agreeable Nez Perce gave Clark's party dried salmon and camas flour, some of which Clark sent back to Lewis and the rest of the expedition with one of his men. Clark and his hunting party accompanied the Nez Perce to their main encampment farther downriver at present-day Orofino. Lewis and the rest of the corps straggled in later.

Among the Nez Perce

Safe and in good hands with the friendly Nez Perce, they established their own camp, called Canoe Camp, just west of the Nez Perce camp, near today's Ahsahka, where they recuperated from their difficult mountain crossing. Besides being a place to recuperate, Canoe Camp was important for another reason. When Lewis and Clark saw the Nez Perce paddling up and down the river, they knew that they could now safely do the same. The expedition members began cutting down ponderosa pines to fashion into canoes, and by October 6, five canoes

were finished and preparations were made to get under way. Under cover of darkness, the expedition members dug a secret hole and buried all their saddles. Then they branded their remaining horses and left them with the Nez Perce, intending to pick them up on their return trip the following spring.

The next day they floated and loaded their canoes and said goodbye to their hosts. Nez Perce Chief Twisted Hair gave Lewis and Clark a map of what lay downriver, and a couple of Nez Perce offered to come along as guides. At last they shoved off. The river's rapids proved difficult, and twice canoes were damaged. But the expedition reached the confluence of the Clearwater and Snake Rivers (site of present-day Lewiston, Idaho, and Clarkston, Washington) on October 10, and paddled on into Washington.

Epilogue

The expedition continued down the Snake to the Columbia River and then down the Columbia to the Pacific Ocean in mid-November. They built Fort Clatsop near present-day Astoria, Oregon, and stayed for the winter.

following the trail of Lewis and Clark on horseback

© IDAHO DIVISION OF TOURISM

On March 23, 1806, they began their return journey by essentially the same route they had come. They picked up the horses and saddles they'd left with the Nez Perce at Orofino. The Indians once again treated them warmly, and the explorers camped near present-day Kamiah for nearly a month while they waited for the snow to melt from the Bitterroots.

Lewis and Clark arrived in St. Louis to a hero's welcome on September 23, 1806. Most people had long since given them up for dead. Lewis served as governor of Louisiana Territory for two years and died under mysterious circumstances—either murder or suicide—in Tennessee on his way to Washington, D.C., in 1809. Sacagawea died in 1812, but not before she and Charbonneau tried homesteading near St. Louis circa 1809–1811. Clark became Superintendent of Indian Affairs for Louisiana Territory and later served as governor of Missouri Territory. He maintained a lifelong trusted relationship with the West's Native Americans and negotiated many Indian treaties before his death in 1838.

The expedition had been a success on many fronts. It had carried out its mission while losing only one man—Charles Floyd, whose appendix ruptured three months into the trip. It had proved an overland route to the Pacific was possible, mapped the land and cataloged its flora and fauna, and established friendly relations with the indigenous peoples. But all those accomplishments contributed to the subsequent flood of white emigrants to the West, an unstoppable wave that would greatly diminish Native American culture and have a profound effect on the land and resources of the Northwest.

THE FUR TRAPPERS
David Thompson

Two years after Lewis and Clark passed through Idaho on their way back home, British fur trappers began working their way into the territory from Canada. One of the first to arrive was geographer David Thompson, an Englishman working for Britain's venerable Hudson's Bay Company. Thompson—today widely considered one of the greatest geographers in history—was an explorer at heart who used fur trapping as a convenient way to fund his true passion. He had come to Canada as a teenage apprentice for Hudson's Bay, and by the time he arrived in Idaho in 1808 he had vast experience in mapmaking and dealing with indigenous peoples. He had also jumped ship, so to speak, leaving Hudson's Bay Company for its Montreal-based British archrival, the **North West Company.**

In 1809, Thompson and his crew built a log house, the first permanent structure built by nonnatives in Idaho, near the present-day town of Hope on Lake Pend Oreille. They named it Kullyspell House after the area's Kalispel Indians—a goodwill gesture guaranteed to grease the wheels of trade with the locals. In the four years Thompson stayed at Kullyspell House, he and his colleagues sent bushel upon bushel of beaver pelts back to England, where beaver-fur hats were all the rage. Also during that period, Thompson explored and mapped much of the Panhandle, established good relations with the Native Americans, and surveyed the passes that would later allow railroads into the area. In doing so he set the stage for further nonnative expansion into the Panhandle.

Andrew Henry

Not to be outdone by the Brits, American interests soon raced west to reap their share of the wealth. First to the scene were members of the St. Louis–based **Missouri Fur Company.** In 1809, Pennsylvania native Andrew Henry, a former lead miner, became a partner in the enterprise. In the fall of the following year, Henry led a party of the company's trappers across the Continental Divide into southern Idaho. There he discovered a big, beautiful lake and encouraging prospects for trapping. Deciding to settle in the area for the winter, Henry headed downstream from the lake several miles and built a fort. What he didn't know was that the area sees some of the coldest, most severe winter weather in the West. The winter of 1810–1811 was no exception. The local deer and antelope hightailed it out of there early to go play on a warmer range, leaving little for Henry's party to hunt and eat. The men were forced to fry up their own horses to survive. As soon as the first spring thaw came, Henry decided Missouri wasn't such a bad place after all and returned home posthaste. While the trip hadn't yielded much in the way of beaver pelts, Henry did get immortality out of it: The big beautiful lake and the river below it are now called **Henry's Lake** and **Henry's Fork,** respectively.

Wilson Price Hunt

The same winter that Andrew Henry huddled shivering and homesick in eastern Idaho, 28-year-old greenhorn Wilson Price Hunt was holed up in South Dakota, leading an expedition for John Jacob Astor's **Pacific Fur Company.** After winter let up, Hunt's party continued west. That fall they made it to Jackson Hole, where they came upon three impressive mountain peaks stacked against the horizon. The sight inspired a couple of French Canadians to name the impressive peaks Les Trois Tétons—"The Three Breasts." Today we know the beautiful mountains as the Grand Tetons.

The party continued over Teton Pass into Idaho, arriving in October 1811 at abandoned Fort Henry, where they made the mistake of leaving their horses behind and attempting to ride the Snake River west. The eastern Snake is a relatively placid affair, today floated by novices, but the flat waters become cantankerous downstream. The expedition portaged around Idaho Falls and American Falls with little difficulty, but then they came to the Milner Reach—a section that even today is run only by experts and fools.

The Hunt party lost a man and equipment on the upper Milner Reach, but the worst was yet to come: a spot so ferocious, so impossibly unforgiving that they named it **Caldron Linn,** or Witch's Caldron Falls. From a safe vantage point today, you can feel some of what Hunt and his men felt. The innocuous river rounds a corner and far too suddenly funnels down a tight rocky gorge, thundering into frothing white madness. The falls spark respect,

if not outright fear. And remember, today the flow is regulated by Milner Dam upriver. When Hunt's party first saw Caldron Linn, the water was racing unbridled down from the Continental Divide. It must have been horrifying. The expedition abandoned thoughts of floating to the Columbia River and began an overland trek along the banks of the Snake. They pressed on forlornly, reaching Fort Astoria at the mouth of the Columbia River in mid-February 1812.

As a footnote, the next year some of the group retraced their route from Astoria to the confluence of the Snake and Boise Rivers, where they intended to set up a trapping base. They might have succeeded, but two years later, in 1814, all but three were killed by Native Americans. It was the first wholesale murder of immigrants by Native Americans in Idaho.

Are Those Bagpipes I Hear?

One of the surviving members of the Hunt expedition was an enormous Scotsman, a Highlander named **Donald Mackenzie.** With flaming red hair and a bulk of over 300 pounds, he must have been an impressive sight.

Mackenzie worked the Snake River and its tributaries for years. His 1818 expedition met with some bad luck that ended up contributing to Idaho's geographic lexicon. In those years, it was common to find Hawaiians among the members of trapping expeditions. When Captain James Cook discovered what he named the Sandwich Islands in 1778, his interpretation of the name the islanders gave themselves was "Owyhees." Subsequently, English vessels working the Pacific would bring these Owyhees to the Northwest to work as laborers. A few of them could usually be found on Mackenzie's expeditions, and the 1818 trip was no exception. At one point, Mackenzie assigned three of them to trap along an unnamed, unexplored river south of the Boise River–Snake River confluence. The men never returned; presumably they were killed by Native Americans. The remaining members of the expedition named the unexplored river after the unfortunate islanders. Today on the map of Idaho you'll find not only the **Owyhee River** but the Owyhee Mountains as well; both are in Owyhee County.

Another Scotsman, seasoned trapper **Finan McDonald,** led an 1823 Hudson's Bay Company expedition from Spokane east into Montana, then back into Idaho over Lemhi Pass. On the upper Lemhi River the expedition was ambushed by a party of Blackfeet. Outnumbered almost three to one, McDonald and company fought a smart battle—the battle of their lives—and miraculously defeated the Blackfeet, losing only six men in the process. The Blackfeet lost 68 of their 75 warriors in the skirmish, which put an irremediable dent into their control of the area. When McDonald got back to Spokane, he vowed never to return to that part of the country. But by vanquishing the Blackfeet, McDonald had succeeded in opening the door to the upper Snake River country for trappers and those who followed.

A New Breed

By the time Canadian **Peter Skene Ogden** took charge of the Hudson's Bay Company Snake River operations in 1824, the Idaho fur-trapping scene had changed drastically from the days of David Thompson's Kullyspell House. Increasing numbers of trappers in the territory were coming into more frequent conflicts with Native Americans, particularly the Blackfeet and Bannock, who were by now well armed. And competition between British and American trappers had increased as the beaver populations had decreased. Ogden's marching orders were to trap out the Snake River country, leaving not a single beaver behind for the Americans. This was easier said than done; although Ogden led profitable expeditions annually until 1830, the regimented bureaucratic machine of the Hudson's Bay Company was giving ground to an American cadre of loosely associated "freelance" trappers well versed in the changing ways of the West.

The earliest trappers had succeeded because they were good explorers, but by the 1820s different skills were needed to succeed in the fur trade. With the land now extensively mapped and traveled, it was more important to be handy with a rifle than a compass. Flexibility and mobility were advantageous when seeking the isolated areas where beavers remained plentiful. The profitability of the Hudson's Bay Company's thoroughly planned, expensive, and massive expeditions—the 1824 brigade numbered 140 people and 392 horses—was challenged by American frontiersmen who could roam freely and relatively easily throughout the territory. But how to organize these independent mountain men into a single economic unit?

William Henry Ashley was among the first to tackle this problem. Ashley hooked up with Andrew Henry and brought together some of the most skilled young mountain men of the day, among them **Jedediah Smith** and **Jim Bridger.** They sent the men out trapping in small teams with instructions to rendezvous at a later date to exchange pelts for payment and new supplies. This strategy proved to be enormously successful, and the **Snake River rendezvous** played a memorable part in Western lore. Imagine a kind of Wild West Mardi Gras—an anything-goes three-day drunk full of white trappers and Native Americans from a number of different tribes, all singing, dancing, gambling, fighting, competing at this or that, and carrying on well into the wee hours of each night. Such was the scene at the many rendezvous that took place nearly annually between 1825 and 1840. Presumably the participants managed to get a little trading done too. A favorite rendezvous location was the Teton Valley, which they called "Pierre's Hole," after "Old Pierre" Tevanitagon, an Iroquois trapper once associated with Hudson's Bay Company.

The Woods!

It may sound like something out of *Fantasy Island,* but it was actually the men of an 1832–1834 expedition led by **Captain Benjamin Louis Eulalie de Bonneville** who famously said, *"Les bois! Les bois!"*—"The woods! The woods!" Bonneville was from a Parisian family that came to the United States in 1803 after Napoleon took control of their homeland. Young Bonneville graduated from West Point and became an Army officer. When he decided to mount his own expedition to the West, the Army graciously gave him some time off to do so.

In 1832, the 110-man expedition left Fort Osage, Missouri, and made it to the Salmon River headwaters before winter set in. The following spring they moved to southeast Idaho, and the year after that, in 1834, they followed the dry and dusty north bank of the Snake River west. After miles and miles of this desert landscape, they topped a small rise and saw to the west a river valley filled with trees, lush and verdant in the distance. The French Canadians could hardly contain themselves.

Today you can drive to the site where they saw the trees—it's just north of I-84—and read a plaque that will tell you that it was the ecstatic Bonneville expedition that gave the Boise River its name. It's a nice story, but actually, the name had at that point been used by trappers on that river for more than 20 years.

Bonneville got an Idaho county, a prehistoric lake, and a modern-day Utah salt flat named for him, but he never really amounted to much as a trapper. You can read all about him in Washington Irving's book *The Adventures of Captain Bonneville*, published in 1837.

The Fur Forts

The year 1834 also saw the establishment of two permanent fur-trading forts on the Snake River: **Fort Boise** in the west, at the confluence of the Snake and Boise Rivers near present-day Parma; and **Fort Hall** in the east, near present-day Blackfoot. Both forts were successful and important for two reasons. First, they led to the eventual end of the rendezvous system by creating what were essentially permanent year-round rendezvous sites. Their strategic placement at either end of the Snake River Plain would make them important way stations along the emigrant trails soon to be established.

Fort Boise (not to be confused with the U.S. Army fort of the same name in today's

city of Boise) was built by the Hudson's Bay Company and run by a jolly French Canadian trapper named **François Payette.** The portly Payette was well known for the hospitality he lavished on visitors to his fort, setting out feasts for his guests and regaling them with tales of his past adventures. The Payette River was named after him.

Fort Hall was built and run by **Nathaniel Wyeth,** a Boston entrepreneur who had been trying unsuccessfully to wring a profit out of the West for some years. The fort was christened with a raucous party on August 5, 1834. Wyeth must have had high hopes that day. Unfortunately, the venture proved only marginally lucrative. After just two full seasons, he sold the fort to the Hudson's Bay Company and moved back to Boston. One might suspect Wyeth's financial disappointments were caused by a lack of business acumen, but for this venture he just had bad luck and bad timing. Although Fort Hall remained in use by the Hudson's Bay Company until 1856, out West, the times were a-changing.

Silk Hats and Wagon Roads

Ah, the fickle finger of fashion. Not long after Fort Hall was built, beaver hats became passé in London and on the East Coast of the United States. Now silk hats were all the rage. Meanwhile, over on the east side of the Mississippi, the population of the United States kept increasing. Over the years, trappers had opened up many passes across the Rockies and had established well-worn trails—including the framework for the Oregon Trail—that could be navigated by wagons.

EARLY MISSIONARIES

When Idaho's indigenous peoples first encountered nonnatives, they must have been amazed at the odd things the pioneers carried with them: guns, medicines, Christianity. In 1831 the Nez Perce decided to send a party of emissaries back to St. Louis to visit their old friend William Clark. After the success of the Corps of Discovery expedition, Clark had taken an assignment with the U.S. government as head of Indian affairs for the West. The Nez Perce may have intended to ask Clark to send them someone to teach them reading, writing, and farming—or they may have sought spiritual assistance in exploring Christianity. Whichever their motivation, word soon spread of the Nez Perce sending representatives all the way to St. Louis in search of a Christian god, and the challenge was quickly taken up.

Henry, Narcissa, Marcus, and Eliza

An enormous new territory, full of heathens and now open to whites: It was the proverbial apple tempting proselytizing Christians to head West and show the natives the path of righteousness. Among the first on the scene were Henry Spalding, Narcissa Prentiss, Marcus Whitman, and Eliza Hart. Hollywood couldn't have written a better script: Henry was enamored of Narcissa, but Narcissa dumped him and married a doctor, Marcus. Henry married Eliza. In 1836, the four Presbyterians loaded up their Bibles and set out west together. You don't suppose there was any tension on *that* wagon train.

Narcissa and Eliza were the first white women to cross the Rockies. That the two women had made the journey and appeared to be faring well was a significant milestone on the road to westward expansion. As long as the Wild West was inhabited only by wild men, it wasn't seen as a place a family could live, but now women had made the trek, survived, and were planning to settle down. The West took on a new stature, as a place one might conceivably call home. Americans back east began to eye the West with more interest.

The two couples eventually went their separate ways. Marcus and Narcissa continued on to Washington Territory, near today's Walla Walla, where they established a mission among the Cayuse people. There the good doctor took in and doctored both sick pioneers and sick Native Americans. When a wagon train of settlers infected with the measles showed up, Whitman's big medicine healed the nonnatives but failed on the Native Americans, who had never before been exposed to the disease. Many Cayuse died under Whitman's care, and the Native Americans understandably concluded that Whitman was killing them. In 1847 the Cayuse raided the mission and killed both Marcus and Narcissa along with 12 other nonnative workers.

The Lapwai Mission

Meanwhile, Henry and Eliza had ended up in Idaho, where they built a mission among the Nez Perce at the confluence of Lapwai Creek and the Clearwater River. By all accounts, the Spaldings were quite a couple. Eliza learned to read and write the Nez Perce language, and soon was teaching locals of all ages to do the same. Word of her successful school reached a Protestant mission in Hawaii, which sent Eliza a printing press so she could print her lessons. In 1838 Eliza had a baby, also named Eliza, the first nonnative child born in Idaho.

Henry was equally busy. First he built a cabin and outbuildings, then taught the locals farming. They got a sizable garden up and sprouting and built a gristmill, a sawmill, and a blacksmith shop. Soon they were up to their ears in corn and up to their eyes in potatoes. The Nez Perce were sufficiently intrigued by the idea of farming to settle around the mission and begin cultivating their own plots. In 1839, Henry put in an irrigation system, the region's first.

Things went well for a few years, but soon the novelty wore off for the Nez Perce. The Spaldings were unable to supply the Native Americans with much in the way of firearms or magic medicinal remedies, and Henry became a strict disciplinarian who was sometimes harsh with the locals. When word got to the Spaldings that Marcus and Narcissa Whitman had been killed, Henry and Eliza decided to leave Lapwai. With a friendly Nez Perce escort to protect them from the Cayuse, they moved to the Willamette Valley and took up farming. Eliza died there in 1851. Henry moved back to Lapwai in 1863, where he died in 1874; both he and Eliza are buried there. The site of the Spaldings' Lapwai mission is today part of Nez

Perce National Historic Park, easily visited off U.S. 12 east of Lewiston.

The Catholic Contingent

Protestants weren't the only ones actively attempting to convert Idaho's indigenous peoples. The first Roman Catholic missionary on the scene was the Belgian priest **Father Pierre Jean de Smet,** who arrived in Idaho's Coeur d'Alene country in 1841. De Smet laid the groundwork for the Mission of the Sacred Heart, which was constructed in its final form and location by **Father Antonio Ravalli** in the early 1850s. The mission was built entirely without nails and still stands today, the oldest extant public building in Idaho. It boldly crowns a hillock along the Coeur d'Alene River east of the city of Coeur d'Alene. The disastrous floods of early 1996 inundated much of the Panhandle, but the old mission stayed high and dry—a credit to Father Ravalli's site selection.

WESTWARD BOUND
South Pass: Gateway to the West

By the 1840s the reports of Lewis and Clark, fur trappers, the Spaldings and Whitmans, and naval explorers off the Pacific coast all confirmed Oregon Country was not a desert wasteland; rather it was a bountiful region of good water and rich soil, ripe for cultivation and settlement. But how to get there? Lewis and Clark, following the Missouri River and its tributaries, had struggled over the Continental Divide at Idaho's Bitterroot Range. Clearly, settlers' wagons could never negotiate the passes that had almost defeated the Corps of Discovery.

The key that unlocked the West to settlers existed but had gone all but unnoticed. In 1824 the great mountain man Jedediah Smith had led a party of trappers working for William Henry Ashley across the Rockies at Wyoming's South Pass. Unlike Idaho's paths across the Rockies, South Pass hardly seems a pass at all. It arcs gently up and over the Continental Divide like a rolling swell on a calm sea. South Pass was reached not by following the

Missouri River to its headwaters in Montana, as Lewis and Clark had done, but by following the Missouri to its confluence with the Platte River (near present-day Omaha, Nebraska). From there, the emigrants followed first the Platte, then the Sweetwater River west to the its headwaters in Wyoming's Antelope Hills, just east of South Pass.

It wasn't until 1841, however, that the first bold party of pioneers hell-bent on settling the West set out from Missouri, headed for South Pass. The group of 70 was led by Thomas Fitzpatrick, who had helped found the Rocky Mountain Fur Company in 1830, and John Bidwell, who split off with about half the settlers at Soda Springs and made his way to California. Among the 70 emigrants was Jesuit Father de Smet, the early Panhandle missionary. Their journey was successful.

The following year, one of the country's great explorers, **John C. Frémont,** headed to Wyoming as a member of an official government survey expedition. The survey party crossed South Pass, and Frémont's rich prosaic reports made the crossing seem like a walk in the park. The following year, Frémont took the trail all the way to Oregon Country. With the benefit of an immensely talented ghostwriter— his wife, Jessie—Frémont described the whole route from St. Louis to Oregon in an enthusiastic and detailed report that was published by Congress and found its way into the hands of many an American contemplating the trek. The route Frémont described—one capable of being negotiated by settlers' wagons—came to be known as the Oregon Trail.

The Great Migration

In 1843 a combination of favorable reports from the West, malaria outbreaks in the Mississippi and Missouri River valleys, and perhaps a desire to participate in history prompted the first major wave of emigrants to pack their wagons. About 1,000 hopefuls set out from Independence, Missouri, that spring. The schedule for the crossing was tight. They couldn't leave the Midwest before the spring grasses had sprouted because they needed the

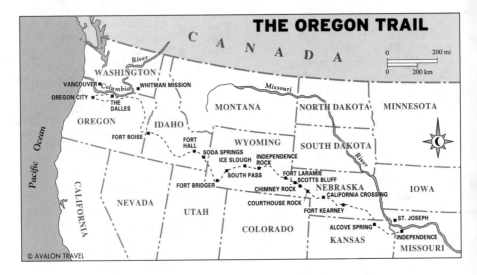

new growth to feed their livestock. Yet they had to be safely across the mountains of Oregon before the first snowfall. The average trip took five months.

The "trail" the pioneers followed was seldom a single set of tracks but rather a braid of parallel trails. Only in the narrow passes and canyons did the various parties funnel into the exact path of their predecessors; in those places, even today, you'll find deep wagon ruts.

Along the way, the Oregon Trail emigrants crossed through the territories of many different indigenous nations between Missouri and Oregon. Some of the Native Americans were friendly, some more hostile. The emigrants were understandably worried about Native American attacks, but that proved the least of their worries. Most who died succumbed to accidents or disease.

Along the Snake River

After crossing South Pass, the original Oregon Trail entered today's southeast Idaho—at the time part of Oregon Territory—near Bear Lake and headed north to Fort Hall, Nathaniel Wyeth's old fur fort on the upper Snake River. In 1837, Wyeth had sold Fort Hall to the Hudson's Bay Company. The British managers,

fearing they'd be driven out by Americans flooding into Oregon, customarily tried to discourage settlers from continuing west. They exaggerated the difficulty of the route, telling emigrants that the rest of the trail to Oregon was impassable by wagons. As a result, many pioneers traded their oxen and wagons for horses for the remainder of the journey.

Like bookends, Fort Hall in the east and Fort Boise in the west were the only two safe harbors along Idaho's stretch of the Oregon Trail. Leaving Fort Boise, the trail followed the south side of the Snake River west through hot, dry, and treeless desert and lava country. Occasionally, emigrants might sight the tantalizing waters of the river, usually out of reach at the bottom of steep, rocky canyons.

At Three Island Crossing, near today's Glenns Ferry, they were faced with a choice: brave the river crossing to easier going on a shorter route down the north side, or continue the long way down the hot and dry south side. Much of the decision depended on how high the Snake was running when they got there. The Snake's south side can be pretty miserable during the dog days of August, even for today's motorists. Imagine what the pioneers felt like, tromping through the dust day after day, with no air-conditioned car or motel room to offer respite. Reaching Fort Boise and the legendary hospitality of François Payette must have felt very good indeed, especially knowing that they were nearing Oregon.

Between 1841 and 1848, most westward-bound pioneers followed this route to Oregon; a far smaller number turned off the trail and headed south to California. Those proportions were reversed dramatically following the discovery of gold in California in 1848. Between 1849 and 1860, about 42,000 pioneers followed the Oregon Trail west to fertile farmland in Oregon's Willamette Valley, while some 200,000 others staked their future on easy money and headed to California, the "Golden State."

The California Trail and Hudspeth's Cutoff

Those pioneers choosing California as their destination followed the Oregon Trail west from Fort Hall only as far as the confluence of the Snake with the Raft River. There they turned south up the Raft River Valley, crossed the divide at City of Rocks, and continued south into Nevada and across the Sierras to the promised land. This route was used primarily until 1849. That year, a group of emigrants led by Benoni Hudspeth tried a shortcut similar to the original route followed by John Bidwell in 1841. From Soda Springs, they turned directly west, crossed four separate north–south-trending mountain ranges, and rejoined the California Trail midway up the Raft River Valley. This route turned out to be 25 miles and two days shorter than the previous route via Fort Hall. After word got out of Hudspeth's successful cutoff, the longer route through Fort Hall was dropped, even by those settlers headed for Oregon. In 1855 the Hudson's Bay Company's Brits packed up and left Fort Hall for good.

Other Routes

In 1859 the federal government commissioned engineer Frederick Lander to build a new wagon road from Wyoming's South Pass directly west to Fort Hall. The **Lander Road** took 100 miles off the length of the Oregon Trail. It also bypassed Fort Bridger, depriving the fort's great mountain-man proprietor, Jim Bridger, of a large chunk of business.

In 1862 another mountain man, Tim Goodale, pioneered a new route from Fort Hall to Fort Boise. Instead of following the hot, dry Snake River Plain west, **Goodale's Cutoff** headed northwest from Fort Hall to the base of the Pioneers. Hopping west from river to river at higher elevations than the routes to the south, Goodale's followers made their way across the Camas Prairie near present-day Fairfield before rejoining the Oregon Trail some 75 miles east of Fort Boise.

The Wood River Valley town of Hailey is named for John Hailey, who pioneered a stagecoach route from Salt Lake City to Boise City in 1869. The **Kelton Road** left Kelton, Utah, passed through the major pioneer-trail intersection at City of Rocks, continued northwest to the little oasis at Rock Creek, then crossed the Snake River and followed the north side of the river into Boise. This was the most important mail and freight route across southern Idaho until the Oregon Short Line railroad was completed in 1883.

CULTURES CLASH

With settlers pouring into age-old Native American territories—including traditional hunting grounds and sacred sites—and competing for often meager resources, tensions were bound to arise. Native American attacks accounted for less than 4 percent of the emigrant deaths on the Oregon Trail. Nevertheless, such attacks made sensational headlines in the Eastern newspapers, fueling the cause of jingoist politicians and business leaders who believed in manifest destiny at any cost.

More than one commentator has noted that when whites killed Indians, the press typically reported the skirmish as a "battle," but when Indians killed whites, it was a "massacre." Such was the case with the three most famous conflicts between settlers and Native Americans in Idaho.

The Ward Massacre

On August 20, 1854, a wagon train of emigrants led by Missourian Alexander Ward was 25 miles east of Boise when it ran into trouble. One of the emigrants caught an Indian horse thief in the act and shot him. Soon the wagon train was attacked full force by the rest of the tribe. Of the 20 people in the wagon train, 18 were killed in a particularly brutal fashion. The Native Americans stole all the livestock and valuables, then apparently went on a shooting spree. A half dozen or more whites in the general area were killed, presumably by the same group. Troops were dispatched from Fort Boise, and the perpetrators were hunted down. Three were shot, three were hanged, and others were jailed. As the episode appeared to involve just one local renegade band, the matter ended quickly.

The Utter-Van Orman Massacre

In September 1860, Owyhee County was the scene of another famous emigrant–Native American conflict. The eight-wagon, 44-person Utter–Van Orman Train was making its way west when it was attacked by Shoshones. Four Fort Hall soldiers came to the rescue but couldn't help much. The initial fight lasted two days. Nine emigrants were killed, and the covered wagons were torched. Some of the emigrants tried to escape and were killed by the Shoshones. The soldiers tried to ride out for help; two were killed. When it was all over, 23 emigrants were dead, and four children had been kidnapped by the Native Americans. Eighteen survivors were left stranded with no food or supplies and tried to walk out of the desert to the north. When a rescue party finally reached them, only 12 were still alive. They had been reduced to dining on their dead. One of the Army officers sent out to look for the kidnapped children tried to keep the situation in perspective. Major John Owen, quoted in Brigham D. Madsen's *The Bannock of Idaho,* summed up succinctly and prophetically the nature of the entire "Indian problem":

These Indians 12 years ago were the avowed friends of the White Man. I have had their young men in my employment as hunters, horse guards, guides, etc. I have traversed the length and breadth of their entire country with large bands of stock unmolested. Their present hostile attitude can in great measure be attributed to the treatment they have received from unprincipled White Men passing through their country. They have been robbed, murdered, their women outraged...and in fact outrages have been committed by White Men that the heart would shudder to record.

The Battle of Bear River

The worst slaughter of Native Americans by U.S. troops in the nation's history took place on the morning of January 29, 1863, about 12 miles north of Franklin. Earlier that winter, a party of miners near Bannack, Montana, had been attacked by Shoshone-Bannocks. One of the miners was killed. Troops from the Army's Camp Douglas, near Salt Lake City, rode north to bring the attackers to justice. Led by Colonel Patrick E. Connor, the troops came upon a band of more than 400 Shoshones camped near the icy Bear River. The Army charged in firing, but the band was determined to fight back, and the battle was bloody. After several hours, the Shoshones realized they were losing. They tried to escape but were brutally cut down. Connor lost 22 men in the battle, while his troops wiped out 200–400 Native Americans, including an estimated 90 women and children. Connor was promoted to brigadier general as a result.

This battle had an effect on the big picture of the relationship between Native Americans and nonnatives in a large part of the West. It broke the spirit of the Native Americans to the extent that most tribes accepted the futility of fighting and resigned themselves to treaty-created reservations. Only one last major conflict occurred in Idaho after the Bear River Massacre, the Nez Perce War of 1877.

MORMON INFLUX
Salmon River Mission

Not to be outdone by the early missionary work of the Presbyterians and Catholics, the Latter-day Saints arrived in Idaho in 1855. That year, Brigham Young sent 27 Mormon men to the Lemhi Valley to work with, and hopefully convert, the local Native Americans. While it lasted, the farming outpost they established—just north of present-day Tendoy, very near where Lewis and Clark crossed into Idaho—was the state's first nonnative agricultural settlement.

The missionaries had selected the site because it was the summer hunting and fishing site for three different tribes—Bannock, Shoshone, and Nez Perce. This very aspect that the Mormons saw as favorable led to the mission's undoing. Although the missionaries succeeded in establishing good relations with all three tribes separately, each tribe came to resent the attentions the Mormons paid to the other two. In the end, many of the Native Americans turned against the Mormons. The mission's horses and cattle were stolen, and a few men were killed. The mission was abandoned in April 1858.

Franklin and Beyond

In April 1860, a group of Mormons once again came north from Salt Lake City, this time founding a settlement just across the Idaho border. They built an irrigation system and began farming the Cache Valley. Before long, a sawmill, a fort, and cabins went up. In June, Brigham Young himself paid a visit, naming the town Franklin after Mormon apostle Franklin Richards. By the end of the year, the town had a population of over 100. Until an official government survey in 1872, the settlers thought they'd built their town in Utah. As it turned out, they'd founded the first town in Idaho.

The Mormons grew onions, potatoes, and wheat, which they shared freely with the area's Native Americans in hopes of ensuring peaceful relations. This strategy was successful for a time. But as more settlers came to town, claimed land, and built cabins, the Native Americans began to feel threatened. The Mormons lost increasing numbers of horses and cattle to thievery, and incidents of violent confrontation escalated. The Mormons were prepared to flee the valley when Colonel Patrick E. Connor and his men came through looking for a fight with the Native Americans. When the Battle of Bear River was over, the settlers helped care for the wounded and frostbitten soldiers and surviving Shoshones alike.

After the battle, the Shoshones signed the Treaty of Box Elder with the government, promising peace in exchange for government help. The government never came through with its side of the bargain, but by that time Connor and the bluecoats were installed at a new fort in nearby Soda Springs, making raids a riskier proposition for the Shoshones. The Fort Hall Indian Reservation was established in 1867, and most of the beleaguered Cache Valley Shoshones resignedly moved onto the reservation. The area was now wide open for nonnative expansion, and the Mormons quickly took advantage of the opportunity. With a religious doctrine encouraging large families, the Latter-day Saints soon expanded their empire across Cache Valley and southeast Idaho. Much of the productive green farmland that today covers vast tracts of Idaho's dry southeast is a result of hard, tenacious work by early Mormon settlers.

GOLD FEVER

Before 1848, the Oregon Trail was the major route, and the California Trail was a smaller spur. Then James Marshall discovered gold at Sutter's Fort, and the two trails swapped places in importance. Gold fever built throughout the West as strikes were made in British Columbia, Nevada, and Colorado.

The first find in Idaho was made by E. D. Pierce in 1860. Pierce was an Irish immigrant who had been a captain in the Mexican

EVOLVING BOUNDARIES

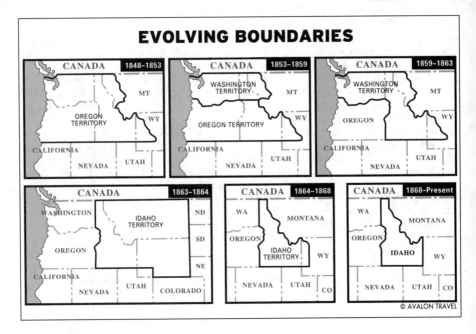

© AVALON TRAVEL

War. In 1852, while trading in north-central Idaho's Nez Perce country, he heard stories of gold in the area. He caught gold fever, but he didn't start prospecting there. News of Canada's Fraser River strikes reached him and he raced north, apparently meeting with little success.

In 1855 the Nez Perce signed a treaty with the U.S. government that created the Nez Perce Reservation. Pierce returned to Idaho's Nez Perce country in 1860 to find that whites were no longer welcome on the lands he had seen. He asked the tribe to let him do some prospecting on the reservation, but the Nez Perce understandably refused. Not to be deterred, Pierce and 10 other men snuck onto the reservation without permission and began searching for riches on the north fork of the Clearwater River. The Nez Perce eventually discovered the miners but restrained themselves from throwing the trespassers out. That fall, one of the Pierce-party miners, Wilbur Bassett, found some very fine gold—*oro fino* in Spanish—in a shovelful of dirt. The Idaho gold rush was on.

The Clearwater Mines and Boise Basin

Soon the Orofino Mining District was formed, and miners rushed into the area. By the summer of 1861, some 3,000 nonnatives had moved in; by the following summer, 10,000. Pierce City and Orofino were founded as the Nez Perce looked on helplessly. The miners spread out, and new mining towns sprouted: Elk City, Newsome, and Florence. Some $3 million worth of gold dust was carried out of the area by the steamships plying the Snake and Columbia Rivers to and from Lewiston.

Named for Meriwether Lewis of Corps of Discovery fame, Lewiston became the rip-roaring supply center for the Clearwater District. Outlaws and vigilantes ran unchecked by any active judicial system. Idaho's first newspaper, *The Golden Age,* started up in Lewiston, and mail service was instituted; the mail was carried on foot between Lewiston and Pierce City, a 10-day trip.

In August 1862, a group of miners discovered gold in the Boise Basin, 30 miles north of today's city of Boise. Idaho City, Placerville, Centerville, and nearby Rocky Bar and Atlanta sprang up to support the hordes of money-hungry hopefuls. Because these communities supported a substantial population of nonnatives, the government decided it needed a fort in the area to protect the miners and their families from hostile Native Americans. The Army selected a site at the foot of the mountains along the Boise River and dedicated Fort Boise on July 4, 1863. (This fort was not connected with the Hudson's Bay Company's famous fur fort of the same name, at the confluence of the Boise and Snake Rivers some 40 miles to the west.) A town was platted around the Army post and grew quickly as the major supply center for the Boise Basin mines, which yielded an estimated $66 million in gold. Today, the basin's boomtowns are ghost towns, relying not on mining but on tourism to keep them alive. Idaho City on Highway 21 is the easiest to reach and the most developed; Atlanta, at the base of the Sawtooths, is the most ghostly.

The Owyhee Mines

Also in 1863, miners discovered gold along Jordan Creek in the Owyhee Mountains, about 50 miles southwest of Boise. The initial finds were streambed placer deposits that soon played out. But then rich seams of gold and silver were discovered up on War Eagle Mountain, and the focus shifted from placer to hard-rock mining. Ruby City was the first major settlement in the area but was soon replaced by Silver City, two miles farther upstream. In the mid-1860s, a constant stream of hopeful miners poured in, giving Silver City a peak population of 2,000. The mines turned out to be among the world's richest, and Silver City became one of southern Idaho's biggest boomtowns.

Unfortunately, it also became one of the most violent. When two competing mining companies discovered they were mining the same seam from opposite directions, an underground mining war broke out. One company's foreman was killed by gunfire deep in the shafts, while mining magnate J. Marion More died when an argument on the porch of

the Idaho Hotel in Silver City got out of control and shots were fired. The territorial governor sent in troops from Fort Boise to quell the disturbance, which ended with no further bloodshed. The Owyhee unrest was a portent of even greater troubles to come in Idaho's mining industry.

Idaho Territory

During the Clearwater, Boise Basin, and Owyhee mining booms, this part of the country was part of Washington Territory, headquartered in Olympia. Fearful that the wealth and population explosion that mining was bringing to the eastern part of the territory would result in a shift of governmental power away from them, Olympians began lobbying to separate the mining districts in a new territory. On March 4, 1863, President Abraham Lincoln signed into law the act creating Idaho Territory. The western boundary of the territory corresponded to today's borders between Idaho on the east and Washington and Oregon on the west. The eastern reaches of the new territory took in parts of Montana and Wyoming.

The territory's name, Idaho, had no particular meaning. In 1859 it had been suggested as the name for a new territory being formed around the Pike's Peak Mining District. At that time, the head of the Senate Committee on Territories explained that Idaho was an Indian word meaning "Gem of the Mountains." When that was proved untrue, the name Colorado Territory was chosen instead. The name Idaho still appealed to some people, however, and was used as the name of a steamship on the Columbia River's Portland–Lewiston run. The steamship supplied the mines up the Clearwater River, which as a result came to be loosely referred to as the Idaho mines. Eventually, the name was applied to the new Idaho Territory.

Lewiston was the only readily accessible city in the fledgling territory, so it was chosen as the temporary territorial capital. The first territorial governor, William Wallace, was a close personal friend of Abe Lincoln. Wallace took office in Lewiston on July 10,

1863, and immediately faced his first crisis. It seems Lewiston wasn't technically in Idaho Territory, but instead squarely on the Nez Perce Reservation, as delineated by the 1855 treaty. The Nez Perce had allowed the miners a primitive staging and supply camp at the site, located at the confluence of the Clearwater and Snake Rivers. But the inch given had turned into a mile taken, and Lewiston had become a full-fledged town in the process. When Wallace and the federal government approached the Nez Perce, asking the Native Americans to once again negotiate away more of their land, including Lewiston, the Nez Perce were divided. One group resigned themselves to a reduced reservation and signed a new treaty; the other group refused. The "nontreaty" Nez Perce didn't make trouble then but 14 years later precipitated the Nez Perce War of 1877.

Just five months after taking office as Idaho's governor, Wallace was elected as a territorial delegate. He resigned as governor and moved to Washington, D.C., in December 1863. His replacement, Caleb Lyon, arrived in Lewiston in August 1864. Lyon soon found himself in the middle of a heated debate over where to put the territory's capital. Since the formation of the territory, the mines served by Lewiston had begun to play out and most of the miners had moved south to the Boise Basin, where mines were beginning to boom. In December 1864, the territorial legislature met in Lewiston and voted to move the capital to Boise City, supply center for the Boise Basin mines and protected from trouble by the U.S. Army's Fort Boise. Lewiston's residents were furious, and Governor Lyon was on the hot seat. Under the pretense of going duck hunting, he fled across the Snake River to Washington and didn't return for a year. In the meantime, territorial secretary C. DeWitt Smith arrived in Lewiston and, with the aid of federal troops, forcibly took possession of the territorial seal and archives and took them south to Boise. From that point on, Boise was entrenched as the territorial capital and later as state capital.

THE NEZ PERCE WAR

Those bands of Nez Perce who refused to sign the 1863 treaty reducing the size of their reservation continued to live as they had before, roaming their traditional homelands. One of these bands, led by Old Joseph, called eastern Oregon's Wallowa Valley home. As the 1860s progressed, more nonnatives began encroaching on Joseph's territory. Since Joseph's band of Nez Perce had not signed the 1863 treaty and had remained peaceful toward settlers, U.S. President Grant signed a proclamation that formally assigned the Wallowa Valley to the Nez Perce. But lobbyists in Washington, intent on developing the region for themselves, raised such an outcry that Grant rescinded the order two years later. On his deathbed, Old Joseph instructed his son Joseph never to give up the Wallowa Valley. Young Chief Joseph took that request to heart.

Joseph's band lived in the Wallowa Valley until 1877, when continued pressure from whites led the Bureau of Indian Affairs in Washington, D.C., to order all nontreaty Nez Perce onto the Lapwai Reservation by June of that year. At a meeting in Lapwai between the Nez Perce and the Army, the Nez Perce argued to no avail that they had not signed the treaty and were not bound by it. Toohoolhoolzote, the Nez Perce's spiritual leader, was defiant. The military man in charge of the U.S. Army's Columbia River district, Gen. Oliver O. Howard, grew frustrated with Toohoolhoolzote's refusal to capitulate. "We do not wish to interfere with your religion," said Howard, "but you must talk about practicable things. Twenty times over you repeat that the earth is your mother, and about chieftainship from the earth. Let us hear no more, but come to business at once." When Toohoolhoolzote responded contemptuously, "What person pretends to divide the land and put me on it?" Howard lost his temper and had Toohoolhoolzote locked up. He was later released, but his arrest angered the Nez Perce. Many young warriors immediately wanted to fight, but Joseph restrained them. The chief faced an agonizing decision.

Joseph chose the path of peace and resigned himself to moving onto the reservation. Returning to Oregon, he gathered his people and moved across the Snake River to the Camas Prairie in preparation for checking in with the Army at Lapwai. Joseph would never again live in his beloved Wallowa Valley and would not set eyes on it again for more than 20 years.

The First Confrontation

On June 2, 1877, the nontreaty bands of Joseph and White Bird were camped at Tolo Lake near present-day Grangeville for a last rendezvous as a free people. Over the course of the next 10 days, frustration grew within the ranks, particularly among the young warriors. One young man from White Bird's band had seen his father murdered by a settler on the Salmon River. Others had also suffered at the hands of the nonnatives but had not sought revenge. As emotions in camp built to a fever pitch, a handful of young warriors broke ranks and went on a rampage, killing several settlers who had treated the Nez Perce poorly. Word got back to General Howard at Lapwai, providing him with a convenient excuse for overreacting. Howard sent two cavalry units racing toward Tolo Lake. The Nez Perce leaders at Tolo Lake, warned of the impending attack, held a meeting. Facing the superior numbers and firepower of the U.S. Army, the leaders knew they had to fight or flee—or both.

The Nez Perce bands moved down to the bottom of White Bird Canyon and prepared for the first assault. The unlucky commander of the cavalry units, Captain David Perry, led his troops down White Bird hill right into a Nez Perce ambush. Thirty-four of Perry's 100 troops were killed; the rest fled back to Fort Lapwai. The Nez Perce packed up and went on the move again. General Howard took Perry's resounding defeat as a personal affront and took charge of the Nez Perce problem himself.

Joseph and White Bird led their group across the Salmon River to the west, then doubled back across the river farther north and sped across the Camas Prairie to hook up with Chief Looking Glass's band near Kooskia. General Howard tried to follow but was unable to make the second crossing of the Salmon and had to retrace his steps, losing several days in the process.

The nontreaty band of Chief Looking Glass, camped near Kooskia, had wanted no trouble. Their land was already on the smaller reservation, so they wouldn't be forced to move. Nevertheless, a contingent of bluecoats and civilian volunteers attacked Looking Glass's camp. The attack was unsuccessful but enraged Looking Glass into joining Joseph and White Bird in the fight. Soon all three Nez Perce bands linked up on the South Fork of the Clearwater River, south of Kooskia, and devised a plan to cross the Bitterroots and enter Crow territory, hoping to receive support from their traditional allies. Howard and his now all-out force of 600 men at last caught up with the Nez Perce. Despite being severely outnumbered, the Nez Perce again managed to hold off Howard's troops and fled—men, women, children, and a whole herd of ponies—east into the Bitterroots. Their superior knowledge of the terrain allowed them to outdistance the Army. When Howard realized the Nez Perce were out of his grasp, he telegraphed General William Tecumseh Sherman and requested Sherman to send a force to cut them off.

The Flight to Canada

After crossing the Bitterroots, Joseph and White Bird knew they were days ahead of Howard, so they stopped to rest at Big Hole, Montana. They didn't know, however, about the telegraph sent by Howard and that Colonel John Gibbon and a large force of bluecoats were galloping toward them at full speed from Fort Shaw, Montana. Gibbon and his troops surprised the Nez Perce in a dawn attack at Big Hole. Both sides sustained heavy casualties. Amazingly, the Nez Perce turned the tables on the Army, forcing them to retreat and pinning them down while the surviving Nez Perce quickly packed up and once again fled south.

Still heading for Crow country, they crossed the Bitterroots again and moved south through

Lemhi Valley and east to Henry's Lake. Howard soon caught up to the recuperating Gibbon and formulated a new plan. Figuring the Nez Perce would turn east through Yellowstone National Park (established in 1872) and head for the plains, Howard devised a scheme to trap the Nez Perce in the park. He was delayed along the way, however, when a party of Nez Perce retraced their steps, snuck into Howard's camp in the night, and stampeded the Army's mules before catching up with the main party. By this time, word of the bravery and incredible evasive tactics of the Nez Perce had made the news back East. Most of the country was following the unfolding drama in the daily papers; no doubt many were rooting for the underdog Nez Perce. When the news came that the Nez Perce had run Howard's mules right out from his camp, Howard became the laughingstock of the country.

Despite the setback, Howard pursued his plan to trap the Nez Perce in the park. The Nez Perce suffered a psychological setback of their own when they found out that Crow scouts were working for General Howard. They realized their last hope was to turn north and head for Canada, where they believed exiled Sioux chief Sitting Bull would welcome them and take them in. They entered Yellowstone, frightening a party of tourists and actually taking them hostage for a time so that they couldn't set Howard on their trail.

Using the telegraph to speed communication, Howard ringed the park's major geographical exits with troops. This time the Nez Perce embarrassed not only General Howard but Colonel Samuel D. Sturgis as well. Sturgis had been assigned to cover the park's northeastern exit along the Clark Fork River. When the Nez Perce didn't show up in his area, Sturgis got impatient and decided that the Nez Perce were instead going to come out to the south, on the Shoshone River. He sent scouts up to find out. The scouts sighted the Nez Perce and watched them apparently head in the direction of the Shoshone River, as Sturgis thought they would. When the scouts returned with the news, Sturgis left his assigned post and

took his troops south. At the Shoshone River, he headed upstream expecting to find the Nez Perce coming down, defeat them, and reap the glory. But the Nez Perce, after being seen by Sturgis's scouts, doubled back and turned down a narrow side canyon headed for the very Clark Fork area that Sturgis had left. They escaped the park, and Sturgis continued all the way up the Shoshone River with no sight of the Nez Perce. General Howard, who had been trailing the Nez Perce and thought he was driving them into Sturgis's waiting trap, was now ahead of Sturgis. Clearly Colonel Sturgis would have some explaining to do. When the press got hold of this news, some papers called for Howard's removal. Others just laughed at the Army and cheered on the Nez Perce, now seen as heroic by much of the nation.

The Nez Perce thought they had once again evaded trouble. Tired of running and thinking themselves days ahead of Howard, they slowed down. But General Howard's boss, General William Tecumseh Sherman, was not pleased. He ordered the ambitious Colonel Nelson Miles to speed northwest from his base at Fort Keogh, Montana, and intercept the Nez Perce before they could reach safety at the Canadian border. Clearly the Nez Perce were headed for Canada, where they would be no threat to the Americans. Why didn't Sherman just let them go? It was part ego—the Nez Perce had made fools of the U.S. Army not once but several times—and part personality. Sherman was an unequivocally ruthless man who had helped win the Civil War for the north by marching across Georgia burning everything in his path. And it was Sherman who, in 1867, said of the country's Native American peoples: "The more we can kill this year, the less will have to be killed the next war, for the more I see of these Indians, the more convinced I am that they all have to be killed or be maintained as a species of paupers."

Last Stand at Bear's Paw

Miles and his troops found the Nez Perce camp at Bear's Paw, southeast of Havre in north-central Montana, less than 40 miles from the

Canadian border. They rushed headlong into an attack, with losses on both sides—among them Toohoolhoolzote. But the Army was unable to defeat the Nez Perce immediately and was forced into a siege of the camp. It was September 28, and the first storms of the season had already descended, leaving the camp cold and covered in snow. Miles was worried, correctly, that in the initial attack a few Nez Perce might have escaped to get help from Sitting Bull. On October 4, General Howard and his troops arrived, making the Nez Perce situation all the more desperate. Joseph, Looking Glass, and White Bird held a council to determine their course of action. By messenger, first Miles, then Howard, had assured the Nez Perce that if they surrendered, they would not be punished and would be returned to the Northwest, though Joseph would not be permitted to resettle in the Wallowa Valley. Joseph saw this as a draw with the Army, not a defeat. But Looking Glass and White Bird didn't trust Howard and decided to try to make a break for Canada and Sitting Bull's camp. Shortly after the meeting was over, Looking Glass was shot in the head and killed by one of Miles's scouts. That was enough for Joseph. On October 6 at 2 P.M., Joseph mounted his horse, rifle across his lap, and rode out to the Army to surrender. He handed his rifle to Miles, and spoke to General Howard through an interpreter: "Tell General Howard I know his heart. What he told me before, I have it in my heart. I am tired of fighting.... My heart is sick and sad. From where the sun now stands I will fight no more forever."

As the surrender commenced, most of the Nez Perce came out of their camp, giving their rifles to the Army in exchange for food and blankets. The Army now treated their foes as respected adversaries who had fought a good battle. After dark, White Bird and his band snuck out of camp and hightailed it for Canada. Along the way they encountered a war party sent by Sitting Bull and told them that it was too late, Joseph had surrendered. They continued on to Sitting Bull's camp and remained in Canada, where White Bird died in 1882.

The Bitter End

Despite the promises of Howard and Miles, the Nez Perce were not permitted to return to the Northwest; General Sherman vetoed that idea. Only public sympathy for the Nez Perce kept Sherman from ordering Joseph executed. Instead the Nez Perce were loaded onto trains and taken to a malarial swamp near Fort Leavenworth, Kansas. They were subsequently shuffled several times to various undesirable spots in the Midwest, many dying of disease at each location. Sherman's intended genocide was coming to fruition, albeit more slowly than he might have wished.

After the war's end General Howard sided with Sherman against any leniency for the Nez Perce, but Colonel Miles constantly advocated for Joseph and his people, probably feeling guilty that his promises to them had been broken. Between Miles's efforts and public outcry, in May 1885 the 268 Nez Perce who were still alive were finally allowed back to the Northwest. The Looking Glass and White Bird followers were returned to Lapwai, while Joseph and his followers were sent to the Colville Reservation in eastern Washington. There Joseph continued his efforts to reclaim his treasured Wallowa Valley homeland, but to no avail. His pleas were refused at every turn, and he died on the Colville Reservation on September 21, 1904. The reservation physician listed the cause of death as a broken heart.

The Dawes Act

With Idaho's Native Americans forced into submission on reservations, the U.S. government came up with one more nail to hammer into the native peoples' cultural coffin. In 1887 Congress passed the Dawes Act, also known as the Allotment Act or the Severalty Act. Under the act, each "civilized" Indian was allotted a private plot of land on their reservation. Any land left over after all the plots had been allotted was thrown open for purchase by white homesteaders.

The act was supported by anti-Indian land-grabbers as well as do-gooders who believed it was in the Native Americans' best interest to become fully integrated into white society. After the allotment process, the Nez Perce people ended up with less than 200,000 acres, down from 7 million acres under the 1855 treaty and down from their original home territory spanning 10 million acres or more. More important, perhaps, the forced relinquishment of the traditional way of life amounted to nothing short of cultural genocide. Subjugation was now complete; "the Indian problem" was solved.

THE IRON HORSE
Idaho's First Railroad

With the driving of the golden spike at Promontory, Utah, on May 10, 1869, the Union Pacific and the Central Pacific Railroads were linked, and a transcontinental rail line became a reality. The rail line passed north of Salt Lake City, but that was no problem for Brigham Young and the Mormons; they formed the Utah Central Railroad and built their own spur north to the Union Pacific Line at Ogden, completing the link in 1870. The following year, the Mormons organized the **Utah Northern Railroad,** planning to build a narrow-gauge line north from Ogden to the gold mines of western Montana. This rail line reached Franklin on May 2, 1874. Here it temporarily ran out of steam, but not before it had become the first railroad into Idaho Territory.

Franklin grew into a major freight center for wagons shipping goods back and forth from the Montana mines, which lay due north over Monida Pass (the route of today's I-15). With all this commerce on the route, it was inevitable that someone would succeed in pushing a rail line through. A new company loosely affiliated with Union Pacific, the **Utah and Northern Railway Company,** grabbed the honor, completing a connection between Franklin and the Northern Pacific line at Garrison, Montana, in 1884. This line had a profound effect on southeast Idaho, as settlements of predominantly Mormon colonists sprang up all along the route. Between 1879 and 1889, many new towns appeared in the

region, among them Menan, Rexburg, Rigby, Sugar City, and Victor.

Tracks Along the Oregon Trail

Scouts for the Union Pacific had investigated possible railway routes along the Oregon Trail as early as 1867. By 1881 the company was ready to build the line. All it needed to do was sidestep government regulations that prohibited it from doing so. Another "loose affiliate" of Union Pacific was formed, and work on the new **Oregon Short Line Railway** began. Construction began off the main Union Pacific line at Granger, Montana, and headed northwest to Montpelier, Pocatello, and Shoshone, where a spur was constructed up to the Wood River Valley mines. The line was completed through to Huntington, Oregon, on November 17, 1884, and hauled both passengers and freight. With transfers at Granger and Huntington, passengers could make an Omaha–Portland trip in three and a half days. The iron horse had made the country smaller.

The line also eased development of the Snake River Plain, as irrigation equipment, seeds, harvested crops, cattle, and laborers could now cross the plain easily and connect with markets across the country. Pocatello, junction of the Oregon Short Line and the Utah and Northern, became an important rail hub, and in 1893 was named the seat of Bannock County.

Northern Routes

Railroad builders in northern Idaho were also hard at work in the 1870s and 1880s. In 1883 the **Northern Pacific Railway** connected eastern Washington with Missoula, Montana, via Sandpoint, resulting in a through line from St. Paul, Minnesota, to Portland, Oregon. In 1887 a branch line was extended up the South Fork Coeur d'Alene River; by 1891 it had crested Lookout Pass and connected through to Montana along the route of today's I-90. This line was later taken over by the Northern Pacific. In 1892, the **Great Northern Railway** connected St. Paul and Seattle via Bonners Ferry, Sandpoint, and

Spokane. The Great Northern was owned by James J. Hill, known as the Empire Builder. Today's Amtrak train of that name follows Hill's old Great Northern route.

Finally, in 1909, the odd **Chicago, Milwaukee, St. Paul, and Pacific Railroad** pushed into Idaho from Montana south of Lookout Pass. It was unusual because a 438-mile segment of the line over the Continental Divide was handled by electric-powered trains. Numerous tunnels and trestles were built to get the trains down from the pass to Avery, Idaho, on the St. Joe River. The now-abandoned railroad grade has become the Route of the Hiawatha, one of the West's coolest mountain-biking trails.

In addition to these main lines, a whole web of spur lines connected all parts of the region in a relatively short time. The timing was fortuitous, because the biggest mining boom in the state's history—the country's history, for that matter—took place in north Idaho at the same time.

SILVER STRIKES
Wood River Mining District

Gold was the initial draw bringing miners into present-day Idaho, but it was silver that created the state's longest-lasting and most lucrative boom. Miners first discovered galena ore—rock rich in silver, lead, and zinc—in the Wood River Valley in 1879. Almost immediately, the boomtown mining camps of Ketchum, Hailey, Bellevue, and others sprouted. By 1880 some 2,000 mining claims had been filed in the valley. The biggest mine in the district, the Minnie Moore, was in the hills west of Bellevue.

In May 1883 the Oregon Short Line spur was completed up the Wood River Valley from Shoshone, allowing major mining equipment to be brought in, and the face of mining began to change. The days of the lone prospector heading out to pan gold in remote creeks were fading. With easy access to the mines provided by the railroad, investors seized the opportunity to bring in modern technology and reap exponentially larger rewards. Professional mining engineers, geologists, and metallurgists replaced grizzled old sourdoughs while mining corporations replaced individual mine owners. Concentrators and smelters were built right in the Wood River Valley, allowing more wealth to stay in the area. The valley became a prosperous place. In 1883, Hailey got the first telephone system in Idaho. Ketchum's smelter enjoyed electric lights. Newspapers, saloons, and social clubs flourished. By all accounts, the Wood River Valley was an orderly and pleasant place in those days. But trouble was on the horizon.

The advent of the mining corporation had turned the average miner from an independent contractor into nothing more than a day laborer, working for wealthy absentee owners. In 1884, in the face of declining lead and silver prices, the Minnie Moore Mine tried to cut wages. The mine's workers went on strike in protest. The mine brought in scabs to replace the strikers, which enraged the townsfolk. A battle broke out, and fighting was stopped only when the territorial governor sent in federal troops from Boise. The mines continued to operate with the scab employees, the price of silver continued to decline, and the mines eventually played out. By 1893 the valley's mining boom had gone bust. But the troubles experienced here foreshadowed worse times to come for Idaho's mining industry.

Noah Kellogg's Lucky Ass

The saga of what would become one of the world's most profitable mining districts began with prospector A. J. Pritchard's discovery of gold along the North Fork Coeur d'Alene River in 1878. Pritchard tried to keep his find quiet, but word got out. By 1883 the rush was on, with Murray and Eagle City the destinations du jour. In contrast to the relatively civilized social scene of the Wood River Valley, the North Fork was a wild, rambunctious place full of drinking, gambling, and prostitutes such as the locally legendary Molly B'Damn.

The easy gold played out by 1885. With the resultant slowdown in construction, 60-year-old carpenter Noah Kellogg found himself unemployed and destitute. Rumors of galena finds across the mountain on the South Fork had circulated through Murray for years. Kellogg figured he'd check them out. He nagged a contractor friend, O. O. Peck, and a doctor named J. T. Cooper into giving him a prospector's grubstake. In this common practice of the day, financiers supplied a prospector with food, tools, and other supplies in exchange for a share of anything the prospector found. Peck and Cooper agreed to give Kellogg a barely adequate grubstake, more to be rid of him than in hopes he might find anything. Kellogg resented the cheapskate stake, but he took it, loaded it on a donkey, and headed for the South Fork.

What happened next is part legend, part mystery. The legend says that while Kellogg was camped up a tributary of the South Fork, near present-day Wardner, his donkey wandered off. When Kellogg found the animal, it was transfixed, staring at a huge glittering outcropping of a prospector's dream come true: high-grade galena ore. This makes a nice myth, and it engendered the former motto of the town of Kellogg: "Discovered by a jackass and inhabited by its descendants." But experts agree that any outcropping of galena ore wouldn't have been shiny but dull and red-streaked from oxidization. There is no doubt, however, that Kellogg had stumbled onto something big.

The mystery involves the chronology of events. Kellogg returned to Murray claiming failure, got another grubstake from a different group of rowdy miner friends, then headed out into the hills again. Did he actually make his find on the first trip or on the second? It seems likely that his first trip produced the find, and Kellogg, resentful of Cooper and Peck's half-hearted support, lied about his "failure" so he could get better terms from a new set of partners. That's certainly what Cooper and Peck thought. They sued Kellogg and were eventually awarded an illogical 25 percent interest in Kellogg's find. As it turned out, the find was a mother lode, and Kellogg and company's Bunker Hill and Sullivan Mine became one of the most profitable mines in world history.

The Coeur d'Alene Mining War of 1892

Almost overnight, every inch of the hills surrounding the valley of the South Fork of the Coeur d'Alene—today called the Silver Valley—swarmed with miners. Shafts were sunk at an incredible pace, and the valley's lush forests were cut down for mine timbers and boomtown buildings. Big mining corporations bought up nearly all the mines and, as they had done in the Wood River Valley, brought in the expensive smelters, mills, and mining engineers necessary to take best advantage of the underground riches.

But the labor strife that had plagued the Wood River Valley also followed the trail to the Coeur d'Alenes. Many of the same miners who had been involved in the Wood River Valley troubles migrated to the Silver Valley and formed a union in 1886. The mine owners responded by forming their own organization in 1889. In 1892, the two groups began to butt heads. Low silver and lead prices, coupled with an increase in freight rates, led the mine owners to ask the miners to accept a pay cut. The miners refused, and in January 1892 the owners shut down the mines, throwing hundreds of miners out of work in the dead of winter.

In spring, the mines attempted to reopen using scab labor. The first efforts were unsuccessful as the townspeople threw the strikebreakers out. But the mine owners retaliated, hiring 54 armed "security guards" out of Lewiston and Moscow to keep the mines open with scabs, and they even employed an agent from the famous Pinkerton Detective Agency to infiltrate the union and work toward its undoing. The mines resumed operation, albeit at a reduced pace.

That summer, the union miners took action. They blew up an abandoned mill, seized a nonunion mine and held the crew hostage, and threatened to dynamite working mills and concentrators. The mine owners appealed to Washington, and President Benjamin Harrison sent in federal troops. The soldiers rounded up all the union miners involved in the incident and temporarily imprisoned them in a large outdoor pen. The nonunion miners went back to work while the union men regrouped for another day.

History Repeats Itself

In 1899, a replay of the Coeur d'Alene mining disputes took place. By this time the strong Western Federation of Miners had been formed, and the union movement had gained strength. The mine owners nevertheless refused to recognize the unions, employing both union and nonunion workers at the same scale.

Union workers marched on the Bunker Hill Mine on April 24, 1899, demanding a uniform $3.50 daily wage for all underground workers and an end to the employment of nonunion miners. The mine owners refused the demands, and some mines ceased operations.

On April 29, the union miners resorted to violence once again. They hijacked a Northern Pacific train in Burke, up Canyon Creek, loaded it with stolen dynamite, and headed for Kellogg. All along the way, miners joined in the procession. When they reached Kellogg, the miners blew up the Bunker Hill offices and an adjacent mill, then reboarded the train and drove it back to Burke. Word reached Idaho governor Frank Steunenberg, who in turn called President William McKinley. Once more federal troops were dispatched. Before they could get there, one of the Bunker Hill employees was shot to death by a miner. At that point, Governor Steunenberg declared martial law.

The troops arrived and again rounded up the union men, arresting about 1,000 of them and incarcerating them in the "bull pen" as before. Steunenberg brought in high-powered lawyers—including William Borah and James Hawley—to prosecute the union leaders, and on July 27, scapegoat and union secretary Paul Corcoran was convicted of second-degree murder in the death of the Bunker Hill man and sentenced to life imprisonment. He was pardoned two years later. Most of the bullpen prisoners were eventually released without trial, and although martial law remained in effect for a year and a half, peace returned to the Silver Valley.

A Tragic Epilogue

Six years after he had ordered troops in to squelch the 1899 Coeur d'Alene mining war, former governor Steunenberg was killed by an assassin's bomb outside his home in Caldwell. The trail of evidence led to Harry Orchard, one of the miners who had been involved in the bombing of the Bunker Hill offices, and a man with high contacts in the Western Federation of Miners. Orchard supposedly confessed to the crime and implicated union officials in a conspiracy to kill Steunenberg. The officials were arrested, and their subsequent trial made national headlines. Two of the greatest American lawyers of the time were pitted against one another: William Borah prosecuted the case, and Clarence Darrow defended the miners. Orchard was convicted and spent the rest of his life in the Idaho Territorial Penitentiary at Boise. The union leaders were acquitted, but even many union miners believed the union brass had somehow been involved. The unions lost credibility among the workers and were dormant for a long time thereafter.

MODERN TIMES
Statehood

Oregon gained statehood in 1859, Nevada in 1864, Washington and Montana in 1889. By 1890, the movement was afoot either to make Idaho Territory a state or to apportion it among neighboring states. The rivalry between the former and the current capital cities, Lewiston and Boise, had continued unabated since C. DeWitt Smith had "stolen" the territorial books from Lewiston in 1865. Lewiston residents wanted nothing more than to separate from Boise. Nevada was looking to annex southern Idaho. Northern Idaho residents were split; Palouse farmers and many others wanted to annex the north state to geographically and economically aligned Washington, while Silver Valley miners preferred annexation to Montana, which they perceived as a more mining-friendly state. Boise politicians fought to retain a unified Idaho with Boise as the capital. Finally, southern Idaho threw northern Idaho just enough of a bone to keep it

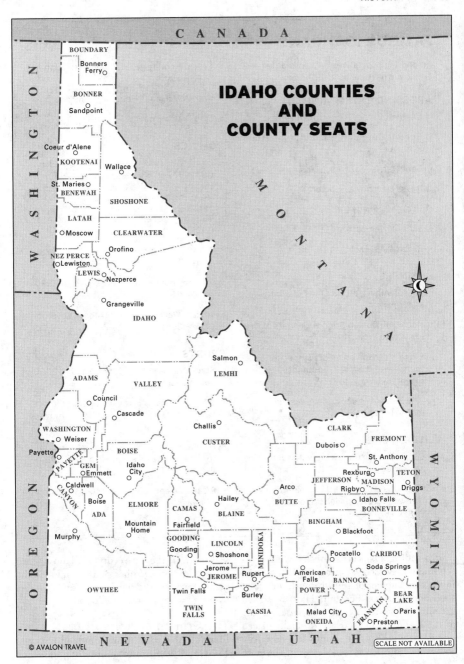

IDAHO COUNTIES
AND
COUNTY SEATS

© AVALON TRAVEL

SCALE NOT AVAILABLE

FAMOUS IDAHOANS

Among famous natives or transplanted residents who have called Idaho home:

ARTS AND ENTERTAINMENT

- Matthew Barney – mixed media artist
- Gutzon Borglum – sculptor of Mount Rushmore
- Gene Harris – jazz musician
- Mariel Hemingway – actor
- George Kennedy – actor
- Lana Turner – actor
- Bruce Willis – actor

BUSINESS

- Joseph Albertson – founder of Albertson's supermarkets
- Nephi and Golden Grigg – founders of Ore-Ida Potato Products
- Harry Morrison and Morris Knudsen – cofounders of the Morrison-Knudsen civil engineering firm
- J. R. Simplot – potato king; was the richest man in Idaho

LITERATURE

- Edgar Rice Burroughs – creator of the *Tarzan* series
- Vardis Fisher – novelist and director of the Works Progress Administration-era Federal Writer's Project

- Ernest Hemingway – Nobel Prize-winning novelist
- Patrick McManus – outdoor humorist
- Ezra Pound – poet

POLITICS

- Cecil Andrus – four-term governor (1971-1977, 1987-1994) and Secretary of the Interior in the Carter administration (1977-1980)
- William Borah – six-term senator (1907-1940)
- Frank Church – four-term senator (1957-1981)
- George Shoup – first state governor, 1890; resigned to become a U.S. Senator
- William Wallace – first territorial governor (1864-1865)

SPORTS

- Stacy Dragila – Olympic pole vaulter; 2000 gold medalist
- Walter Johnson – record-setting pitcher for the Washington Senators; played 1907-1927
- Harmon Killebrew – home-run champ for the Minnesota Twins; played 1954-1975
- Picabo Street – Olympic skier; 1998 gold medalist

from seceding: plans for a university in northern Idaho at Moscow. Northern Idaho agreed to the deal and got behind the push for Idaho statehood. President Benjamin Harrison signed the bill creating Idaho, the 43rd state, on July 3, 1890, and Idaho's star was officially placed on the nation's flag the following day, July 4. Emma Edwards Green designed the state seal in 1891, the University of Idaho opened in Moscow on October 3, 1892, and Idaho granted women the right to vote in 1896, becoming the fourth state to do so.

The Growth of Agriculture

Idaho's population nearly doubled between 1890 and 1900, and more than doubled between 1900 and 1910. The reason was agriculture. First the timber barons—men such as Frederic Weyerhaeuser, who had made a fortune wiping out the forests of the Great Lakes region—came west and discovered the great pine forests of Idaho. The U.S. government had given much of Idaho's forest lands outright to the railroads, supposedly to encourage westward expansion. Given the cozy relationship between the era's politicians and business leaders, one suspects their motives were rather less principled and more self-serving. The timber companies snapped up this land for a song, since the railroads knew their trains would haul the logs out of the forests. It was a classic case of mutual back-scratching. Loggers flooded into the state to partake in the conversion of green to gold.

Next, dry farmers turned the Palouse into a profitable sea of green. Between the fertile farmland there and the new university, the population of north-central Idaho swelled. But the biggest factor in increasing Idaho's population after the turn of the century was the development of irrigation on the Snake River Plain. A whole network of privately financed canals laced southwest Idaho by 1900, and settlers rushed in to try their luck at farming. These canals made use of the region's many tributaries of the Snake River. The mass volumes of water in the Snake River itself weren't fully exploited until the completion of major government-sponsored irrigation projects in the early 1900s.

In 1894 the federal government passed the Carey Act, which granted federally owned arid lands to the states if they would undertake and complete irrigation projects on those lands within 10 years. Private companies built the irrigation systems on the state land, and when those systems were completed, the lands were offered for sale. Farmers bought parcels of irrigated land from the state and bought water rights to that land from the irrigation companies.

Nowhere was this public-private partnership more successful than in south-central Idaho. Led by Twin Falls entrepreneur Ira B. Perrine, the region's movers and shakers completed Milner Dam in 1905 along with a network of canals that eventually irrigated 244,000 acres. Farms soon blanketed the once dry, desert region, which as a result of its incredible transformation was nicknamed the Magic Valley. Along with subsequent similar projects under the Carey Act, 850,000 arable acres were created, and Idaho's population increased by 50,000 as a result.

The Reclamation Act of 1902 brought the federal government in on the irrigation efforts in a big way. The U.S. Reclamation Service, forerunner of the Bureau of Reclamation, built huge, earth-filled Minidoka Dam near Rupert between 1904 and 1906. The dam included the region's first major hydroelectric power plant. Other federal Reclamation Act dams included Arrowrock Dam on the Boise River—at the time the world's highest—and American Falls Dam. As a result of irrigation, nearly the entire Snake River Plain was rapidly settled, and Idaho became one of the country's premier agricultural states.

World War I and the 1920s

Following the outbreak of World War I in 1914, the state's agricultural potential was tapped to its fullest as farmers geared up to supply food for Allied troops. Nearly 20,000 Idahoans served in the armed forces during the war, and 782 of those lost their lives. Patriotism ran high, spawning occasional bouts of anti-German backlash. Interestingly, the state's governor during this period and his wife were German immigrants. Moses Alexander was elected in 1914 as the nation's first Jewish governor. Perhaps because he was Jewish, or because he was not especially sympathetic to other German immigrants enduring suspicion bordering on persecution in the state, Alexander's loyalties were considered above reproach.

At the end of the war, returning GIs brought home victory but also a particularly virulent strain of influenza dubbed the Spanish flu. The virus swept through the world's population; 500,000 Americans died from the disease, and Idaho was not exempt. The epidemic lasted until spring 1919.

The Roaring '20s didn't do much roaring in Idaho. After the war, agricultural exports tapered off as European farmers returned to their fields. The resultant farm-commodity surplus sent prices plummeting; many farmers suddenly found themselves struggling. In a prelude to the Great Depression, small independent banks that dealt virtually exclusively in loans to farmers began to go under as farmers found it increasingly difficult to make their loan payments. Labor groups like the radical socialist Industrial Workers of the World (IWW), cofounded by Big Bill Haywood of Coeur d'Alene Mining War fame, tried to take advantage of the economic downturn by organizing strikes and advocating labor control of industry. But conservative Idahoans would have none of it in light of Russia's Bolshevik Revolution of 1917 and its aftermath, and fearing that the Wobblies, as IWW members were known, were working to overthrow the U.S. government.

Highways and automobiles made steady inroads into Idaho during the 1920s. The Prohibition era came, along with talkies, but worsening economic conditions caused a population exodus from the state.

The Great Depression

No sooner had Idaho dug itself out from the economic trough of the 1920s than the whole country was thrown into the Great Depression of the 1930s, precipitated by the stock market crash of October 1929. With drought exacerbating dried-up markets, Idaho's farm economy crashed. Farm prices dropped to their lowest point in a century, and between 1929 and 1932 the state's total farm income dropped 65 percent. Farmers lost their farms to foreclosure; bank runs caused many banks to fail. Firefighters in southwest Idaho deliberately set fires to provide themselves with employment; Idaho's governor had to call out the National Guard and close off all public access to the forests. Drought had stricken the Midwest as well,

bringing refugees into Idaho and other Western states in search of work and better conditions. But conditions weren't any better in Idaho, and the influx of economic refugees added to the burden of the state's relief agencies.

Soon after his inauguration in 1933, President Franklin D. Roosevelt initiated his New Deal program of federal spending in an effort to jump-start the nation's economy. Many of the New Deal programs greatly aided Idaho. The Civilian Conservation Corps (CCC) put young men to work in Idaho's expansive national forests. They helped control the blister rust devastating Idaho's vast tracts of white pine; fought forest fires; planted trees; built roads, trails, and fire-lookout towers; and constructed public facilities such as those in Heyburn State Park. The Rural Electrification Administration strung power lines across the state, benefiting schools, industries, and residences. The Public Roads Administration improved some 1,650 miles of Idaho roadways. The Works Progress Administration (WPA), whose name was later changed to the Work Projects Administration, constructed bridges, water supplies, sewer systems, and recreational facilities. A similar program, the Public Works Administration, helped build roads in and near Idaho's national forests, develop the state's infrastructure for irrigated agriculture, and construct dozens of school buildings. And the Federal Writers Project, led in Idaho by Vardis Fisher, produced the WPA *Guide to Idaho*, the first of the WPA state guides. A total of $331 million in New Deal aid money went to Idaho.

In the meantime, some entrepreneurs found ways to succeed without federal help. Harry Morrison and Morris Knudsen started their famous civil engineering firm in 1912; it went on to become one of the biggest such companies in the world. And in 1936, railroad baron and sometime statesman W. Averell Harriman founded his Sun Valley Ski Lodge, which enjoyed immediate success as an escape from the tribulations of the era and spawned the world's first chairlifts for skiers.

World War II

Roosevelt's New Deal spent somewhere in the neighborhood of $24 billion over seven years in an attempt to bolster the American economy. But in the first year alone of its involvement in World War II, the United States spent more than double that amount. Defense spending skyrocketed, and Idaho benefited in several areas. The Defense Department kept Morrison-Knudsen busy building airfields and roads in the Pacific theater. The Navy built Farragut Naval Training Center on the shores of Lake Pend Oreille in the Panhandle and used it to train recruits for submarine duty. Construction of the base put 22,000 men to work nearly round-the-clock. Pocatello got an ordnance plant, Boise an airfield for bombers. Mountain Home's airbase was built, and Sun Valley Lodge was taken over by the Navy as a hospital.

Of the 60,000 Idahoans who served in World War II, nearly 1,800 died, eight were declared missing in action, and 31 were captured as prisoners of war. As it had in World War I, Idaho's agricultural industry provided much of the food the GIs ate during the conflict; the war started Idahoan J. R. Simplot on the road to riches when he began dehydrating potatoes and selling them to the military. In addition, as more high-tech armaments were developed, Idaho's supplies of strategic minerals were tapped. Cobalt, tungsten, and antimony mines worked overtime to satisfy defense-industry requirements.

A prisoner-of-war camp for German soldiers was established at Farragut Naval Base. And following the Japanese attack on Pearl Harbor, Japanese Americans living on the West Coast were rounded up and incarcerated at several concentration camps farther inland, including one near Minidoka. Between September 1942 and October 1945, this "relocation center" was the eighth-largest "city" in Idaho, holding about 10,000 internees. Morrison-Knudsen built the camp, the construction of which helped pull south-central Idaho out of the Depression.

The war had exacted a horrible price in human lives but, as elsewhere in the country, had gotten the state's economy back on track.

Postwar Growth

Following World War II, mining for strategic metals continued to enjoy defense-industry support as the Korean, Cold, and Vietnam Wars raged on. Other industries that had fueled the war effort turned their knowledge and experience to civilian uses. J. R. Simplot went from selling dehydrated potatoes to the military to selling French fries to McDonald's.

In 1949 the U.S. Departments of Defense and Energy established the National Reactor Testing Station in Idaho, where physicists and nuclear engineers developed the world's first nuclear power plant, EBR-1, and first sent fission-produced electricity through the wires to provide electricity for municipal needs, supplying the town of Arco for a couple of hours on July 17, 1955. The site also developed fission reactors for the U.S. Navy's nuclear needs.

Entering a New Century

The last part of the 20th century saw Idaho transitioning from its traditional natural resources–based economy: While agriculture remains strong and pockets of mining and timber activity continue, technology and tourism have become increasingly important.

Idaho has embraced advanced technology in a big way. Hewlett-Packard established a Boise division in the 1970s, and Micron Technology—a semiconductor company begun in Boise in 1978—is now the state's largest private employer. Although the economic downturn in the early 21st century meant tech-industry layoffs, especially in Boise, Idaho's pro-business climate means good long-term prospects for the industry. The state's recreational riches, meanwhile, have proven a drawing card both for tourists and for entrepreneurs who like to mix business and leisure.

People and Culture

DEMOGRAPHICS

Idaho's population is 87 percent white, 8 percent Hispanic, 1 percent Native American, and 4 percent others.

Hispanics

Traveling through some parts of Canyon County, you might think you were in Mexico. The fields of the Treasure Valley are worked chiefly by migrant farm workers, most of them of Mexican descent; nearly 20 percent of the county's residents are Hispanic. If you're a fan of Mexican food, you'll find restaurants in Nampa and Caldwell that are some of the most authentic and delightful in the country.

Native Americans

After relegating Idaho's native peoples to reservations, the federal government gave them only minimal aid. Unemployment and poverty became epidemic, forcing the tribes to look for income in nontraditional places. When they hit upon gambling, they struck the mother lode. Today, revenues from bingo halls, casinos, and lotteries bring in large sums of money for the tribes, helping turn the tables on poverty. In 2003, Idaho voters approved a measure allowing expanded Indian gaming, despite strong opposition that was rooted—no surprise—in south-central Idaho, a region closely aligned with the border-town destination of Jackpot, Nevada.

The **Coeur d'Alene** tribe is setting aside a percentage of the profits from its gaming operations to reacquire land that was first granted and then taken away by successive treaties with the nonnatives. The tribe is also putting substantial amounts into both remedial action and court fights to clean up and gain control of the waters and shores of Coeur d'Alene Lake that have been ravaged by heavy-metal pollution from a century of mining. The Coeur d'Alene Reservation is in north-central Idaho, surrounding the south side of Coeur d'Alene Lake.

Other Indian reservations in the state include

Basque dancers

© IDAHO DIVISION OF TOURISM

SPEAKING IDAHONIAN

So many names of places and things in Idaho are pronounced differently than you'd expect that it sometimes seems as if there is a plot to confound the outsider. Here is a list of the most common odd pronunciations. Many result from their origins as Native American or French words, reflecting the state's multilingual history. Memorize them or risk being branded a tourist.

- Boise: "BOY-see," not "BOY-zee," and certainly not the French "bwah-ZAY"

- Coeur d'Alene: butchered French "core-duh-lane"

- creek: always rhymes with "sick," with the one exception being the Sandpoint catalog company and retailer Coldwater Creek (rhymes with "seek").

- Dubois: "doo-BOYCE" (from Fred Dubois), not the French "doo-BWAH" ("from the woods")

- Kamiah: "KAM-ee-eye"

- Kooskia: "KOO-skee"

- Kootenai: "KOOT-nee"

- Lochsa: "LOCK-saw"

- Montpelier: "mahnt-PEEL-yer," never the French "moan-pale-YAY"

- Moscow: "MOS-coe"

- Moyie: "MOY-yay"

- Nez Perce: "nezz purse," never the French "NAY-pare-SAY"

- Owyhee: "o-WHY-hee"

- Pend Oreille: close to the original French, "PON-der-ray"

- root: always rhymes with "foot"

- Sawtooths: never Sawteeth

- Weippe: "WEE-yipe"

the Shoshone-Bannock **Fort Hall Reservation** in southeast Idaho; the Shoshone-Paiute **Duck Valley Reservation,** straddling the Nevada border in southwest Idaho; and the **Nez Perce Reservation,** in north-central Idaho, home to the headquarters of Nez Perce National Historic Park.

The Kootenai tribe doesn't have its own reservation, but it owns the **Kootenai River Inn** in Bonners Ferry. You can support the descendants of Idaho's indigenous Kootenai and learn a little about their culture by staying at the inn on your way through the area.

Basques

Their homeland is in northern Spain, but many Basque immigrants make their home in Idaho. Boise has the largest Basque population in the United States and offers plenty of opportunities for the visitor to learn about this unique culture. You can eat Basque food at a number of restaurants across the state—try Boise's Bar Gernika, where chances are good you'll overhear the unusual Basque language being spoken while you eat. Boise is also the site of the annual Festival of San Inazio and the Jaialdi, an international blowout that draws Basque people from all over world once every five years.

POLITICS

Idaho is one of the most Republican states in the country. Sixty-one percent of Idahoans voted for John McCain in the 2008 presidential election. The Gem State is not an easy place for Democrats to win office; Idaho hasn't had a Democrat for governor since Cecil Andrus in 1995. Even more remarkable, Idaho hasn't had a Democrat as a First Position U.S. Senator since Bert Miller in 1949, and a Second Position U.S. Senator since Frank Church in 1981. Idaho has recently had Democrats as U.S. Representatives, but currently both are Republicans. The state legislature continues to be overwhelmingly GOP.

Idaho Statesman columnist Dan Popkey recalls that during the era of U.S. Senator Frank Church and Governor Cecil Andrus, the 1960s through the 1980s, Democrats "shared power in Republican Idaho through force of intellect and personality." But these days the only areas where Democrats prevail are Sun Valley, Pocatello, and Boise; the latter elected former Democratic state legislator Dave Bieter as mayor in 2003 in a four-way race in which Bieter polled more than 50 percent. Bieter still holds office as Boise's mayor.

Many Idahoans are firmly entrenched in the mind-set of the Sagebrush Rebellion: "It's our land to do what we want with, and the federal government should mind its own business." In other words, the Tea Party movement is alive and well in Idaho.

THE ARTS
Performing Arts

Boise is not exactly New York City, but it is home to the excellent Boise Philharmonic, Boise Opera, Boise Master Chorale, and Ballet Idaho as well as the premier Idaho Shakespeare Festival. In addition to performances by those groups, the rock-and-roll clubs, country-music emporiums, and small but growing jazz scene make for an entertainment calendar busy enough to satisfy all but the most ardent city-dweller.

Most of Idaho's other major cities also offer community orchestras, and both major cities and many small towns have community theater groups. The quality is usually first-rate, and what you lose in cutting-edge talent and training are more than made up for in down-home heart, as people take pride in performing for their friends and neighbors.

Look for plentiful student performances and active nightlife scenes at Idaho's college towns: Boise, home of Boise State University; Moscow, home of the University of Idaho; and Pocatello, home of Idaho State University. On those campuses, you'll likely find a film club screening great foreign films and independent fare at budget prices.

Visual Arts and Crafts

Mountain landscapes, wildlife, and Western themes dominate the subject matter of much of the state's two-dimensional artwork. Native American crafts—primarily beadwork and leatherwork—are also widespread across the state. Visitors to the big Shoshone Bannock Indian Festival and Rodeo, at Fort Hall the second week in August, will be faced with an enormous array of craftworks.

The biggest art towns in the state are Ketchum, Boise, and Sandpoint, in that order. Ketchum is a gallery prowler's paradise; some blocks have several galleries, all filled with quality work. Boise's galleries run the gamut from traditional to avant-garde, while Sandpoint's venues display a delightful mix of regionally famous artists and local hopefuls. Boise Art Museum is the state's premier public art repository. The museum hosts traveling shows of merit and houses a respectable permanent collection.

ESSENTIALS
Getting There and Around

BY AIR
Major Airlines
No international flights serve Idaho directly. Boise has the state's largest airport, served by **Horizon Air** (800/547-9308, www.horizonair.com), an affiliate of Alaska Airlines, with nonstop service to and from Seattle; **Delta Air Lines** (800/221-1212, www.delta.com), regionally based in Salt Lake City; **Southwest Airlines** (800/435-9792, www.southwest.com), which offers direct flights between Boise and many western U.S. cities; and **United** (800/241-6522, www.united.com), which flies direct to and from San Francisco, Chicago, and Denver.

Travelers headed into and out of southeast Idaho generally book flights through the airport in Salt Lake City, Utah, 161 miles south of Pocatello. Those headed for the Panhandle book flights into Spokane, Washington, 33 miles west of Coeur d'Alene.

Commuter Airlines
Once you've arrived in Idaho, you can avail yourself of smaller airlines of the turboprop sort to fly you to and among the smaller cities. **Horizon Air** (800/547-9308) maintains an extensive route system across the Northwest and California. From Boise, Horizon flies to about a dozen cities around the West. Delta-

© IDAHO DIVISION OF TOURISM

affiliated **SkyWest Airlines** (800/221-1212, www.skywest.com) also serves Idaho Falls, Pocatello, Sun Valley, and Twin Falls with nonstop service from Salt Lake City. **Salmon Air** (800/448-3413, www.salmonair.com) has weekday flights from Salmon to McCall and Boise.

Backcountry Charters

To fly into one of Idaho's many rural burgs, or to remote airstrips in the state's expansive backcountry, you'll need to hire an air taxi service. A number of companies do a booming business shuttling rafters, backpackers, and anglers into the wilderness. For starters, try **McCall Aviation** (800/992-6559, www.mccallaviation.com), which offers branches in McCall, Stanley, and Salmon.

BY TRAIN

Train service in Idaho is now limited to the *Empire Builder,* an Amtrak (800/872-7245, www.amtrak.com) route that runs between Chicago and either Portland or Seattle via Wisconsin, Minnesota, North Dakota, Montana, north Idaho, and Spokane, Washington. The train was named for the nickname of James Jerome Hill (1838–1916), a Canadian-born railroad magnate who founded the Great Northern Railway; the Great Northern's line between St. Paul, Minnesota, and the Pacific opened up the Northwest at the turn of the 20th century. Today's Amtrak train makes one run daily in each direction. Its only Idaho stop is in the Panhandle at Sandpoint, where it creeps through in the middle of the night (11:49 P.M. westbound, 2:32 A.M. eastbound).

BY BUS

Greyhound (800/231-2222, www.greyhound.com) goes almost everywhere in this great country. **Northwestern Trailways** (800/366-3830, www.northwesterntrailways.com) connects Boise with McCall, Lewiston, Grangeville, and Spokane, Washington. **Sun Valley Express** (877/622-8267) offers service between Boise Airport and Sun Valley. **Rocky Mountain Trails/Salt Lake Express** (800/356-9796, www.saltlakeexpress.com)

backcountry flying

© IDAHO DIVISION OF TOURISM

offers daily van shuttle service between Salt Lake City and the Idaho communities of Rexburg, Rigby, Idaho Falls, Blackfoot, and Pocatello.

BY CAR

Driving is the easiest and most efficient way to make your way around Idaho, but with some caveats. Except in and around major cities and on the interstates, all Idaho highways have two lanes and are undivided. To make matters worse, few are equipped with Botts' dots—those bumpy, reflective lane markers that wake you up if you drift out of your lane. This can make driving a challenge, particularly on dark rainy nights. If you can't see the lanes clearly, slow down.

All the major national car-rental companies are represented in Idaho, including at the major airports.

Traffic Laws

Here are a few of the common Idaho traffic laws you ought to know before you start the car. First, you'll need to possess and carry a valid driver's license from your home state or country, or a valid international driver's license. You must also possess and carry proof of liability insurance. Your vehicle must also be currently registered. Finally, before you turn the key, buckle up—it's the law; you must wear your seat belt in Idaho. All children under 40 pounds must be strapped into a car seat.

Once out on the road, a couple of rules are worthy of special mention. First, in the United States, you drive on the right side of the road. Unless posted otherwise, you are permitted to make a right turn on a red light after coming to a complete stop. You can also

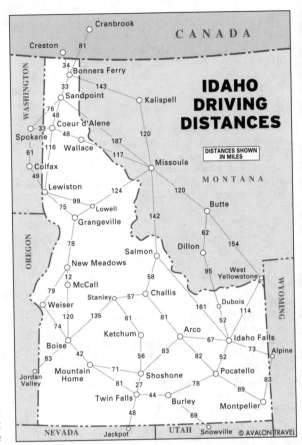

IDAHO DRIVING DISTANCES

DISTANCES SHOWN IN MILES

make a U-turn at a controlled intersection if no sign specifically prohibits it, and then only if you can do so safely, in one continuous movement (no three-point turns). Unless posted otherwise, the maximum speed limit on city streets is 35 mph. And be careful of horses; horseback riders are permitted on most public roads.

A special note for you RVers: Idaho law requires you to pull over if you are holding up three or more vehicles.

Drinking and Driving

The drinking age in Idaho is 21. If you're 21

or over, you're considered legally drunk if your blood-alcohol level is 0.08 percent or above. If you're under 21, you can't have any alcohol in your system while operating a motor vehicle on Idaho's roads. These laws are strictly enforced.

Winter Driving

Old Man Winter is always ready to get you if you don't watch out, so just say "slow." You'll see plenty of signs warning of **frost heaves,** places where water beneath the pavement has frozen and expanded, buckling the road. Hitting one of these at too high a speed on a rain- or snow-slickened road can throw you instantly out of control.

The weather in Idaho can be unpredictable, and much of the state gets at least some snow in winter. You'd be wise to carry chains in your trunk October–April. Also in the trunk should go a short-handled shovel so you can dig yourself out of that snow bank, and blankets, a sleeping bag, and extra food and drinking water just in case you get stranded. Winter and summer, carry emergency flares and a flashlight or headlamp. If you do break down in a snowstorm, stay with the car. Don't try to walk for help unless you can see that it's very close; many people have died of hypothermia in the attempt.

Summer Driving

Much of the state swelters in summer—particularly at low elevations on the Snake River Plain and in the canyons of western Idaho. Make sure your radiator is in good working order, and carry a couple of extra gallons of coolant in the trunk. As in winter, also carry extra food and water in the trunk, in case you get stuck out in the middle of nowhere. And even in summer, carry blankets. Idaho summer days may get hot, but nights can still get plenty cold in many parts of the state, even in mid-July. If you're renting a car, make sure it has a functioning air conditioner—you'll need it. As in winter, keep emergency flares and a flashlight or headlamp handy at all times.

As summer opens up many roads into high mountain country, roadside encounters with wildlife become more common. In your travels through the state, you'll see many dead deer and other animals on the roadsides. To avoid a collision with an animal, never outdrive your headlights at night, use your high beams whenever possible, and immediately slow down as soon as you spy any animal even remotely close to the road.

Getting Off the Pavement

Half the fun of exploring the state is leaving the highway behind and heading out into the desert or deep into the mountains. Special precautions apply, however, since often these roads will take you a day's hike or more away from the nearest fellow human being. Four-wheel-drive vehicles are really in their element here, but if you go slowly enough, most of Idaho's dirt roads are passable in the family sedan.

Southern Idaho's deserts are especially desolate—plan on being on your own. If ever a case could be made for carrying not one but two spare tires, this would be it. Make sure your jack works and you know how to use it. Two jacks could even come in handy. Carry a shovel to dig yourself out of the sand or mud, and some boards—two-by-fours or whatever you can fit in the trunk—to put under your stuck wheels for traction.

In the mountains, you'll have to contend with **logging trucks,** which often barrel down narrow one-lane roads and around blind corners at high speed with seeming disregard for everything in their path. The best advice is to just stay out of areas being actively logged; stop at the nearest ranger station to find out where these areas are. If you must enter an active area, it helps to have a CB radio. Usually, a communication channel is posted on the entrance to every logging road where a visitor might wander in. If you have a CB, tune to the posted channel and let everyone know you're on that road, or at least listen in to find out who else is out there.

Further Information

To find out the current status of the roads along your intended route, call the Idaho Transportation Department's 24-hour recorded **road conditions** report (511 or 888/432-7623, www.511.idaho.gov). RVers can obtain a list of RV **dump stations** in the state by contacting the RV Program Supervisor, Idaho Department of Parks and Recreation (5657 Warm Springs Ave., Boise, 208/334-4199).

Sports and Recreation

STATE PARKS

Each of Idaho's 26 state parks highlights a different Idaho natural wonder, but they all feature well-kept facilities, and many offer outstanding interpretive programs. Most parks charge a $5 motor-vehicle entry fee (no charge for walk-ins or bike-ins). For $40, you can buy a calendar-year pass that provides unlimited entry to all the state parks that year (however, it doesn't include camping fees); a second vehicle can be covered for just $15 more. To purchase this pass, call 888/922-6743 or go to www.parksandrecreation.idaho.gov.

Many of the parks are designed for camping. You'll generally find RV-suitable campsites with water and electric hookups for $18–26 per night, or water only for $12–18 per night. The first-rate restroom facilities are kept clean, and most parks have showers as well; noncampers can use the showers for a small fee. Several parks have camper cabins that sleep up to six and rent for around $50 per night. The cabins have electricity and heat along with a cooking grill outside. You'll also find larger cabins at Harriman, Heyburn, and Ponderosa as well as year-round yurts at Harriman, Ponderosa, and Winchester State Parks. Pets are allowed on a leash at most parks but must be kept enclosed within your RV or tent at night.

Reservations are taken for some campsites and cabins for $10. Call the park of your choice, or go to www.reserveamerica.com. Some parks offer campsites on a first-come, first-served basis.

For more information, contact the **Idaho Department of Parks and Recreation** (5657 Warm Springs Ave., Boise, 208/334-4199).

NATIONAL FORESTS

Idaho encompasses all or part of 13 different national forests, which together cover most of the state, so it's no surprise that national forest campgrounds are the most numerous of any type in Idaho. The big popular ones with developed drinking-water sources are usually managed by private companies under contract with the U.S. Forest Service. At these campgrounds, you'll typically find a campground host who keeps the place picked up and collects fees from campers. Fees commonly run $10–15 per site per night for up to two vehicles. Some of these campgrounds are on a **central reservation system;** make reservations through ReserveAmerica's National Recreation Reservation Service (NRRS, 877/444-6777, www.recreation.gov). A reservation fee is charged.

Other, free Forest Service campgrounds are scattered throughout the state. These are usually found in less popular or more remote areas either too small for practical fee collection or lacking potable water. At these campsites, you'll usually find an outhouse, picnic tables, and fire rings or grills, but you'll often be on your own for drinkable water. As a good many of these campgrounds are found along lakes or streams, this is not much of a problem for anyone with a water filter.

One other Forest Service option is available: rental guard stations and lookout towers. Air surveillance today has largely replaced the staffed lookouts, so the Forest Service offers the buildings to the public as backcountry accommodations. Almost by definition, these will have terrific views and be ensconced in remote and wild landscapes. The rentals are by and large primitive and sleep anywhere from a pair of cozy friends to a whole college football team. Many are accessible only on skis or snowmobiles in winter.

BUREAU OF LAND MANAGEMENT LANDS

Most of the 12 million acres of Bureau of Land Management (BLM) land in Idaho are found on and around the Snake River Plain in the southern portion of the state. BLM campgrounds are generally free, primitive, minimally maintained, and minimally used. Depending on your perspective, that could be good or bad. They tend to be near areas offering recreation opportunities such as rivers, lakes, and remote hiking areas. The BLM maintains a number of district offices in Idaho (see www.blm.gov/id for more information).

SUMMER SPORTS
White-Water Rafting and Kayaking

Idaho ranks as king of the Lower 48 when it comes to wild white water, boasting about

1,000 more white-water miles than runner-up California. The Snake River through Hells Canyon, the Salmon River and its Middle Fork, and the Lochsa, Selway, and Payette are the state's most notorious rivers. The Snake and the main Salmon offer big-water thrills; the Lochsa and Payette offer challenging runs through narrower gorges; and Middle Fork and the Selway provide a wilderness experience par excellence. Many more Idaho rivers await white-water enthusiasts, however, ranging from the remote desert canyon run of the Jarbidge near the Nevada border to the lushly forested run of the Moyie near the Canadian border.

If you go with a commercial guide service, you won't need to worry about a permit. Otherwise, you must obtain a permit from the U.S. Forest Service for private noncommercial trips on the Middle Fork of the Salmon, the main Salmon, the upper Selway, and the Snake River through Hells Canyon. Only a limited number of permits, awarded through the Four Rivers Lottery, are issued each season. You need to fill out an application form, available October 1 for the next summer, and submit it December 1–January 31 for the following

rafting the Payette River

© IDAHO DIVISION OF TOURISM

season. You can specify your preferred rivers and launch dates. For Middle Fork permits, contact the **Middle Fork Ranger District** (U.S. 93 N., P.O. Box 750, Challis, ID 83226, 208/879-4101); for main Salmon permits, contact **North Fork Ranger District** (U.S. 93, P.O. Box 180, North Fork, ID 83466-0180, 208/865-2700); for Selway permits, contact the **West Fork Ranger District** (6735 West Fork Rd., Darby, MT 59829, 406/821-3269); for Snake permits, contact **Hells Canyon National Recreation Area** (P.O. Box 699, Clarkston, WA 99403, 509/758-1957). Applications can also be downloaded online at www.fs.fed.us/r4/sc/recreation/4rivers.htm, but you must mail or fax them in before January 31.

Other Water Sports

With lakes and reservoirs scattered from one end of the state to the other, you'll never be too far from **waterskiing** and **windsurfing.** Especially popular for the latter are the windy reservoirs of the Snake River Plain, notably American Falls Reservoir and Lake Walcott. Others take their boards up to Redfish Lake in the Sawtooths, where the winds can be erratic but the views are world-class. In the state's southeastern corner, Bear Lake is popular with water-skiers, as are Lakes Coeur d'Alene and Pend Oreille in the Panhandle and Payette Lake at McCall. **Sailing** is best on Payette Lake and Lakes Coeur d'Alene, and Pend Oreille. **Scuba diving** is a limited proposition in Idaho; check out Brownlee Reservoir, on the Snake River west of Cambridge, in spring.

Mountain Biking

For mountain bikers, Idaho is nirvana. Look at all that national forest land with all those national forest roads ripe for the pedaling. Yes, mountain biking is big virtually everywhere up here.

In Boise, the **Boise Front** is practically right behind the state capitol—head out on

---

INTERNATIONAL SCALE OF RIVER DIFFICULTY

- **Class I: Very Easy.** Small regular waves and riffles. Few or no obstructions. Little maneuvering required.

- **Class II: Easy.** Waves up to three feet. Wide, clear channels that are obvious without scouting. Low ledges; small rock gardens. Some maneuvering required.

- **Class III: Medium.** Rapids with numerous high, irregular waves capable of swamping an open canoe. Strong eddies. Narrow passages that often require complex maneuvering. May require scouting from shore.

- **Class IV: Difficult.** Long difficult rapids with powerful, irregular waves, dangerous rocks, boiling eddies, and constricted passages that require precise maneuvering in very turbulent waters. Scouting from shore is necessary and conditions make rescue difficult. Generally not possible for open ca-

noes. Boaters in covered canoes and kayaks should be able to Eskimo roll.

- **Class V: Very Difficult.** Long, violent rapids with wild turbulence and highly congested routes that must be scouted from shore. Rescue conditions are difficult, and there is significant hazard to life in event of a mishap. Ability to Eskimo roll is essential for paddlers in kayaks and covered canoes.

- **Class VI: The Limits of Navigation.** Difficulties of Class V carried to the extreme limits of navigability. Nearly impossible and very dangerous. For teams of experts only, after close study and with all precautions taken. Rarely run and a definite hazard to your life.

If water temperature is below 50°F, or if the trip is an extended trip into a wilderness area, the river should be considered one class more difficult than normal.

8th Street and just keep going. At **Bogus Basin,** ride up the hill and take off on the forest roads.

If you're in southwest Idaho and ready for multiday solitude, head for the **Owyhee County Backcountry Byway;** if you'd rather go out for the day and come back to a brew, head up to McCall and explore the **Payette National Forest** or the lift-served trails at **Brundage Mountain.**

There's lots to choose from in the southeast. The **Mink Creek** trails outside Pocatello make for a good workout, or try the lift-served biking at **Grand Targhee.**

The high country is total mountain biker heaven. Just about anywhere in the **Wood River Valley** you'll find dirt roads heading off into the mountains. Or cross over Galena Summit and bike into the **White Cloud Peaks,** an airy realm of sheer craggy summits and wildflower-filled meadows.

In the north-central area, **McCroskey State Park** north of Moscow is a little-known state park used more by mountain bikers than by cars. The park offers sweeping views of the Palouse. When you're done, head east to Harvard and up into the **Palouse Range,** where mighty forests of white pine once covered the land and where you still might ride past a big tree or two.

For Panhandle biking, first try the **Route of the Hiawatha** near Lookout Pass, for thrills negotiating the tunnels and trestles of an abandoned railroad grade. After that, head for **Priest Lake,** where you can ride from the northwest edge of the lake all the way to Canada.

Road Biking

Although many Idaho roads are narrow, with little or no shoulder, paved trails are popping up all over. The **Boise River Greenbelt** offers a beautiful traffic-free path long enough to give the average cyclist a workout. The **Wood River Valley** makes the list for its extensive network of bike paths. The **Palouse,** east of Moscow, offers gently rolling hills through scenic farmland. But the best road-biking

experience of all is the 72-mile **Trail of the Coeur d'Alenes,** a recent rails-to-trails conversion that is tied with Minnesota's Willard Munger State Trail to make the longest continuous paved bikeway in North America. It crosses the Idaho Panhandle from Mullan in the east to Plummer in the west.

Fishing

You'll need to purchase an Idaho state fishing license before you head out to try your luck. Idaho residents pay $25.75 adults, $13.75 ages 14–17. Nonresident anglers pay $12.75 for the first day, $6 for each additional consecutive day. You can get a license at sporting goods stores, many convenience stores, or any office of the Idaho Department of Fish and Game.

Old fly-fishers never die, they just find heaven in Idaho at **Silver Creek,** in south-central Idaho, and at **Henry's Fork** and the **South Fork Snake** in the southeast. Fishing lodges in these parts are sometimes booked years in advance. Meanwhile, the Rambo types among the angling crowd prefer to wrestle the enormous primeval-looking **sturgeon** (no harvest), which inhabits the lower Snake River. Others find **steelhead** fishing on the Clearwater River to hold the biggest thrills.

To find out up-to-the-minute information about fishing conditions in various parts of Idaho, contact the **Idaho Department of Fish and Game** (600 S. Walnut St., Boise, 208/334-3700, www.fishandgame.idaho.gov).

Golfing

At last count, Idaho had about 100 golf courses. Many courses in southwest Idaho and south-central Idaho stay open year-round. Linksters will find many modest nine-hole courses in small towns throughout the state as well as several world-class megacourses. Among the most impressive are the Robert Trent Jones Jr. courses in the Sun Valley area and the luxurious Coeur d'Alene Resort course with its novel floating green. Statewide, prices range from around $12 to well over $150 per round.

Hiking and Backpacking

With all that public land at their disposal, hikers will find no shortage of trails to explore. Start with the wilderness areas for a pristine experience free from exhaust fumes and chainsaws. For sheer scenic beauty, it's hard to top **Sawtooth Wilderness,** which offers peaks and lakes galore. Nevertheless, the **Hells Canyon Wilderness,** with its exquisitely beautiful Seven Devils Range, gives the Sawtooths a run for their money. If you really want to get lost for a couple of weeks, head out into the vast **Frank Church-River of No Return Wilderness** or the adjacent **Selway-Bitterroot Wilderness.** Both take you about as far from the madding crowd as you can get in the state.

Those looking for the ultimate Idaho trek can attempt the 1,200-mile **Idaho Centennial Trail,** which runs the length of the state, south to north. The trail starts near Murphy Hot Springs on the Nevada border and follows the Jarbidge and Bruneau Rivers north, crossing I-84 near Glenns Ferry. It works its way into the Sawtooths, then traverses both the Frank Church and Selway-Bitterroot Wildernesses, crossing U.S. 12 near the Lochsa Historical Ranger Station. From there it bears east to the high Bitterroots, following the Continental Divide along the Idaho-Montana border for a time before sliding off the divide to head west into the Cabinet Mountains and over to Priest Lake. At Priest Lake, the trail makes a short hop, skip, and jump north to the Canadian border. Signage of the trail has been completed in recent years.

Hot Springs

Thanks to its geology, Idaho is blessed with more hot springs by far than any other state in the West. The lion's share lie in the state's central mountains, in an area bounded roughly by U.S. 12 and U.S. 20 on the north and south and U.S. 95 and U.S. 93 on the west and east. No matter what your style—developed or primitive, clothing mandatory or clothing optional, easy access or remote—you'll find a hot spring to suit you. Many of the springs taunt the nose with that characteristic sulfur smell; many do not. True hot-springs believers come to appreciate the smell and can follow their nose to hot-soaking delights.

The best-developed family hot springs in Idaho is the state-run **Lava Hot Springs** resort, in the laid-back little resort town of Lava Hot Springs, southeast of Pocatello. The facility is immaculate, the setting beautiful, and the fumes sulfur-free. Fans of developed yet rustic geothermal-pool facilities will surely like **Burgdorf Hot Springs** outside McCall. Here you can soak in a sand-bottomed pool, stay in a rustic old pioneer's cabin, and watch elk feed under the stars. For a personal spiritual retreat, head for **Murphy Hot Springs.** It's remote, quiet, and magical—out in the middle of nowhere in Owyhee County.

Idaho has so many undeveloped natural hot springs that it's beyond the scope of this guide to describe each and every one; whole books are devoted to the topic. A couple of favorites: **Chattanooga Hot Springs** in Atlanta and **Elk Bend Hot Springs** south of Salmon off U.S. 93. The award for the most social natural hot springs goes to **Jerry Johnson Hot Springs,** off U.S. 12 east of Lowell, where you'll just about always find good conversation with your soaking companions.

Rock Climbing and Mountaineering

Rock jocks will find world-class climbing centers at **City of Rocks/Castle Rocks** in south-central Idaho, a massive area of rock towers up to 600 feet high; in the **Sawtooth Range,** on sheer granite spires and big-wall faces; and in the Panhandle's **Selkirk Range,** which climbers share with grizzlies and woodland caribou.

Mountain ranges literally cover most of the state. There's no end to the peak-bagging possibilities. The highest peak in the state is **Borah Peak** (12,662 feet) in the Lost River Range near Mackay. It's an easy Class 2–3 climb, but airy in places; it makes a comfortable solo for the experienced mountaineer and a great place to take your neophyte partner for his or her first big summit. Borah isn't a particularly impressive peak to look at, but others in the range are.

Ketchum, in close proximity to the Soldiers, Smokies, Pioneers, Boulders, Sawtooths, and White Clouds, is the hub of a strong mountaineering scene. The area has enough peaks to keep you busy well into your next life. Among the biggest: **Castle Peak** in the White Clouds tops out at 11,815 feet; **Hyndman Peak** in the Pioneers juts up into the thin air at 12,009 feet.

WINTER SPORTS
Alpine Skiing

In a state with so many mountains, ski resorts are understandably ubiquitous, with 16 alpine ski areas from Magic Mountain in the extreme south to Schweitzer Mountain in the extreme north. Powder-hounds should take Idaho's climatology into consideration; for better powder, go higher or drier. The best powder skiing in the state isn't even in the state but just across the border in Wyoming at **Grand Targhee,** accessible only through Driggs, Idaho. Here, continental weather patterns produce colder, drier storms than the maritime-influenced storms of the more northerly and westerly resorts.

Sun Valley is the West's oldest, grandest ski resort, offering a zillion fast lifts up a big mountain and luxurious pampering at every turn. It's also the state's priciest resort. **Schweitzer Mountain** outside Sandpoint, **Silver Mountain** at Kellogg, **Brundage Mountain** near McCall, and **Bogus Basin** outside Boise are medium-size areas offering lots of fun skiing at reasonable prices. Schweitzer has a beautiful base lodge and hotel; Silver Mountain boasts the world's longest gondola; Brundage offers some of the best facilities for kids in the state and the liveliest ski-town atmosphere; and Bogus Basin has killer night skiing.

Smaller than those resorts but offering good skiing at a budget price are several locals-oriented areas, including **Soldier Mountain** (Sawtooth Country); **Pebble Creek, Kelly Canyon,** and **Lost Trail Powder Mountain** (Southeast); and **Lookout Pass** (Panhandle).

skiing at Brundage Mountain

© IDAHO DIVISION OF TOURISM

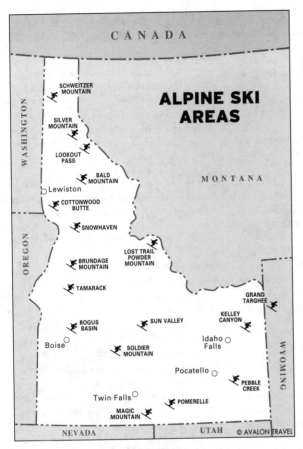

ALPINE SKI AREAS

CANADA

WASHINGTON

SCHWEITZER MOUNTAIN

SILVER MOUNTAIN

LOOKOUT PASS

BALD MOUNTAIN

Lewiston

COTTONWOOD BUTTE

SNOWHAVEN

OREGON

LOST TRAIL POWDER MOUNTAIN

BRUNDAGE MOUNTAIN

TAMARACK

MONTANA

GRAND TARGHEE

BOGUS BASIN

SUN VALLEY

KELLEY CANYON

Boise

SOLDIER MOUNTAIN

Idaho Falls

WYOMING

Pocatello

PEBBLE CREEK

Twin Falls

POMERELLE

MAGIC MOUNTAIN

NEVADA

UTAH

© AVALON TRAVEL

Cross-Country Skiing

Across the state, from Boise to Bonners Ferry, you'll find **Park N' Ski areas** established by the Idaho Department of Parks and Recreation. To use the Park N' Ski areas, you must first buy a permit ($25 for an entire season, $7.50

for three days). Theoretically, this is supposed to get you plowed trailhead parking and groomed trails, but grooming can be sketchy in some areas. For more information on the Park N' Ski areas, contact the Idaho Department of Parks and Recreation (5657 Warm Springs Ave., Boise, 208/334-4199, www.parksandrecreation. idaho.gov).

In a class by themselves are the public-private partnership **Wood River Valley** trails. Two separate systems in the lower and upper parts of the valley offer a vast network of meticulously groomed trails. The lower valley system is free, courtesy of Blaine County. The North Valley trails require a $15 daily permit, which is easily worth three times as much. The North Valley system culminates in the trails at Galena Lodge, the ultimate intimate cross-country ski chalet.

Snowshoeing

Most of the state's cross-country ski areas welcome snowshoers too—just be careful not to step on the groomed tracks. The great thing about snowshoeing is you don't need a trail; you can set off across any snowy patch of land. Some ski areas and other parklands offer guided snowshoe treks, which can be a great way to learn animal tracks and other winter ecology.

Festivals and Events

Something is going on somewhere in Idaho every weekend year-round. If you're traveling through an area of the state and want to find out what's happening, consult the travel chapters of this guide; many major events have been listed in the city sections.

If, on the other hand, you're planning a trip to Idaho around a big event, here's a list of some of the biggest and best.

CULTURE

- **Festival of San Inazio:** Boise, last weekend in July. Boise's Basque community pulls out all the stops for this cultural celebration; look for food, dancing, and contests of strength and skill.

- **Shoshone Bannock Indian Festival and Rodeo:** Fort Hall, second week of August. One of the biggest powwows in the West, drawing Native Americans and visitors from all over the continent for dancing, drumming, rodeo, and arts and crafts.

MUSIC

- **Lionel Hampton Jazz Festival:** Moscow, late February. How can this many jazz masters show up in one place at the same time? Don't miss it.

- **National Oldtime Fiddlers' Contest:** Weiser, third full week of June. The finest fiddlers in the country compete, and a party atmosphere prevails day and night.

- **Festival at Sandpoint:** Sandpoint, early August. Expect performances by many big-name rock and jazz musicians.

RODEO

- **Dodge National Circuit Finals Rodeo:** Pocatello, early April. All the big names show up for the country's second-largest points-qualifying rodeo.

- **Snake River Stampede:** Nampa, mid-July. A venerable southwest Idaho institution and one of the country's top 25 rodeos, this one draws upward of 40,000 spectators.

- **Caldwell Night Rodeo:** Caldwell, mid-August. The Snake River Stampede may be bigger, but this one is the most rip-roarin' fun.

SPORTS

- **Boulder Mountain Nordic Ski Classic:** Ketchum, early February. Idaho's biggest Nordic ski race held on the Wood River Valley's magnificent Boulder Mountain Trail.

- **Race to Robie Creek:** Boise, mid-April. Thousands of legs thrash madly up and over Adalpe Summit in the Northwest's toughest half-marathon.

- **Sun Valley Ice Show:** Sun Valley, mid-June–September. All the big names perform on the ice at the ritzy Sun Valley Lodge.

- **Payette Whitewater Roundup:** Banks, July. Idaho's largest kayak competition features scores of brightly colored boats and competitors from all across the country.

GENERAL FUN

- **Winter Carnival:** McCall, late January–early February. The state's funnest winter carnival in the state's funnest town—snow monsters, ice sculptures, sleigh rides, and a parade.

- **Western Days:** Twin Falls, late May. Check out this down-home festival with one of Idaho's biggest parades, a carnival, food booths, and music.

- **Teton Valley Summer Festival:** Driggs, July 4 weekend. Brightly colored balloons speckle the sky with the Tetons in the background. How scenic can you get?

Accommodations and Food

ACCOMMODATIONS

Idaho has every kind of hotel and motel chain possible. If you're looking for your favorite one, just call its toll-free number, or check the website for a location finder.

Generally peak-season accommodation rates are listed in this guide. Peak-season rates can run rather high in Idaho's resort towns, but many of these places offer great deals in the off-season or the in-between seasons. For example, many hotels in the Sun Valley area (during spring and fall slack) and McCall (during spring and fall shoulder) offer discounted rates when things slow down, sometimes up to 30 percent off peak-season rates. Coeur d'Alene's peak season is summer, so look for big discounts there during the winter months.

Guest Ranches and Fishing Lodges

Most of Idaho's 20 or so guest ranches provide a bit of Old West adventure with their accommodations. Typically rustic and remote, these lodgings put an emphasis on outdoor activities such as fishing, hunting, swimming, and horseback riding. Rates are usually based on stays of a week and generally include all meals and recreation. Some are working ranches; some operate in summer only while others are open year-round.

Also usually offering weeklong packages but replacing horseback activities with guided fishing are Idaho's numerous fishing lodges. Most of these are found along the Henry's Fork and the South Fork Snake River in southeast Idaho.

Many guest ranches and fishing lodges are members of the **Idaho Outfitters & Guides Association** (208/342-1438, www.ioga.org) in Boise.

Bed-and-Breakfasts

Idaho's B&Bs fall into two camps. Many are converted residences, where you'll be sharing a family's home and living space with them. Others are more like small hotels, designed as guest accommodations from the ground up and generally offering more privacy at higher prices. Breakfast is included in the rates, but if it makes a difference to you, be sure to inquire what sort of breakfast is served; a few B&Bs offer only a light continental breakfast, while others serve a big homespun breakfast. It's also important to remember that many B&Bs don't allow children, at least young ones.

The Panhandle has the majority of Idaho's bed-and-breakfast inns, especially in the Coeur d'Alene area. To check listings, see the North Idaho Bed & Breakfast Association's website (www.nibba.com).

FOOD AND DRINK

Idaho is a meat-and-potatoes state. Steakhouses are standard, but particularly in rural areas, vegetarians will make good use of grocery stores. The larger cities all provide a range of fare. In Boise you can get nearly every ethnic food imaginable, and in nearby Canyon County you'll find some of the best Mexican restaurants this side of Los Angeles. As Idaho has a large Basque population, many towns, particularly in the southwest, have Basque restaurants. And cowboy cooking is dear to the heart of many Idahoans; Dutch-oven cookouts and grilled steaks are the prime offerings of many tourist resorts and excursion providers. Chefs in mountain resort towns make good use of hand-foraged foodstuffs such as morel mushrooms and huckleberries as well as farm-raised elk and trout.

Idaho has several excellent farmers markets where shoppers can score impeccably fresh organic produce, natural meat products, alfalfa honey, and eggs. Among the best are the Capital City Public Market in Boise, the Kootenai County Farmers Market in Coeur d'Alene, and the Moscow Farmers Market, the oldest of its kind in the state.

Southwest Idaho holds the state's best vineyards, in the newly designated Snake River Valley American Viticultural Area, while microbreweries producing excellent handcrafted beer dot the state.

Tips for Travelers

TRAVELING WITH CHILDREN

State parks, national parks and monuments, and Forest Service ranger district offices all have a multitude of resources for children. Interpretive centers with interesting exhibits and short films, outdoor programs, travel brochures, and free coloring books and other fun swag can help to keep kids happy while on the road. (My children love the Smokey the Bear comic books and Frisbees given to them by friendly Forest Service employees.)

Rest stops also are a saving grace when traveling with kids. The main interstates (I-84, I-86, and I-15) have relatively clean rest stops with some green space about every 40 miles or so. The two-lane highways (U.S. 20, U.S. 95) also have rest stops, but these are fewer and farther between. Most convenience stores don't have a problem letting travelers use their restrooms, especially if you buy something, and nearly every town you'll pass through has a city park with restrooms and picnic areas.

TRAVELERS WITH DISABILITIES

While resources are getting better for disabled folks in Idaho, it still falls below the national average for accessibility for those with mobility issues. Wheelchair ramps and wheelchair-accessible restrooms aren't always where you need them to be, especially in older districts and in small towns. But Idaho has made great strides to improve accessibility in its state park system. For general information and resources about accessible travel, contact **Access-Able Travel Source** (303/232-2979, www.access-able.com).

SENIORS

Elderhostel (800/454-5768, www.roadscholar.org), also known as Road Scholar, is a nonprofit organization that focuses on worldwide recreational and cultural programs for travelers ages 55 and over. In Idaho, Elderhostel offers white-water rafting trips on the Salmon River and skiing adventures at Sun Valley Resort. Contact the organization for a free catalog of its global destinations and programs.

GAY AND LESBIAN TRAVELERS

In Boise, especially downtown and in the city's North End, a progressive attitude prevails about gays and lesbians. But as you get farther out into the small towns and even larger cities in southeast Idaho, the feeling can quickly change to one of intolerance. Thankfully, physical violence toward gays and lesbians is not the norm, but public displays of affection with your partner could result in having some Bible verses shouted at you, or worse, some f-bombs. Smaller towns where this likely wouldn't happen are the liberal bastions of Ketchum and Moscow—both have big out gay and lesbian communities.

An excellent travel resource for gay and lesbian sojourners worldwide is www.purpleroofs.com, which has some Idaho listings.

Health and Safety

EMERGENCIES

For extreme emergencies, **dial 911** to summon medical or law enforcement help. The 911 system is installed almost universally throughout Idaho. If 911 doesn't work, dial 0 (zero) for the operator, who will patch you through to either the ambulance or a law enforcement agency.

PLANTS TO AVOID

A few plants in Idaho can cause discomfort if they come into contact with your skin. **Poison ivy** is common in the state; look for small white-to-yellow berries and large, waxy, ternate (three to a bunch) leaves. Poison ivy likes water, so be especially careful on overgrown trails around creek beds. **Stinging nettle** has broad, coarse-toothed leaves and also grows near water. Unlike poison ivy, you'll know you've encountered stinging nettle soon after contact. Yes, it stings. If any of these plants contact your skin, wash the area with soap and water and try not to scratch. This is easier said than done, no doubt. Once the area is thoroughly washed, you can't spread the rash by scratching, but you can scratch the skin open, inviting infection. Calamine lotion or mudpacks may offer some relief.

PARASITES
Giardia

The *Giardia lamblia* intestinal parasite has spread throughout the backcountry of the West in the past 20 years, lurking in streams and lakes, just waiting for the thirsty, unsuspecting hiker to come along. You should assume *all* water in the backcountry is contaminated, no matter how crystal clear and pure it may appear. Once inside you, the giardia parasite attaches itself to the intestinal wall, causing symptoms including severe fatigue, cramps, nausea, diarrhea, and gas. To ensure that none of the little buggers gets inside you, you'll have to boil (10 minutes minimum at sea level; longer at altitude), chemically treat (iodine, halazone, or other water-purification tablets), or

filter your water. If you go with a filter, be sure to get one with a pore size of less than one micron (one millionth of a meter) in diameter. That's the maximum width that will safely filter out *Giardia*.

Schistosomes

Shallow waters at the edges of lakes commonly harbor the larvae of these parasitic flatworms. The larvae can penetrate human skin, and after doing so will die, but not before causing **swimmer's itch**. The itchy red spots or welts will go away after about a week. Some people are more susceptible than others, for some reason, but who wants to find out into which camp you fall? To avoid the possibility of contracting the bug, swim in water away from the shore and towel off as soon as you get out of the water.

INSECTS
Ticks

These creepy crawlers cling to brush and hop a ride on any warm-blooded animal that happens by. Inserting their barbed mouthparts into the skin, the ticks clamp on tight and begin sucking merrily away. Contrary to the commonly held misconception, you do not remove a tick by unscrewing it, burning it out, or covering it with nail polish or petroleum jelly in an attempt to suffocate it. Instead, get a pair of tweezers and grab it as close to the head as possible, then pull it out with slow, steady pressure. Wash the area with soap and water and check to see if any part of the tick broke off under the skin. If so, best check with your doctor or at least monitor your condition closely for any signs of illness. Ticks have been linked to the spread of Lyme disease and Rocky Mountain spotted fever, but such cases are rare. Ticks are most prevalent in late spring–early summer. To avoid them, tuck your shirt into your pants and your pant legs into your socks or boots. Wearing a DEET-based insect repellent is an additional safeguard. Check your clothes often during your hike, and do a thorough body check when you get back to your home base.

Mosquitoes

The joke about mosquitoes being the state bird could apply in some parts of Idaho, although the dry Snake River Plain doesn't seem to get as many. With lots of wild backcountry with lots of water, Idaho grows 'em big and bountiful. Summer is prime time for skeeters; a hike in the woods in mid-July–August will invite a bloodthirsty bombardment. Repellents containing DEET work the best.

Mosquitoes infected with **West Nile virus** have been detected in Idaho, and many cases of the virus have been reported in humans and horses since it first hit the state in 2004. Most of the human cases have involved older people with compromised immune systems, but younger folks have contracted it too. Luckily the infection rate is going down as the awareness level rises. To avoid being bitten, especially dusk–dawn, take these precautions: Apply DEET or another Environmental Protection Agency–approved insect repellent, wear a long-sleeved shirt, long pants, and socks, and always cover infant carriers with mosquito netting.

Yellow Jackets

The picnickers' pariah, these unwelcome intruders will inevitably crash your outdoor party, buzzing around your soda can, your sandwich, and you. They're incredibly persistent, and the more agitated you get, the more persistent they seem to become. The best advice may be just to ignore them. Or you can try creating a "sacrifice area" by opening a couple of cans of soda and making a really gooey ham sandwich with lots of mustard, then setting it all out at some distance from your table. If you're lucky, the yellow jackets will go for the easy grub and leave you alone. Of course, if you're allergic to their sting, you should just retreat to the safety of the Buick rather than risk anaphylactic shock. In the end, you just can't win with these buggers.

BEARS

While bear attacks are extremely rare in Idaho, they do happen from time to time, especially in grizzly country on the state's east side. Black bears, which are prevalent throughout Idaho, generally are smaller than grizzlies, and they have tall, pointed ears, whereas grizzlies tend to be larger and have a pronounced shoulder hump. Some experts say that attacks from black bears can be just as vicious as grizzly attacks, since the latter often bluff-charge people. Either way, keep your distance from these beautiful but powerful animals. Follow these general rules when hiking or camping in bear country: Never hike between dusk and dawn when bears are most active; keep a clean campsite, and don't put food in your tent; make loud noises along the trail and by streams; and never mess with a dead animal (like a deer or elk carcass) that you might encounter—this could be a bear's dinner. It's a good idea to carry bear spray if you're backpacking in Idaho. If a black bear attacks, use bear spray, throw rocks at the animal, or shout commands with a loud, firm voice. In other words, fight back. It's the opposite for grizzly attacks, though, where you should not try to fight the animal. It's recommended that you drop to the ground, lay flat on your stomach, and clasp your hands behind your neck. In other words, play dead.

COUGARS

Cougar attacks are even rarer than bear attacks, but keep your wits and your kids close to you when hiking in big cat country, which is the entire state. Like bears, cougars are highly active at night and in the early morning, so pay close attention on hiking trails during these hours. Cougars are incredibly fast and stealthy, and if one does attack, fight it with every available weapon, like a hiking stick or a big rock. Pepper spray works well on cougars.

RATTLESNAKES

These venomous pit vipers inhabit Idaho, generally at elevations below 5,000 feet, but

rattlesnake at Hells Canyon

you'll probably never see one. They crawl into cool places under rocks and logs in the heat of day, and even if they're out and about, they'll generally avoid humans if possible. Your greatest chance of encountering one along the trail would be in early morning or evening, or in turning over the wrong rock. Scrambling up rocks is also risky, as you tend to grab above your head in places you can't see. If you do get bitten, the current medical consensus seems to be to get to a doctor as soon as possible, rather than trying the incision-and-suction method formerly recommended. It seems many people did more damage than the snake by slicing themselves or their friends open incorrectly. The best advice is to be cautious and avoid contact in the first place. If you come around a bend in the trail to find one staring you down and rattling at you, just back off a safe distance and wait for it to crawl away. And never invite trouble by poking at a rattler with a stick or otherwise harassing it. If you do, you'll get what you deserve.

MINES

One place you might indeed encounter a rattlesnake at midday is a place to be avoided for other reasons as well. Idaho is full of old abandoned mines. Rattlers come in for the cool darkness. You come in to explore and wind up getting bitten by the snake, falling down a hidden shaft, getting knocked unconscious by a falling rotten timber, and buried alive in the ensuing cave-in. What do you think you're going to find, anyway? Golf ball-size gold nuggets lying on the ground? Just stay out.

HANTAVIRUS

This nasty virus attracted a lot of attention several years ago after a major outbreak in the Four Corners area of the Southwest. It can be fatal, and it's worth mentioning because it is spread by deer mice and other rodents common to Idaho. The virus is found in the animals' urine, saliva, and feces. You can get it by handling contaminated materials, being bitten by a rodent, or, most commonly, by breathing in the virus in contaminated dust or airborne mist from urine. Household disinfectants such as bleach and alcohol will kill the virus. If you rent a backcountry cabin and find telltale signs of rodent habitation, the safest course of action would be to spray the area down with bleach, then mop it up. Don't sweep mouse droppings up without spraying them with disinfectant first. And don't invite rodents into your camp by leaving food out carelessly or intentionally attempting to feed them. Cases of hantavirus infection in humans are fortunately rare.

CRIME

Idaho's relatively small population makes for a relatively low crime rate. Homicides and other violent crimes are thankfully rare and still make front-page news, even in Boise. Part of this can be attributed to Idaho's overall strong sense of community. People know their neighbors more than in many other parts of the West. But burglaries from cars and other property crimes do happen in Idaho, so don't leave valuables in plain sight on the front seat of your parked car.

Information and Services

TOURIST INFORMATION

If, heaven forbid, you can't find the answer to your question somewhere in this guide, contact the **Idaho Department of Commerce/ Idaho Travel Council** (700 W. State St., Boise, 800/847-4843, www.visitid.org).

MEDIA

The best of the state's mainstream daily newspapers are Boise's **Idaho Statesman** (www. idahostatesman.com), the largest-circulation paper in the state, and Lewiston's **Lewiston Morning Tribune** (www.lmtribune.com). The Spokane-based **Spokesman-Review** (www. spokesmanreview.com) also offers comprehensive coverage of north Idaho.

Also in the state capital, the **Boise Weekly** (www.boiseweekly.com) stands out as a highly credible liberal rag featuring excellent reporting and writing. The *Weekly* is available free around Boise.

National Public Radio junkies will find affiliates in Boise at KBSU (90.3 FM), KBSX (91.5 FM), and KBSU (730 AM); in Cottonwood at KNWO (90.1 FM); in McCall at KBSM (91.7 FM); in Moscow at KRFA (91.7 FM); in Rexburg at KRIC (100.5 FM); and in Twin Falls at KBSW (91.7 FM).

MONEY

Automatic teller machines (ATMs) are found at most Idaho banks and at many grocery stores and other locations; with a debit or credit card you can get cash at any time of day or night. If you need to deal with a human, you'll find that most banks are open longer hours than they once were, typically 9:30 A.M.–5:30 P.M., with some open on Saturday as well.

TELEPHONES

Here's a relief to visitors from other areas of the country where new telephone area codes seem to be spawning faster than cockroaches. The area code for all of Idaho is **208.** That means that when you're calling someplace in Idaho that is distant from where you are, you must dial 1-208 before the standard seven-digit telephone number you're trying to reach. If you're calling someplace near where you are, you need only dial the seven-digit number. If you're not sure how "distant" your intended number is, just dial the seven-digit number. If it's too far away, a disembodied voice will tell you to try it the other way.

You'll notice many numbers in this guide listed with an 800, 888, 877, or 866 area code. These are toll-free area codes—no charge to you. You have to dial a 1 before the area code.

For telephone **directory assistance,** call 208/555-1212.

Cell phone coverage can be spotty in Idaho, especially deep in the mountains and far out in the desert, but coverage is clear most everywhere else.

TIME ZONES AND SYSTEMS

Idaho is shared by two different time zones. Northern Idaho is on **Pacific time.** Down around Riggins, the time zone changes to **mountain time,** an hour ahead of Pacific time. As with most places in the country, Idaho follows the daylight saving convention. In spring (the second Sunday in March) daylight saving time goes into effect, and everyone sets their clocks an hour ahead. In fall (the first Sunday in November) the clocks go back an hour to standard time. Remember the ditty: "spring forward, fall back."

RESOURCES

Suggested Reading

DESCRIPTION AND TRAVEL

Alt, David D., and Donald W. Hyndman. *Roadside Geology of Idaho.* Missoula, MT: Mountain Press, 1998. A great overview for the layperson, this book describes in easy-to-understand fashion just what you'll be looking at as you drive the roads of Idaho. The introduction provides a crash course in plate tectonics.

Conley, Cort. *Idaho for the Curious.* Cambridge, ID: Backeddy Books, 1982. Although some descriptions are dated, this massive tome is tailor-made for travel down the highways of Idaho. Organized by region and highway number, this monster masterwork provides historical context for virtually every sight of significance you'll come across. Conley pulls no punches in his observations, lustily attacking the greedy magnates and bungling bureaucrats who have done damage to his precious home state. How about a new edition, Cort?

Johnson, Frederic D. *Wild Trees of Idaho.* Moscow, ID: University of Idaho Press, 1995. A comprehensive guide to Idaho's trees and shrubs, with abundant large drawings and a helpful set of color plates. Johnson taught Forest Resources at the University of Idaho.

Shallat, Todd, ed. *Snake: The Plain and Its People.* Boise: Boise State University, 1994. Expertly written by a group of Idaho professors and other academics, lushly illustrated with both modern and historical photographs, and superbly laid out and edited, this book is a must-read for those who want to learn more about southern Idaho and its central feature: the Snake River. Obviously a labor of love, the book provides an intimate understanding of life on the Snake River Plain.

HISTORY AND POLITICS

Arrington, Leonard J. *History of Idaho.* Moscow, ID: University of Idaho Press, 1994. Commissioned for Idaho's 1990 centennial celebration, this is the definitive Idaho history text. Arrington was an Idaho native and a lifelong student of Idaho history. The two-volume set covers all the bases succinctly and points the way toward further research with copious footnotes. It's highly readable—not too dry—and boasts some great historical photos. Highly recommended.

Derig, Betty. *Roadside History of Idaho.* Missoula, MT: Mountain Press, 2009. Put out by the same folks who publish the Roadside Geology series, this book is a must-have for history buffs traveling around Idaho. Historian Betty Derig, a longtime Idahoan, takes readers on a fact-filled tour of the state, by region, offering insight and Western colloquialisms like "The old town relaxed like a burro at the hitching post and hardly twitched a muscle until 1936." The book also offers well-researched facts about lesser-known areas.

Josephy, Alvin M. *The Nez Perce Indians and the Opening of the Northwest.* Boston: Houghton Mifflin Company, 1965; abridged edition

1997. Josephy tells the whole sad story of the Nez Perce from their welcoming encounter with Lewis and Clark in 1805 to their defeat at the hands of the U.S. Army in 1877. This account is recommended by the Nez Perce.

Lukas, J. Anthony. *Big Trouble: A Murder in a Small Western Town Sets Off a Struggle for the Soul of America.* New York: Simon & Schuster, 1997. At 880 pages, this sprawling account of Idaho labor strife and the 1905 assassination of former governor Frank Steunenberg is no light read. Pulitzer Prize–winning journalist Lukas killed himself after completing *Big Trouble*, feeling he wasn't living up to his reputation, but the book still offers an unmatched look at early Idaho politics and class warfare.

Moulton, Gary. *The Definitive Journals of Lewis & Clark: Volume 5—Through the Rockies to the Cascades* and *Volume 7—From the Pacific to the Rockies.* Lincoln, NE: University of Nebraska Press, 2003. Volume 5 covers the expedition's arduous summer 1805 travels through Idaho; Volume 7 details the explorers' return trek and long camp with the Nez Perce in 1806. Both are packed with high drama—and unbelievably bad spelling.

Stapilus, Randy. *The Idaho Yearbook.* Boise, ID: Ridenbaugh Press, 2002. Although produced somewhat irregularly, this is the bible of Idaho politics, media, business, and a who's who of the state. Stapilus was also author and publisher of *Paradox Politics* (Ridenbaugh Press, 1988), probably the best-ever assessment of Idaho's political culture.

LITERATURE

Blew, Mary Clearman, ed. *Written on Water: Essays on Idaho Rivers.* Moscow, ID: University of Idaho Press, 2001. Many of the state's best-known writers offer celebrations of Idaho rivers, including the Snake, Clearwater, Salmon, St. Joe, and others. Read this and you'll understand why, to many Idahoans, rivers are a religion.

Fisher, Vardis. *Children of God.* Boise: Opal Laurel Holmes, 1939; revised edition 1977. Arguably Fisher's most famous work, this historical novel chronicles the development of the Mormon religion from the first vision of Joseph Smith in 1820 until after the death of Brigham Young in 1877. Along the way, Fisher—raised a Mormon—takes an unflinching look at the controversies surrounding the church, most troublesome among them the Mormons' early adoption of polygamy. Fisher's prose is eminently readable, and this book won the Harper Prize for fiction.

McCunn, Ruthanne Lum. *Thousand Pieces of Gold.* Boston, MA: Beacon Press, 1981; latest edition 2004. This beautifully written historical novel follows the life of Polly Bemis, a Chinese woman sold into slavery as a teenager by her father in the mid-19th century. She was brought to the United States and forced into prostitution in Idaho mining camps before meeting Charlie Bemis, an Idaho saloon owner who treated her with dignity. She ended up running a boardinghouse and restaurant in the mining town of Warren, where she became a local legend.

McFarland, Ronald E., and William Studebaker, eds. *Idaho's Poetry: A Centennial Anthology.* Moscow, ID: University of Idaho Press, 1989. The editors—themselves well-known Idaho poets—have pulled together a stunning anthology of the best poetry written by Idahoans, from early Native Americans and settler-era poets to their contemporaries. The book is out of print but easy to find at used bookstores.

McManus, Patrick F. and Patricia McManus Gass. *Whatchagot Stew: A Memoir of an Idaho Childhood.* New York: Henry Holt, 1989. This is one of many great books by outdoor writer and humorist Patrick McManus native and longtime columnist for *Field & Stream* and *Outdoor Life* magazines. The book offers hilarious stories about his childhood spent in the Panhandle. There are also lots of useful homespun recipes in the book, using Idaho foodstuffs like wild game, trout, and huckleberries, compiled by McManus and his sister, who lives in Sandpoint.

Parkinson, Heather. *Across Open Ground*. New York: Bloomsbury, 2002. This impressive first novel by Parkinson, an Idaho native, is set in the Wood River Valley in 1917. If the two principal characters, a young sheepherder and his love interest, seem older than their years, maybe it's because people had to grow up fast on the Idaho frontier and during World War I.

MAPS
National Forest Maps

The U.S. Forest Service publishes detailed maps to each of Idaho's national forests—an invaluable resource for backcountry users. The maps cost $6 each. You can obtain a particular national forest's map from the office for that forest, but if you're interested in several different forests, it's easier to deal with the Forest Service regional offices. For maps of the forests in the southern half of the state, including the Bitterroot, Boise, Caribou, Payette, Salmon-Challis, Sawtooth, and Caribou-Targhee National Forests, write to the Forest Service Intermountain Region office (324 25th St., Ogden, UT 84401, 801/625-5306).

Idaho Atlas and Gazetteer

DeLorme Mapping (P.O. Box 298, Yarmouth, ME 04096, 800/452-5931, www.delorme. com) publishes detailed atlases to many Western states, including Idaho. These are not detailed city street maps, à la Thomas Bros., but rather partially topographic maps that show Forest Service roads, campgrounds, and natural features across every inch of the state. They are indispensable for off-the-beaten-path travel in Idaho.

RECREATION

Bingham, Dave. *City of Rocks, Idaho: A Climber's Guide*. Hailey: Dave Bingham, 2004. The classic guide to the rock-climbing destination;

the latest edition includes information on Castle Rocks State Park, just next door.

Carrey, Johnny, and Cort Conley. *The Middle Fork: A Guide*. Cambridge, ID: Backeddy Books, 1992. After a thorough introduction to the history of the Middle Fork's early explorations, the authors take you on a mile-by-mile trip down the river, exhaustively detailing the history of every point along the way. Read this one before your float trip to add an additional layer of richness to the experience.

Daly, Katherine, and Ron Watters. *Kath and Ron's Guide to Idaho Paddling: Flatwater and Easy Whitewater Trips*. Pocatello, Idaho: The Great Rift Press, 1999. Here's a wonderful guide for novice and family boaters, featuring practical advice for canoeing and kayaking nearly 100 routes (up to Class II) throughout the state. This book is sometimes out of stock, but it's a good read if you can find it.

Litton, Evie. *Hiking Hot Springs in the Pacific Northwest*. Helena, MT: Falcon Publishing, 2005. This well-researched book is geared toward wilderness springs that you need to hike in to. The descriptions provide information about the hikes as well as about the springs you'll find at the end of the trail. Maps and photos accompany the text; about 120 springs are described.

MacMillan, Daniel. *Golfing in Idaho & Montana*. Carnation, WA: MAC Productions, 2000. An indispensable guide for linksters, this book describes about 100 courses in the state, providing course ratings, course layouts, slopes, hazards, distances, greens and cart fees, and particularly challenging holes for each course. It's small and light enough to put in your golf bag.

Maughan, Ralph, and Jackie Johnson Maughan. *The Hiker's Guide to Idaho*. Helena, MT: Falcon Publishing, 2001. From the Selkirks up near the Canadian border to the

Bear River Range in Idaho's southeast corner, this book provides selected proven hikes across the entire state. The 100 trail descriptions are thick and prosy, and are accompanied by good maps and photos.

Stone, Lynne. *Adventures in Idaho's Sawtooth Country.* Seattle: The Mountaineers, 1990. This book, now out of print, describes 63 trips for hikers and mountain bikers in the Sawtooth, White Cloud, Boulder, Smoky, Pioneer, and Salmon River Mountain Ranges. Stone is a Sun Valley resident, so these mountains are in her backyard. The book is well laid out and includes a useful appendix that can help you quickly select a trip to suit your time and ability.

STATE PUBLICATIONS
Idaho Highway Historical Marker Guide. Ever notice how all of those many roadside historical markers you pass in your travels through Idaho are numbered? This catalog describes them all, providing the text of that sign you just passed and were too lazy to pull over and read. It's available for $5 (send a check or money order) from the Idaho Transportation Department, Office of Communications (P.O. Box 7129, Boise, ID 83707-1129, 208/334-8000).

Idaho Official Travel Guide. The state's tourism folks put out this lush and lovely guide to the state every year. It's got a wealth of information on sights, lodgings, and recreation opportunities, accompanied by stunning color photography. Best of all, it's free. Request a copy from the Idaho Travel Council, Administrative Office, Idaho Department of Commerce (700 W. State St., P.O. Box 83720, Boise, ID 83720-0093, 208/334-2470).

Internet Resources

These websites can help you explore Idaho, both from afar and once you arrive. fun, Lewis and Clark, mountain biking, fishing, and more.

STATE SERVICES AND INFORMATION
State of Idaho
www.accessidaho.org
Idaho's official website has all the usual links to state agencies, plus some truly useful and fun stuff. You can check road conditions, get fishing license information, and even learn all about Larry LaPrise, the Idaho man who wrote *The Hokey Pokey,* for example.

Idaho State Travel Planner
www.visitidaho.org
A handy itinerary planner, calendar of events, and lodging guide are among the features of the state's official tourism site. Be sure to look at the "Vacation Deals" section, where package deals are available in more than a dozen categories, including romantic getaways, family

Idaho Transportation Department
www.itd.idaho.gov
One of the most practical sites for visitors, where you can check winter road conditions in Idaho and neighboring states, learn about road closures and detours, and get forecasts from the National Weather Service.

Idaho State Library
www.lili.org
Use this site to find a local library and search catalogues statewide.

ACCOMMODATIONS AND FOOD
In Idaho Reservations
www.inidaho.com
This private McCall-based company is a handy place to research and book accommodations

and activities throughout the state. It features good package deals too, including some you won't see on the official state website.

North Idaho Bed-and-Breakfast Association
www.nibba.com

The website offers information and links to bed-and-breakfast inns in the Panhandle.

Idaho Eats
www.idahoeats.com

This is a great online guide to Boise-area restaurants. While it doesn't provide detailed descriptions, it does offer addresses and phone numbers of eateries, broken into 25 categories.

Northwest Food News
www.northwestfoodnews.com

If you want to stay current on thought-provoking food topics in the Northwest, check out this website produced by Guy Hand, a Boise-based food journalist and host of the National Public Radio series *Edible Idaho*.

Idaho Grape Growers and Wine Producers Commission
www.idahowines.org

You will find tons of information about Idaho's burgeoning wine country, including winery listings, touring advice, history, and other winery resources.

CULTURE AND HISTORY

Idaho Commission on Hispanic Affairs
http://icha.idaho.gov

Idaho's growing Latino community can look to this site for information on Spanish-language media, upcoming events, job postings, and more.

Idaho Tribal News
www.shobannews.com

The online edition of the tribal newspaper for the Fort Hall Reservation near Pocatello offers a glimpse into modern Native American life as well as links to other Indian news sources.

Lewis and Clark in Idaho
www.lewisandclarkidaho.org

Look here for information on the famous expedition's travels through Idaho, where it crossed the rugged Lolo Trail in fall 1805 and returned to camp among the Nez Perce on the way home in 1806.

MEDIA

Idaho Statesman
www.idahostatesman.com

The online edition of this Boise-based newspaper, Idaho's largest, is a great place to learn what's going on in the state, especially the Boise metro area. There are also links to the paper's superb entertainment section and its archive of restaurant reviews.

Boise Weekly
www.boiseweekly.com

For an irreverent, informative look at life in and around Boise, check out this alternative weekly's site. See the "Eight Days Out" section for upcoming events around town.

RECREATION

Idaho State Parks and Recreation
www.parksandrecreation.idaho.gov

Learn about Idaho's state parks and make online camping reservations.

National Park Service
www.nps.gov

The website has links to such Idaho attractions as Craters of the Moon National Monument and City of Rocks National Reserve, along with Yellowstone National Park, a small part of which is in Idaho.

U.S. Forest Service
www.fs.fed.us

Search for Idaho on the main page, then follow the links to all of Idaho's dozen national forests and one national grassland. The agency administers more than 20 million acres throughout the state. This is also a good place to get forest fire information.

Bureau of Land Management
www.blm.gov/id
The BLM manages 11,836,481 acres in Idaho—close to one-quarter of the state's total land. This site has information on BLM-related recreation sites as well as a list of field offices throughout the state.

Idaho Outfitters and Guides Association
www.ioga.org
Plan an outdoor Idaho adventure on this site, which showcases the state's licensed outfitters and guides in hunting, fishing, river running, trail rides, mountain biking, and more.

ReserveUSA
www.recreation.gov
Reserve campsites, cabins, and fire lookout stays in nearly 100 U.S. Forest Service and Corps of Engineers locations across Idaho.

As with the state parks' online reservations, the only drawback is a fairly stiff reservation fee—though it's a small price to pay for a guaranteed campsite on busy holidays and weekends.

OTHER WEBSITES
Idaho Conservation League
www.idahoconservation.org
Of the many environmental groups working in Idaho, this homegrown organization ranks among the oldest and best. Its website has regularly updated information on every major environmental issue facing the state, from salmon runs to forest health and efforts to preserve such places as the Boulder-White Cloud Mountains, Owyhee Canyonlands, and even the Boise Foothills.

Digital Atlas of Idaho
http://imnh.isu.edu/digitalatlas
A wonderful compendium of knowledge about all the natural sciences in Idaho. Whether you're trying to identify a bird or learn more about the state's weird geology, you'll find it here.

Index

List of Maps

Acknowledgments

First off, I'd like to thank Don Root and Julie Fanselow for laying the groundwork for this edition. Big thanks also go to Patrick McManus for contributing to the book and to Bethine and Chase Church, who so graciously invited me into their home. Wine country shout-outs go to Ron Bitner, Greg Koenig, and Steve and Leslie Robertson.

Additional thanks go to Diane Norton at the Idaho Division of Tourism, Brad Arendt at *The Arbiter,* and Dr. Dan Morris for being a great soundboard.

And most importantly, I owe much gratitude to my lovely wife, Dana, who handled driving responsibilities (so I could take copious notes) as we crisscrossed the state, not to mention for taking so many beautiful photos for the book — and for putting up with me. I would be remiss if I failed to thank my kids, Nolan and Audra, for being wonderful backseat navigators.

www.moon.com

DESTINATIONS | ACTIVITIES | BLOGS | MAPS | BOOKS

MOON.COM is ready to help plan your next trip! Filled with fresh trip ideas and strategies, author interviews, informative travel blogs, a detailed map library, and descriptions of all the Moon guidebooks, Moon.com is all you need to get out and explore the world—or even places in your own backyard. While at Moon.com, sign up for our monthly e-newsletter for updates on new releases, travel tips, and expert advice from our on-the-go Moon authors. As always, when you travel with Moon, expect an experience that is uncommon and truly unique.

MOON IS ON FACEBOOK—BECOME A FAN!
JOIN THE MOON PHOTO GROUP ON FLICKR